"Maui No Ka Oi"

(Maui is the Best)

Dedicated to Maren and Jeffrey, two terrific travelers.

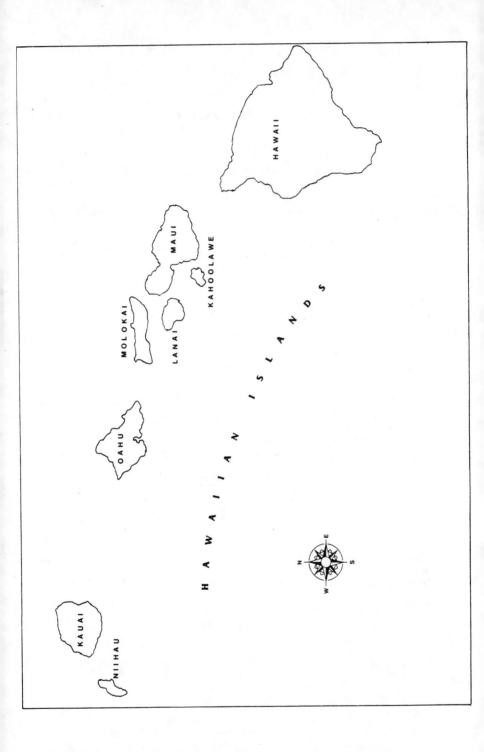

HAWAIIAN ISLANDS

HAWAII

MAUI

KAHOOLAWE

MOLOKAI

LANAI

OAHU

KAUAI

NIIHAU

MAUI

AND LANA'I

Making the Most of Your Family Vacation

by Christie Stilson & Dona Early

Prima Publishing in affiliation with
Paradise Publications

MAUI and Lana'i, Making the Most of Your Family Vacation
Copyright © 1997 Paradise Publications, Portland, Oregon

First Edition: Dec 1984   Fifth Edition: Oct 1992
Second Edition: May 1986   Sixth Edition: Nov 1994
Third Edition: May 1988   Seventh Edition: Nov 1996
Fourth Edition: May 1990

Illustrations: Janora Bayot
Maps: Greg Stilson, Janora Bayot
Layout & Typesetting: Paradise Publications
Published By Prima Publishing, Rocklin, California

Library of Congress Cataloging-in-Publication Data

Stilson, Christie
        Maui and Lana'i, Making the most of your family vacation / Christie Stilson & Dona Early -- 7th ed.

        p.   cm. (Paradise Family guides)
        Includes bibliographical references and index
        ISBN 0-7615-0655-1
        1. Maui (Hawai'i)-Guidebooks. 2. Lana'i City (Hawai'i)-Guidebooks.
        I. Early, Dona. II. Title. III. Series
        DU628.M3S76   1996
        919.69'21044--dc20   96-9164
                                               CIP

    98 99 00 01 02 AA 10 9 8 7 6 5 4
Printed in the United States of America

WARNING-DISCLAIMER
Prima Publishing in affiliation with Paradise Publications has designed this book to provide information in regard to the subject matter covered. It is sold with the understanding that the publishers and authors are not liable for the misconception or misuse of information provided. Every effort has been made to make this book as complete and as accurate as possible. The purpose of this book is to educate. The author, Prima Publishing and Paradise Publications shall have neither liability nor responsibility to any person or entity with respect to any loss, damage, or injury caused or alleged to be caused directly or indirectly by the information contained in this book. They shall also not be liable for price changes, or for the completeness or accuracy of the contents of this book.

HOW TO ORDER
Quantity discounts are available from the publisher, Prima Publishing, PO Box 1260BK, Rocklin, CA 95677; telephone (916) 632-4400. On your letterhead include information concerning the intended use of the books and the number of books you wish to purchase.

TABLE OF CONTENTS

AIR TOURS

VII.   THE ISLAND OF LANA'I

VIII.   RECOMMENDED READING

IX.   INDEX

X.   READER RESPONSE - ORDERING INFORMATION

LOKELANI

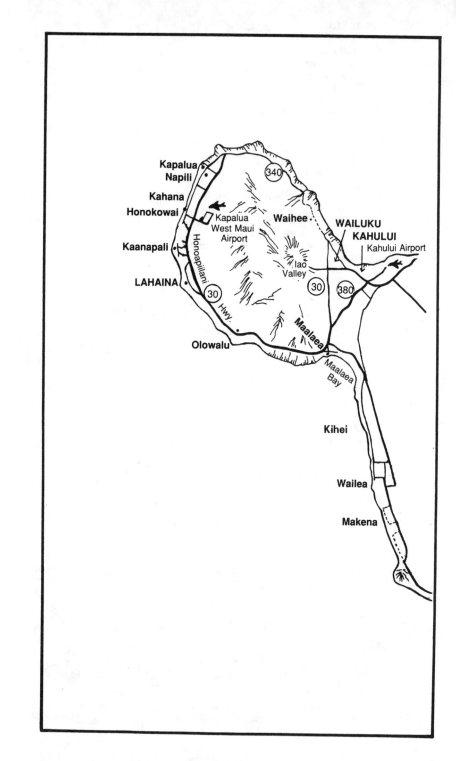

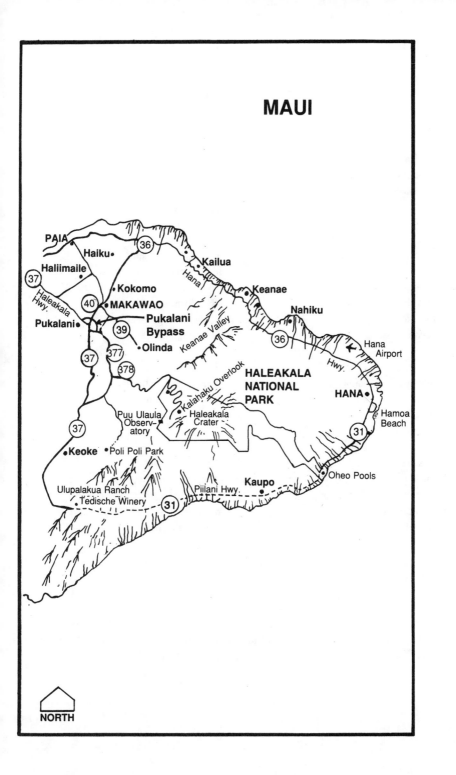

MAUI

PAIA
Haiku
Haliimaile
Kailua
(37)
(36)
Haleakala Hwy.
Kokomo
Keanae
(40) MAKAWAO
Nahiku
Pukalani
Pukalani Bypass
(39)
Olinda
Keanae Valley
(36)
Hana Hwy.
Hana Airport
(37)
(377)
(378)
Kalahaku Overlook
HALEAKALA NATIONAL PARK
HANA
Hamoa Beach
Puu Ulaula Observatory
Haleakala Crater
(37)
Keoke
Poli Poli Park
(31)
Ulupalakua Ranch
Tedische Winery
Piilani Hwy.
Kaupo
Oheo Pools
(31)

NORTH

9

KAWAIPUNAHELE

No e Kawaipunahel	For you Kawaipunahele
Ku'u le aloha mae'ole	My never-fading lei
Pili hemo'ole, pili pa'a pono	Never separated, firmly united
E huli ho'i kaua	Come, let's go back
E Kawaipunahele	O Kawaipunahele
Ku 'oe me ke ki'eki'e	You stand majestically
I ka nani a'o Wailuku	In the splendor of Wailuku
Ku'u ipo henoheno,	My cherished sweetheart
ju'u wehi o ka po	My adornment of the night
E huli ho'i kaua	Come, let's go back
E Kawaipunahele	O Kawaipunahele
Eia ho'i 'o Keali'i	Here is Keali'i
Kali'ana i ka mehameha	Waiting in loneliness
Mehameha ho'i au, 'eha'eha ho'i au	I am lonely, I hurt
E huli ho'i kaua	Come, let's go back
E kawaipunahele	O Kawaipunahele
Puana 'ia ke aloha	Tell of the love
Ku'u le aloha mae 'ole	Of my never-fading lei
Pili hemo'ole, pili pa'a pono	Never separated, firmly united
Ke pono ho'i kaua	When it's right, we'll go back
E Kawaipunahele	O Kawaipunahele

Music and lyrics by Keali'i Reichel, Arrangement by Moon Kauakahi. Used with he permission of Punahele Productions, Wailuku, Maui. From Keali'i Reichel's CD recording, *Kawaipunahele*.

INTRODUCTION

Congratulations on choosing Maui as the site of your vacation. You will soon see why it has the deserved slogan, *Maui No Ka Oi* (Maui is the Best). The sun and lush tropicalness, and some of the finest accommodations, blend sublimely together to create a perfect holiday paradise - a place both magical and beautiful.

While this guide is dubbed a *Family Travel Guide* -- it is aimed for any kind of family, from a single traveler to a family reunion. It is for you the traveler who wishes to be in control of his/her vacation plans. From the family values "buzz words" of the 90's we know that "family" can mean anything. *Ohana*, the Hawaiian word for relative or family, is also used for an extended family of friends, neighbors or co-workers. Even visitors who share a common love and respect for the islands are often described as "part of the *ohana*." Your co-authors for this book have felt this "*ohana*" ever since they first visited the islands. In 1983, Dona moved to Maui to live permanently. Christie first visited the islands in 1978, and became so infatuated that she kept returning each year.

As authors who travel in very different modes (Christie, who travels with a family with two children, and Dona as a single adult), we can share our island experiences from different "family" viewpoints. Maui offers a perfect location for a romantic interlude, a vacation with family or a wonderful destination to spend time relaxing with friends. There is plenty of information on traveling with children, as well as older adults who might be a part of your family. (If you don't have children or seniors to travel with, you might want to consider renting one after you read up on some of the freebies & discounts they get!)

We work continually to update our information, discover new things, rediscover old things and to thoroughly enjoy the tropical energy and seductive charm of Maui. While first-time visitors will delight in the diversity of activities that Maui has to offer, those making a return visit can enjoy discovering new sights and adventures on this magnificent island.

The chapters on accommodations and sights, restaurants, and beaches are conveniently divided into areas with similar characteristics and indexes are provided for each chapter. This allows a better feel for, and access to, the information on the area in which you are staying, and greater confidence in exploring other areas. Remember that except for Hana, most of the areas are only a short drive and worth a day of sightseeing, beach exploring, or a meal at a fine restaurant.

Maui can be relatively inexpensive, or extravagantly expensive, depending on your preference in lodgings, activities, and eating arrangements. Therefore, we have endeavored to give complete and detailed information covering the full range of budgets. The opinions expressed are based on our personal experiences, and while the positive is emphasized, it is your right to know, in certain cases, our bad experiences. To aid you, a **BEST BET** summary is included at the beginning of the General Information Chapter. Refer to individual chapters for additional best bets and check for ★'s which identify our special recommendations.

Our guide is as accurate as possible at the time of publication, however, changes seem extremely rapid for an island operating on "Maui Time." Ownerships, managements, names, and menus do change frequently, as do prices. For the latest information on the island, Paradise Publications has available *THE MAUI UPDATE*, a quarterly newsletter. We invite you to receive a complimentary issue or to order a yearly subscription; see ORDERING INFORMATION at the back of this guide. If your itinerary includes visits to the other islands, the Paradise Family Guide Series includes *Kauaʻi, A Paradise Family Guide* by Dona Early and Christie Stilson and *Hawaiʻi: The Big Island, A Paradise Family Guide* by John Penisten. These essential travel accessories not only contain information on all the condos, hotels, restaurants, along with specific recreational activity information, but also inside information that most visitors never receive, shared by an author who knows and loves the islands. Each of these titles also feature update newsletters.

Although the islands have changed greatly during the century since Mark Twain visited the islands, there remains much to fall in love with. The physical beauty and seductiveness of the land remains despite what may seem rampant commercialism, and the true aloha spirit does survive. We are confident that as you explore these islands, you too will be charmed by their magic. Keep in mind the expressive words used by him nearly 100 years ago when he visited and fell in love with Hawaiʻi.

"No alien land in all the world has any deep strong charm for me but that one, no other land could so longingly and so beseechingly haunt me, sleeping and waking, through half a lifetime, as that one has done. Other things leave me, but it abides; other things change, but it remains the same. For me its balmy airs are always blowing, its summer seas flashing in the sun; the pulsing of its surfbeat is in my ear; I can see its garlanded crags, its leaping cascades, its plumy palms drowsing by the shore, its remote summits floating like islands above the cloud wrack; I can feel the spirit of its woodland solitudes, I can hear the splash of its brooks; in my nostrils still lives the breath of flowers..."

A special mahalo to Maren Stilson, Jody van Aalst, Andrew Nordby, Marie Ganesmer, Cyndie Fischborne, and Kim Morris for their assistance and patience with the many sundry tasks which are required to put the pieces of a book together. Their support and encouragement with the preparation of this edition has been invaluable. Our thanks also to all of you who have written sharing your trip experiences. (Yes! we read them all.) It is a delight to be invited to share your trip through your letters.

Aloha and happy travels to you! *Christie and Dona*

GENERAL INFORMATION

OUR BEST BETS

BEST FOOD SPLURGE: Sunday Brunch at the Prince Court (Maui Prince Resort in Makena) or at Sound of the Falls (Westin Maui at Kaanapali). A fabulous dinner at the Lodge at Koele on the island of Lana'i or a sumptuous seafood buffet at the Garden Restaurant at Kapalua. Dinner at Prince Court at the Maui Prince Resort in Makena or Raffles in Wailea. Close seconds include Swan Court at the Hyatt Regency in Kaanapali or Kincha in Wailea.

BEST SUNSET AND COCKTAILS: West Maui - Kapalua Bay Lounge; South Maui - Maui Prince Resort, Molokini Lounge.

BEST SUNSET DINING VIEW: West Maui - The Plantation House Restaurant at Kapalua. South Maui - Joe's Bar & Grill, SeaWatch or Seaside in Wailea.

BEST SUSHI BAR: Sansei Restaurant and Sushi Bar - sushi and sashimi are served along with Pacific Rim appetizers at the bar or at a table to mix and match - the best of both worlds.

BEST DAILY BREAKFAST BUFFET: Swan Court at the Hyatt Regency.

BEST LUAU VALUE: Check the Maui newspaper for advertisements listing local luaus that might be held by churches or other organizations as fund raisers. A great value and you're sure to enjoy some great food!

MOST UNUSUAL BREAKFAST BUFFET: Auntie Aloha's Breakfast Luau at the Kaanapali Beach Hotel is a Hawaiian buffet with eye-opening mai tai's (at 8 am!) and entertainment for $13.95 offered Monday thru Thursday. It is a promotional and informational buffet where they also discuss island tours and activities.

BEST SALADS: Gado Gado and Chinese Chicken Salad at Avalon restaurant in Lahaina. We keep trying others, but we keep coming back for more of these!

BEST AMBIANCE: Gerard's restaurant in Lahaina and Seaside at Four Seasons. Sound of the Falls and Swan Court are also lovely. And if you want oceanside dining in West Maui, it doesn't get any better than Hula Grill at Kaanapali.

BEST SALAD BAR: It is tough to find a salad bar on Maui! The Embassy Suites' North Beach Grille has one with only basic ingredients, but the freshness and quality are excellent. A more extensive selection can be found at the Kihei Prime Rib and Seafood House and though somewhat smaller, the Royal Ocean Terrace at Kaanapali's Royal Lahaina offers an interesting variety.

MOST UNUSUAL SALAD: Tiki Salmon Salad is a signature dish at Avalon and consists of a layered "tower" salad of mashed potatoes, eggplant, salmon, greens, mango and tomato salsa with a plum vinegarette.

BEST DINNER VALUES: Early bird specials are offered at a number of island restaurants. There are generally more specials offered during the summer months and the price may also reflect the time of year. Some of the better early bird offerings are at the Marriott's Moana Terrace at Kaanapali which is available year round. Kihei Prime Rib and Seafood House or Chuck's in Kihei in south Maui also have early bird specials. Kaanapali Mixed Plate at the Kaanapali Beach Hotel has an Early Bird (4-7 pm) Prime Rib Buffet. Also check in some of the brochures and booklets around town for dinner specials.

BEST FAMILY DINING VALUES: Koho Grill and Bar in Kahului and Napili is a good stop with plenty of selections on the menu. Kaanapali Mixed Plate is one of the best values on Kaanapali Beach with buffet breakfast or lunch for $7.95 and early bird prime rib for $9.95. Peggy Sue's in Kihei has a fun, splashy atmosphere like a 50's diner and malt shop. We also recommend reading the chapter on dining in Wailuku to get the most for your vacation restaurant dollar and experience some wonderful ethnic meals.

BEST FAMILY DINING EXPERIENCE, COST IS NO OBJECT: The older youth will probably insist on a trip to one of the "cool" restaurants, such as Hard Rock Cafe, Cheeseburger in Paradise or Planet Hollywood. Cheeseburger offers great open air, oceanview dining. Planet Hollywood is just plain neat.

BEST PIZZA: Shaka Sandwich and Pizza in Kihei. BJ's Chicago Pizzeria in Lahaina. (And readers have frequently mentioned that Pizza Hut in Lahaina is great! We'll take their word for it!)

MOST OUTRAGEOUS DESSERTS: The Lahaina Provision Company's Chocoholic Bar at the Hyatt Regency Maui and the artistic mastery served in dessert form at The Ritz-Carlton, Kapalua is worth savoring even before you eat it!

BEST SEAFOOD RESTAURANTS: The Waterfront Restaurant in Maalaea or Mama's Fish House in Paia. And while it isn't a strictly seafood restaurant, some of the best fresh island fish we've enjoyed has been at Gerard's restaurant in Lahaina.

BEST TAKE-HOME FOOD PRODUCTS: Take Home Maui, Inc. at 121 Dickenson St., Lahaina. Ship it home or enjoy it here.

ALOHA WEAR: The traditional tourist garb is available in greatest supply at the 17,000 square foot Hilo Hattie's factory in the Lahaina Center at the Kaanapali end of Lahaina.

BEST SHOPPING: Affordable and fun - Kahului Swap Meet each Saturday. Lahaina waterfront at any time; Practical - Kaahumanu Shopping Center in Kahului; Extravagant - Any of the gift shops at the fine resorts on Maui; Odds 'n Ends - Long's Drug Store, Kahului, Lahaina and Kihei and Costco, K-mart or Woolworth's in Kahului. For the adventurous there is a Salvation Army in Kahului and Lahaina. Least fun - Whalers Village has gone off the deep end. Most of the shops here are now designer boutiques with little for the average visitor.

MOST SPECTACULAR RESORT GROUNDS: The Hyatt Regency Maui at Kaanapali and the Grand Wailea Resort & Spa in Wailea tie for first place. The Westin Maui is a close second.

BEST EXCURSIONS: *Most spectacular* - a helicopter tour. *Most unusual* - a bike trip down Haleakala or around Upcountry. *Best adventure on foot* - a personalized hike with Hike Maui. *Best sailing* - a day-long snorkel and picnic to Lana'i with the congenial crew of the Trilogy.

BEST BEACHES: Beautiful and safe - Kapalua Bay and Ulua Beach. Unspoiled - Oneloa (Makena) and Mokuleia (Slaughterhouse) Beaches. For young kids - try Puunoa Beach near Lahaina.

BEST RECREATION AND TOURS: See beginning of Recreation & Tours chapter for ideas!

BEST MAUI GET AWAY FROM IT ALL RESORT: Lodge at Koele or Manele Bay Resort on Lana'i. Hotel Hana Maui in Hana, Maui.

MOST INTIMATE ACCOMMODATIONS: The Lahaina Hotel in Lahaina is a step back into time. No ocean view here (or televisions for that matter) but wonderful and romantic.

BEST CONDOS IF YOU CAN SPLURGE: South Maui - Makena Surf is a terrific, luxury property. Elegant, ideally located and beautifully appointed units. You can really get away from it here. West Maui - The Kaanapali Alii has long been one of our favorites.

BEST ACCOMMODATIONS DISCOUNT: Entertainment book coupon discounts continue to offer half price at several Maui hotels and condominiums. The *Entertainment book* is printed in most major cities around the country and contains coupons for dining and activities in that area. In addition, they carry discounts for accommodations in other regions of the U.S., including Hawai'i. The books are published and are usually sold by non-profit organizations as fund-raisers. Check your phone book under Entertainment, Inc. There is also a Hawai'i edition which carries coupons for dining and attractions, largely for O'ahu, but the outer islands are included as well. The current edition for our state (Oregon) lists several Aston properties and a few other condominiums around the island at 50% off the standard rate. Properties listed currently include Aston Kaanapali Shores, Aston Kamaole Sands, Aston Maui Kaanapali Villas, Aston Maui Park, Colony's Napili Shores, Embassy Suites Resort, Kahana Beach Condominium, Kahana Villa Maui, Kea Lani Hotel & Suites, Mahana at Kaanapali, Maui Beach Hotel, Maui Coast Hotel, Maui Eldorado Resort, Maui Hill, Maui Lu, Maui Marriott, Maui Palms, Maui Sunset, Maui Vista, Papakea Resort, Royal Lahaina Resort, Maui Hill and Paki Maui. Restrictions are plenty, with limited times for availability and allowable only on certain categories of rooms. For example, the Aston properties are only valid January 3-31, April 1-June 30 and September 1-December 22. Others are less restrictive, disallowing only a few key weeks a year. They only offer a few rooms at these discounts, so make your travel plans well in advance to take advantage of this vacation bargain! On Maui they can be purchased through the American Lung Association or Lahaina Business and Professional Women's Association. A portion of the proceeds goes to benefit these organizations. For information contact *Entertainment Publications* at their Honolulu office at (808) 737-3252 or write them at 4211 Waialae Ave., Honolulu, HI 96816. There is a fee for these books (about $40.)

The new *Destination 2000* card also offers accommodation discounts and anywhere from 5 to 50% off dining, shopping, personal care, activities and professional services all in Maui. There are enough good restaurants listed that, given a moderate stay on Maui, this might well pay for itself. The accompanying booklet provides detailed maps and descriptions. The card is $39 and is valid for one year with unlimited usage. Call Destination 2000 on Maui at (808) 875-9405.

Island Savings currently offers an all island guide for $19.95 plus shipping and handling. Individual island books (Maui, Kaua'i, Hawai'i or O'ahu) are available for $14.95. Restaurants, excursions, discounts on admissions. Shipping rates $3-15. Contact: Island Savings, PO Box 5587, Ventura, CA 93305 or call 1-800-475-3728 ext. 011. Internet: Http://www.altonet.com:90/~islesav/.

BEST BODY SURFING: Slaughterhouse in winter (only for experienced and strong swimmers).

BEST SURFING: Honolua Bay in winter (for experienced surfers only!)

BEST SNORKELING: North end - Honolua Bay in summer. Kapalua area - Kapalua Bay and Namalu Bay. Kaanapali - Black Rock at the Sheraton. Olowalu at Mile Marker 14. Wailea - Ulua Beach. Makena - Ahihi Kinau Natural Reserve. Island of Lana'i - Hulopoe Beach Park. And Molokini Crater.

BEST WHALE WATCHING: From the shore it is definitely the Pali on the road to West Maui and Lahaina. While whale watch boat excursions are great, you'll be in for a real thrill if you can view them from a helicopter! Sign up for a helicopter excursion to Molokai which crosses the Pailolo (which translates to "slap crazy") Channel. You won't believe your eyes!

BEST WINDSURFING: Hookipa Beach Park (for experienced windsurfers).

MOST UNUSUAL VISUAL ADVENTURES: The Hawaii Experience Domed Theater in Lahaina and Incredible Journeys, the new indoor helicopter flying experience at the Hyatt Regency.

BEST NIGHT SPOTS: Lively evenings are available at Tsunami, the nightclub at the Grand Wailea Resort & Spa and the Blue Tropix Nightclub in Lahaina. More nightlife information is listed at the conclusion of the restaurant chapter.

BEST POSTCARD HOME: Pick up a coconut at Hana Gardenland. Add your personal greeting and surprise someone back home. Sometimes they are also available at the swap meet. Cost is about $10 for a plain one, $15 for a painted coconut.

UNUSUAL GIFT IDEAS: For the green thumb, be sure to try Dan's Green House on Prison Street in Lahaina for a Fuku-Bonsai planted on a lava rock. They are specially sprayed and sealed for either shipping or carrying home.

Maui Crafts Guild at 43 Hana Highway in Paia (579-9697) has some unusual handcrafted, albeit expensive, gifts.

Antique maps and prints make an unusual and prized gift for yourself or a family member or friend. Visit one of the Lahaina Printsellers galleries for a piece of history.

If you'd like to share a little Hawai'i with friends back home, consider a CD of Hawaiian music. A good selection and the best prices in town are at Costco in Kahului. We'd recommend any of Keali'i Reichel's albums; also Hapa is great.

The Maui Onion Cookbook ($4.95) is a great little book, die-cut in the shape of an onion and filled with recipes from Maui chefs and residents. It's unusual, inexpensive and easy to pack - or mail! Bring home a few Kula onions to go with it!

If you love Kona coffee, you'll love the coffee bean jewelry made by Heart Springs of Maui. They make earrings out of real Kona coffee beans, but add a variety of stones so you don't have to wear brown clothes all the time. They're $9.95 and you can find them at all of The Coffee Store locations (Kahului, Kihei, Napili), at Anthony's in Paia or Makani Hou Gifts in Haiku at the Pauwela Cannery.

MORE UNUSUAL GIFT IDEAS: And if you can wear coffee, why not cook and serve your food with a coconut? The Coconut Cookery collection includes ladles, spoons, spatulas, bowls - even chopsticks - all made from the shell of a coconut. Pieces and prices vary. Ka Honu Gift Gallery (Whalers Village, Kaanapali), Maui to Go (Lahaina), Tiger Lily or Cost Less (Kahului), Island Memories (Kihei), Home Collections (Makawao), Hana Treasures and Lamont's Sundries (Kea Lani or Hyatt Regency) and both Lanai hotels.

BEST FLOWERS: For best flower values visit the Kahului Swap Meet (and make your own arrangements). Leis are sometimes available here also. Check Ooka's grocery in Wailuku (enroute to the airport) for fresh flowers and leis to take home. The last Thursday of each month leis are available in front of the Baldwin Home in Lahaina from AARP. Safeway in Lahaina also has a fair selection.

BEST T-SHIRTS: Our favorites are Crazy Shirts, more expensive than the run of the mill variety, but excellent quality and great designs. There is a Crazy Shirts outlet at most malls and several in Lahaina. (If you're ever caught in the rain, stop in at Crazy Shirts' Wharf location in Lahaina and you can buy a rain poncho for $1.50.) A huge selection of inexpensive shirts are available at the T-Shirt Factory near the Kahului Airport. Sizes range from infants to XL adults and, with plenty to choose from, it is easy to mix and match styles and sizes. Also check the Kahului Swap Meet.

BEST FREE (OR ALMOST FREE) STUFF: *Around the island* - Free introductory scuba instruction offered poolside at many of the major resorts. A self-guided tour of the Grand Wailea, Hyatt Regency Maui or Westin Maui Resorts. Public beaches with their free parking. Lahaina Divers has a map of some of the most popular beach diving and snorkeling sights on Maui. It advises divers as to the special features and facilities of each beach and the suitability for diving or snorkeling. And the best news is the map is free! Stop by the headquarters of Lahaina Divers at 143 Dickenson St. in Lahaina, or contact them at (808) 667-7496. Maui Dive Shop in Kihei, Lahaina and Kahului offers a free snorkel guide. Free hikes with Sierra Club. See Annual Events for more *free* activities!

Lahaina-Kaanapali - Friday night is "art night" in Lahaina. Stroll through the Lahaina Galleries when they offer special attractions, such as an opportunity to meet the artists and possibly get some free refreshment! Visit Pioneer Inn, now an official U.S. Historic Landmark. Canoe races held at Honokaoo Park. Halloween Parade in Lahaina or in June, the Kamehameha Day Parade on Front St. The free shuttle buses in West Maui are now $1, but the routes have been extended for travel between Lahaina, Kaanapali and the Ritz-Carlton. Free admission to Wo Hing Temple in Lahaina. There are free Hawaiian shows and musical entertainment around Maui. The times and days change, so please check. Watch Hula Kahiko (Ancient Dance) at the Kapalua Shops (669-5433) every Thursday at 10 am or enjoy Plantation Days, the third Thursday of the month, offering arts & crafts, pineapple cutting as well.

At Whalers Village (661-4567) hula is performed Monday, Wednesday and Friday at 7 pm. A whale slide presentation is shown Tuesday and Thursday, at 7 pm. The Lahaina Center has hula shows Wednesday and Friday at 2 pm (667-9216). At the Lahaina Cannery Mall (661-5304), keiki (children ages 5-16) perform the hula on Sundays at 1 pm with Polynesian entertainment at 7 pm. Strolling musicians perform on Wednesday afternoons or you can take a complimentary crafts class. There's island style jazz on Tuesdays and a Polynesian show on Thursdays, both at 7 pm.

Free Hula Show nightly at 6 pm at the Kaanapali Beach Hotel. They offer complimentary Hawaiian quilting demonstrations on Mondays from 1-3 pm. Whale presentations with naturalist Phil Secretario are presented seasonally (whale season, of course!) For information call the Kaanapali Beach Hotel, 661-0011 ext. 7145. The Whalers Village Whaling Museum at Kaanapali is great and free to the public. The Crazy Shirts shop located on the north end of Lahaina town has a ng display of whaling memorabilia and a big cannon sits out behind the shop. Inside the Hobie Sports store at the Cannery shopping center is a great display of old surfing long boards. Free tour of the artwork at the Westin Maui. "Live on the Beach" -- a free concert of contemporary Hawaiian music at Whalers Village the last Sunday of the month.

Kihei-Wailea-Makena - Wailea Shopping Village (879-4465) features demonstrations of Hawaiian art and a Polynesian Show at no charge each Tuesday at 1:30 pm and free hula lessons on Wednesdays. A string trio entertains evenings in the courtyard at the Maui Prince Resort. Free guided tour, twice weekly, of the artwork at the Grand Wailea Resort.

Wailuku-Waikapu-Kahului - Visit the Iao Needle located near Wailuku. Watch windsurfing at Ho'okipa Beach on Maui's windward shore. See the Maui Botanical Gardens in Wailuku. Ooka's Market in Wailuku is worth a visit just to see the varied island foods available, from breadfruit to flying fish eggs! The Maui Tropical Plantation has free admission to their marketplace; a charge to tour their grounds. Free behind-the-scenes tours of the Maui Arts & Cultural Center, Wed. 11 am.

Upcountry - No charge to visit Hui No'eau Visual Arts Center in Makawao; special events may require a fee (572-6560). Visit Hot Island Glass Studio in Makawao to see glass blowing and tour their art shops. The Makawao Parade held the Fourth of July weekend. Free Square Dancing in Upcountry at the Upcountry Community Center every Tuesday at 7:30 pm. Call 572-1721 for more information. Country Western Dancing at locations island-wide. Nominal charge. Call 669-4946 for schedule. Free natural & cultural history programs and guided hikes at Haleakala (572-9306). Free admission to Sunrise Protea. Free tour and sampling at Tedeschi Winery.

BEST GIFT FOR FRIENDS TRAVELING TO MAUI: A copy of *MAUI, A PARADISE FAMILY GUIDE* and, of course, a subscription to the quarterly *MAUI UPDATE* newsletter!

HISTORY

Far beneath the warm waters of the Pacific Ocean is the Pacific Plate, which moves constantly in a northwest direction. Each Hawaiian island was formed as it passed over a hot vent in this plate. Kaua'i, the oldest of the major islands in the Hawai'i chain was formed first and has since moved away from the plume, the source of the lava, and is no longer growing. Some of the older islands even farther to the northwest have been gradually reduced to sandbars and atolls. The Big Island is the youngest in the chain and is continuing to grow. A new island called Lo'ihi (which means "prolonged in time"), southeast of the Big Island is growing and expected to emerge from the oceanic depths in about a million years.

It was explosions of hot lava from two volcanos that created the island of Maui. Mauna Kahalawai (Ma-ow-na Ka-HA-la-why) is the oldest, creating the westerly section with the highest point (elevation 5,788 ft.) known as Pu'u Kukui (Poo'oo koo-KOO-ee). The great Haleakala (HAH-leh-AH-kuh-LAH), now the world's largest dormant volcano, created the southeastern portion of the island. (The last eruption on Maui took place about 1789 and flowed over to the Makena area.) A valley connects these two volcanic peaks, hence the source of Maui's nickname, "The Valley Isle."

The first Hawaiians came from the Marquesa and Society Islands in the central Pacific. (Findings suggest that their ancestors came from the western Pacific, perhaps as far away as Madagascar.) The Polynesians left the Marquesas about the 8th century and were followed by natives from the Society Islands sometime between the 11th and 14th centuries. The Hawaiian population may well have been as high as 300,000 by the 1700's, spread throughout the chain of islands. Fish and poi were diet basics, supplemented by various fruits and occasionally meat from chickens, pigs and even dogs.

Four principal gods formed the basis of their religion until the missionaries arrived. The stone foundations of Heiaus, the ancient religious temples, can still be visited on Maui.

The islands were left undisturbed by western influence until the 1778 arrival of James Cook. He first spotted and visited Kaua'i and O'ahu and is believed to have arrived at Maui on November 25 or 26, 1778. He was later killed in a brawl on the Big Island of Hawai'i.

The major islands had a history of independent rule with, at times, open warfare. On Maui, Kahului and Hana were both sites of combat between the Maui islanders and the warriors from neighboring islands.

Kamehameha the First was born on the Big Island of Hawai'i about 1758. He was the nephew of Kalaiopi who ruled the Big Island. Following the King's death, Kalaiopi's son came to power, only to be subsequently defeated by Kamehameha in 1794. The great chieftain Kahekili was Kamehameha's greatest rival. He ruled not only Maui, but Lana'i and Moloka'i, and also had kinship with the governing royalty of O'ahu and Kaua'i. King Kahekili died in 1794 and

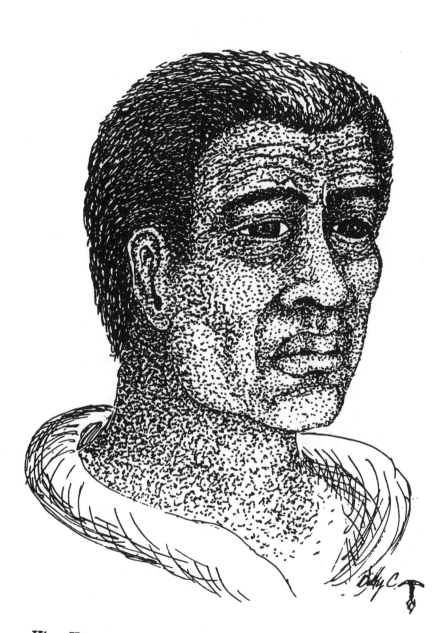

King Kamehameha the First

left control of the island to his son. A bloody battle (more like a massacre since Kamehameha used western technology, strategy, and two English advisors) in the Iao Valley resulted in the defeat of Kahekili's son, Kalanikupule, in 1795. Kamehameha united all the islands and made Lahaina the capital of Hawai'i in 1802. It remained the capital until the 1840's when Honolulu became the center for government affairs. Lahaina was a popular resort for Hawaiian royalty who favored the beaches in the area. Kaahumanu, the favorite wife of Kamehameha was born in Hana, Maui, and spent much of her time there. (Quiet Hana was another popular spot for vacationing royalty.)

Liholiho, the heir of Kamehameha the Great, ruled as Kamehameha II from 1819 to 1824. Liholiho was not a strong ruler so Kaahumanu proclaimed herself prime minister during his reign. She ended many of the kapus of the old religion, thus creating a fortuitous vacuum which the soon-to-arrive missionaries would fill. These New England missionaries and their families arrived in Lahaina in the spring of 1823 at the invitation of Queen Keopuolani. They brought drastic changes to the island with the education of the natives both spiritually and scholastically. The first high school and printing press west of the Rockies was established at Lahainaluna. Built just outside of Lahaina, it now houses a museum, and is open to the public. Liholiho and his wife were the first Hawaiian royalty to visit the United States. When their travels continued to Europe, they succumbed to the measles while in London. Liholiho was succeeded by Kauikeaouli (the youngest son of Kamehameha the Great) who ruled under the title of Kamehameha the III from 1824 to 1854.

Beginning in 1819 and continuing for nearly 40 years, whaling ships became a frequent sight, anchored in the waters off Lahaina. The whalers hunted their prey north and south of the islands, off the Japanese coast and in the Arctic. Fifty ships were sometimes anchored off Lahaina, and during the peak year of whaling, over 400 ships visited Lahaina with an additional 167 in Honolulu's harbor. Allowing 25 to 30 seamen per ship you can quickly see the enormous number of sailors who flooded the area.

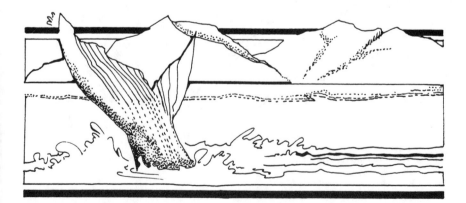

While missionaries brought their Christian beliefs, the whaling men lived under their own belief that there was "No God West of the Horn." This presented a tremendous conflict between the sailors and missionaries, with the islanders caught right in the middle. After months at sea, sailors arrived in Lahaina anxious for the grog shops and native women. It was the missionaries who set up guidelines that forbade the island girls to visit the ships in the harbor. Horrified by the bare-breasted Hawaiian women, the missionary wives quickly set about to more thoroughly clothe the native ladies. The missionary women realized that their dresses would not be appropriate for these more robust woman and using their nightwear as a guideline, fashioned garments from these by cutting the sleeves off and enlarging the armholes. The muumuu was the result, and translated means "to amputate or to cut short."

In 1832, a coral fort was erected near the Lahaina harbor following an incident with the unhappy crew of one vessel. The story goes that a captain, disgruntled when he was detained in Lahaina for enticing "base women," ordered his crew to fire shots at the homes of some Lahaina area missionaries. Although the fort was demolished in 1854, remnants of the coral were re-excavated and a corner of the old fort reconstructed. It is located harborside by the Banyan Tree.

An interesting fact is reported in the 1846 Lahaina census. The count included 3,445 Hawaiians, 112 foreigners, 600 seamen, 155 adobe houses, 822 grass houses, 59 stone and wooden houses, as well as 528 dogs!

The *whaling era* strengthened Hawaii's ties with the United States economically, and the presence of the missionaries further strengthened this bond. A combination of things brought the downfall of the whaling industry: The onset of the Civil War depleted men and ships, (one Confederate warship reportedly set 24 whaling vessels ablaze), and the growth of the petroleum industry lessened the need for whale oil. Lastly, the Arctic freezes of 1871 and 1876 resulted in many ships being crushed by the ice. Lahaina, however, continues to maintain the charm and history of those bygone whaling days. The last monarch was Liliuokalani, who ruled from 1891 to 1893. Hawai'i became a territory of the United States in 1900 and achieved statehood in 1959.

Sugar cane brought by the first Hawaiians was developed into a major industry on Maui. Two sons of missionaries, Henry P. Baldwin and Samuel T. Alexander, as well as Claus Spreckels played notable roles and their construction of a water pipeline to irrigate the arid central isthmus of Maui secured the future of the sugar industry and other agricultural development on the island.

Pineapple, another major agricultural industry, has played an important role in the history of Maui. Historians believe that pineapple may have originated in Brazil and was introduced to the modern world by Christopher Columbus on return from his second visit to the Americas. When it arrived in the islands is uncertain, but Don Francisco de Paula y Marin writes in his diary on January 21, 1813 that "This day I planted pineapples and an orange tree." The first successful report of pineapple agriculture in Hawai'i is attributed to Captain James Kidwell, an English horticulturist. He brought the smooth cayenne variety of pineapple from Jamaica and began successfully raising and harvesting the fruit on O'ahu in 1886.

23

History

Since the fresh fruits perished too quickly to reach the mainland, Captain Kidwell also began the first cannery, called Hawaiian Fruit and Packing Company, which operated until 1892 when it was sold to Pearl City Fruit Company. James Dole, a young Harvard graduate, arrived on Oʻahu from Boston in 1899, and by 1901 had established what has today become known as the Dole Pineapple Company.

Grove Ranch and Haleakala Ranch Company both began pineapple cultivation on Maui in 1906. Baldwin Packers began as Honolua Ranch and was owned by Henry Baldwin who started it in 1912. The Grove Ranch hired David T. Fleming as company manager and began with several acres in Haiku which soon increased to 450 acres. W. A. Clark succeeded Fleming as Grove Ranch manager and while the acreage increased, for some unknown reason the pineapples failed. For ten years the fields were leased to Japanese growers who were successful.

During these early years Haleakala Ranch Company continued to expand their acreage and to successfully produce pineapples. J. Walter Cameron arrived from Honolulu to become manager of Haleakala Ranch Company in about 1925. In 1929 the ranch division was divided from the pineapple division and the company became Haleaakala Pineapple Company. In 1932 the Company and Grove Ranch merged, forming Maui Pineapple Company Limited and thirty years later in 1962, Baldwin Packers merged with Maui Pineapple Company to form what we know today as Maui Land and Pineapple. Maui Land and Pineapple continues to raise pineapples as well as develop land into the fine resort area known as Kapalua. The company owns 29,800 acres of land and uses 7,300 acres for company operations while employing approximately 1,800 people on a year-round or seasonal basis. While competition from abroad (particularly Thailand) has been fierce, Maui Land and Pineapple has chosen to maintain their market by supplying a quality product. Maui Land and Pineapple Company is the only 100% Hawaiian producer of canned pineapple in the world.

It was about 100 years ago that the first macadamia nut trees arrived from Australia. They were intended to be an ornamental tree, since they had nuts that were extremely difficult to crack. It was not until the 1950's that the development of the trees began to take a commercial course. Today, some sugar cane fields are being converted to macadamia. It is a slow process, taking seven years for the grafted root (they do not grow from seed) to become a producing tree. While delicious, beware of their hazards: 1/2 ounce of nuts contains 100 calories!

The Kula area of Maui has become the center for many delicious fruits and vegetables as well as the unusual Protea flower, a native of South Africa. Wineries have also made a comeback with the success of the Tedeschi Winery at Ulupalakua. They started by producing an unusual pineapple wine followed by a champagne in 1984 and a red table wine in 1985.

Be sure to also sample the very sweet Kula onions raised in this area (these are not the same as "Maui onions" that can be grown anywhere in Maui County) and are available for shipping home. In recent years coffee has proved to be a successful and popular new crop for Maui. Amfac is currently developing 500 acres in Kaanapali for coffee production.

MAUI'S NAMES AND PLACES

Haiku (HAH-ee-KOO) abrupt break
Haleakala (HAH-leh-AH-kuh-LAH) house of the sun

Hali'imaile (HAH-LEE-'ee-MAH-ee-leh) maile vines spread
Hana (HAH-nuh) rainy land

Honoapiilani (HOH-noh-AH-PEE-'ee-LAH-nee) bays of Pi'ilani
Honolua (HOH-noh-LOO-uh) double bay

Hookipa (HOO-keep-pah) welcome
Iao (EE-AH-oh) cloud supreme, name of star

Kaanapali (KAH-AH-nuh-PAH-lee) land divided by cliffs
Kahana (Kuh-HAH-nuh) meaning unknown, of Tahitian origin

Kaho'olawe (kuh-Ho-'oh-LAH-veah) taking away by currents
Kahului (Kah-hoo-LOO-ee) winning

Kapalua (KAH-puh-LOO-uh) two borders
Kaupo (KAH-oo-POH) night landing

Ke'anae (keh-'uh-NAH-eh) the mullet
Keawakapu (Keh-AH-vuh-KAH-poo) sacred harbor

Kihei (KEE-HEH-ee) shoulder cape
Kula (Koo-la) open country, school

Lahaina (LAH-HAH-ee-NAH) unmerciful sun
Lana'i (LAH-NAH-ee) meaning lost

Maalaea (MAH-'uh-LAH-eh-uh) area of red dirt
Makawao (mah-kah-wah-oh) forest beginning

Makena (Mah-KEH-nuh) abundance
Napili (NAH-PEE-lee) pili grass

Olowalu (oh-loh-wah-loo) many hills
Paia (PAH-EE-uh) noisy

Pukalani (poo-kah-lah-nee) sky opening
Ulupalakua (OO-loo-PAH-luh-KOO-uh) ripe breadfruit

Waianapanapa (WAH-ee-AH-NAH-puh-NAH-puh) glistening water
Wailea (WAH-ee-LEH-uh) water Lea (Lea was the canoe maker's goddess)

Wailua (WAH-ee-LOO-uh) two waters
Wailuku (WAH-ee-LOO-KOO) water of slaughter

25

HAWAIIAN WORDS - MEANINGS

alii (ah-lee-ee) chief
aloha (ah-loh-hah) greetings

hale (Hah-lay) house
hana (HAHA-nah) work

Heiau (heh-ee-ah-oo) temple
ipo (ee-po) sweetheart

kai (kye) ocean
kahuna (kah-HOO-nah) teacher, priest

Kamaaina (Kah-mah-AI-nuh) native born
kane (kah-nay) man

kapu (kah-poo) keep out
keiki (kayee-kee) child

lanai (lah-nah-ee) porch or patio
lomi lomi (loh-mee-LOH-mee) to rub or massage

luau (loo-ah-oo) feast
mahalo (mah-ha-low) praise, thanks

makai (mah-kah-ee) toward the ocean
mauka (mah-oo-kah) toward the mountain

mauna (MAU-nah) mountain
mele (MAY-leh) Hawaiian song or chant

menehune (may-nay-hoo-nee) Hawaiian dwarf or elf
moana (moh-ah-nah) ocean

nani (NAH-nee) beautiful
ono (oh-no) delicious

pali (PAH-lee) cliff, precipice
paniolo (pah-nee-oh-loh) Hawaiian cowboy

pau (pow) finished
pua (POO-ah) flower

puka (POO-ka) a hole
pupus (poo-poos) appetizers

wahine (wah-hee-nay) woman
wiki wiki (wee-kee wee-kee) hurry

WHAT TO PACK

When traveling to paradise, you won't need too much. Comfortable shoes are important for all the sightseeing and shopping! Sandals are the norm for foot-wear. Dress is casual for dining. Many restaurants require men to wear sport shirts with collars, but only one or two require a tie. Clothes should be light-weight and easy care. Cotton and cotton blends are more comfortable for the tropical climate than polyesters. Shorts and bathing suits are the dress code here! A lightweight jacket with a hood or sweater is advisable for evenings and the occasional rain showers.

The only need for warmer clothes is if your plans should include hiking or camping in Haleakala Crater or seeing the sunrise. While it may start out warm and sunny, the weather can change very quickly Upcountry. Even during the daytime, a sweater or light jacket is a good idea when touring Upcountry. (The cooler weather here is evidenced on the roofs of the homes where chimney stacks can be spotted.) Tennis shoes or hiking shoes are a good idea for the rougher volcanic terrain of Haleakala or hiking elsewhere as well. Sunscreens are a must. A camera, of course, needs to be tucked in. Many visitors are taking their memories home on video tape. Binoculars are an option and may be well used if you are traveling between December and April when the whales arrive for their winter vacation. Special needs for traveling with children are discussed in the next section. Anything that you need can probably be purchased once you arrive. Don't forget to leave some extra space in those suitcases for goodies that you will want to take back home!

TRAVEL WITH CHILDREN

Traveling with children can be an exhausting experience for parents and children alike. There are a number of direct flights to Maui out of Seattle, San Francisco, Los Angeles, Chicago and Dallas, which saves stopping over in Honolulu. These flights are very popular and fill up well in advance.

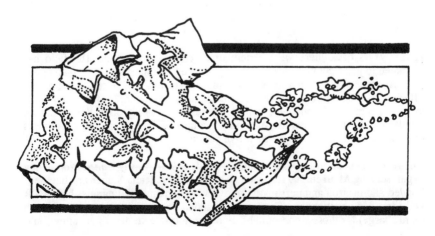

Packing a child's goody bag for the long flight is a must. A few new activity books or toys that can be pulled out enroute can be sanity-saving. Snacks (boxes of juice or Capri Sun are a favorite with our children) can tide over the little ones at the airport or on the plane while awaiting your food/drink service. A thermos with a drinking spout works well and is handy for use during vacations. A change of clothes and a swim suit for the kids can be tucked into your carry-on bag. (Suitcases have been known to be lost or delayed.) Another handy addition is a small nightlight as unfamiliar accommodations can be somewhat confusing for children during the bedtime hours. And don't forget a strong sunscreen!

Young children may have difficulty clearing their ears when the plane lands. Many people don't realize that cabins are pressurized to approximately the 6,000 foot level during flight. To help relieve the pressure of descent, have infants nurse or drink from a bottle, and older children may benefit from chewing gum. If this is a concern of yours, consult with your pediatrician about the use of a decongestant prior to descent.

CAR SEATS: By law, children under 4 must travel in child safety seats in Hawai'i. While most rental agencies do have car seats for rent, you need to request them well in advance as they have a limited number. The one, and only, car seat we have rented had seen better days, and its design was only marginal for child safety. Prices run about $24 per week, $36 for two weeks or $6 per day. You may wish to bring your own with you. Several styles are permitted by the airlines for use in flight, or it may be checked as a piece of baggage.

BABYSITTING: Most hotels have some form of babysitting service which runs about $10 an hour. Check with your condo office as they sometimes have numbers of local sitters. As you can easily figure from the rates, spending much time away from your children can be costly. Consider the feasibility of bringing your own sitter, it may actually be less expensive, and certainly much more convenient (and your sitter will love you forever). This has worked well for us on numerous occasions. With any of these agencies, or through your hotel, at least a 24 hour notice is requested. We suggest phoning them *as soon* as you have set up your plans. At certain times of the year, with the limited number of sitters available, it can be nearly impossible to get one. If you can plan out your entire vacation babysitting needs, it might also be possible to schedule the same sitter for each occasion.

A few years back there were a number of childcare services. The field has dwindled to just a couple. One reason might have been simply too much competition. Another might be the increased number of resorts and hotels that are now offering half and full day childcare programs year round. A few even offer evening programs. Previously, many of the resorts had only offered them during holidays and summer months. With only a couple of exceptions, most programs don't accept children younger than five years.

Our recommendation for your childcare needs is *The Nanny Connection.* They began serving Maui in 1991. Owners Thomas and Patricia Seider are licensed, bonded and insured and personally interview each nanny. All nannies have CPR and First Aid certification. They recently added a personal pager service (at an extra charge) for those who would be more comfortable knowing the nanny could reach them. Rates are $10 per hour for one or two children with a three hour minimum. Extra child from the same family is an additional $1 per hour, from a different family $3 per hour per child. No travel fee, no tax. Extra charge past midnight or holidays. PO Box 477, Puunene, Maui, HI 96784. (808) 875-4777.

CRIBS: Most condos and hotels offer cribs for a rental fee that may vary from $2 to $10 per night. Companies such as Maui Rent (877-5827) charge $6 a day, $30 a week and $36 for two weeks. For an extended stay you might consider purchasing one of the wonderful folding cribs that pack up conveniently. There are several varieties which fold up into a large duffle bag. At around $60, and depending on the length of your stay, they might be worth bringing along.

EMERGENCIES: There are several clinics around the island which take emergencies or walk-in patients. Your condominium or hotel desk can provide you with suggestions, or check the phone book. Kaiser Permanente Medical Care Facilities are located in Wailuku (243-6000) and in Lahaina (661-7400). See the section on Helpful Information for additional numbers. Calling 911 will put you in contact with local fire, police and ambulances.

BEACHES - POOLS: Among the best beaches for fairly young children are the Lahaina and Puunoa beaches in Lahaina, where the water is shallow and calm. Kapalua Bay is also well protected and has fairly gentle wave action. Remember to have children well supervised and wearing flotation devices for even the calmest beaches can have a surprise wave. Several of the island's beaches offer lifeguards, among these are the Kamaole I, II, and III beaches in Kihei. Kamaole III Park also has large open areas and playground equipment. In the Maalaea area, follow the road down past the condominiums to the public access for the beach area. A short walk down the kiawe-lined beach - to the small rock jetty with the large pipe - and you'll discover a seawater pool on either side that is well protected and ideal for the younger child. Another precaution on the beach that is easily neglected is the application of a good sunscreen; reapply after swimming.

A number of complexes have small shallow pools designed with the young ones in mind. These include the Marriott, Kaanapali Alii, Sands of Kahana, Grand Wailea Resort and the Kahana Sunset. We recommend taking a life jacket or water wings (floaties). Packing a small inflatable pool for use on your lanai or courtyard may provide a cool and safe retreat for your little one. Typically Maui resorts and hotels DO NOT offer lifeguard services. Older children will be astounded by the labyrinth of pools and rivers at the Grand Wailea Resort. During slow season, non-hotel guests are invited to enjoy the pool for a day with an admission charge of $65 for adults and $50 for children. Guests of the Four Seasons Resort receive a reduced admission of $50 adults and $35 children.

A number of children's programs at resorts around the island are open to non-resort guests. Some of these youth programs are seasonal, offered just summer, spring and Christmas holidays. Many are available year round. During summer vacation (July-August), The Gemini, a 64-foot catamaran with glass bottom view ports used by the Westin Maui, operates a program for youths ages 14-19. The two-hour Teen Sail includes pizza, music, and swimming. It departs every Friday at 4:30 pm. Reservation phone 661-2591.

ENTERTAINMENT: The 112 acre *Maui Tropical Plantation* has become one of the top visitor attractions in the state. We find it "touristy," but an interesting stop anyway. Surrounding the visitor center are acres planted in sugar cane, macadamia, guava, mango, banana, papaya, pineapple, passion fruit, star fruit, and coffee in addition to an array of flowers. There are also displays of the Hawai'i's agricultural history throughout the grounds. Admission to the plantation market and restaurant are free, but there is a charge for the tram which takes visitors through the working plantation.

There are plenty of great free opportunities to enjoy Polynesian performances. See Our Personal Best Bets at the beginning of this chapter for this listing.

There is a six-plex cinema at the Kaahumanu Center and a four-plex in Kihei. The Wharf Shopping Center in Lahaina has a tri-cinema with first run movies and another set of four theaters opened at the Lahaina Center in 1995. Both offer a $4 early admission (first show of the day only), seniors are $3.50 all day. You'll also find a single-screen theater at the Kahului Shopping Center. There are a number of video stores which rent movies and equipment. See the listing under Best Bets for other free things to do with kids!

The Napili Kai Beach Club's Sea House Restaurant has for years been involved with local performers. They offer a Friday evening dinner show where children perform Hawaiian songs and dances. The Napili Kai Foundation Dinner Show costs $35 for adults and $20 for children.

Try *The Sky's The Limit's Ultimate Trampoline.* Located in the courtyard of the Lahaina Marketplace and they promise more than a mere trampoline experience. Cost is $6 per jumping session. 9:30 am-9:30 pm. (808) 283-6042.

The *Maui Zoological and Botanical Gardens*, located in Kahului, no longer has animal exhibits, but the playground and garden are open to the public free of charge. It's still a great stop-off so bring along a picnic lunch! For more information see WHERE TO STAY - WHAT TO SEE, Wailuku & Kahului. The Hawai'i Nature Center at Iao Valley offers guided "themed" hikes for children on Saturday afternoons. There is also a bowling alley in Wailuku.

The *Whaling Museum,* renovated and better than ever, at Whalers Village in Kaanapali is a most informative stop. Also see the Best Bets information in the front of the book for additional suggestions! The annual *Keiki Fishing Tournament* is held sometime during July each year in Kaanapali. The large pond in the golf course is stocked with fish for the event.

In the Lahaina-Kaanapali area, the colorful *Sugar Cane Train* runs a course several times a day along Honoapiilani Highway from Kaanapali to Lahaina. Transportation can be purchased alone or in combination with one of several excursions in Lahaina. After arrival in Lahaina, you will board a red, double decker bus for the short drive to the Lahaina Harbor. (See Land Tours for additional details.) There is time for a stroll or a visit to the Baldwin missionary home before returning to the train for the trip home or combine your train excursion with a trip to the Hawaiian Experience Omni Theater.

The *Hawaiian Experience Omni Theatre* is an interesting, educational and "cool" way to spend an hour on a warm Lahaina afternoon. *Incredible Journeys,* the new indoor helicopter flying experience at the Hyatt Regency, is about as close to Disneyland as you get on Maui. A little spendy, but surprisingly realistic. Several submarines and a number of boats offer the young and young at heart a chance to tour the underwater wonders of the Pacific without getting wet. The boats depart from Lahaina Harbor, see water activities for more details. During July and August, *Gemini Charters* offers a Kaanapali Teen Sail for 14-19 year olds. A two hour evening of sailing, swimming, music and pizza. 661-2591.

Theatre Theatre Maui is a community and youth oriented theater organization in West Maui. Adult programs are held in the spring and there are summer workshops for children and teens in the summer. For more information contact Nancy Sherman (661-1168) 505 Front St., #226 (PO Box 12318), Lahaina, Maui, HI 96761. With the long-awaited *Maui Arts & Cultural Center* in full operation in Kahului, there are some great opportunities to enjoy a variety of family entertainment. Among performance groups is the *Maui Academy of Performing Arts*. For schedules call 244-8760. See Theater for more information.

The Embassy Suites, in Honokowai above Kaanapali, has an 18-hole *miniature golf course* on their roof-top. The only such course on the island is open 9 am to 10 pm daily, $5 for adults, $2.50 for guests 12 and under. 661-2000.

The local bookstores offer a wealth of wonderful *Hawaiian books* for children. There are some delightful books with factual information designed to stimulate each child with a fundamental knowledge of Hawaii's birds, reptiles, amphibians and mammals. A collection of colorful Hawaiian folk tales may be a perfect choice to take home for your own children to enjoy or as a gift for others.

Many restaurants offer a *keiki* (children's) menu. There are also an assortment of Burger Kings and McDonald's on the island.

Flashlights can turn the balmy Hawaiian evenings into adventures! One of the most friendly island residents is the Bufo (Boof-oh). In 1932 this frog was brought from Puerto Rico to assist with insect control in the cane fields. Today this large toad still emerges at night to feed or mate and seems to be easier to spot during the winter months, especially after rain showers. While they can be found around most condominiums, Kawiliki Park (the area behind the Luana Kai, Laule'a and several other condominium complexes with access from Waipulani Road off South Kihei Road) seems to be an especially popular gathering spot. We suggest you don't touch them, however. The secretions may cause skin irritation. We also enjoy searching for beach crabs and the African snails which have shells that may grow to a hefty five inches. The other Hawaiian creature that cannot go without mention is the gecko. They are finding their way into the suitcases of many an island visitor, in the form of tee-shirts, sun visors and jewelry. This small lizard is a relative of the chameleon and grows to a length of three or four inches. They dine on roaches, termites, mosquitos, ants, moths and other pesky insects. While there are nearly 800 species of geckos found in warm climates around the world, there are only about five varieties found in Hawaii. The house gecko is the most commonly found, with tiny rows of spines that circle its tail, while the mourning gecko has a smooth, satiny skin and along the middle of its

31

back, it sports pale stripes and pairs of dark spots. The mourning gecko species is parthenogenic. That means that there are only females which produce fertile eggs -- no need for a mate! The stump-toed variety is distinguished by its thick flattened tail. The tree gecko enjoys the solitude of the forests, and the fox gecko, with a long snout and spines along its tail, prefers to hide around rocks or tree trunks. The first geckos may have reached Hawai'i with early voyagers from Polynesia, but the house gecko may have arrived as recently as the 1940s, along with military shipments to Hawaii. Geckos are most easily spotted at night when they seem to enjoy the warm lights outside your door. We have heard they each establish little territories where they live and breed so you will no doubt see them around the same area each night. They are very shy and will scurry off quickly. Sometimes you may find one living in your hotel or condo. They're friendly and beneficial animals and are said to bring good luck, so make them welcome.

Except for two male snakes on display in the Honolulu zoo, Hawai'i has no snakes!

If you headquarter your stay near the Papakea Resort in Honokowai, you might take an adventurous nighttime reef walk. If an evening low tide does not conflict with your children's bedtime, put on some old tennis shoes and grab a flashlight. (Flashlights that are waterproof or at least water resistant are recommended.) The reef comes right into shore at the southern end of Papakea where you can walk out onto it like a broad living sidewalk. Try and pick a night when the low tide is from 9-11 pm (tide information is available in the Maui News or call the recorded weather report) and when the sea is calm. Searching the shallow water will reveal sea wonders such as fish and eels that are out feeding. Some people looked at us strangely as we pursued this new recreation, but our little ones thought it an outstanding activity. Shoes (we recommend old sneakers) are a must as the coral is very sharp. Afterwards, be sure to thoroughly clean your shoes promptly with fresh water or they will become horribly musty smelling.

Check with your resort concierge for additional youth activities. During the summer months, Christmas holidays and Easter, many of the resort hotels offer partial or full day activities for children. Rates range from free to $65 per day. Following are a few of the programs offered by some Maui resorts. Please be sure to check with the resort to see the current status and prices for their children's programs. Be sure to call for current schedules, availability and prices.

As we mentioned previously, some of these *children's programs* are available to non-hotel or resort guests. Among those are the Ritz-Kids at The Ritz Carlton, Kapalua, and Camp Grande at the Grand Wailea Resort & Spa. Even more good news is the fact that more and more of them appear to be heading to year-round programs.

Aston Kaanapali Shores Resort features a year-round program for children ages 3 - 10 years. "Camp Kaanapali" is offered from 8 am - 3 pm Monday thru Friday. A $10 initial registration covers you regardless of the length of your stay and includes a camp T-shirt. Three sessions available each day and the cost is $5 per session. Choose a morning 8-11 am session, or a lunch 11 am-noon session, or afternoon activities 12-3 pm. Activities are all held on property grounds and include hula and crafts. Program available for resort guests only. 667-2211.

Aston Wailea Resort (formerly Maui Inter-Continental) in Wailea offers the "Keiki's Club Gecko Program" for children age 5 and older. Cost is $40 per day and includes lunch, snacks and T-shirt. Second child in same family at half price. Activities include Hawaiian arts & crafts, and off-property tours. Special activities for holidays. Children's menus available in restaurants. The program is open to guests and non-guests. Programs Tues., Thurs. and Sat. 9 am-3 pm. Contact 879-1922.

Embassy Suites children's program, "Beach Buddies," operates year round, seven days a week from 8:15-2:30 pm. Activities are designed to keep the children entertained as well as acquainting them with the Hawaiian way of life. Learning to count in Hawaiian, coconut decorating, beach combing, lei making, leaf painting, nature walks and swimming are among the experiences for kids 4 - 10 years of age. The daily rate is $20 and includes a t-shirt and lunch. 661-2000.

The Four Seasons Wailea features "Kids for all Seasons," a daily complimentary program for youths age 5 - 12 years with year round supervised activities from 9 am-5 pm. Hawaiian songs, lei-making, hula, beach games. 874-8000.

Grand Wailea Resort & Spa offers the most incredible 20,000 sq. foot space devoted to their youthful guests. The program is also available to non-resort guests for an additional $10 fee.

When we called to inquire about the current rate schedule, hours of operation etc. they suggested that they fax me the information. A half mile of fax paper later... well, okay, it was only seven pages... I had enough information to start another book! They have it all covered, including handicapped children, illnesses, early or late drop offs, and even swim requirements. So here is a synopsis. The day camp (9 am-3 pm) is $65 including lunch. A half day rate (9 - 12 including lunch, or noon - 4 pm) runs $40 for each session. There is an evening camp, one to three times each week, depending on the season, (5 - 10 pm) which includes dinner for $50.

Packages are available at a special rate and must be purchased in advance. The program has structured activities in the morning and free play in the afternoon.

To participate in the Grand Wailea program, children must be ages 4-12 (although exceptions will be made for three year olds on a trial basis). The camp area has a video room, arts & crafts center, special kiddie pool and movie theater. Guests of the resort may accompany (and stay) with their children and enjoy the facilities of Camp Grande, but you still pay the child's camp fees.

They also offer workshops from 3-4 pm. The cost is $30. Workshops include authentic lei making, computer graphics, pottery, tile painting and more. Nanny services can be arranged.

The Camp Video Arcade and Escapades are open several days a week from 1 - 4 pm. Kids can enjoy playing with Nintendo, Super Nintendo, and Sega. Candy, chips, juice and ice cream can be purchased. Parental supervision is required for children under 10 years of age. The arcade is complimentary to hotel guests.

The whale wading pool, playground & kiddieland is complimentary to hotel guests, accompanied by their children! Check with the hotel regarding hours and days of the week that this is available. For information on camp, teen programs or classes at the Grand Wailea call 875-1234.

Hyatt Regency Maui operates Camp Hyatt, for youth age 3 - 12 years, daily from 9 am - 3 pm. The $55 charge per child per day to attend includes lunch and snacks. Camp is also offered nightly from 6 pm - 10 pm. Evening activities include table games, movies, video games and light snacks. Cost is $10 per hour per child. 661-1234.

Kaanapali Beach Hotel features a Kalo (Taro) Patch Kids program. This is offered only seasonally (summer & holidays). The cost is $15 per child. Activities include movies, picnics, table games, as well as Hawaiian arts and crafts. 661-0011.

Kapalua Bay Hotel and Villas offers Camp Kapalua for youth between the ages of 5 and 12 years. Each "kamper" receives lunch at The Pool Terrace. The program runs Monday to Friday, year-round, for Kapalua guests. Activities include nature walks, tide pool exploration, Hawaiian games, snorkeling, and Hawaiian arts and crafts. The charge is $25 per child, or $45 for two children in the same family. 669-5656.

Kea Lani Hotel offers "Keiki Lani" (Heavenly Kids) for youths age 5 - 11 years. This program services hotel guests year-round, seven days a week, from 9 am-3 pm and includes lunch and snack, plus a T-shirt on the first day. Cost is $25 per day. Available only to guests of the Kea Lani. 875-4100.

Maui Marriott Resort offers their "Kaanapali Kids" a children's activity and adventure program, is offered Monday-Friday, year round, for guests aged 6 - 12 years. Fee includes lunch, transportation and a camp T-shirt. Kaanapali Kids is $45 per child per day. Marriott guests only. 8 am - 2 pm. 667-1200.

Maui Prince Hotel offers a program year-round called the "Prince Kids Club." Children ages 5 - 12 years can have hours of fun with activities such as bamboo pole fishing, sand castle building, pool swims, Hawaiian arts and crafts, or treasure hunts. Three sessions are offered to hotel guests throughout the day. A morning session 9 am - noon which is free. An afternoon session noon until 3 pm for $15 which includes lunch. Or combine the two sessions for a full day. For an additional $20 guests have the option of adding one of several amenities to the package. For example one option is their Kahakai or "beach" amenity package which includes a Maui Prince Hotel beach mat, sunscreen, kid-sized beach towel, T-shirt and tote bag. These gift packages are a nice option which keeps the program a very affordable one. 874-1111.

Renaissance Wailea Beach Resort (formerly Stouffer) provides "Camp Wailea" for kids 5 - 12 years. Currently offered five days a week, 9 am - 1 pm. The $35 price per day includes lunch at the Maui Onion Restaurant. Some of the programs take place on property, but others venture to the Maui Tropical Plantation or the Hawai'i Nature Center in the Iao Valley. 1-800-468-3571 or (808) 879-4900.

The Ritz-Carlton Kapalua provides a children's program for hotel and non-hotel guests. One of the few to do so. (We'd recommend that non-hotel guests call to confirm). Their "Ritz Kids" program explores the earth, sea and sky with full-day and half-day programs for keikis 5 - 12 years of age. The theme varies each day of the week with topics such as Whale Day, Ocean Day or Volcano Day setting the focus for the activities. The program is available from 9 am - 4 pm and is $60 for hotel guests, including lunch, $75 for other guests. The half-day program, from 9 to noon or from 1 to 4 pm is $40 for hotel guests, $55 for other guests. 669-6200.

Wailea Golf Course has golf instruction for youth twice weekly, summer only, for 6 - 12 year olds. The 6 week program runs two hours per session. 879-2966.

Wailea Resort Company offers junior tennis clinics and golf lessons during various weeks in the summer months, as well as tennis camps. Ages 4 - 13 years, the program charges a $35 registration fee and $10 each session. Some single lessons or play. 879-1958.

Westin Maui offers Kamp Kaanapali for 5 - 12 year olds. The program runs daily from 9 am - 3 pm. The participation fee is $45 for the first child and $35 for each additional sibling. Activities include a visit to Lahaina's Omni Theater, a ride on the Sugar Cane Train or a sail on the 64-foot Gemini Catamaran. An evening program is also offered. Charge is $15 for the first child and $10 for additional siblings. 667-2525.

The Whaler on Kaanapali Beach provides a program during summer, Christmas and spring break sessions. Call for current information. 661-4861.

TRAVEL TIPS FOR THE
PHYSICALLY IMPAIRED

Make your travel plans well in advance and inform hotels and airlines when making your reservations that you are a person with a disability. Most facilities will be happy to accommodate. Bring along your medical records in the event of an emergency. It is recommended that you bring your own wheelchair and notify the airlines in advance that you will be transporting it. There are no battery rentals available on Maui. Other medical equipment rental information is listed below.

Additional information can be obtained from the State Commission on Persons with Disabilities, c/o State Department of Health, 54 High St., Wailuku, Maui 96793. 984-8219 V-TT; fax 808-984-8222, or the State Commission on Persons with Disabilities (Also area code 808) 586-8121 V-TT; fax 808-586-8129). They offer a book entitled *Aloha Guide to Accessibility* which is divided into sections that provides services information and advises persons with disabilities of the accessibility features of hotels, beaches & parks, theaters & auditoriums, shopping centers and visitor attractions. They will send specific sections or the entire guide for the cost of postage. ($3-5 per section; $15 complete).

ARRIVAL AND DEPARTURE: On arrival at the Kahului airport terminal, you will find the building easily accessible for mobility impaired persons. Parking areas are located in front of the main terminal for disabled persons. Restrooms with handicapped stalls (male and female) are also found in the main terminal.

TRANSPORTATION: There is no public transportation on Maui (although there is an airport shuttle) and taxi service can be spendy. The only car rental companies providing hand controls are Avis and Hertz. See the Rental Car listing for phone numbers. They need some advance notice to install the equipment. Wheelers of Hawai'i offers car and van rentals with hand controls and delivery and pick up of island visitors. Phone 1-800-303-3750, 879-5521 or fax 879-0649. Hawai'i Care Van Shuttle and Tour (Kapalua Executive Transportation) at 85 Alo Alo Place, Lahaina, HI 96761 offers airport transports island-wide and tour services. Phone 669-2300 or fax 669-3811. The Maui Economic Opportunity Center operates a van with an electric lift for local residents.

ACCOMMODATIONS: Each of the major island hotels offer one or more handicapped rooms including bathroom entries of at least 29" to allow for wheelchairs. Due to the limited number of rooms, reservations should be made well in advance. Information on condominium accessibility is available from the Maui Commission of the Handicapped Office. Wheelers of Hawai'i also has condo listings as well as additional information on the availability of roll-in showers.

ACTIVITIES: Wheelers of Hawai'i and Hawaii Care Van Shuttle and Tour, both listed above, offer wheelchair accessible touring and can provide information on recreational activities for the traveler. Among the options are wheelchair tennis or basketball, bowling and swimming. Contact them in advance of your arrival. Wheelchair access to some of the tourist attractions may be limited.

MEDICAL SERVICES AND EQUIPMENT: Maui Memorial Hospital is located in Wailuku and there are also good clinics in all areas of the island. Check the local directory. Several agencies can assist in providing personal care attendants, companions, and nursing aides while on your visit. Maui Center for Independent Living 242-4966 provides personal care attendants, as does Aloha International Employment Service Interim Health Care and Personnel 871-6373, and Interim Home Health Care 877-2676.

Lahaina Pharmacy, Old Lahaina Center 661-3119 has wheelchairs, crutches, canes, and walkers with delivery by special arrangement. Gammie Home Care, located in the Kahului Commercial Center, 355 Hukilike St. #103, Kahului, HI 96732 can provide medical equipment rentals, from walking aides to bathroom accessories or wheelchairs 877-4032 or Fax 877-3359. It is again recommended that you contact them well in advance of your arrival.

Wheelers of Hawai'i Accessible Van Rentals, Activity & Travel Agency is the only travel, tour and activity agency on Maui that specializes in assisting the disabled traveler. "Imagination is your limit" they report when it comes to the activities they offer. They can assist in making reservations at a condominium or hotel to fit the needs of the traveler, make airport arrangements including wheelchair-accessible vans with lifts and arrange for personal care such as attendants, pharmacists, or interpreters. They can arrange for rental cars with hand controls, make airport arrangements including ticketing, and provide "doctors on call." Owner David McKown is a one-stop shopping connection for the disabled traveler and the Maui (and State of Hawaii) Representative for Wheelers Accessible Van Rentals. As for recreation, how about snorkeling, scuba diving, helicopter tours, bowling, golf, horseback riding, boating, luaus, tennis (disabled opponent available), tours, jet skiing, or ocean kayaking! Wedding and honeymoon arrangements, too. Maui County has made the beaches more accessible for disabled travelers. A $200,000 grant in December 1993 paved the way for work on parking lots at beaches with handicapped designations, sidewalks and curb cuts, comfort stations, picnic tables, beach showers, and an accessible pathway onto the beach. Wheelers of Hawai'i can also provide sand/beach wheelchairs with big inflatable rubber tires. Currently beaches that have been made accessible include Kamaole I, II and III, Hanakaoo Beach and Kanaha Beach. Contact David for updated information as improvements continue to progress. Write or call for their free brochure: 186 Mehani Circle, Kihei, Maui, HI 96753. (808) 879-5521 or (800) 303-3750 for reservations. Fax: 808-879-0649

WEDDINGS - HONEYMOONS

If a Hawaiian wedding (or a renewal of vows) is in your dreams, Maui can make them all come true. While the requirements are simple, here are a few tips, based on current requirements at time of publication, for making your wedding plans run more smoothly. We advise you to double check the requirements as things change!

Both bride and groom must be over 18 years of age; birth certificates are not required, but you do need a proof of age such as a driver's license or passport. You do not need proof of citizenship or residence. If either partner has been divorced, the date, county and state of finalization for each divorce must be

37

verbally provided to the licensing agent. If a divorce was finalized within the last three months, then a decree must be provided to the licensing agent. The bride will need to have a rubella blood test and must bring proof of the screening test from her state of residence. However, the test is not required if the female has had rubella immunization, has had rubella in the past, has had sterilization, is past menopause or has other reasons for inability to conceive. A health certificate attesting to one of these reasons for not having the test is required. There is no blood test required for the groom. On Maui the test can be done at the Maui Medical Group in Lahaina or the Maui Reference Lab in Wailuku. A license must be purchased in person in the state of Hawaii. Call the Department of Health (808) 984-8210 for the name of a licensing agent in the area where you will be staying. The fee is currently $25. (For $3 you can buy a package with a booklet and information on planning a wedding.) There is no waiting period once you have the license. Check with the Chamber of Commerce in Kahului (808) 871-7711 for information regarding a pastor. Many island pastors are very flexible in meeting your needs, such as an outdoor location, etc. For copies of current requirements and forms, write in advance to the State of Hawaii, Department of Health, Marriage License Section, 1250 Punchbowl St., Honolulu, HI 96813. (808) 586-4545. The Maui Visitors Bureau (808) 244-3530 or 1-800-525-MAUI also can provide a copy of the requirements for weddings. Included in the information are some free public wedding locations at Hawai'i State and National Park. The Court is located at 2145 Main St. in Wailuku. To book a marriage ceremony with a judge, call (808) 244-2852.

As for other wedding items: Formal wear rentals for the gents in your party can be obtained from Gilbert's Formal Wear at 104 Market St. in Old Wailuku Town, 244-4017. Rental wedding gowns, formal dresses, and bridesmaid dresses are available through Maui Fashion Center at 341 N. Market St., Wailuku HI 96793. 244-3875. If you'd like to have your food catered try Glorious Food 879-1332, Clambake Catering Service 808-242-5095 or An Absolute Affair 667-7154. Hawai'i Video Memories will capture your special day on video tape. 173 Alamaha St., Suite 4, Kahului, HI 96732. 871-5788.

SEASIDE CHAPEL, GRAND WAILEA RESORT

A basic package costs anywhere from $300 - $400. Although each company varies the package slightly, it will probably include assistance in choosing a location and getting your marriage license, a minister and an assortment of extras such as champagne, limited photography, cake, leis, and a bridal garter. Video-taping, witnesses, or music are usually extra. Phone numbers are area code (808).

A Maui Wedding 879-2355 or 1-800-993-0576 at 2439 S. Kihei Rd., Suite 205B, (mailing address PO Box 116, Kihei, HI 96753). Beachside, tropical garden and small historic church settings. Contact Jan Lyle.

A Wedding Made in Paradise 879-3444 or 1-800-453-3440 US mainland or PO Box 986, Kihei, Maui, HI 96753. Contact Alicia Bay Laurel, the "Martha Stewart of wedding planners."

A Dream Wedding Maui Style 143 Dickenson St. #201, Lahaina, HI 96761. 661-1777 or 1-800-743-2777. Personalized, one-on-one service, from simple to exotic. Tracy Flanagan, Consultant.

Arthur's Limousine Service 871-5555, 1-800-345-4667 from the US mainland or FAX 808-877-3333, 296A Alamaha St., Kahului, Maui, HI 96732. They offer limousine service for weddings, but no packages.

Beautiful Beginnings 874-6444, PO Box 307, Kihei, HI 96753. Location video available. Can also provide formal wear. Contact Sandy Barker.

Grand Wailea 875-1234. The extraordinary Grand Wailea has constructed a seaside wedding chapel on their grounds. The picturesque white chapel features stained-glass windows, designed by artist Yvonne Cheng, that depict a royal Hawaiian wedding. Woods of red oak, teak and cherry dominate the interior which is accented by three hand-crafted chandeliers from Murano, Italy. Outside the chapel is a flower-filled garden with brass-topped gazebos. A beautiful indoor location for your wedding!

Hyatt Regency 661-1234. As a part of their $11 million renovation in 1996, they have added a wedding gazebo. Designed from ohia wood from the Big Island, it will be set amid tropical Hawaiian gardens and waterways.

John Pierre's Photographic Studio 667-7988, 143 Dickenson St., Lahaina, Maui, HI 96761. Eighteen years of providing wedding photo packages; John Pierre recently won the Fuji Masterpiece award for his photography.

Royal Lahaina Resort 661-3611. They have a new wedding gazebo. It features six open air windows and is located in the cottage courtyard. Rows of pink and white hibiscus line the walkways leading to the courtyard and gazebo. The Royal Lahaina resort has introduced a unique new wedding custom, they provide stepping stones engraved with the bride and groom's name and wedding date. Wedding coordinator, Diana Smith, notes that they hope to sometime have all of the walkways paved with these stones. She comments, "In the future, the stepping stones should provide a memorable opportunity for couples to return to the site of their ceremony and renew their vows or simply reminisce." Honeymoon packages are also available.

Royal Hawaiian Carriage Co. (808) 669-1100 has four carriages, six passengers each and eight trained draft type horses which pull the carriages. The company does wedding transportation to and from the ceremony and/or reception and provides pick up island-wide. They are based at The Ritz-Carlton, Kapalua. Minimum charge is $150 per hour, depending on the location and the number of carriages. PO Box 10581, Lahaina, HI 96761. They also provide restaurant transportation and other romantic excursions.

Royal Hawaiian Weddings 1-800-659-1866 US or Canada or (808) 875-0625, PO Box 424, Puunene, HI 96784. Andrea Thomas and Janet Renner have been putting together the ceremonies for the most special occasions since 1977. Choose from dazzling beachside sunsets, private oceanfront settings, tropical gardens, sleek yachts or remote helicopter landings. Name your dream.

Special Services and Accommodations (808) 244-5811, 252A Awapuhi Place, Wailuku, Maui, HI 96793. Burt and Linda Freeland offer a range of wedding services in traditional or remote locations.

Tropical Gardens of Maui (808) 244-3085, RR 1, Box 500, Wailuku, Maui, HI 96793. They provide a garden area in the Iao Valley. They can provide tables, tents, buffet tables, chairs, and flowers. Furnish your own food.

Weddings the Maui Way (808) 877-7711, 353 Hanamau St., Suite 21, Kahului, Maui, HI 96732. Contact Beth Lovell or Richard Dickinson. Can provide wedding services in Japanese.

The Westin Maui (808) 667-2525, Kaanapali Beach, has their own resident Director of Romance who will assist you with your wedding and honeymoon plans.

The social directors of the major resorts can assist you with your wedding plans and there are a variety of locations on the grounds of these beautiful resorts to set the scene for your very special wedding. For a shipboard wedding see information in on *American Hawai'i Cruises*.

HORSE AND CARRIAGE

ESPECIALLY FOR SENIORS

More and more businesses are beginning to offer special savings to seniors. RSVP booking agency offers special rates for seniors who book their accommodations through them. They are listed in the *Rental Agents* section of our accommodations chapter. Whether it is a boating activity, an airline ticket or a condominium, be sure to ask about special senior rates. And be sure to travel with identification showing your birthdate.

Check the yellow pages when you arrive on Maui for senior discount program logos. Look for a black circle with a white star and in the ad. Remember that AARP members get many travel discounts for rooms, cars and tours.

A number of airlines have special discounts for seniors. Some also have a wonderful feature which provides a discount for the traveling companion that is accompanying the senior. Coupon books for senior discounts are also available from a number of airline carriers.

HELPFUL INFORMATION

INFORMATION BOOTHS: Booths located at the shopping areas can provide helpful information and lots of brochures! Brochure displays are everywhere.

MAUI VISITORS BUREAU: 1727 Wili Pa Loop, PO Box 580, Wailuku, Maui, HI 96793. Phone (808) 244-3530, 1-800-525-MAUI or FAX 808-244-1337.

RADIO: Our favorite, KPOA 93.5 FM plays great old and new Hawaiian music, with a daily jazz program 8 pm to 1 am. Tune in and catch the local disk jockeys "talking story"! KKUA 90.7 has Hawai'i Public Radio and classical music. KDLX 94.3 has country music, KAOI on either 95.1 (or Upcountry 96.7) has contemporary rock, KMVI 98.3 has Maui's rock, KNUI 99.9 (or Upcountry 99.3) light rock/Hawaiian and KLHI 101 is adult contemporary. On the AM dial KMVI is at 550 with island music, KNUI 900 oldies and Hawaiian music and KAOI 1110 with contemporary rock.

TELEVISION: Maui Today, on Channel 6, is a service of Hawaiian Cable and features information, calendar of events, special programs of historical and cultural interest broadcast only in West Maui. The Paradise Network, shown island-wide on Channel 7, is designed especially with visitors in mind. Information is provided on recreation, real estate, shopping, restaurants, history, culture and art. If you prefer to get your information from a computer screen, the Paradise Network now operates Maui "On-Line," a kind of electronic guide book that provides a menu of hotels, beaches, activities, sports, services as well as updated columns on dining, entertainment and community events. If you have a modem, you can log-on by dialing (808) 661-9700 or you can reach them on the Internet at: *http://maui.net/~mol/molhome.html*

PERIODICALS: This Week Maui, Maui Gold, Maui (Rent A Car) Drive Guide, Maui Island Guide, The Kaanapali Beach Guide, The Kihei/Wailea Beach Guide, The Makena Beach Guide, Lahaina Historical Guide, Menu, Real Estate Maui Style, The Maui Island Guide, Maui Visitor and Maui Menus are all free publications available almost everywhere. Both the Maui Quick Guide and Today Magazine have some good shuttle schedules and maps.

Most of these free publications offer lots of advertising. However, they do have coupons which will give you discounts on everything from meals to sporting activities to clothing. It may save you a bit to search through these before making your purchases.

There are also a number of newspaper-style publications which offer helpful and interesting information:

The Maui Bulletin - This is a free newsprint booklet with classified ads and television listings. *South Maui Times* - Free weekly. Less touristy, more local stories. *Haleakala Times* - Regional newspaper serving the Upcountry area. Lahaina News - A small weekly newspaper. It contains local and West Maui news, columns and lots of advertisements. Fee is 25 cents. *Maui News* - This is the primary Maui newspaper, published Monday thru Friday and Sunday, available for 50 cents, and $1.50 for the larger Sunday edition. A good source of local information. The Thursday *Scene* supplement has entertainment and dining news.

SUN SAFETY: The sunshine is stronger in Hawai'i than on the mainland, so a few basic guidelines will ensure that you return home with a tan, not a burn. Use a good lotion with a sunscreen, reapply after swimming and don't forget the lips! Be sure to moisturize after a day in the sun and wear a hat to protect your face.

Exercise self-control and stay out a limited time the first few days, remembering that a gradual tan will last longer. It is best to avoid being out between the hours of noon and three when it is the hottest. Be cautious of overcast days when it is very easy to become burned unknowingly. Don't forget that the ocean acts as a reflector and time spent in it equals time spent on the beach.

FOR YOUR PROTECTION: Do not leave valuables in your car, even in your trunk. Many rental car companies urge you to not lock your car as vandals cause extensive and expensive damage breaking the locks. Many companies also warn not to drive on certain roads (Ulupalakua to Hana and the unpaved portion of Hwy. 34) unless you are willing to accept liability for all damages.

TELEPHONE BASICS: The area code for the entire state is (808). Calls anywhere on Maui are considered local calls. At a pay phone it will cost you twenty-five cents. If you are calling another island, you must do so by dialing 1-808-plus the phone number and it is long distance. Note that most resorts charge between seventy-five cents and one dollar for each local call you make and an additional surcharge for long distance.

HELPFUL PHONE NUMBERS:

EMERGENCIES: Police - Ambulance - Fire 911

NON-EMERGENCY POLICE:
  Lahaina 661-4441
  Hana 248-8311
  Wailuku 244-6400

Poison Control (on Oʻahu) 1-800-362-3585
Helpline (suicide & crisis center) 244-7407
Red Cross 244-0051
Consumer Protection 984-8244
Visitor Complaint Hotline (Activity Owner's Association) . 871-7947
Directory Assistance:
  Local . . . . (1) 411
  Inter-island . . . . 1-(808)-555-1212
  Mainland . . . . 1-(area code)-555-1212
Hospital (Maui Memorial):
  Information 242-2036
  Emergency 242-2343
Camping Permits:
  State Parks 984-8109
  County Parks 243-7389
Maui Visitors Bureau 244-3530
Time of Day 242-0212
Information - County of Maui (Gov't info & complaint) . . 243-7866
Haleakala National Park Information (recording) 572-9306
Haleakala Weather 871-5054
Oheʻo Headquarters Ranger Station (10am-4pm) 248-7375
Carthaginian 661-8527
Baldwin Home (9am-5pm) 661-3262
Weather:
  Maui 877-5111
  Marine (also tides, sunrises, sunsets) 877-3477
  Recreational Area 871-5054

The Aloha pages in the front of the phone book have various hotline numbers to call for community events, entertainment, etc. While the call is free, the companies pay to be included, so information is biased.

COSTS PER HOUR: Did you ever wonder what something was costing in relation to the time spent? This is what we came up with based on approximate lengths of time with average prices.

$300/hr	Parasail (based on $50 for a 10 min. ride)
$165.00	Maui helicopter tour (1 hour trip)
$80.00	Sailboat charter (usually 4 - 8 hrs.)
$80.00	Limousine service
$60.00	Round trip (straight) coach airfare LA to Maui (11 hrs.)
$55.00	Dinner for two at a top restaurant (2 hrs.)
$50.00	Fishing boat charter (8 hrs.)
$35.00	Horseback rides
$33.33	18 holes of golf at a resort course ($100 greens fee - 3 hrs of play)
$17.50	Introductory scuba dive (3 hrs.)
$16.50	Molokini snorkel trip (4 hrs. - $66)
$16.00	Lanaʻi snorkel/sail/tour (8 hrs.)
$13.75	Haleakala bike trip (8 hrs. - $110)
$11.85	Deep sea fishing - Shared boat (8 hrs.)
$9.38	Hotel room ($225/day)
$7.00	Diver certification course (36 hrs.)
$6.20	Haleakala sunrise van tour (6 hrs.)
$6.00	Hana van tour (10 hrs.)
$5.00	Moderate condominium ($120/day)
$1.25	Rental car ($30/day)

GETTING THERE

The best *airline* prices can generally be arranged through a reputable travel agent who can often secure air or air with car packages at good prices by volume purchasing. Prices can vary considerably, so comparison shopping is a wise idea. All have senior citizen and companion fare discounts. The major American carriers that fly from the mainland to The Honolulu International Airport on Oʻahu in Hawaiʻi are:

AMERICAN AIRLINES - 1-800-433-7300 in Honolulu (808) 833-7600, or on Maui (808) 244-5522. Through flights to Maui from San Francisco and Los Angeles and direct from Dallas.

AMERICA WEST AIRLINES - 1-800-235-9292 offers service to Honolulu through its major mainland hubs of Las Vegas and Phoenix with connecting service to over 67 cities nationwide.

CANADIAN AIRLINES INTERNATIONAL - 1-800-426-7000; Nineteen weekly flights from Vancouver to and from Honolulu. Then connecting inter-island carriers to Maui.

CONTINENTAL AIRLINES - 1-800-525-0280; in Honolulu, (808) 836-7730. Mainland to Honolulu with connecting service to Maui only via inter-island carriers.

DELTA AIR LINES - 1-800-221-1212; Flight information 1-800-325-1999. They fly out of Atlanta, stopping in Los Angeles, then direct flights to Maui. They also have one flight direct from Dallas-Fort Worth to Honolulu.

HAWAIIAN AIRLINES - 1-800-367-5320; in Honolulu, (808) 838-1555; on Maui 808-871-6132. Flies DC10's with regularly scheduled flights servicing Tahiti, Samoa and the Mainland: Los Angeles, Las Vegas, San Francisco, Portland and Seattle.

NORTHWEST AIRLINES - 1-800-225-2525; Flies into Honolulu (808-955-2255.) No direct Maui flights. No Maui phone number.

PLEASANT HAWAIIAN HOLIDAYS ★ - 1-800-242-9244. We were informed by one of our readers that they saved over $150 per ticket (over the lowest rate quoted by another airline) using an "airfare only" package from Pleasant Hawaiian. The flight was from San Francisco direct to Maui using American Trans Air and they tell us it was as good, if not better, than the service they've had on United. They even had a separate audio channel oriented towards small children. They added that the seat configuration on the L-1011 is 3-4-3 and they recommend tall people staying away from the middle 4 seats, which seemed to have less leg room.

TWA - Call 1-800-221-2000 from Hawai'i or the Mainland. Honolulu only.

UNITED AIRLINES - United has more flights to Hawai'i from more U.S. cities than any other airline. UAL Reservations 1-800-241-6522. Flight information 1-800-824-6200. They have a number of direct flights to Maui from Los Angeles and San Francisco as well as through (but not direct) flights from Denver, Chicago and Philadelphia. No local Maui phone number. United Airlines offers a free round trip ticket for 5,000 mileage plus miles on Aloha Airlines. If you have miles to use, check United for the price of their O'ahu flight. Sometimes they can be less expensive than the direct flight to Maui. A little more inconvenience, but you could then use your mileage plus miles for the inter-island portion of your trip. On one occasion recently we were able to get a $224 ticket to O'ahu (by meeting certain restrictions and flying on specific days) as compared with a $550 price tag on the direct to Maui flight.

The direct flights available on United, Delta, and American Airlines save time and energy by avoiding the otherwise necessary stopover on O'ahu. Travel agents schedule at least an hour and a half between arrival on O'ahu and departure for Maui to account for any delays, baggage transfers, and the time required to reach the inter-island terminal.

If you do arrive early, check with the inter-island carrier. Very often you can get an earlier flight which will arrive on Maui in time to get your car, and maybe some groceries, before returning to pick up your luggage when it arrives on your scheduled flight.

The inter-island carriers that operate between Honolulu and Maui are:

ALOHA AIRLINES - They fly only jets - all 737s. 1-800-367-5250 U.S. and Canada. Their Honolulu number is 808-484-1111, on Maui 808-244-9071. This airline tends to have more respect for its schedule than the others. They fly 1,300 flights weekly with their fleet of 15 Boeing 737s. Also weekly charter service to Johnson Island and long range charters upon request.

When making your reservations, you might inquire about any special promotions, passes, AAA membership discounts or coupon books that are currently available. During slower times of the year they offer assorted discounts. Typical inter-island one way is $74. If you are an AAA member and have your membership card, you can purchase a ticket for $58. Coupon books are great if you plan lots of inter-island excursions or have a family you might inquire about their six or ten coupon books. They also have 7, 10 and 14 day pays. If you have United Mileage plus miles you can receive a free round trip ticket for 5,000 miles!

ISLANDAIR - Their fleet consists of 2 - 37 seat Dash 8's and 4 - 18 passenger twin engine deHavilland Dash 6 Twin Otters (turbo-prop) aircraft. They fly 80 flights daily servicing Kahului and Hana and are the only airlines that currently fly in and out of the Kapalua West Maui Airport to Lanai City, Princeville, Molokai and Honolulu. From Hawai'i the toll free number is 1-800-652-6541, (808) 484-2222 in Honolulu or 1-800-323-3345 U.S. Charters available.

HAWAIIAN AIRLINES - They fly DC9's on the hour and half-hour from Maui to Honolulu. Toll free 1-800-367-5320; on Maui (808) 871-6132.

MAHALO AIR - Up to 83 inter-island flights daily with 6 - ATR-42 Turboprop seating 44 to 48 passengers each. Aware of their status as the new kid in the sky, they offer frequent specials and tend to keep their fares low. Call 1-800-4-MAHALO (U.S. and Canada); 1-800-277-8333 (Hawaii); or (808) 833-5555 in Honolulu.

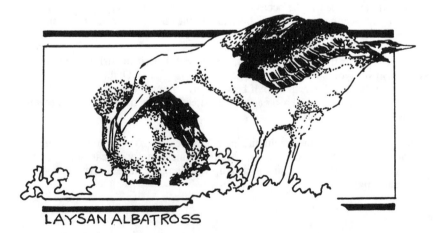

LAYSAN ALBATROSS

TRANS AIR - Began passenger service in 1994 servicing Honolulu and Moloka'i from Kapalua West Maui. They also offer executive charters, cargo and express package service plus business or vacation excursions. (1-800-634-2094) or (808) 833-5557 in Honolulu.

Most visitors arrive at the **Kahului Airport**, via direct or inter-island flights. The Kahului Airport has been transformed over the past few years into an attractive new passenger center. (What was once the entire airport is now just the baggage claim area!) No longer do you disembark from your plane and trudge down the runway to the airport terminal, although the walk within the terminal building from the United Airlines gate to the baggage claim area is quite a distance. There is now a regular baggage claim carousel and a restaurant that even offers runway views. The Kahului Airport has emerged from the stone age with a terminal to be proud of! They have improved the parking and there is an on-site rental car area.

From the airport it is only a 20-30 minute drive to the Kihei-Wailea-Makena areas, but a 45 to 60 minute drive to the Kaanapali/Kapalua areas. If your destination is West Maui from O'ahu, Kaua'i, or Hawai'i, it might be more convenient to fly into the **Kapalua West Maui Airport**. This small, uncrowded airport is serviced by IslandAir and, with slightly less frequency, Trans Air.

In addition to inter-island commuter flights, there are several options to shuttle between islands by water. **Expeditions** (661-3756) departs from Lahaina to the island of Lana'i five times daily. Cost is $50 round trip adults, $40 children. The **Maui Princess** travels between Lahaina on Maui and Kaunakakai on Moloka'i once each day, departing at 7 am and returning at 5:30 pm. $50 adults, $25 children. The **Maui Princess** (661-8397) also offers cruise/drive, golf, mule ride and overnight excursions. 1-800-833-5800 from the mainland US.

One pleasant way to see the Hawaiian islands is aboard the **American Hawai'i Cruises** ship *Independence*. They currently are operating with only one cruise ship. The other ship, the *Constitution*, was taken out of service in 1995 for repairs. A year later it was determined that the repair costs were so high that it was not feasible to have the ship refurbished. They announced that at this time they do not have plans to add a second ship to their Hawaiian fleet. For now the *Independence* is a comfortable 700-foot (800 passenger) ship which provides accommodations and friendly service during the seven day sail around the islands. In 1993, American Hawaii Cruises was acquired by The Delta Queen Steamboat Co. and some great new ideas have been initiated. Hawaiian costumes, onboard hands-on Hawaiian museum exhibits, cabins receiving Hawaiian names, traditional Hawaiian church services, menus filled with Hawaiian specialties, tropical flowers in every room, are among the changes which bring the essence of Hawaii on board. American Hawaii has recently added on board Kumus (Hawaiian teachers) to teach passengers about the culture and history of Hawaii. A Kumu's Study with historic artifacts has been developed off the central lounge. Fully handicap-accessible suites will be created and all passenger cabins will be stripped and redecorated. Direct cellular telephone service are available from each cabin.

Also available on the *Independence* are a number of "Theme Cruises" which range from Big Band cruises to one which combines with the island's Aloha Festival. The ships come into port at each of the major islands for a day (or in some cases two) of touring.

Wedding ceremonies can be performed on board with the purchase of a special $595 wedding package. The package includes a minister/judge fee, a Hawaiian lei and haku for the bride and matching lei or boutonniere for the groom, 24 photos in an album, live Hawaiian music, champagne with two keepsake glasses, and an individual wedding cake for two. Anniversary couples can arrange to renew their vows in a ceremony performed by the Captain himself. See GENERAL INFORMATION chapter for information on tests and licenses.

They also offer a special six-day package which begins on Sunday, especially convenient for those folks who have mainland weddings on Saturdays and then fly to the islands the following day. These packages include a choice of spending Sunday and Monday at a hotel on Maui (they have several to choose from) and begin their cruise on Tuesday by calling at the ports of Kona and Hilo on the Big Island before disembarking in Honolulu on Saturday. Anniversary and Honeymoon packages are available. American Hawaii also offers you the option of extending your stay on land following a seven-day cruise.

American Hawaii also offers shore excursions which include opportunities for passengers to discover the "hidden" Hawaii. Trips include the opportunity to relax in an authentic polynesian-style outrigger canoe as a personal tour guide paddles through tropical landscapes and by exotic wildlife, or hike through a rain forest to discover a hidden waterfall.

The idea of a cruise is to give you a taste of each of the islands without the time and inconvenience of traveling by plane in-between islands. In fact, it would be impossible to see all the islands in a week in any other fashion.

For additional information write American Hawai'i Cruises and Land Vacations, 550 Kearny St., San Francisco, CA 94108. Phone 1-800-765-7000 from the U.S. or Canada. In San Francisco phone (415) 392-9400.

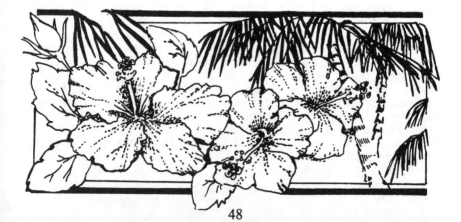

GETTING AROUND

FROM THE AIRPORT: After arriving, there are several options. Taxi cabs, because of the distances between areas, can be very costly (i.e., $50 from Kahului to Kaanapali). There are several bus/limo services available also. Arthur's Limousine Service currently commutes to most resorts from the Kahului airport. The limited around-the-island public transportation that did exist is very limited and it is expensive ($10-15 one way). There are some local area shuttles. The best option may be a rental car unless your resort provides transportation. The phone number for cab service, *Alii Cab*, (808) 661-3688.

Trans Hawaiian 1-800-566-7000 U.S., 1-800-231-6984 inter-island, (808) 877-7308, provides the Kahului Airport with service to Lahaina and Kaanapali. No charge for first two bags, additional charge for more. The shuttle currently departs every hour from 8 am until 4 pm (no 9 am shuttle). Service from Kahului to Lahaina-Kaanapali-Kapalua is $13 one-way. (Call to verify current schedules and price.) Check in by baggage claim area #3. *SpeediShuttle* offers door-to-door airport service that fits your schedule. Pick up anytime and to any location in their 11 and 14 passenger vans. Especially economical for a family. Call ahead for reservations (808) 875-8070. *Airport Shuttle* (808) 661-6667.

Travel in style with one of the limousine services. Rates between them are competitive, $60 and up per hour plus tax and gratuity. Minimum 2 hours. See transportation section for a list of the limo services. Also available with some companies are chauffeurs as drivers for your own car.

LOCAL TRANSPORTATION: If you don't choose a rental car, you will find Maui offers no public transportation. There are several shuttles offering service between Lahaina and Kaanapali. Two of them continue on to Kapalua making alternating stops at shopping centers and condos along the way. Fare is $1 each way with transportation to other parts of the island available for $10-15 one way. These are not part of a public system, but instead are subsidized by various business or tourism agencies. Two free publications, *Today Magazine* and *Maui Quick Guide*, have listings of several of the schedules or you can call Trans Hawaiian at 877-0380 for information.

The free Kaanapali Trolley services the resort area operating only between the area hotels and golf course. Kapalua has a shuttle running 6:15 am to midnight between the condos and the hotel. Call the front desk to request it. Most van tours offer pickup at your hotel or condo.

In Wailea there is a shuttle that offers transportation between the hotels, restaurants and shopping. Check with the front desk or concierge at the property at which you stay.

RENTAL CARS AND TRUCKS: It has been said that Maui has more rental cars per mile of road than anywhere in the nation. This is not surprising when you realize that Maui has no mass transit, a population of over 100,000 (1995 figures for Island of Maui), and 2.3 million visitors per year. Recently, shuttles have been initiated to help alleviate this problem. A choice of more than 30 car rental companies offer luxury or economy and new or used models. Some are local island operators, others are nation-wide chains, but all are very competitive. The rates may vary between high and low season and the best values are during price wars, or super summer discount specials. Given the status of public transportation on Maui, a rental car is still the best bet and sometimes the only way to get around the island and, for your dollar, a very good buy. Prices are approximated as follows: Vans $65-80, Jeeps $52-80, Mid-size $35-$62, Compacts $30-$50.

The least expensive choice is a late-model compact or economy. Often these cars are only 2 - 3 years old and in very good condition. Also available from specialty car rental agencies are a variety of luxury cars. A Porsche or Mercedes will run $200 plus per day.

Vans are available from a number of agencies, but camping in them is not allowed. We advise that you bring your own camping equipment.

Many of the rental companies have booths next to the main terminal building at the Kahului Airport. There is also a large courtesy phone board in the baggage claim area. This free phone is for those rental agencies not having an airport booth, or for regular shuttle service, so that you can call for a pick up. A few agencies will take your flight information when your car reservation is made and will meet you and your luggage at the airport with your car. The policies of all the rental car agencies are basically the same. Most require a minimum age of 21 to 25 and a maximum age of 70. All feature unlimited mileage with you buying the gas ($1.75 - $1.99 per gallon). Be sure to fill up before you return your car, the rental companies charge about $2.50 or more per gallon to do it for you. A few require a deposit or major credit card to hold your reservation. Insurance is an option you may wish to purchase which can run an additional $14-18 a day. A few agencies will require insurance for those under age 25. Most of the car rental agencies strongly encourage you to take the additional insurance coverage. Hawai'i is a no-fault state and without the insurance, you are required to take care of all the damages before leaving the island. We suggest you check with your own insurance company before you leave to verify exactly what your policy covers. You should also check your credit card benefits: some "gold" cards offer enough coverage to allow you to waive the additional insurance. Add to the rental price a 4% sales tax and a $2 per day highway road tax.

A few of Maui's roadways are rough and rugged. The rental agencies recommend that cars not traverse these areas (shown on the map they distribute) and that if these roads are attempted, you are responsible for any damage. Some restrict driving to Haleakala due to drivers riding the brakes down the steep road.

Discounts are few and far between. You might be able to use some airline award coupons, but they are often very restrictive. If you are a member of AAA you can receive a discount on rental cars. Sunscapes offers the best prices we've seen in sometime. They handle Alamo, Dollar and Avis with prices beginning at $132 for 2 dr. economy during value season. Island hopping rates (a REAL bonus) are available also.

RENTAL CAR LISTING:

ADVENTURES
RENT A JEEP
877-6626

ALAMO
RENT A CAR
1-800-327-9633
Kahului 871-6235
Lahaina 661-7181

ANDRES
RENT A CAR
Kahului 877-5378

ARTHUR'S
LIMOUSINE SERVICE
1-800-345-4667
Kahului 871-5555

ATLAS CAR RENTAL
1-800-367-5238
Kahului 871-2860

AVIS
1-800-331-1212
Kahului 871-7575
Kaanapali 661-4588
Kihei 879-4077

BUDGET
1-800-527-0700
Kaanapali 661-8721
Wailea 874-2831
Kahului 871-8811

DOLLAR
1-800-800-4000
Kahului 877-2731
Kaanapali 667-2651
Interisland
1-800-342-7398

ISLAND RIDERS
Lahaina 661-9966
Kihei 874-0311
Rent an A/C Cobra, a Ferrari 348
TS, Porsche 911 Cabriolet, a
Corvett, a Dodge Viper, a Harley
Motorcycle. Other cars, boats, and
mountain bikes available.

HERTZ
1-800-654-3131
Kahului 877-5167
Kaanapali (Marriott) 661-3195
(Westin) 667-5381

KIHEI RENT-A-
CAR
Kihei 879-7257

NATIONAL
1-800-227-7368
Kahului 871-8851
Kaanapali 667-9737

SEARS
contracts with Budget
1-800-451-3600

SUNSCAPE
1-800-225-7978
See above information

SURF RENTS TRUCKS
(flat beds, pick-ups)
Wailuku 244-5544

WHEELERS OF HAWAII
(Handicapped
    Accessible Vans)
1-800-303-3750
FAX 808-879-0649

WORD OF MOUTH
RENT A CAR
Kahului 877-2436

GROCERY SHOPPING

Grocery store prices may be one of the biggest surprises of your trip. While there are some locally grown foods and dairies, most of the products must be flown or shipped to the islands. The local folks can shop the advertisements and use the coupons, but it isn't so easy when traveling. To give you an idea of what to expect at the supermarket, here are some grocery store prices. Bread $2.39, Bananas $.99 lb., baby food $.55-69 per jar, Chicken $1.69 per pound, hamburger $1.99 lb., mayonnaise $3.79, Bumble Bee Tuna $1.29 per can, diapers $6.69 in the 12-24 count size, ketchup $2.29, skim milk $4.59 per gallon.

The three major grocery stores in Kahului are Foodland, Safeway and Star Market (all accept Visa or Mastercard) and Star Market. In Lahaina you can choose between Foodland or Nagasako at the Old Lahaina Center, or the Safeway at Lahaina Cannery Mall. In Kihei the major markets are Foodland and Star Market. These larger stores offer the same variety as your hometown store and the prices are better than at the small grocery outlets. In Hana there is Hasegawa's and the Hana Ranch Store. Long's Drug Stores carry some food items as do K-Mart and Costco.

Azeka's (879-0611) at Azeka's Place in Kihei closed its market in the summer of 1994. It is now an Ace Hardware, but with an outside take-out window on the side where you can still get Azeka's famous ribs as well as teriyaki beef and chicken.

The Farmers' Market is a group of people who bring produce down from the Kula area. They set up roadside shopping, and you can't find it fresher. Their locations seem to change each time we visit. Just look for the green sandwich board signs that are set up roadside.

Take Home Maui (661-8067) is located just off Front Street in Lahaina and offers a selection of fruits and vegetables for shipment home. *Fresh Island Fish* (244-9633 or 242-6532) is located near the dock at Maalaea Harbor, open Mon.-Sat. 10-5. They offer a wonderful selection of fresh island fish and a cafe, open 10 am-8 pm (see restaurants). The *Nagasako Fish Market* on Lower Main Street in Wailuku have what may be the most diverse selection of fresh seafood from reef fish to live clams and crabs.

Local grocery shopping is a little more adventuresome. The largest local stores are in Wailuku and Kahului. In addition to the regular food staples they often have deli sections which feature local favorites and plate lunches. *Takamiya's* at 359 N. Market St. in Wailuku has a huge deli section with perhaps more than 50 cooked foods and salads as well as very fresh meats. *Ah Fook's* at the older Kahului Mall has a smaller deli section with plate lunches running about $3. *Ooka* is the largest of the three. The packed parking lot and crowded aisles prove its popularity and low prices. Besides the usual sundry items, they have a fascinating and unusual array of foods. How about a tasty fresh pig ear ($1.29 lb.), pig blood ($1.99 lb.), tripe ($3.99), calf hoof or tongue? In the seafood aisle check out the Opihi ($25 lb.), cuttlefish ($13 lb.), Tobikko (Flying Fish Roe, $14.29 lb.), lomi salmon ($3.78 lb.) and whole or filets of fresh island fish like whole catfish ($3.99 lb.) or Onaga ($5.95 lb. is a great price!).

ANNUAL MAUI EVENTS

JANUARY/FEBRUARY
- Celebration of the Whales at the Four Seasons Wailea
- WhaleFest - Week-long events in Lahaina and West Maui
- Chinese New Year celebrations with Lion Dancers in Lahaina and Wailea with many restaurants (Ming Yuen) and hotels (Four Seasons) offering special holiday meals
- Marine/Art Expo in Wailea (Hotel to be announced)
- Professional surfing at Honolua Bay

MARCH
- Annual Maui Marathon from Kahului to Lahaina, sponsored by the Valley Isle Road Runners
- Annual Kukini Run along the Kahakuloa Valley Trail
- The 26th is Prince Kuhio Day, a state holiday
- Held February or March, the LPGA Women's Kemper Open at the Kaanapali Golf Course
- East Maui Taro Festival in Hana with entertainment, exhibits, demonstrations and samplings
- St. Patrick's Day Parade - Kaanapali Parkway
- Wild and Wonderful Whale Regatta/Whale Day
- Just Desserts fundraiser for Maui Humane Society

APRIL
- David Malo Day at Lahainaluna High School includes Hawaiian entertainment and local food
- Hui No'eau Visual Arts Center, "Art Maui" - an annual juried show with works by island artists. Free admission
- Budlight Triple Crown Softball Tournament - teams from Hawai'i and the mainland compete in Wailuku and Kihei
- Annual Maui Marathon, 10K Run in Iao Valley, sponsored by Valley Isle Road Runners
- The Ritz-Carlton "Celebration of the Arts"
- "The Ulupalakua Thing" is an Agricultural Trade Show with Maui product booths, entertainment, cooking contests, chef's demonstrations and lots of free samples. Held at Ulupalakua Ranch/Tedeschi Winery
- Kihei Sea Fest - canoe races, music, food and crafts

MAY
- Lei Day celebration in Lahaina and Wailea (check with hotels for their events)
- Pineapple Jam on Lana'i - a two-day festival with arts, crafts, entertainment, cooking contests and samplings
- Seabury Hall in Makawao sponsors their annual craft fair the Saturday prior to Mother's Day
- Annual Lei Festival at Aston Wailea Beach Resort
- Annual Hard Rock Cafe World Cup of Windsurfing at Hookipa Beach Park
- On Molokai, the Molokai Ka Hula Piko, a celebration of the birth of hula on Molokai
- Tedeschi Vineyard 10K run through Upcountry Maui. Entry fee
- Annual Bankoh Kayak Challenge, Molokai to Oahu, 41 mile kayak race

JUNE
- Maui Chamber Music Festival (formerly Kapalua Music Festival) - a week of Hawaiian and classical music at Sacred Hearts Mission Church in Kapalua
- Obon Season (late June through August) - Bon Odori festivals are held at the many Buddhist temples around the island. They are announced in the local newspapers and the public is invited
- King Kamehameha Day Celebration - Front St. parade with pa'u riders and floral floats
- Maui Upcountry Fair, Eddie Tam Center, Makawao
- Hard Rock Cafe Rock N Roll, 10K run
- Makeke Fair at the Hana Ballpark - Hawaiian music, hula, crafts, food & games
- Kapalua Wine and Food Symposium - seminars and tastings culminating in the Kapalua Seafood Festival, a one day event featuring goodies from the best chefs from the best restaurants from all the islands
- Taste of South Maui - Kihei and Wailea chefs offer their best at this food festival to raise money for the Kihei Youth Center

JULY
- All-American Fourth of July celebration with fireworks at Aston Wailea Beach Resort
- Fireworks on the Green, an Independence Day fireworks display at Kaanapali Golf Course
- Annual 4th of July Rodeo & Parade in Makawao
- Friday Night is Art Night Anniversary Celebration - street party with food, entertainment, art in action and gallery displays
- Pineapple Festival - Kaahumanu Center, free tastings, games, entertainment and historic photo and label displays from Maui Pineapple Co.
- Canoe races at Hookipa State Park
- Maui Jaycees Carnival at Maui War Memorial Complex, Wailuku
- Annual Sausa Cup races in Lahaina, sponsored by the Lahaina Yacht Club
- Victoria to Maui Yacht Race
- Keiki Fishing Tournament at Kaanapali
- Annual Wailea Tennis Open Championship at the Wailea Tennis Club

AUGUST
- Run to the Sun Marathon, a grueling trek from sea level up to the 10,000 foot level of Haleakala Crater
- Ice Cream Festival at Maui War Memorial Complex, Wailuku
- Maui Onion Festival at Whalers Village, Kaanapali
- The 21st is Admissions Day, a state holiday
- Earth Maui Nature Summit Environmental Festival. This three-day Kapalua arts and music event includes hands-on activities & workshops as well as hiking, snorkeling and a Rainbow Music Festival

SEPTEMBER
- Maui Music Festival - weekend of jazz and contemporary music at Kaanapali
- Maui County Rodeo in Makawao
- Aloha Festivals (events stretch into October)
- Labor Day Fishing Tournament

SEPTEMBER (Continued)
- The Annual Maui Writers Conference, Labor Day Weekend at The Grand Wailea Resort
- Maui Academy of Performing Arts annual Garden Party
- "Taste of Lahaina" Friday Chef's Dinner followed by two-day Food Festival at Lahaina Center. Maui's biggest food event with over 30 participating restaurants. Proceeds from the festival donated to designated charity each year
- Haku Mele O Hana sponsored by the Hotel Hana-Maui. Traditional song, chant and dance
- Terry Fox Run and Simply Pasta Dinner raises funds for cancer research. Sponsored by Four Seasons Wailea

OCTOBER
- Maui County Fair at the War Memorial Complex in Wailuku
- Open Pro-Am Golf Championship
- Polo Season Begins at the Olinda Polo Field (808) 572-2790
- Parade and Halloween festivities in Lahaina, "The Mardi Gras of the Pacific"
- Lahaina Coolers Historic Fun Run. A 5K run/walk with Lahaina's history with entertainment and re-enactments at each landmark. In conjunction with the Aloha Festival
- Wailea Celebration of Aloha - at Wailea Shopping Village. Cultural festival featuring food and entertainment
- Hawai'i Winter League Season opens at Wailuku Baseball Stadium (242-2950)

NOVEMBER
- Lincoln-Mercury Kapalua International Championship of Golf
- Queen Kaahumanu Festival at the Maui High School
- Hawai'i International Film Festival at Maui Arts & Cultural Center
- Thanksgiving weekend - The Molokai Ranch Rodeo, a statewide event held on the island of Moloka'i combined with the Great Molokai Stew Cook Off and Arts & Crafts Festival
- Thanksgiving weekend
- Santa arrives at Kaahumanu Center
- La Hoomaikai - Thanksgiving luau celebration at Aston Wailea Beach Resort

DECEMBER
- First part of December, Maui's Largest Gala Treelighting Ceremony at The Ritz-Carlton Kapalua, featuring a tree of lights to honor people around the world. Proceeds benefit Maui's Ka Hale A Ke Ola Homeless Resource Center
- Kapalua/Betsy Nagelsen Pro-Am Tennis Invitational
- Bridges Family/Whales Alive Pro-Celebrity Tennis Tournament at Wailea Tennis Club. Celebrity tournament to raise funds for Whales Alive.
- The Na Mele O Maui Festival celebrates Hawai'i's music heritage throughout the Kaanapali Resort. Children's song contest, hula festival, arts and crafts fair.
- Festival of Lights, Lahaina - Santa Claus, holiday treats, festive lights.
- Christmas House at Hui Noeau, near Makawao, is a non-profit organization featuring pottery, wreaths, and other artwork
- Santa arrives by outrigger canoe at Wailea Beach - First Night Maui at Maui Arts & Cultural Center - alcohol-free, family festival to celebrate the New Year

For the exact dates of many of these events, write to the Hawai'i Visitors Bureau, 2270 Kalakaua Avenue #801, Honolulu, HI 96815, and request the Hawai'i Special Events Calendar. The calendar also gives non-annual information and the contact person for each event.

A more complete listing for Maui events can be obtained from the Maui Visitors Bureau, PO Box 580, Wailuku, HI 96793. Check the local papers for dates of additional events.

WEATHER

When thinking of Hawaii, and especially Maui, one visualizes bright sunny days cooled by refreshing trade winds, and this is the weather at least 300 days a year. But what about the other 65 days? Most aren't really bad - just not perfect.

Although there are only two seasons, summer and winter, temperatures remain quite constant. Following are the average daily highs and lows for each month and the general weather conditions.

January	80/64	May	84/67	September	87/70
Feb.	79/64	June	86/69	October	86/69
March	80/64	July	86/70	November	83/68
April	82/66	Aug.	87/71	December	80/66

Winter: Mid October thru April, 70 - 80 degree days, 60 - 70 degree nights. Tradewinds are more erratic, vigorous to none. Kona winds are more frequent causing wide-spread cloudiness, rain showers, mugginess and even an occasional thunderstorm. 11 hours of daylight.

Summer: May thru mid October, 80 degree days, 70 - 80 degree nights. Tradewinds are more consistent keeping the temperatures tolerable. When the trades stop, however, the weather becomes hot and sticky. Kona winds are less frequent. 13 hours of daylight.

Summer type wear is suitable all year round. However, a warm sweater or lightweight jacket is a good idea for evenings and trips to cooler spots like Haleakala.

If you are interested in the types of weather you may encounter, or are confused by some of the terms you hear, read on. For further reference consult *Weather in Hawaiian Waters*, by Paul Haraguchi, 99 pages, available at island bookstores.

TRADE WINDS: Trade winds are an almost constant wind blowing from the northeast through the east and are caused by the Pacific anti-cyclone, a high pressure area. This high pressure area is well developed and remains semi-stationary in the summer causing the trades to remain steady over 90% of the time. Interruptions are much more frequent in the winter when they blow only 40 to 60% of the time. The major resort areas of South and West Maui are situated in the lee of the West Maui Mountains and Haleakala respectively. Here they are sheltered from the trades and the tremendous amount of rain (400 plus inches per year) they bring to the mountains.

KONA WINDS: The Kona Wind is a stormy, rain-bearing wind blowing from the southwest, or basically from the opposite direction of the trades. It brings high and rough surf to the resort side of the island - great for surfing and boogie-boarding, bad for snorkeling. These conditions are caused by low pressure areas northwest of the islands. Kona winds strong enough to cause property damage have occurred only twice since 1970. Lighter non-damaging Kona winds are much more common, occurring 2 - 5 times almost every winter (Nov-April).

KONA WEATHER: Windless, hot and humid weather is referred to as Kona weather. The interruption of the normal trade wind pattern brings this on. The trades are replaced by light and variable winds and, although this may occur any time of the year, it is most noticeable during the summer when the weather is generally hotter and more humid, with fewer localized breezes.

KONA LOW: A Kona low is a slow-moving, meandering, extensive low pressure area which forms near the islands. This causes continuous rain with thunderstorms over an extensive area and lasts for several days. November through May is the most usual time for these to occur.

HURRICANES: Hawai'i is not free of hurricanes. However, most of the threatening tropical cyclones have weakened before reaching the islands, or have passed harmlessly to the west. Their effects are usually minimal, causing only high surf on the eastern and southern shores of some of the islands. At least 21 hurricanes or tropical storms have passed within 300 miles of the islands in the last 33 years, but most did little or no damage.

GINGER

57

Hurricane Dot of 1959, Hurricane Iwa of 1982 and Hurricane Iniki in 1992 caused extensive damage. In each case, the island of Kaua'i was hit hardest, with lesser damage to southeast O'ahu and very little damage to Maui, except for the beaches. Kaua'i has been much slower to recover from the damage caused by the September 1992 Hurricane Iniki, and more than four years following the devastation, there are still several major island resorts that have not yet begun restoration. Some of the difficulties in restoring real estate have been collecting on insurance and finding new companies to insure against future natural disasters.

TSUNAMI: A tsunami is an ocean wave produced by an undersea earthquake, volcanic eruption, or landslide. Tsunamis are usually generated along the coasts of South America, the Aleutian Islands, the Kamchatka Peninsula or Japan and travel through the ocean at 400 to 500 miles an hour. It takes at least 4 1/2 hours for a tsunami to reach the Hawaiian Islands. A 24-hour Tsunami Warning System has been established in Hawai'i since 1946. When the possibility exists of a tsunami reaching Hawaiian waters, the public will be informed by the sound of the attention alert signal sirens. This particular signal is a steady one minute siren, followed by one minute of silence, repeating as long as necessary. If you hear it, turn on a TV or radio immediately; all stations will carry CIV-Alert emergency information and instructions with the arrival time of the first waves. Do not take chances - false alarms are not issued. Move quickly out of low lying coastal areas that are subject to possible inundation. The warning sirens are tested throughout the state on the first working Monday of every month at 11 am. The test lasts only a few minutes and CIV-Alert announces on all stations that the test is underway. Since 1813, there have been 112 tsunamis observed in Hawai'i with only 16 causing significant damage.

Tsunamis may also be generated by local volcanic earthquakes. In the last 100 years there have been only six (the last one was November 29, 1975) affecting the southeast coast of the island of Hawaii. The Hawaiian Civil Defense has placed earthquake sensors on all the islands and, if a violent local earthquake occurs, an urgent tsunami warning will be broadcast and the tsunami sirens will sound. A locally generated tsunami will reach the other islands very quickly. Therefore, there may not be time for an attention alert signal to sound. Any violent earthquake that causes you to fall or hold onto something to prevent falling is an urgent warning, and you should immediately evacuate beaches and coastal low-lying areas. For additional information on warnings and procedures in the event of a hurricane, tsunami, earthquake or flash flood, read the civil defense section located in the forward section of the Maui phone book.

TIDES: The average tidal range is about two feet. Tide tables are available daily in the Maui News or by calling the marine weather number, 877-3477.

SUNRISE AND SUNSET: In Hawaii, day length and the altitude of the noon sun above the horizon do not vary as much throughout the year as at the temperate regions because of the island's low latitude within the sub-tropics. The longest day is 13 hours 26 minutes (sunrise 5:53 am, sunset 7:18 pm) at the end of June, and the shortest day is 10 hours 50 minutes (sunrise 7:09 am and sunset 6:01 pm at the end of December). Daylight for outdoor activities without artificial lighting lasts about 45 minutes past sunset.

WHERE TO STAY
WHAT TO SEE

INTRODUCTION

Maui has more than 16,000 hotel rooms and condominium units in vacation rental programs, with the bulk of the accommodations located in two areas. These are *West Maui*, a 10-mile stretch between *Lahaina* and *Kapalua*, and the South shore of *East Maui*, which is also about ten miles of coastline between Maalaea and Makena, and including *Kihei* and *Wailea*. On the northern side, in the *Kahului/-Wailuku* area, as well in *Upcountry* Maui, accommodations are more limited. In *Hana* there are a number of agencies that provide homes for rent and a few condominiums. This chapter contains a list of essentially all of the condominiums that are in rental programs, as well as the island's hotels. Bed and Breakfast homes are sprinkled around the island, and we have included a few of these along with agencies that have additional listings.

If you are physically impaired, please see our section in the General Information chapter. While many accommodations do have facilities to accommodate the physically impaired, you may encounter difficulty with some of the tourist attractions. Access to many of them is limited.

HOW TO USE THIS CHAPTER: For ease in locating information, the properties are first indexed alphabetically following this introduction. In both South and West Maui, the condominiums have been divided into groups that are geographically distinct and are laid out (sequentially) as you would approach them arriving from the Kahului area. These areas also seem to offer similar price ranges, building style, and beachfronts. At the beginning of each section is a description of the area, sights to see, shopping information, best bets and a sequential listing of the complexes. For each complex, we have listed the local address and/or PO Box and the local, fax and toll-free phone numbers. Often times the management at the property does reservations, other times not.

In many cases there are a variety of rental agents handling units in addition to the on-site management and we have listed an assortment of these. We suggest that when you determine which condo you are interested in that you call all of the agents. Be aware that while one agent may have no vacancy, another will have several. The prices we have listed are generally the lowest available (although some agents may offer lower rates with the reduction of certain services such as maid service on check in only - that means your room is clean when you arrive - rather than daily maid service). Unfortunately, we've had at least one occasion where the cheaper rate resulted in a condo that needed not only a good cleaning, but complete renovation. On the other hand, a reputable rental agent will not let a unit fall into disrepair. We can recommend ***Maui & All Island Condominiums***. Be sure to ask about their seasonal specials! ***Kihei Maui Vacations*** is a also very good with their broad range of properties in South Maui, and ***Whalers Realty*** in West Maui offers moderate to expensive properties at rates lower than the posted rack rates. At the end of the accommodations chapter is an alphabetical listing of rental agents and the properties they handle. Prices can vary, sometimes greatly, from one agent to another, so we suggest again that you contact them all.

Prices are listed to aid your selection and, while these were the most current available at press time, they are subject to change without notice. As island vacationers ourselves, we found it important to include this feature rather than just giving you broad categories such as budget or expensive. After all, one person's "expensive" may be "budget" to someone else!

For the sake of space, we have made use of several abbreviations. The size of the condominiums are identified as studio (S BR), one bedroom (1 BR), two bedroom (2 BR) and three bedroom (3 BR). The numbers in parenthesis refers to the number of people that can occupy the unit for the price listed and that there are enough beds for a maximum number of people to occupy this unit. The description will tell you how much it will be for additional persons over two, i.e. each additional person $10/night. Some facilities consider an infant as an extra person, others will allow children free up to a specified age. The abbreviations o.f., g.v., and o.v. refer to oceanfront, gardenview and oceanview units.

The prices are listed with a slash dividing them. The first price listed is the high season rate, the second price is the low season rate. A few have a flat yearly rate so there will be only be a single price.

All listings are condominiums unless specified as a (Hotel). Condos are abundant, and the prices and facilities they offer can be quite varied. We have tried to indicate our own personal preferences by the use of a ★. We felt these were the best buys or special in some way. However, it is impossible for us to stay in or view all the units within a complex, and since condominiums are privately owned, each unit can vary in its furnishings and its condition.

WHERE TO STAY: As for choosing the area of the island in which to stay, we offer these suggestions. The Lahaina and Kaanapali areas offer the visitor the hub of the island's activities, but accommodations are a little more costly. The beaches are especially good at Kaanapali.

The values and choice of condos are more extensive a little beyond Kaanapali in Honokowai, Kahana (Lower Honoapiilani Hwy. area) and further at Napili. However, there are fewer restaurants here with slightly cooler temperatures, and, often times, more rain. Some of the condominiums in this area, while very adequate, may be a little overdue for redecorating. While many complexes are on nice beaches, many are also on rocky shores.

Kapalua offers high class and high price condominium and hotel accommodations. Maalaea and Kihei are a half-hour drive from Lahaina and offer some attractive condo units at excellent prices and, although few are located on a beach, there are plenty of easily accessible public beach parks.

Many Maui vacationers feel that Kihei offers better weather in the winter months, and this may be true with annual rainfall only about 3" on Maui's southern shore.

There are plenty of restaurants here and an even broader selection by driving the short distance to Wailuku.

The Wailea and Makena areas are just beyond Kihei and are beautifully developed resort areas. The beaches are excellent for a variety of water activities, however, it is significantly more expensive than the neighboring Kihei. The introductory section to each area offers additional information.

HOW TO SAVE MONEY: Maui has two price seasons. High or "in" season and low or "off" season. Low season is generally considered to be April 15 to about December 15, and the rates are discounted at some places as much as 30%. Different resorts and condominiums may vary these dates by as much as two weeks and a few resorts are going to a flat, year round rate. Ironically, some of the best weather is during the fall when temperatures are cooler than summer and there is less rain than the winter and spring months. (See GENERAL INFORMA-TION - Weather for year round temperatures). For longer than one week, a condo unit with a kitchen can result in significant savings on your food bill. While this will give you more space than a hotel room and at a lower price, you may give up some resort amenities (shops, restaurants, maid service, etc.). There are several large grocery stores around the island with fairly competitive prices, although most things at the store will run slightly higher than on the mainland. (See GENERAL INFORMATION - Shopping.)

Money can be saved by using the following tips when choosing a place to settle. First, it is less expensive to stay during the off or low season. Second, there are some areas that are much less expensive. Although Kahului has some motel units, we can't recommend this area as a place to headquarter your stay. The weather is wetter in winter, hotter in summer, generally windier than the other side of the island, and there are few good beaches. Two renovated old hotels in Wailuku now offer serviceable, basic and affordable accommodations for the budget minded, and they should especially appeal to the windsurfing community with nearby Hookipa Beach. There are a couple of hostel type accommodations also in this area. There are some good deals in the Maalaea and Kihei areas, and the northern area above Lahaina has some older complexes that are reasonably good values. Third, there are some pleasant condo units either across the road from the beach or on a rocky, less attractive beach. This can represent a tremendous savings, and there are always good beaches a short walk or drive away. Fourth, hotel rooms or condos with garden or mountain views are less costly than oceanview or oceanfront rooms. We find the mountainview, especially in Kaanapali, to be, in fact, superior. The mountains are simply gorgeous and we'd rather be on the beach than look at it!

Most condominiums offer maid service only on check-out. A few might offer it twice a week or weekly. Additional maid service may be available for an extra charge. A few condos still do not provide in-room phones or color televisions, and fewer still have no pool. (A few words of caution: condominium units within one complex can differ greatly and, if a phone is important to you, ask!) Many are adding microwaves to their kitchens. Some may also add up to $1 per in-room local call, others have no extra charge for local calls. Some units have washers and dryers in the rooms, while others do not. Many have coin-operated laundry facilities on the premises.

61

Travel agents will be able to book your stay in the Maui hotels and also in most condominiums. If you prefer to make your own reservation, we have listed the various contacts for each condominium and endeavored to quote the best price generally available. Rates vary between rental agents, so check all those listed for a particular condominium. We have indicated toll free 800 numbers for the U.S. when available. For additional Canadian toll free numbers, check the rental agent list at the end of this chapter. Look for an 808 area code preceding the non-toll free numbers. You might also check the classified ads in your local newspaper for owners offering their units, which may be a better bargain.

Although prices can jump, most go up only 5-10% per year. Prices listed do not include the sales tax which is over 9%.

GENERAL POLICIES: Condominium complexes require a deposit, usually equivalent to one or two nights stay, to secure your reservation and insure your room rate from price increases. Some charge higher deposits during winter or over Christmas holidays. Generally a 30 day notice of cancellation is needed to receive a full refund. Most require payment in full either 30 days prior to arrival or upon arrival, and many do not accept credit cards.

The usual minimum condo stay is three nights with some requiring one week in winter. Christmas holidays may have steeper restrictions with minimum stays as long as two weeks, payments 90 days in advance and heavy cancellation penalties. It is not uncommon to book as much as two years in advance for the Christmas season. ALL CONDOMINIUMS HAVE KITCHENS, TV'S., AND POOLS UNLESS OTHERWISE SPECIFIED.

Monthly and often times weekly discounts are available. Room rates quoted are generally for two people. Additional persons run $8 - $15 per night per person with the exception of the high class resorts and hotels where it may run as much as $25 to $35 extra. Many complexes can arrange for crib rentals. (See GENERAL INFORMATION - Traveling with Children.)

We have tried to give the lowest rates generally available, which might not be through the hotel or condo office, so check with the offices as well as the rental agents. When contacting condominium complexes by mail, be sure to address your correspondence to the attention of the manager. The managers of several complexes do not handle any reservations so we have indicated to whom you should address reservation requests at these properties. If two addresses are given, use the PO Box rather than street address.

BED AND BREAKFAST

An alternative to condominiums and hotels are the Bed and Breakfast organizations. They offer homes around the island, and some very reasonable rates. *Bed & Breakfast Hawai'i* is among the best known. To become a member and receive their directory (which also includes the other islands) contact: *Bed and Breakfast Hawaii*, Directory of Homes, Box 449, Kapaa, HI 96746. Another organization, *Bed and Breakfast Maui Style* can be reached at PO Box 886, Kihei, HI 96753 or (808-879-7865) or (808-879-2352). *Go Native Hawai'i* also features bed and breakfast vacation accommodations. Contact them at PO Box 13115, Lansing, MI 48901, phone (517-349-9598). Following are just a few of the Bed and Breakfast selections offered on Maui (you can book the following directly).

Ahinahina Farm Vacation Bungalows, 210 Ahinahina Place, Kula, HI 96790. (808-878-3294), FAX (808) 878-3927 ext. 5. Located upcountry, they offer studio and cottage rentals. Two night minimum. No smoking. No children under age 12. 50% deposit, full payment on arrival. Fourteen day cancellation. They accept traveler's checks, Visa and MasterCard. Rates are 1-2 persons $95, cottage 1-2 persons $115, 3-4 persons $150. The studio can accommodate one or two. The two bedroom cottage can accommodate up to four. Both units have queen beds, full bath, TV and private deck.

Ann & Bob Babson's B & B Vacation Rentals, 3371 Keha Drive, Kihei, Maui, HI 96753. (808) 874-1166, fax (808) 879-7906 or toll free from the mainland 1-800-824-6409. The Babson's offer four vacation rentals with panoramic Pacific Ocean views in Maui Meadows, a residential area, located above Wailea on the Southwest side of Maui. All rentals include cable TV, telephone, and washer/dryer. The main house is situated on a half acre and offers a Bougainvillea Suite (bedroom with private bath), Molokini Master Suite (Master BR with private bath & jacuzzi) or Hibiscus Hideaway Apartment (1 BR 1 BTH w/ kitchen) $70-85. 2BR 2BTH cottage w/kitchen $105 single/double, each additional person $10 up to maximum of 6 persons.

Banyan Tree House, 3265 Baldwin Avenue, Makawao, HI 96768. (808-572-9021) FAX (808) 573-2842. Located upcountry they offer plantation house bedrooms with private bathrooms and a studio cottage with open lanai and kitchen. Rates from $85 per night include full breakfast. (Editors note: Few B&B's in Hawai'i really serve a cooked breakfast, so this is a treat!) Your hosts are Anthony Edington & Yasamin Alarab, who also happen to be a French-trained chef and a massage therapist. Also available are lunches "to-go" and special dinners and banquets by arrangement. They are currently offering a once a month evening supper club. Each course is accompanied by wine. We heard a rave review by one who recently attended.

WATER LILY

Bed & Breakfast

Blue Horizons, PO Box 10578, Lahaina, HI 96761. (808) 669-1965 or 1-800-669-1948. Located between Kaanapali and Kapalua they offer a one bedroom apartment, studio or traditional bed and breakfast room. Kitchen, lap pool, laundry facilities, air conditioning. Rates $60-75. Hosts: Jim and Beverly Spence.

Garden Gate, PO Box 12321, Lahaina, Maui, HI 96771. (808-661-8800), FAX (808) 667-7999. Hosts Ron & Welmoet Glover began their B&B in 1991 after spending time at B&B's on a trip to Europe. Their garden is filled with plumeria, pikake, ginger and other tropical flowers and a six-person hot tub sits beneath a large coral tree. They offer a 500 sq. foot garden studio with its own private entrance, private lanai with fountain, kitchen, bathroom, queen bed and sleeper sofa. Room rate is $95 for two. Their Molokai Room is $55 for two and located in the home and is a more traditional B&B. It offers a full size bed with a private bathroom across the hall. The room offers a small refrigerator, fan and air conditioning with use of phone and TV in the main house. Their Molokai Room offers a full bed and private bath. Children accepted. Located at 67 Kaniau Road, just outside of Lahaina.

Halfway to Hana House, PO Box 675, Haiku, HI 96708. (808-572-1176). FAX (808) 572-3609. They offer a studio with breakfast $65 double, $55 single, or without breakfast $55 double, $50 single. Two night minimum, 10% weekly discounts. The studio offers a private entrance, bathroom, double bed, mini-kitchen and outdoor covered patio.

Hamoa Bay Bungalow, PO Box 773, Hana, HI 96713. 1-808-248-7884. FAX (808) 248-8642. This 600 sq. ft. studio cottage has a fully equipped kitchen, including a blender, ice maker and even a coffee maker with grinder. A king-size bed, jacuzzi bath for two, CD/tape player, VCR with mini movie library, micro-wave, phone, laundry facilities, and filtered drinking water. Rate includes breakfast, $135 for two.

House of Fountains, 1579 Lokia Street, Lahaina, HI 96761. (808-667-2121) 1-800-789-6865. Located between Lahaina and Kaanapali, three blocks from the beach. Accommodations in their 7,000 square foot home. Rooms furnished with queen bed, private bath, air conditioning, $90 and up.

Maluhia Hale, PO Box 687, Haiku, HI 96708. (808-572-2959). Located at Twin Falls, about 25 miles past the airport. Diane Garrett rents a private plantation style cottage. The cottage is furnished with a king-size bed and additional double bed in the sitting room. The furnishings are antiques that reflect the plantation era. There is a kitchenette stocked with coffee and tea and they serve a light breakfast of fruit and muffins on your first morning. There is a glassed-in sitting room and a screened veranda for indoor/outdoor sitting and relaxing. $75 per night, two night minimum.

Kula Cottage, Write: 380 Hoohana St., Kahului, HI 96732. (808-871-6230 or 878-2043.) FAX (808) 871-9187. Cecilia and Larry Gilbert offer an upcountry cottage. The one bedroom cottage offers a queen size bed. Other amenities include a wood-burning fireplace (yes!), a full kitchen, TV and VCR, private driveway, and barbecue. Two night minimum stay. One night deposit. $85 per night.

Kula View B & B, PO Box 322, Kula, HI 96790. (808-878-6736). Located on two acres in the cool Upcountry region on the slopes of Haleakala. They offer private room, bath and deck with own entrance. $85 single or double occupancy. Your host, Susan Kauai, is descended from a kamaaina Hawai'i family.

Kula Lynn Farm, PO Box 847, Kula, HI 96789. (808-878-6176) or FAX (808) 878-6320. Your hosts are a part of the Coon family (Trilogy Excursions) and they offer several rooms, two full baths, kitchen (with a refrigerator stocked with breakfast fixings) and living room, on the ground level of their home. The home is located on the slopes of Haleakala, in lower Kula. $85 single or double, $10 each additional person, max. 6 persons. Three night minimum.

Maui-What A Wonderful World, Bed & Breakfast (808-879-9103) or cellular (808-283-1414). Jim and Eva Tantillo share their Hawaiian style pole home with island visitors. They have two one bedroom/one bath suites and one studio suite, all with complete cooking facilities, private baths and entrances, along with phones. Additional amenities include air conditioning, TV/VCR, hot tubs, and BBQ grill. Kamaole II beach is 1/2 mile away. They also offer guests the use of beach towels, chairs, coolers, snorkel gear, and boogie boards.

Old Lahaina House Bed & Breakfast, PO Box 10355, Lahaina, HI 96761. (808-667-4663), 1-800-847-0761, FAX (808) 667-5615. Hosts John and Sherry Barbier offer rooms in their home in the historic Lahaina area. Their $60 rooms with two twin beds, air conditioning, phone, television and private baths $60-69. They have a new room that will have either a queen size sleeper sofa, or double bed, air conditioning, TV, phone, private bath and private entrance at $60-69. Two rooms with private bath, king size bed, air-conditioning, refrigerator at $95. Swimming pool, Hawaiian continental breakfast. They are across the street from a neighborhood beach and four blocks from Lahaina Harbor.

Pilialoha Bed & Breakfast Cottage, 2512 Kaupakalua Rd., Haiku, HI 96708. (808-572-1440). Hosts Bill & Machiko Heyde offer a cottage with fully equipped kitchen, phone, and washer/dryer. Rate is $95 for single/double occupancy, $10 each additional person. Located in Upcountry Maui, near Makawao.

Silver Cloud Upcountry Guest Ranch, Old Thompson Rd., RR2 Box 201, Kula, Maui, HI 96790. (808-878-6101). FAX (808) 878-2132. Silver Cloud Ranch was originally part of the Thompson Ranch, which had its beginnings on Maui in 1902. The nine-acre ranch is located at the 2,800 ft. elevation on the slopes of Haleakala.

Owners Mike and Sara Gerry have done major renovations and now offer 12 rooms, suites and cottages, each with private bathrooms and most with private lanais and entrances. The King Kamehameha and Queen Emma suites are located in the main house with a private lanai and view of the lush Upcountry. The Lana'i Cottage offers total privacy with a complete kitchen, clawfooted bathtub, and woodburning stove surrounded by a lovely flower garden and lanai. The Paniolo Bunkhouse has studios that are furnished in Hawaiian motif. They offer kitchenettes and lanais. The Bunkhouse's Haleakala suite is a larger facility with a bedroom, separate living area, fireplace and complete kitchen. All room rates include breakfast and use of the main house and kitchen. No minimum stay, and discounts for seven nights or longer. Plantation Home Bedrooms with private baths $75-$95 and suites $110. Paniolo Bunkhouse Suites $95-$135. Lanai Cottage $135.

Tony's Place, 13 Kauala Rd., Lahaina, Maui, HI 96761. (808-661-8040). Located at the corner of Kauala Rd. and Front Street. Lodging with kitchen privileges in a simply furnished home. He offers three rooms with double or twin beds, but notes "that some couples have opted to put the two twins in their room together while guesting here instead of staying elsewhere. I don't think the room is attractive that way but if they are happy, usually, so am I." Tony Mamo, a would-be writer moved from Alaska to Hawai'i in 1990 and in addition to running his guest home he works as a journeyman electrician. Complimentary Kona coffee each morning, continental breakfast $4.50. Tax included $45 single, $55 double. Two night minimum stay. Visa and mastercard accepted.

Wai Ola, PO Box 12580, Lahaina, HI 96761. (808-661-7901 fax/phone) 1-800-492-4652. Host Julie Frank offers a 500 sq. ft. studio and a one bedroom apartment. Both include full kitchens, queen bed. Pool, jacuzzi, air conditioning, and private phone. Located two blocks to beach. Rates run $60-100.

PRIVATE RESIDENCES

For a large family, a couple of families, or a group of friends, a vacation home rather than a condo, may be a more spacious and cost effective option. Homes are available in all areas of the island. Following are a list of agents.

Bello Realty-Maui Beach Homes, PO Box 1776, Kihei, Maui, HI 96753. (808-879-2598). 1-800-541-3060 U.S. & Canada. Condos and homes rented by the day, week or month. Specializing in the Kihei area.

Elite Properties Unlimited, PO Box 5273, Lahaina, Maui, HI 96761. 1-800-448-9222 U.S. & Canada, (808-665-0561). Family homes and luxury estates (3-7 bedrooms) available on all four major islands. Weekly and monthly rentals. One week minimum. Maid service, chefs and concierge services available.

Hana Alii Holidays, PO Box 536, Hana, Maui, HI. 1-800-548-0478 or (808-248-7742). They handle rental homes and condos in Hana, Maui.

Hana Bay Vacation Rentals, Stan Collins offers eight homes in the Hana area. Contact Hana Bay Vacation Rentals, PO Box 318, Hana, Maui, HI 96713. (808-248-7727).

Hana Plantation Houses, PO Box 249, Hana, Maui, HI 96713. 1-800-228-HANA. (808-248-7049). They offer rental houses on Moloka'i and in Hana, Maui.

Hawaiian Apartment Leasing Enterprise, 479 Ocean Ave., Suite B., Laguna Beach, CA 92651. 1-800-472-8449 California, 1-800-854-8843 U.S. except California, 1-800-824-8968. 150 plus homes and 90 condominium properties on all islands.

Kathy Scheper's Maui Accommodations, (808-879-8744), 1-800-645-3753, FAX (808) 879-9100. Kathy offers a beach cottage and studio located on her property in Kihei. The rates are hard to beat!

The cottage sleeps four. The studio is suited for one or two on a budget. It includes a small refrigerator, microwave oven, color TV and a half bath. A private tropical garden patio has a private outdoor shower. The beach is a short walk away. She also rents units at the Kai Nani Beach Condo. Beach Cottage $80/65, Studio $49/39.

Kihei Maui Vacations, 1-800-542-6284 US, 1-800-423-8733 ext. 4000 Canada (808-879-7581). In addition to condos they offer homes and cottages in the Kihei, Wailea and Makena areas.

Maui and All Islands, PO Box 1089, Aldergrove, BC V0X 1A0. U.S. Mailing address PO Box 947, Lynden, WA 98264. 1-800-663-6962 from B.C. and Alberta, Canada. (604) 533-4190. Approximately 150 homes rented weekly, bi-weekly and monthly on Kaua'i and Maui.

Maui Condo and Home Realty, PO Box 1840, Kihei, Maui, Hi 96753. 1-800-822-3309 U.S., 1-800-822-4409 U.S. & Canada, (808-879-5445). Homes and condos rented daily, weekly and monthly. They currently have 400 individual units at 17 properties in Kihei and Wailea.

Maui Dream Cottages, 265 W. Kuiaha Rd., Haiku, HI 96708. (808-575-9079), FAX (808) 575-9477. Gregg Blue offers several rental cottages and homes. Halelea, (House of Joy), is a 3,650 square foot home with three bedrooms, four baths and includes a self-contained pool house cottage with kitchen and bath. It rents for $350 per night with a one week minimum. He also has two "Dream Cottages" located in Haiku.

Windsurfing West, Ltd., PO Box 1359, Haiku, HI 96708 1-800-782-6105. (808-575-9228), FAX (808-575-2826). They have continued to broaden and diversify their list of rental condominiums to cover the North Shore, South Shore and Upcountry properties. Along with condos they have rental homes and cottages. Even if you're not a windsurfer, you might want to check into their Accommodations Only packages! For their windsurfing guests they can arrange equipment rentals and lessons.

LONG-TERM STAYS

Almost all condo complexes and rental agents offer the long term visitor moderate to substantial discounts for stays of one month or more. Private homes can also be booked through the agents listed above.

CONDOMINIUM & HOTEL INDEX

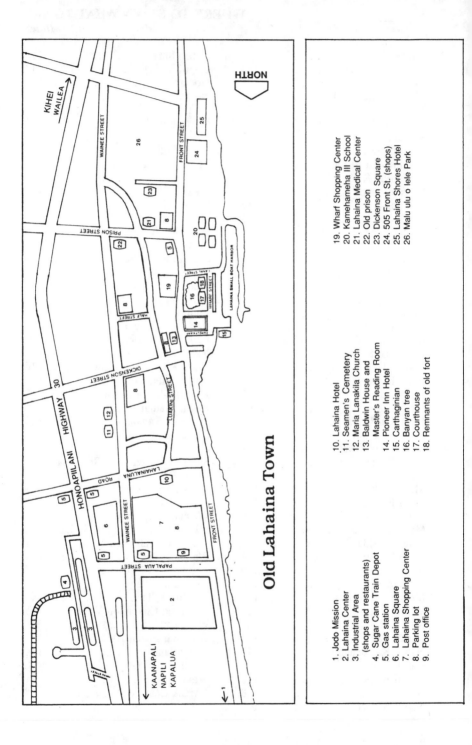

Old Lahaina Town

1. Jodo Mission
2. Lahaina Center
3. Industrial Area
   (shops and restaurants)
4. Sugar Cane Train Depot
5. Gas station
6. Lahaina Square
7. Lahaina Shopping Center
8. Parking lot
9. Post office
10. Lahaina Hotel
11. Seamen's Cemetery
12. Maria Lanakila Church
13. Baldwin House and
    Master's Reading Room
14. Pioneer Inn Hotel
15. Carthaginian
16. Banyan tree
17. Courthouse
18. Remnants of old fort
19. Wharf Shopping Center
20. Kamehameha III School
21. Lahaina Medical Center
22. Old prison
23. Dickenson Square
24. 505 Front St. (shops)
25. Lahaina Shores Hotel
26. Malu ulu o lele Park

LAHAINA

INTRODUCTION

As you leave the Kahului area on Hwy. 38, you plunge immediately into Maui's central valley. The rugged and deeply carved valleys of the West Maui mountains are on the right, and on the left is the dormant volcano, *Haleakala*. Its broad base and seemingly gentle slopes belie its 11,000 foot height, and no hint of its enormous moon-like crater is discernible from below. On a clear day the mountains are so distinct and sharp-edged they appear to have been cut out with giant scissors. The drive across the isthmus ends quickly as you pass Maalaea Harbor where the gently swaying sugar cane gives way to rugged sea cliffs and panoramic Pacific vistas. Across the bay is the South Maui coastline and in the distance the islands of Kaho'olawe and Lana'i. Construction of this road was to accommodate the new resort developments at Kaanapali that began in the 1960's. Traffic must have been far different on the old road which is still visible in places along the craggy cliffside of the pali. The pull off along the roadside offers an ideal vantage point from which to do a little whale watching December through April. A hiking trail over the pali was recently refurbished. The tunnel, built in 1951, is the only one on Maui. Just beyond it are enormous metal chain blankets hanging along the rocky cliffs above the road. Termed a protective measure by some and an eyesore by others, they were installed in 1987.

As you descend from the cliffs, the first glimpse of the tropical and undeveloped West Maui coastline is always a thrill. Stretching as far as the eye can see are sugar cane fields hugging the lower slopes of the mountains and a series of narrow, white sand beaches lined by kiawe trees and coconut palms. For several miles the constant stream of traffic is the only clue to the populated areas ahead. The first sign of civilization is Olowalu, a mere hamlet along the roadside and an unusual location for one of the island's best restaurants, Chez Paul. Public beaches line the highway and the unobstructed view of the ocean is a visual feast.

A few homes to the left and the monolithic smoke stack of the Pioneer Mill announce your arrival to *Lahaina*, the now bustling tourist center of Maui. It has maintained the aura of more than a century ago when it was the whaling capitol of the world. Located about a 45 minute drive from the Kahului Airport (depending on traffic), this coastal port is noted for its Front Street, which is a multi-block strip of shops and restaurants along the waterfront. The Lahaina Harbor is filled with boats of varying shapes and sizes, eager to take the visitor aboard for a variety of sea excursions.

The oldest accommodation on the island, Pioneer Inn, is located here. Still popular among many a visitor, it offers a nostalgic and rustic atmosphere, and reasonable prices. Other accommodations include a luxuriously expensive condominium complex, several priced in the moderate range, two charming country-style inns and a number of bed & breakfasts. Although several complexes are located oceanfront, the beaches in Lahaina are fronted by a close-in reef which prohibits swimming. Only Puamana has a beach suitable for swimming. If you want to be in the midst of the action on Maui, you might want to investigate staying in this area.

WHAT TO DO AND SEE

There is much to see and do in busy Lahaina Town. The word *Lahaina* means "merciless sun," and it does tend to become quite warm, especially in the afternoon with little relief from the tropical trade winds. Parking can be somewhat irksome. Several all day lots are located near the corner of Wainee and Dickenson (only a couple of blocks off Front Street) and the charge is about $5 for all day. One nearer to Front Street charges $7 per day. The inexpensive lots fill up early in the day. The Old Lahaina Center (formerly Lahaina Shopping Center) has a three hour (free) parking area, but it is always very crowded. New Lahaina Center, across the street from the Lahaina Shopping Center, has pay parking, validated with purchase from one of the stores. If you don't mind a short walk, parking is available across the road from the 505 Front Street shops. (See the Lahaina map for locations of other parking areas.) On-street parking is very limited and if you are fortunate enough to find a spot, many are only for one hour. BEWARE: the police here are quite prompt and efficient at towing.

There is no longer any free shuttle service. In West Maui there is one private company which offers bus service between Kapalua and Lahaina with lots of stops in-between. Transhawaiian, aka the Maui Shopping Express travels along West Maui making stops at most of the major hotels. The *Maui Shopping Express* (877-0380) also offers shuttle service to Kaahumanu Center, K-Mart and Costco, Kihei Town, Wailea Resort, Makena Resort and Kahului Airport. They offer a one-day pass for unlimited travel at $30. A trip from Lahaina/Kaaanpali to Kaahumanu Center is $20 round trip. Transportation between Lahaina and any stop up to Kapalua is $1 for adults. They operate 9:30 am-7:30 pm.

Now that you have arrived, let's get started. Historical memorabilia abounds in Lahaina. The Lahaina Restoration Foundation has done an admirable job restoring and maintaining many historical landmarks. If you have questions, contact their office at 661-3262. The historical landmarks have all been identified by numbered markers. A free walking tour map of Lahaina can be found in a copy of the Lahaina Historical Guide. Look for free copies of this pocket-size guide on corner display racks in Lahaina Town. Then enjoy your walking tour of the Baldwin House, *the Brig Carthaginian*, Masters Reading Room, and Wo Hing Temple.

CARTHAGINIAN

The Banyan Tree is very easy to spot at the south end of Lahaina adjacent to Pioneer Inn on Front Street. It was planted on April 24, 1873 by Sheriff William Owen Smith, it was to commemorate the 50th anniversary of Lahaina's first Protestant Christian Mission. You may find art shows or other events happening under the cool, shady boughs of this magnificent arbor. With its long, heavy limbs supported by wood braces and 12 solid trunks that have re-rooted themselves over a 200-foot area, visitors find it hard to believe that this is all one tree!

The stone ruins of *The Old Fort* can be found harborside near the Banyan Tree. The fort was constructed in the 1830's to protect the missionaries' homes from the whaling ships and the occasional cannonball that would be shot off when the sailors were too rowdy. The fort was later torn down and the coral blocks reused elsewhere. A few blocks have been excavated and the corner of the fort was rebuilt as a landmark in 1964. On the corner near the Pioneer Inn is a plaque marking the site of the 1987 Lahaina Reunion Time Capsule, which contains newspapers, photos and other memorabilia.

Pioneer Inn is the distinguished green and white structure just north of the Banyan Tree. It was a haven for inter-island travelers during the early days of the 20th century. Built back in 1901, it managed to survive the dry years of prohibition, adding a new wing, center garden and pool area in 1966. Two restaurants operate here and accommodations are available. The history of Pioneer Inn is an interesting one and is discussed under the accommodation information which follows. (See RESTAURANTS - Lahaina and WHERE TO STAY - Lahaina for additional information.)

The *Lahaina Courthouse* was built in 1859, at a cost of $7,000, from wood and stone taken from the palace of Kamehameha II. You'll find it near the Lahaina Harbor. Recently the county council approved $600,000 toward renovation of this historic landmark. No decision has been made as to the use of the renovated second floor space. The first floor houses the Lahaina Art Society on one side and the *Lahaina Visitors Center* on the other. The Lahaina Visitors Center is open from 9 am - 5 pm. They dispense information that is "free, friendly and unbiased." There is also a small gift shop and a rack of brochures.

In front of Pioneer Inn is the *Lahaina Harbor*. You can stroll down and see the boats and visit stalls where a wide variety of water sports and tours can be arranged. (See RECREATION AND TOURS) *The Brig Carthaginian,* anchored just outside the harbor, is a replica of a 19th century square rigger, typical of the ships that brought the first missionaries and whalers to these shores. The first *Carthaginian* sank on Easter Sunday, April 2, 1972. It had been built in 1921 in Denmark as a schooner and the 130 foot vessel had sailed the world as a cargo ship. She was purchased by Tucker Thompson and sailed to Hawai'i in 1964. Her original name was *Wandia*, but was rechristened *Carthaginian* in Honolulu with a bottle of passion fruit juice. The ship was used in the South Pacific for a time and later was restored to resemble a whaling vessel for the movie version of Michener's *Hawai'i*. The Lahaina Restoration Foundation worked to acquire the *Carthaginian* for $75,000. The ship found a home at the Lahaina wharf, becoming an exhibit of the whaling era. On June 20, 1971 it was discovered by the ship's skipper, Don Bell, that the vessel was sinking. The ship was pumped and a large hole was patched, the cause seeming to be dry rot.

It was decided the following year to tow her to Honolulu for repairs in dry dock. However, 150 yards from dock she became lodged on the reef and valiant efforts to save her were not successful. An immediate search began for a replacement and it was found in the Danish port of Soby. The ship was a 97 foot steel hulled freighter that had originally been a schooner, but had been demasted. The ship called *Komet* had been built in the shipyards in Germany in 1920 and was purchased for $20,500.

An all-Lahaina crew sailed via the Panama Canal and arrived in Hawai'i in September, 1973. Volunteers set to work transforming the ship to the proud vessel it is today and it was christened *Brig Carthaginian* on April 26, 1980. Today the ship features video movies and recorded songs of humpback whales and an authentic 19th century whale boat. All items are on display below deck. The ship is open daily from 10 am-4:30 pm. Admission $3 adults, seniors $2 and children free.

Whale watching is always an exciting pastime in Lahaina. The whales usually arrive in December to breed and calve in the warm waters off Maui for several months.There is also a number to call to report any sightings you make: WHALE WATCH HOTLINE at 879-8811. Numerous whale watching excursions are available. (See RECREATION AND TOURS.)

Adjacent to the *Carthaginian* is the oldest Pacific lighthouse. "It was on this site in 1840 that King Kamehameha III ordered a nine foot wooden tower built as an aid to navigation for the whaling ships. It was equipped with whale oil lamps kept burning at night by a Hawaiian caretaker who was paid $20 a year." In 1866 it increased to 26 feet in size and was again rebuilt in 1905. The present structure of concrete was dedicated in 1916. (Information from an engraved plaque placed on the lighthouse by the Lahaina Restoration Foundation.)

The Hauola Stone or Healing Rock can be found near the Lahaina Harbor. Look for the cluster of rocks marked with a Visitors Bureau "warrior" sign. The rock, resembling a chair, was believed to have healing properties which could be obtained by merely sitting in it with feet dangling in the surf. Here you will also find remnants of the **Brick Palace** of Kamehameha the Great. Vandals destroyed the display which once showed examples of the original mud bricks.

The Baldwin Home is across Front Street from Pioneer Inn. Built during 1834-1835, it housed the Reverend Dwight Baldwin and his family from 1837 to 1871. Tours of the home, furnished as it was in days gone by, are given between the hours of 10 am and 4:30 pm. Adults are $3, seniors $2, no charge for children or a family rate of $5. The empty lot adjacent was once the home of Reverend William Richards, and a target of attack by cannonballs from angry sailors during the heyday of whaling. On the other side of the Baldwin Home is the Masters' Reading Room. Built in 1833, it is the oldest structure on Maui. Its original purpose was to provide a place of leisure for visiting sea captains. It is not open to the public at this time.

Hale Paahao (The Old Prison) on Prison Street just off Wainee is only a short trek from Front Street. Upon entry you'll notice the large gate house which the Lahaina Restoration Foundation reconstructed to its original state in 1988. Nearby is a 60 year old Royal Palm, and in the courtyard an enormous 150 year old breadfruit tree. The cell block was built in 1852 to house the unruly sailors from the whaling vessels and to replace the old fort. It was reconstructed in 1959. In 1854 coral walls (the blocks taken from the old fort) were constructed. The jail was used until the 1920s when it was relocated to the basement of the Lahaina Court House next to the Harbor. While you're at Hale Paahao be sure to say hello to the jail's only tenant, George. He is a wax replica of a sailor who is reported to have had a few too many brews at Uncle Henry's Front Street Beer House back in the 1850's, then missed his ship's curfew and was tossed into jail by Sheriff William O. Smith. George will briefly converse with you by means of a taped recording. The grounds are open to the public daily, no charge.

The construction of the *Waiola Church* began in 1828 on what was then called the Wainee Church. The original church was made of stone and was large enough to accommodate 3,000 people. Hale Aloha was built in 1858 as a branch of the Wainee Church and was used as a school. It was named House of Love as a way of giving thanks that the citizens of Lahaina did not suffer in a smallpox epidemic that ravaged the island of O'ahu during 1853. The Waiola Church is now a United Church of Christ with worship in Hawaiian and English.

In 1951 a fierce wind, called a Kaua'ula wind, seriously damaged the church and Hale Aloha. The wind is named for a narrow valley in the mountains above Lahaina called Kaua'ula, through which the wind blows and gains force. Legend has it that the wind blows when the ali'i die. Among the damage incurred during the wind of 1951 was the loss of the Hale Aloha belfry. Hale Aloha and the church were both sold to the county in the 1960s. In 1996 the bellfry was restored as a result of efforts of the Lahaina Restoration Foundation. The bell should be arriving one of these days. *Hale Aloha* is now fully restored and used as a framing shop for Lahaina Printsellers.

In the neighboring cemetery you will find tombs of several notable members of Hawaiian royalty, including Queen Keopuolani, wife of Kamehameha the Great and mother of Kamehameha II and III. The church is located on Wainee and Shaw Streets. The *Maria Lanakila Church* is on the corner of Wainee and Dickenson. Built in 1928, it is a replica of the 1858 church. Next door is the Seamen's Cemetery.

The *Hawaiian Experience Omni Theatre* ★ at 824 Front Street occupies what was once the site of the old Queen's Theatre and has been recycled into a theatre once again. The seating for 150 persons is such that everyone gets an unobstructed view of the 180 degree screen which curves up and to the sides of the auditorium. The history of the islands is narrated as the viewer is thrilled to a bird's eye view of the remote Hawaiian leeward islands of Tern, Nihoa and Necker. Travel through the jungles and volcanoes of the major islands as well as the underwater world of the Pacific. The adults in our group found the show realistic enough to cause an occasional "seasick" sensation (especially the bike ride down Haleakala), but the kids were riveted and motionless for the 40 minute show. The film, "Hawaii: Island of the Gods," is an informative as well as entertaining show and the air-conditioned comfort is a pleasant break from the warm sidewalk shopping in Lahaina. The show is offered hourly from 10 am - 10 pm. $6.95 adults, children 4 - 12 $3.95, under 3 are free. Phone 661-8314.

The Wo Hing Temple on Front Street opened following restoration in late 1984. Built in 1912, it now houses a museum which features the influence of the Chinese population on Maui. Hours are 10 am - 4:30 pm with a $1 admission donation appreciated. The adjacent cook house has become a theater which features movies filmed by Thomas Edison during his trips to Hawai'i in 1898 and 1906. In 1993 a new Koban information booth was added near the Wo Hing Temple.

A small, but interesting **Whaling Museum** is located in the Crazy Shirts shop on Front Street. No admission is charged.

Follow Front Street towards Kaanapali to find **The Seamen's Hospital**. This structure was once a hideaway for King Kamehameha III and a gaming house for sailors of Old Lahaina. Now it houses The Paradise Television Network, a local television station.

Hale Pa'i is on the campus of Lahainaluna school. Founded in 1831, Lahainaluna is the oldest school and printing press west of the Rockies. You will find it located just outside of Lahaina at the top of Lahainaluna Road. The hours fluctuate depending on volunteers, so call the Lahaina Restoration office at 661-3262 for current schedule. No admission fee. Donations welcomed.

The Lahaina Jodo Mission is located on the Kaanapali side of Lahaina, on Ala Moana Street near the Mala Wharf. The great Buddha commemorated the 100th anniversary of the Japanese immigration to the islands which was celebrated at the mission in 1968. The grounds are open to the public, but not the buildings. The public is welcome to attend their summer O'Bon festivals, usually in late June and early July. Check the papers for dates and times.

WHERE TO SHOP

Shopping is a prime fascination in Lahaina and it is such a major business that it breeds volatility. Shops change frequently, sometimes seemingly overnight, with a definite "trendiness" to their merchandise. It was a few years back that visitors could view artisans creating scrimshaw in numerous stores. The next few years saw the transformation to T-shirt stores. There still are plenty of clothing stores and a little price comparison can be worthwhile. The next theme was art, art and more art. Galleries sprang up on every corner. It was a wonderful opportunity to view the fine work of many local artists and international ones as well. Original oils, watercolors, acryclics, carvings and even pottery were all on display. Rather like a museum without any admission fee! Since the last edition of this guide, we have seen a decline in art galleries. With the prices on these original pieces of artwork in the $$$$$$$ figures, perhaps there were more lookers than buyers. Unfortunately, the transition we now see are the eruption of numerous tour and activity book agents. We find that they have infiltrated every nook and cranny, even a corner of one ice cream shop. While some are pleasant enough, others are obnoxious and extremely pushy. More editorial opinion on this in the RECREATION AND TOURS section. In thinking back, only a few of the same shops have remained in operation along Front Street since we began this book some 13 years ago!

Here are a few shops that we feel are worth the mention:

Environmental awareness has arrived at the *Endangered Species Store* at 707 Front St. It's filled with T-shirts, collectibles, books and toys that all focus on endangered wildlife worldwide. Next door is a fun store with a novel idea that certainly makes this shop memorable from the many others that line Front Street. Step through the door of *The Gecko Store* and take a look at what is under your feet! We'll let you be surprised!

Lahaina Galleries at 728 Front Street, plus galleries in Kaanapali and Kapalua. Begun in 1976, their art falls in the $500 - $30,000 (and up) range. The works by local artists are the most popular.

Some of the larger ones are the David Lee Galleries, Galerie Lassen Maui, and The Village Galleries. A number of "retired" movie and television stars have turned artist and you'll see the work of Tony Curtis, Red Skelton, Anthony Quinn, Buddy Ebsen and Richard Chamberlain. Originals, numbered lithographs and poster prints by popular Hawaiian artists Pegge Hopper, Diana Hansen-Young and others can be found in many shops as well. The best representation of local artists may be found at the Lahaina Galleries located at 728 Front Street in Lahaina and at the Kapalua Shops at 123 Bay Drive. The Lahaina Arts Society is a non profit organization featuring work by Maui artists with two locations in the Old Lahaina Courthouse: the Old Jail Gallery and the Banyan Tree Gallery. Open 10 am-5 pm daily, they also feature arts and craft shows on Saturday.

Friday night in Lahaina is ART NIGHT! Participating galleries feature a special event between 6 and 9 pm that might include guest artists and refreshments.

Island Sandals is tucked away in a niche of the Wharf Cinema Center near the postal center at 658 Front Street, Space #125, Lahaina, Maui, HI 96761, (661-5110). Michael Mahnensmith is the proprietor and creator of custom-made sandals. He learned his craft in Santa Monica from David Webb who was making sandals for the Greek and Roman movies of the late 50's and early 60's. He rediscovered his sandal design from the sandals used 3,000 years ago by the desert warriors of Ethiopia. He developed the idea while living in Catalina in the 1960's and copyrighted it in 1978. The sandals are all leather, which is porous and keeps the feet cool and dry, with the exception of a non-skid synthetic heel.

The sandals feature a single strap which laces around the big toe, then over and under the foot, and around the heel, providing comfort and good arch support. As the sandal breaks in, the strap stretches and you simply adjust the entire strap to maintain proper fit (which makes them feel more like a shoe than a sandal). They are clever and functional. His sandals have been copied by others, but never duplicated. So beware of other sandals which appear the same, but don't offer the fit, comfort or function of Michael's! The charge is $85 for the right shoe and the left shoe is free. Charges may be slightly higher for men's sandals over size 13. Anyone who gets shoes from Island Sandals becomes an agent and is authorized to trace foot prints of others. Commissions are automatic when your sales reach the "high range." (However, you must like coconuts and bananas.) Michael stresses the importance of good footwear, so stop in upon your arrival! Sandals can also be ordered by sending a tracing of both feet and both big toes, including the spaces in-between (or by having an "authorized agent" do so) along with $85 to Island Sandals. Michael can also assist with leather repair of your shoes, purses, bags, or suitcases.

A three-screen movie theater is located on the upper level of the **Wharf Cinema Center** with seating capacity for 330 people (special first show of the day prices are currently $4). The **Fun Factory** is located in the lower level with video games and prize-oriented games. **Maui Sea Chest, Lahaina Golf, Island Swimwear** and **Parrots International** are a few of the shops. **Hawaiiana Arts & Crafts**, where you can watch artists at work and buy all Maui-made gifts is a new addition to the center. A new addition to the Hawaiiana Arts & Crafts is the *Paper Airplane Museum and the Tin Can Man*. The airplane models are all shapes and sizes. Ray Roberts is continually expanding his airplane museum and is in search of airline artifacts to display. Highlighted is the history of aviation on Maui since 1917. Ray Roberts is the Tin Can Man of Maui and has fashioned some incredible pieces out of cans. A number of restaurants are also found throughout the center.

Dickenson Square (On Dickenson St. off Front St.) bears a strong resemblance to Pioneer Inn. Lahaina Gourmet Deli & Cyber Cafe, hairdresser, quick stop market, art gallery and Lahaina Coolers restaurant are located here.

Walking south on Front Street you'll pass the Banyan Tree and Kamehameha III School before you come to **Kamehameha Iki Park** (also known as Armory Park) on your right. This park is being developed and will be maintained as a Hawaiian cultural park. The aim is for both the local population and visitors to gain an insight into the culture of Hawai'i through "hands-on" experiences. The focus of the work will be the design, construction, sailing, and maintenance of magnificent Hawaiian double-hulled sailing canoes constructed along traditional lines. The **Hui O Wa'a Kaulua** is working with the County of Maui in the development of this park. They will involve the youth of the community through programs with the Department of Education, the County of Maui and private organizations. Their ultimate goal is to teach skills, ethics, and values that will benefit all of Maui and Hawai'i. Two *Hale Wa'a*, or canoe houses will be constructed. They will be thirty-seven feet tall, forty-one feet wide and one-hundred feet long. The two *Hale Wa'a* will house three double-hulled canoes on the ground floor with

room in the ceiling for smaller or lighter canoes. A 62 foot double-hulled canoe of traditional design with a single sail has recently been constructed. The canoe is named *Mo'okiha*, which means sacred lizard/dragon. They also have a 42.5-foot canoe called *Mo'olele*.

Some modern building techniques are used so that these vessels will be lighter, faster, safer, and easier to handle than the canoes of ancient Hawaii. Both traditional and instrument navigation techniques and seamanship will be taught. Construction of a thirty-one foot double-hulled cane will be a teaching aid for the keiki and new member program. The canoe will also be used as a support vessel for larger canoes that may have to be anchored outside of the Lahaina reef. The canoe will have a small sail for teaching sailing techniques.

Final phases of the project include the construction of a building with open sides to serve as a covered picnic area and space for working and teaching of Hawaiian crafts, arts and other demonstrations. They also plan on the construction of a Board of Health approved kitchen, wood and craft workshop, and maintenance storeroom. Landscaping of the park will include vegetation that will serve the Hawaiian activities, such as ti, taro, bamboo, Hawaiian medicinal plants and bananas.

They anticipate completion of these projects within the next five years. *Hui O Wa'a Kaulua* (the assembly of the double hulled canoe) is a nonprofit organization. If you are interested in membership, contact them at *Hui O Wa'a Kaulua*, 525 Front Street, Lahaina, HI 96761. Family membership is $50, adult dues $25.

505 Front Street is next door to the park. Originally developed to be a shopping center (then unsuccessfully converted into condominiums) it has now been restored into busy shops and restaurants. The *Old Lahaina Luau* is held on the beachfront and restaurants include *Hecocks, Pacific'O*, and the *Old Lahaina Cafe*. *Scaroles Village Pizzeria* or *Eden's Garden* offer a respite for the hungry shopper! (Shops here change faster than we can keep track!)

Dan's Green House at 133 Prison Street (661-8412) has a variety of beautiful tropical birds for sale as well as an array of plants for shipping home. Their specialty is Fuku-Bonsai "Lava Rock" plants. These bonsai are well packaged to tolerate the trip home.

Lahaina Center, on the Kaanapali end of Lahaina, is composed of two parts. The Lahaina Shopping Center is newly renovated and now called *"Old Lahaina Center."* The *"New Lahaina Center"* is located across the street, a low level, pioneer type architecture and has a paid parking area. *Hilo Hatties* has relocated here with a 17,000 square foot location. Hatties is famous around the islands for its aloha wear. The *Hard Rock Cafe* is a major attraction. There is also a multi-screen movie theater and a *Liberty House*, but it is a scaled down version of its Kahului counterpart.

An area slightly removed from Lahaina's Front Street is termed the industrial area. Follow Honoapiilani Road and turn by the Pizza Hut. *The Sugar Cane Train* (661-0089) offers a nostalgic trip between Kaanapali and Lahaina. Round trip fare for adults is $12, children 3-12 years is $6. They have several package options that combine the train ride with another Lahaina experience. The prices on the packages offer a bit of a discount if you were to price the two activities separately. The Lahaina Town Package includes a tour of the Wo Hing Temple, the *Carthaginian* and the Baldwin House. The ***Hawaiian Experience Omni Theatre*** Packages includes admission to the 40-minute theater presentation. The Nautilus Package includes a trip out of the Lahaina Harbor on the semi-submersible Nautilus. Make your plans early as space is limited and sometimes the return trips are booked. The red double decker bus will transfer you from the Sugar Cane Depot to the Wharf Shopping Center and in front of Pioneer Inn. You can catch the bus back to the train depot from these same locations.

Also in the industrial area, ***The Bakery*** is a personal favorite for some really fine pastries and breads. ***MGM, Maui Gold Manufacturing*** (661-8981), not only does standard repairs, but designs outstanding jewelry pieces. They can design something to your specifications, or choose a piece from one of their many photograph books. A limited number of pieces are ready made for sale as well. ***J.R.'s Music Shop*** (661-0801), on the back side of The Bakery building, has a large selection of Hawaiian tapes and records as well as just about any other type of music.

Just on the Kaanapali side of Lahaina, a drive of less than a mile, is ***The Lahaina Cannery Shopping Center*** which opened in 1987. The original structure, built in 1920, was used as a pineapple cannery until its closure in 1963, and this new facility was built to resemble its predecessor. It's easy to spot as you leave Lahaina heading for Kaanapali. A large parking area makes for convenient access.

This enclosed air-conditioned mall is anchored by Safeway and Long's Drug Store. Within the mall are several fast food eateries, as well as sit down dining at Compadres restaurant. Other shops include Waldenbooks, Lahaina Printsellers, a coffee house, jewelry, clothing and sporting goods stores. The surf board display at *Hobie Sports* is worthy of a stop.

BE FOREWARNED!!! If you have the time, do a lot of window shopping before you buy. Prices can vary significantly on some items from one store to another.

ACCOMMODATIONS - LAHAINA

Puamana	Plantation Inn
Lahaina Shores Beach Resort	Lahaina Inn
Pioneer Inn	Lahaina Roads
Maui Islander Hotel	Puunoa

BEST BETS: Puamana - A nice residential type area of two-plex and four-plex units, some oceanfront. ***Lahaina Shores*** - A moderately priced colonial style high rise right on the beach and within walking distance of Lahaina shops. ***Lahaina Inn*** is tastefully done with all the elegance of bygone days.

PUAMANA ★

PO Box 11108, Lahaina, Maui, HI 96761. (808-667-2551) 1-800-628-6731. Rental Agent: Klahani 1-800-669-MAUI. 228 units in a series of duplexes and four-plexes in a garden setting. This large oceanside complex resembles a residential community much more than a vacation resort. The variation in price reflects location in the complex, oceanfront to gardenview. Limited maid service. $300 deposit, weekly/monthly discounts, three night minimum.

1 BR (4) $125-175 / $100-150
2 BR (6) $160-250 / $140-200
3 BR (6) $300-350

LAHAINA SHORES BEACH RESORT ★

475 Front Street, Lahaina, Maui, HI 96761. (808-661-4835 Hotel only, no reservations). Agents: Classic Resorts 1-800-628-6699. 200 oceanfront units in this seven-story building of plantation style offer air-conditioning, lanais, full kitchens, daily maid service, and laundry facilities on each floor. The beach here is fair and the water calm due to offshore reefs, but shallow with coral. Lahaina town is only a short walk away, plus this complex neighbors the 505 Front Street Shopping Center which offers several restaurants and a small grocery/convenience store. Car/condo packages also available.

SBR(2;max 3) mt.v.-o.f. $120-150 /110-130
1BR(2;max 4) mt.v. $160/135
1BR(2;max 4) o.f. $190/160
PENTHOUSE(2;max 5) mt.v. $200/170
PENTHOUSE(2;max 5) o.f. $225/195

PIONEER INN (Hotel)

658 Wharf St., PO Box 243, Lahaina, Maui, HI 96764. 1-800-457-5457, FAX 1-808-667-5708, (808-661-3636). George Freeland, a robust 300 pound, 6 ft. 5 inch Englishman, had relocated to Vancouver, Canada and become a Royal Canadian Mountie. He was sent to Hawai'i in 1900 to capture a suspect, but failing to do so, chose to make Maui his home. He formed the Pioneer Hotel Co., Ltd and sold $50 shares of stock. In October of 1901 he constructed the hotel as accommodations for the inter-island travelers. Similar to the plantation house of the Maunalei Sugar Company on Lana'i, the total cost of constructing the hotel was $6,000.

(Note: On Lana'i we heard a report that the Maunalei Plantation House was transported to Maui and became Pioneer Inn, but this was not accurate. Apparently, years ago, the *Honolulu Star-Bulletin* printed an article to this effect. George Alan Freeland, son of Pioneer Inn's founder George Freeland spoke with Lawrence Gay, the owner of most of Lana'i at the turn of the century, and was told that when the construction of Pioneer Hotel was completed, the similar-designed building on the island of Lana'i was still standing.) Soon George Freeland opened the Pioneer saloon, the Pioneer Grange, the Pioneer Wholesale Liquor Company and in 1913 the Pioneer Theater. The Pioneer Theater ran silent movies to packed crowds and had stage shows and plays in the theater as well. George Freeland died on July 25, 1925, survived by his wife, a Hawaiian woman, three sons and four daughters. His eldest son, George Alan Freeland, ran the business until the early 1960's. His grandson, George "Keoki" Freeland, is now the Director of the Lahaina Restoration Foundation.

In the late 1960's the inn was expanded and at that time the theater was torn down. A complete history of the Pioneer Inn is available along with their brochure. A guest in 1901 would have been required to adhere to the following bizarre "house rules:"

> *"You must pay you rent in advance. You must not let you room go one day back. Women is not allow in you room. If you wet or burn you bed you going out. You are not allow to gamble in you room. You are not allow to give you bed to you freand. If you freand stay overnight you must see the mgr. You must leave you room at 11 am so the women can clean you room. Only on Sunday you can sleep all day. You are not allow in the down stears in the seating room or in the dinering room or in the kitchen when you are drunk. You are not allow to drink on the front porch. You must use a shirt when you come to the seating room. If you cant keep this rules please dont take the room."*

With such a colorful history, Pioneer Inn remains a nostalgic Lahaina landmark. We recently toured one of the renovated rooms. It was simple, unenhanced by wallpaper, pictures or the like. The rates have doubled since the last edition of this guide, and based on the new room prices, we cannot recommend this property as a good vacation value. The Lahaina Inn, just up the street, offers elegant rooms with a continental breakfast at the same price. If you are still inclined to say, and are a AAA member, they discount the rooms.

Rooms are divided into three categories: Courtyard, Front Street and Banyan Side. All rooms are air conditioned with private baths and a single queen bed in all rooms. No televisions, no pool. All rooms $120 plus tax.

MAUI ISLANDER HOTEL
660 Wainee Street, Lahaina, Maui, HI 96761. (808) 667-9766, 1-800-367-5226. FAX (808) 661-3733. 372 rooms include hotel rooms with refrigerators. Studio and 1 BR suites w/ kitchens. Located in the heart of Lahaina town, less than a 5 minute walk to the sea wall, yet far enough away to be peaceful. The back of the building borders the Honoapiilani Hwy., so there may be more traffic noise in those units - request the front units. Daily maid service, air-conditioning, laundry facilities, tennis courts, pool. Group rates available. Two night deposit. Add $9 per night for high season.
Room with refrigerator - no kitchen (2) $75
Studio with kitchen (3) $87-95, 1 BR (4) $105, 2 BR (6) $157

PLANTATION INN ★
174 Lahainaluna Rd., Lahaina, Maui, HI 96761 (808-667-9225) 1-800-433-6815, FAX 1-808-667-9293. This 18 room building has all the charm of an old inn, while all the benefits of modernization. Filled with antiques, beautiful Victorian decor, hardwood floors, and stained glass, they also offer air-conditioning, refrigerators and even VCR's. Some units have kitchens and jacuzzi tubs. Located a block from the ocean in the heart of Lahaina, it also has a 12 foot deep tiled pool, and a spa. An added bonus is the outstanding Gerard's Restaurant,

which provides guests with discounts for breakfast and dinner. Some suites include kitchens and jacuzzis. Honeymoon and car packages available.
Room rates range: High season $119-219; low season $104-195.

LAHAINA INN ★ (Hotel)

127 Lahainaluna Rd., Lahaina, Maui, HI 96761. (808-661-0577), FAX (808) 667-9480, 1-800-669-3444. This history of this property is an interesting one. Built in 1938 by Tomezo Masuda for his general store, Maui Trading Company, it was apparently a popular place for World War II army men to "hang loose." Dickie, the Masuda's black German Shepherd, became legendary for his mail run. He would make the trip to the Lahaina post office to fetch the store's mail.

In 1949, the Tabata family purchased the business from Masuda, but by the early 1960's the business failed and the building was placed at public auction. George Izaki purchased the property and made the street level store into four business spaces and transformed the second floor to a hotel.

A fire destroyed the business in the mid 1960's. The interior was reconstructed the Lahainaluna Hotel was developed in the second story level. There were 19 rooms and three baths. The hotel gradually deteriorated.

In the early 1980's when we toured the property for the first edition of this guidebook, the Lahainaluna was renting for $20 a night. And that was a lot for what you got.

In 1986 Rick Ralston, who also owns Crazy Shirts, undertook renovations at this ideally situated location and the transformation was dramatic. Gone are the cheap "rustic" units. The fully air-conditioned hotel has 13 rooms for single or double occupancy only. The hotel has been restored exactly as if it were sent into a time warp between 1860 and 1900. (That means no televisions, too!) No details have been overlooked from the authentic antiques to the ceiling moldings. All the furnishings have come from Rick Ralston's personal collection so each room is different. The headboards and footboards are intricately carved as are the highboy

ORCHIDS

dressers. Each room is unique with lush wallpaper in deep greens, burgundy, blues and golds and offers a small, but adequate private bathroom. Each has its own lanai complete with rocking chairs. Other amenities include in-room bottled water and classical music piped into the rooms if you choose. In-room phones offer free local calls. Considering you are in the center of town, the rooms are surprisingly quiet. The rooms are not only beautifully decorated, but the maintenance of them is superb. In the morning, a few steps down the hall will lead you to the buffet with steaming hot coffee, fresh fruit and muffins or croissants. If you can do without the oceanview, we can't imagine a more romantic, charming and intimate way to spend your Maui vacation. Manager Ken Eisley has been with the hotel since it's inception and his dedication and energies show through. Adjacent is the David Paul's Lahaina Grill. Parking $5 per day. Honeymoon packages. *Standard rooms with full size bed or two twin-size m.v. $89. Harbor view with full-size bed $99. Makai Room with full-size bed and harbor view $129. Mauka Room, queen-size bed, with Harbor & m.v. $129. Lahainaluna Room, m.v., king-size bed $129.*

LAHAINA ROADS
1403 Front St., Lahaina, Maui, HI 96761. (808-661-3166) No bookings available from the resident manager. Agent: Klahani Resorts 1-800-669-0795. 42 ocean-view units, covered parking and elevator to upper levels. Microwaves, washer/dryer, cable TV. Maid service available for an extra charge. A very unpretentious, non-resort looking property. Additional person $10/night, three night minimum, two nights deposit, deposit forfeited on cancellation if unit not re-rented. Weekly and monthly discounts.
1 BR (2,max 4) $115/95, 2 BR (4,max 6) $150/130, Penthouse (4) $200/150

PUUNOA BEACH ESTATES
45 Kai Pali Place, Lahaina, Maui, HI 96761. Agents: Classic Resorts (808-667-1400) 1-800-642-MAUI. Amenities include full size swimming pool, jacuzzi, his and hers sauna, and paddle tennis courts. Units include laundry rooms, lanais, master bath with jacuzzi, full bar and daily maid service. These luxury units are located on Puunoa Beach in a residential area just north of Lahaina. Beautiful and spacious air-conditioned units, convenient to restaurants and shops. The beachfront has a coral reef which makes for calm conditions for children, but swimming or snorkeling are poor due to the shallowness and coral. A full size rental car is included. Three night minimum.
2 BR 2 bath o.f. (4) $580/550, 2 BR with loft (6) $695/580
3 BR o.f $730/605, 3 BR with loft (8) $800/665

KAANAPALI

INTRODUCTION

The drive from Lahaina is quick (unless it's rush hour). All that is really visible from the highway are a couple of gas stations, the old mill, a few nondescript commercial buildings, and a Pizza Hut. Old Lahaina and the waterfront a couple of large blocks off to the left, cannot be seen. The large shopping center on the left is the Cannery, described above. As you leave Lahaina, the vista opens with a view of the Hyatt Regency and the beginning of the Kaanapali Beach Resort a mile off in the distance. The resort is beautifully framed by the West Maui mountains on the right, the peaks of Moloka'i, appearing to be another part of Maui in the background, the island of Lana'i off to the left, and of course, the ocean. The name Kaanapali means "rolling cliffs" or "land divided by cliffs" and refers to the wide, open ridges that stretch up behind the resort toward Pu'u Kukui, West Maui's highest peak. The beaches and plush resorts here are what many come to Hawai'i to find.

Kaanapali began in the early 1960s as an Amfac Development with the first hotels, the Royal Lahaina and the Sheraton Maui, opening in late 1962 and early 1963 respectively. The Kaanapali Beach Resort, 500 acres along three miles of prime beachfront, is reputed to be the first large-scale planned resort in the world. There are six beachfront hotels and seven condominiums which total more than 5,000 rooms and units, two golf courses, 37 tennis courts, and a shopping village.

Now that the Kaanapali Airport has been closed, there are another 700 acres available for development. Construction has been awaiting a number of things, including the road improvements in the Kaanapali to Lahaina area. The resort boasts the most convention space of any of the neighboring islands, with the Maui Marriott, Westin Maui and the Hyatt Regency being popular locations. All the hotels are located beachfront, although some of the condos are situated above the beach in the golf course area. All are priced in the luxury range. The wide avenues and the spaciousness of the resort's lush green and manicured grounds are most impressive. No on-street parking and careful planning have successfully given this resort a feeling of spaciousness. Nestled between a pristine white sand beach and scenic golf courses with a mountain range beyond, this may be the ideal spot for your vacation.

This may be paradise, but traffic congestion between Kaanapali and Lahaina may have reminded you more of L.A. in the past few years. Non-synchronized traffic lights, roads designed for 20 years ago, and greatly increased traffic, caused the three mile transit through Lahaina to Kaanapali (or Kaanapali to Lahaina) to consume over an hour during the afternoon rush (most other times there was only light traffic). Of deep concern to the government, residents and business interests alike, this situation was eased considerably with the completion of four lanes from Kaanapali to Lahaina. The two Kaanapali to Lahaina shuttles have also somewhat eased congestion. The major bottleneck is now at the first Kaanapali entrance where the four lanes end. Getting past this point in either direction can be difficult. Hopefully, the four lanes will extend up to at least Napili or Kahana in the near future.

WHAT TO DO AND SEE

The Hyatt Regency Maui and *The Westin Maui* must be put at the top of everyone's list of things to see. Few hotels can boast that they need their own wildlife manager, but upon entry you'll see why they do. Without spoiling the

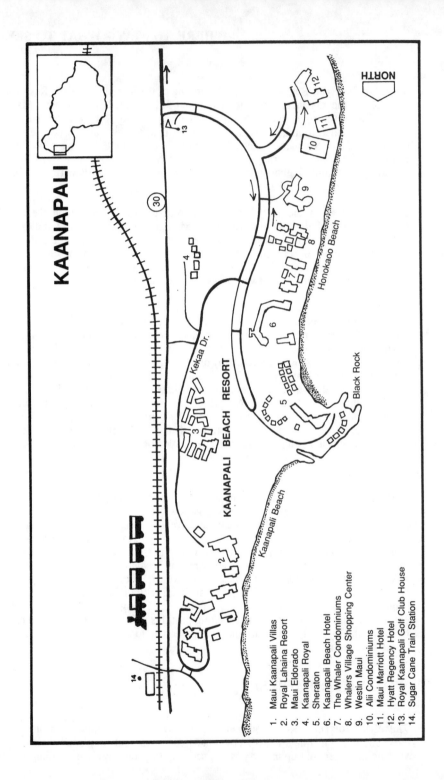

KAANAPALI

KAANAPALI BEACH RESORT

Kekaa Dr.

Kaanapali Beach

Honokaoo Beach

Black Rock

NORTH

1. Maui Kaanapali Villas
2. Royal Lahaina Resort
3. Maui Eldorado
4. Kaanapali Royal
5. Sheraton
6. Kaanapali Beach Hotel
7. The Whaler Condominiums
8. Whalers Village Shopping Center
9. Westin Maui
10. Alii Condominiums
11. Maui Marriott Hotel
12. Hyatt Regency Hotel
13. Royal Kaanapali Golf Club House
14. Sugar Cane Train Station

surprises too much, just envision the Hyatt with palm trees growing through the lobby, peacocks strolling by, and parrots perched amid extraordinary pieces of Oriental art. The lagoon and black swans are spectacular. And did we mention there are penquins, too? The pool area occupies two acres and features two swim-through waterfalls and a cavern in the middle with a swim up bar. A swinging bridge is suspended over one of the two pools and a water slide offers added thrills particularly for the young traveler.

The Westin Maui had a major renovation a few years ago. To appreciate this property, a little background may be necessary. The Maui Surf was the original hotel with the single curved building and a large expanse of lush green lawn and two pools. The transformation has been extraordinary. The pool areas are unsurpassed, with five swimming pools on various levels fed by waterfalls and connected by two slides. There are exotic birds afloat on the lagoons which greet you upon your arrival and glide gracefully by two of the hotel's restaurants. The Oriental art collection surpasses even the Hyatt's. Both resorts feature glamorous shopping arcades, with prices to match of course. Both developments were designed by the remarkable, champion hotel builder of Hawaii, Chris Hemmeter. We are anxious to see the transformations made to the Sheraton Maui when it reopens in 1997.

WHERE TO SHOP

Whalers Village shopping center is located in the heart of Kaanapali. Some part or other of this center always seems to be under construction or renovation. It offers a small for grocery items, restaurants and a food court. Recent renovations have brought in very "high end" specialty and boutique shops. These designer clothing stores and jewelry stores (including Tiffany's) offer little for the average shopper. There are still a couple of clothing stores, including a Crazy Shirts outlet. Other shops include Waikiki Aleo, Elepahnt Walk, The Body Shop, Lahaina Printsellers, an art gallery, and several novelty stores. The mall is a pleasant place for an evening stroll and shop browsing, before or after dinner, followed by a seaside walk back to your accommodations on the paved beachfront sidewalk.

Hale Kohola (House of the Whale) is a museum located on the upper level. Admission is free, but donations are welcome. They recently expanded in size and have a wonderful exhibition of the great whales with special emphasis on the Humpback Whale. The information director gives lectures on topics from scrimshaw to the life of a sailor. Call for times at 661-5992. Private group lectures are also a possibility.

Restaurants include The Rusty Harpoon, Leilani's, and Hula Grill. All are good options for breakfast, lunch or dinner. The Food Court offers several additional dining options.

A multi-level parking structure is adjacent to the mall and parking is $1 for the first two hours or fraction thereof, and 50 cents for each additional half hour, with a $10 maximum charge. Restaurants can provide validation or you can find 2-hours free coupons in many of the visitor publications.

ACCOMMODATIONS - KAANAPALI

Hyatt Regency Maui	Royal Lahaina Resort
Maui Marriott Resort	Maui Kaanapali Villas
Kaanapali Alii	Kaanapali Plantation
Westin Maui	International Colony Club
The Whaler	Maui Eldorado
Kaanapali Beach Hotel	Kaanapali Royal
Sheraton Maui	

BEST BETS: *Hyatt Regency Maui* - An elegant and exotic setting with a wonderful selection of great restaurants. *Maui Marriott Resort* - Beautiful grounds with a nice pool area and attractively decorated rooms. *Westin Maui* - A gorgeous resort and a pool aficionados paradise. *Kaanapali Alii* - One of only three condominiums that are oceanfront. Luxurious, expensive and spacious. (Our choice to purchase a unit with future lottery winnings!). *Royal Lahaina Resort* - A beautiful property on sandy Kaanapali Beach. *The Whaler* - Condominiums on the heart of Honokaoo Beach adjacent to the Whalers Village Shopping Center. NOTE: Some resort hotels have begun charging guests a daily parking fee.

HYATT REGENCY MAUI ★ (Hotel)
200 Nohea Kai Drive, Lahaina, Maui, HI 96761. (808-661-1234) 1-800-223-1234. This magnificent complex is located on 40 beachfront acres and offers 815 rooms and suites. The beach is beautiful, but has a steep drop off. Adjoining Hanokaoo Beach Park offers a gentler slope into deeper water. The pool area is an impressive feature, covering two acres and resembling a contemporary adventure that Robinson Crusoe could only have dreamt. The pool is divided by a large cavern that can be reached on either side by swimming beneath a waterfall. The more adventurous can try out their waterslide. One side of the pool is spanned by a large swinging rope bridge. The kids just love walking back and forth with the swaying motion! Penguins, jewel-toned koi, parrots, swans, cranes and flamingos around the grounds require full time game keepers. The lobby is a blend of beautiful pieces of oriental art and paths that lead to the grounds.

The tropical birds are so at home here that some are reproducing, a rarity for some of these species in captivity! Non-guests should definitely visit the Hyatt for a self guided tour of the grounds, the art, the elegant shops and for an opportunity to enjoy one of this resort's fine restaurants which include Swan Court, Spats, Lahaina Provision Company, Pavilion and the lua'u show. It's worth coming here just to look around! Parking $8 per day, validated parking for diners.

The newest addition is the outdoor wedding gazebo. Made of natural ohia wood from the Big Island, it is set amid a tropical Hawaiian garden overlooking the ocean. A $12 million renovation was recently completed. Guest rooms in the Atrium, Napili and Lahaina towers were enhanced with new carpeting and wood finishing, and bathrooms were augmented with new Italian marble tile. The Regency Health Club was expanded to more than triple its previous size. All rooms offer complimentary access to the health club. The addition of an outdoor jacuzzi is also a part of the renovation.

Another novel activity is the *Hyatt's Tour of the Stars*. Shows are three times nightly on the hotel rooftop. Seating is limited to 10 persons per show, cost is $12 adults, $6 children 12 and under.

So it's a rainy day. Here is a suggestion. *Incredible Journeys!* is Maui's newest, and the world's first simulated helicopter attraction. You can view Maui from a birds-eye-view without leaving the ground. This indoor option gives you the opportunity to buzz across the fields of Maui, drop into the crater of Haleakala and zip past waterfalls without ever leaving the ground. This is no mere movie, but an amusement ride. The show is reminiscent of "Back to the Future" at Universal Studios and is very realistic. A 10-minute flight briefing is given before guests are invited into the seven seat helicopter, equipped to include even air sickness bags. The tour is narrated and features a 180 degree screen that is designed to resemble the experience of looking out windows. While a real helicopter tour lasts nearly an hour, this one is an edited version lasting 20 minutes. It is cheaper than the real thing, but still a pricey $39.95 per person.

The Regency Club at the Hyatt consists of two floors that feature special services, including continental breakfast, evening cocktails and appetizers. Room rates are based on single/double occupancy (for additional persons 13 years or older $25 charge per night/Regency Club level $45 charge per night). 3 adults or 2 adults 2 children maximum per room.
Terrace $245, golf/mtn.v. $310, o.f. $335-370; Suites: Ocean $600, Dlx $900, Regency $1,400, Presidential $3,000; Regency Club (mtn.v.) $400, (o.f.) $430

MAUI MARRIOTT ★ (Hotel)
100 Nohea Kai Drive, Lahaina, Maui, HI 96761. (800-228-9290) 1-808-667-1200, FAX (808) 667-8300. This 720 room complex has a large, open lobby in the middle featuring an array of fine shops. Although not as exotic as its neighbor the Hyatt, this is still a very attractive, upscale property. The pool area is large and a keiki (children's) wading pool is a welcome addition for families. Their "Keiki Kamp," a children's activity and adventure program, is offered Monday thru Friday for guests aged 6-12 years. Fee includes lunch, transportation and a camp T-shirt. On site restaurants are Nikko Japanese Steak House, Lokelani, Moana Terrace and the Kau Kau Grill. Inquire regarding their current package

plans, one package now available offers a Two for Breakfast or a Room and Car Package at $199 for Mountain View, $219 for Ocean View and $249 for Deluxe Ocean View. Their "Everything Under the Maui Sun Package" includes a rental car, daily breakfast buffet for two, and other amenities including lei greeting and welcome gift, free parking, free tennis, free beach rentals and discounts for $239-$289 per night. Currently their advance purchase rates are being offered which begin at just $169 for a mountain view room.
Non-Package Rates run: Mtn. view $270, o.v. $290, deluxe o.v. $320. Maximum four persons per room. Additional persons add $25. They charge $7 per day parking.

KAANAPALI ALII ★
50 Nohea Kai Dr., Lahaina, Maui, HI 96761. 1-800-367-6090. Agents: Classic Resorts 1-800-642-MAUI or FAX (808) 661-0147, Whalers Realty 1-800-676-4112, Hawaiian Apt. Leasing 1-800-854-8843, 1-800-472-8449 CA. All 264 units are very spacious and beautifully furnished, with air-conditioning, microwaves, washer/dryer, and daily maid service. Other amenities include security entrances and covered parking. The 1-bedroom units have a den, which actually makes them equivalent to a 2-bedroom. Three lighted tennis courts, pool (also a children's pool), and exercise room. No restaurants on the property, but shops and restaurants are within easy walking distance. A very elegant, high-class and quiet property with a very cordial staff and concierge department. They charge for local phone calls from room, as do most hotels. Three night min., extra person $15/night. The following rates are through Whalers Realty.
1 BR (2) g.v. $210/180; o.v. $240/205
2 BR (4) partial ocean $295/240; o.f. $400/360

WESTIN MAUI ★ (Hotel)
2365 Kaanapali Parkway, Lahaina, Maui, HI 96761. (808-667-2525). Westin Central Reservations 1-800-228-3000. Under the direction of Chris Hemmeter, champion hotel builder in Hawaii, this gorgeous resort offers 761 deluxe rooms, including 28 suites. The Westin Maui has an ocean tower of 11 stories with 556 guest rooms and a beach tower with 206 guest rooms and suites. Guest rooms are available for those with disabilities as well as non-smoking floors. The rooms have been designed in comfortable hues of muted peach and beige. The top two floors of the new tower, house the Royal Beach Club, which offers guests complimentary continental breakfast buffet, afternoon cocktails, evening cocktails and hors d'oeuvres, and a private concierge. Complimentary shuttle service is offered to the Royal Lahaina Tennis Ranch, the largest tennis facility on Kaanapali with 11 tennis courts and 6 courts lit for night play. Conference and banquet facilities are available as well as an array of gift, art, and fashion shops. The focal point of this resort is the 55,000 square foot aquatic playground, complete with meandering streams, 15 - 20 foot waterfalls, and a 25,000 square foot pool area featuring five free-form pools, two waterslides and a swim-up Jacuzzi hidden away in a grotto. The pool areas are spacious and well arranged. Eight restaurants and lounges overlook the ocean, waterfalls and pools. The hotel exercise room includes complete exercise and weight rooms, with sauna and whirlpool.

The Westin offers three tours to help guests learn more about their resort. Tour the grounds with a guide to learn more about the Westin's family of birds and their tropical surroundings. This resort's 2.5 million art collection could put a museum to shame and each piece was carefully selected and placed personally by Chris Hemmeter. An art collection tour, as well as a self-guide book, are available. Another option is to take a personalized stroll around the manicured 12-acre grounds of the resort to learn more about the flora and fauna found on this resort property.

One of the features we like best are the numerous nooks with comfortable chairs and art work that provide intimate conversation areas.

Parents may enjoy a brief respite while the kids enjoy the resort's Westin Kids Club Keiki Camp for youth ages 5-12 years. It runs daily from 9 am - 3 pm. The participation fee is $45 for the first child and $35 for additional siblings. Activities include a visit to Lahaina's Omni Theater, a ride on the Sugar Cane Train or a sail on the 64-foot Gemini Catamaran. A night program is offered evenings. Participation is $15 for the first child and $10 for additional siblings.

For those planning a wedding on Maui, the Westin has their own Director of Romance to assist you with your wedding or honeymoon plans. On property restaurants include Sound of the Falls (open only for Sunday Brunch), The Villa Restaurant, Sea Dogs, Cook's at the Beach and Sen Ju Sushi Bar.

Rates are based on single or double occupancy. Third person add $25, to Royal Beach Club add $45 (maximum 3 persons to a room). Family Plan offers no extra charge for children 18 or under sharing the same room as parents. A 25% discount is available for additional rooms occupied. Complimentary valet parking. *Terrace $245, garden view $285, golf or mtn. view $310, oceanview $350, deluxe ocean view $380, ocean front $410, Royal Beach Club o.v. $450, Suites $650-$2,750*

THE WHALER ★
2481 Kaanapali Parkway, Lahaina, Maui, HI 96761. (808-661-4861) Managed by Village Resorts 1-800-367-7052, FAX (808) 661-8315. Agents: Whalers Realty 1-800-367-5632, Hawaiian Apt. Leasing 1-800-854-8843 (U.S. except California), 1-800-472-8449 Calif., RSVP 1-800-663-1118, Kumulani 1-800-367-2954. Choice location in the heart of Kaanapali next to the Whalers Village shopping center and on an excellent beach front. A large pool area is beachfront and they provide a children's program during the summer. Underground parking. $200 deposit, 2-night minimum except over holidays, balance on check-in. 2-week refund notice. Garden view studios begin with Whalers Realty slightly less money.

S BR 1 bath (2) o.v. $195/185,	*g.v. $180/170*	*Cribs $12/night*
1 BR 1 bath (4) o.v. $275/250,	*g.v. $225/210*	*Rollaway beds $15/night*
1 BR 2 bath (4) o.v. $285/260,	*g.v. $230/220,*	*o.f. $355/325*
2 BR 2 bath (6) o.v. $385/370,	*o.f. $465/430*	

KA'ANAPALI BEACH HOTEL ★ (Hotel)
2525 Kaanapali Pkwy, Lahaina, Maui, HI 96761 (808-661-0011), 1-800-262-8450, FAX (808) 667-5616 guests, or (808) 667-5978 administration.

The 430 room Ka'anapali Beach Hotel has earned the reputation as Maui's most Hawaiian hotel. There are four wings to this property which embrace a tropical courtyard that features gardens, walkways, a whale-shaped swimming pool and an outdoor bar and grill. Each room is decorated with airy, island decor, offers a private balcony or lanai, air conditioning, mini-refrigerator, color cable TV, in-room safes and coffee maker. Non-smoking rooms are available. Four rooms are equipped for the disabled traveler. The hotel offers two restaurants plus a poolside grill.

A variety of Hawaiian activities are scheduled daily. Among them are lau printing, ti-leaf skirt making, hula classes, lei making, and lauhala weaving. They have an Aloha Friday crafts fair and special employee entertainment on Monday, Wednesday and Friday. A complimentary sunset hula show is performed nightly in the Tiki Terrace Courtyard. Coin operated laundry facilities on the property. A seasonal Kalo (Taro) Patch Kids program is offered.

Located on Kaanapali Beach near Black Rock and Whalers Village Shops, this hotel has been welcoming guests since it opened in 1964. And there is no doubt that it continues to be the best hotel value on Kaanapali Beach. A great location, but not a "posh" resort. The hotel could use a bit more freshening up, but then it would also be reflected in the prices! This is Maui's most Hawaiian hotel where the staff are actually instructed in Hawaiiana.

Cribs available at no charge. Roll-away bed $15 per night, additional person $25 per night. Children under 17 free when sharing room with parents using existing bedding. Special package rates include complimentary daily breakfast, complimentary compact rental car, golf and special rates for guests 50 years of age or older.

Garden $145, Courtyard $165, Partial Ocean View $175, Ocean View $190, Oceanfront $225, Suites $190-535.

SHERATON MAUI (Hotel)

2605 Kaanapali Parkway. (808-661-0031) 1-800-325-3535. One of the first properties to be built along Kaanapali, the property opened in January of 1963. The resort closed in April 1994 for a $150 million renovation. Sheraton announced that the grand re-opening is scheduled for November 1996. As we've seen before, and will no doubt see again, these completion dates are not always accurate, nor is advance information about the property. Items such as the names of the restaurants often have last minute revisions. Given fair warning, here is the information we currently have received from Sheraton.

The new 510-room resort will stretch over the 23 beachfront acres. The rooms will include 16 luxury suites, 30 junior suites, 15 accessible rooms and 10 rooms designated for hearing impaired. The resort will feature the Coral Reef Restaurant, serving Hawaii-Pacifica specialties and Teppan-Yaki Dan, with meals prepared to order tableside. The open-air Kekaa Terrace will provide all day dining with a view of the resort's lagoon and oceanfront. There will also be the Lagoon and Sundowner bars, Reef's Edge Lounge and the Honu Snack Shop.

In making better use of their beachfront property, the garden cottages are being replaced with several high-rise structures. Each is named as a *hale*, which is Hawaiian for house. The main structure of the original property remains, but the *makai* wing (nearer the ocean) will be Hale Nalu (House of the Surf) while the *makua* portion will be Hale Anuenue (House of the Rainbow). The Hale Moana (House of the Ocean) is being built on the point at black rock. The Hale Lahaina and Hale Ohana are in the middle of the property. Standard guest rooms feature air conditioning, lanai (patio), small refrigerator, iron and ironing board, along with coffee maker, TV with remote and guest safe. A 140 yard freshwater swimming pool and kiddie pool will be available for resort guests and they promise to continue their nightly cliff-diving ceremony. Their Keiki Aloha children's program will be available June through August. This program is complimentary for resort guests. Children must be ages 5-12 years.

Following are the 1996-1997 scheduled room rates (subject to change!) *Large Luxury (Hale Koku) $490, Junior Suites "Family Rooms" $465, Luxury Ocean Front (Hale Moana, Hale Hoku) $465, Deluxe Ocean (Hale Lahaina) $425, Ocean Front (Hale Nalu) $390, Ocean View (Hale Anuenue) $360, Mountain View (Hale Anuenue) $320, Garden View (Hale Anuenue) $270, Alii Suite (Hale Hoku) $3,000, Prestige Ocean Suites (Hale Hoku) $950 and Ocean and Executive Suites $550-700.*

ROYAL LAHAINA RESORT ★
2780 Kekaa Drive, Lahaina, Maui, HI 96761. (808-661-3611) 1-800-44-ROYAL. 592 units located on excellent Kaanapali Beach just north of Black Rock. Located on 27 tropical acres, all cottage suites have kitchens and are situated around the lush, spacious grounds. A mini-shopping mall is conveniently located on the property. Amenities include ten tennis courts, three swimming pools. Restaurants on the property are the Royal Ocean Terrace (which features a very good Sunday Brunch), Basil Tomatoes and Beachcomber's. Made in the Shade is a poolside restaurant and the Royal Scoop is an ice cream and sandwich shop. Nightly luaus are offered in the luau gardens. Children under 17 sharing parents room in existing beds are free. Three swimming pools. Additional amenities include beach cabanas for half or full day rental and beach rental equipment. The Royal Lahaina Tennis Ranch offers hour rates of $5 per person, full day rates of $7.50 and weekly passes at $30 per person, $50 per couple, $75 per family. Racquets, ball machine and even tennis shoes are available for rent.

Our brief stay in one of the bungalow/cottages that are scattered around the grounds was a relaxing one. It offered an opportunity for the kids to run around the grassy area that stretched beyond our patio. There, they made fast friends with a very friendly rabbit that they named Lettuce. This rabbit definitely had friends, since he was the most robust, hearty and all around enormous rabbit we'd ever seen. We inquired with the General Manager who was aware of this unusual resort resident. Apparently he had been a pet that an employee had let loose and that they had plans to round him up. However, the rabbit has received much admiration from resort guests as the GM noted that many have reported that they look forward to visiting with Mr. Rabbit on return visits. (My kids included.) And, they recently added 17 garden and oceanfront Ehu Kai Suites to their collection of secluded cottage-style guest accommodations.

The resort also has a new wedding gazebo. It features six open air windows and is located in the cottage courtyard. Rows of pink and white hibiscus line the walkways leading to the courtyard and gazebo. The resort has introduced a unique new wedding custom, they provide stepping stones engraved with the bride and groom's name and wedding date. Wedding coordinator, Diana Smith, notes that they hope to one day have all of the walkways paved with these stones. She comments, "In the future, the stepping stones should provide a memorable opportunity for couples to return to the site of their ceremony and renew their vows or simply reminisce." Honeymoon packages are also available.

The Royal Lahaina offers some wonderful values and with a location on one of Maui's best beaches, it is a vacation oasis.
Garden $175-195; Ocean View $213-235; Deluxe Ocean Front $275-295; Garden Cottage $235-400; Garden Front Cottage $295-315; Suites $550-1500.

MAUI KAANAPALI VILLAS
2805 Honoapiilani Hwy., Lahaina, HI 96761 (808-667-7791). Agents: Aston 1-800-221-2558, Whalers Realty 1-800-367-5632, Hawaiian Apt. Leasing 1-800-854-8843 (U.S. except CA.), 1-800-472-8449 CA, RSVP 1-800-663-1118, Kumulani 1-800-367-2954, Located on fabulous, sandy Kaanapali Beach, this was once a part of the Royal Lahaina Resort, and before that the Hilton, prior to being converted into condos.The units are all air-conditioned and have kitchen facilities (except the hotel rooms). Three swimming pools, beach concessions, store nearby. Walking distance to Whalers Village shops an restaurants and adjacent to the Royal Kaanapali Golf Course. *Hotel Room (2) $145/125, Studio w/kitchen (2) $180-200/155-180, 1 BR (4) $220-255/195-230*

KAANAPALI PLANTATION
150 Puukolii Rd., (PO Box 845) Lahaina, Maui, HI 96761. No rental units available at this time from on-site management. 62-unit one, two and three bedroom units in a garden setting overlooking golf course and ocean.

INTERNATIONAL COLONY CLUB
2750 Kalapu Dr., Lahaina, Maui, HI 96761 (808-661-4070), FAX (808) 662-5856. 44 low-rise single family cottages on 10 lush acres, across Honoapiilani Hwy. from the beach. Lanais, most have washer/dryers and coin-op laundry on site. Limited maid service. Two heated swimming pools. It is a bit of a walk to the beach. 3-day minimum low season, 7 day high. NO CREDIT CARDS.
1 BR (1-4) $105, 2 BR (1-4) $125, 3 BR (1-6) $150.

MAUI ELDORADO
2661 Kekaa Drive, Lahaina, HI 96761. (808-661-0021) 1-800-367-2967, Canada 1-800-663-1118. Agents: Hawaiian Apt. Leasing 1-800-472-8449 CA, 1-800-854-8843 U.S. except CA, Castle Group 1-800-367-5004, Hawaiian Pacific Resorts 1-800-367-5004. Marc Resorts 1-800-535-0085. 204 air-conditioned units located on golf course. Private lanais with free HBO and Disney cable TV. Daily maid service. Three pools. Free shuttle to cabana on nearby beachfront.
Hotel Room g.v. (1-2) $119

S BR (1-2) g.v. $149, o.v. $179	*Extra persons $15*
1 BR (1-4) g.v. $185, o.v. $219	*5-day minimum, weekly/monthly discounts.*
2 BR (1-6) g.v. $255, o.v. $295	*Rollaways $15 and cribs $5 day*

KAANAPALI ROYAL ★
2560 Kekaa Dr., Lahaina, Maui, HI 96761. (808-661-8687). Agents: Outrigger
Hotels Hawaii 1-800-OUTRIGGER, Whalers Realty 1-800-367-5632, Hawaiian
Apt. Leasing 1-800-472-8449 CA, 1-800-854-8843 U.S. except CA, RSVP 1-
800-663-1118, Kumulani 1-800-367-2954, Pali Kai 1-808-879-8550. These very
spacious condos, 1,600 - 2,000 sq. ft., offer air-conditioning and lanais and are
situated on the 16th fairway of the Kaanapali golf course overlooking the Kaanapali resort and Pacific Ocean. Daily maid service. Washer/dryers. Note that while
all units have two bedrooms, they may be rented as a one bedroom based on
space availability. One bedroom reservations may be wait listed outside of 30
days of arrival. No minimum stay, except Christmas holiday. One night deposit.

1 BR (2,max 4) garden or golf view $165/150, o.v. or dlx golf view $185/165
2 BR (2,max 6) garden or golf view $190/175, o.v. or dlx golf view $220/195

HONOKOWAI

INTRODUCTION

As you leave the Kaanapali Resort there is a stretch of yet undeveloped beachfront on the left is no longer cultivated, but wild cane now continues to grow
sporadically. This was the site of the old Kaanapali Airport. Resorts will be
stretched along this beach within the next few years.

Ahead, four large condo complexes signal the beginning of Honokowai, which
stretches north along Lower Honoapiilani Highway. Accommodations are a mix
of high and low-rise, some new, but most older. The beachfront is narrow and
many complexes have retaining walls. A close-in reef fronts the beach and comes
into shore at Papakea and at Honokowai Park. Between the reef and beach is
generally shallow water unsuitable for swimming or other water activities. The
only wide beach and break in the reef for swimming and snorkeling is at the
Kaanapali Shores and Embassy Suites.

In late 1987, several condominiums made a major investment in saving the
beachfront by building a seawall beneath the sand to prevent winter erosion and
it appears to have been successful. A number of the condominiums are perched
on rocky bluffs with no sandy beach.

Many people return year after year to this quiet area, away from the bustle of
Lahaina and Kaanapali and where condo prices are in the moderate range. A
couple of small grocery stores are nearby. For dining out there is the Beach Club
restaurant at the Kaanapali Shores and The Embassy Suites offers three restaurant
choices.

The condominiums are individually owned for the most part, and the quality and
care of each (or lack of) is reflected by the owner. Perhaps it is the shape of the
sloping ridges of Mauna Kahalawai that cause this area to be slightly cooler and
cloudier with more frequent rain showers in the afternoon than at neighboring
Kaanapali.

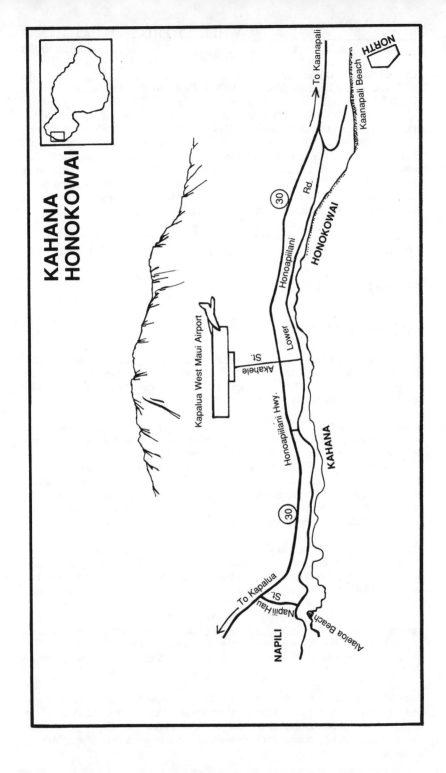

KAHANA
HONOKOWAI

NORTH

To Kaanapali

Kaanapali Beach

Honoapiilani Rd.

30

HONOKOWAI

Kapalua West Maui Airport

Lower

Akahele St.

Honoapiilani Hwy.

KAHANA

30

To Kapalua

Napili Hau St.

Alaeloa Beach

NAPILI

ACCOMMODATIONS - HONOKOWAI

Mahana Resort	Hale Kai	Hale Ono Loa
Maui Kai	Pikake	Lokelani
Embassy Suites	Hale Maui	Hale Mahina
Kaanapali Shores	Apt. Hotel	Beach Resort
Papakea	Nohonani	Hoyochi Nikko
Maui Sands	Kulankane	Kuleana
Paki Maui	Makani Sands	Polynesian Shores
Honokowai East	Kaleialoha	Mahinahina Beach
Maui Parkshores	Hale Royale	Mahina Surf
Honokowai Rsrt. Apts.	Hono Koa	Noelani

BEST BETS: Kaanapali Shores - A high-rise surrounded by lovely grounds on the best beach in the area. *Papakea* - A low-rise complex with attractive grounds and pool. *Embassy Suites Resort* - A mix between a condo and a hotel, spacious rooms and breakfast is included, a good sandy beach.

MAHANA
110 Kaanapali Shores Place, Lahaina, Maui, HI 96761. (808-661-8751) Agents: Aston 1-800-922-7866, Whalers Realty 1-800-676-4112, RSVP 1-800-663-1118, Hawaiian Apt. Leasing 1-800-854-8843 in U.S. except CA, 1-800-472-8449 CA, Kumulani 1-800-367-2954, Pali Kai 1-808-879-8550. Mahana means "twins" as in two towers. All units oceanfront. Two twelve-story towers with two tennis courts, heated pool, central air-conditioning, saunas, elevators, small pool area. Located on narrow beachfront with offshore coral reef precluding swimming and snorkeling. A better swimming area is 100 yards up the beach. This is a rather drab looking condominium on the outside, the pool sits out on a slab of cement without much in the way of atmosphere. We haven't stayed here, but over the years have heard from many of our readers that they wouldn't stay anywhere else. The earlier problems with beach erosion seems to have been remedied. Three night minimum.
S BR 1 bath (1-2) $130-160/105-135
1 BR 1 bath (1-4) $165-195/140-170
2 BR 2 bath (1-6) $240-170/270-300

MAUI KAI
106 Kaanapali Shores Pl., Lahaina, Maui, HI 96761. (808-661-0002) 1-800-367-5635. Agents: Blue Sky Tours 1-800-678-2787, Classic Resorts 1-800-642-6284, (808) 667-1400. A single ten-story building with 79 units. Two night deposit, two-night minimum. Units offer central air-conditioning, private lanais, full equipped kitchens. Property amenities include swimming pool, jacuzzi, laundry facilities, free parking. Some studio units may be available. Weekly/monthly discounts.
SBR (2) o.f. $125-135/99-114
1 BR (2) o.f. $145-155/125-135
1 BR (2) Corner o.f. $155-165/135-145
2 BR (4) o.f. $220-240/200-220

97

EMBASSY SUITES RESORT ★
104 Kaanapali Shores Place, Lahaina, Maui, HI 96761. (808-661-2000). 1-800-462-6284 U.S. and Canada. On 7 1/2 acres, this pink pyramid structure with a three-story blue waterfall cascading down the side can't be missed. This accommodation blends the best of condo and resort living together. The pool (which is heated) area is large and tropical with plenty of room for lounge chairs. In the past there were problems here with beach erosion, but they seem to have remedied it with erosion control measures. The lobby is open air and their glass enclosed elevators will whisk you up with a view! Atop the resort, families can now enjoy their miniature golf course, open daily 9 am-9 pm, price is $5 per person, $2.50 for youths under 12 years.

Each one bedroom suite is a spacious 820 sq. ft; two bedroom suites are 1,100 sq. ft. Each features lanais with ocean or scenic views. Master bedrooms are equipped with a remote control 20" television and an large adjoining master bath with soaking tub. The living room, decorated in comfortable hues of blue and beige, contains a massive 35" television, stereo receiver, VCR player and cassette player. Living rooms have a sofa that makes into a double bed. A dining area with a small kitchenette is equipped with a microwave, small refrigerator and sink. Ironing equipment available upon request. One phone in the living room and another in the bedroom connect to a personal answering machine for your own recorded message. Suite rates include complimentary full American breakfasts and daily two-hour Manager's cocktail reception.

Their two presidential suites are 2,100 sq. ft. and offer two bedrooms, two full baths and a larger kitchen. One features an Oriental theme, the other is decorated with a contemporary California flare.

On property restaurants include North Beach Grille for evening dining, Ohana Grill for casual breakfast, lunch, and snacks and the Deli Planet for deli sandwiches and sundries. Video rentals are available.

Their children's program, Beach Buddies, is dedicated to perpetuating and preserving the heritage of the islands. "As a *Keiki O Ka Aina Ika Pono* (child of the land), let us share with you a 'Hawaiian Experience' rich in culture and tradition." Activities include hula class, lei making, coconut weaving and crafts, beachcombing and pool time. The program is designed for children 4 to 10 years and operates year round, seven days a week, Monday through Friday from 8:30 am - 2:30 pm. The participation fee is $20 per child per day. The fee includes lunch and T-shirt. Their health facility was recently furnished with state-of-the-art exercise equipments. The facilities are open daily from 8 am - 10 pm, seven days a week at no charge to Embassy Suites guests. They also offer salon and spa services. The resort has a gazebo for wedding ceremonies as well as a 13,000 sq. ft. meeting facility.

1 BR scenic view $240, o.v. $300, dlx. o.v. $375
2 BR suite $475, Presidential Suite $1,200
Package plans also available.

KAANAPALI SHORES ★
100 Kaanapali Shores Place, Lahaina, Maui, HI 96761, (808-667-2211). Agents: Aston 1-800-922-7866, Whalers Realty 1-800-676-4112, RSVP Reservations 1-800-663-1118, Kumulani 1-800-367-2954. 463 units, all offer telephones, free tennis, daily maid service, and air-conditioning. Nicely landscaped grounds and a wide beach with an area of coral reef cleared for swimming and snorkeling. This is the only resort on north Kaanapali Beach that offers a good swimming area. Putting green, jacuzzi and the Beach Club Restaurant located in the pool area. The Aston Kaanapali Shores Resort features a year-round program for children ages 3 - 10 years. Camp Kaanapali is offered from 8 am - 3 pm, Monday thru Friday. A $10 initial registration covers you regardless of the length of your stay and includes a camp T-shirt. Three sessions available each day and the cost is $5 per session. Choose a morning 8-11 am session, or a lunch 11 am-noon session, or afternoon activities 12-3 pm. Activities are all held on property grounds and include hula and crafts. Program for resort guests only. 667-2211.
Hotel Room w/ refrigerator $150/130
S BR (1-2) g.v., partial o.v. $170-195/145-170
1 BR (1-4) g.v. $300/260, o.v. $360/310, o.f. $410/360
Aloha Oceanfront suite (1-6) $500
Penthouse Suite with kitchen (1-6) $650

PAPAKEA ★
3543 L. Honoapiilani, Lahaina, Maui, HI 96761. (808-669-4848) 1-800-367-5037. Agents: Maui Resort Management. 1-800-367-5037, Whalers Realty 1-800-676-4112, Village Resorts 1-800-367-7052, RSVP 1-800-663-1118, Hawaiian Apt. 1-800-472-8449 CA, 1-800-854-8843 U.S. except CA., Maui Network 1-800-367-5221, More Hawaii 1-800-967-6687. 364 units in five four-story buildings. Two pools, two jacuzzis, two saunas, tennis courts, putting green, washer/dryers, and BBQ area. A seawall was installed in an effort to prevent further beach erosion. The shallow water is great for children due to a protective reef 10-30 yards offshore, but poor for swimming or snorkeling. A better beach is down in front of the Kaanapali Shores. One of the nicer grounds for a condominium complex, Papakea features lush landscaping and pool areas. A comfortable, and quiet property that we recommend especially for families. No smoking units available. Crib or roll-away $6/day. Christmas holiday 14-day minimum with no refunds after October 1. Seven day refund notice, $250-$300 deposit. Cribs available. Rates shown are through Maui Resort Management and reflect the discount they give on their "base rates."
S BR (2) garden & partial o.v. $100/70, o.f. $112/80
1 BR 1 BTH (4) garden & partial o.v. $115/104, o.f. $130/117
1 BR 2 BTH LOFT (4) garden & partial o.v. $130/115
2 BR 2 BTH (6) garden & partial o.v. $140/112, o.f. $165/150
2 BR 2 BTH LOFT (6) garden & partial o.v. $150/130

MAUI SANDS
3559 L. Honoapiilani, Lahaina, Maui, HI 96761. (808-669-9007) Maui Resort Management 1-800-367-5037, Klahani 1-800-669-MAUI. All 76 units have air-conditioning and kitchens. Limited maid service. Microwaves, coin-op laundry facility, rollaway & cribs available $9 night. A very friendly atmosphere where

old friends have been gathering each year since it was built in the mid-sixties. They feature a large central laundry facility and a large pool area with barbecues. Large boulders line the beach. A good family facility. Extra persons $9/night. 15% monthly discounts.

1 BR (2,max 4) std. $80/68, g.v. $105/85, o.f. $135/115
2 BR (2,max 6) std. $100/81, g.v. $130/108, o.f. $160/135

PAKI MAUI

3615 L. Honoapiilani, Lahaina, Maui, HI 96761. (808-669-8235) Agents: Marc Resorts Group, 1-800-535-0085. This complex surrounds a garden and waterfall. No air-conditioning. Daily maid service. Pay phones located on the main level.

S BR (1-2) o.f. $149	*2-nite deposit*
1 BR (1-4) g.v. $159; o.f. $179	*cribs $5/nite*
2 BR (1-6) o.f. $219-249	*children under 2 free*

HONOKOWAI EAST

3660 L. Honoapiilani Hwy., Lahaina, Maui, HI 96761 (808-669-8355) 51 units, mostly studios, in a 4-story building. Long term property.

MAUI PARK

3626 L. Honoapiilani Hwy., Lahaina, Maui, HI 96761. (808-669-6622) Agents: RSVP Reservations 1-800-663-1118, Maui Condominiums 1-800-663-6962 US & Canada. Located across the road from Honokowai Beach Park which lacks a sandy shoreline. A quiet area of West Maui with nearby grocery store. All units have complete kitchen. Coin-op laundry facility. Air conditioned with lanais.. Originally built as residential apartments they offer phones, and daily maid service. Because of its original intention, this property does resemble a residential area more than a vacation resort. Some units are now, once again, being rented on a long term basis. All units are garden view. Cribs or rollaways $15.
S BR (1-2) $119-125/99-105, 1 BR (4) $135-145/115-125,
2 BR 1 BTH (6) $169/159

'ILIMA

HONOKOWAI PALMS RESORT
3666 L. Honoapiilani, Lahaina, Maui, HI 96761. (808-669-6130) Agent: Klahani 1-800-669-MAUI. 30 units across road from Honokowai Beachfront Park. Built of cement blocks this property lacks a great deal of ambience as a vacation retreat. Perhaps for the budget conscious it would be suitable, but it is a very basic, functional complex. $300 deposit.
1 BR (2,max 4) $65, 2 BR (2,max 6) $75. Extra person $6.

HALE KAI
3691 L. Honoapiilani Hwy., Lahaina, Maui, HI 96761. (808-669-6333) 1-800-446-7307 U.S. and Canada. FAX (808) 669-7474. 40 units in a two-story building. The units do have lanais, kitchens, and a pool, but the beach is somewhat rocky. A simple and quiet property. Three-night minimum except Christmas. $250 deposit. Minimum 3 nights. 10% monthly discounts.
1 BR (2) $100/90, 2 BR (4) $130-135/120-125, 3 BR (6) $160/135-145 - Extra persons over 3 years $10/night

PIKAKE
3701 L. Honoapiilani, Lahaina, Maui, HI 96761. (808-669-6086) 1-800-446-3054. A low-rise, two-story, Polynesian style building with only twelve apartments completed in 1966. Private lanais open to the green lawn or balconies, with a beach protected by sea wall. Central laundry area. Light housekeeping provided after two week's stay. Three-night deposit, three-night minimum, extra persons $10/night. NO CREDIT CARDS. *1 BR (2,max 4) $70, 2 BR (4,max 6) $85*

HALE MAUI APARTMENT HOTEL
PO Box 516, Lahaina, Maui, HI 96761. (808-669-6312). Limited maid service. Coin-operated washer/dryer. BBQ. Weekly and monthly discounts. Three-day minmum, seven-day during Christmas. Extra persons $10/night
1 BR (2, max 5) $65-95

NOHONANI
3723 L. Honoapiilani, Lahaina, Maui, HI 96761. (808-669-8208) 1-800-822-7368, FAX (808) 822-RENT. Agent: Klahani 1-800-669-0795. Two 4-story buildings containing 22 oceanfront two-bedroom units and 5 one-bedroom units. Complex has large pool, telephones, and is one block to grocery store. Extra persons $15/night. $200 deposit with 60-day refund notice, three-day minimum stay. Weekly/monthly discounts. NO CREDIT CARDS taken from on-site reservations.
1 BR (1-2) $108/98-113, 2 BR (1-4) $134/118

KULAKANE
3741 L. Honoapiilani (PO Box 5236), Lahaina, Maui, HI 96761. (808-669-6119), FAX (808) 669-9694. 1-800-367-6088. 42 oceanfront units with fully equipped kitchen, laundry facilities on premise. Lanais overlook ocean but no sandy beach. $10 extra person. Three night minimum low season, five night high season. $150 deposit. 10% monthly discounts.
1 BR 1 bath (1-2) $90-95, 2 BR 2 bath (1-4) $135

MAKANI SANDS

3765 L. Honoapiilani Hwy., Lahaina, Maui, HI 96761. (808-669-8223). Agents:
Nai'i Properties, Inc. 1-800-300-5399. Thirty units in a four-story building.
Dishwashers, washer/dryers, elevator. Oceanfront with small sandy beach.
Weekly maid service. Deposits vary, weekly and monthly discounts, three-night
minimum, extra persons $10/night. Seasonal discounts may apply.
1 BR (2) $95, 2 BR (4) $135, 3 BR (6) $155

KALEIALOHA

3785 L. Honoapiilani, Lahaina, Maui, HI 96761. Kaleialoha Rental agent - (808-
669-8197) 1-800-222-8688. Agents: Nai'i Properties, Inc. 1-800-300-5399, More
Hawaii 1-800-967-6687. Sixty-seven units in a four-story building. Three night
minimum. Deposit equal to three nights stay, $7.50 extra persons over age two.
Refundable if cancelled 45 days prior to arrival. Washer/dryers. Weekly discounts. Credit cards accepted.
Studio (1-2) mtn.v. $75, 1 BR (1-4) o.v. superior $95-100, deluxe $85-90

HALE ROYALE

3788 L. Honoapiilani, Lahaina, Maui, HI 96761. (808-669-5230). No short term
rental units available at this time.

HONO KOA

3801 L. Honoapiilani, Lahaina, Maui, HI 96761. (808-669-0979). This property
is no longer vacation rental, time share only. 28 units in one four-story building.
Washer/dryer, dishwasher, microwave, BBQ. Pool with jacuzzi.

HALE ONO LOA ★

3823 L. Honoapiilani, Lahaina, Maui, HI 96761. (808-669-6362) Agents: Nai'i
Properties, Inc. 1-800-300-5399, More Hawaii 1-800-967-6687 U.S. & Canada,
Klahani 1-800-669-MAUI (U.S. & Canada), Maui Accommodations 1-800-252-
MAUI (U.S.) 67 oceanfront and oceanview units. Maid service extra charge.
Beachfront is rocky. The units we toured were roomy and nicely furnished with
spacious lanais. The grounds and pool area were pleasant and well groomed. A
good choice for a quiet retreat. Grocery store nearby.
1 BR 1 bath (4) garden or ocean view $75-85
2 BR 2 bath (6) g.v. $150, o.v. 160, o.f. $170

LOKELANI

3833 L. Honoapiilani, Lahaina, Maui, HI 96761. (808-669-8110) 1-800-367-
2976. Three 3-story 12 unit buildings with beachfront or oceanviews. The 1
bedroom units are on beach level with lanai, two bedrooms units are townhouses
with bedrooms upstairs and lanais on both levels. Units feature washer/dryers and
dishwashers. Weekly discount, three night minimum low season, seven night high
season, extra persons $10, $25 cancellation fee. Three night deposit, balance due
two weeks prior to arrival. *1 BR (1-2) $95, 2 BR (townhouses) (1-4) $145*

HALE MAHINA BEACH RESORT

3875 L. Honoapiilani, Lahaina, Maui, HI 96761. (808-669-8441) 1-800-367-8047
ext. 441. Agents: Maui Network 1-800-367-5221, Pali Kai 1-808-879-8550.

Hale Mahina means "House of the Pale Moon" and offers 52 units in two, four-story buildings and one two-story building featuring lanais, ceiling fans, microwaves, washer/dryer. BBQ area, jacuzzi. Extra persons $10/night. 3-day minimum, deposit within two weeks of reservations, balance on arrival.
1 BR (1-2) $115/100, 2 BR (1-4) $135/120

HOYOCHI NIKKO
3901 L. Honoapiilani, Lahaina, Maui, HI 96761. (808-669-8343) 1-800-487-6002. Agents: Klahani 1-800-669-MAUI. 18 one-bedroom oceanview units (on a rocky beachfront) in two-story building bearing an oriental motif. Underground parking, "Long Boy" twin beds, some with queens, half size washer and dryers in units. Maid service on check-out only. $300 deposit with 30-day refund notice low season, 60-day high season. Prepayment required. NO CREDIT CARDS through property. Agent Klahani will take MC or Visa.
1 BR $95/75 - extra persons $10/night

KULEANA
3959 L. Honoapiilani, Lahaina, Maui, HI 96761. (808-669-8080) or 1-800-367-5633. 118 one bedroom units with queen size sofa bed in living room. Large pool with plenty of lounge chair room and tennis court. A short walk to sandy beaches. Weekly and monthly discounts. Three night minimum stay. Extra persons $7.50. Children under 2 free. Cribs $4/night, rollaways $6. Three night deposit refundable with 14 day notice. *1 BR o.v. $85/80, o.f. 95/90*

POLYNESIAN SHORES
3975 L. Honoapiilani, Lahaina, Maui, HI 96761. (808-669-6065) 1-800-433-6284, from Canada toll free 1-800-488-2179. 52 units on a rocky shore but nice grounds with deck overlooking the ocean. Additional persons $10 each. 10% monthly discount. 60 days cancellation notice for refund. $300 deposit, 3-day minimum, seventh night free.

1 BR 1 bath (2) $95-105/85-95, 2 BR 2 bath (2) $100-120 / $95-105
2 BR 2 Bath End (4) $160/140,   3 BR 3 bath (4) $175/160

MAHINAHINA BEACH
4007 L. Honoapiilani, Lahaina, Maui, HI 96761. Units only through owners.

MAHINA SURF
4057 L. Honoapiilani, Lahaina, Maui, HI 96761 (808-669-6068) 1-800-367-6086, FAX (808) 669-4534. 56 one-bedroom and one-bedroom with loft units. Dishwashers, maid service available at hourly charge. Located on rocky shore, the nearest sandy beach is a short drive to Kahana. Large lawn area around pool offers plenty of room for lounging. $300 deposit, four-week refund notice. AAA and AARP discounts available. Extra persons $8/night including children. Weekly and monthly discounts.

1 BR 1 bath (2,max 4) $110/95
2 BR 1 bath $125/100, 2 bath $130/105-125

NOELANI

4095 L. Honoapiilani, Lahaina, Maui, HI 96761. (808-669-8375) 1-800-367-6030, FAX (808) 669-8374. Agent: Condominium Connection 1-800-423-2976. 50 oceanfront units in one 4-story building and two 2-story structures. Kitchens with dishwashers and washer/dryers only in 1, 2, and 3-bedroom units. Three bedroom units feature a sunken living room as do the two bedroom units on the third floor. Complex has two pools and maid service mid-week. Located on a rocky shore, nearest sandy beach is short drive to Kahana. Weekly and monthly discounts. Extra person $7.50 day. 3 day minimum low season/7 day high season. AAA approved. 7th night free during low season.

S BR 1 bath (1-2) $87-97, 1 BR 1 bath (1-2) $110   *3-night deposit*
2 BR 2 bath (1-2) $140,   3 BR 3 bath (1-6) $170   *2-wk refund notice*

KAHANA

INTRODUCTION

To the north of Honokowai, and about seven miles north of Lahaina is a prominent island of high-rise condos with a handful of two-story complexes strung along the coast in its lee. This is Kahana. The beach adjacent to the high-rises is fairly wide, but tapers off quickly after this point. Several of the larger complexes offer very nice grounds and spacious living quarters with more resort type activities than in Honokowai. The prices are lower than Kaanapali, but higher than Honokowai. In the past we have reported a continuing problem in the Honokowai to Kapalua areas with algae. The algae bloom which clusters in the ocean offshore seems to come and go, causing problems to a greater or lesser degree for reasons yet unknown. State officials continue their investigation but a cause or reason for this condition has not yet been determined. Of late, the problem seems to have improved. The algae doesn't appear to be any health risk, just an annoyance for swimming and snorkeling.

WHERE TO SHOP

There are several shops in the lower level of the Kahana Manor as well as Kahana Gateway. Shops include gift and dive shops, a gas station and Whalers General Store, beauty salon, children's fashion store, a laundry, McDonald's, Roy's, Nicolina as well as Kafe Kahana and Fish and Games Sports Bar.

ACCOMMODATIONS - KAHANA

Kahana Beach Resort	Valley Isle Resort	Kahana Reef
Kahana Villa	Royal Kahana	Kahana Outrigger
Kahana Falls	Hololani	Kahana Village
Sands of Kahana	Hawaii Kalani	Kahana Sunset

BEST BETS: Sands of Kahana - Spacious units on a nice white sand beach.
Kahana Sunset - Low-rise condos surrounding a secluded cove and beach.

KAHANA BEACH RESORT

4221 L. Honoapiilani, Lahaina, Maui, HI 96761. (808-669-8611) Agent: Pleasant Hawaiian Holidays 1-800-242-9244. All units offer oceanview. The studios sleep up to four and have kitchenettes. The 1 bedroom units have kitchens, 2 lanais, living room with queen-size loveseat sleeper, bedroom with 2 king beds, 2 full-size baths, dressing room, and will accommodate 7. Coin-op laundry on premises. Nice, white sandy beach fronting complex. Previously this was Pleasant Hawaiian Holidays Maui property and only available through one of their packages. While packages are still available, you can also rent it as a land option only. *Studios partial o.v. $110, o.f. $120; Suites o.f. $210*

KAHANA VILLA

4242 L. Honoapiilani, Lahaina, Maui, HI 96761. (808-669-5613) Agents: Marc Resorts Group 1-800-535-0085, RSVP 1-800-663-1118. Across the road from the beach. Units have microwaves, washer/dryers, telephones. Daily maid service. Sauna, tennis courts, store, restaurants. Cribs $5, rollaway $15.
Studio $115, 1 BR 1 bath g.v. (1-4) $149, o.v. $169, o.v. deluxe $179
2 BR 2 bath g.v. (1-6) $189, o.v. $219, o.v. deluxe $239

KAHANA FALLS

4260 Lower Honoapiilani Hwy., Lahaina, Maui, HI 96761. 36 2-bedroom 2-bath units and 24 1-bedroom units. This property is time share. No rental units.

SANDS OF KAHANA ★

4299 L. Honoapiilani, Lahaina, Maui, HI 96761. Agents: Village Resorts 1-800-367-7052, (808-669-0400), Hawaiian Apt. Leasing 1-800-854-8843 (1-800-472-8449 CA), RSVP 1-800-663-1118, Pali Kai 1-808-879-8550. 96 units on Kahana Beach. Underground parking. If you're looking to be a little away from the hustle of Lahaina/Kaanapali, with quarters large enough for a big family, and luxuries such as microwaves and full-size washer/dryers then this may be just what you seek. Located on a sandy beachfront and only a couple miles from Kaanapali, it is also less than a mile from the West Maui Airport. Four 8-story buildings surround a central restaurant and a dual pool area.

NAUPAKA KAHAKAI

Sands of Kahana is family oriented from the size of their rooms to their children's playground. Spacious 1, 2 or 3 bedroom units have enormous kitchens and beautifully appointed living rooms. Moloka'i is beautifully framed in the large picture windows of the oceanview units, or select among the slightly less expensive garden view units. There was plenty of fun in the sun here with a beachside volleyball court filled each afternoon, and the large three foot deep children's pool was popular as was another larger and deeper pool with jacuzzi, three tennis courts and a putting green.

Most complexes restrict the use of snorkel gear or flotation equipment in the pool, however, here it is allowed to the delight of the children. A small children's play area offers diversion while parents make use of several garden area charcoal barbecues. Across the street is a full size grocery store and several restaurants are within walking distance. Cribs $10 per night/$60 per week, rollaway $15 per night.

1 BR 1 bath o.v. (4) $215/175,   o.f. $255/210,   courtyard $185/155
2 BR 1 bath o.v. (6) $270/240,   o.f. $320/285,   courtyard $250/205
3 BR 2 bath o.v. (8) $335/310,   o.f. $365/335,   courtyard $320/290

VALLEY ISLE RESORT
4327 L. Honoapiilani, Lahaina, Maui, HI 96761. (No front desk phone) Agents: Klahani 808-669-5511, Hawaiian Apartment Leasing 1-800-854-8843 US except CA). Partial air-conditioning. Located on Kahana Beach. On site restaurant and grocery store. Payment in full 30 days prior to arrival. Weekly maid service.
S BR 1 bath (2) o.f. $110/85   Extra persons $10, under 3 free
1 BR 1 bath (2) o.v. $1155/100, o.f. $125/110
2 BR 2 bath (4) o.v. available through some rental agents.

ROYAL KAHANA
4365 L. Honoapiilani, Lahaina, Maui, HI 96761. (808-669-5911) 1-800-447-7783, FAX (808) 669-5950. Agents: Hawaiian Apartment Leasing 1-800-854-8843 US except CA), Marc Resorts Group, 1-800-535-0085. 12 story high-rise complex built in 1975 with 236 oceanview units on Kahana Beach. Underground parking and air-conditioning. Daily maid service. A nice pool area with sauna. Tennis courts. Units have full kitchens and microwaves. Nearby grocery stores, restaurants and shops. Rollaways and cribs $6/per day.
Rates from Marc Resorts: Studio (1-3) o.v. $169, 1 BR 1 bath (1-2) o.v. $189, 2 BR 2 bath (1-6) g.v.-o.v.-o.f. $239-289

HOLOLANI
4401 L. Honoapiilani, Lahaina, Maui, HI 96761. (808-669-8021), 1-800-367-5032, FAX (808) 669-7682. Agents: Nai'i Properties, Inc. 1-800-300-5399, More Hawaii 1-800-967-6687. Twenty-seven oceanfront units on sandy, reef protected beach. Covered parking. Grocery store. Seven-day/three-day minimum. Monthly discounts. $250 deposit, full payment 60/30 days prior to arrival. Children under five free. NO CREDIT CARDS. Extra persons $10/night, no charge for infants under three years.
2 BR 2 bath (2,max 6) $125-165 / $125-135

HAWAII KAILANI

4435 L. Honoapiilani, Lahaina, Maui, HI 96761 (808-669-6994), FAX (808) 669-4046. Agent: Hawaii Kailani 206-676-1434. Hawaii Kailani is the rental portion of the Pohailani. The Hawaii Kailani offers a mixture of two-bedroom and studio apartments. The larger units are situated around eight park-like acres, while the studio units sit directly on the beach. Walking distance to restaurants and grocery stores. Swimming pool, tennis courts, laundry facilities. TV cable and TV rental are available for each unit, but cannot be requested prior to arrival. Full kitchens in both studio and two bedroom units. Twice weekly maid service. Extra person $5 day. Monthly rates available. Deposit varies. A good value for this area.

S BR o.f. (2, max 3) $75, 2 BR g.v. (2, max 5) $75. Weekly rates $455 for either

KAHANA REEF ★

4471 L. Honoapiilani, Lahaina, Maui, HI 96761. (808-669-6491), 1-800-253-3773, FAX (808) 669-2192. 88 well-kept units. Limited number of oceanfront studios available. Laundry facilities on premises. 15% monthly discounts. Maid service daily except Sunday. NO CREDIT CARDS. Room and car packages. $200 deposit, extra persons $8/night. A good value.

Studio $100/95, 1 BR 1 bath (2,max 5) $110/100, 2 BR $200/174

KAHANA OUTRIGGER

4521 L. Honoapiilani, Lahaina, Maui, HI 96761. (808-669-6550) 1-800-987-8494. Sixteen spacious three bedroom oceanview condo suites in low-rise complex on a narrow sandy beachfront. Units have microwaves, washer/dryers and are appointed with Italian tile. These are rented as a vacation "home" and no on-property service provided. $250 deposit. *3 BR 2 bath (6) $185/155*

KAHANA VILLAGE ★

4531 L. Honoapiilani, Lahaina, Maui, HI 96761. (808-669-5111) 1-800-824-3065. Agents: Kumulani 1-800-367-2954, RSVP 1-800-663-1118. Attractive townhouse units. Second level units are 1,200 sq.ft.; ground level three bedroom units have 1,700 sq.ft. with a wet bar, sunken tub in master bath, Jenn-aire ranges, microwaves, lanais, and washer/dryers. They offer a heated pool and attractively landscaped grounds. Nice but narrow beach offering good swimming. 5-day minimum. Bi-weekly maid service. NO CREDIT CARDS. $300 deposit, balance due prior to arrival. Monthly discounts. Additional person $20.

2 BR o.v. $180/150, o.f. $220/180, 3 BR o.v. $230/190, o.f. $280/230

KAHANA SUNSET ★

PO Box 10219, Lahaina, Maui, HI 96761. (808-669-8011) 1-800-669-1488, FAX (808) 669-9170. Agents: RSVP 1-800-663-1118, Whalers Realty 1-800-676-4112, Hawaiian Apartment Leasing 1-800-854-8843 US except CA).

Ninety units on a beautiful and secluded white sand beach. Units have very large lanais, telephones, and washer/dryers. Each unit has its own lanai, but they adjoin one another, adding to the friendly atmosphere of this complex. One of the very few resorts with a heated pool, heated children's pool and BBQ. You can drive up right to your door on most of the two bedroom units making unloading easy (and with a family heavy into suitcases that can be a real back saver). These are not luxurious units, but it is a location that is difficult to beat.

Extra persons $8/night including infants, 10% monthly discounts. The Kahana Sunset offers condo/car packages also. Kahana Sunset rates, room only:
1 BR 1 bath (2) o.v. $150, 2 BR 2 bath (2) o.v. $185, o.f. $235

Following rates for Kahana Sunset are thru Whalers Realty, 1-800-676-4112.
2 BR 2 bath (2) o.v. $165/150

NAPILI

INTRODUCTION

This area's focal point is the beautiful Napili Bay with good swimming, snorkeling and boogie boarding, and it even has tide pools for children to explore. The condominium units here are low-rise, with prices mostly in the moderate range, and are clustered tightly around the bay. A number are located right on the beach, others a short walk away. The quality of the units vary considerably, but generally a better location on the bay and better facilities demand a higher price. The complexes are small, most under 50 units, and all but one has a pool. At the nearby Napili Plaza shopping center you'll find a full-size grocery store, restaurants and shops.

WHERE TO SHOP

Napili Plaza may be within walking distance, depending on the location of your condominium. It includes Subway Sandwiches, Stanfield's West Maui Floral, Maui Tacos, The Coffee Store, Pizza People, All Star Video, Boss Frog's Dive Shop, First Hawaiian Bank, Napili Market and Koho Grill and Bar.

ACCOMMODATIONS - NAPILI

Honokeana Cove	Napili Bay
Napili Ridge	Napili Sunset
Coconut Inn	Hale Napili
Napili Point	Napili Village Suites
Napili Shores	Mauian
Napili Surf	The Kahili Maui
	Napili Kai Beach Club

BEST BETS: *Napili Sunset* - Centered right on the edge of Napili Bay, rooms are well kept. *Napili Kai Beach Club* - A quiet facility on the edge of Napili Bay. Large grounds and a restaurant are on site. Resort activities are offered.

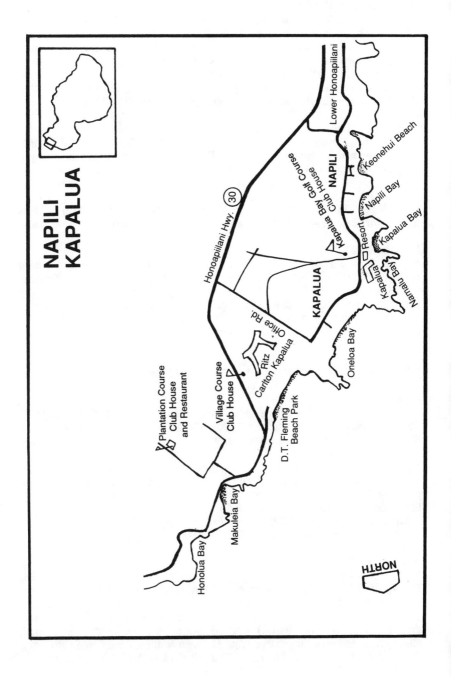

NAPILI
KAPALUA

Honoapiilani Hwy. (30)

Lower Honoapiilani

Keonehui Beach

Napili Bay

NAPILI

Kapalua Bay Golf Course

Kapalua Bay Club House

Kapalua Bay

Resort

KAPALUA

Namalu Bay

Kapalua Bay

Oneloa Bay

Office Rd.

Ritz Carlton Kapalua

Village Course Club House

Plantation Course Club House and Restaurant

D.T. Fleming Beach Park

Makuleia Bay

Honolua Bay

NORTH

HONOKEANA COVE

5255 L. Honoapiilani, Lahaina, Maui, HI 96761. (808-669-6441) 1-800-237-4948. Agent: Nai'i Properties, Inc. 1-800-300-5399. Thirty-eight oceanview units on Honokeana Cove near Napili Bay. Attractive grounds. Three night minimum, three night deposit (except Christmas). NO CREDIT CARDS.

1 BR 1 bath (2) $ 105, 1 BR 2 bath (2) $115
2 BR 2 bath (4,max 4) $147, 3 BR 2 bath (6,max 6) $175, Townhouse (4) $165
Weekly and monthly discounts, extra persons (all ages) $10-$15/nite

NAPILI RIDGE

Hui Rd. "F," Lahaina, Maui, HI 96761. (808-669-6911) 44 studios and 88 one-bedroom units in 11 two-story buildings. Pool, BBQ. Short walk to nearby Napili Market, bus stop and beach. Long term stays only, no vacation rentals.

COCONUT INN

Hui Rd. "F," PO Box 10517, Napili, Maui, HI 96761. (808-669-5712) 40 units in two-story retreat about 1/4 mile above Napili Bay. Long term residents only.

NAPILI POINT

5295 L. Honoapiilani, Lahaina, Maui, HI 96761. Napili Point Resort Rental (808-669-5611) 1-800-669-6252. Agent: Hawaiian Apartment Leasing 1-800-854-8843 US except CA). Located on rocky beach, but next door to beautiful Napili Bay. Units have washer/dryer, full kitchens including dishwasher, direct dial phones, daily maid service. King or queen size beds in one bedroom units. No air conditioning, most units have ceiling fans. No wheelchair facilities. Cribs available. Two pools. In some suites the second bedroom is loft-style.

1 BR 1 bath (4) o.v. $164/144, o.f. $184-204 / $164-184
2 BR 2 bath (6) o.v. $204/184, o.f. $224-244 / $104-224

NAPILI SHORES

5315 L. Honoapiilani, Lahaina, Maui, HI 96761. (808-669-8061) FAX (808) 669-5047. Agents: Colony Resorts 1-800-367-6046, Outrigger Resorts Hawaii 1-800-OUTRIGGER, Hawaiian Apt. Leasing 1-800-854-8843, RSVP 1-800-663-1118. 152 units on Napili Bay. Rooms offer lanais and the one-bedroom units have dishwashers. Laundry facilities on premises as well as two pools, adult hot tub, croquet, and BBQ area. Restaurant, cocktail lounge and grocery store on property. Extra persons $15/night, no minimum stay, daily maid service. Studios have one queen and one twin bed. Crib $8, rollaway $15/per day.

S BR (2,max 3) g.v. $140/125, o.v. $170/155, o.f. $190/180
1 BR (2,max 4) g.v. $175/165, o.v. $200/190

NAPILI SURF

50 Napili Place, Lahaina, Maui, HI 96761. (808) 669-8002. 1-800-541-0638. FAX (808-669-8004). 53 units on Napili Bay. Two pools, BBQ, shuffleboard, lanais, daily maid service, and laundry facilities. Ten percent monthly discount, $300-500 deposit, 30-day refund notice, five night minimum except ten day during Christmas, NO CREDIT CARDS. Rates based on double occupancy. Children six and under no charge. Add $15 each additional person. *S BR (2,max 3) g.v. $95/79, o.v. $130-140/125-130; 1 BR (2,max 5) $155-185/150-175*

NAPILI BAY RESORT

33 Hui Drive, Lahaina Maui, HI 96761. (808-669-6044). Agents: Whalers Realty 1-800-676-4112, Hawaiian Apt. Leasing 1-800-854-8843 (1-800-472-8449 CA). This older complex on Napili Bay is neat, clean and affordably priced. Studio apartments offer one queen and two single beds, lanais, kitchens, daily maid service. Coin-op laundromat with public phones. Extra persons $8/night, children under 12 free. Three night minimum, two night deposit, seven day refund notice, weekly and monthly discounts. *Studio (2,max 4) g.v. $75, partial o.v. $80*

NAPILI SUNSET ★

46 Hui Rd., Lahaina, Maui, HI 96761. (808-669-8083) 1-800-447-9229 U.S.A. or 1-800-223-4611 Canada, FAX (808) 669-2730. Forty-one units located on Napili Bay. Daily maid service. Ceiling fans, no air conditioning. These units have great oceanviews and are well maintained. A very friendly atmosphere. Kitchens have microwaves. Deposits vary. 15 day notice for full refund. 10% monthly discount. Three day minimum. $12 charge per extra person, children two and under are free. Deposits $280-690.
Studio (2) g.v. $85, 1 BR 1 bath (2) o.f. $159, 2 BR 2 bath (4) o.f. $249

HALE NAPILI

65 Hui Rd., Napili, Maui, HI 96761. (808-669-6184) 1-800-245-2266, FAX (808) 665-0066. 18 units oceanfront on Napili Bay. Lanais. Daily maid service except Sunday. Ceiling fans, microwaves, laundry facilities on property. No pool. Three night minimum. $300 deposit, 30-day refund notice, monthly discounts. *Studio (2) g.v. $90, o.f. $115, 1 BR (2) o.f. $135*

NAPILI VILLAGE SUITES

5425 Honoapiilani, Lahaina, Maui, HI 96761. (808-669-6228) 1-800-336-2185, FAX (808-669-6229) U.S. & Canada. All rooms have king or queen size beds, daily maid service. Free laundry facilities on premises. Located a short walk from Napili Bay. Extra persons $8/night, three night deposit. Deposit $250, 14 day refund notice. *Studio (2) $89/79*

MAUIAN

5441 Honoapiilani, Lahaina, Maui, HI 96761. (808-669-6205) 1-800-367-5034, FAX (808-669-0129). Studio apartments on Napili Bay. Kitchen plus microwave, one queen and two twin day beds. BBQ area. Two public phones on property, one courtesy reservation phone. Television only in recreation center. Daily maid service. Three day minimum, 14-day refund notice. 5% discount for stays of two weeks or longer. No charge for crib use. Children 12 and under free. Extra person $9 night, fourth person $6. The rates quoted when reservation is made are guaranteed. Many of their guests have been returning to vacation at this quiet corner of Napili for 30 years or more. Advance deposit of $300 at time reservation is made. Cancellation 60 days before arrival will be charged 10% service fee, 14 days before arrival will result in loss of deposit. They cannot guarantee any specific room number, however, they will make every attempt to accommodate those guests requesting a particular building location (ocean view, ocean front or garden view).
Studios are g.v., o.v. and o.f. $115-140/95-125

THE KAHILI MAUI
5500 Honoapiilani Hwy., Lahaina, HI 96761. (808) 669-5636, 1-800-SUNSETS.
Thirty studio and one-bedroom units. Currently converting to time share.

NAPILI KAI BEACH CLUB ★
5900 Honoapiilani, Lahaina, Maui, HI 96761. (808-669-6271) 1-800-367-3030
FAX (808) 669-0086. Units feature lanais, kitchenettes and telephones. Complimentary tennis equipment, beach equipment, putters, and snorkel gear. Daily coffee and tea party in Beach Club. Sea House Restaurant located on grounds. Four pools and Hawaii's largest jacuzzi. The key here is location, location, location. The grounds are extensive and the area very quiet. A relaxed and friendly atmosphere, a great beach, and a wide variety of activities may tempt you to spend most of your time enjoying this very personable and complete resort. A popular location for family reunions! A summer kids program is offered during the summer months for youth between the ages of six and thirteen. The Napili Kai Keiki Club features an hour or two of free activities daily for children of the resort's guests. Activities include Hawaiian games, hula and lei making, nature/ecology walks, hot dog barbecues and more. Two night deposit. 14-day refund notice. NO CREDIT CARDS.
S BR (2) luxury g.v. no kitchen $160, with kitchen $180, suites $300-450
S BR deluxe o.v. $195, suites $230-400, dlx. o.f. $205, suites $245-280
S BR luxury o.v. no kitchen $195, with kitchen $215, suites $365-522220
S BR luxury o.f. $230-250, suites $250-475
Suites 2-4 persons, S BR 1-2 persons. Extra person $5. Package rates available.

KAPALUA

INTRODUCTION

The story of **Kapalua** begins in ancient times, for it is said that Mauna Kahalawai, the immense volcano that formed the West Maui Mountains, is the juncture between Heaven and Earth. Hawaiians settled in this region in abundance, they built their *lo'i*, or flooded fields for growing their staple crop, taro. They harvested fish, *'ama'ama*, *moi*, *akule* and *opelo* from the clear waters, never taking more than they needed, and always giving thanks. It was an area rich in blessing, much of it sacred. There was a temple of medicine and one for astronomy. The highest chiefs and their families gathered for sports and games in this place, which they deemed their special retreat and playground. They built *holua* sleds for sliding down the grassy slopes. They rolled lava balls in their game of ulu maika, lawn bowling. They wrestled, competed in spear hurling, swam, and surfed the waves at Honolua on giant koa boards. Ruins of ancient temples, fishing shrines and agricultural terraces can still be seen along the streams and shores and people who sometimes find huge lava balls, marvel at the prowess of the ancient bowlers. In earlier times, the Hawaiian lands were divided into *ahupua'a*. These pie-shaped land sections traverse from forest to sea. They give each person access to various elevations for different crops, and an outlet to the ocean for fishing. There were seven beautiful *ahupua'a* called Honolua, Honokahua, Honokawai, Honokohau, Kahana, Mahinahina and Mailepai. Later they were joined to form Honolua Ranch, and parts later became Kapalua resort.

The most important historic site at Kapalua is the Honokahua Burial Grounds which were unearthed when digging began for The Ritz-Carlton, Kapalua. As the significance of the discovery became apparent, the entire hotel was redesigned and moved inland. The mound, which contains over 900 ancient Hawaiian burials dating between 610 and 1800, has been recognized as a sacred site. The mound is now carpeted in lush grass and bordered by native naupaka bushes. Also at this site is a portion of the sixteenth century Alaloa or King's Trail, a footpath that once encircled the island.

The modern day history of Kapalua dates back to 1836 when the Baldwin family of New England settled on the island of Maui as missionaries. The Baldwin family home is now an historical landmark in Lahaina. After seventeen years of service, Doctor Baldwin was given 2,675 acres, the lands of Mahinahina and Kahana *ahupua'a*, to use for farming grazing. By 1902 the area known as Honolua ranch had grown to 24,500 acres as a result of marriages, purchases and royal grants. The ranch crops included taro, mango, aloe and coffee bean and fishing along with cattle raising took place here. Kapalua became a bustling enclave on the island, with a working ranch that supplied pork and beef to the port of Lahaina. David Fleming arrived from Scotland and became the ranch manager. He experimented with a new fruit, *hala-kahili*, or pineapple, and planted four acres. The ideal environment produced a very sweet pineapple. It was determined that the coffee operation should be moved upland to make room for a pineapple cannery, homes and bungalows for workers. The area grew to include a railroad, store, churches, a golf course, tennis courts and a new house for Fleming. Honolua Ranch became Baldwin Packers, the largest producer of private label pineapple and pineapple juice in the nation. In the years that followed, Kapalua's acres of grassy slopes were transformed into geometric patterns of silver-blue pineapple fields and the first crop of this fruit was harvested in 1914. By 1946 the cattle operation had ceased. In the next two decades, Baldwin Packers merged with Maui Pineapple and in 1969 became Maui Land and Pineapple Company, Inc. Before his death, Colin Cameron, a fifth generation descendent of the Baldwin family, envisioned Kapalua as a sanctuary for man and nature.

In the 1970's a new master plan for Kapalua began to take place when Colin Cameron chose 750 acres of his family's pineapple plantation for the development of this up-scale resort. The result is the Kapalua Bay Hotel and Villas which opened in 1979 and the surrounding resort area that includes a residential community, golf courses, and The Ritz-Carlton Kapalua resort. Today the resort area encompasses 1,500 acres surrounded by 23,000 acres of pineapple plantation and open fields.

Perhaps the most unusual program that Maui Land & Pineapple Company, Inc. has undertaken is to develop a home for Koko, the gorilla. Dr. Francine "Penny" Patterson has been working with Koko for 23 years teaching her communication through sign language. Koko is expected to arrive to her new 70 acre enclosure in the West Maui mountains by the end of 1998. The compound will be called the Allan G. Sanford Gorilla Preserve in memory of the son of Mary Cameron Sanford, chair of Maui Land & Pineapple. Koko will be joined by two male companions, Michael and Ndume. For more information contact The Gorilla Foundation at 1-800-63-GO-APE.

The mood reflected at the Kapalua Bay Hotel and The Ritz-Carlton, Kapalua is serene. Their philosophy of quality of food and service in a resort setting offers the ultimate in privacy and luxury living. The grounds are spacious with manicured lawns and an oasis of waterfalls and gardens and a butterfly-shaped pool located nearer the beachfront. More than 400 condominium units are located in the Ridge, Golf and Bay Villas; about 125 are available as vacation rentals. There are three 18-hole championship golf courses, a tennis garden, a shopping area with a myriad of boutiques and sushi bar and restaurant. The Ritz-Carlton Kapalua, which opened October 1992, offers an outstanding luxury resort. There are several excellent restaurants in the area from which to choose. Kapalua Bay is a small cove of pristine white sand, nestled at the edge of a coconut palm grove. It has been named among the top beaches in the world. The protected bay offers good snorkeling and a safe swimming area for all ages. This area of Maui tends to be slightly wetter than in neighboring Lahaina, and the winds can and do pick up in the afternoon.

WHAT TO SEE AND DO

Kapalua, "arms embracing the sea," is the most north-western development on Maui. The logo for Kapalua is the butterfly, and with a close look you can see the body of the butterfly is a pineapple. One might enjoy a stop at the elegant Kapalua Bay Hotel. The lobby bar is ideally situated for evening refreshment, music, and sunset viewing. The resort has a small shopping mall located just outside the Kapalua Bay Hotel and there are shops at The Ritz-Carlton, Kapalua.

The road beyond Kapalua is paved and in excellent condition, and offers some magnificent shoreline views. Slaughterhouse Beach is only a couple of miles beyond Kapalua and you may find it interesting to watch the body surfers challenge the winter waves. Just beyond is Honolua Bay where winter swells make excellent board surfing conditions. A good viewing point is along the roadside on the cliffs beyond the bay.

Continuing on, you may notice small piles of rocks. This is graffiti Maui style. They began appearing a few years ago and these mini-monuments have been sprouting up ever since. There are some wonderful hiking areas here as well. One terrain resembles a moonscape, while another is windswept peninsula with a symbolic rock circle formation. See RECREATION & TOURS "Hiking" for more details. There is plenty to see along the way. Some of the cliffs have incredible scenic viewpoints. You will also pass the village of *Kahakuloa*. Some of the residents living here are descendents from the original settlement some 1,500 years ago. It was not many years ago that electricity finally arrived, but much is still done in the way of old Hawai'i. Tours are available. See RECREATION & TOURS "Land Tours". Travel time from Napili to Wailuku is about 1 1/2 hours. The road beyond is a slow and scenic drive and many parts of the road are windy with room enough for only one car. However, don't venture on if you are in a hurry. On occasion, parts of the road have been washed away, closing it. Some rental car companies may restrict your travel on this route.

Kapalua is home to a number of outstanding annual events. The Kapalua Tennis Jr. Vet/Sr. Championship is held each May. In June both the Maui Chamber Music Festival and Kapalua Wine and Food Symposium are held at the Kapalua Resort. The Kapalua Open Tennis Tournament is in September and the Kapalua Betsy Nagelson Tennis Invitational is held the end of November and/or the first part of December. The nationally televised Kapalua International is held in November when top PGA golfers try their skills on Kapalua's Plantation Course. The Ritz-Carlton sponsors some wonderful events. Every Easter weekend they hold the Celebration of the Arts and throughout the year they host an Artists-in-Residence program. In August Kapalua hosts the Earth Maui Nature Summit, presented by Kapalua Nature Society, an event designed to foster an appreciation of Maui's natural environment. In 1996 the Kapalua Resort became the first Audubon Heritage property in the world.

WHERE TO SHOP

The *Kapalua Shops* offers a showcase of treasures. Here you will find *The Kapalua Logo Shop* (669-4172) where everything from men's and women's resort wear to glassware displays the Kapalua butterfly logo. *Kapalua Kids,* features fashions for infants through boys and girls size 7 (669-0033).

ACCOMMODATIONS - KAPALUA

Kapalua Bay Hotel & Villas	The Ritz-Carlton	Ironwoods
Kapalua Bay and Golf Villas	The Ridge	

BEST BETS: The Kapalua Bay Hotel & Villas - This resort offers quiet elegance, top service and great food with all the amenities. Any of the condominium units in this area would be excellent, however, they are not all located within easy walking distance of the beach. A shuttle service is available. The condominiums at Kapalua offer spacious living and complete kitchen facilities. Rental information for the Kapalua Villas is in three different sections, and there are a number of rental agents. The Kapalua Hotel handles rentals of these luxurious condominiums. Also see the listing below for "Kapalua Bay Villas" and "Ridge Villas" for other rental management companies. *The Ritz-Carlton Kapalua*, which opened in October 1992, is an outstanding resort.

KAPALUA BAY HOTEL & THE KAPALUA VILLAS ★

One Bay Drive, Kapalua, Maui, HI 96761. (808-669-5656) 1-800-367-8000. FAX (808) 669-4694. 194 hotel rooms plus 100 villa condominiums. Hotel rooms have service bars and refrigerators, no kitchens. All rooms have air-conditioning and ceiling fans with decor in warm neutral shades of taupe, rose and muted terra cotta. The villas are private and expansive, rather like a home away from home. Five-star restaurants include The Bay Club and The Garden. Lovely grounds, excellent beach and breathtaking bay. The resort includes The Bay Course and The Village Course, two 18-hole championship golf courses designed by Arnold Palmer, and the third and newest, the Plantation Course designed by Cooke & Crenshaw. A tennis garden with ten plexipave courts, four lighted are available for guest use. The pool is butterfly-shaped, located near the ocean. The expanse of lawn gives way to lush tropical foliage, waterfalls, pools and gardens. This is elegance on a more sophisticated scale than the glitter and glitz of the Kaanapali resorts. Other amenities include coffee and tea service from 6:30-10:30 am in the Lobby Terrace and afternoon tea is also served there daily from 3-5 pm. As the sun sets Hawaiian musicians and dancers entertain in the open air lobby.Children 14 or younger free if sharing room with parent. Extra persons $35 high season, $25 low season. Cribs available at no charge. Three night deposit high season, one low season. 14-day refund notice. Modified American Plan is available at $65 per person.

Kapalua Bay Hotel rates:
g.v. $260, o.v. $325-375, o.f. $450
1 BR suite $760-960, 2 BR suite $1,060-1,260

Villa rates:
Bay-o.f. 1 BR $395, 2 BR $495; o.v. 1 BR $340, 2 BR $440;
Golf & Ridge Villas (fairway or o.v.) 1 BR $200-235, 2 BR $235-285
Third day maid service on Ridge and Golf villas. Extra person add $35.

THE RITZ-CARLTON, KAPALUA ★

One Ritz Carlton Drive, Kapalua, Maui, HI 96761. (808) 669-6200. The 550 room oceanfront resort opened in the fall of 1992 at D. T. Fleming Beach and follows in the same quality and high standards set for all of Kapalua. A Hawaiian motif with a plantation feel features native stonework throughout the hotel. Accommodations include 320 kings, 172 doubles, 58 executive suites and two Ritz-Carlton suites.

Amenities include twice daily made service, in-room terry robes, complimentary in-room safe, multilingual staff, babysitting, and full service beauty salon. Ten tennis courts plus a 10,000 sq. ft., three level swimming pool are among the amenities. Restaurants include The Anuenue Room Restaurant and Lounge, the Terrace Restaurant, the Banyan Tree poolside restaurant. See the Kapalua chapter on restaurants for further information.

The Ritz-Carlton is certainly another jewel for West Maui. We enjoyed a couple of days at this property and experienced their Club Floor for the first time. These special floors, available at many of the finer properties on Maui, have added security. A special key was required in the elevator to reach your floor. A special "Club" lounge area offered snacks almost continually. The continental breakfast was more than one would expect with some wonderful cereals, pastries, freshly squeezed juices and fresh fruits. The mid-day snack included sandwiches, and fresh vegetables or fruits. The early evening hours provided appetizers and wine or mix your own drinks. After dinner (which we missed because we were either too tired or too full) were chocolates and cordials. There were also cold drinks and hot coffee available all day. The lounge/dining room was elegant, yet homey and the balconies provided entertaining views of golfers playing the course. The kids really enjoyed running down for a snack whenever they felt like it. In fact, they seldom were hungry at mealtimes and probably could have survived for weeks on the goodies served on the Club Floor. While it is more expensive, judging by the number of people in the lounge, it certainly appears to be a popular option and we can see why! This is the way to be pampered in paradise! The guest rooms are spacious and beautifully appointed.

The Ritz-Kids program is a half or full-day program that is distinctly Hawaiian. Geared for ages 5-12 years, counselors teach hula, basket weaving, jewelry-making with shells and other arts and crafts, along with T-shirt painting, tennis and board games. A full-day program is $60 for hotel guests, $75 for other guests. The program includes a Ritz Kids tee shirt, keepsake membership card, access to the international pen pal program, and birthday cards mailed to the home each year. The half-day program is $40 for resort guests, $55 for non-resort guests.

Wedding packages can be arranged to include the use of the historic Kumulani Chapel. Construction on the 60-seat New England style plantation church began in the late 1930's, but due to the war, it was not completed until 1951. The chapel was renovated in 1994. Wedding packages run $1,375-6,989 for the Polynesian Experience which includes a lu'au buffet and Polynesian revue. The resorts Honeymoon Coordinator can arrange that the newlywed couple are truly indulged! How about rose petals on the bed or a side by side massage?

Garden Mt. $285, partial o.v. $325, o.v. $400, o.f. $455, The Ritz-Carlton Club $495 1 BR executive suite $625, 1 BR executive Club Suite $750, 1 BR o.f. suite $900 The Ritz-Carlton Suite $2,500, The Ritz-Carlton Club Suite $2,800

KAPALUA BAY VILLAS ★
500 Office Road, Kapalua, Maui, HI 96761, Kapalua, Maui, HI 96761. (808) 669-8088, 1-800-545-0018 U.S. and Canada. AGENTS: Kapalua Hotel 1-800-367-8000, Kapalua Vacation Rentals (808) 669-4144, 1-800-326-6775, Kapalua Hotel (808) 669-0244, 1-800-367-8000, Hawaiian Apt. Leasing 1-800-854-8843 (1-800-472-8449 in California, 1-800-824-8968 in Canada). Ridge Rentals handles only Ridge villas (808) 669-9696, 1-800-326-6284 in U.S. and Canada. There are over 400 units in the villages and each is spacious and beautifully appointed.

Wonderful units for several couples or a larger family. They feel much more like a home than a condominium. Units include kitchens, washer/dryers, and daily maid service. Several pools and tennis courts. Extra persons $35 per night. Three night deposit high season, two night low season. The Kapalua Hotel, which is among the rental agents which handles the property, currently has gone to a flat year round rate, no discounts for low season. However, Kapalua Villas (808) 545-0018 are the company we have dealt with and they do have discounts for low season. The following prices are a mix of the high and low prices we surveyed from several different agents for high season. Differences in prices are also reflected by location and view. A little calling may be worth your while. We'd suggest starting with a call to Kapalua Villas.
1 BR (4, max 6) fairway v. $175-275, o.v. $225-315, o.f. $250-375
2 BR (4, max 6) fairway v. $225-375, o.v. $250-415, o.f. $375-475

THE RIDGE ★
Agents: Kapalua Hotel 1-800-367-8000, Ridge Rentals Realty 1-800-326-6284, Kumulani 1-800-367-2954. Part of the Kapalua condominiums, these are also well appointed but slightly less expensive. With its location above the hotel in the golf course area it is quite a walk to the beach. However, if you book through the Kapalua Hotel, you may pay more, but services include the use of the Kapalua pool, grounds, shuttle service etc. These amenities do not apply if you rent through other agencies. Prices shown below are through Ridge Rentals Realty. 5-day minimum (10 at Christmas), $200 deposit, 14-day notice of cancellation between 12/15 and 4/15, other dates 48 hours. Maid service only on check-in. Weekly and monthly rates available.
1 BR 2 bath o.v. (1-4) $165/115
2 BR 3 bath o.v. (1-6) $240/175

IRONWOODS
Beautiful and very expensive oceanview homes. Currently no rentals available.

THE RITZ-CARLTON   KAPALUA, MAUI

MAALAEA

INTRODUCTION

Maalaea to many is just a signpost enroute to Kaanapali, or a harbor for the departure of a tour boat. (Some even think that Buzz's Wharf, with its more visible and prominent sign, is the real name of the town!) However, Maalaea (which means "area of red dirt") is the most affordable and centrally located area of the island. A short 10 minutes from Kahului, 30 minutes from Lahaina and 15 minutes from Wailea makes it easy to see all of the island while headquartered here. You can hop into the car for a beach trip in either direction. Even better is the mere six-mile jaunt to Kahului/Wailuku for some of Maui's best and most affordable eateries. This quiet and relaxing area is a popular living area for local residents. Seven of the ten condominium complexes are located on a sea wall on or near the harbor of Maalaea, while the other three are on one end of the three mile long Maalaea Bay beach. The two end complexes, Maalaea Mermaid and the Maalaea Yacht Marina are actually within the harbor.

The ocean and beach conditions are best just past the last condo, the Makani A Kai. There is less turbidity providing fair snorkeling at times, good swimming and even two small swimming areas protected by a reef. These are found on either side of the small rock jetty with the old pipe. This length of beach is owned by the government and is undeveloped, providing an excellent opportunity for beach walkers who can saunter all the way down to Kihei. The condominium complexes are small and low-rise with moderate prices and no resort activities. The vistas from many of the lanais are magnificent, with a view of the harbor activity and the entire eastern coastline from Kihei to Makena, including majestic Haleakala, as well as Molokini, Ka'aholawe and Lana'i. The view is especially pleasing at night and absolutely stunning when a full moon shimmers its light across the bay and through the palm trees with the lights of Upcountry, Kihei and Wailea as a backdrop. No other part of the island offers such a tranquil and unique setting. Another plus are the almost constant trade winds which provide non air-conditioned cooling as opposed to the sometimes scorching stillness of the Lahaina area. Summer in Maalaea is time for surfing. Summer swells coming into the bay reportedly create the fastest right-breaking rideable waves in the world and are sometimes referred to as "the freight train." The local kids are out riding from dawn to dusk. Winter brings calmer seas with fair snorkeling over the offshore reef. The calm conditions, undisturbed by parasailing and jet-skiing, also entice the Humpback whales into the shallow waters close to shore.

Local eating options are limited. One particular restaurant, The Waterfront, at the Milowai condominiums is excellent! In addition to sandwiches at the Maalaea Mermaid market, a limited number of snacks are available at the Maalaea store. Casual seafood lunch and dinners are served Monday through Saturday at the Island Fish Market. Buzz's Wharf sits at the end of the Harbor and is open for lunch, dinner and cocktails.

Under development is the new Maalaea Fishing Village. Plans call for a shopping center about as large as the Lahaina Cannery. The two-story plan calls for a design

119

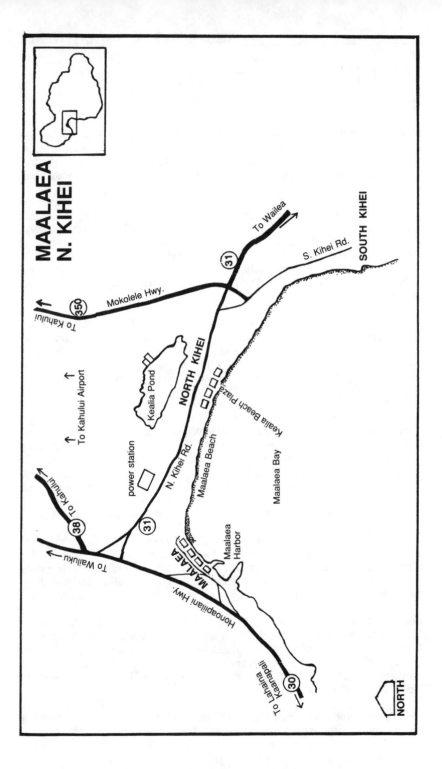

that will incorporate a local Hawaiian theme with lots of small shops and vendors selling fresh produce and island crafts. Five or six restaurants are being figured into the preliminary reports. There is also mention that the Maui Historical Society is reportedly considering a museum and museum shop. It will be located across from the harbor near the old fishing shrine. All in all, Maalaea is a quiet and accessible choice. It is not for those seeking the hub of activity or convenient fine dining, but for the independent and modest traveler. Undecided about where to stay? Maybe you should try Maalaea!

WHAT TO DO AND SEE

The Maalaea Harbor area is a scenic port from which a number of boats depart for snorkeling, fishing and whale watching. Also in this area is Buzz's Wharf Restaurant, open for lunch and dinner. Fresh Island Fish Company, a seafood market is open Monday thru Saturday 10 am-5 pm. In 1994 Maalaea Harbor is under consideration as a site for a new *aquarium project* by Coral World International, Inc. Plans for the proposed Maui Ocean Center would include an 18 acre site where the aquarium would be part of a new shopping center. Note: the mailing address for the Maalaea Village condos DOES list the town as Wailuku.

ACCOMMODATIONS - MAALAEA

Maalaea Mermaid	Island Sands
Maalaea Yacht Marina	Maalaea Banyans
Milowai	Kana'I A Nalu
Maalaea Kai	Hono Kai
Lauloa	Makana A Kai

BEST BETS: Kana'i A Nalu - Attractive complex with all two-bedroom units on a sandy beachfront, affordably priced. *Lauloa* - Well designed units oceanfront on the seawall. *Makani A Kai* - Located on a sandy beachfront, two bedroom units are townhouse style.

MAALAEA MERMAID
20 Haouli St., Wailuku, HI 96793. No rental information available. Located within the Maalaea Seawall. Small market on the ground floor.

MAALAEA YACHT MARINA
30 Hauoli St., Wailuku, Maui, HI 96793. (808-244-7012). Agents: Maalaea Bay Rentals 1-800-367-6084, Kihei Maui Vacations 1-800-541-6284, Hawaiian Apt. Leasing 1-800-854-8843 (1-800-472-8449 CA).

All units are oceanfront, a beach is nearby. The units we viewed were pleasant with a wonderful view of the boats from most units, and the added plus of having security elevators and stairways. Many of the units have no air-conditioning and laundry facilities are located in a laundry room on each floor. A postage stamp size grassy area in front and a small, but adequate pool.
Oceanfront Reef Units: 1 BR (2) $85/75, 2 BR (4) $120/80

121

MILOWAI
50 Hauoli St., Wailuku, Maui, HI 96793. Agents: Milowai Rentals (808-242-1580), FAX (808) 242-1634, Kihei Maui Vacations 1-800-541-6284, Maalaea Bay Rentals 1-800-367-6084. One of the larger complexes in Maalaea with a restaurant on location, The Waterfront. They offer a large pool area, with a BBQ along the seawall. The corner units are a very roomy 1,200 square feet with windows off the master bedrooms. Depending on condo location in the building, the views are of the Maalaea harbor or the open ocean. The one bedroom units have a lanai off the living room and a bedroom in the back. Washer/dryer. Weekly/monthly discounts. *1 BR (2) $85/70, 2 BR (4) $100-125/80-100*

MAALAEA KAI
70 Hauoli St., Wailuku, Maui, HI 96793. (244-7012). Agents: Maalaea Bay Rentals 1-800-367-6084. 70 oceanfront units. Laundry facilities, putting green, BBQ, and elevator to upper levels. Located on the harbor wall, the rooms were standard and quite satisfactory. Some do not have washer and dryers in the rooms. There is a pool area and large pleasant grounds in front along the harbor wall. A few blocks walk down to a sandy beach. Monthly discounts. *Oceanfront reef: 1 BR (2) $85/75, 2 BR (4) $120/80*

LAULOA ★
100 Hauoli Street, Wailuku, Maui, HI 96793. (808-242-6575). Agent: Maalaea Bay Rentals 1-800-367-6084. Forty-seven 2-bedroom, 2-bath units of 1,100 sq. ft. One of the Lauloa's best features is their floor plan. The living room and master bedroom are on the front of the building with a long connecting lanai and sliding glass patio doors which offer unobstructed ocean views. A sliding shoji screen separates the living room from the bedroom. Each morning from the bed you have but only to open your eyes to see the palm trees swaying and a panoramic ocean view. The second bedroom is in the back of the unit. These two bedroom units are spacious (only two bedroom units are currently available in the rental program) and are in fair to good condition (depending on the owner). Each has a washer/dryer in the unit. The pool area and grounds are along the seawall. With a stairway in the sea wall, there often are local fishermen throwing nets and lines into the ocean. $200 deposit. Five night minimum. Maid service extra charge. Monthly discounts. *2 BR 2 bath (4) Oceanfront Reef $130/85*

ISLAND SANDS
150 Hauoli St., Wailuku, Maui, HI 96793. Island Sands Resort Rentals 1-800-826-7816, (808) 244-0848, FAX (808) 244-5639. Agent: Condominium Rentals Hawaii 1-800-367-5242, (808) 879-2778. Eighty-four units in a 6-story building. One of Maalaea's larger complexes located along the seawall. Offers a Maui shaped pool, a grassy lawn area, BBQ. Many of these units also have a lanai off the master bedroom, however, the lanais have a concrete piece in the middle of each railing which somewhat limits the view while sitting or laying in bed. (Okay, so we got a little spoiled at the Lauloa!) Washer/dryers, and air-conditioning. Elevators. Extra person $7.50/night. Weekly and monthly discounts. 4-night minimum, $200 deposit with 15-day refund notice. Children under three free. *Studio (2) $80/65, 1 BR 1 Bath (2) 100/85, 2 BR 2 Bath (4) $130/100*

MAALAEA BANYANS

190 Hauoli St., Wailuku, Maui, HI 96793. (808-242-5668). Agents: Maalaea Bay Rentals 1-800-367-6084, Oihana 1-800-367-5234, Real Hawaii 1-800-967-6687, Maui Condo & Home 1-800-822-4409. Seventy-six oceanview units with lanai and washer/dryer. Weekly and monthly discounts. Oceanfront on rocky shore, short walk to beach. Pool area, jacuzzi, BBQ's. Extra persons $10/night. Seven night minimum. NO CREDIT CARDS. *1 BR Oceanfront Reef (2) $85/75, 2 BR (4) Oceanfront Reef $120/80*

KANA'I A NALU ★

250 Hauoli Street, Wailuku, Maui, HI 96793. Agents: Maalaea Bay Rentals 1-800-367-6084. 80 units with washer/dryers in four buildings with elevators. No maid service. This is the first of the three condominiums along a sandy beachfront. Its name means "parting of the sea, surf or wave."

The complex is V-shaped with a pool area in the middle. Nicely landscaped grounds, a decent beach and only a short walk along the beach to the best swimming and playing area along this section of coastline. While over the last couple of years the high season prices have jumped a bit, the low season rates have consistently remained an excellent value. Overall one of the best values in the Maalaea area.

Have you wondered where the authors of this guide stay? If we aren't moving around the island, sampling different properties, you'll find us catching our breath here, and enjoying the sunny shores and gentle breezes of Maalaea.

5-day minimum, $200 deposit, 30-day refund notice. Weekly discounts.
2 BR (4) o.v. $145/100, o.f. $175/125

HONO KAI

280 Hauoli St., Wailuku, Maui, HI 96793. (244-7012) Agent: Maalaea Bay Rentals 1-800-367-6084. Forty-six units located on the beach. Choice of garden view, oceanview or oceanfront. Laundry facilities, BBQ, pool. This is one of many Maalaea properties managed by Maalaea Bay Rentals. This complex is on the beach and bears attention for the budget conscious traveler, but don't expect any frills. Five day minimum stay.
1 BR $80-100/$60-75, 2 BR $110-125/77-88, 3 BR $150/93

MAKANI A KAI ★

300 Hauoli St., Wailuku, Maui, HI 96793. Agent: Maalaea Bay Rentals 1-800-367-6084. These deluxe o.f. or o.v. units are on the beach. Laundry room on property, pool, BBQ. This is the last property along the beach in Maalaea. Beyond this is a long stretch of sandy beach along undeveloped state land and about a four mile jaunt down to North Kihei. Great for you beach walkers! The two bedroom units are townhouse style. This is a very pleasant place to headquarter your Maui vacation!
1 BR $95-130 / $70-95, 2 BR $145-175 / $100-125   5-day minimum stay

NORTH KIHEI

INTRODUCTION

North Kihei is 15 minutes from the Kahului Airport and located at the entrance
to South Kihei. The condominiums here stretch along a gentle sloping white sand
beach. The small Kealia Shopping Center is located between the Kihei Sands and
Nani Kai Hale. Another small shopping area is found at the Sugar Beach Condominiums. Several snack shop restaurants can be found along Kihei Road in this
area. A little to the south down Kihei Road are additional restaurants, grocery
stores and large shopping areas.

Along with Maalaea, this is one of our favorite places to stay because of the good
units, central but quiet location, nice beach, cooling breezes and certainly some
of the island's best vacation buys.

ACCOMMODATIONS - NORTH KIHEI

Kealia	Kihei Kai
Sugar Beach	Maalaea Surf
Kihei Sands	Kihei Beach Resort
Nani Kai Hale	

***BEST BETS: Kealia** and **Maalaea Surf**.*

KEALIA ★
191 N. Kihei Rd., Kihei, Maui, HI 96753. (808-879-9159) 1-800-367-5222.
Fifty-one air-conditioned units with lanais, washer/dryers, and dishwashers. Maid
service on request. The one bedroom units are a little on the small side, but
overall a good value. Well maintained and quiet resort with a wonderful sandy
beach. Shops nearby. Extra person $10. 10% monthly discount. $125 deposit,
$10 cancellation fee. 100% payment required 30 days prior to arrival. Seven day
minimum winter, four day in summer. NO CREDIT CARDS. *Studio (2) $70/55,
1 BR o.v. (2) $90/75, 1 BR o.f. (2) $100/85. Limited number of 2 BR units
available.*

SUGAR BEACH RESORT
145 N. Kihei Rd. Kihei, Maui, HI 96753. (808-879-7765). Agents: Maui Condo
& Home 1-800-822-4409, Hawaiian Apt. Leasing 1-800-854-8843 (1-800-472-
8449 CA), Maui Condos 1-800-663-6962 US & Canada, RSVP 1-800-663-1118,
More Hawaii 1-800-967-6687, Rainbow Rentals 1-800-451-5366, (808) 874-0233,
Condo Rental HI 1-800-367-5242. 215 units in several six-story buildings with
elevators. Air-conditioning. Jacuzzi, putting green, gas BBQ grills. Sandwich
shop and quick shop market on location. A nice pool area and located on an
excellent swimming beach.
1 BR o.v. $125/90, o.f. $140/1055, 2 BR o.v. $200/150

124

KIHEI SANDS
115 N. Kihei Rd., Kihei, Maui, HI 96753. (808-879-2624). Thirty oceanfront air-conditioned units, kitchens include microwaves. Shops and restaurant nearby. Seven night minimum high season/4-day minimum low season, $100 deposit with 20% cancellation fee. 50% of balance due 30 days prior to arrival, balance on arrival. No maid service or room phone. Coin laundry area. NO CREDIT CARDS. Extra persons $6/night.
1 BR (2) $90-115 / $69-90, 2 BR (4) $108-138 / $80-103

NANI KAI HALE ★
73 N. Kihei Rd., Kihei, Maui, HI 96753. (808-879-9120) 1-800-367-6032. Agents: Maui Condo & Home 1-800-822-4409, Hawaiian Apt. Leasing 1-800-854-8843 (1-800-472-8449 CA), Kumulani 1-800-367-2954, Maui Condominiums 1-800-663-6962 US & Canada. 46 units in a six-story building. Under building parking, laundry on each floor, elevator. No maid service, no room phones. Patio and BBQ's by beach. Lanais have ocean and mountain views. Prices based on seven day/three day minimum stay. $100 deposit. Monthly discounts. Children under five years no charge. Extra person $10 per night. *Some studios available, 1 BR 2 bath (2) standard $100/75, o.v. $115/80, o.f. $135/100; 2 BR 2 bath (2) std. $135/110, o.f. $170/150*

KIHEI KAI
61 N. Kihei Rd., Kihei, Maui, HI 96753. (808-879-2357) 1-800-735-2357. Twenty-four units in a two-story beachfront building. Recreation area, laundry room, units have air-conditioning or ceiling fans. BBQ. On seven-mile stretch of sandy beach, near windsurfing, grocery stores. A good value. Minimum seven days winter, four days summer. $100 deposit per week. NO CREDIT CARDS. Extra persons $5/night. Weekly discounts. *1 BR (2,max 4) $90-105 / $80-95*

KIHEI BEACH RESORT
36 S. Kihei Rd., Kihei, Maui, HI 96753. (808-879-2744) 1-800-367-6034, FAX (808) 875-0306. Agents: Maui Network 1-800-367-5221, Maui Condo & Home 1-800-822-4409, Maui Condo 1-800-663-6962 Canada. 54 beachfront units with oceanview, microwaves, phones. Resort offers central air-conditioning, recreation area, elevator, maid service. Minimum 3 nights. Extra person $10/night. Weekly and monthly discounts. *1 BR (2,max4) $120/105; 2 BR (4,max 6) $155/135*

MAALAEA SURF ★
12 S. Kihei Rd., Kihei, Maui, HI 96753. (808-879-1267) 1-800-423-7953. Sixty oceanview units in 8 two-story oceanfront buildings. These townhouse units have air-conditioning and microwaves. Daily maid service, except Sundays and holidays. Two pools, two tennis courts, shuffleboard. Laundry facilities in each building. Very attractive and quiet low-rise complex on a great beach. In this price range, these spacious and attractive units, along with five acres of beautiful grounds, are impressive and hard to beat. Extra persons $8/night. NO CREDIT CARDS. $200-300 deposit. High season balance due 30 days prior to arrival, low season on arrival. 60-day refund notice with $10 cancellation fee during high season, 30-day notice low season.

SOUTH KIHEI

INTRODUCTION

South Kihei began its growth after that of West Maui, but unfortunately with no planned system of development. The result is a six-mile stretch of coastline littered with more than 50 properties, nearly all condominiums, with some 2,400 units in rental programs. Few complexes are actually on a good beach. However, many are across Kihei Road from one of the Kamaole Beach Parks. A variety of beautiful beaches are just a few minutes drive away.

The drive from Maalaea to Kihei is but a few miles. There is a mix of sugar cane which blends into the mudflats of Maalaea on your right and a rather indistinguishable flatland on your left. The area on your left can best be seen from an aerial perspective. It is the enormous Kealia pond which recently became Hawai'i's second-largest national wildlife refuge. The federal government paid $6.9 million for ownership of the 437 acre pond and another 263 acres were donated as a federal wildlife easement by Alexander & Baldwin. Plans are underway to create a boardwalk which will allow visitors to view the endangered wildlife while protecting their habitat. Among the endangered species currently making their home in the pond are the Hawaiian coot and Hawaiian stilt.

This section of East Maui has a much different feel than West Maui or Lahaina. There are no large resorts with exotically landscaped grounds, very few units on prime beachfront, and more competition among the complexes making this area a good value for your vacation dollar. (And a good location for extended stays.) Kihei always seemed to operate at a quieter and more leisurely pace than that of Kaanapali and Lahaina, but the last couple of years has seen a significant upsurge of development, not of condos, but of shopping complexes. Sadly, in 1994 what was beginning of shopping in Kihei, the Azeka Market closed its doors. Progress has pushed out a Kihei institution.

Even parts of South Kihei Road have been repaved and regular curbs installed. These changes indicate the increasing tourist activity along with a corresponding loss of Kihei's once laid-back charm. Restaurant selections have expanded as well, giving visitors many options for dining, other than their condominium kitchens. Most needs can be filled locally at one of several large grocery stores or the growing number of small shopping centers. Kahului, Wailuku, Wailea and Lahaina remain an easy drive for additional shopping and dining out.

WHAT TO DO AND SEE

The only historical landmark is a totem pole near the Maui Lu Resort which commemorates the site where Captain Vancouver landed.

WHERE TO SHOP

Every corner of Kihei is sprouting a new shopping mall. The complexes all seem to have quick markets, video stores and a T-shirt shop.

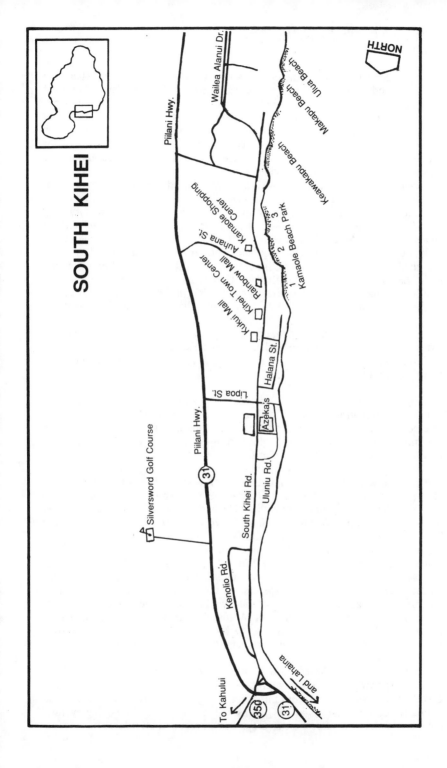

SOUTH KIHEI

NORTH

Wailea Alanui Dr.

Piilani Hwy.

Makapu Beach

Ulua Beach

Keawakapu Beach

Kamaole Shopping Center

Auhana St.

1
2
3

Kamaole Beach Park

Rainbow Mall

Kihei Town Center

Kukui Mall

Halana St.

Lipoa St.

Azeka's

Piilani Hwy.

Silversword Golf Course

4

31

South Kihei Rd.

Uluniu Rd.

Kenolio Rd.

To Kahului

and Lahaina

350

31

Traveling down Kihei Road, the first center is *Azeka Place* (874-8400) where Bill Azeka opened his first store in 1950. *Azeka's Market* closed in September 1994 and *Ace Hardware* has relocated in that space. The *Azeka Snack Shop* continues to offer great deals on island style plate lunches. The *International House of Pancakes, Royal Thai Cuisine, Pizza Hut, Taco Bell* and a *Blimpie* sandwich shop are among the restaurants here as well as *Crazy Shirts* and assorted tourist shops which vary each year. Newer arrivals to the mall include *Old Dayes Antiques & Collectibles* and *Tilt*, which is a video arcade. *Liberty House* is across the street at *Azeka Place II* and the good news is they have their discount store, *Penthouse*, is here as well! You can find great buys on out-of-season or one of a kind items! Also located here are several jewelry and clothing stores, a baby accessory shop *Paradise Swimwear* and a Chinese restaurant, *Panda Express*. *The Coffee Store* and *A Pacific Cafe* (a fabulous restaurant) seem to form a dividing line in this mall. Beyond these two stores, is another portion of the mall which has a sign that reads *"Longs Drugs Kihei Center."* Here you'll find a children's clothing store, *Little Polynesians, Maui Sporting Goods, Eel Skin and Gifts* along with eateries that include *Sushi Paradise, Peggy Sue's, The Kal Bi House and Stars & Stripes Yogurt and Shave Ice*. Opposite this mall is the ever popular *McDonald's*.

If you're traveling toward Wailea, on your right will be Star Market and on your left a Chevron Station and behind this is Paradise Plaza. Behind the service station is *Shaka Pizza*. They have fabulous N.Y. subway style pizza, so be sure to give them a try!

The *Lipoa Shopping Center* is a block down Lipoa Street and is home to the new micro brew/restaurant/cigar bar called *Hapa*s Brew Haus*. Gourmet Italian is offered alongside a microbrewery that serves "upscale" burgers and pizza with live music six nights a week. Also located in this center are *Kaipuni Japanese Restaurant* and *Henry's Bar and Grill*.

Just past the Kapulanikai condominiums, the *Kukui Mall* at 1819 S. Kihei Rd., (244-8735) gets our vote for the most attractive mall. This large complex is done in a Spanish style of architecture with a wide assortment of shops. The multi-plex theater offers a good selection of first run movies. *Subway Sandwiches* is a handy stop for lunch enroute to one of Wailea's fine beaches or stop by *Pair O Dice Pizza*. *Tony Roma's Ribs* is a dining option here and you can follow up your rib dinner with a cool treat there's *I Can't Believe It's Yogurt*. The *Waldenbooks* has a great selection of books on just about any subject (and hopefully our Paradise guides!). The kids might want to spend some time on a rainy afternoon at the *Fun Factory*. They have an assortment of video and arcade games. A number of gift and sundry shops round out this mall. Across the street from the Kukui Mall is an open air shopping area. *The Aloha Market* is kind of a junky swap meet style tourist trap. Lots of jewelry, tee-shirts, and the like. No great deals.

A bit farther is *The Kihei Town Center* which offers a selection of shops including sporting goods, novelty, grocery, and clothing. The restaurants here are *Chuck's* and *Hirohachi*. Across the street is a great little row of eateries. The *Lone Star Cafe* specializes in BBQ items with a young crowd enjoying evening entertainment. *Alexanders Fish & Chips* has a great and affordable menu. The fish is prepared either deep fried or broiled. In addition to island seafood, they import oysters from Puget Sound. The best shave ice in town and a MUST STOP for all visitors is here at *Tobi's*. (Tobi is no longer the owner though as she is spending her time rearing her new twins!) Next door at *Kihei Caffe* you can get a generous meal for a reasonable price.

The next few shopping areas run almost together. The **Dolphin Plaza**, 2395 S. Kihei Rd., across from Kamaole I Beach is one of the shopping centers. Here you'll find *The New York Deli, Senor Tacos*, a sushi bar and a pizza restaurant.

Between the Dolphin Plaza and Rainbow Mall is the **Kamaole Beach Center**, 2411 S. Kihei Rd. Here you'll find *Hawaiian Moons Natural Foods*. They offer health foods, vitamins, and organically grown produce. Adjacent is *Hawaiian Moons Pizza and Deli*. Not quite the same ambiance as the old Paradise Fruits (Hawaiian Moons actually has a floor) but a great new addition to Kihei. Other eateries at this center are the *Sports Page Grill and Bar* and the popular *Maui Tacos*.

The Rainbow Mall is a small center also located on the mauka side (towards the mountain) of South Kihei Road. They offer a stand that serves shave ice and espresso, a sub style sandwich shop and video rental store. *Restaurant Cairo*, upstairs, is a new African restaurant. *Thai Chef*, towards the back of the mall, is another dining option.

Kamaole Shopping Center is one of the larger new malls and offers several restaurant selections. *Denny's* includes *Gator's Good Times Tavern* and *Canton Chef*. The *Cinnamon Roll Faire* has wonderful, huge and decadent cinnamon buns. There is also a *Maui Dive Shop*, a *Whalers General Store* and several clothing shops.

The last shopping center in Kihei, across from Kamaole III Beach, is the **Nani Kai Center**. *Kai Ku Ono Bar & Grill, Kihei Prime Rib & Seafood, The Greek Bistro and Sunyside Cafe and Deli* are the restaurants which make up this complex. There is also a mini-market.

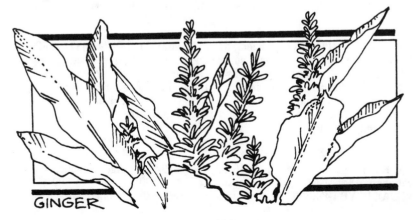

GINGER

ACCOMMODATIONS - SOUTH KIHEI

Nona Lani	Punahoa
Kihei Holiday	Beach Club Apts.
Wailana Sands	Lihi Kai Cottages
Maui Isana	Maui Vista
Pualani	Kamoa Views
Sunseeker Resort	Kamaole One
Maui Lu Resort	Maui Coast Hotel
Kihei Bay Vista	Kamaole Beach
Kihei Bay Surf	Royale
Menehune Shores	Kihei Alii Kai
Kihei Resort	Royal Mauian
Koa Lagoon	Kamaole Nalu
Koa Resort	Hale Pau Hana
Kauhale Makai	Kihei Kai Nani
Leinaala	Kihei Akahi
Luana Kai	Maui Banyan
Maui Schooner	Haleakala Shores
Maui Sunset	Maui Parkshore
Leilani Kai	Kamaole Sands
Kihei Garden	Hale Kamaole
Hale Kai O Kihei	Maui Kamaole
Waiohuli Beach	Maui Hill
Kihei Beachfront	Kihei Surfside
Kapulanikai	Mana Kai Maui
Island Surf	Maui Oceanfront
Kihei Park Shores	Hale Hui Kai
Shores of Maui	

BEST BETS: Maui Hill - Situated on a hillside across the road from the ocean, some units have excellent ocean views. The three-bedroom units here are roomy and a good value for large families. ***Haleakala Shores*** - Across from Kamaole III Beach Park. ***Mana Kai Maui*** - One of Kihei's larger resorts, the units are fair but an extra plus is that they are some of only a few located on good beaches.

NONA LANI
455 S. Kihei Rd., (PO Box 655) Kihei, Maui, HI 96753. (808-879-2497), 1-800-733-2688. Eight individual cottages with kitchens, color TV, queen bed plus two day beds, full bath with tub and shower, and lanais. Large grounds, public phone, two BBQ's, and laundry facilities. Located across the road from sandy beach. Extra person $7 night. Full payment 30 days prior to arrival. Cancellation penalty. NO CREDIT CARDS. *1 BR (2) $68; $455 weekly low season, higher rates December 16-April 1.*

KIHEI HOLIDAY
483 S. Kihei Rd., Kihei, Maui, HI 96753. (808-879-9228) Agents: Kihei Maui Vacations 1-800-541-6284, Hawaiian Apt. Leasing 1-800-854-8843 (1-800-472-8449 CA), RSVP 1-800-662-1118. Units are across the street from the beach and

have lanais with garden views. Pool area jacuzzi and BBQ's. $100 deposit, full payment 30 days prior to arrival. Maid service on request. NO CREDIT CARDS. *1 BR $90/75, 2 BR (4) $110/85*

WAILANA SANDS
25 Wailana Place, Kihei, Maui, HI 96753. 10 units, overlook courtyard and pool area, in a two-story structure. Quiet area on a dead end road one block from the beach. No rental rates available.

PUALANI TOWNHOUSES
15 Wailana Place, Kihei, Maui, HI. No rental units available.

MAUI ISANA RESORT
515 S. Kihei Road, Kihei, Maui, HI 96753 (808-879-7800), 1-800-633-3833. Agent: Kihei Maui Vacations 1-800-541-6284. These 51-one-bedroom units are decorated in muted beige and blues and are complete down to an electric rice cooker and china dishes. A spacious pool area is the focal point of the central courtyard. Located across the road from the beach. Washer/dryer, cable TV., maid service. Extra person $15. *1 BR 1 BTH (1-3) $120, 2 BR 2 BTH (1-5) $160.*

SUNSEEKER RESORT
551 S. Kihei Rd. (PO Box 276) Kihei, Maui, HI 96753. (808-879-1261) 1-800-532-MAUI, FAX (808) 874-3877. Units include studios with kitchenettes, one bedrooms with kitchens. Monthly discounts available. No room phones, no pool. Across street from beach. Popular area for windsurfing. Minimum stay three days. Three night deposit. NO CREDIT CARDS. Milt & Eileen Preston are the Owner/Managers. *S BR $60/55, 1 BR $70/65, Extra person $6*

MAUI LU RESORT
575 S. Kihei Rd., Kihei, Maui, HI 96753. (808-879-5881) Agent: Aston 1-800-922-7866. 180 units on 26 acres. Pool is shaped like the island of Maui. Many of the hotel rooms are set back from South Kihei Road and the oceanfront units are not on a sandy beachfront. One of the first resorts in the Kihei area and unusual with its spacious grounds. Extra persons $12, under 18 no charge. The *Ukulele Grill* restaurant is located on site.
Hotel rooms (2) g.v., o.v., o.f. $119-205/99-185

KIHEI BAY VISTA
679 S. Kihei Rd., Kihei, Maui, HI 96753.(808-879-8866). Agents: Outrigger Hotels Hawaii 1-800-OUTRIGGER, Hawaiian Apt. Leasing 1-800-854-8843 or 1-800-472-8449 from CA., Kihei Maui Vacations 1-800-541-6284. Built in 1989, this complex offers pool, spa, jacuzzi, putting green, air-conditioning, washer/dryer, lanais and full kitchens. A short walk across the road to Kamaole I Beach. Overlooking Kalepolepo Beach.
1 BR g.v. and o.v. units $95-110 / $85-100

KIHEI BAY SURF
715 S. Kihei Rd. (Manager Apt. 110), Kihei, Maui, HI 96753. (808-879-7650) Agents: Kihei Maui Vacations 1-800-541-6284, Maui Condominiums 1-800-663-

6962 US & Canada, Maui Network 1-800-367-5221, Island Discount Rentals 1-808-879-1466, Hawaiian Apt. Leasing 1-800-854-8843. Kihei Bay Surf offers 118 studio units in 7 two-story buildings. Pool area, jacuzzi, recreational area, gas BBQ, laundry area, tennis. Across the road from Kamaole I Beach. Phones. Weekly discounts. *Studios $70/60*

MENEHUNE SHORES
760 Kihei Rd., Kihei, Maui, HI 96753. (808-879-0076) Agents: Menehune Reservations, PO Box 1327, Kihei, Maui, HI 96753, (808-879-3428), 1-800-558-9117 US & Canada, FAX (808) 879-5218. RSVP 1-800-663-1118, Kihei Maui Vacations 1-800-541-6284. 115 units with dishwashers, washer/dryers and lanais in a six story building. Recreation room, roof gardens with whale-watching platform, and shuffleboard. The ocean area in front of this condominium property is the last remnant of one of Maui's early fish ponds. These ponds, where fish were raised and harvested, were created by the early Hawaiians all around the islands. Extra persons $7.50/night, $200 deposit. Five day minimum stay. $25 cancellation charge. NO CREDIT CARDS.
1 BR 1 bath (2) $100/ 75, 1 BR 2 bath (2) $120/88.50
2 BR 2 bath (2) $130/100, 3 BR 2 bath (6) $140-160/120-140

KIHEI RESORT
777 S. Kihei Rd., Kihei, Maui, HI 96753. Agents: Kihei Maui Vacations 1-800-541-6284, RSVP 1-800-663-1118, Rainbow Rentals 1-800-451-5366, Hawaiian Apt. Leasing 1-800-854-8843. Sixty-four units, two-story building, located across the street from the ocean, BBQ's, pool area jacuzzi. NO CREDIT CARDS.
1 BR (2) $ 85/70   7-nite minimum, $100 deposit, 10-day refund notice
2 BR (4) $105/90   Extra persons $7/night, 10% monthly discount

KOA LAGOON
800 S. Kihei Rd., Kihei, Maui, HI 96753. RENTAL AGENT: Bello Realty, 1-800-541-3060, (808-879-3328), FAX (808) 879-3329. 42 oceanview units in one six story building. Washer/dryers. Pool area pavilion, BBQ's. Located on a small sandy beach that is often plagued by seaweed which washes ashore from the offshore coral reef. This stretch of Kihei is very popular with windsurfers. Extra person $10 additional. $250 deposit, full payment 45 days prior to arrival. 45-day cancellation notice. 14-day minimum stay during Christmas holiday. $45 cleaning charge for stays of 4 days or less. NO CREDIT CARDS.
1 BR 1 bath (2,max 4) $110/80, 2 BR 2 bath (4,max 6) $130/100

KOA RESORT
811 S. Kihei Rd., Kihei, Maui, HI 96753. (808-879-1161) 1-800-877-1314, FAX (808) 879-4001. 54 units (2,030 sq.ft.) on spacious 5 1/2-acre grounds in 2 five-story buildings across road from beach. Two tennis courts, spa, jacuzzi, putting green. Units have washer/dryers. 10% monthly discount. Cash discount. Extra persons $10/day, children under two free. Five night minimum. $100 deposit.
1 BR 1 bath (2,max 4) $100/85, 2 BR 1 bath (4,max 4) $120/100,
2 bath (4,max 6) $130/110, 3 BR 2 bath (6,max 8) $155/135, 3 bath (6,max 8) $180/160

KAUHALE MAKAI (Village by the Sea)
930-938 S. Kihei Rd. Kihei, Maui, HI 96753. (808-879-8888). Agent: Maui Condominium & Home Realty 1-800-822-4409, (808-879-5445), FAX (808) 874-6144, Maui Condominiums 1-800-663-6962 US & Canada, RSVP 1-800-663-1118, Kihei Maui Vacations 1-800-541-6284, Rainbow Rentals 1-800-451-5366. 169 air-conditioned units in 2 six-floor buildings with phones. Complex features putting green, gas BBQ's, children's pool, sauna, laundry center. The beach here is usually strewn with coral rubble and seaweed. $5 additional person. 4-night minimum through Maui Condo.
Studio (2) $75/60, 1 BR (2) $90/70, 2 BR (4) $120/85

LUANA KAI ★
940 S. Kihei Rd., Kihei, Maui, HI 96753. (808-879-1268), 1-800-669-1127, FAX (808) 879-1455. AGENTS: Kihei Maui Vacations 1-800-541-6284, Hawaiian Island Resorts 1-800-367-7042. 113 units on 8 acres with washer/dryers are located adjacent to a large oceanfront park with public tennis courts. The beach, however, is almost always covered with coral rubble and seaweed. The grounds are nicely landscaped and include a putting green, BBQ area, pool area, sauna and jacuzzi. Maid service available for extra fee. Children under 12 free. Extra person $10. Deposit $300/$100 with $25 cancellation fee. 7-night minimum holiday, three night minimum high season.

Rates from Hawaiian Island Resorts: 1 BR (2) g.v./o.v. $100-125/75-110, 2 BR (6) g.v. or o.v. $130-155/95-130, 3 BR (8) g.v. $160/210.

MAUI SCHOONER RESORT
980 S Kihei Rd, Kihei, Maui HI 96753. (808-879-5247) Reservations phone weekdays during business hours 1-800-877-7976. These 58 units are fully furnished complete with equipped kitchens, TV, VCR, washer/dryer and private lanai. Only one building has an elevator to the upper floors. Fronting these condos is a public park with 4 tennis courts and a beach (that is seasonally strewn with coral rubble). Swimming pool, sauna, and hot tub. Now a time share resort, but offering rentals as well. Check-ins are Friday, Saturday and Sunday. Check in is 4 pm, check out is an early 10 am.
Weekly rates: 1 BR (4) $750, 2 BR (6) $925, 3 BR $1100

LEINAALA
998 S Kihei Rd, Kihei, Maui, HI 96753. (808-879-2235) 1-800-334-3305 U.S. & Canada, FAX (808) 879-8366. 24 one and two bedroom units in a 4-story building. Tennis courts at adjoining park. Pool, cable color TV. Oceanview. This property is fronted by a large grassy park which stretches out to the ocean. The beach is usually covered with coral rubble and much better beach activities would be enjoyed a short drive down to one of the Kamaole Beach Parks in Kihei. Weekly/monthly discounts. $200 deposit with 30-day refund notice. NO CREDIT CARDS. Extra persons $10 night. Four night minimum. AARP and AAA discounts.
Studio/no view (2) $65, 1 BR (2) $95/85, 2 BR (4) $115/100

WAIPUILANI
1002 S. Kihei Rd., Kihei, Maui, HI 96753. (808-879-1465). 42 units in three 3-story buildings. No vacation rentals. Only long term.

MAUI SUNSET
1032 S. Kihei, Rd., Kihei, Maui, HI 96753. (808-879-0674) Reservation Assistance 1-800-843-5880. Agents: Kihei Maui Vacations 1-800-541-6284, Kumulani 1-800-367-2954, Maui Network 1-800-367-5221, Hawaiian Apt. Leasing 1-800-854-8843 (1-800-472-8449 CA), RSVP 1-800-663-1118, Maui Condo & Home 1-800-822-4409. 225 air-conditioned units in two multi-story buildings. Tennis courts, pitch and putt golf green, and sauna. Large pool, exercise facility, barbecues. Located on beach park with tennis courts, however, this beach is generally covered with seaweed and coral rubble. Extra persons $7/night.
1 BR $105/85, 2 BR $145/110, Some 3 BR $185-205/155-175

LEILANI KAI
1226 Uluniu St., (PO Box 296) Kihei, Maui, HI 96753. (808-879-2606). Eight garden apartments with lanais. $200 deposit. Extra person $7.50. Full payment 30 days prior to arrival. Three day minimum stay. NO CREDIT CARDS. Monthly discounts.
Studio (2) $75/60, 1 BR (2) $100/75, 1 BR dlx (4) $115/85, 2 BR (4) $125/90

KIHEI GARDEN ESTATES
1299 Uluniu St., Kihei, Maui, HI 96753. (808-879-5785), 1-800-827-2786. Agents: Kihei Maui Vacations 1-800-541-6284, Maui Condominiums 1-800-663-6962 US & Canada. 84 units in eight 2-story buildings. Jacuzzi, BBQ's. Across road and short walk to beaches. Monthly discounts. $100 deposit, full payment 30 days prior to arrival. NO CREDIT CARDS. Rates for 4-6 nights. Weekly discounts. *1 BR (2,max 4) $90-100/ 75, 2 BR (4,max 6) $110/85*

HALE KAI O KIHEI
PO Box 809, 1310 Uluniu Rd., Kihei, Maui, HI 96753. (808-879-2757), 1-800-457-7014, FAX (808) 875-8242. 59-oceanfront units with lanais in 3-story building. Sandy beachfront. Shuffleboard, putting green, BBQ's, laundry, recreation area. Maid service on request for extra charge. Extra person $10/night. 10% monthly discount. $200 deposit. 60-day/30-day cancellation notice (less $20 handling fee). NO CREDIT CARDS. Daily rates upon request.
1 BR (2) $660/455 weekly, 2 BR 2 bath (4) $835/625 weekly

WAIOHULI BEACH HALE
49 West Lipoa St., Kihei, Maui, HI 96753. Rental Manager: (808-879-5396) FAX (808) 875-7626. Agents: Kihei Maui Vacations 1-800-541-6284, Pali Kai 1-808-879-8550, Paradise Realty 1-808-874-8074. 52 units in four two story buildings. Large pool, gas BBQs. Located on beachfront that is poor for swimming or snorkeling, often covered with coral rubble and seaweed. Spacious park-like lawn area around pool. Weekly and monthly discounts available.
1 BR o.v. (2) $95/70; 2 BR o.v. (4) $115/100; Dlx 2 BR o.v. (4) $129/114
1 BR o.f. (2) $95/80; 2 BR o.f. $120/120. Weekly and monthly discounts.
Additional guests $10 per night, children 12 and under $5 per night.

KIHEI BEACHFRONT RESORT

Located at end of Lipoa St. Agent: Maui Condos & Homes 1-800-822-4409. Eight oceanview two bedroom units with washer/dryers, microwaves, dishwashers, and air-conditioning in a single 2-story building. Large lawn area fronting units. Lanais on upper level. No elevator. Pool area jacuzzi. Five night minimum stay or cleaning fee required. $200 deposit. $10 additional person. Weekly, monthly discounts. *2 BR o.v./g.v. $130/100, 2 BR o.f. (4) $165/135*

KAPULANIKAI APTS

73 Kapu Place, PO Box 716, Kihei, Maui, HI 96753. Agent: Bello Realty 1-800-541-3060. 12 units are oceanview with private lanais or open terraces. Beachfront is poor for swimming or snorkeling. Grassy lawn area in front. BBQ's, laundry facilities, pay phone on property. *1 BR 1 bath $80/65*

ISLAND SURF

1993 S. Kihei Rd., Kihei, Maui, HI 96753. This property once had vacation units, but is now primarily commercial or residential.

KIHEI PARK SHORES

The only rental agent we have found is Pali Kai 1-808-879-8550. They have a one bedroom, one bath oceanfront *$75/65*

SHORES OF MAUI

2075 S. Kihei Rd., Kihei, Maui, HI 96753. (808-879-9140) 1-800-367-8002. 50-unit two-level complex in garden setting offers BBQ's, tennis courts, and spa. Located across the street from a rocky shoreline and 1½ blocks north of Kamaole I Beach Park. $100 deposit, 30-day cancellation notice, full payment 30 days prior to arrival. Extra persons $8/night, monthly discounts. Three day minimum (Christmas holiday 1-week minimum). Monthly discounts. Credit cards accepted if arrival date within 60 days of reservation date. *1 BR $90/65, 2 BR $115/90*

PUNAHOA

2142 Iliili Rd., Kihei, Maui, HI 96753. (808-879-2720) 1-800-564-2720. 15-oceanview units with large lanais, telephones. No pool. Elevator, laundry facilities, beaches nearby. NO CREDIT CARDS. $400/200 deposit, 60-day refund notice. Extra persons $12/night, under age 2 free. Weekly/monthly discounts. 5-day minimum or pay $50 service charge.
Studio (2) $81/62, 1 BR (2,max 4) $106-109/79-82,
2 BR (2,max 6) $87-110 / $120-140

BEACH CLUB APARTMENTS

2173 Iliili Rd., Kihei, Maui, HI 96753, (808-874-6474). Long term rentals only.

LIHI KAI COTTAGES

2121 Iliili Rd., Kihei, Maui, HI 96753. (808-879-2335) 1-800-544-4524. Nine beach cottages are one bedroom and one bath with kitchen and lanai. Self-service laundromat. Next to Kamaole I Beach. $100 deposit, three day minimum, 60/30 day refund notice. Maid service at additional fee. NO CREDIT CARDS.
1 BR (2) $69/64

MAUI VISTA
2191 S. Kihei Rd., Kihei, Maui, HI 96753. (808-879-7966) 1-800-367-8047 ext.330. Agents: Kihei Maui Vacations 1-800-541-6284, RSVP 1-800-663-1118, Maui Condo & Home 1-800-822-4409, Maui Condominiums 1-800-663-6962 US & Canada (Maui Condos had lower rates than those listed below.) 280 units in three 4-story buildings, across from the beach. Some units have air-conditioning, some have washer/dryers. All have kitchens with dishwashers. The two bedroom units are fourth floor townhouses. Some oceanview units. Six tennis courts, three pools, BBQ's. We had some problem with sound carrying from a neighboring unit. Extra persons are $12 per night.
1 BR 1 Bath (2,max 4) $105-120/95-110,
2 BR 2 Bath (2,max 6) $145-160/125-140
Some studios may be available through some rental agents.

PACIFIC SHORES
2219 S. Kihei Rd. (808-874-3461). Residential and long term rentals only.

KAMOA VIEWS
2124 Awihi Place. (808-879-5335). Long term rentals only.

KAMAOLE ONE
2230 S. Kihei Rd., Kihei, Maui, HI 96753. (808-879-4811 or 808-879-2449), FAX (808) 874-3744. Two story building. Twelve units, currently nine are available for vacation rental. No elevators or pool, covered parking. Beachfront. Nice location on Kamaole I Beach. Telephones, microwaves, washer/dryers, air-conditioning, ceiling fans and cable TV. One week minimum stay. $200 deposit. NO CREDIT CARDS. No swimming pool, but as Jean Simpson, manager, notes in her explanation, "we felt it redundant here on Kamaole #1 Beach."
2 BR ground or second floor $160-170/140-150

MAUI COAST HOTEL (Hotel)

2259 S. Kihei Rd., Kihei, Maui, HI 96753. (808-874-MAUI), FAX (808) 875-4731. Reservations: 1-800-426-0670. Operated by West Coast Hotels, they opened in February 1993 and offer 264 guest rooms and 216 sleeping rooms -- 114 of them suites. The hotel offers a pool area, two outdoor whirlpools, the Kamaole Bar & Grill in front, two night lit tennis courts and complimentary laundry facilities. We found this to be a great concept, a more affordable hotel with some condominium conveniences. The in-room refrigerator was stocked with a couple of complimentary cans of juice daily and there was a coffee maker with the fixings.

Located across the road from the Kamaole Beach Parks, the pool area was pleasant and an international mix of people seemed to be staying at the property during our visit. We heard both Chinese and Italian spoken at the pool. We inquired as to how some of the other guests had discovered this hotel. One group was from a large company. They had needed a large cluster of rooms and wanted hotel amenities, but weren't interested in the $300 mega-resort rates. One couple was staying two nights at the hotel before they moved to another mega-resort in Wailea that couldn't accommodate them upon their arrival. Another advantage here is for the short term island visitor. Many of the condominiums have a four day or even a week minimum stay. The standard room we had was a little crowded with one king bed and the two kids on a sofa bed. No frills, but nicely appointed. Currently they offer an extra value "Meals" or "Wheels" package. Enjoy a $25 daily food and beverage credit at the Kamaole Bar & Grill or a free daily car rental, priced at $119 per day.

Standard Hotel Room: Terrace $119, Partial Ocean View $129; Alcove Suite: Terrace $139, Partial Ocean View $149. Standard One Bedroom suite $165; Deluxe One Bedroom Suite $179; Standard Two Bedroom Suites $225-250.

KAMAOLE BEACH ROYALE

2385 S. Kihei Rd., Kihei, Maui, HI 96753. (808-879-3131), 1-800-421-3661, FAX (808) 879-9163. 64 units with washer/dryers and single or double lanais in a single seven story building across from Kamaole I Beach. Recreation area, elevator, roof garden. 10% monthly discount, 5-day minimum, $200 deposit, balance due 30 days prior to arrival. $25 cancellation service charge. NO CREDIT CARDS. Management notes that all units have been recently upgraded.
1 BR 1 bath (2) $ 95/70   Extra person $10 per night
2 BR 2 bath (2) $110-115 / $85-90
3 BR 3 bath (2) $120/95

KIHEI ALII KAI

2387 S. Kihei Rd., Kihei, Maui, HI 96753. (808-879-6770), 1-800-888-MAUI. Agents: Leisure Properties (PO Box 985, Kihei, 96753) 1-800-888-MAUI, Pali Kai 1-808-879-8550, RSVP 1-800-663-1118, Kihei Maui Vacations 1-800-541-6284, Rainbow Rentals 1-800-451-5366. 127 units in four buildings. All units have washer/dryers. No maid service. Complex features pool, jacuzzi, sauna, two tennis courts, BBQ. Across road and up street from beach. Nearby restaurants

and shops. Extra persons $7/night. $100 deposit, 3 night minimum. Full payment 30 days prior to arrival.
1 BR (2) $90/65, 2 BR (4) $105-115 / $80-90, 3 BR (6) $130/110

ROYAL MAUIAN
2430 S. Kihei Rd., Kihei, Maui, HI 96753. (808-879-1263) 1-800-367-8009, FAX (808) 367-8009. 107 units with lanai, washer/dryer, in a six story building. Complex has shuffleboard, carpeted roof garden, and is next to the pleasant Kamaole II Beach Park. $15 extra person, five night minimum, $350 deposit with $50 cancellation fee. Maid service twice weekly. Following are high season rates.

1 BR 1 bath or 2 bath (2) $137
2 BR 2 bath (2) $150-175, 3 BR (4) $220
Side wing two bedroom, two bath units are $120

KAMAOLE NALU
2450 S. Kihei Rd., Kihei, Maui, HI 96753 (808-879-1006) 1-800-767-1497. FAX (808) 879-8693. Thirty-six two bedroom, two bath units with large lanai, dishwasher, and washer/dryer in a 6-story building. Located between Kamaole I and II Beach Parks with all units offering oceanviews. Weekly maid service during high season. $12-15 extra person. Three day minimum. $400/200 deposit with $25 cancellation fee. Summer specials offered.
2 BR 2 bath (2) o.v. $125/110, o.f. $160/125

HALE PAU HANA
2480 S. Kihei Rd., Kihei, Maui, HI 96753. (808-879-2715) 1-800-367-6036, FAX (808) 875-0238. Agent: Maui Condo & Home 1-800-822-4409. Seventy-eight oceanview units in four buildings. Laundry area, elevator. Located on Kamaole II Beach. NO CREDIT CARDS. Weekly and monthly discounts. Extra person $10-12. No charge for children 5 years and younger. $250 deposit. $100 cancellation fee. Inquire about condo/car packages and summer specials.
1 BR 1 or 2 BATH (2,max 4) $155-165/110-120
2 BR 2 bath (2,max 4) $155

KIHEI KAI NANI
2495 S. Kihei Rd., Kihei, Maui, HI 96753. (Front desk: 808-879-1430), reservations 1-800-473-1493, Reservations FAX (808) 879-8965. Agents: Kihei Maui Vacations 1-800-541-6284, Maui Condominiums 1-800-663-6962 US & Canada, Hawaiian Apt. Leasing 1-800-854-8843.

180 one-bedroom units with lanai or balcony in a two and three story structure. This complex is one of the older ones along Kihei Rd. Laundry room and recreation center. Across from Kamaole II Beach. $7 extra person. Senior discount 10% low season. Three night minimum, $100 deposit, balance due 30 days prior to arrival. NO CREDIT CARDS thru front desk reservations. Car-/condo packages and weekly discounts available thru front desk office.
1 BR (2) $80/65

MAUI BANYAN
2575 S. Kihei Rd. Agents: Kihei Maui Vacations 1-800-541-6284, Kumulani 1-800-879-9272, Maui Condo & Home 1-800-822-4409, Maui Condominiums 1-800-663-6962 US & Canada. Overlooking Kamaole II Beach Park, these suites feature kitchens, washer/dryer, lanai, air-conditioning, cable TV and telephone. Facilities include tennis court, pool and jacuzzi, BBQ. Hotel rooms have no kitchens or telephones. Daily maid service.
Hotel Room (1-2) g.v. $90/75, partial o.v. $95/80
1 BR (max. 4) g.v. $125/110, partial o.v. $135/120, o.v. $145/130
2 BR (max. 6) g.v. $165/150, partial o.v. $175/160, o.v. $190/175
3 BR (Max. 8) g.v. $200/185, partial o.v. $215/205

KIHEI AKAHI
2531 S. Kihei Rd., Kihei, Maui, HI 96753. (808-879-1881) Agents: Maui Condo & Home Realty 1-800-822-3309, Maui Condominiums 1-800-663-6962 US & Canada, Kihei Maui Vacations 1-800-541-6284, RSVP 1-800-663-1118. 240 units with washer and dryers. 2 pools, tennis court, BBQ's. Across from Kamaole II Beach Park. Weekly & monthly discount. Extra person $12. 4-day minimum, $125 deposit, full payment 30 days prior to arrival. NO CREDIT CARDS. *Studio (2) $80/65, 1 BR 1 bth (2) $95-100/75-80, 2 BR 2 bth (4) $120/90*

HALEAKALA SHORES ★
2619 S. Kihei Rd., Kihei, Maui, HI 96753. (808-879-1218) 1-800-8888869-1097. Seventy-six, 2-BR units in two four story buildings. Located across the road from Kamaole III Beach. Washer/dryer. Covered parking. A good value! Winter season seven night minimum, $200 deposit except Christmas season which requires a two week minimum with non-refundable full payment in advance. Summer season five night minimum, $100 deposit, 5% weekly discount. NO CREDIT CARDS. *2 BR (1-4) $115/85*

MAUI PARKSHORE
2653 S. Kihei Rd., Kihei, Maui, HI 96753. (808-879-1600. Agent: Oihana Properties 1-808-244-7685. Sixty-four, two bedroom, two bath oceanview condos with washer/dryers, and lanais in a 4-story building (elevator) across from Kamaole III Beach. Pool area sauna. 10% monthly discount. $150 deposit, payment in full 30 days prior to arrival. Four night minimum. NO CREDIT CARDS. Extra person $10 per night. *2 BR 2 bath (4) $100/80*

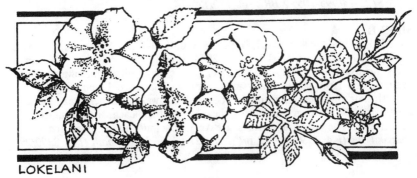

LOKELANI

KAMAOLE SANDS
2695 S. Kihei Rd., Kihei, Maui, HI 96753. (808-874-8700), FAX (808) 879-0666. Agents: Kihei Maui Vacations 1-800-541-6284, Hawaiian Apt. Leasing 1-800-854-8843 (1-800-472-8449 CA), Kumulani 1-800-367-2954, Maui Condo & Home 1-800-822-4409, Castle Group 1-800-367-5004, Hawaiian Pacific Resorts 1-800-367-5004, Maui Condominiums 1-800-663-6962 US & Canada, Kihei Maui Vacations 1-800-541-6284. 440 units in 10 four-story buildings. Includes daily maid service. 4 tennis courts, wading pool, 2 jacuzzi's and BBQ's. Located on 15 acres across the road from Kamaole III Beach. In 1996 they began a refurbishment of the units including bedspreads, carpets, drapes as well as new microwaves. Other upgrades in the kitchen and bathrooms as needed.
Hotel room w/refrigerator $199/109, Studio w/ kitchen $159-179/129-149, 1 BR 2 bath (1-4) $125-160/110-135, 2 BR 2 bath (1-6) $170-225/155-205, 3 BR 3 bath (1-7) $250-275/240-250

HALE KAMAOLE
2737 S. Kihei Rd., Kihei, Maui, HI 96753. (808-879-2698) 1-800-367-2970. Agents: Kumulani 1-800-367-2954, Maui Condo & Home 1-800-822-4409, Maui Condominiums 1-800-663-6962 US & Canada. 188 units in 5 buildings (2 & 3-story, no elevator) across the road from Kamaole III Beach. Laundry building, BBQ's, 2 pools, tennis courts. Some units have washer and dryers. Courtesy phone at office. One time cleaning fee for stays less than 5 nights. $100 deposit per week, balance due 30-60 days before arrival. 3 night minimum stay. Monthly discounts. NO CREDIT CARDS. Extra person $8, no charge for children under twelve. *1 BR (2) $89/67, 2 BR 2 bath (4) $129/87*

MAUI KAMAOLE
2777 S. Kihei Rd., Kihei, Maui, HI 96743. (879-7668). Agents: Kihei Maui Vacations 1-800-541-6284, Maui Condo & Home 1-800-822-4409, Pali Kai 1-808-879-8550, Maui Condominiums 1-800-663-6962 US & Canada. The newest development on South Kihei Road is on a bluff overlooking the ocean and across the street and a short walk down to Kamaole III Beach Park or Keawakapu Beach. 1 BR units are 1,000 - 1,300 sq.ft. and 2 BR units are 1,300 -1,600 sq.ft. Some have oceanviews. This is a four phase development that will eventually have 316 residential units on 23 acres. They are low-rise, four-plex buildings grouped into 13 clusters, each named after Hawaiian flora.
1 BR $125-140/95-105, 2 BR $160-180/125-140

MAUI HILL ★
2881 S. Kihei Rd., Kihei, Maui, HI 96753. (808-879-6321) Agents: Aston Hotels 1-800-922-7866, Kumulani 1-800-367-2954, RSVP 1-800-663-1118. 140 attractively furnished units with washer/dryers, air-conditioning, microwaves, dishwashers, and large lanais. Daily maid service. There are 12 buildings with a Spanish flair clustered on a hillside above the Keawakapu Beach area. There is a moderate walk down and across the road to the beach. Upper units have oceanviews. The 3-bedroom units are very spacious. Large pool and tennis courts. *1 BR (1-4) $190/160, 2 BR (1-6) $210/185, 3 BR 3 bath (1-8) $300/270*

KIHEI SURFSIDE
2936 S. Kihei Rd., Kihei, Maui, HI 96753. (808-879-1488) 1-800-367-5240. Agents: Maui Condo & Home 1-800-822-4409. 83 units on rocky shore with tidepools, a short walk to Keawakapu Beach. Large grassy area and good view. Coin-op laundry on premise. No maid service. Extra persons $10. Children free during summer. Three night minimum, three day deposit, 14-day cancellation notice. Monthly discount. This property has a three rate system. Summer, fall and winter are each priced at a slightly different rate.
1 BR 1 bath (2) $125/80-94, 1 BR 1½ bath (2) $135/88-105,
2 BR 2 bath (4) $160/130

MANA KAI ★
2960 S. Kihei Rd., Kihei, Maui, HI 96753. (808-879-1561), 1-800-525-2025, FAX (808) 874-5042. Agents: Kumulani 1-800-367-2954, Castle Group 1-800-367-5004, Maui Condo & Home 1-800-822-4409, Hawaiian Pacific Resorts 1-800-367-5004. 132 rooms in an eight story building. The studio units have a room with an adjoining bath. The one bedroom units have a kitchen and the two bedroom units are actually the hotel unit and a one bedroom combined, each having separate entry doors. Some of the units need a bit of sprucing up and some minor refurbishment.

This complex has laundry facilities on each floor, an oceanfront pool, and a restaurant off the lobby. Daily maid service. The Mana Kai is nestled at the end of Keawakapu Beach, and offers a majestic view of the blue Pacific, the 10,000 foot high Haleakala and Upcountry Maui. It is the only major facility in Kihei on a prime beachfront location. Keawakapu Beach is not only very nice, but generally very under used. One night deposit, balance due 30-60 days in advance of arrival. 14-day cancellation notice. The rates include a late model car with unlimited mileage. Car user must be 21 years of age.

S BR 1 bath (2) $ 95/ 90, includes breakfast & car (no kitchen)
1 BR 1 bath (2) $175/155, includes car
2 BR 1 bath (2) $195/175, includes car

MAUI OCEANFRONT
2980 S. Kihei Rd., Kihei, Maui, HI 96753. (808-879-7744). Hawaiian Pacific Resorts 1-800-367-5004. 88 units on Keaweakapu Beach. They were unable to show us units following their renovation. No pool, located on Keaweakapu Beach, but only the front unit has an oceanview. Several two-story buildings, no lanais.
Standard $85 (3), Superior $90 (2), Deluxe $100 (2), 1 BR $160 (5)

HALE HUI KAI
2994 S. Kihei Rd. Kihei, Maui, HI 96753. On-site property rental agent (808-879-1219), FAX (808) 879-0600, 1-800-809-MAUI. Oceanfront on Keawakapu Beach. Five night minimum, $200 deposit. Extra person $15-20.
All 2 BR 2 bath:
Rates from $95-160 May 1-Dec. 15; from $120-180, Dec.16-April 30.

141

WAILEA

INTRODUCTION

Wailea is a well planned and well manicured resort on 1,500 acres just south of Kihei developed by Alexander and Baldwin. In addition to a selection of outstanding luxury resorts and condominiums, there are a fine selection of championship golf courses, a large tennis center and a shopping village. The spacious and uncluttered layout is impressive, as are its series of lovely beaches.

There is a shoreline paved trail that travels between the Kea Lani up to the Grand Wailea Resort, making it a wonderful option for a stroll, day or night.

Besides visiting resorts and beaches, there isn't much to do. There is a small shopping center which will satisfy most basic needs. Tuesdays at 1:30 pm they feature a free Hawaiian show in the central courtyard of the Wailea Shopping Center that is quite good. Bring a towel or mat to sit on. You can pick up a cold drink, an ice cream cone or a sandwich to enjoy during the show.

The first two resort hotels were the 550-room Aston Wailea Resort (they opened as the Maui Inter-Continental Resort and changed management in 1996) which opened in 1976, and the 350-room Renaissance Wailea Beach Resort (formerly the Stouffer Wailea Beach Resort that originally opened as a Westin) which opened in 1978. The Palms at Wailea is located at Wailea's entrance. The Four Seasons Resort opened in the spring of 1990 and was followed by the September 1991 opening of the neighboring, 812 room Grand Wailea Resort & Spa, which originally opened as a Hyatt. Kea Lani, an all-suites resort, opened in November of 1992 with 450 rooms and 37 oceanfront villas on Polo Beach. The Diamond Resort, a private, primarily Japanese guest hotel, is located in the foothills above Wailea. The Wailea condominium villages are divided into four locations: two are beachfront while two are adjacent to the golf course. The newest of these villages is the Grand Champion Villas which opened in 1989. The Polo Beach condominiums are located adjacent to Wailea resorts on Makena Road. An exclusive property, Wailea Point, has no vacation rentals.

WHAT TO SEE AND DO

The lovely Wailea beaches are actually well-planned and nicely maintained public parks with excellent access, off-street parking and most have restrooms and rinse-off showers. Ulua Beach is our personal favorite. Don't miss visiting one of Wailea's wonderful beaches! And, be sure you spend some time strolling through the imaginative grounds of the Grand Wailea Resort & Spa.

WHERE TO SHOP

Wailea Shopping Village is located at the southern end of Wailea. It offers a small pantry market, a mall of shops, and a restaurant. Each of the Wailea resorts also has an assortment of gift shops.

ACCOMMODATIONS - WAILEA

The Palms at Wailea
Wailea Villas:
  Ekolu Village
  Ekahi Village
  Elua Village
  Grand Champion Villas
Renaissance Wailea Beach Resort

Aston Wailea Resort
Diamond Resort
Grand Wailea Resort & Spa
Four Seasons Resort Wailea
Kea Lani Hotel
Polo Beach Club

BEST BETS: It's hard to go wrong in wonderful Wailea. Affordable accommodations are not what the visitor will find here, but there are a variety of excellent condominiums and hotels among which to choose. Each is different, each is lovely and in fact there is not one property that we would not recommend. The choice is up to the personal preference of the guest. Here is a quick synopsis of each.

Wailea Villas - Our choice among the four areas would be the Elua Village. These are more expensive, of course, but beach aficionados will love having Ulua Beach at their front door.

Aston Wailea Resort - Previously The Maui Inter-Continental, Aston took over management in February 1996. A lovely property featuring a tropical flavor with spacious grounds, excellent restaurants, and two great beaches. They are continuing to develop a wonderful Hawaiiana program. We're hoping that Aston will include some guest room renovations in their plans. While very nice, they could use a little freshening up. Ask about second room discounts for kids.

Renaissance Wailea Beach Resort - Formerly Stouffer Wailea Beach Resort. This complex is smaller, and more intimate -- as resorts go -- it has lush, tropical grounds, and it is fronted by one of the island's finest beaches.

The ***Grand Wailea Resort and Spa*** - This is an enormous resort, but also enormous fun! The pools are incredible, but if you prefer the ocean, there is excellent Wailea Beach. There is something to do for everyone in the family. Just walking the grounds and touring the $40 million art collection could fill up a day!

Four Seasons Resort - This resort is purely and simply elegant. From it's white porte cochere you enter a tranquil and serene environ. Simply sit by the pool or enjoy a day on the beach. No need to go further!

The ***Kea Lani Hotel*** - This is an all-suites resort, a blend of the best of resorts and the comforts of a condominium, all on Polo Beach. Want to really indulge? Then how about one of their private oceanfront villas with private swimming pool?

Polo Beach - Luxury condominium units with easy access to two small but good beaches.

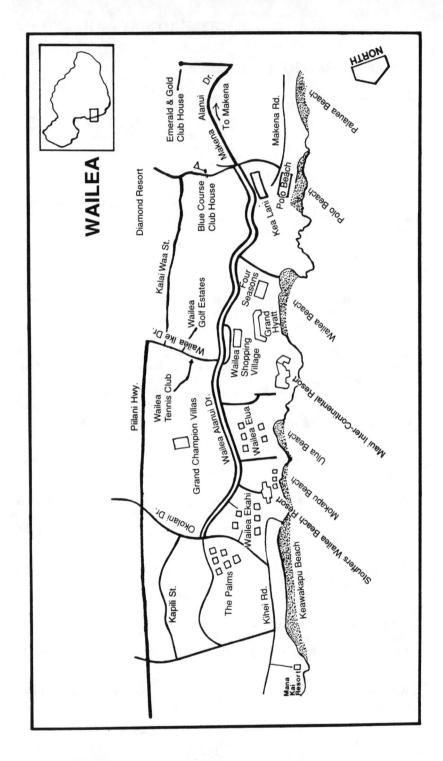

WAILEA

NORTH

Emerald & Gold Club House

Alanui Dr.

Makena

To Makena

Makena Rd.

Palauea Beach

Diamond Resort

Blue Course Club House

Kea Lani

Polo Beach

Polo Beach

Kalai Waa St.

Wailea Golf Estates

Four Seasons

Grand Hyatt

Wailea Beach

Wailea Ike Dr.

Wailea Shopping Village

Maui Inter-Continental Resort

Piilani Hwy.

Wailea Tennis Club

Wailea Alanui Dr.

Wailea Elua

Ulua Beach

Grand Champion Villas

Mokapu Beach

Okolani Dr.

Wailea Ekahi

Stouffers Wailea Beach Resort

Kapili St.

The Palms

Kihei Rd.

Keawakapu Beach

Mana Kai Resort

THE PALMS AT WAILEA
3200 Wailea Alanui Drive, Wailea, Maui, HI 96753 (808) 879-5800. Agents: Outrigger Hotels Hawaii 1-800-OUTRIGGER, Maui Condo & Home 1-800-822-4409 (Rates: 1 BR $130/100). Luxury units located with oceanviews in Wailea. One and two bedroom condominiums on a bluff overlooking the Wailea area with view of the islands of Kaho'olawe and Lana'i. Each unit features air-conditioning, washer/dryer. Guests have use of the recreation center which includes a pool and jacuzzi. As part of the Wailea, this property offers access to the two Wailea golf courses and tennis complex. Daily maid service.
1 BR g.v. (4) $160/150, o.v. $190/175, 2 BR (6) g.v. $190/165, o.v. $225/205

WAILEA VILLAS
3750 Wailea Alanui, Wailea Maui, HI 96753. (808-879-1595) 1-800-367-5246. Agents: Destination Resorts Wailea (808-879-1595) 1-800-367-5246, Maui Condo & Home (Grand Champion & Ekolu) 1-800-822-4409, Kumulani (only Ekahi condos) 1-800-367-2954, Pali Kai (only Ekolu units) 1-808-879-8550. Some agents may have a limited number of units for slightly better prices than those quoted below. The price range reflects location in the complex. Children under 16 free in parent's room.

EKOLU VILLAGE - Located near the tennis center and the Wailea golf course.
1 BR (2) $160/135, 2BR (4) $200/160

EKAHI VILLAGE - On the hillside above the south end of Keawakapu Beach, some units are right above the beach.
S BR (2) $140/120, 1 BR (2) $170-190/140-160, 2 BR (4) $275/225

ELUA VILLAGE - Located on Ulua Beach, one of the best in the area. We would recommend these units.
1 BR (2) g.v.-o.v. $195-230/165-200, o.f. $300/250
2 BR (4) g.v.-o.v. $275-315/225-270, o.f. $400/340
3 BR (6) g.v. only $375/300, o.f. $500/440

GRAND CHAMPION VILLAS - Located at 155 Wailea Iki Place, Wailea, HI 96754. The fourth and newest of the Wailea Villas, this is a sportsman's dream, located between Wailea's Blue Golf Course and the "Wimbledon West" Tennis Center. Agent: Destination Resorts 1-800-367-5246, Maui Network 1-800-367-5221, Kihei Maui Vacations 1-800-541-6284. 188 luxury condominium units on 12 lush acres with garden view, golf view or oceanview units. Only booking through Destination Resorts Hawaii offers services which include daily maid service, grocery delivery and concierge service. Golf, tennis and/or car packages available. *1 BR (2) $140-160/120-135, 2 BR (4) $180-200/150-160*

RENAISSANCE WAILEA BEACH RESORT ★ (Hotel)
3550 Wailea Alanui, Wailea, Maui, HI 96753. (808-879-4900) 1-800-992-4532, FAX (808) 874-5370. 347 units including 12 suites. This luxury resort (formerly Stouffer Wailea) covers 15.5 acres above beautiful Mokapu Beach. Each guest room is 500 sq.ft. and offers a refrigerator, individual air-conditioner, a stocked mini-bar, and private lanai. The rooms are decorated in soothing rose, ash and

blue tones. An assortment of daily guest activities are available as well as a year children's program called Camp Wailea. The program operates five days per week from 9 am - 1 pm for youth ages 5-12 years. Participation is $35 per child.

Fat City is an unusual attraction here. This "multi-colored cat of undetermined lineage" has become the unofficial resort resident. In fact, she has endeared herself to so many guests that she receives mail on a regular basis.

The Mokapu Beach Club is a separate beachfront building with 26 units that feature open beamed ceilings and rich koa wood furnishings, plus a small swimming pool. The resort's restaurants are the Maui Onion, a pool-side gazebo; Palm Court, serving international buffets in an open air atmosphere; Raffles', an award-winning gourmet restaurant and Hana Gion, serving authentic Japanese cuisine. The Sunset Terrace, located in the lobby area, offers an excellent vantage point for a beautiful sunset and nightly entertainment 5:30 pm-8:30 pm. The beach offers excellent swimming. The best snorkeling is just a very short walk over to the adjoining Ulua Beach. The grounds are a beautiful tropical jungle with a very attractive pool area which was recently expanded to include additional lounging areas and more jacuzzi pools. They also offer several "breakation" options. These include a combination of room and car, room and golf or honey-moon options.
Deluxe mountainside $275, Deluxe Oceanside (Floors 1-4) $315, Deluxe Oceanview $380, Mokapu Beach Club $485, Makai Suites (1 bdr/2 bdr) $760-1140, Alii Suites (2 bedrooms) $1900, Aloha Suite (2 bedrooms) $2,600.

ASTON WAILEA RESORT ★ (Hotel)
3700 Wailea Alanui, Kihei, Maui, HI 96753. (808-879-1922), FAX (808) 874-8331), 1-800-367-2960. The porte cochere greets your arrival with a grand entry and ocean view. Beautiful koa rockers tempt guests to sit, relax and enjoy the tranquil, gorgeous view. Just beyond, the main stairway descends down and winds past a lily pond (a popular wedding site) to the central pool area. The oceanview, 34,000 sq. ft. conference pavilion is a topped with a rooftop observatory. Take the elevator or walk up for a panoramic view and an perfect vantage point for whale watching. The lobby design is unpretentious, old Hawaiian and classic. The artwork is subtle. Chests from Japan, huge stone mochi bowls, spirit houses from Thailand, roof finials from New Guinea, and calabashes from the Big Island. Located on 22 acres they have 1/2 mile of oceanfront property and access to two great beaches, Ulua and Wailea. There are three pools, a seven-story tower and six low-rise buildings. The wonderful layout of this resort allows 80% of all guest rooms to have an ocean view and the grounds are spacious and sprawling. No "packing them in" feel here! The main pool area has two pools. One deeper and one a 4 1/2 foot depth all over. There is also a pint-size slide into a small pool that is perfect for the pint size members in your family. Nothing exotic or fancy, just plain good water fun. A separate pool in the luau area is often uncrowded. The units located nearest the beach afford wonderful private ocean views. The restaurants in this lovely resort include Hula Moons and the Lana'i Terrace which offers a very good Sunday Champagne Brunch and a weekly Seafood Buffet. Laundry facilities are coin-op and located in several areas on property. The resort offers a *Hoolokahi* program which are a series of Hawaiian

classes available to guests and non-guests for a nominal fee. This is also home to one of the Maui's best luaus. Live entertainment from 5:30-7:30 in the Kai Puka Bar. A number of exciting annual events are sponsored by the resort. Golf, tennis and honeymoon package plans also available.

We have a small complaint regarding their $8 "resort fee." We were told this was an Inter-Continental policy that Aston continued when they took over management. One front desk representative asked if we had a car and we replied that we did. She said that normally the parking fee was $7, but for an extra $1 you received added amenities. These include a small in-room coffee pot, daily paper, free local calls, one-hour complimentary rental of snorkeling equipment and discounts on the children's program. This was not an "optional" fee. When we inquired what it was if we did not have a car, we were told by another desk agent that it was not a parking fee, but a resort fee and it was the same whether you had a car or not. While some island resorts have begun adding a parking fee to cover the construction of new enlarged and secured parking areas, this parking lot (at least as of this writing) is not a gated, secured parking area. This resort fee struck a bit of disharmony with these editors. Perhaps it was the manner in which it was presented, but this non-optional fee was made, by the desk agents, to sound as if it were some great deal. However, many of the island resorts, in this price range, offer at least some of these amenities at no charge. Personally, we felt that if this increase was necessary, it should be added to the cost of the rooms. Somehow having a room that costs $200 plus a night and then being told you owe an extra $8 for a resort fee does not present a visitor friendly "Aloha Spirit." We have presented our "opinions" to the Public Relations Department for Aston properties. We'll see if anything changes. We also hope Aston has plans to freshen up the guest rooms. They are very pleasant, but some new bedspreads would really liven up the rooms.

Garden View $245; Mountain View $275; Ocean View $325; Oceanfront $375; Deluxe Oceanfront $405; Junior Suite $475; Aloha Suite $825; Maka'i Suite $1,000; Alii Suite $1,350. Rate information notes a $8 per room per day "resort service fee." Rates are singe/double occupancy. Extra person charge $30 daily (maximum 4 persons).

DIAMOND RESORT (Hotel)

555 Kaukahi St., Wailea, Maui, HI 96753. (874-0500) This private resort, an extension of the Diamond Resort Corporation which manages a chain of 20 resorts throughout Japan, is located on 14.5 acres just above the Wailea Golf Course. The spa facility which includes a men's and women's daiyokujo (traditional Japanese bath), a waterfall to gently massage your neck and shoulders as well as a soothing Finlandia sauna is one of the resort's highlights. Recently, Diamond Resort has implemented the Diamond Spa Club program. Membership in the club provides the opportunity to experience the luxurious spa and spend a peaceful night in one of the exclusive hotel rooms. For rates and more information, contact a Spa Club representative. Their Restaurant Taiko and Le Gunji are both fine dining restaurants. See the RESTAURANTS-Wailea section, for descriptions.

WAILEA POINT

4000 Wailea Alanui, Wailea, Maui, HI 96753. 136 luxurious oceanview and oceanfront condominiums arranged in four-plexes which are laid out in a residential plan on 26-oceanfront acres. Privacy is maintained by a gate guard at the entrance. Unfortunately, no rental properties available here!

GRAND WAILEA RESORT & SPA ★

3850 Wailea Alanui Drive, Wailea, Maui, HI 96753 (808) 875-1234, Reservations only 1-800-888-6100. The Grand opened their 767 room resort in September 1991 (originally it was a Hyatt Property) at a cost of $600 million with an additional $30 million in fine artwork. Quite frankly when we first heard the concepts planned for this mega-resort we were concerned it would be another Kaua'i Lagoons, or take on aspects of Orlando or Anaheim. Wrong! The resort is a bit overwhelming, but it is tasteful, innovative and truly spectacular. Beautifully appointed with great attention to detail make it is a must-see, even if you aren't lucky enough to stay! In fact, make at least two trips... a second at night to enjoy dinner and tour the grounds when they are alight like a fairy land.

The sea remains the theme throughout the resort. Guests are greeted by a huge waterfall flowing down from Mt. Haleakala as they arrive. Look closely for the Hawaiian sea spirits which are hidden amid this interesting aquatic cascade. Each of the many Hawaiian sculptures has a legend or history -- King Kamehameha stands out near the entry and was created by Herb Kane, a noted specialist on Polynesian culture and history. He also created many of the mermaids, dancers and fisherman found by the resort's lagoons and streams. Inside the resort you'll find Hena, the mother of the demigod Maui. In the open air walkway of the Molokini Wing. There are 18 bronzes around the grounds that were sculpted by world-famous artist Fernard Leger. Jan Fisher sculpted ten life-size pieces for the resort including the maidens bathing and the Fisher's two-trios of hula dancers at the entry of the atrium. Be sure to take note of the beautiful relief painting on the walls of the Grand Dining Room. The murals were painted by Doug Riseborough and depict his version of the legend of the demigod Maui. In the center of the dining room is a sculpture done by Shige Yamada, entitled "Maui Captures the Sun." Just outside the dining room is a small stage with a fabulous

148

WHERE TO STAY - WHAT TO SEE

Hawaiian mosaic. The resort offers a complimentary art tour twice weekly led by an island art expert. The center courtyard is called the Botero Gallery. These sculptures seem to be getting the most discussion - both good and bad! Fernando Botero is a contemporary artist from Colombia and his work is "oversized." The huge Hawaiian woman reclining on her stomach (smoking a cigarette in the buff) weighs 600 pounds and is appraised at $2 million. If you're on the upper levels, be sure to look down to see her from another.... uh, interesting, perspective!

Over $20 million was spent on the waterfalls, streams, rapids, slides, reflecting pools, swimming pools, river pool, scuba pool, salt water lagoon and spa features. This is one of the most high-tech aquatic systems in the state. Strikingly beautiful, the formal reflecting pool leads you to the sweeping Wailea Beach. Beyond this pool is a formal swimming Hibiscus pool made of Mexican glass tile with gold leaf. This adults only pool is lined with wide Mediterranean-style cabanas. The "action pool" (The Wailea Canyon Activity Pool) is a million gallon, 23,500 square foot pool with five large, free-form pools at various levels beginning at a height of 40 feet and dropping to sea level. Painted tiles depicting turtles & tropical fish in varying shades of green and blue line the bottom and sides, while huge rocks and landscape features line the pools. At one end of the pool is an incredible waterslide, a 225 foot twisting ride that drops three stories. The "jungle pool," another part of the Wailea Canyon Activity pool, offers a rope swing. The pools are connected by a 220 foot river which carries swimmers at varying current speeds, ranging from white water rapids to a lazy cruise. Along the way are hidden grottoes, whirlpools and saunas, six slides, six water-falls and a bumpy white water rapids that has been created by the use of special aquatic devices. At the bottom of the river is a one-of-a-kind water elevator which lifts the swimmers back up to the top again. Below the rocky waterfall is the scuba pool which gets prospective divers in the mood with an underwater mural featuring a coral reef, and sea life made of tiles. Streams and pools also meander through elaborate gardens in Hawaiian and Japanese themes throughout the resort. It takes 50,000 gallons of water a minute to sustain their aquatic system. The pool may be used by non-resort guests for a daily fee of $65 for adults and $50 for children. A reduced rate for guests staying at the neighboring Four Seasons Resort run $50 adults and $35 for children.

Spa Grande is Hawai'i's largest spa, and spans 50,000 square feet in the atrium wing of the resort. It is designed with Italian marble, original artwork, Venetian chandeliers and inlaid gold. It provides a blend of European, Japanese and American spa philosophies. The spa's central concept is based on a longevity program which allows guests to enjoy fitness, beauty and health treatments as well as working out a regimen that will continue once their vacation has ended. An in-house physician works with guests, providing medical and fitness evalua-tions. Hawaiian therapies include a ti leaf wrap, limu (seawood) bath and a lomi lomi massage. The "Terme Wailea" is a 30-minute circuit on the spa's "wet" level which begins with a loofah scrub, followed by a trip to the Roman tub for a cool dip followed by a choice of specialty baths. The masso, thermo and hydrotherapy treatments are available in 42 individual rooms. Also available are a sonic relaxation room, cascading waterfall massage, authentic furo soaking tubs and white and black sand body treatments. An aerobics studio, weight room, plus cardiovascular room, racquetball and squash court (the only ones on Maui), a full-service beauty salon, and game room are among the many spa options.

The *Tsunami Nightclub* (what a great name!) offers 10,000 square feet of high tech lounge with black marble. Five restaurants give guests plenty of choices. Kincha features very authentic and expensive Japanese cuisine and is set amid a beautiful Japanese Garden. The Grand Dining Room Maui, situated 60 feet above sea level, offers a panoramic view of the Pacific, the gardens and Molokini Island from inside or on a lovely outdoor eating veranda. Currently they can only be enjoyed at breakfast. Cafe Kula features family style foods. Humuhumunukunuku (Humuhumu for short) is named for the Hawaiian state fish. It sits surrounded by a saltwater lagoon filled with tropical fish. It is definitely worth a stop just to see this restaurant which serves expensive Pacific Rim/seafood cuisine. Bistro Molokini serves California and Italian items and the Volcano Bar provides light dining and snacks. There is also a swim up bar. The Food & Beverage Department has created an interesting assortment of original drinks. A Reeses peanut butter smoothie may be just the thing for sipping around the pool, or a liliokoi and orange juice splashed with champagne, the ideal before dinner drink.

Now the rooms! There are 787 oceanfront rooms each 650 square feet and 53 suites. The Presidential suite (5,500 sq. ft.) is priced at a mere $8,000 per night and features what is lovingly referred to as the Imelda Marcos shoe closet, a private sauna, a room-sized shower with ocean view in one bathroom and a black marble and teak soaking tub in the other. Lots of marble is used throughout all the rooms with subtle marbleized wallpapers in earthen hues. The resort was designed so that each room would provide an ocean view.

This may be the one resort that your kids will INSIST you come back to again and again. After you visit the kids' camp you will, at least momentarily, wish you could pass for a 10 or 11 year old. The 20,000 square foot Camp Grande operates year-round, as well as older kids. A huge area is designed with crafts complete with pottery kiln. Adjacent is a kid's dining dream, resembling a 1950's style soda fountain. An outdoor area offers a toddler-size whale-shaped pool, cushy soft grass-like play yard and playground equipment. Another room houses the computer center, another the video arcade and yet another has a Hawaiian version of F.A.O Schwartz that will guarantee that your kids will not be glad to see you upon pickup time. The price is $65 per day (9am-3pm) for children ages three years (and potty-trained) to fifteen years of age and includes lunch with an evening schedule including dinner. Package rates are available. Babysitters may be arranged through the children's program. Parents are invited to bring and supervise their own children at Camp Grande at no charge.

The 28,000 sq. ft. ballroom is a convention planner's dream, with concealed projection screens, specialized audio equipment -- the works! The ballroom also has three huge, beautiful and unique artworks in gold and silver leaf which depict the story of Pele, the fire goddess, and her two sisters. Don't neglect a look up at the 29,000 pound Venetian glass chandelier imported from Italy.

We, frankly, are fascinated by the interesting blend of mega resort glitz and Hawaiian themes tempered with outstanding craftsmanship. It seems to work. There is actually a great deal of fine craftsmanship (notice the twisted ohia wood rails that line the pathways) and we especially like the attention to the Hawaiiana aspects. The resort is visually very stimulating and each time you stroll the grounds you're sure to see something new. The chapel, set in the middle of the grounds, however, leaves us a bit puzzled. Looking as though it were snatched from Reno and transplanted to the beach in Wailea, we wonder why anyone would choose to be married inside, where the view of the ocean is obscured by stained glass, when there are so many more beautiful sites around the hotel grounds or on the beach. However, you should still inspect the Chapel. The woodwork and stained glass windows are absolutely beautiful, and take note of the chandeliers, priced at $100,000 each!

All-in-all, if you're seeking an action-packed resort vacation, you'll find it all here. Not everyone wants the activity of a resort, but this one certainly has something for everyone.

Terrace $380, Premier $445, Deluxe Ocean $495, 1 BR suites 1,100-$1,600. Napua Tower: This is a private tower with two private lounges, complimentary continental breakfast, afternoon tea, and cocktails available in the evening: Napua Club $580; Napua Suites $1,400-$1,800; Napua Royal $2,500-$3,000; Grand Suite $10,000.

THE FOUR SEASONS RESORT WAILEA ★
3900 Wailea Alanui, Wailea, Maui, HI 96753. (808-874-8000) (National reservations 1-800-332-3442). 380 over-sized guest rooms (600 sq. ft) on eight floors encompassing 15 beachfront acres on the beautiful white sand Wailea Beach. A full service resort featuring two pools, (one large, one smaller lava pool) and a jacuzzi on each end of the main pool, one of which is set aside for children only. The layout of the grand pool provides shelter from the afternoon breezes. In addition there are two tennis courts at the resort, a croquet lawn, health spa, beauty salon, three restaurants and two lounges. The public areas are spacious, open and ocean oriented. (If we had a category for "Best Bathrooms," These would be the winners. They are elegantly decorated and each stall is like a "mini" suite!) A very different atmosphere from other Maui resorts, the blue tiled roof and creamy colored building create a very classical atmosphere. Even the grounds, although a profusion of colors with many varied Hawaiian flora, are more structured in design with a vague resemblance to a Mediterranean villa. The focus of the resort is water. Throughout the resort's gardens and courtyards are an array of attractive formal and natural pools, ponds, waterfalls and fountains.

Their guest policy features real aloha spirit, with no charge for use of the tennis courts or health spa and complimentary snorkel gear, smash or volleyball equipment. Guest services, which distinguish the Four Seasons from other properties, include their early arrival/late departure program. These guests have their luggage checked and are escorted to the Health Club where a private locker is supplied for personal items. The resort makes available for these guests an array of casual clothing from work-out gear to jogging suits or swim wear.

For the meeting planner, the Four Seasons features a 7,000 square foot ballroom, two banquet rooms and five conference areas situated adjacent to a 3,000 square foot hospitality suite. The suite offers a large living room, two bedrooms, another living space designed for private meetings, kitchen, and a 1,000 square foot lanai.

Our stay at the *Four Seasons Resort* climaxed one of our island vacations and proved to be the highlight of our entire trip. It was restful and elegant. The pool was nothing exotic or elaborate, but it didn't make it any less enjoyable for our children. A "children's only" hot tub allowed the second adult hot tub to be a peaceful respite. There are plenty of cabanas around the pool area and on the beach to enjoy the day while staying out of the sun. Pool and beach staff are on their toes providing prompt attention for guests in setting up their lounge chairs with towels and providing chilled lemon towels or spritzers to cool the face. A poolside restaurant (with espresso) and bar make it easy to spend the entire day without leaving your lounge chair. The chilled coffee drinks are wonderful and there are plenty to choose from.

The snorkeling is best out to the left near the rocky shoreline, but go early in the day. Like clockwork, about noon the wind picks up and the water clarity rapidly deteriorates.

Another plus for the Wailea area is the walkway that spans along the shoreline between resorts. It is a pleasant walk over to the neighboring southern resort, the Kea Lani, and the Grand Wailea, to the north, is definitely worth a stroll (go during the day and again at night for a very different experience). The Four Seasons is truly geared for the family. A full-time, year-round children's program is complimentary to hotel guests. Milk and cookies are delivered to the room for those young guests upon arrival. Sylvester Stallone, a guest of the hotel during our visit, made a couple of poolside appearances.

Amenities for guests on the Club Floor* include a private lounge, 24 hr. concierge, complimentary breakfast, afternoon tea, evening cocktails and after dinner liqueurs.

Numerous special package offers include a room and car, golf, romance and family packages. (Note: The Golf package offers play at the exclusive new private Waikapu course.) Complimentary, year-round "Kids for All Seasons" program designed for hotel guests aged 5 - 12 years. Restaurants include Pacific Grill, Seaside and Seasons.

Package programs currently available include a Bed & Breakfast package, Golf for Two, Room & Car, Family, Romance for all Seasons or Romantic Interlude.

Five night minimum required for stays over the Christmas holiday.

*Mountain View $295, Garden View $320, Partial Ocean View $375, Ocean View $450 (Club floor $570), Ocean View Prime $490 (Club Floor $610), Four Seasons Executive Suite, Garden View $515, Four Seasons Executive Suite Ocean View $655 (Club Floor $775). *Club floors include added amenities. Third adult in room $80 night, club floors $120 per night. Under age 18 complimentary when sharing same room with parents, except on club floor, add $60 per night per child ages 5 - 17. Adjoining children's room is available for $250 when parents pay standard room rate, except on club floors. Oceanview and oceanfront, one bedroom suites $710 and up. Two and three bedroom suites are also available. The Maile, oceanfront three bedroom suite runs $5,500.*

KEA LANI HOTEL, SUITES & VILLAS ★

4100 Wailea Alanui Drive, Wailea, HI 96753. (808) 875-4100 or 1-800-882-4100. 413 suites plus 37-one, two and three BR oceanfront villas. Designed after Las Hadas in Manzanillo, the name means "White Heavens." Its Mediterranean-style architecture received many mixed reviews when it opened years ago. It seems to us that perhaps this might be the home of a Sultan with a dramatic style set on 22 acres and a bit out of place in Wailea. However, the tropical lushness has grown and softened the look of the resort. You enter a drive lined with Norfolk pines and beyond the porte cochere there is a large open lobby area with a fountain covered by nine domes. Decorations are in Hawaiian florals, with mosaic tile ceilings and floors.

There are 413 spacious (840 sq. ft.) one-bedroom suites, each with a private balcony. Views are garden, partial ocean, and ocean, and deluxe ocean view. Each has a sunken marble tub, an enormous walk-in shower, king or two double beds, two closets, decorated in hues of cream and white. A cotton kimono is provided for guests. The living room features a state of the art compact and laser disc system, 27 inch television and video cassette player. Fresh ground coffee and coffee maker is provided daily in the suite and a mini-kitchen offers a microwave, a small sink, and mini-bar. An iron and ironing board are also available in each room. The exercise room is complimentary for guests.

The Caffe Ciao II is a casual dining establishment offering indoor and alfresco seating. They feature an assortment of Italian dishes including pastas and pizzas, which are baked to order in an outdoor brick oven fired by kiawe wood. They are open for lunch and dinner. Polo Beach Grille & Bar has an outdoor setting under a canopy of coconut palm trees and serves kiawe grilled meats, seafood, salads, specialty ice creams and tropical drinks. The Kea Lani Restaurant offers breakfast in a casual setting and fine dining featuring Euro-Pacific cuisine for dinner. The indoor and outdoor dining room overlooks the formal pool. The 22,000 sq. ft. pool area is be a series of pools connected together. The upper level pool adjoins a swim up pool bar.

In addition to the suites, there are also 37 townhouse style villas which overlook Polo Beach. A 100 sq. ft. one bedroom villa costs $795-895, a 1,800 sq. ft. two-bedroom villa runs $895-995 a night, and a 2,200 sq. ft three-bedroom unit runs

$1,095-1,195. A little spendy, but it would be easy to feel at home here! Each has a private lanai, huge walk-in closets, full size kitchen and washer and dryer, and are decorated in very muted mauves. Each has a generous living room and eating area. If you don't want to make that walk to the beach, you can just meander out onto the lanai and take a dip in your private swimming pool. That's right. Each villa has its own pool!

Other interesting amenities include complimentary daily golf clinics. For those who prefer to be "Beach Bound" they offer beach rental equipment, everything from a single kayak to a pool float. Beach Butlers are on hand to ensure you have a great day at the beach. Also available are beach cabanas! For a small fee the resort offers "Keiki Lani" (Heavenly Kids) for youths aged 5 to 11 years of age. Offered year-round 9am until 3pm includes snack, lunch and a Keiki Lani t-shirt. Activities range from face painting to sailing, picnics to hula and off-property excursions. Children's menus available in the restaurant. Honeymoon, wedding, family, and golf packages are available.

1 BR suite scenic view (4) 265, o.v. (4) $350, deluxe o.v. (4) $450
1 BR villa (1-4 persons) o.v. $795, o.f. $895
2 BR villa (1-6 persons) o.v. $895, o.f. $995
3 BR villa (1-8 persons) o.v. $1,095, o.f. $1,195

POLO BEACH CLUB ★

20 Makena Rd., Wailea, Maui, HI 96753. (808-879-8847) Agents: Destination Resorts 1-800-367-5246 is the on-site rental agent, Hawaiian Apt. Leasing 1-800-854-8843 (1-800-472-8449 CA) Kumulani, 1-800-367-2954. 71 apartments in a single 8-story building located on Polo Beach. The units are luxurious and spacious. Underground parking, pool area jacuzzi. This once very secluded area is soon to be "discovered." Located next to the Kea Lani Resort.
Additional persons (over 4) $20 each. Three night minimum.
1 BR (2) o.f. $275-325 / $200-240,
2 BR 2 bath (max 6) o.f. $275-325 / $225-275

KEA LANI

MAKENA

INTRODUCTION

This is area just south of Wailea is Makena, and one of the newer resort developments on Maui. The project began with the completion of an 18-hole golf course in 1981. The Makena Surf condominium project opened in 1984. The Japanese conglomerate, Seibu, has a magnificent new resort, the Maui Prince Hotel, located at Maluaka Beach. Also in this area are several beaches with public access. They include Oneloa, Puuolai, Poolenalena, Palauea and Maluaka beaches. Since the area is not fully developed the end results remain to be seen.

WHAT TO DO AND SEE

Here are the last really gorgeous and undeveloped recreational beaches on Maui. Consequently, development in this area has met with a great deal of ongoing controversy. The paved road (Makena Alanui) runs from Wailea past the Makena Surf and Maui Prince Hotel, exiting onto the Old Makena Rd. near the entrances to Oneuli (Black Sand) Beach and Oneloa (Big Makena)-Puuolai (Little Makena) Beaches. Past Ahihi Kinau Natural Reserve on Old Makena Rd. you will traverse the last major lava flow on Maui which still looks pretty fresh after some 250 years and continues to La Perouse Bay. (See BEACHES)

The Keawala'i Church, founded in 1832, was once the cultural and spirtual center of the community. The structure, completed in 1854 is 3 feet thick and made of melted coral gathered from the sea. It is surrounded by ti leaf which is planted because of Hawaiian belief that it provides protection and healing. This charming historical churc sits quietly along the ocean in Makena and is home to an active Protestant congregation. Service is given in both English and Hawaiian.

Captain James Cook may have been the first Western explorer to visit and map the Hawaiian islands, but he failed to even see Maui during his first voyage. On his second trip in 1779 he spotted the northeast coastline of Maui, but a rugged and rocky shore prevented him from landing. It was Admiral Jean-Francois de Galaup, Comte de La Perouse, who was the first western explorer to set foot on Maui. Seven years after Cook had anchored offshore of Maui, Perouse departed from the Easter Island and arrived in the Sandwich Isles in May of 1786. His two frigates, the Astrolabe and the Boussole sailed around the Hana coast searching for a location to land. Discovering Maui's south shore, he decided to land at Keone'o'io to conduct trading with the Hawaiians. He was greeted by local Hawaiians that were friendly and eager to trade. They exchanged gifts and La Perouse visited a total of four villages. This brief, three hour visit, resulted in the Keone'o'io Bay being called La Perouse Bay.

Hiking beyond La Perouse affords some great ocean vistas. You'll see trails made by local residents in their four wheel drive vehicles, and fishermen's trails leading to volcanic promontories overlooking the ocean. You may even spot the fishing pole holders which have been securely attached to the lava boulders.

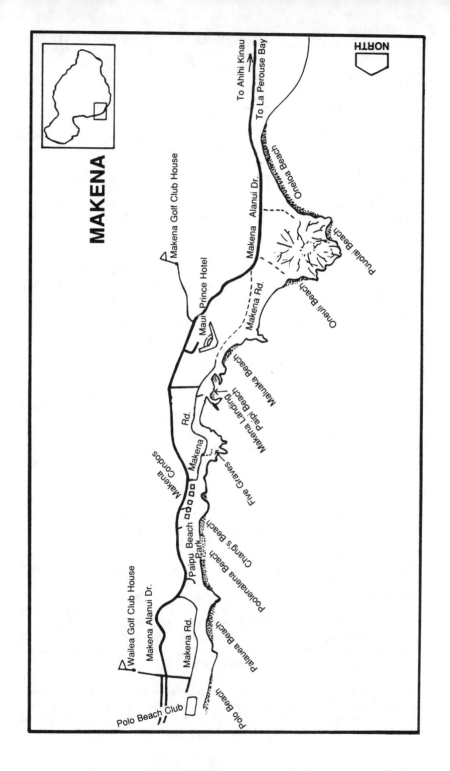

MAKENA

NORTH

To Ahihi Kinau
To La Perouse Bay

Makena Golf Club House

Maui Prince Hotel

Makena Alanui Dr.

Makena Rd.

Oneloa Beach

Puuolai Beach

Oneuli Beach

Maluaka Beach

Makena Landing
Paipu Beach

Five Graves

Makena Rd.

Makena Condos

Paipu Beach Park

Chang's Beach

Poolenalena Beach

Palaua Beach

Wailea Golf Club House
Makena Alanui Dr.

Makena Rd.

Polo Beach Club

Polo Beach

The Hoapili Trail begins just past La Perouse Bay and is referred to as the King's Highway. It is believed that at one time the early Hawaiians made use of a trail that circled the entire island and this is a remnant of that ancient route. The state Forestry and Wildlife Division and volunteers worked together recently putting in place stone barricades to keep the four wheel drive vehicles and motorcycles from destroying any more of the trail.

ACCOMMODATIONS - MAKENA

BEST BETS: The Maui Prince Hotel and *Makena Surf* - Both are first class, luxury accommodations on beautiful beaches.

MAKENA SURF ★
96 Makena Alanui Rd., Makena, Maui, HI 96753., Destination Resorts 1-800-367-5246, Jim Osgood (206) 391-8900 or check out his web page on the internet at (http://www.officefinder.com/makena.htm), Kihei Maui Vacations 1-800-541-6284, Kumulani 1-800-367-2954, Hawaiian Apt. Leasing 1-800-854-8843. Located 2 miles past Wailea. All units are oceanfront and more or less surround Paipu (Chang's) Beach. These very spacious and attractive condos feature central air-conditioning, fully equipped kitchens, washers and dryers, wet bar, whirlpool spa in the master bath, telephones and daily maid service. Two pools, and four tennis courts are set in landscaped grounds. Three historic sites found on location have been preserved. We recently had the opportunity to stay, for the first time, at this property. It was even better than we had imagined. When they were first built it seemed that the Makena Surf was so out of the way and removed from the rest of the Wailea area. That isn't the case any more, but this property is still very private. The units are well maintained and luxuriously appointed. Looking out from the oceanfront units it is hard to imagine that this isn't your own private island. Pull up a lounge chair, open that bottle of wine and watch the whales frolic as the sun sets gloriously in the Pacific beyond them. It doesn't get any better than this! Destination Resorts is the management company for this property, so they handle most of the rental units.

1 BR (2) $250-325 / $200-275   Prices listed are 2 or 3 nights
2 BR (2) $300-375 / $240-315   Discounts for 4 nights or longer
3 BR (4) $450 / $395   Extra person $15/night

MAUI PRINCE ★
5400 Makena Alanui, Makena, Maui, HI 96753. (808-874-1111) Reservations: 1-800-321-6284. In sharp contrast to the ostentatious atmosphere of some of the Kaanapali resorts, the Maui Prince radiates understated elegance. Its simplicity in color and design, with an Oriental theme, provides a tranquil setting and allows the beauty of Maui to be reflected. The central courtyard is the focal point of the resort with a lovely traditional water garden complete with a cool cascading waterfall and ponds filled with gleaming koi. The rooms are tastefully appointed in cool neutral hues and equipped with the comfort of the guests in mind. The units have two telephones and a small refrigerator. Terry robes are available for use during the guest's stay. A 24-hour full room service adds to the conveniences. They currently offer the Prince Kids Club program year around to youth ages 5- 12 years. Three sessions are offered throughout the day. The morning session 9am - noon is free. Afternoon session noon to 3 pm includes lunch and is $15, full session 9am - 3pm is $15 and includes lunch.

There is plenty of room for lounging around two circular swimming pools or in a few steps you can be on Maluaka (Nau Paka) Beach with its luxuriously deep, fine white sand and good snorkeling, swimming and wave playing.

The resort comprises 1,800 acres including two championship golf courses. The first 18-holes were built in 1981, they were divided and each half was combined with nine new holes to create the North and South Courses. The South Course opened in August 1993 and the North Course on November 23, 1993. The courses were designed by Robert Trent Jones, Jr.

Restaurants include Prince Court serving Hawaiian Regional dishes (and one of the island's best Sunday brunches), al fresco dining in Cafe Kiowai and the Japanese restaurant and sushi bar at Hakone.

Partial o.v. $230, o.v. $290, o.v. prime $330, o.f. $380, Suites $420-820
No charge for third person using existing beds.

Package plans include Single Golfer Package, Room & Meal Package, Sporting Clays Package, Tennis for Life package, Sunset Romance Package, Unlimited Golf Package and more.

WAILUKU AND KAHULUI

INTRODUCTION

The twin towns of Wailuku and Kahului are located on the northern, windward side of the island. Wailuku is the county seat of Maui while Kahului houses, not only the largest residential population on the island, but also the main airport terminal and deep-water harbor. There are three motel-type accommodations around Kahului Harbor, and while the rates are economical, and the location is somewhat central to all parts of the island, we cannot recommend staying in this area for other than a quick stopover that requires easy airport access. This side of the island is generally more windy, overcast and cooler with few good beaches. Except for the avid windsurfer, we feel there is little reason to head-quarter your stay in this area; however, there are good reasons to linger and explore.

WHAT TO DO AND SEE

Kahului has a very colorful history, beginning with the arrival of King Kamehameha I in the 1790's from the big island of Hawai'i. The meaning of Kahului is "winning" and may have had its origins in the battle which ensued between Kamehameha and the Maui chieftain. The shoreline of Kahului Bay began its development in 1863 with the construction of a warehouse by Thomas Hogan. By 1879, a landing at the bay was necessary to keep up with the growing sugar cane industry. Two years later, in 1881, the Kahului Railroad Company had begun. The city of Kahului grew rapidly until 1900 when it was purposely burned down to destroy the spreading of a bubonic plague outbreak. The reconstruction of Kahului created a full-scale commercial harbor, which was bombed along with Pearl Harbor on December 7, 1941. After World War II, a housing boom began with the development of reasonably priced homes to house the increasing number of people moving to the island. The expansion has continued ever since. Wailuku is the county seat of Maui and has been the center of government since 1930. It is now, slowly, experiencing a rebirth. It is often overlooked by visitors who miss out on some wonderful local restaurants and interesting shopping.

Market Street in Old Wailuku Town is alive with the atmosphere of Old Hawai'i. The area, rich in history, was built on the site of ancient Heiaus and witnessed decisive Hawaiian battles. Later the area hosted the likes of Mark Twain to Robert Redford. It is no wonder that such an area should re-emerge in the modern day with shops of a cultural nature. One-of-a-kind items can be found here, gathered from around the world and eras gone by. Such is the case with Old Wailuku Town and the cluster of interesting antique shops along Market Street.

Set against the lush backdrop of the Iao Valley and the West Maui Mountains, this area offers a quaint alternative to the hustle-bustle vacation centers of Lahaina and Kihei. Surrounding this area is a multitude of wonderful and inexpensive ethnic restaurants. So don't limit your excursion to the few shops on the corner of Market and Main streets.

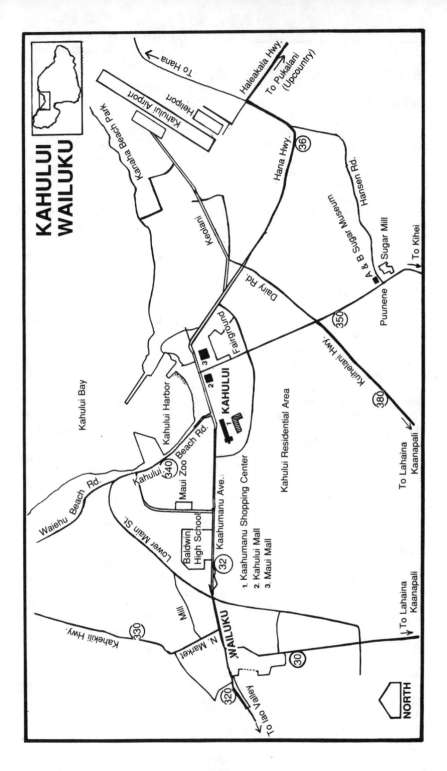

KAHULUI
WAILUKU

To Hana

Haleakala Hwy.

To Pukalani
(Upcountry)

Heliport

Kahului Airport

Kanaha Beach Park

Hana Hwy.

36

Hansen Rd.

Keolani

A & B Sugar Museum

Sugar Mill

To Kihei

Puunene

Dairy Rd.

Kahului Bay

Fairground

KAHULUI

350

Kuihelani Hwy.

380

To Lahaina
Kaanapali

Kahului Harbor

3

2

1

Kahului Residential Area

Kahului Beach Rd.

Kahului 340

Maui Zoo Beach Rd.

Waiehu Beach Rd.

Kaahumanu Ave.

Lower Main St.

Baldwin
High School

32

1. Kaahumanu Shopping Center
2. Kahului Mall
3. Maui Mall

To Lahaina
Kaanapali

Kahekili Hwy.

330

Mill

N. Market

WAILUKU

30

320

To Iao Valley

NORTH

Emura's at 49 Market Street has consistently proven to be the spot for the best buys of eel skin items from wallets and purses, to shoes and attaches. Pay cash and get an extra discount! Antique row can be found along Market Street as well. The following are a couple of our favorites. Located next to the historic Iao Theater is *Traders of the Lost Art* (62 North Market St.). This shop is operated by Tye Hartall and features a variety of native carvings and primitive art which he brings back from the Sepik River area of Papua in New Guinea. The shop also offers antiques including Hawaiiana items, jewelry and vintage clothing. A bit farther down the road is *Memory Lane* and adjacent is *Ali'i Antiques* (158 North Market St.) which features Hawaiiana, Christmas items, and military memorabilia, among other antiques items. A short drive down Market Street is *Takamiya Market*. They have a large selection of ready cooked foods. *Ooka's Super Market* on Main Street, another grocery store, has some of the best grocery values from produce to meats. They also have some interesting local foods!

Kaahumanu Church, Maui's oldest remaining church was built in 1837 at High and Main Streets in Wailuku. Hale Hoikeike in Wailuku houses the *Bailey House Museum* (circa 1834). To reach it, follow the signs to Iao Valley and you will see the historical landmark sign on the left side of the road. It's open from 10 am - 4 pm, and a small admission is charged. (The third Saturday of the month is Family Day with freee admission from 1:30-2:30 pm if you call for a reservation at 244-3326.) Here you will find the Bailey Gallery, (once a dining room for the female seminary that was located at this site), with paintings of Edward Bailey done during the 19th century. His work depicts many aspects of Hawaiian life during earlier days. Also on display are early Hawaiian artifacts and memorabilia from the missionary days. The staff is extremely knowledgeable and friendly. They also have for sale an array of Hawaiian history, art, craft and photographic books. Originally, the Royal Historical Society was established in 1841, but it was not until 1956 that it was reactivated as the Maui Historical Society. The museum was dedicated on July 6, 1957, then closed for restoration on December 31, 1973 and reopened on July 13, 1975. Of special interest are the impressive 20 inch thick walls that are made of plaster using a special missionary recipe which included goat hair as one ingredient. (Talk about recycling!) The thick walls provided the inhabitants with a natural means of air conditioning.

KAAHUMANU CHURCH

The *Maui Jinsha Mission* is located at 472 Lipo Street, Wailuku. One of the few remaining old Shinto Shrines in the state of Hawai'i, this mission was placed on the National Register of Historic Places in 1978.

The *Halekii and Pihana State Monuments* are among Maui's most interesting early Hawaiian historical sites. Both are of considerable size and situated on the top of a sand dune. These temples were very important structures for the island's early Ali'i. Their exact age is unknown, although one resource reported that they were used from 1765 to 1895. The Halekii monument is in better condition as a result of some reconstruction done on it in 1958. Follow Waiehu Beach Road across a bridge, then turn left onto Kuhio Place and again on Hea Place. Look for and follow the Hawai'i Visitors Bureau markers. Some say the Pihana Heiau (temple) was built by the menehunes (Hawai'i's little people), others believe the construction was done under the guidance of Maui chieftain, Kahekili.

The Iao Valley is a short drive beyond Hale Hoikeike. Within the valley is an awesome volcanic ridge that rises 2,250 feet and is known as the Iao Needle. A little known fact is that this interesting natural phenomena is not a monolithic formation, but rather what you are viewing is the end of a large, thin ridge. A helicopter view will give you an entirely different perspective! Parking facilities are available and there are a number of hiking trails. The *Tropical Gardens of Maui* is a botanical garden that features the largest selection of exotic orchids in the Hawaiian islands. For a small fee you can stroll the grounds where they grow, and visit their gift shop filled with tropical flowers and Maui made products. Plants can be shipped home. Snack bar and picnic tables available. Phone 244-3085. Admission is $3. *The Heritage Garden - Kepaniwai Park* is an exhibit of pavilions and gardens which pay tribute to the culture of the Hawaiians, Portuguese, Filipinos, Koreans, Japanese and Chinese. Picnic tables and BBQ's are available for public use. They are located on Iao Valley Road. Free admission, open daily. A public swimming pool for children is open daily from 9 am - 11:45 and again from 1 until 4:30. The newly remodeled pool is open only weekends and holidays. They may consider opening on a daily basis if use increases. The pool is free, but it is cold! Also a popular site for weddings and other functions, it is available for rent from the Maui Parks Dept. A deposit is required. The Wailuku permit office (1580 Kaahumanu Avenue, Wailuku, Maui (808) 243-7389 can provide the forms.

Just outside Wailuku on Hwy. 30, between Wailuku and Maalaea, is Waikapu, home of the *Maui Tropical Plantation and Country Store*. This visitor attraction has become one of the top ten most heavily visited in the state of Hawai'i. The fifty acres, which opened in 1984, have been planted with sugar cane, bananas, guava and other island produce. A ten-acre visitor center includes exhibits, The Country Store (a marketplace), nursery and restaurant. There is no admission for entry into the store or the restaurant. However, there is an $8.50 adults, $3.50 children (5-12 years) charge for admission for the narrated tram ride around the fields. The tram ride departs every forty-five minutes between 10 am and 4 pm. The trip includes several stops for samples of fresh fruit. The Country Store is open daily from 9 am - 5 pm. Several nights a week, the Maui Tropical Plantation features a Hawaiian Country Barbecue and dinner show which features the

Rodney Arias Paniolo Show. Current price is $51.95 adults, $19.95 children 5-17 years and toddlers free. For reservations call 244-7643.

Baldwin Beach - See the section on BEACHES for Baldwin Beach and others

The Maui Zoological and Botanical Gardens closed in late 1995. During the following year efforts were being made to find new homes for the animals. The Botanical Gardens continue to be maintained and are open to the public from 9 am - 4 pm daily. Go up Kaahumanu to Kanaloa Street and turn by the Wailuku War Memorial Center. No admission fee is charged.

The Kanaha Wildlife Sanctuary is off Route 32, near the Kahului Airport, and was once a royal fish pond. Now a lookout is located here for those interested in viewing the stilt and other birds which inhabit the area.

A popular Saturday morning stop for local residents and visitors alike is *The Swap Meet* ★ (877-3100) held at grounds around the Christ the King Church, next door to the Post Office off Pu'unene Hwy. 35. You'll find us referring to this event for various reasons throughout this guide. For a fifty-cent admission (children free) you will find an assortment of vendors selling local fruits and vegetables, new and used clothing, household items and many of the same souvenir type items found at higher prices in resort gift shops. We recently discovered one fellow selling "designer" sunglasses and handbags. At one third the price of retail stores, he professed they were the real thing, not knock-offs. The Swap Meet is also a great place to pick up tropical flowers and for only a few dollars you can lavishly decorate your condo during your stay. Protea are seasonally available here, too, for a fraction of the cost elsewhere. This is also the only place to get true spoonmeat coconuts. These are fairly immature coconuts with deliciously mild and soft (to very soft) meat and filled with sweet coconut milk. We stock up on a week's supply at a time. These coconuts are the ones that are trimmed off the trees while still green and far different than the hard brown ones in the supermarkets. One booth we discovered recently had coconuts that could be inscribed with a message and mailed home as a postcard. Plain were around $10 including postage, painted were $15. Another "must purchase" are goodies from Four Sisters Bakery! Hours are 8 am - noon.

The *Alexander and Baldwin Sugar Museum* ★ is located at 3957 Hansen Road, in Puunene. Puunene is on Highway 35 between Kahului and Kihei. The tall stacks of the working mill are easily spotted. The museum is housed in a 1902 plantation home that was once occupied by the sugar mill's superintendent. Memorabilia include the strong-box of Samuel Thomas Alexander and an actual working scale model of a sugar mill. The displays are well done and very informative. Monday thru Friday 9:30 am - 4 pm. Admission charge: $4 adult visitors, $2 students 6-17. Children under 6 are free. 871-8058. A *historic tunnel of trees* once lined the Puunene Road between the mill and Kahului. The trees were taken down to make room for state and county road improvements. The earpods and monkeypods were more than 65 years old, but had suffered from time and were frankly rather pitiful. There will be 35 new monkeypods trees planted on both sides of the road to replace them.

WHERE TO SHOP

There are three large shopping centers in Kahului, all on Kaahumanu Avenue. The *Maui Mall* is only a two-minute drive from the airport. It offers Woolworth's and Star Market and Safeway across the street. This Longs Drugs is great for picking up sundry items and souvenir items as well. They also have a variety of small shops and restaurants. The older, local style *Kahului Shopping Center* is lined with monkey pod trees and is filled with local residents playing cards. Check out Ah Fook's grocery for their bentos. The largest shopping center is *Kaahumanu Center,* recently expanded to more than double in size with a new second level which includes a food court. Three major department stores, Penney's, Sears and Liberty House anchor this mall with the island's largest selection of clothing and gift shops in between. New additions to the mall are The Disney Store, Waldenbooks, The Gap, Sharktooth Brewery and Steak House and a six-plex cinema operated by Consolidated Theatres. If you don't have accommodations with a kitchen, you might want to pick up a styrofoam type ice chest at one of these centers and stock it with juices, lunch meats and what not to enjoy in your hotel room and for use on beach trips or drives to Hana and Haleakala. (Check with your hotel regarding small in-room refrigerators.) *K-Mart* opened in 1993 at the intersection of Dairy Road and the Hana Hwy and next door is *Costco*. Costco is a wholesale membership warehouse, but the membership is good at any of their Hawai'i or mainland stores. Certain qualifications are required for membership. Costco has some great deals and some not as great deals. We'd recommend checking out their Hawaiiana CD music and books. Not a complete selection, but the prices are great for those items that they do stock. K-Mart has some very good values on everyday items such as sandals. The downside is that the combination of Costco and K-Mart has really increased the traffic on Dairy Road! The proposed 110,000 square foot *Triangle Square Factory Stores* will be located at the intersection of Hana and Haleakala Highway in Kahului. The mall will have a plantation theme with space for 40 stores. Except for the Beak and Fin Restaurant, most of the mall was not open as we go to press.

Wailuku has no large shopping centers, but as we mentioned earlier, a cluster of shops down their Main Street makes for interesting strolling.

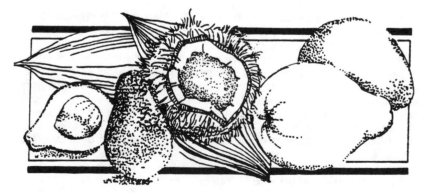

ACCOMMODATIONS - WAILUKU

BANANA BUNGALOW MAUI - Hotel & International Hostel
310 North Market Street, Wailuku (808) 244-5090, 1-800-8-HOSTEL. Previously the old Happy Valley Inn and Valley Isle Lodge. They describe their accommodations as an international budget hotel and hostel, with clean and comfortable accommodations with a social atmosphere attracting budget travelers, windsurfers and international backpackers. Rooms are equipped with closet, chair, mirror and night stand. Bathrooms are shared. They have recently added a jacuzzi.

The lounge offers a cable TV, refrigerator and pay phone. Laundry facilities on property. Free beach or airport shuttle, complimentary coffee and tea. They do take Visa, Mastercard and American Express.

Shared room (sleeps 2-3) $13 per person
Single room with double bed $29 single/35 double

NORTHSHORE INN
2080 Vineyard St., Wailuku (808) 242-8999. This hotel offers fifty beds that are used as shared accommodations, with each room sleeping four or six persons. There are several private rooms available for one or two persons.

Each room has a ceiling fan and a small refrigerator, some rooms have air-conditioners. The bathrooms are shared by all. A kitchen is available for use by everyone and a TV lounge area offers a VCR. There is a locked storage area for the guests' windsurfing equipment, and a washer and dryer is on the premise. Shuttle trips are provided to and from the airport.

The Inn features an informal, international atmosphere with windsurfers and budget backpackers from around the world staying as guests. Their motto is "Fun is Number 1 - come as guests, leave as friends." The garden in the back of the building is gone, but there are still plenty of great ethnic restaurants up and down the street. Reservations accepted. Weekly discounts. *Shared rooms (sleep 4-6) $14.95 per night, single $29.95, double $39.95*

ACCOMMODATIONS - KAHULUI

One advantage to choosing this area for headquarters is its proximity to the Kahului Airport and its somewhat central location to all other parts of the island. The motels are clustered together on the Kahului Harbor.

MAUI PALMS   (Hotel)
170 Kaahumanu Avenue, Kahului, Maui, HI 96732. (808-877-0051) Agent: Hawaiian Pacific 1-800-367-5004. This property is a 103 unit low-rise hotel with Polynesian decor. Restaurant on premises. They offer free airport pickup. *Room rates (3) $67-80/57-70*

MAUI BEACH HOTEL (Hotel)
170 Kaahumanu Avenue, Kahului, Maui, HI 96732.(808-877-0051) Agent:
Hawaiian Pacific 1-800-367-5004. Renovated in 1991, this two story, 152 room
hotel is located oceanfront on Kahului Bay. All rooms have air-conditioning, TV,
some balconies. Complimentary airport shuttle. *Rates (3-4) $85-120/75-110*

MAUI SEASIDE (Hotel)
100 Kaahumanu Avenue, Kahului, Maui, HI 96732. 1-800-367-7000 U.S., 1-
800-654-7020 Canada, FAX (808) 922-0052. The older Maui Hukilau has been
combined with the much newer Maui Seaside to form one property called the
Maui Seaside. You might want to inquire when booking here about which of the
buildings you will be in. Vi's Restaurant is right next door. Add $10-15 per day
for car. *Rates rates (2) $85-110/75-100. Extra person $12. Children 17 and under
free.*

UPCOUNTRY
and onward to HALEAKALA

INTRODUCTION

The western slopes of Haleakala are generally known as Upcountry and consist
of several communities including Makawao and Pukalani. The higher altitude,
cooler temperatures and increased rainfall make it an ideal location for produce
farming. A few fireplace chimneys can be spotted in this region where the nights
can get rather chilly. Accommodations are limited to two small lodges in Kula
and a few cabins which are available with the park service for overnight use
while hiking in the Haleakala Wilderness Area. (It is actually not a crater, rather
an erosional valley.) *Refer to the Maui map at the beginning of the guidebook for
the highways and roads discussed in this section.*

WHAT TO DO AND SEE

Enroute to Upcountry is *Pukalani*, meaning "opening to the sky," which is the
last stop for gas on the way to Haleakala. There are also several places to enjoy
a hearty meal. (See RESTAURANTS.)

Haleakala means "house of the sun" and is claimed to be the largest dormant
volcano in the world. While it rises 10,023 feet above sea level, the greater
portion of this magnificent mountain lies below the ocean. If measured from the
sea floor, Haleakala would rise to a height of nearly 30,000 feet. The volcano is
truly awesome and it is easy to see why the old Hawaiians considered it sacred
and the center of the earth's spiritual power. The Haleakala National Park was
created in 1916, but the first ranger did not arrive until March 1935. In July of
1945 the park, concerned about vandalism of the endangered plants, began
checking visitors cars. The park encompasses two districts, the Summit District
and the Kipahulu District. The Kipahulu District is on the South Shore near
Hana, and will be discussed later. The charge for entry to the summit district is
$4 per car. U.S. residents age 62 and older enter free.

The most direct route is to follow Hwy. 37 from Kahului then left onto Hwy. 377 above Pukalani and then left again onto Hwy. 378 for the last 10 miles. While only about 40 miles from Kahului, the last part of the trip is very slow. There are numerous switchbacks and bicycle tours doing the 38-mile downhill coast. Two hours should be allowed to reach the summit.

Sunrise at the summit is a popular and memorable experience, but plan your arrival accordingly. Many visitors have missed this spectacular event by only minutes. *The Maui News*, the local daily, prints sunrise and sunset times. The park offers a recording of general weather information and viewing conditions which can be reached by calling 572-7749. The park headquarters number is 572-9306. Be sure you have packed a sweater as the summit temperature can be 30 degrees cooler than the coast and snow is a winter possibility. Early to mid-morning from May to October generally offers the clearest viewing. However, fog (or vog) can cause very limited visibility and a call may save you a trip.

At the park headquarters (open 7:30 am-4 pm), you can obtain hiking and camping information and permits. Day-hike permits are not required. Keep in mind that this increased elevation may affect your endurance! Short walks include the 1/2 mile Hosmer Grove Nature Trail Lookout, the 1/4 mile trek to the Leleiwi Overlook, the 1/2 mile hike to White Hill and a 2/3 mile hike to the first switchback on the Sliding Sands Trail. Day Hikes include the 2.2 mile hike from Halemau'u to the valley rim, and the Sliding Sands to Ka Lu'u o ka 'o'o, which is a distance of 5 miles with a 1,400 change in elevation each way. For the hiker with more stamina, there is the 10 mile Halemau'u to Silversword Loop and the Sliding Sands to Halemau'u Trailhead which traverses 11 miles. The first stop is Park Headquarters. Here you can see an example of the rare *silversword* which takes up to 20-50 years to mature, then blooms in a profusion of small purplish blossoms in July or August. It then withers and dies in the fall. Some years many silverswords may flower, in other years they may be none. The Hawaiian word for silversword is *'ahinahina*. Hina is the goddess of the moon. Once the silverswords grew in abundance. They were used on floats for parades in the early part of the 1900's and wild cattle, goats and sheep found them so appealing that by the 1930's there were only a few thousand silversword plants remaining. Keep your eye out for the many nene geese which inhabit the volcano.

KAMEHAMEHA BUTTERFLY

Exhibits on Haleakala history and geology are in the Haleakala Visitors Center located at an elevation of 9,745 feet. It is open daily from sunrise - 3 pm, hours may vary. A short distance by road will bring you to the Summit Building located on the volcano rim. This glassed-in vantage point (the Puu Ulaula outlook) is the best for sunrise and is the highest point on Maui.

The rangers give morning talks here at 9:30, 10:30 and 11:30. The view, on a good day, is nothing short of awesome. The inside of the volcano is seven miles long, two miles wide, and 3,000 feet deep. A closer look is available by foot or horseback (see RECREATION AND TOURS - Horseback riding). A 2 1/2 hour hike down Sliding Sands Trail into the Haleakala Volcano is offered by the park service regularly. Check bulletin boards for schedules. They depart from the House of the Sun Visitor Center. A hike featuring native Hawaiian birds and plants is scheduled regularly. Again, check with the ranger headquarters 572-9306 to verify trips, dates and times.

The park service maintains 30 miles of well-marked trails, three cabins and two campgrounds. All are accessible only by trail. The three cabins are Holua, Kapalaoa and Paliku, all located within the Haleakala Wilderness Area. The closest cabin is about seven miles away from the observatory. Arrangements for these cabins need to be made 90 days in advance and selection is made 60 days prior to the dates requested by a lottery-type drawing. For more information, write: Superintendent, Haleakala National Park, PO Box 369, Makawao, Maui, HI 96768. Rates are currently being revised, but are a minimal charge per person. A deposit is required to hold reservations. Maximum cabin occupancy is 12. For current rates call 572-9306.

Short walks might include the three-fourth mile Halemau'u Trail to the volcano rim, one-tenth mile to Leleiwi Overlook, or two-tenth mile on the White Hill Trail to the top of White Hill. Caution: the thin air and steep inclines may be especially tiring. (See RECREATION AND TOURS - Hiking.)

Haleakala Observatories can be seen beyond the visitor center, but it is not open to the public. It houses a solar and lunar observatory operated by the University of Hawaii, television relay stations, and a Department of Defense satellite station.

To get a better visual idea of Haleakala, see the back of the book for ordering information on the full-color, inexpensive, pictorial book on Haleakala.

If time allows, there is more of Upcountry to be seen! The *Kula* area offers rich volcanic soil and commercial farmers harvest a variety of fruits and vegetables. Grapes, apples, pineapples, lettuce, artichokes, tomatoes and, of course, Maui onions are only a few. It can be reached by retracking Hwy. 378 to the Upper Kula Road where you turn left. The protea, a relatively recent floral immigrant from South Africa, has created a profitable business.

The Kula Botanical Gardens (878-1715) charges an admission of $4 for adults, and children 6-12 years $1. Open 9 am - 4 pm.

The *Enchanting Floral Gardens*, on Hwy. 37 in Kula, charges \$4 for adults, \$2.50 for children for a self-guided botanical tour. 878-2531.

The *Sunrise Protea Farm* (876-0200) in Kula has a small, but diverse, variety of protea growing adjacent to their market and flower stand for shipment home. Dried assortments begin at about \$25. Picnic tables available and no charge for just looking!

Be sure and stop in Keokea at *Grandma's Coffee House*. This wonderfully cozy, restaurant is the place for some freshly made, Maui grown coffee, hot out of the oven cinnamon rolls or a light lunch. If you stop in, will you check and see if they've found Christie's coffee cup yet? See Upcountry restaurants.

Poli Poli Springs Recreational Area, this state park is high on the slopes of Haleakala, above Kula at an elevation of 6,200 feet. Continue on Hwy. 377 past Kula and turn left on Waipoli Rd. If you end up on Hwy. 37, you've gone too far. The sign indicating Poli Poli may be difficult to spot, so you could also look for the sign indicating someone's home that reads WALKER (assuming it is still there). It's another 10 miles to the park. Fortunately, the road has been paved making accessibility easy. The 10-acre park offers miles of trails, a picnic area, restrooms, running water, a small redwood forest and great views. This is an excellent trail for the non-athlete or family. Keep your eye out for earth that appears disturbed. This is an indication of one the wild boars at work. While not likely, we still advise you to keep your ears alert, you don't want to encounter one. On one occasion we heard them rumbling through the brush near the trail. A single cabin, which sleeps up to 10, is available through the Division of Parks, PO Box 537, Makawao, Maui, HI 96768. Cabin rental is \$45 for 1-4 persons per day, \$5 each additional person. For more information see the "Hiking" section in the RECREATION AND TOURS chapter.

Approximately nine miles past the Kula Botanical Gardens on Hwy. 37 is the *Ulupalakua Ranch. The Tedeschi Vineyards* (878-6058), part of the 30,000 acre ranch, made its debut in 1974. The tasting room is located at the Ranch in the old jail and provides samples of their pineapple, champagne and red table wines. Free daily guided tours are offered between 10 am and 5 pm. The tour begins at the Tasting Room, then continues on to view the presses used to separate the juice from the grapes, the large fermenting tanks, the corking and the labelling rooms.

If you continue on past the ranch on Hwy. 37 it's another very long 35 miles to Hana with nothing but beautiful scenery. Don't let the distance fool you. It is a good 3-hour trip (each way), at least, over some fairly rough sections of road, which are not approved for standard rental cars. During recent years this road has been closed often to through traffic due to severe washouts. Check with the county to see if it is currently passable. We'd recommend doing just the first part of the road, driving as far as Kaupo. (See Hana section for more information.)

If you are not continuing on, we suggest you turn around and head back to Pukalani and Makawao. Unfortunately, the Ulupalakua Road down to Wailea has been closed for years due to a dispute between the Ranch and the county. It is hoped that this or some other access between Upcountry and the Kihei/Wailea area will someday be developed. On the way down you can go by way of Makawao, the colorful "cowboy" town, and then on to Paia or Haliimaile. Both have several good restaurants. (See RESTAURANTS - Upcountry).

WHERE TO SHOP

The town of Makawao offers a western flavor with a scattering of shops down its main street, along with a few restaurants and grocery stores. We recommend the *Komoda Store* for its popular bakery, but get there early if you want any of their famous cream puffs! The *Pukalani Shopping Center* has a grocery store, and some small shops and restaurants. A number of good restaurants will allow for a diverse selection of dining options.

Viewpoints Gallery, 3620 Baldwin (572-5979) is a fine co-operative gallery featuring local artists and a clustering of interesting gift shops -- a must see in Makawao.

WHAT TO SEE AND DO

The *Hui Noeau Visual Arts Center* may, at first, seem a little out of place, located at 2841 Baldwin Avenue, down the road from Makawao. However, there could not be a more beautiful and tranquil setting than at this estate, called Kaluanui, which was built in 1917 by famous Honolulu architect C.W. Dickey for Harry and Ethel Baldwin. The house was occupied until the mid-1950's and in 1976 Colin Cameron (grandson of Ethel Baldwin) granted Hui Noeau the use of Kaluanui as a Visual Arts Center.

Near the entrance to the nine-acre estate are the remains of one of Maui's earliest sugar mills. It utilized mule power and was the first Hawaiian sugar mill to use a centrifuge to separate sugar crystals. What were once stables and tack rooms are now ceramic studios.

MAKAWAO   JBAYOT

A gift shop is open year round and the first part of December they have a special Christmas boutique. Daily 9 am - 1 pm. (572-6560).

Fourth of July weekend is wild and wonderful in Makawao. Festivities include a morning parade through town and several days of rodeo events. Check the local paper for details.

ACCOMMODATIONS - UPCOUNTRY

Accommodations are limited in Upcountry. Five and one-half miles past Pukalani is the Kula Lodge. See listings at beginning of Accommodations section for information on Upcountry bed & breakfast facilities.

KULA LODGE
RR 1, Box 475, Kula, Maui, HI 96790 (808-878-2517) 1-800-233-1535. FAX (808) 878-2518. Five rustic chalet-like cabins located at the 3,200 foot elevation. Restaurant on the property. Full advance deposit required. $25 cancellation fee.
Chalet 1 & 2 $150 (queen bed, fireplace, lanai, stairs to loft with 2 twin beds)
Chalet 3 & 4 $120 (queen bed, ladder to loft with two futons)
Chalet 5 $100 (single story with double bed and studio couch)
An additional amount of $30 will be charged for more than two guests

KULA SANDALWOODS B&B
Haleakala Hwy., RR 1, Box 469, Kula, Maui, HI 96790. 1-808-878-3523, FAX (808) 878-3194. Non-smoking cottage, maximum 2 persons, $135 per night single or double occupancy. Includes breakfast at their Kula Sandalwoods Restaurant. Visa, Mastercard or Discover cards only.

HANA

INTRODUCTION

If you've heard any discussion at all about Maui it has probably included a mention of the Hana Highway. The twisted, narrow route follows the windward shore down to Hana, located on the southern coast of the island. *Hana* is about as far away as you can get from "tourism." More native Hawaiians live in this area than in any other part of Maui. A substantial reason for the isolation of Hana, is the Hana Highway. Hana attracts the average traveler who yearns to get a taste of real Hawai'i as well as the celebrity attempting to find a little seclusion as well. Leaving Wailuku along Highway 36 you will continue to mile marker 16 and at this point Highway 365, also known as Kaupakulua Road, intersects. This is where the mile markers return to zero, and in our opinion, is the official start of the Hana Highway.

As we discuss later, it is a lengthy drive and will require a full day. If you do not plan an extended stay in Hana, you might consider at least an overnight stop at one of the many varied accommodations to break up the long drive to this isolated east coast of Maui.

Insider's secret! Hana can best be enjoyed before and after the throngs of visitors who daily make this drive, so plan a stay in Hana of several days or at least overnight! The best travel days are Saturday and Sunday, since road crews are generally not at work and you won't encounter the many delivery trucks which keep Hana supplied with all their goods. Here is a different Maui from the sunny, dry resort areas on the leeward coast. The windward coast here is turbulent with magnificent coastal views, rain forests, and mountain waterfalls that create wonderful pools for swimming. However, DO NOT drink the water from these streams and falls. The water has a high bacteria count from the pigs which live in the forests above. The beaches along the Hana Hwy. are unsafe for swimming.

The trip to Hana by car from Kahului will take at least three hours, one way, which allows for plenty of time to make some stops, enjoy these waterfalls up close and experience this unique coastline. Add another 45-60 minutes for travel from Lahaina/Kapalua areas.

Accommodations vary from hotel/condo to campgrounds and homes at a variety of price ranges. Several moderately priced condominiums and inexpensive cottages and homes are available from several Hana rental agents. A bit more luxurious accommodation can be found at the 7,000 acre **Hotel Hana Maui** at Hana Ranch has achieved their goal of creating an "elegant ranch atmosphere."

Waianapanapa State Park, just outside Hana, has camping facilities and cabins. (See the Camping section for more information.) Ohe'o also has a tent camping area; bring your own drinking water.

Hana offers a quiet retreat and an atmosphere of peace (seemingly undisturbed by the constant flow of tourist cars and vans) that has lured many a prominent personality to these quiet shores. Restaurant choices are extremely limited. The diversity between eating at Tutu's at Hana Bay and the fine dining of the Hotel Hana Maui is quite striking! Shopping is restricted to the Hasegawa General Store, the Hana Ranch Store or a few shops at the Hana Hotel. The original Hasegawa store burned down a few years back, and they reopened in another location. It is almost as wonderful and cluttered as the old version. Plans were recently announced that they will be rebuilding in the original location.

WHAT TO SEE AND DO

PAIA - ALONG THE ROAD TO HANA
There are a couple of good resources you might consider taking along on your drive. If you'd like a self-guided, yet narrated tour, consider renting one of the "Best of Maui" cassette tours. The $25 charge includes a tape player, Hana Highway guidebook, blossoms of Hawai'i guide book, tropical flower identification card, detailed route map and sometimes a special premium offer of a free T-shirt! The tape allows you to drive at your own pace while listening to information on the legends and history of the islands. You pick up the tape and player on Dairy Road, in Kahului, just off Puunene Ave. For information or reservations phone 871-1555. You can also purchase a Hana cassette tour at local tourist and drug stores for $19.95. *Maui's Hana Highway*, by Angela Kay Kepler, runs

about $12 at local bookstores and it's eighty information-filled pages include plenty of full color photos of the area -- especially good for identifying the flora and fauna.

A little beyond Wailuku, and along the highway which leads to Hana, is the small town of *Paia*. The name Paia means "noisy," however, the origin of this name is unclear. This quaint town is reminiscent of the early sugar cane era when Henry Baldwin located his first sugar plantation in this area. The wooden buildings are now filled with antiques, art and other gift shops to attract the passing tourist. (See RESTAURANTS for more information.) The advent of windsurfing has caused a rebirth in this small charming town and a number of new restaurants have recently appeared over the last few years with more to come.

The *Maui Crafts Guild*, a group of local artisans own and operate this store. Koa furniture, pottery, weaving, wall sculptures, wood serving pieces, prints and basketry are featured: very lovely, but expensive, hand-crafted items.

Accommodations in Paia are a little scarce. There may be some bed & breakfast options and there has been talk now and again of a lodging in the town of Paia, but that is still in the discussion stages.

MAMA'S VACATION RENTALS (KUAU COVE RENTALS) - 799 Poho Place, Paia, Maui, HI 96779. (808) 579-9764. FAX (808) 579-8594. They have a one bedroom apartment with queen bed, kitchen and laundry facilities. Located across the street from the beach at $75 per day. Also available are two-bedroom duplex cottages located on a spacious lawn which faces the beach. Completely equipped kitchens, stereo, TV/VCR, private lanai $150 per night. 20% discount at Mama's Fish House. Minimum 3 night stay. Limited parking. Weekly maid service. Major credit card required for telephone service (to cover long-distance charges.)

HANA
Anyone who endures the three-hour (at least) drive to *Hana* deserves to sport the "I survived the Road to Hana" T-shirts which are sold locally. While it may be true that it is easy to fall in love with Hana, getting there is quite a different story. Even with greatly improved road conditions (as a result of repaving) the drive to Hana is not for everyone. It is not for people who are prone to motion sickness, those who don't like a lot of scenery, those who are in a hurry to get somewhere or those who don't love long drives. However, it is a trip filled with waterfalls and lush tropical jungles (which flourish in the 340-inch average annual rainfall).

Maps are deceiving. It appears you could make the 53-mile journey in much less than three hours, but there are 617 (usually hairpin) curves and 56 miniature bridges along this narrow road. And believe it or not, each of these bridges has its own Hawaiian name! You'll note in places that the road is so narrow there isn't even room to paint a center line! With drivers visually exploring the many scenic wonders, you may find cars traveling in the middle of the road, thus making each turn a potentially exciting experience.

The Hana Hwy. was originally built in 1927 with pick and shovel, which accounts for its narrowness, to provide a link between Hana and Kahului. There can also be delays on the road up to two hours if the road is being worked on. In days gone by when heavy rains caused washouts, it is said that people would literally climb the mud barricades and swap cars, then resume their journey. Despite all this, 300-500 people traverse this road daily, and it is the supply route for all deliveries to Hana and the small settlements along the way.

Now, if we haven't dissuaded you and you still want to see spectacular undeveloped scenery, plan to spend the whole day (or even better, stop overnight) in Hana. If you are driving, be sure to leave as early in the morning as possible. You don't want to be making a return trip on this road in the dark. Be sure to get gas; the last stations before Hana are in Kahului or Paia. Be sure you pack your own food and drink. With the exception of an occasional fruit stand, there is no place to eat and only limited stops for drinking water. *Picnic's* in Paia is a popular stop for a picnic lunch. For something a little more unusual try packing along some local style foods or a bento (box lunch). Takamiya's Market on Lower Market Street has an unbelievable assortment of cooked, pre-packaged food made fresh daily, including fried calamari, tako poki (raw octopus), kalbi ribs, baked yams, and much, much more. If you plan on arriving in Hana after 5 pm, make sure you have either dinner plans at the Hotel Hana Maui or some food for your evening meal. The Hana Ranch Restaurant is open only a couple of a nights a week for dinner. All other local restaurants close by 5 pm, as does the *Hasegawa General Store*. Whether you are planning a day or an extended visit in Hana, packing some rain gear and a warm sweater or sweatshirt is a precaution against the sometimes cooler weather and rain showers. Don't forget your camera, but remember not to leave it in your car unattended. We strongly recommend you take along some mosquito repellent.

We also might recommend that if you drive, select a car with an automatic transmission (or else be prepared for constant shifting). Another choice is to try one of the affordable van tours (or splurge with a company such as *Temptation Tours*) which go to Hana and leave the driving to them. Be aware that the driver of your car will be so busy watching the road, they won't have much opportunity to enjoy the spectacular scenery. If you don't wish to retrace your route along the windward shore's Hana Highway, check to see whether the tours are operating their vans around the other, leeward side of the island. This route follows the Piilani Highway and travel will depend on the road conditions. And you thought the Hana Highway was rugged? This route can be traveled in your personal vehicle, but rental car disclaimers warn against or prohibit travel along the Piilani Highway. The exception is some companies which rent four wheel drive vehicles. Check with the rental companies for their guidelines and restrictions. The scenery along the Piilani Highway, on this dry leeward side, is strikingly different from the windward coastal rain forests. Good tour guides will also be able to point out the sights of interest along the way that are easy to miss! Another alternative is to drive to Hana and then fly out of Hana's small airport back to Kahului.

Just past one of the best seafood restaurants on Maui, *Mama's Fish House*, you should be able to spot what appear to be colorful butterflies darting along in the ocean offshore. This is *Ho'okipa*, located two miles past Paia, thought by some to offer the world's best windsurfing. There won't be much activity in the morning, but if you are heading back past here in mid to late afternoon when the winds pick up, you are sure to see numerous windsurfers daring both wind and wave. These waves are enough to challenge the most experienced surfers and are not for the novice except as a spectator sport. You'll note that on the left are the windsurfers while the waves on the right are enjoyed by the surfers! A number of covered pavilions offer shaded viewing and the beach, while not recommended for swimming, has some tidepools (of varying size depending on the tidal conditions) for children to enjoy a refreshing splash. This beach is also a popular fishing area for local residents and you may see some folks along the banks casting in their lines.

At mile marker 11 (another turn off is 2.4 miles farther) there is a turn off to Haiku and Makawao. Haiku is a couple of miles inland. *Haiku* is noted for its two canneries that have been converted into local, Hawaiian-style mini-malls. The first is the *Haiku Cannery*, the second is farther up and is the *Pauwela Cannery*. The Hawaiian translation for the word Haiku is "abrupt break." It is not unusual to experience some overcast, rainy weather here. At the first cannery you can stop at *Haiku Pizza* for some very good Italian pies, and at the second you'll find homemade breakfast and lunch at the *Pauwela Cafe*. Traveling back down to Highway 36, a half mile past milemarker 15 is Ulumalu Road. A detour up there will take you to *Maui Grown Market* that professes to have the island's best sandwiches, or your money back. Highway 36 ends just past mile marker 16. At this point Highway 365, also known as Kaupakulua Road intersects. The Hana Highway continues at this point, but it is now Highway 360 and the mile markers begin again at zero! So begins the Hana Highway you have heard and read about!

Just past the 2 mile marker you will reach the new Hoolawa Bridge. You will probably spot a few cars parked along the roadside. You will need to climb over the gate to begin your trek up the one-mile trail to the waterfall. This area, known as *Twin Falls*, offers a pleasant spot for swimming. The first pool has two waterfalls, but by hiking a little farther, two more pools of crystal clear water created by waterfalls can be easily reached. This is a fairly easy hike, so a good one for the entire family. Remember, don't drink the stream water! Mosquitos can be prolific so pack bug spray. There are no safe beaches along this route for swimming, so for a cool dip, take advantage of one of the fresh water swimming holes provided.

The picnic area and nature trail 1/3 mile past the roadside marker is *Kolea Koolau State Forest Reserve*. It has no restrooms or drinking water. This area is noted for its stands of majestic bamboo, and you are sure to see wild ginger and huge ferns. Bamboo picking is allowed here with a permit.

Puohkamoa Falls is located near roadside marker #11. There is a pull off area with parking only for a couple of cars. This small picnic area offers one covered (in the event of one of the frequent windward coast rain showers) table. A short tunnel trail through lush foliage leads to a swimming hole beneath the waterfall.

175

Kaumahina State Wayside is located just past roadside marker #12. Here you'll find a lovely park. This area overlooks the spectacular Honomanu Gulch, the rugged Maui coastline and in the distance a view of the Ke'anae Peninsula. This is a good opportunity to make use of the restroom facilities.

Located a half mile past mile marker 16 is the ***YMCA's Camp Ke'anae***. It offers overnight accommodations for men and women (housed separately). The rate is $10 a night. Arrival is requested between 4 pm and 6 pm. Bring your own food and sleeping bag. On site phone 248-8355. Reservations and information available through the Maui YMCA office at 250 Kanaloa Ave., Kahului, HI 96732 or phone 242-9007.

Just past Camp Ke'anae is the ***Ke'anae Arboretum***. This free six-acre botanical garden is managed by the Department of Land and Natural Resources and is home to a myriad of tropical plants. A number of the plants have been labeled for your assistance in identification. Traveling farther up the trail you can view taro patches and beyond, hike into the rainforest.

Just past the arboretum is a dead end which turns off makai (to the sea). Follow it down to the ocean and enjoy some spectacular pinnacle lava formations along this peninsula. With the azure Pacific pounding onto the volcanic coastline, it is truly spectacular. The small island off-shore is ***Mokumana Island***, a sanctuary for seabirds. Located here is the small ***Ke'anae Congregational Church***. The church was built in 1860 of lava and coral and invites visitors to come in and sign their guest book. The ***Ke'anae Peninsula*** was formed by a massive outpouring centuries ago from the volcano, Haleakala. The lava poured out of the volcano, flowed down the Koolau Gap and into this valley. Today it is an agricultural area with taro the principal crop. The taro root is cooked and mashed and the result is a bland, pinkish brown paste called poi. Poi was a staple in the diets of early Hawaiians and is still a popular local food product which can be sampled at luaus or purchased at local groceries. Alone, the taste has been described as resembling wallpaper paste, (if you've ever tried wallpaper paste) but it is meant to be eaten with other foods, such as kalua pig. It is a taste that sometimes needs time to acquire. We understand island grandmothers send fresh poi to the mainland for their young grandbabies. Poi is extremely healthy, full of minerals and well tolerated by young stomachs.

At mile marker 17 you'll find ***Uncle Harry's***. The snack shop is named for Harry Kunihi Mitchell and is now operated by his family. Harry was an advocate for Hawaiian Rights. The road just past this stand is Wailua Road. Turn makai (left) and you'll reach the main attraction in Wailua, Our Lady of Fatima Shrine, also known as ***The Miracle Church***. This historical landmark has a fascinating history. In the mid-1800's the community lacked building materials for their church. The common practice was for men to dive into the ocean and bring up pieces of coral. Obviously, this was very laborious and time consuming. Quite suddenly a huge storm hit and, by some miracle, deposited a load of coral onto the beach. The story continues that following the construction of the church, another storm hit and returned the remaining coral back to the sea. Now painted, the coral church walls are still standing today. Upcoming around a bend in the road near mile marker 19 is the ***Wailua Wayside Lookout***. Look carefully for the turnoff on the right. Park and follow the tunnel made by the hau plants, up the steps to the Lookout. The short trek up is worth the excellent view. Back up to the highway and a few hundred yards to the next lookout. Here you can take a few photos of the incredible Ke'anae Peninsula. There are no signs, but it is easy to spot this gravel area on the left of the roadside. The ***waterfalls*** are spectacular along the road, but consider what they are like from the air! We had no idea of the vastness of this tropical forest until we experienced it from a bird's eye view. Almost every waterfall and pool are preceded by another waterfall and pool above it, and above it there are yet others. The slice of this green wonderland seen from the winding Hana highway is just a small piece of the rugged wilderness above. A half-mile past marker 22 is ***Puaa Kaa State Wayside***. This state park offers two waterfalls and pools that are only a short walk from the roadside. This picture-perfect little park is a favorite stop for a picnic lunch. The waterfalls and large pool have combined with this lush tropical locale to make you feel sure a *menehune* must be lurking nearby. Restrooms and drinking water are available here too. Keep your eye out for mongoose. They have been "trained" by some of the van tour guides to make an appearance for a handout at some of these wayside stations. The best place to get a look at them is usually near the garbage cans. Toss a little snack and see if anyone is home. If you don't spot a mongoose, you'll probably meet one of many stray cats. They seem to subsist on the garbage that the visitors leave here.

TARO

With a little effort a sharp observer can spot the open ditches and dams along the roadside. These are the *Spreckles Ditches* built over 100 years ago to supply water for the young sugar cane industry. These ditches continue to provide the island with an important part of its supply of water.

Just before mile marker 31, the road begins to straighten out. Look for a flag and flagpole on your left and the turn off to *Hana Gardenland* is on your right. Browse through their gift shop, enjoy their exotic birds and view the flower displays. The Hana Gardenland is one of Hana's best eateries. Open for breakfast and lunch this is a Hana-style cafe. Order at the counter and then pick out your favorite picnic table. They gained tremendous notoriety when Hillary Clinton and her daughter, Chelsea, visited Hana. They enjoyed their first meal here so much, they came back again the next day! The plants sold here include the "rare and beautiful" and are available for shipping anywhere. They also have one of the island's best deals for a unique Hawaiian-style postcard. A whole coconut can be shipped to your favorite person with a personalized message. Cost is about $10 for a plain coconut, slightly more for a painted one. Owners of the Gardenland also operate Hana Plantation Houses, so if you are staying in one of their rental units, this is where you will check in and pick up your keys.

The *National Tropical Botanical Garden* operates the *Kahanu Gardens*. The headquarters of the non-profit NTBG is on Kaua'i, where they operate three gardens with another garden in Florida. The 126-acre Kahanu Garden is reached by turning makai (toward the sea) on Ulaino Road, just past mile marker 31. It is 1.5 miles to the entrance of the garden. The gardens are located at Kalahu Point, which is also the location of Hawai'i's largest heiau. The Pi'ilanihale Heiau is six centuries old and was constructed by a Maui chief, Piilani. The gardens are open on a limited basis by appointment and for special events, but they plan to open more frequently in the near future. An admission fee is charged. They host a variety of events, although not all are held annually. Events might include an Open House at the Kahanu Garden or a Breadfruit Cook-off, a most appropriate event as Kahanu is home to the world's largest breadfruit collection. Contact the NTBG headquarters on Kaua'i for appointments and events at this Maui location. 332-7324.

Waianapanapa (pronounced WHY-A-NAHPA-NAHPA) *State Park* is four miles before Hana at mile marker 32. It covers an area of 120 acres. Translated Waianapanapa means "glistening water." This area offers a number of historical sites, ancient heiaus (temples) and early cemeteries. You can spot one of the many lava rock walls used by the early Hawaiians for property boundaries, animal enclosures and also as home foundations. Waianapanapa is noted for its unusual black sand beach made of small, smooth volcanic pebbles. From the rocky cliff protrudes a natural lava arch on the side of Pailoa Bay. This can be reached by following the short path down from the parking lot at the end of the road. The ocean here is not safe for swimming, but there is plenty of exploring! Don some mosquito repellent, tennis shoes are a good idea, and follow the well marked trails to the Waianapanapa Caves. The trail is lined with thick vines, a signal left by the early Hawaiians that this area was *kapu* (off limits). The huge lava tubes have created pools of cold, clear water. An ancient cave legend tells of a beautiful Hawaiian princess named Popoalaea who fled from Kakae, her cruel husband. She hid in the caves, but was discovered and killed. At certain times of the year the waters turn red. Some say it is a reminder of the beautiful slain princess, while others explain that it is the infestation of thousands of tiny red shrimp.

In ancient times there was a coastal trail that circumnavigated the entire island along a coastal route. Known as the King's Highway, it once traversed 138 miles. Maui is the only island to have had a trail which inter-connected the entire island. Remnants of the King's Highway can be found from here to La Perouse Bay. Examining the King's Highway you can almost imagine the Hawaiians of years gone by traveling over these same smooth stones. The stones were placed on top of the sharp lava rock for obvious reasons. The effort it took to place these many stones must have been tremendous. You can follow this trail east toward Hana, passing a blowhole as well as heiau ruins and ending near Hana town at Kainalimu Bay. The trail also goes north toward the Hana Airport for a short distance.

Camping is allowed at Waianapanapa in their rustic cabins available for rent at a modest charge. (See ACCOMMODATIONS - Hana, which follows).

The Helani Gardens is now closed to the public. It was created by Howard Cooper, and opened in 1970 after thirty years of development. The lower area consists of five acres with manicured grounds and a tropical pool filled with jewel-colored koi. The upper sixty-five acres are a maze of one-lane dirt roads through an abundant jungle of amazing and enormous flowering trees and shrubs. Also closed is Alii Gardens.

Now, back in the car for a drive into downtown Hana, but don't blink, or you might miss it. *Hana Cultural Center* (248-8622) opened in August of 1983. It contains a collection of relics of Hana's past in the old courthouse building and a small museum. Open Monday through Sunday 10 am - 4 pm. Located on Uakea Road Street near Hana Bay, watch for signs. *Editors' warning:* Watch out for the little terrier that lives around the corner. He apparently has a hankering for rubber! He dashes out onto the street to run into your car and bites at the tires. He's amazingly proficient at this. We thought the "thud" was the car hitting the terrier, when in fact it was the other way around. It took a year off *this* editor's life! Amusingly, this terrier seems to be known around Maui for his hobby.

Hana Bay has been the site of many historical events. It was a retreat for Hawaiian royalty as well as an important military point from which Maui warriors attacked the island of Hawaii, and then were, in turn, attacked. This is also the birthplace of Ka'ahumanu (1768), Kamehameha's favorite wife. (See BEACHES for more information.)

The climate on this end of Maui is cooler and wetter, creating an ideal environment for agricultural development. The Ka'eleku Sugar Company established itself in Hana in 1860. Cattle raising, also a prominent industry during the 20th century, continues today. You can still view the paniolos (Hawaiian cowboys) at work at nearby Hana Ranch. There are 3,200 head of cattle which graze on 3,300 acres of land. Every three days the cattle are moved to fresh pastures. Our family was thrilled when a paniolo flagged us to stop on the road outside Hana, while a herd of cattle surrounded our car enroute to greener pastures.

Hana has little to offer in the way of shopping. However, the *Hasegawa General Store* offers a little bit of everything. It has been operated since 1910, meeting the needs of visitors and local residents alike. Several years ago the original structure was burned down, but they reopened in the old Hana Theatre location. Hours are Monday thru Saturday 8 am - 5 pm and Sunday 9 am - 5 pm. This store has even been immortalized in song. You may even run into one of the celebrities who come to the area for vacation. They have plans for a rebuilding of the store in the original location. The *Hana Ranch Store* is open daily and the Hana Resort has a gift shop and boutique. The oldest building in town, built in 1830, currently houses the laundry facility for the Hana Hotel.

SOME LOCAL HANA INFORMATION:

St. Mary's Church (248-8030) Sat. Mass 5 pm, Sun. 9 am
Wananalua Protestant Church (248-8040) Established in 1838. Church services are held 10 am Sundays
Hana Ranch Store (248-8261) 7:00 am-7 pm daily
Hasegawa General Store (248-8231) 8 am-5:30 pm, Mon.-Sat., Sun. 9 am-4:30
Hana Medical Center (248-8294) Emergencies 24 hours. Mon., Tues., Wed.,
  Fri. 8 am-noon and 2 pm-5 pm. Thurs. & Sat. 8 am-noon. Closed Sunday.
Bank of Hawaii (248-8015) Mon.-Thur. 3-4:30 pm and Fri. 3-6 pm
(As you can see Hana is the place where they coined the term "Banker's Hours."
Library (248-7714) Tues.-Thurs 8-5 pm, Mon. 8-8 pm, Fri 9 am - 5 pm., Closed Saturday and Sunday
Post Office (248-8258) 8 am-4:30 pm, Mon.-Fri.

On *Lyon's Hill* stands a 30 foot tall lava-rock cross in memory of Paul Fagan. It was built by two Japanese brothers from Kahului in 1960. Although the access road is chained, the front desk of the Hotel Hana will provide a key. The short

COMMON 'AMAKIHI

trip to the top will reward the visitor with a spectacular panoramic view of Hana Bay and the open pasture land of the Hana Ranch. About a quarter of a mile up toward the cross you'll find the beginning of a jogging/walking trail that follows the track of the old narrow-gauge railroad once used on the plantation. The path runs for about 2 1/2 miles.

Kaihalulu Beach (Red Sand Beach) is located in a small cove on the other side of Kauiki Hill from Hana Bay and is accessible by a narrow, crumbly trail more suited to mountain goats than people. The trail descends into a lovely cove bordered by high cliffs and is almost enclosed by a natural lava barrier seaward. (For more details see BEACHES.)

Hamoa Beach is a gorgeous beach that has been very attractively landscaped and developed by the Hotel Hana Maui in a manner that adds to the surrounding lushness. The long sandy beach is in a very tropical setting and surrounded by a low sea cliff. As you leave Hana toward the Pools of Ohe'o, look for the sign 1½ miles past the Hasegawa store that says "Koki Park - Hamoa Beach - Hamoa Village." Follow the road, you can't miss it.

You quickly pass fields of grazing world-famous Maui beef and re-enter the tropical jungle once more. Numerous waterfalls cascade along the roadside and after ten curvy, bumpy miles on a very narrow two-lane road (and a 45-60 minute drive) you arrive at one of the reasons for this trip, the ***Kipahulu Valley*** and ***Haleakala National Park***. The Kipahulu Ranger Station offers cultural demonstrations, talks, and guided walks. For more information call 248-7375.

Looking for the Seven Sacred Pools? They don't exist! The National Park Service notes that the term "Seven Sacred Pools" has been misused for this area for more than 50 years. The name was first promoted in 1946 by the social director of a newly developed hotel in Hana to attract visitors to the area. Along the stream there are actually more than 24 large and many small pools along the one mile length of the gulch, so even the term "Seven Pools" is misleading and inaccurate.

For the last few years, these sparkling mountain pools, one of Hana's most sought after tourist sights, fundamentally, had no name. One may properly refer to the area as Kipahulu or Haleakala National Park - Kipahulu. However, a name for these pools has been elusive. Ever since our first Maui guide was published in 1983, this area, for all essential purposes had no real name. Sort of like the artist formerly known as Prince. This area was formerly (and in this case, inaccurately) known as the Seven Sacred Pools.

The term 'Ohe'o refers to the name of the area where the Pipiwai Stream enters the ocean. When the Kipahulu District was acquired by Haleakala National Park in 1969, park rangers interviewed native Hawaiians born and raised in the area to document its history. Without exception all local residents claimed that none of the pools was ever considered sacred. In public hearings in 1974 and 1975, local people strongly expressed that original Hawaiian names be used in place of romantic English terms. Highway signs were changed in 1977 and then in 1982 the incorrect labels were removed by the U.S. Geological Survey from its maps.

181

In 1996 the confusion was solved when the Haleakala National Park finally settled on a name which will appear in their publications and maps. So now when you head to Kipahulu you can visit the *"Pools of 'Ohe'o."* And imagine that, it only took 50 years to figure out a name!

Waterfalls cascade beneath the narrow bridge (a great place for a photo) flowing over the blue-gray lava to create these lovely lower pools. The pools you see below the bridge are just a few of the more than 20 that have been formed as the water of this stream rushes to the ocean. When not in flood stage, the pools are safe for swimming so pack your suit, but no diving is allowed. Swimming off the black sand beach is very dangerous and many drownings and near-drownings have occurred here. The best time to enjoy the park may be in late afternoon, when the day visitors have returned to their cars for the drive home. (This is another good reason to make Hana an overnight trip.) The bluff above the beach offers a magnificent view of the ocean and cliffs, so have your camera ready.

This area is of historical significance and signs warn visitors not to remove any rocks. A pleasant hike will take you to the upper falls. The falls at *Makahiku* are 184 feet high and is a fairly easy half mile hike that passes through a forest. *Waimoku Falls* is another mile and a half. Three to four hours should be allowed for this hike which traverses the stream and through a bamboo forest. Heavy rains far above in the mountains can result in flash floods. Avoid swimming in these upper streams or crossing the stream in high water. Check with the park rangers who keep advised as to possible flooding conditions. Also check with the park service (248-7375) to see when the free ranger-guided hikes are available. Cultural demonstrations are given daily; check the bulletin boards for schedules.

Camping at Kipahulu is available at no charge. Be advised there is no drinking water. Bottled water may be available for a minimal cost at the ranger station, but we suggest you arrive with your own supply.

One interesting fact about Kipahulu is that many of the marine animals have evolved from saltwater origins. Others continue to make the transition between the ocean's salty environment and the fresh water of the Palikea stream. One of the most unusual is the rare oopu which breeds in the upper stream, migrates to the ocean for its youth and then returns to the stream to mature. After a glimpse of the many waterfalls, this appears to be a most remarkable feat. The ingenious oopu actually climb the falls by using its lower front fins as a suction cup to hold onto the steep rock walls which form the falls. Using its tail to propel itself, the oopu travels slowly upstream.

The upper *Kipahulu Valley* is a sight visitors will never see. Under the jurisdiction of the park service, it is one of the last fragments of the native rain forests. The native plants in the islands have been destroyed by the more aggressive plants brought by the early Hawaiians and visitors in the centuries which followed. Some rare species, such as the green silversword, grow only in this restricted area. Two miles further on is the *Charles Lindbergh grave*, located in the small cemetery of the 1850 *Kipahulu Hawaiian Church*. He chose this site only a year prior to his death in 1974, after living in the area for a number of years. However, he never envisioned the huge numbers of visitors that would come to Hana to enjoy the scenery and visit his gravesite. A little know fact are the graves behind Lindbergh's that bear a single name. We were told these are the graves of monkeys. Sam Pryor, the President of Pan American Airways was instrumental in encouraging Lindbergh to relocate to Hana following the death of Lindbergh's young child. Pryor apparently had an affection for those primates, and his pets are buried in this churchyard as well. Please respect the sanctity of this area.

It is sometimes possible to travel the back road from Hana through Upcountry and back to Kahului. The trip from Hana to Ulupalakua is a rugged 37 miles. This is Maui's desert region and it is a vivid contrast to the lush windward environs. As your island representatives, we deemed it necessary to attempt the perilous trek around the south coast of Maui on this "primitive" route. You will be following Hwy. 31 (Piilani Hwy.) from Hana along the southern coast until you gradually move inland and begin the ascent up the slopes of Upcountry, joining Hwy. 37 or the Kula Highway.

While some consider this road "an adventure," others term the drive "fool-hardy." In our opinion, they are both probably correct. Keep in mind the rental car companies have restrictions on travel along this route. Namely, if you get stuck or break down, it is your problem. These restrictions may not apply if you rent a four wheel drive vehicle, but check with the specific rental car company to be sure. It is very important to determine the current condition of the road and the current and future weather is a key factor.

While very parched, this route presents a hazard which can take visitors unaware. Flash floods in the mountains above, which are most likely during November to March, can send walls of water down the mountain, quickly washing out a bridge or overflowing the road. The road is sometimes closed for months due to serious washouts. Check with the county to see the current status of this route. Another good source of road information are the local folks in Hana. Although their viewpoints might differ, they generally seem to be well informed about the road conditions. We checked with no fewer than ten people before ascertaining that we might make it through. Recent rains can cause part of this "road" (that term is used loosely) to become huge oozing, muddy bogs. Currently the road is only seriously eroded for about two or three miles. But travel is reduced to about five miles an hour, or less, over these portions. Another two or three miles are marginally better. The "Drive Slowly" signs that are posted are quite sincere (but hardly necessary)!

The first section of the road past the Oʻheo area seems easily navigable. However, fairly quickly you may wonder if you made an incorrect turn and ended up on a hiking trail. This section of the unimproved road lasts about 4 1/2 VERY LONG miles. You'll be challenged by steeply dropping cliffs to your left, and the rocky walls on your right, chiseled just enough to let only a single car go by. However, if you have second thoughts at this point, you may be out of luck. There isn't even room to turn around! The most harrowing portions, besides the huge muddy ruts, are the blind corners. During our adventurous trek we heard the rumbling of the huge rock truck before we saw it. It is recommended that you honk as you prepare to navigate these corners. With the sound of the truck pressing down upon as we furiously attempted to find the horn (you know those rental imports) out of sheer panic we started hollering, "honk, honk." (As if that would do any good -- it's one of those things that is probably only funny if you were there.) The area wildlife must have thought these two odd women were absurdly imitating geese. We were successful in locating the horn and eased into a rocky crevice awaiting the rock truck to zoom by. (Apparently, those "drive slowly" signs don't pertain to multi-ton vehicles.)

Traffic was very light, and the few cars that passed us, having negotiated the road from Upcountry toward Hana, all seemed to gaze at us with a grin that implied, "Good luck, fools." Obviously, we did make the journey, and we honestly think they need a tee-shirt stating "I SURVIVED THE PIILANI HIGHWAY." All in all, we were glad we made the journey, maybe a little amazed at our fortitude, but even with a four-wheel drive vehicle, we couldn't recommend it. The drive from Kaupo to Upcountry is fairly decent, and we would suggest if you want a minor adventure try this. Drive from Upcountry, past the Tedeschi Winery and continue down to Kaupo. The scenery is wonderful and you'll have the opportunity to see Maui from a little different viewpoint and have the opportunity to enjoy lunch and "talk story" with Auntie Jane.

But, we're jumping ahead a little. Returning to "the back road," the condition of the road improves marginally and you'll pass the *Hui Aloha Church*, built in 1859. Continue on to *The Kaupo Store*. It has been operating since 1925 and is open based upon the whim of the management. If they are open, you can head to the back of the store and choose from one of several refrigerators for a cool soda, or the freezer for an ice cream. The walls are lined with an assortment of antiques, none of which are for sale. There are old bottles, an impressive collection of old cameras, radios and antique drug store items.

Continue on another 100 yards and visit with Auntie Jane of *Auntie Jane's Fine Foods*. She has her trailer set up in a vacant field with a picnic table or two under a shady tree. She will cook you up a burger "her way," so don't even bother asking for it your way. Her way means something different each day. Perhaps

TEDESCHI WINERY

tomorrow it will be fiddle ferns or seaweed on the burger, or another day minced onion mixed in with the ground beef. On "our day" it was leaf lettuce and potato salad topping the burger. At $5 they are quite possibly the heartiest and best local-style burger on the island. She also serves up some great Maui-made ice cream along with floats. If she's in the mood, she might have banana bread or lumpia for sale as well. Auntie Jane has an opinion on most everything, and most of them are pretty sound. One "Auntie-ism" is that in Hawaii you don't eat until you're full, you eat until you're tired. This wonderful woman seems to have lived by that motto. She'll show you her wedding picture and tell you about her husband Charlie who works at Ulupalakua Ranch. However, the love of her life is apparently her stove and she confessed that when she dies, she wants to be buried with it. She reported that Charlie was a little bewildered about where he would be buried. She suggested that if there was room he could go beside her, otherwise he could go in the oven. This lady is what the "real" Hawai'i is all about. Finally, after an hour of laughter talking story with Auntie, it is time to head out and continue your journey to Upcountry.

The scenic attractions are pretty limited for the next few miles. A half mile past Auntie's is *St. Joseph's Church*, built in 1862. Take note of the many lava rock walls along the roadside. This area supported a large native Hawaiian population and these walls served as boundaries as well as retaining walls for livestock, primarily pigs. The walls are centuries old and unfortunately have suffered from visitor vandalism and destruction by the range cattle. Cattle are now the principal area residents. However, more people are gradually moving into this area. You'll note the remnants of an old church on a bluff (makai side) overlooking the ocean. This is the headquarters of *Ka'ohana O Kahikinui*. This self help organization is attempting to put the Hawaiians back on Hawaiian land. As you enter Upcountry and civilization once more, look for the *Tedeschi Winery*. Located at the Ulupalakua Ranch, it offers tasting daily from 9 am-4 pm. They began in 1974 and produced only pineapple wine until 1983 when they harvested their first grapes. They also offer a champagne and a red table wine. On the way back down you might stop at *The Maui Botanical Gardens* which feature a look at the unusual protea flowers. Admission is charged. (See Upcountry)

ACCOMMODATIONS - HANA

Aloha Cottages	Heavenly Hana Inn
Hana Alii Holidays	Hotel Hana Maui
Hana Bay Vacation Rentals	Waianapanapa State Park
Hana Plantation Houses	YMCA Camp Ke'anae

ALOHA COTTAGES
PO Box 205, Hana, Maui, HI 96713 (808-248-8420). No telephones; messages will be taken. TVs in 3 units only. Daily maid service. All balance must be paid on arrival by cash or traveler's checks. NO CREDIT CARDS. *1 BR Cottages $75 per night double/single occupancy. Add $5 for 2 people, 2 bedrooms. $10 for each additional person. Larger Houser $75 double/single, 1 bedroom, add $5 for two people, 2 bedrooms, 2 baths, $15 for each additional person. Studio $60 single/double occupancy, $10 per extra person.*

HAMOA BAY BUNGALOW
PO Box 773, Hana, HI 96713. 1-808-248-7884. FAX (808) 248-8642. This 600 sq. ft. studio cottage has a fully equipped kitchen, including a blender, ice maker and even a coffee maker with grinder. A king-size bed, jacuzzi bath for two, CD/tape player, VCR with mini movie library, microwave, phone, laundry facilities, filtered drinking water. Rate includes breakfast $135 for two.

HANA ALII HOLIDAYS VACATION RENTALS ★
PO Box 536, Hana, Maui, HI, (800) 548-0478 or (808) 248-7742. They have a number of home and condominium rentals. The Hana Kai Condominiums are oceanfront one bedroom and studio units overlooking Hana Bay, kitchens, daily maid service. Rates start at $80 per night. Deluxe one bedroom ocean front condo sleeps 4 $170. Also available are several cottages, hillside homes and oceanfront locations. The Popolana Liilii is a tropical one bedroom cottage, with pullout queen size sofa in the living room. Washer/dryer. $95. The Hamoa Hale Kai is a two-bedroom ocean view home within walking distance of Hamoa Beach. Sleeps six. $95 per night for 2, additional persons $10. Ekena is a hillside suite with panoramic views. Ekena Luna has two master bedroom/bath suites, full kitchen, TV, washer/dryer $275/night while Ekena Elua has two bedrooms, two baths, full kitchen at $120 for two, $180 for three or four guests. Other units $90-$165.

HANA AAA BAY VACATION RENTALS ★
Stan Collins, PO Box 318 Hana, Maui, HI 96713 (808-248-7727) FAX (808) 959-7727. They offer cabins, cottages and houses in and around the Hana area. All units have full kitchens, linens and utensils. Some have jacuzzi hot tubs. They offer daily or weekly rates, maid service at extra charge.

HANA PLANTATION HOUSES ★
Blair Shurtleff is once again running this operation and continuing to improve and add to the number of rental properties. Current rental options include: The Hale Kipa, House of Hospitality, located in the town of Hana, a short walk to Hana Bay. This two story plantation style house is located on grounds that include a private spa. Hale Kipa has two separate accommodations, each with its own entrance. The upstairs is a split level that sleeps four with one bedroom, one bath, kitchen, private sundeck, while the downstairs sleeps two. Upstairs rents for $135, downstairs for $100. Their Waikoaloa Beach House is a mile from the town of Hana and this solar-powered home accommodates up to four guests. Rental rate for the Beach House is $160.

Full payment is required in advance. They have several condos on Moloka'i, too! For information on their Maui or Moloka'i accommodations contact them at PO Box 249, Hana, Maui, HI 96713. 1-800-228-HANA.

HOTEL HANA-MAUI AT HANA RANCH ★
PO Box 8, Hana, Maui, HI 96713 (808-248-8211) 1-800-321-HANA. FAX (808) 248-7202. This is the most secluded Maui resort, and a Hana landmark that has been called an island on an island. Five plantations were consolidated when Paul Fagan saw that the end of the sugar industry in Hana was close at hand.

There had been 5,000 residents in Hana in 1946, and only 500 remained when he began the hotel and cattle ranch which rejuvenated Hana. Approximately 1/3 of Hana's population of over 1,000 are employed in some fashion by the hotel, ranch or flower nursery. Hotel Hana Ranch opened for public use in 1947 and was later renamed Hotel Hana Maui.

The 93-room hotel resembles a small neighborhood with the single story units scattered about the grounds. The rooms are simple but elegant with hardwood floors and tiled bathrooms with deep tubs and "walk-in" showers. Wicker and bamboo are also prominent in a harmony of texture and design. The wet bar offers a selection of coffees and teas along with a grinder and cache of fresh beans. The resort prides itself on the fact that it has no televisions or room air-conditioning. Newer additions are the 47 lovely sea ranch cottages located oceanview at Kaihalulu Bay. These resemble the early plantation style houses. These cottages include oceanview and the majority offer spas on the lanais.

The following are the published rates: Garden accommodations $395, Garden Jr. suites $450, Waikaloa Garden Suites $495; Sea Ranch Cottages $525; Sea Ranch Cottage Suites $795. They also offer a Family and Friends-Suite program. Two night minimum stay is required, maximum of 8 persons including children. Available only in the Waikaloa Garden Suite category. The first room is charged the published rate of $495, the second suite at a special rate of $100. Significant discounts on extended stays. Any guest staying a minimum of five nights is entitled to 33% off the published rate in any category.

The Wellness Center offers a range of health related activities. Complimentary guest activities include twice daily aquacise classes. Step aerobics and yoga are offered at a nominal fee. Personal training is available by the hour. Nature walks, nutritional counseling, and even creative visualization are available. Other wellness activity packages includes the Ali'i Massage Sampler, The Wellness Sampler, The Great Outdoors-Hana Style package.

The Historic Plantation House has been restored to its original elegance. Built in 1928, the 4,000 square foot building was the home of August Unna, Hana's first plantation owner. The surrounding four acres are filled with beautiful plants and trees that are more than 100 years old. The Plantation House is available as a guest home and offers two bedrooms and baths, a large living room with fireplace, dining room, library, bar and complete kitchen. To provide the latest technology for private business gatherings and meetings, it has been equipped with electronic data transmission equipment and audio-visual equipment that includes a large screen closed circuit television system. An adjacent pavilion and covered deck area add outdoor meeting areas. The site is also the location of the Hotel Hana Maui's weekly Manager's cocktail party.

Activities include a weekly luau, many trails for hiking or horseback riding, or cookouts at Hamoa beach. A shuttle provides convenient transportation for the three mile trip to beautiful Hamoa Beach with private facilities for hotel guests. Tours are also available to 'Ohe'o Stream. Two swimming pools are located on the hotel grounds. They also offer a dining room as well as an informal family dining restaurant. (Restaurant dining and the weekly luau are available to non-hotel guests on a space available basis. Call for reservations.) Children's activities and overnight sitters are available. A bar with a large fireplace and an open deck with a quiet lounge adjoining invite guests to enjoy a peaceful atmosphere for conversation or reading. The restaurant has a 35-foot ceiling with skylight, hard-wood floors and a deck opening to a magnificent oceanview and excellent food. The library contains rare volumes of early Hawaiiana as well as popular novels. There is also a small boutique with resort fashions and jewelry in addition to a beauty salon. The "golf adventure" is three holes in the midst of the resort. The Club Room has a television, and evening lectures are sometimes given here. A more tranquil setting is difficult to imagine.

WAIANAPANAPA STATE PARK
54 S. High Street, First Floor, Wailuku, Maui, HI 96793. (808-243-5354) The State Park Department offers cabins that sleep up to six people. The units have electric lights and hot water, showers and toilet facilities. There is a living room and one bedroom with two bunks in the bedroom and two singles in the living-room. Completely furnished with bedding, bath towels, dish cloth, cooking and eating utensils. Electric range (no oven) and refrigerator. No pets are allowed and bring your own soap!

A five-day maximum stay is the rule and guests are required to clean their units before departure, leaving soiled linens. A 50% deposit is required for reservations and they are booked way ahead (six months to one year). Children are considered those ages 11 and under, adults are counted as being 12 years and above. A pro-rated list of rates will be sent to you by the Parks Department on request.

The beach is unsafe for swimming. However, there are some interesting trails, pools, and lava tubes. The beach is not sand, but actually very small, smooth black pebbles. Mosquito repellent is strongly recommended, even for a short walk through the pool area. Six persons maximum. Following are a few sample prices. *Lodging rates are $45 for 1-4 persons, $5 for each additional person.*

YMCA CAMP KE'ANAE
In Ke'anae. (808-248-8355) Bring your own sleeping bag and food. Separate facilities for men and women. Accommodations are dormitory style. *$10 a night.* Reservation number (808) 242-9007.

HEAVENLY HANA INN
PO Box 790, Hana, Maui, HI 96713. (808-248-8442) 4 units in a Japanese-style inn. Each two bedroom suite has a Japanese style bath, a lanai and a private entrance. The inn is entirely non-smoking. No personal checks or charge cards. 1 or 2 persons $175; 3 persons $205; 4 persons $235. Additional person add $30. Tax not included in prices. Payment in full must be received 10 days prior to reservation and according to the brochure, it must be paid by money order or cashier's check.

ACCOMMODATIONS
- RENTAL AGENTS

AA OCEANFRONT CONDO RENTALS
2439 So. Kihei Rd., #102A
Kihei, HI 96753
1-800-488-6004
(808) 879-7288
FAX (808) 879-7500

Cleaning fee for less than 5 nights. Focuses on South Shore, Wailea & Kihei area properties

ASTON HOTELS & RESORTS
2255 Kuhio Avenue
Honolulu, HI 96815
1-808-931-1400 1-800-321-2558
From Canada 1-800-445-6633

Kaanapali Shores
Kaanapali Villas
Kamaole Sands
The Mahana
Maui Hill
Maui Lu Resort

BELLO REALTY
PO Box 1776
Kihei, Maui, HI 96753
1-800-541-3060
(808) 879-3328
FAX (808) 879-3329
Variety of South Shore condos and home rentals.

CASTLE GROUP
745 Fort St.
Honolulu, HI 96813
1-800-367-5004

Kamaole Sands
Mana Kai-Maui
Maui Beach Hotel
Maui Eldorado Resort
Maui Palms Hotel
Maui Oceanfront Hotel

CLASSIC RESORTS
50 Nohea Kai Drive
Lahaina, Maui, HI 96761
1-800-642-6284 (808-667-1400)
FAX (808) 661-1025

Kaanapali Alii
Lahaina Shores
Puunoa

COLONY RESORTS
32 Merchant St.
Honolulu, HI 96813
1-808-523-0411 or 1-800-777-1700

Napili Shores

CONDOMINIUM RENTALS HAWAII
362 Huku Lii Place, #204
Kihei, Maui, HI 96753
1-808-879-2778 or 1-800-367-5242
Canada: 1-800-663-2101

Sugar Beach
Hale Pau Hana
Maui Kamaole
Hale Kamaole
Kihei Akahi
Island Sands

DESTINATION RESORTS ★
3750 Wailea Alanui
Wailea, Maui, HI 96753
1-800-367-5246 or 1-808-879-1595

Makena Surf
Polo Beach Club
Ekahi Village
Elua Village
Ekolu Village
Grand Champion Villas

ELITE PROPERTIES
PO Box 5273,
Lahaina, Maui, HI 96761.
1-800-448-9222 U.S. & Canada,
808-665-0561
FAX (808) 669-2417

Private homes (3-7 bedrooms) and
luxury estates. Maid service, chefs
& concierge services available.

HANA ALII HOLIDAYS
PO Box 536
Hana, Maui, HI
(800) 548-0478
(808) 248-7742

Rental homes and condos
in Hana, Maui

HANA PLANTATION HOUSES
PO Box 249
Hana, Maui, HI 96713
1-800-228-HANA
(808) 248-7049

Rental houses on Moloka'i and in
Hana, Maui.

HAWAIIAN APT. LEASING
479 Ocean Avenue, Suite B
Laguna Beach, CA 92651
1-800-472-8449 CA
1-800-854-8843 U.S. except CA
1-800-824-8968 Canada

Hale Mahina
Kaanapali Alii
Kaanapali Royal
Kaanapali Shores
Kaanapali Villas
Kahana Outrigger
Kahana Sunset
Kamaole Sands
Kauhale Makai
Kihei Akahi
Kihei Bay Surf
Mahana

Makena Surf
Luana Kai
Mana Kai
Maui Banyans
Maui Kamaole
Menehune Shores
Papakea
Palms at Wailea
Polo Beach Club
Royal Kahana
Sands of Kahana
Sugar Beach
Wailea Villas
The Whaler

**HANA AAA BAY
VACATION RENTALS ★**
PO Box 318
Hana, Maui, HI 96713
1-808-248-7727

Stan Collins has a great alternative
to condo vacationing. Choose one
of his Hana cottages or homes.

HAWAIIAN PACIFIC RESORTS
1150 South King St.
Honolulu, HI 96882
1-800-367-5004
FAX 1-800-477-2329

Kamaole Sands   Mana Kai
Maui Beach   Maui Eldorado
Maui Palms   Maui Oceanfront

**KATHY SCHEPER'S
MAUI ACCOMMODATIONS**
1587 N. Alaniu Pl.
Kihei, HI 96753
(808-879-8744),   1-800-645-3753,
FAX (808) 879-9100.

Private studio & cottage

**HOMES & VILLAS
IN PARADISE**
116 Hekili St. #201
Kailua, HI 96734
1-800-282-2736

Kapalua Bay Villas
Maui Eldorado
Private homes

KIHEI MAUI VACATIONS ★
PO Box 1055
Kihei, Maui, HI 96753
(808-879-7581)
1-800-541-6284
FAX (808) 879-2000

Grand Champions	Maalaea
Kamaole Sands	Yacht Marina
Kauhale Makai	Makena Surf
Kihei Akahi	Maui Banyan
Kihei Alii Kai	Maui Kamaole
Kihei Bay Surf	Maui Isana
Kihei Garden	Maui Sunset
Kihei Holiday	Maui Vista
Kihei Kai Nani	Menehune Sh.
Kihei Resort	Milowai
Luana Kai	WaiohuliBeach
	Hale

Also homes and cottages. KMV has a good range of South Maui properties. Something for every budget.

KLAHANI
PO Box 11108
Lahaina, Maui, HI 96761
1-800-669-MAUI (U.S. & Canada)
FAX (808) 661-5875

Hale Ono Loa
Honokowai Palms
Hoyochi Nikko
Lahaina Roads
Maui Sands
Puamana
Nohonani
Valley Isle

KUMULANI
PO Box 1190
Kihei, Maui, HI 96753
1-800-367-2954 U.S. & Canada
1-808-879-9272

Kaanapali Royal
Kaanapali Shores
Kamaole Sands
Mahana
Makena Surf

**MAUI & ALL ISLAND ★
CONDOMINIUMS & CARS**
PO Box 1089
ALDERGROVE, BC,
CANADA V4W 2V1
PO BOX 947 LYNDEN, WASH
98264
Local Canadian # 856-4190
1-800-663-6962 Canada & U.S.
Fax (604) 856-4187

Hale Kamaole
Kamaole Sands
Kauhale Makai
Kihei Akahi
Kihei Bay Surf
Kihei Garden Estates
Kihei Kai Nani
Maui Banyan
Maui Kamaole
Maui Vista
Nani Kai Hale
Sugar Beach

MAUI CONDO & HOME
PO Box 1840
Kihei, Maui, HI 96753
1-800-822-3309
(808) 879-5445

Homes & Condos
Primarily Kihei/Wailea

MAUI NETWORK LTD.
PO Box 1077
Makawao, Maui, HI 96768
1-800-367-5221
1-808-572-9555

They manage the following &
have access to most others:

Grand Champions
Hale Mahina
Kihei Beach Resort
Kihei Bay Surf
Maui Sunset
Papakea

**MAUI RESORT
MANAGEMENT**
3600 Lower Honoapiilani Hwy.
Suite C
Lahaina, HI 96761
(808) 669-1902
1-800-367-5037

Papakea
Maui Sands
Sands of Kahana

MORE HAWAII FOR LESS
1200 Quail St. #290
Newport Beach, CA 92715
1-800-967-6687 U.S. & Canada

Hale Ono Loa
Honolani
Kaleialoha
Maalaea Banyans
Papakea
Sugar Beach
Also other properties

NAI'A PROPERTIES, INC.
3823 Lower Honoapiilani Hwy.
Lahaina, HI 96761
1-800-300-5399
1-808-669-0525
FAX (808) 669-0631

Hale Ono Loa
Hololani
Honokeana Cove
Kaleialoha
Kulakane
Makani Sands

**OIHANA PROPERTY
MANAGEMENT**
840 Alua
Wailuku, Maui, HI 96793
1-808-244-7684 or 1-808-244-7491
1-800-367-5234 U.S. & Canada

Kealia
Maalaea Banyans
Maui Parkshore

OUTRIGGER HOTELS HAWAII
2335 Kalakaua Ave.
Honolulu, HI 96715-2941
1-800-OUTRIGGER
(303) 369-7777

Kaanapali Royal
Kihei Bay Vista
Napili Shores
Palms at Wailea

PALI KAI INC. REALTORS
1993 S. Kihei Rd.
Kihei, Maui, HI 96753
1-808-875-4927,   1-800-544-6050,
FAX (808) 879-2790

They handle a limited number of
units at Kihei Alii Kai, Wailea
Ekolu, Kihei Park Shores, Kaanapali Royal, Hali Mahina, Mahana
and Sands of Kahana.

PLEASANT HAWAIIAN HOLIDAYS
2404 Townsgate Rd.
W estlake Village, CA 91361
1-800-242-9244
U.S. Mainland & HI

Bookings are for package plans or land only options.

They have expanded to include several fine properties on Maui.

RSVP
1575 W. Georgia St., 3rd Floor
Vancouver, BC Canada V6G 2V3
1-800-663-1118 U.S. and Canada

Following is a partial list of properties. Ask about specials they may have for free rental cars, senior rates etc.

Kaanapali Royal	Maui Hill
Kaanapali Shores	Maui Park
Kahana Sunset	Maui Sunset
Kahana Villa	Maui Vista
Kahana Village	Menehune Shores
Kauhale Makai	Napili Shores
Kihei Akahi	Paki Maui
Kihei Alii Kai	Papakea
Kihei Holiday	Sands of Kahana
Kihei Resort	Sugar Beach
Mahana	The Whaler

RAINBOW RENTALS CONDOMINIUM MGNT.
PO Box 1893
Kihei, Maui, HI 96753
1-800-451-5366 U.S. Mainland
1-808-874-0233

Kauhale Makai	Luana Kai
Kealia	Maalaea Surf
Kihei Alii Kai	Sugar Beach
Kihei Resort	

RAINBOW RESERVATIONS INC.
PO Box 11453
Lahaina, Maui, HI 96761-6453
1-800-367-6092 U.S. & Canada
1-808-669-5550
Hololani ResortKuleana
Kahana Outrigger Valley Isle

RIDGE REALTY RENTALS ★
10 Hoohui Rd. Suite 301
Kahana, HI 96761
1-800-326-6284 U.S. & Canada
1-808-669-9696

The Ridge (Kapalua)

VILLAGE RESORTS
3478 Buskirk Avenue Suite 275
Pleasant Hill, CA 94523
(510) 988-2800
(510) 939-6644
Papakea
Sands of Kahana
The Whaler

WHALERS REALTY ★
Whalers Village, Suite A-3
2435 Kaanapali Parkway
Lahaina, Maui, HI 96761
1-800-676-4112
1-808-661-8777

Kaanapali Alii
Kaanapali Royal
Kaanapali Shores
Kahana Outrigger
Kahana Sunset
Lahaina Shores
Maui Kaanapali Villas
Napili Bay
Papakea
Puamana
The Whaler
(They offer high quality condos at fair prices)

WHEELERS OF HAWAII
186 Mehani Circle
Kihei, Maui, HI 96753
(808) 879-5521
(800) 303-3750 Fax: 808-879-0649

Specializes in assisting the disabled
traveler with any physical limita-
tions. They can assist with rental
accommodations, tours, or personal
care.

WINDSURFING WEST, LTD
PO Box 1359
Haiku, Maui, HI 96708
1-800-782-6105
(808) 575-9228
FAX (808) 575-2826

Not limited to just windsurfers!
Condo, home and cottage properties
available. For their windsurfing
guests they can arrange rental
equipment and lessons.

GINGER &
ANTHURIUMS

RESTAURANTS

INTRODUCTION

Whether it's a teriburger at a local cafe or a romantic evening spent dining next to a swan lagoon, Maui offers something for everyone. We're confident that you will enjoy exploring Maui's diverse dining options as much as we have!

The majority of *restaurants* in the Maalaea to Makena and Lahaina to Kapalua areas have been included and for the adventurer or budget conscious traveler, take special note of the wonderful local dining opportunities in Kahului and Wailuku.

Needless to say, we haven't been able to eat every meal served at every restaurant on Maui, but we do discuss with a great many people their experiences in order to get varied opinions. As we go to press there are nearly a dozen new restaurants due to open so we have only been able to give you a general preview of what's in store. Many others have disappeared, only to reappear with new owners, names and menus -- just before they closed again! We've done our best to keep track and to inform you of all the new places that we think will become a permanent part of the Maui dining scene. Sharktooth Brewery Steakhouse is a welcome addition to Kaahumanu Center, Haliimaile's Bev Gannon has opened Joe's Grill & Bar in Wailea and Sansei Restaurant and Sushi Bar has brought a new sushi bar and restaurant concept to Kapalua. There are also a lot of new small, local eateries in Wailuku and there's even African cuisine in Kihei! We look forward to hearing your comments on these newcomers, as well as your experiences with some of the old favorites.

Following this introduction, the restaurants are first indexed alphabetically and then also by food type. The restaurants are then divided by geographical area, separated by price range, and listed alphabetically in those price ranges. These are: "INEXPENSIVE" mostly under $15, "MODERATE" most items $15 to $25, and "EXPENSIVE" $25 and above. As a means of comparison, we have taken an average meal (usually dinner), excluding tax, alcoholic beverages and desserts, for one person at that restaurant. The prices listed were accurate at the time of publication, but we cannot be responsible for any price increases.

For quick reference, the type of food served at the restaurant described is indicated in *Italic* type next to the restaurant name. Sample menu offerings are also included as a helpful guide.

An important postscript here is to reiterate the rapidity with which some island restaurants open and close, change names and raise prices. Our quarterly newsletter, THE MAUI UPDATE, will keep you abreast of these changes.

There are numerous fast food/chain restaurants, but we have only included the larger, more "restaurant-like" ones in key locations. We have also tried to include all the locally-owned places; the inexpensive little "finds" you won't see back home. Among those not listed are Subway, McDonald's, Pizza Hut, Taco Bell,

195

KFC, and Dairy Queen. The only Wendy's and Arby's are in Kahului as is the Little Caesar's mini pizza station inside K-Mart. They all serve the same food you'd expect, but most have slightly higher prices than the mainland. Keep an eye out for special offers and promos as they tend to be the same price as the mainland. The Burger King in Lahaina has a very good location on Front St. with patio seating across from the Banyan Tree and a view of the ocean beyond it. The McDonald's have the usual fare, but with some unusual items added in: for breakfast you can have Portuguese sausage with rice and chase it down with a chilled guava juice then for lunch, try a big bowl of saimin!

Dinner cruises are covered in the Recreation and Tour section of this book.

Our favorite restaurants are generally either a real bargain for the price, or serve a very high quality meal, and are indicated by a ★.

BEST BETS

TOP RESTAURANTS
Our criteria for a top restaurant are excellence of food preparation and presentation, a pleasing atmosphere and service that anticipates or responds promptly to one's needs. While the following exemplify these criteria, they are also all "deep pocket" restaurants, so expect to spend at least $70-$100 or more for your meal, wine and gratuity for two. Generally, anything you have will be excellent. Remember, even the best restaurants may have an "off" night, but these are seldom. Also, chefs and management do change, rendering what you may have found to be excellent on one occasion quite different the next. However, the following have proven to be consistent through the years. Enjoy your meal, enjoy being a little bit spoiled, and remember that muumuus are great for covering up all those calories!!

David Paul's Lahaina Grill
Hakone, Maui Prince Hotel
Koele Lodge - Island of Lana'i
Prince Court, Maui Prince Hotel
Raffles', Renaissance Wailea Beach Resort
Spats Trattoria, Hyatt Regency at Kaanapali
Swan Court, Hyatt Regency at Kaanapali
The Anuenue Room, The Ritz-Carlton, Kapalua

TOP RESTAURANTS IN A MORE CASUAL ATMOSPHERE
While some of these restaurants are slightly less expensive, it is still easy to spend $60 or more for dinner for two. They serve a superior meal in a less formal atmosphere.

A Pacific Cafe, Kihei
Avalon, Lahaina
(The) Garden Restaurant, Kapalua Bay Hotel
Haliimaile General Store, Haliimaile
Longhi's, Lahaina

TOP RESTAURANTS IN A MORE CASUAL ATMOSPHERE (Continued)
Mama's Fish House, Paia
Plantation House, Kapalua
Roy's Kahana Bar & Grill, Kahana
Roy's Nicolina, Kahana
SeaWatch, Wailea
The Villa, Westin Maui
Waterfront, Maalaea

RESTAURANTS WITH THE BEST VIEW
Plantation House Restaurant at Kapalua
SeaWatch, Wailea
Seaside at Four Seasons

LA CUISINE FRANCAISE
Maui's French restaurants fall in the "champagne" price range. Both *Gerard's* in Lahaina and *Chez Paul* in Olowalu offer outstanding fare, although the atmosphere at Gerard's is one of our favorites.

BEST SEAFOOD / BEST SEAFOOD BUFFET
Among the best seafood restaurants are: *Mama's Fish House* in Paia, *Gerard's* in Lahaina (though not a seafood restaurant, their fresh fish is outstanding) and *Waterfront* Restaurant in Maalaea. *The Villa* restaurant at the Westin Maui has an extensive selections of fresh fish on the menu each evening and usually a lobster special. *Fish and Games Sports Grill* in Kahana has a fresh oyster bar combined with a fresh seafood market with live lobster and crab and a very good selection of fresh fish. A number of excellent sushi bars are available around the island with sushi and sashimi appearing on most restaurant appetizer menus.

All of the top restaurants have wonderful seafood, but an All-You-Can-Eat buffet is a seafood lover's dream come true! A number of seafood buffets are available around the island: *The Moana Terrace* at the Maui Marriott has a Saturday seafood buffet that may not be as elaborate as the others with it's relatively low price of $21.95. The Westin Maui offers a seafood mixed grill buffet nightly at their *Villa Terrace*. It is served outside in a casual clambake-style setting for $27.95. The Kapalua Bay Resort was one of the first to offer a Friday seafood buffet in their *Garden Restaurant* ★ and they offer it at the regular price of $26.95, or if you arrive between 5:30 and 6pm, it's only $21.95. The Ritz-Carlton offers a good seafood buffet at their *Terrace Restaurant* for $29. The Aston Resort Wailea has a seafood buffet with four rotating menus at their *Lanai Terrace* ★ each Friday for $28.95. *Palm Court* at the Renaissance Wailea Beach features a $35 seafood buffet each Friday. The Maui Prince offers their Friday seafood buffet at *Cafe Kiowai* for $30.

BEST BREAKFAST / BRUNCH BUFFETS
Buffets are a good way to enjoy a great meal with a wide selection of food at a moderate price. And you may not have to eat for the next two days! The best Sunday brunches in South Maui are *Prince Court* at the Maui Prince Resort in Makena $31.95 and the *Lanai Terrace* at Aston Wailea Resort $29.

In West Maui, Kapalua's *Garden Restaurant* at the Kapalua Bay Resort also has a wonderful brunch, as does *Sound of the Falls*. The best value for a Sunday brunch goes to the Kaanapali Beach Hotel's *Tiki Terrace* and adjoining Plantation Room.

Daily breakfast buffets:
In South Maui, the *Grand Dining Room* at the Grand Wailea has an outstanding daily breakfast buffet for $19 adult, $9.50 children. *Lanai Terrace* at the Aston Wailea Resort offers a daily breakfast buffet for $17 adults, children half price; daily continental breakfast buffet is $13.

In West Maui the *Swan Court* ★ features a lovely breakfast buffet daily, 7-11:30am, til 12:30pm on Sundays. Adults are $16.95, children $7.95. The elegant atmosphere and macadamia nut pancakes earn this one a star. The *Pool Terrace* at the Kapalua Bay Hotel offers a daily breakfast buffet $14.95; continental buffet $11.95.

Sunday brunches:
LAHAINA: Reilley's in Kaanapali offers a Sunday Brunch menu, but it is not a buffet. *Sound of the Falls* ★ (Westin Maui, Kaanapali) serves an elegant Sunday champagne brunch in a beautiful atmosphere. Some people come just for the sushi bar! 10am-2pm priced at $22.95. *Swan Court* ★ (Hyatt Regency, Kaanapali) offers their lovely breakfast buffet for an additional hour on Sunday, until 12:30pm. *The Garden Restaurant* ★ (Kapalua Bay Hotel) features an artistic presentation and unusual variety of gourmet specialties in an open-air setting for Sunday brunch buffet 9:30am-1:30pm. Prices are $24.95 (or $29.95 with champagne) and early or late (9:30-10 or 12-12:30) specials, $20.95 (or $25.95 with champagne). The most Hawaiian Sunday brunch is held in the Kaanapali Beach Hotel's *Tiki Terrace* and adjoining Plantation Room from 9am-2pm. There is live Hawaiian music and the price is $19.95; $1 per year for children.

PLANTATION HOUSE RESTAURANT

WAILEA: *Lana'i Terrace* (Aston Wailea Resort) has a fine Sunday Champagne buffet brunch in a casual setting. 11am-1:30pm, $29 adults, under age 12 are $14.50.

MAKENA: *Prince Court* ★ (Maui Prince Hotel) features a spectacular display of over 160 food choices at the Sunday Champagne buffet brunch, each arranged as a work of art, and best of all, each tastes as good as it looks! 9:30am-1:30pm, $31.95, under 12 are $23, under age 5 are free.

UPCOUNTRY: *Haliimaile General Store* in Upcountry has a great a la carte Sunday brunch menu, but not a buffet.

BEST DINNER BUFFETS
Moana Terrace ★ at the Maui Marriott has for years offered among the best dinner values. Their buffets are no exception. Their Friday night prime rib buffet is still a value at $13.75, their Saturday evening seafood buffet is $21.95 and if you go on "Italian Pasta and Sundae" Sunday, it's only $11.25.

Monday-Oriental, Wednesday-Italian, Friday-Seafood and Saturday-Paniolo are the $29 buffets at *The Ritz-Carlton, Kapalua.*

Lana'i Terrace at the Aston Wailea Resort offers a $19.95 pasta buffet on Wednesdays, $28.50 seafood on Fridays and $23.50 prime rib on Saturdays. All are from 5-9pm.

Palm Court (Renaissance Wailea Beach Resort) serves a dinner buffet every night: Monday-Pacific Rim ($28), Tuesday and Saturday-prime rib ($30), Wednesday-Italian ($26), Thursday-Southwestern ($28) and Friday-Seafood ($34). Overall, the priciest of the island buffets.

An in-between buffet is at the *Kamaole Bar & Grill* at the Maui Coast Hotel. A selection of hot and cold pupus are offered from 4-6pm Thurs.-Sat. for $5.95.

BEST SALADS/BEST SALAD BARS
The winners are the Chinese chicken and gado gado salads, both available at *Avalon* restaurant in Lahaina. There's also their signature Tiki Salmon Salad, but technically, it's more of an entree. A good salad bar is at *Kihei Prime Rib & Seafood House* which offers a bread and cheese station along with a large selection of salad items.

TOP "LOCAL" RESTAURANTS (Kahului/Wailuku)
We have delighted in exploring the many small, family-owned "local" restaurants in Kahului, and especially in Wailuku. The food in these establishments is not only plentiful and well prepared, but also very inexpensive. The service is often better and friendlier than at many of the resort establishments.

A Saigon Cafe (Vietnamese) 243-9569
Aki's Hawaiian Food and Bar (Hawaiian) 244-8122
Bangkok (Thai) 579-8979

RESTAURANTS
Best Bets

Fujiya's (Japanese) 244-0206
Mama Ding's (Puerto Rican) 877-5796
Mel's Lunch To You (Local Style) 242-8271
Mushroom (Local style) 244-7117
Nhu Y' Restaurant (Vietnamese) 244-2167
Saeng's Thai Cuisine (Thai) 244-1567
Sam Sato's (Japanese/noodles) 244-7124
Siam Thai (Thai) 244-3817
TC Restaurant (Formerly Tasty Crust) (Home style) 244-0845
Tokyo Tei (Japanese) 242-9630

BEST PIZZA
One of our personal favorites is *Shaka Pizza and Sandwich* in Kihei, a New York subway style pizza that is wonderful and very cheesey. The pizza at *BJ's Chicago Pizzeria* on Front St. has a crust that's thick, yet light with fresh, flavorful toppings. Some readers continue to rave about the *Pizza Hut* in Lahaina, so we'll pass the advice along to you!

BEST SANDWICHES
Dona's favorite is the Peking Duck sandwich at *Longhi's* in Lahaina or try the lobster salad sandwich at the *Pacific Grill*, Four Seasons Resort. *Kamaole Bar & Grill* at the Maui Coast Hotel in Kihei and *Reilley's* in Kaanapali have an interesting and varied selection. And *Maui Grown Market* is confident enough to offer the best sandwich or your money back. (Sort of like putting their money where your mouth is!)

BEST HAMBURGER WITH A VIEW
Best hamburger with a view goes to *Cheeseburger in Paradise*. *Kimo's* in Lahaina is another best bet with a view. Neither is inexpensive!

BEST HAWAIIAN
Aki's, located on Market Street in Wailuku, is small, quaint, and very inexpensive or sample Hawaiian fare for lunch at *Dani's Catering* at *Takamiya's* store in Wailuku. In West Maui check out the *Old Lahaina Cafe* at 505 Front St. *Pukalani Country Club Restaurant* offers a Hawaiian plate and several Hawaiian dishes. *Tiki Terrace* at the *Kaanapali Beach Hotel* offers a genuine Hawaiian menu of Kulaiwi Cuisine as well as a set meal modeled after the Native Hawaiian Wainae Diet. Also check into the section on luaus.

GOOD AND CHEAP *(EARLY BIRD)*
Some restaurants continue to offer a discounted meal for early diners. Hours vary with the restaurant, but usually begin between 5-5:30pm and ends 6-6:30pm. Generally, the meals are almost the same ones that you would pay more for an hour later, but you are limited in your selections. The following are ones we recommend. Some are good values, others are mediocre fare. Offers vary and discounts may range from expensive to moderate or moderate to cheap. Call to verify their hours and to make sure they still have a discount.
China Boat, Kahana 669-5089
Erik's Seafood Grotto 669-4806

Friday Seafood Buffet at Kapalua's Garden Restaurant ★ 669-5656
Kihei Prime Rib and Seafood House ★ 879-1954
Kobe Japanese Steak House 667-5555
Lahaina Fish Company 661-3472
Lokelani ★ 667-1200
Moose McGillycuddy's, Lahaina 667-7758
Nikko Japanese Steak House at Maui Marriott ★ 667-1200
Old Lahaina Cafe ★ 661-3303
Orient Express, Napili 669-8077
Sea House at Napili Kai 669-1500

Kaanapali Mixed Plate at the Kaanapali Beach Hotel has a $9.95 all-you-can-eat prime rib dinner buffet from 4-7pm; from 7-9pm it's $11.95. A different themed buffet lunch including salad bar, beverages and dessert is offered daily for $7.95.

BEST FAST "LOCAL STYLE" FOODS
Sushiya's in Lahaina on Prison Street offers inexpensive local plate lunches. The new *Saigon Sandwiches*, in Kahului, makes French-style Vietnamese sandwiches!

BEST SHAVE ICE
"Shave ice" had almost disappeared on Maui, but a few places have revived it. Shaved ice, however, should not, in our opinion, be confused with a "snow cone." Both are cold and sweet, but a shave ice should be fine bits of ice crystals. *Lappert's*, with two locations in Lahaina, serves what they call a "shaved ice," but we thought it should have been called a snow cone! They aren't the REAL thing. Fortunately, there are a few better options. *Tobi's Shave Ice* ★ in Kihei offers a small, friendly atmosphere, 1913 South Kihei Rd., 879-7294.

We're also told that *W & F Washerette Snack Bar* at 125 S. Wakea in Kahului has shaved ice. *Ashley's Yogurt* at Kahana Gateway claims they do, but we haven't sampled it. *The Snack Shop* at Suda's Store sells shaved ice only between 1 and 5pm after the main store closes 61 S. Kihei Rd., 875-4633.

MOST OUTRAGEOUS DESSERT
The *Lahaina Provision Company's* Chocoholic Bar at the Hyatt Regency Kaanapali is a chocolate lover's dream come true. This dessert buffet features soft, self-serve vanilla and chocolate ice cream and an array of toppings. Hot fudge, hot milk chocolate sauce, or hot caramel, strawberries, bananas, shredded coconut, M&M's, fresh fruits, granola, nuts, lady fingers, and they've added some candy bars, cookies, mousse and even chocolate truffles. You can make the trip through as many times as you or your waistline can tolerate. Served 6-11pm, $7.95 a la carte, or $5.95 with dinner.

BEST BAKERIES
The Bakery, in Lahaina, 991 Limahana Place, 667-9062, is a good early morning stop that will ensure you the best selection of their wonderful French pastries. Cheese and luncheon meats are also available. The atmosphere isn't quite as fresh as it could be.

In central Maui, don't miss a stop at the *Home Made Bakery* ★ on Lower Main Street 244-7015. Their bread pudding is fantastic.

And be sure to stop at the *Four Sisters Bakery* ★ at Vineyard St. at Hinano in Wailuku. Melen, Mila, Beth and Bobbie arrived from the Philippines around 15 years ago. Their father had operated a Spanish Bakery in Manila for 15 years before moving the family to Maui. Not a large selection, but the items are delicious and different. One sweet bread is filled with cinnamon pudding, a sponge cake with a thin layer of butter in the middle of two moist pieces. The butter rolls are very good and the Spanish sweet and cinnamon rolls delicious. They sell their items only at this location and at the Swap Meet each Saturday morning. Hours are Monday thru Friday 4am-8pm. 244-9333

The Casey who owns *Casey's Bakehouse* ★ is Casey A. Logsdon, the award-winning pastry chef from Roy's, Kapalua and Four Seasons. He recently opened this bakery in the Kihei Industrial area. 879-7295.

Komoda Store and Bakery in Makawao is famous for their cream puffs throughout the state and beyond. Arrive past noon and you'll likely not get any! 572-7261.

The Maui Bake Shop features fancy pastries and cakes and is operated by Jose and Claire Fujii Krall. Jose was previously the executive pastry chef at the Maui Prince Hotel in Makena. Located at 2092 Vineyard, 242-0064.

BEST VEGETARIAN
The Vegan restaurant in Paia has probably the largest vegetarian menu.

BEST LUAU (See luau section which follows)
West Maui - Old Lahaina Luau
South Maui - Aston Wailea Resort and Grand Wailea Resort and Spa
Most authentic - Old Lahaina Luau

NOTE: As a rule, we do not list cocktail lounges and poolside snack bars in the index, but we have included a few that offer more extensive menus.

There are several food courts around the island. We won't be individually reviewing these, but will include them under a general heading of Food Court. For example: For Ganso Kawara Soba, Pizza Paradiso and Yakiniku Hahn, see Food Court at Whalers Village. Edo Japan, Little Cafe Siam, Mama Brava, Maui Tacos, Panda Express and Yummy Korean BBQ are listed under Food Court at Kaahumanu Center. Siu's Chinese Kitchen, SW Bar-B-Q, Harvest House and Tasaka Guri Guri are the smaller food outlets in the Maui Mall listing.

ALPHABETICAL INDEX

FOOD TYPE INDEX

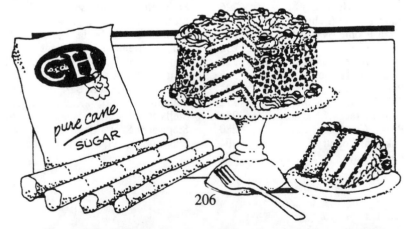

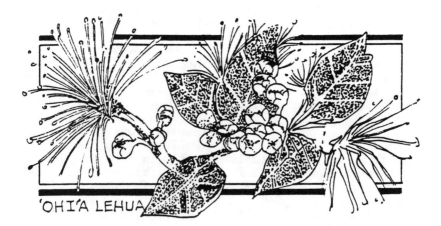

'OHI'A LEHUA

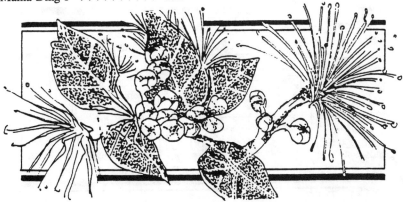

TUTU'S

CATERING

A TABLE FOR TWO
Owner/chef Paul Alkire offers "an intimate dining experience" whether on a romantic beach or in your private condo. Catering service from his set menu of appetizers, salads, pasta, entrees and desserts or request an item you'd like. Sample choices include sushi, potstickers, warm goat cheese salad, gnocchi, fusilli pesto, duck in port sauce with fruit, scampi, four preparations of fresh fish plus crepes, bananas or pineapples foster or chocolate mousse in a white chocolate seashell. Can accommodate most dietary requirements such as low fat, low sodium, or heart healthy. Picnic baskets, too. 516 Lower Kimo Dr., Kula, HI 96790. 878-1350.

AN ABSOLUTE AFFAIR
General catering services for 2-2,000 people for weddings and all occasions. 667-7154 or FAX 667-7155.

CLAMBAKE HAWAIIAN STYLE, INC.
A full catering service providing breakfast, brunch, lunch, dinner and cocktail parties. Per person breakfasts $7-8.75; lite lunches include BBQ or clambake $7.50-14.75; meat or seafood pupu platters priced per pound or choose a "theme" bar with oysters, sushi, pasta, crab, Thai chicken or baron of beef. Pupu parties for 25 people run $181.75-382.50. Clambakes are their specialty with combinations of lobster tails, clams, crab, bouillaibaise, sesame chicken, grilled steaks and corn on the cob $15.50-21.95. Meals are cooked on location in their self-contained steam cookers and grill. All seafood is cooked in its shell with Hawaiian salt and butter. Prices include paper products, utensils, buffet service, set up and clean up. No delivery charge for a minimum of 20 people. Children's prices available. RR 1 Box 52, Wailuku, HI 96793. 242-5095.

DANI'S CATERING
If you've never been to the Takamiya Market, you're missing a culinary experience. Dani's is the kitchen for Takamiya's market and they specialize in American, Japanese, Hawaiian and even some Filipino foods. Pupus include won ton, teri meatballs, spring rolls and tempura, lomi salmon, kalua pig, and chicken long rice. Sushi, chow mein, pork adobo and chicken hekka are a few of the entree choices. Catered parties have a 20-person minimum. They also provide Central Maui delivery at no charge. Set menus range from $10.75 to $11.25 per person and include warmers, plates, napkins, chopsticks; no beverages or wait service. Takamiya Market has been in business for over 50 years now and the catering operation has been around for 12 of those! They have take-out and eat-in lunches with daily specials like chicken curry, pork cutlet, stuffed cabbage $2.25-6.50 Takamiya is at 359 N. Market, Wailuku, HI 96793. (242-6652)

GLORIOUS FOOD
The catering services of Kathy and Robin Williams range from dinners for two to "theme" corporate dinners for 10,000. Hollywood celebrities, Wailea families, incentive groups, wedding parties and banquets for film crews are some of the diversified clients that use Glorious Food for Pacific Rim and Italian catering.

211

Duck tacos, drunken prawns, Italian spicy sausages, gnocchi, bruschetta, Thai opakapaka, veal parmigiana and apricot dijon chicken are some of the culinary possibilities from Kathy's kitchen. Robin will also take care of a site, theme, props, staff, lighting, florals or music -- depending on your needs. Sample wedding dinner with five appetizers, salad, full entree, cake, wine or champagne, beer and non-alcoholic beverages plus service, special lights and dinner setting for $75 per person. PO Box 329, Paia, HI 96779. (879-1332)

PORTABLE CHEFS OF MAUI
Nutritionist Louise Link, Ph.D specializes in gourmet preparations that cater to your health: vegetarian and "heart smart" meals low in fat, salt and cholesterol. She uses organic foods whenever possible and no chemicals, MSG or artificial preservatives. Entrees include poached paradise salmon, honey guava chicken, roast duck in orange-ginger sauce, rack of lamb with papaya chutney $30-35 per person; and vegetarian offerings of mock clam linguini, Thai noodles, walnut pate and mock chicken tofu $16-22. Soups, salads and desserts $6-10. In-home cooking or catering for large parties and banquets. PO Box 1224, Makawao, HI 96768. (573-3777)

TOO HAUTE
Chef Randall Bouck provides personal cuisine and personal chef service in your home, vacation condominium or exotic location of your choice. Too Haute's modern approach incorporates healthy cuisine with fine, gourmet dining for anniversaries, birthdays, weddings, business luncheons, holiday parties or romantic dinners for two. Prices and menus are customized to meet each client's individual needs. 150 Puukolii, Suite #25, Kaanapali, HI 96761. (661-3537)

In addition, many restaurants on Maui will be happy to provide catering service.

A FEW WORDS ABOUT FISH

Whether cooking fish at your condominium or eating out, the names of the *island fish* can be confusing. While local shore fishermen catch shallow water fish such as Goatfish or Papio for their dinner table, commercial fishermen angle for two types. The steakfish are caught by trolling in deep waters and include Ahi, Ono, and Mahi. The more delicate bottom fish include Opakapaka and Onaga which are caught with lines dropped as deep as 1,500 feet to ledges or shelves off Maui's west shoreline.

A'U - The broadbill swordfish averages 250 lbs. in Hawaiian waters is a "steakfish." Hard to locate, difficult to hook, and a challenge to land.

AHI - The yellow fin tuna (Allison tuna) is caught in deep waters off the Kaua'i coast. The pinkish red meat is firm yet flaky. This fish is popular for sashimi. They weigh between 60 and 280 pounds.

ALBACORE - This smaller version of the Ahi averages 40 - 50 pounds and is lighter in both texture and color.

AKU - This is the blue fin tuna.

EHU - Orange snapper

HAPU - Hawaiian sea bass

KAMAKAMAKA - Island catfish, very tasty, but a little difficult to find.

LEHI - The silver mouth is a member of the snapper family with a stronger flavor than Onaga or Opakapaka and a texture resembling Mahi.

MAHI - Although called the dolphin fish, this is no relation to Flipper or his friends. Caught while trolling and weighing 10-65 lbs., this is a seasonal fish which causes it to command a high price when fresh. *Beware*, while excellent fresh, it is often served in restaurants having arrived from the Philippines frozen and is far less pleasing. A clue as to whether fresh or frozen may be the price tag. If it runs less than $10-15 it is probably the frozen variety. Fresh Mahi will run more! This fish has excellent white meat that is moist and light. It is very good sauteed.

MU'U - We tried this mild white fish at the Makawao Steak House years ago and were told there is no common name for this fish. We've never seen it served elsewhere in restaurants.

ONAGA (ULA) - Caught in holes that are 1,000 feet or deeper, this red snapper has an attractive hot pink exterior with tender, juicy, white meat inside.

ONO - Also known as Wahoo. ONO means "very good" in Hawaiian. A member of the Barracuda family, its white meat is firm and more steaklike. It is caught at depths of 25-100 fathoms while trolling and weighs 15 to 65 pounds.

'OPAE - Shrimp

OPAKAPAKA - Otherwise known as pink snapper and one of our favorites. The meat is very light and flaky with a delicate flavor.

PAPIO - A baby Ulua is caught in shallow waters and weighs 5-25 lbs.

UKU - The meat of this grey snapper is light, firm and white with a texture that varies with size. It is very popular with local residents. This fish is caught off Kaua'i, usually in the deep Paka Holes.

ULUA - Also known as Pompano, this fish is firm and flaky with steaklike, textured white meat. It is caught by trolling, bottom fishing, or speared by divers and weighs between 15 and 110 pounds.

LUAUS AND DINNER SHOWS

For a local luau, check the Maui News. You may be fortunate to find one of the area churches or schools sponsoring a fund-raising luau. The public is welcome and the prices are usually half that of the commercial ventures. You'll see wonderful spontaneous local entertainment.

Most of the luaus are large, with an average of 400 - 600 guests, with one of the smallest being the Old Lahaina Luau with only 280. Most serve traditional Hawaiian foods. The entertainment ranges from splashy Broadway-style productions to a country barbecue, or a more authentic Hawaiian dance and song. In general there are a few standard things to be expected at most luaus. These are shell leis, photos (for an additional fee), an imu ceremony, the Hawaiian wedding song, mai tai's (a name which means "the very best" in Tahitian), kalua pig, poi, and haupia (coconut pudding). Upon arrival there may or may not be some waiting in line before it's your turn to be greeted with a shell lei and a snapshot of your group (available for purchase after the show).

It is very difficult to judge these luaus due to their diversity. While one reader raves about a particular show, another reader will announce their disappointment with the same event. Read the information provided, carefully keeping in mind that the performers do come and go. Luau prices run $55 - $58 for adults, most have youth prices discounted by about half.

OVERALL BEST BETS

Best Atmosphere, Food and Luau - South Maui:
Aston Wailea Resort and Grand Wailea Resort & Spa
Best Atmosphere: Food and Luau - West Maui: Old Lahaina Luau
Most Authentic Luau: Old Lahaina Luau

ASTON WAILEA RESORT ★

The Aston Wailea Resort refers to their luau as "Wailea's Finest Luau" and we'd have to agree. The fabulous outdoor setting in their luau garden is both beautiful and spacious with a sublime ocean view. The stage is set up to offer the ocean and beautiful sunset as backdrop. An open bar is available. Dinner moves swiftly through several buffet lines serving sauteed fish with lemon macadamia nut butter, teriyaki steak and kalua pig (which was the best of the all the luaus with good flavor, solid but juicy texture and chunks of meat). The dessert table remains the best of the luaus, now better than ever with a bigger selection of cream pies and cakes, tropical fruit cobbler and macaroons.

The show begins just as the sun is setting with the music of Ka Poe o Hawai'i and Paradyse. First is a kahiko hula which is followed by a paniolo number, traditional love songs, Tahitian numbers and finally the fire-knife dancer, Ifi So'o, who proved to be the best out of all the luaus. He did stunts, somersaults across the stage and even seemed to twirl much faster. After a half dozen luaus, it is pretty hard to be impressed, but this guy was impressive. (Apparently the judges in Honolulu thought so too: he just won the World Championship Fire-Knife Dancer competition -- twice!) The final song is from an album by Keali'i Reichel, a talented kumu hula and singer. This luau continues to rate in our book as the best overall luau in a close tie with the Grand Wailea. This luau is $6 less, with excellent food though not quite as "gourmet" as the Grand. This show features a good range and quality of entertainment with one of the best outdoor settings. And, an outstanding fire-dancer! For overall food, entertainment and setting, this is a great luau. Tues.-Thur.-Fri., 5-8pm. Adults $52, children 6-10 $26. Phone 879-1922.

GRAND WAILEA RESORT & SPA ★

In Wailea, there is always room for another good luau. The Grand Ohana luau at the Grand Wailea was the last to join the many varied luaus around the island and, at one time, it was the most expensive. There are a few less amenities, but now their Monday and Wednesday shows are right in line at $58A/$38C with a cocktail show for $30A/$20C. Luau guests are asked to meet in the front lobby at 5:15pm (the show is 5:30-8:30) where you are greeted by the entertainers who come up to meet you and do a pre-show in the lobby bar. Some hula and even a bit of a fire-knife dance are performed. Not only does this get people in the mood, but it is a good advertisement for those wandering around the resort. This is also a good way to ensure that the guests don't get lost enroute to the luau grounds. Located in an area past their HumuHumu restaurant, the luau grounds are near the ocean, which you can see through the hedges.

A shell lei is provided along with a drink (mai tai's or punch) as you are set up for your picture. Entering through a thatched hut, the area is nicely decorated in Hawaiian style with nets and fresh fruit and tables with real chairs. They have a cocktail-only show (from 7-8:30) with a separate seating (if the luau doesn't sell out). A Hawaiian trio entertains and at 6:15pm they light the torches and the dancers escort the guests to the imu ceremony. This one IS a ceremony, with the pig placed on a tray with long handles surrounded by fruit and leaves and carried from the imu with honors. The pig is served at the table family style.

215

There are two buffet lines which speeds serving. The food was good, the salads were classy and included local style such as lomi lomi, ahi poke, and poi along with a fancy mixed greens. Hot dishes included saffron rice salad with seafood, sweet potato with macadamia nuts and coconuts, stir-fried vegetables (made in a wok on the luau grounds), teriyaki chicken breasts (which we had with a tangy orange peel and hoisin sauce), mahi mahi in papaya butter sauce, teriyaki steak and a big pan of shellfish steamed in champagne and black bean sauce. Taro and nori (the seaweed stuff used for sushi) rolls were unusual, flavorful and very fresh. The dessert table had haupia (coconut pudding) along with trays of pineapple, melons, and strawberries, assorted miniature cakes and coffee cheesecake. Their Hawaiian sweet bread pudding was topped with fresh thick whipped cream. Very good gourmet food for a luau.

The luau show was a cut above too, with no tired lounge show type MC. There were some songs and hula during dinner before the big production which included dances from Samoa and Tahiti, Kahiko hula warriors, and spear dancing with some battle scenes. An explanation of the tatoos on their faces and what they meant was an interesting touch. There was also a fire-knife dancer. Most luaus have audience participation of some kind which is often times just a chance to make the audience members look foolish. The audience did participate at the very end, in a kind of Tahitian finale, which wasn't as bad as some. Just as the show ended, the full moon was beginning to rise behind the stage, and was silhouetted by palm trees. Of course this isn't an every night happening, but it certainly added a special touch to the end of a very enjoyable evening. In summary, the food was a highlight, except for the steaks which were terrible compared to the rest of the food. The MC was somewhat duller than most, but all in all, there was excellent food and an enjoyable show. 875-1234.

HAWAIIAN COUNTRY BARBECUE-TROPICAL PLANTATION
Waikapu. Currently on Tuesday, Wednesday and Thursday 4:30-7:30pm. The theme is a combination of Hawaiian and cowboy country and it works well musically and visually. The dancers wear muu muus made out of gingham and bandanna prints. When they wear jeans, they also wear hakuleis or have flowers in their hair. The music is lively and fun with Rodney Arias as the headliner. The food was, in some cases, surprisingly good, with steaks grilled on an outdoor BBQ and an all-American selection on the buffet table. BBQ chicken thighs, chili, cornbread and chips served with salsa and an excellent homemade guacamole. The dessert table was mediocre fare. mai tai's and sodas were available during the meal. A nice addition was the real silverware and set tables! The audience appeared to have fun and clapped along with the show. Pre-show dance music with The Posse. Adults $51.95, children 5-17 years $19.95, under five no charge. Transportation available for fee. 244-7643.

HOTEL HANA-MAUI AT HANA RANCH
Hamoa Beach Luau is held at Lehoula Beach on Tuesdays at 6pm. Open to non-hotel guests based on availability for $50. Guests of the hotel are transported on horseback or by van to the beachfront luau location. A very local and family-oriented production. Many of those involved in the entertainment are folks you might see working in another capacity around the hotel. Phone 248-8211.

HYATT REGENCY

Hyatt Regency Kaanapali. The "Drums of the Pacific" is more a dinner show than a luau format. It is held on the grounds of the Hyatt, however, there is no ocean view. The show is from 5-8pm and there is usually a bit of a line. Pictures are taken while waiting prior to admission to the grounds, where you are greeted with a lei and taken to a table by your server. The dinner buffet features ono with a nice Hollandaise-type sauce and tropical salsa. The steaks were cooked to order on the grill and were very good. Big slices of Kula potato were unusual and tasty, as was the kim chee. The desserts were a cut above: the haupia had good texture and coconut flavor, the hot bread pudding was baked with a meringue topping and the macadamia nut cream pie didn't have that awful synthetic taste that cream pies sometimes do. The show starts off with a welcome chant by Cliff Ahue who also does the free hula show at the Kapalua Shops. His voice is beautiful and enchanting and his choreography has always been very Hawaiian and very authentic. The kahiko hula followed the chant and had a very effective smoke-like mist surrounding the dancers. The Imu ceremony was short and nondescript, but did have the "Pig Procession" carrying his piggly majesty through the center aisle of the audience. A separate side stage for solo dances made things visually interesting. Perhaps the best number was the Maui Waltz, a pretty song with girls in high collared white Victorian blouses and colored skirts. Chief Fa'a, the fire dancer, continues to be one of the best. A good, professional, fast-paced production, although the Wayne Newton-like MC may be to your liking or annoyance. They sometimes offer a cocktail-only show at 7pm, usually during the slower season. All in all, it was a show worth seeing. Currently five-six nights a week. Prices $55 for adults, children $25. Cocktail seating $29 adults, $20 for children. 661-1234.

KAANAPALI BEACH HOTEL (Tiki Terrace)

Auntie Aloha's Breakfast Luau is a bit out of the ordinary. It's primarily an orientation breakfast for hotel guests, but anyone can attend. Auntie Aloha has been a vacation briefer for over ten years with both American Express and Pleasant Hawaiian Holidays and her goal is to guide visitors toward the most exciting and sometimes unpublicized things to do. Visitors can enjoy mai tai's, live music, a hula show and Auntie Aloha's comedy review along with a Hawaiian breakfast buffet of eggs, pancakes, fresh fruit, cereal, biscuits & gravy, Portuguese sausage and sweet bread French toast at 8:15 am, Mon.-Thurs., $13.95. Not personally reviewed...Mainly because Dona is not a morning person! 661-0011.

MAUI MARRIOTT RESORT

Daily, $57 for adults, children $25. Fruit punch and mai tai's are available from 4:30pm while guests can enjoy, and participate in, Hawaiian games and crafts from 5-6pm. The regular bar is open from 5-7:30pm while the fruit punch and mai tai's are available throughout the show (until 8) from a self-service table. The imu ceremony is held following the games and crafts and the show begins with Auntie Betsy Hinau. She is both a talented singer and hostess and comes through naturally. While guests line up for the buffet, Betsy narrates a fashion show with muu muus, pareaus and the like. The food lines move quickly past the selection of kalua pig, teriyaki beef steak, sweet and sour chicken, mahi mahi, fried rice and more. The show begins with Barry Kim as MC. The presentation is a lively one, with Fiji warriors doing lots of high jumps, a Hollywood hula segment, Maori men from New Zealand and girls with poi balls doing an effective number. The fire-knife dancer is the finale. Although we think Betsy would have been a wonderful warm MC for the entire show, Barry seemed to keep the crowd well entertained. This is one of those luaus that offered nothing truly exceptional or extraordinary, but it certainly had everything you go to for a luau for, so nothing was lacking or disappointing. 667-1200.

OLD LAHAINA LUAU ★
The Old Lahaina Luau at 505 Front Street in Lahaina is situated right on the beach and offers the most beautiful luau setting. A celebration of aloha in the traditional Hawaiian style is emphasized as guests are greeted with a fresh flower lei (the only ones that we know of!) and offered a choice between table seating or mats on the ground. The many young Hawaiians that form their helpful and friendly staff are dressed in colorful Hawaiian garb. One beautiful young lady demonstrates the crafts of weaving, tapa, kukui and flower leis by the water's edge. They provide a souvenir program which they can be personalized for each party attending and even add Happy Anniversary or Congratulations salutations, too. This luau is one of Maui's smallest, with a maximum of 280 people. Following the imu ceremony, it's time to visit the buffet with a pleasing array of half a dozen salads (including a taro leaf and a seafood salad) and entrees of BBQ sirloin steaks, chicken, fish and, of course, kalua pig! Their beverage service offers more than the usual mai tai's with premium well drinks and a choice of alcoholic or non-alcoholic tropical coolers like pina coladas and chi chis. There are four buffet lines which speed the guests through smoothly. Get your cameras ready as the show begins with a bit of a surprise. The show changes from time to time, but it is strictly Hawaiian, no fire-knife dancers here. Auntie Eileen and Piilani Jones perform the duties of show hostesses; Larry Carvalho is your MC. For food, atmosphere and good Hawaiian entertainment this luau rates as the best in West Maui. Make sure you make your reservations in advance, as they have become quite popular and may be sold out. They have received top honors from the "Keep it Hawaii" Kahili Awards program sponsored by the Hawai'i Visitors Bureau. There are plans for another location sometime in the near future. Held nightly at 5:30pm. Phone 667-1998. Adults $57, children $28.50.

RENAISSANCE WAILEA BEACH RESORT
The Renaissance (formerly Stouffer's) luau has resumed operation since our last edition and is now held every Monday in the Luau Gardens. It begins at 6 pm with a hosted cocktail reception accompanied by a Hawaiian trio followed by the imu ceremony, buffet and Polynesian show with fire-knife dancer and ending at approximately 8:30. The buffet includes green salad, Chinese chicken salad, chow mein salad, fresh fruit salad, pineapple spears, macaroni/potato salad, poi, lomi lomi salmon, kalua pig, grilled fish with coconut flakes, huli huli chicken, char-broiled teriyaki steaks, Hawaiian yams, fried rice, sweet bread and for dessert pineapple upside-down cake and banana cake with chocolate frosting. Seating at round tables of 10. There is table service from the open bar throughout the evening. $51 adults, $29 children 5-12, under 5 free. Not reviewed. 879-4900.

ROYAL LAHAINA RESORT

In Kaanapali. Nightly at 5:30 or 6pm (changes seasonally), $55 adults, $28 children 5-12 years, under 5 free. The ready-made mai tai's, fruit punch, open bar and shell leis were the first order of business, but they have a new twist on the photographs. They take two of them, one with your party and male and female greeters, and the other is a circle inset in a picture of the luau performers on stage, making it an effective souvenir. The luau grounds are near the ocean, but without an ocean view (unless you peek over the hedge). Seating is at padded picnic table benches. The imu ceremony was the shortest and some people hadn't even reached the pit before it was over! While people were settling in, hostess Makalapua welcomed guests.

Dinner began at 6:45 with four tables and eight lines allowing people to flow quickly through. Real "glass" glasses for drinks were a pleasant surprise, although the coffee cups were plastic. Large wooden trays offered plenty of room to pile on the teri beef, kalua pig, pineapple chicken, lomi lomi salmon, poi and salad bar with an interesting selection. The desserts included haupia, pineapple upside-down cake and the coconut cream cake was particularly good. Frank Hewitt, a prominent kumu hula and songwriter, is the choreographer and he wrote all the songs in the show (except the Hawaiian Wedding song). There was just the right amount of audience interaction with Makalapua providing a short hula lesson with instructions about moving and wiggling your papayas and bananas, which was sort of cute. A fashion show followed and the production began with the blowing of the conch shell and kahiko hula, the male dancers making a nice entrance through the audience to be joined by the female dancers on stage. Co-MC Warren Molina sang a lively tune which was followed by several more very entertaining numbers. The song and hula about the legend of the rain resulted in a very fine water spray reaching the front of the audience. They still have the Hollywood number which is a fun piece, followed by a romantic Hawaiian song. The finale was the fire-knife dance.

Drawbacks at this luau included the gravel covered dirt ground which made annoying crunching sounds as people got up throughout the show to pick up a drink at the bar, which remained open during the show. This is another good, but not great luau. A nice touch is the original music and choreography. They have the advantage of moving their luau into their indoor Alii Room if the weather is uncooperative. 661-3611.

Here are some facts and figures you may not want to know!

Luaus are definitely not low-calorie dining options. So eat and enjoy, but just in case you are interested, here is the breakdown! Kalua Pig 1/2 cup 150 calories, Lomi Lomi salmon 1/2 cup 87 calories, Poi 1 cup 161 calories (but who could eat that much!), fried rice 1 cup 200 calories, fish (depending on type served) 150-250 calories, chicken long rice 283 calories, haupia 128 calories, coconut cake 200-350 calories, Mai Tai 302 calories, Pina Colada 252 calories, fruit punch 140 calories, Blue Hawai'i 260 calories, Chi Chi 190 calories.

LAHAINA

INEXPENSIVE

ARAKAWA   *Japanese Fast Food*
736 Front St., at the Wainee St. end of the Kishi Mall. (661-8811) HOURS: 11am-2pm; 5-7:30pm (Closed every 1st and 15th to do errands!) SAMPLING: Yakitori teriyaki, hekka - tofu, chicken, vegetables, chicken katsu, breaded mahi, chicken katsu curry, katsu don, California roll sushi $4.50-5. Fried noodle, fried rice, manapua, vegetable egg roll, macaroni salad, rice, pot sticker, chicken stick $.50-$3. COMMENTS: This a great little hole-in-the-wall, a little tricky to find, but worth the effort. There are always several locals and a few visitors waiting to order and the general consensus seems to be that the yakitori chicken sticks are the best. A very small counter, so most get their local-style food items to go.

ATHENS GREEK RESTAURANT   *Greek*
Located inside the Lahaina Cannery Mall (661-4300) HOURS: 9:30am-9pm daily. A fast food Greek restaurant that features gyros, falafel and souvlaki shish kebab $5.59; $7.59 with salad and pita bread. Moussaka and pastichio $6.15-8.15; Greek salad $3.25-5.65; spanakopita $1.99. COMMENTS: Limited seating.

BJ'S CHICAGO PIZZERIA ★   *Italian*
730 Front St. (661-0700) HOURS: 11am-11pm, same menu all day (additional pizza specials at lunch). SAMPLING: Pizzas for the small, medium or large appetite include specialties like BBQ Chicken (grilled chicken breast, BBQ sauce, red onions and cilantro) $14.65-21.75, or basics like cheese and tomato $7.45-12.45 to add your own toppings. B.J. specialty salads include chopped Italian or sesame chicken $4.95-7.45, pasta dishes $6.95-10.95, homemade sandwiches on B.J.'s freshly baked rolls: meatball, roast beef, sausage and grilled chicken $6.50-6.95. COMMENTS: The landmark Front Street location reopened in 1994 and is filled with woodwork, murals and historic photographs that recreate the look and feel of its former incarnation as The Blue Max. This is the ninth restaurant in the B.J. chain and they came to Maui with a good reputation. Their deep-dish Chicago-style pizza has a crust that is thick, while surprisingly light, and the toppings are fresh and innovative. Try an appetizer like Brie and Papaya Quesadilla, Charleston Crab Cakes, Fried Provolone, Roasted Peppers or Toasted Raviolis. But leave room for dessert. You won't be able to resist the Pizookie n' Cream: a chocolate chip or white chocolate and macadamia cookie baked fresh in a mini-pizza pan and served warm with vanilla ice cream.

THE BAKERY ★   *French/American*
911 Limahana (turn off Honoapiilani Hwy. by Pizza Hut) (667-9062) HOURS: Mon.-Fri. 5:30am-3pm; Sat. 5:30am-2pm; Sun. 5:30am-noon. SAMPLING: Chocolate almond and whole wheat cream cheese croissants. Ham or turkey-stuffed croissants or small sandwiches such as turkey dijon. Huge fresh fruit tortes, fudge, and fresh breads (the newest is natural grain raisin-walnut) are made here daily. COMMENTS: There's a small deli case with meats and cheeses, but no seating area. Arrive early in the day to insure getting the best

selections. They're all delicious and it's well worth the stop if you are a pastry lover. Try their stuffed Tongan bread with savory combinations of mushrooms, onions and chicken!

BLUE LAGOON TROPICAL BAR AND GRILL *American*
658 Front. St. Located on the lower level of the Wharf Cinema Center (661-8141) HOURS: 6am-10:30pm. SAMPLING: Omelettes, pancakes, waffles and full English, American, Spanish and Continental breakfasts $3-8.50. Sandwiches include burgers, chicken, fish, turkey, ham or club sandwiches in various combinations with soups and salads $5.95-8.50 plus steak, chicken, mahi mahi and chicken entrees $8.95-15.95. BLT and club sandwiches served until 5pm, all other menu items available all day. COMMENTS: Seating is in the courtyard of the shopping center surrounded by waterfalls and koi ponds or inside a recessed area recently renovated by the new owners with bamboo and koa wood to make it look like a Polynesian hut. The bar is out in the courtyard where you can order a Lahaina Sunrise and other tropical creations. (There's a keiki menu that has non-alcoholic versions!) They have a small salad bar $7.95 including some tropical fruit items offered free with certain entrees, half-price with others.

CAPTAIN DAVE'S ARCTIC WAVE *Fish & Chips*
Lahaina Marketplace off Front. St. (667-6700) HOURS: 10:30am-9pm. SAMPLING: Ono & chips, prawns & chips, clams & chips, calamari & chips or combination platter $5.95-7.95. Grilled ono or chicken sandwich $5.95-6.95 COMMENTS: All main menu fish items served with French fries and Maui coleslaw (with pineapple) and homemade tartar or cocktail sauce. They use 100% canola oil in all their cooking. With recent expansion, they now offer malasadas for breakfast, salad lunches and salmon dinners with Caesar salad.

CHEESEBURGER IN PARADISE ★ *American*
811 Front St., Lahaina (661-4855) HOURS: Lunch/dinner served 11am-11pm. SAMPLING: Select from their classic BLT, Philly-chicken & Swiss or cajun chicken sandwich, jumbo cheese dog, their famous "Cheeseburger in Paradise" and a number of vegetarian dishes including a grilled cheese and tofu or garden burger $5.95-6.95. Entree salads, fish sandwich or coconut shrimp $6.95-9.95; stuffed baked potatoes $5.95. Chili cheese or seasoned fries, fried calamari & scallops or onion rings $3.50-6.50. COMMENTS: A casual and fun atmosphere with open-air dining and wonderful views of the Lahaina Harbor and Front Street from the upstairs loft. The cheeseburgers are good and you get the view at no charge! Live music nightly 4-7pm and 8-11pm. Make sure your try some of their tropical drinks, the Lahaina Sunburn, the Lahainaluna Swirl or Trouble in Paradise. (Or if you want to stay *out* of trouble, try the thick and chunky non-alcoholic Oreo cookie smoothie!) It can be crowded at meal times, but the lines move quickly.

CHUN'S KOREAN RESTAURANT *Korean*
658 Front St., Wharf Cinema Center. (661-9207) HOURS: Lunch 10am-3pm, dinner 10am-10pm. SAMPLING: Lunch menu includes chicken katsu, pot stickers, BBQ meats or kook soo $6.50-7.95. Beef, chicken or pork bul ko gi (thinly sliced BBQ marinated meat), beef jun (BBQ beef in egg batter), bi bim

naeng myun (cold buckwheat noodles with beef and vegetables), yuk ke jang (spicy beef soup with vegetables and rice noodle) and spicy pork or calamari bok kum $9.25-14.50. COMMENTS: The BBQ dishes are cooked on the table with a grill in the center. The owners recently opened Isana restaurant in Kihei.

DENNY'S *American*
Lahaina Square Shopping Center (667-7898) HOURS: Open 24 hours a day. SAMPLING: Traditional Denny's burgers, sandwiches, salads and dinners plus island favorites like saimin, mahi sandwich, teri burger, spam & eggs, local-style plate lunches and a new dessert special: macadamia nut caramel cream cheese pie. Fresh catch dinner includes soup or salad, potato, vegetable and rolls for $11.95. Prices from $4 (pancakes) to $12.75 (prime rib). Breakfast served anytime. Senior specials available. COMMENTS: Wine & beer. Second location in Kihei has Gator's Good Times Tavern & Sports Bar.

EDEN'S GARDEN *Vegetarian*
505 Front St. #142, Lahaina (667-5727) HOURS: 9am-9pm Mon.-Sat., til 6 on Sunday. SAMPLING: Smoothies and freshly squeezed juices (including wheat grass) $2-4.75. Specialties include vegetarian chili nachos, burrito, garden burger, tofu melt, chili-cheese potatoes $3.75-5.95. Tofu, avocado, pasta, fruit salads $4.25-5.50. Daily hot entrees. COMMENTS: Homemade and healthy desserts, too. Try the mango pie when it's in season.

GOLDEN PALACE *Chinese*
Old Lahaina Center (661-3126) HOURS: Lunch 11am-2pm, dinner 5-9pm. Also take out. SAMPLING: A large variety of selections with Cantonese and some Szechuan dishes. Pressed duck, shrimp fu yung, chicken fritters, steamed pork hash, beef with bitter melon, chop suey and chow mein $4.50-8.25 COMMENTS: Beer, cocktails, and Chinese wine are also available. This place is an institution on Maui, in business now for over 30 years.

HARD ROCK CAFE ★ *American*
New Lahaina Center, 900 Front St. (667-7400) HOURS: 11:30am-10pm. SAMPLING: Grilled burgers or chicken breast sandwiches $6.95-7.95, lime BBQ chicken $10.95, HRC baby rock watermelon ribs $12.95. Chicken, beef or combination fajitas $11.95. Newer additions include grilled vegetable or Chinese chicken salad, chicken Caesar sandwich or roasted turkey wrap (in a tortilla). $6.95-9.95. COMMENTS: A lively atmosphere, if the music isn't too loud for you. Fun and interesting memorabilia around the room, such as a Steinberger guitar signed by Ziggy Marley, a bustier worn by Madonna during her 1989 world tour, or an autographed bass drum skin by Fleetwood Mac. And not to worry, they can provide you with a brochure to serve as a self-guided tour of this rock-n-roll memorabilia that covers the restaurant walls AND the bathrooms, too. Great prices, good food and a trendy reputation makes this a very popular eatery, so there may be a waiting line to get in during peak dining hours. This is one of the places the kids will want to be sure visit, if not to eat, then to get a T-shirt!

IL BUCANIERE *Italian*
666 Front St. (661-3966) HOURS: Lunch 11am-2:30pm, dinner 5:30-10pm.

SAMPLING: Salads and antipasto $4.25-5.75; pizzas $8.95-9.95. Assorted pastas come with clams, mussels, home-made sausage, mushrooms, shrimp, vegetables and gorgonzola $10.75-14.95. Dinner entrees of pork chops, rosemary chicken, steak and fish include scalloped potatoes or rice and vegetable $12.95-18.95. COMMENTS: Located upstairs in the old Whale's Tale location overlooking Front St. Live music nightly. Casual, family-style atmosphere.

LAHAINA BROILER *Seafood/American*
887 Front St. (661-3111) HOURS: Lunch 11am-2pm, late lunch 2-5pm, dinner 5-10pm. SAMPLING: Lunch sandwiches, burgers, salads, appetizers, pizzas or hot entrees $4.95 - $10.95. Dinners also offer a variety of burgers or foot long hot dog $5.50-7.95 and pizzas with teriyaki or shoyu chicken, crab meat, veggies or shrimp $6.95-10.95. Entrees include steaks, fish, shrimp Tahitian, baby back ribs, oriental or pineapple-teriyaki chicken and crab legs $10.95-20.95. COMMENTS: A wonderful, open ocean view setting done in hues of grey, green and mauve. While the atmosphere is great the food has not proven to be outstanding. An ideal location for an evening beverage, however.

LAHAINA GOURMET DELI & CYBER CAFE *Sandwiches plus*
180 Dickenson St., Located at Dickenson Square, the corner of Wainee and Dickenson. (661-4455) HOURS: 6 am to 10 pm for breakfast, lunch and dinner. SAMPLING: Breakfast sandwiches, oven-baked French toast and omelettes run from $3.59-3.99 while plate lunches featuring anything from beef stir-fry to pork chops and gravy are $2.99 or $5.99 depending on how many scoops of rice or macaroni salad. They offer two homemade soups daily ($2.99) and salads include Caesar, cobb, spinach, fruit and a pasta-with-greens carbo salad for $5.99. Mile-high, mega-bite sandwiches with lettuce, tomato and onion are stuffed with roast beef, hot pastrami, smoked or oven-roasted turkey breast, lean corned beef, black forest ham, kosher bologna, Italian dry salami or teriyaki chicken breast and come with a choice of side salad for $5.99. Choose from a variety of breads and rolls or add one of a half dozen cheeses for $1. COMMENTS: Limited seating, a few tables outside and inside. The deli opened in June '96, but at press time they were not yet on the net. By the end of summer, they planned to expand into the space next door with their Cyber Cafe lounge area (with more seating and extended menu) along with three new computers and their own home page. (You can also get information the old fashioned way: if you'd like an update on the day's daily specials, just call 661-4455.)

LAHAINA TREEHOUSE RESTAURANT *Homecooking*
Lahaina Market Place on Front St. (661-3235) HOURS: 11:30am-10pm. SAMPLING: Appetizers include Treehouse baby nest (shrimp cradled in flaky pastry) and mini mahi mahi log wrapped in Maui onion dough $4.95-6.95, plus salads of black bean, grilled chicken or sauteed shrimp offered with chips or an assortment of freshly baked breads $6.95-12.95. Lunch selections include a burger, herbed chicken sandwich and a peanut butter club sandwich layered with home-made peanut butter and choice of jelly, cheese, banana or any other of your favorite childhood memories $4.95-9.95! For dinner, pork is cooked in an underground imu and served in a Hawaiian hut of buttery dough (accompanied by long rice and taro); creamy seafood is served in a pastry bowl surrounded by fresh

vegetables or you can order the grilled tenderloin or an assortment of vegetables, grilled and served on an edible plate $14.95-19.50. Top off the meal with original dessert creations like the "Hawaiian" chocolate eclair or passion fruit "Napoleon." $2.75-3.75. Served all day: spaghetti, chili or a pizza platter of fresh pizza toppings served on a variety of savory homemade breads $6.95-8.95. COMMENTS: The tree is still there and it comes right up through the third floor where you can enjoy your meal and look across town. New owners show their bakery background with dishes embellished by freshly-baked pastry, doughs and breads. Sauces and dressings are made from scratch, too.

LANI'S PANCAKE COTTAGE ★ *American Breakfast*
658 Front St., Wharf Cinema Center, across from the Banyan Tree (661-0955) HOURS: Breakfast 6am-noon. (Becomes Gekko Japanese Restaurant in the afternoon and evening.) SAMPLING: Macadamia nut, chocolate chip, and a variety of fruit pancakes, waffle, French toast $3-5.95, biscuits & gravy $2.95, cereals $2.25, breakfast meats and egg dishes $3.95-8.95 including the "Chef's Mess Omelette" $10.95-15.95 with enough fillings for one or two people. In addition to the popular breakfast fare they offer entrees such as fish and chips or chili burgers $4.50 - $6.50. COMMENTS: As popular as ever and always busy. Seating indoors or on the patio.

LOCAL FOOD *Healthy Hawaiian*
Anchor Square, 888 Wainee St. (667-2882) HOURS: Mon.-Fri 10am til whenever they run out of food! SAMPLING: Local dishes like shoyu chicken from $5; Hawaiian Plate with lomi lomi salmon, lau lau, chicken long rice, poi or rice $8.50. COMMENTS: Hawaiian food made healthy for the 90's. Little or no salt, no sugar, light oil.

THE MAUI GOURMET *Sandwiches/Pastries*
505 Front St. (667-4051) HOURS: 10am-9pm SAMPLING: Danish, muffins, scones. cinnamon rolls, bread pudding $1.75-2.50. Greek, Caesar, pesto pasta, fruit salads $4-6.95. Turkey, tuna, ham, club and specialty Balé sandwiches and spaghetti or lasagna $5.95-7.95. COMMENTS: A good selection of coffee drinks, juices, Italian sodas -- even a root beer float! Cheesecake, brownies, chocolate cake, cookies and other desserts. The new owners have introduced the Balé sandwich made with deli meats (ham, pate or steamed pork), cucumber, pickled carrots, cilantro and gourmet mayo on French bread $3.50-3.90.

MAUI LU-WOW *Hawaiian Sandwiches*
757 Luakini St. (662-6284) HOURS: 10am-10pm. SAMPLING: Shrimp, mahi, beef pork, chicken or turkey "Aki" sandwich $3.75-5.75 or combos $5.75-7.25. Coffee drinks or passion-guava and orange-pineapple "tropicals" $2.25-2.50; Volcano dessert (ice cream shaped like a volcano with lilikoi and other flavor "lava") $3.25. COMMENTS: Aki sandwich on Maui baked flat bread is filled with shredded cabbage and piled high with meat, fish or shrimp then topped with BBQ, teriyaki, hot mustard or tartar sauce. Combos include choice of two sides: sticky rice, macaroni salad, sauteed green beans or vegetable tempura. Tropicals are their version of an Orange Julius updated for the 90's. Attractive building designed and painted in the old Pioneer Inn style. Opened June, 1996.

MAUI SWISS CAFE   *Swiss-Continental*
640 Front St. (661-6776) HOURS: 8am-7pm; from 10am Sunday. SAMPLING: Swiss breakfast of sliced ham, cheeses, salami, fruit, hard boiled egg, croissant $5.25; other pastries $1.25-4.25. Hot and cold Sandwiches $5.50-7.25 and Kaseschnitten: open faced hot cheese sandwiches $7. Raviolis and penne pastas $7.50-9 and pizzas $6.50 plus toppings. COMMENTS: Hot and iced coffee drinks plus ice cream in a variety of ways: scoops, sundaes, shakes, smoothies and tropical drinks. Imported swiss chocolates for sale. Limited outdoor seating.

MAUI TACOS   *Healthy Mexican*
Lahaina Square (661-8883) HOURS: 10am-9pm. SAMPLING: Potato enchiladas, hard or soft tacos, quesadillas, chimichangas and over a dozen varieties of special hand-held burritos $1.99-6.95. COMMENTS: Guacamole and salsa made fresh every day. No lard, no msg -- they use only vegetable oil, fresh beans and lean meats. The complimentary salsa bar offers several choices with jalapenos, onions, cilantro, hot sauce and more. Good values! They now have outlets in Kihei and Kaahumanu Food Court as well as the original in Napili Plaza, all owned and operated by Mark Ellman of Avalon.

MR. SUB   *Sandwiches*
129 Lahainaluna Rd. (667-5683) HOURS: Mon.-Fri. 7am-5pm; Sat. til 4. Closed Sunday. SAMPLING: Sandwiches with one or two items like turkey, tuna, egg salad, roast beef and Danish ham $3.95-5.25. Specialties offer larger combinations with 4-5 meats and cheeses as well as chicken salad, turkey and bacon, garden burger and French dip $4.75-7.25. Caesar, tossed, garden and fruit salads and chicken or tuna in half a papaya $3.25-5.75. COMMENTS: Choice of breads include wheat, onion or Italian seasoning roll, French baguette or crunch wheat bread.

ORANGE JULIUS   *American/Sandwiches*
Wharf Cinema Center, lower level (661-1579) HOURS: Daily 9:30am-9:30pm. SAMPLING: Owner Kris Krewson has gone far beyond the usual OJ, so we feel they merit a listing. A variety of hot dogs include the more unusual nacho, pepperoni or Reuben dog $1.75-2.90; tacos, egg rolls, mozarella sticks and 4 kinds of nachos $1.55-4.25; jalapeno, chili, teri, western and other burgers $2.95-5; hamburger, seafood, shrimp plate lunches $5-6.50 and daily specials like beef stroganoff, turkey enchilada, lasagna, corned beef & cabbage, pot roast, lau lau, buttermilk chicken and a once-a-month "Thanksgiving" turkey dinner $5.50-6.50. Homemade soups and tacos, oriental and grilled chicken salads round out the menu $2-6.50. Seasonal Julius flavors include guava-passion, mango, pina colada or Tropical Julius. Yum!

PANIOLO COFFEE CO.   *Coffee Drinks/Light Meals*
Lahaina Center, 900 Front St. (661-8488) HOURS: Breakfast 7:30-11am, from 8:30am Sat.-Sun., lunch 11-4:30pm. SAMPLING: Breakfast burrito, egg croissant sandwich, homemade oatmeal, banana mac nut or gingerbread pancakes (sounds interesting!), scones, banana bread and cinnamon buns $1.95-5.25. Turkey, veggie or tuna sandwich, pizza bread, Caesar salad, soup, veggie chili and rice or quesadilla and Mexican pizza $2.75-5.75. COMMENTS: Sample

225

coffee drinks, smoothies, milkshakes $2.75-3.50 served all day. Small coffee bar with counter seating. Cowboy-western motif inside with an "awning" of cool mist around the outside. The food items are all new (as of Summer '96), previously it was just coffee and pastries.

PIZZA HUT *Italian*
127 Hinau, Lahaina, (661-3696). HOURS: 11am-10pm daily; Fri. and Sat. until 11pm. They now have seven locations on Maui from Honokowai to Kihei and from Kahului up to Pukalani. We've heard some good reports on their salad bar and their $6.99 lunch buffet. COMMENTS: For years we have driven by, and never stopped. After all, we have Pizza Huts at home, so why eat here? So, we still have never stopped, but we keep getting letters from those of you who do that the pizza is great and so is the salad bar. In fact we probably get more letters about this single restaurant than any other.

PIZZA PEOPLE *Italian*
Lahaina Center, 900 Front St. (667-7700) HOURS: 11am to midnight. SAMPLING: The usual pizza toppings plus extras like fresh broccoli, Maui onions, sweet banana peppers and pineapple with choice of tomato or pesto sauce and white, sesame seed or whole wheat crust. Medium and large $13.44-24.00. Also salads, hot and cold submarine sandwiches, ice cream and a selection of coffee drinks. COMMENTS: The dough is made fresh every day and hand-tossed the traditional way. Also at Napili Plaza.

PLANET JUICE AND JAVA ★ *Juice/Coffee/Light meals*
Lahaina Square Shopping Center HOURS: 5:30am-8pm. SAMPLING: Juiced to order carrot, spinach, celery, apple, orange juice $3-4; wheatgrass juice $2-3.50; pineapple, mango, papaya, blueberry smoothies $3.75. One drink booster included in all smoothies. Espresso, latte, mocha, Italian soda $1.75-3.25. Daily selection of soups, salads, pastas and baked goods. Wrappers and rice pots $4.50-6.00 COMMENTS: Not only are the smoothies wonderful, but so is the food!

Pita sandwiches of tuna or chicken curry salad $4-4.50. Salads $5.95-6.50. Their wrappers are whole wheat tortillas overstuffed with yummy stuff (i.e. rice, vegetables, non-fat yogurt and peanut sauce) and served with an unusual assortment of sweet potato, taro and other chips. These juice bars seem to be a new trend. An alternative to the coffee houses! Dining indoors or out.

S&E FILIPINO VARIETY STORE *Filipino*
Anchor Square, 888 Wainee St. (667-5486) HOURS: 9am-5pm (or until they run out - whichever comes first). SAMPLING: Plate lunches with two scoops of rice. Three daily specials: 2 items, $3.95; 3 items $4.50. To go only.

SAENG'S THAI ★ *Thai*
1312 Front St. (667-0822) HOURS: Lunch Mon.-Fri. 11am-2pm, dinner nightly 5-9:30pm. As we go to press, Siam Thai has just cclosed. Coconut Grove will be opening in the same location.

SANDWICH ISLAND *Sandwiches*
Lahaina Cannery Mall (661-6128) HOURS: 9:30am-9pm daily. SAMPLING: Ham, turkey, pastrami, roast beef, egg salad, tuna and vegetarian sandwiches $4.95; Caesar, Oriental, somen and cold pasta salads $4.95-5.25; cheese ravioli, spaghetti or freshly made pasta of the day $5.25. Clam chowder and saimin $2-3.50; plate lunch specials $6.50.

SCAROLES VILLAGE PIZZERIA *Italian*
At 505 Front St. (661-8112) HOURS: 11am-10pm. SAMPLING: Pizza is available in Neapolitan style (thin crust) or Sicilian (thick crust). A 14" plain pizza starts at $12, a combo of 4 items at $17. Calzone and pasta items (lasagna, ravioli, ziti) $6.95-12.95. Meatball, sausage & peppers, chicken or veal parmigiana sandwiches served with pasta $6.75-8.75 COMMENTS: The clam and garlic pizza is a specialty here along with cannoli, spumoni, tiramisu and other homemade Italian desserts. Wine and coffee drinks, too.

SIR WILFRED'S ESPRESSO CAFE *Sandwiches/coffee*
Lahaina Cannery Mall, Kaanapali side of Lahaina (667-1941) HOURS: 9am-9pm. SAMPLING: Limited menu includes quiche, lasagna, sandwiches $3.95-5.95. Pastries, cookies, cheesecake to enjoy with a great cup of coffee or an espresso drink. Also available is 100% Kona coffee by the pound. They also have the only walk-in humidor on Maui, so you cigar and pipe smokers will be delighted! COMMENTS: A very small, pleasant eatery. Gourmet coffees, Hawaiian name mugs and tropical jams & jellies available for purchase.

SONG'S ORIENTAL KITCHEN *Chinese-Hawaiian*
658 Front St. at the Wharf Cinema Center (667-1990) HOURS: Daily for lunch and dinner. SAMPLING: This is an okazuya style buffet with chicken adobo, kim chee, stir-fry vegetables and more. After viewing the selections in the display case, your plate is dished up for you. Only a few tables near the door offer seating or get yours to go. Saimin, lomi lomi, stuffed cabbage. Chow Fun $2.50, plate lunches $5, sides from $1.20.

227

SUNRISE CAFE   *Sandwiches/Light meals*
693A Front St. (661-3326) HOURS: 6am-10:30pm SAMPLING: Homemade soups, salads, plate lunches, salads, quiche, also espresso drinks and bakery items $2-7.95. Dinner specials $9.95 plus daily Hawaiian specials. COMMENTS: This is a very small, quaint eatery with food available to go. Entertainment nightly.

SUSHIYA ★ *Japanese*
117 Prison Street (661-5679). HOURS: Mon.-Fri. 6am-4pm, take out available. SAMPLING: Beef teri plate $5.50, chicken teri plate $5.25, hamburger $3.95, a la carte items include saimin $2.25, kim chee, corned beef hash, macaroni salad from $.60-1.35. Plate lunches and daily specials $3.95-5. COMMENTS: This place is a real find in West Maui. We've tried for 10 years to try out this hole-in-the-wall restaurant, and they were either closed or on vacation. In operation for over 30 years, the daughter-in-law took over the family business about 17 years ago. Visitors are discovering what the locals have known for years. Inside you'll find family style tables and benches. It's a clean, comfortable self-service restaurant with no frills. Some interesting selections too -- how about a side order of sweet potato, eggplant or spam tempura for just 60 cents? So escape the hustle and bustle of in-town Lahaina and take a short walk for some local-style dining.

TAKE HOME MAUI   *American*
121 Dickenson (661-8067 or 661-6185). From the mainland 1-800-545-MAUI. HOURS: 6am-5:30pm. SAMPLING: Fresh fruit smoothies $3.25, sandwiches $4.80-5.95, salads $3.25-5.95, ice cream and sodas in the freezer. Papayas, pineapples, onions and Hawaiian coffee are among the items to be shipped or taken home. They offer free airport or hotel delivery. They also do catering. COMMENTS: Limited seating. The staff is helpful and friendly. Fruit smoothies are delicious and their sandwiches are good, too!

THAI CHEF   *Thai*
Old Lahaina Center (667-2814) HOURS: Lunch 11am-2:30pm Mon.-Fri., dinner from 5pm nightly. SAMPLING: Entrees such as Thai crisp noodles, sateh, green papaya salad, Thai toast, Evil Prince and garlic squid are $4.95-11.95. COMMENTS: A very lengthy menu ranging from noodle dishes to salads, seafoods, vegetarian fare and curry dishes. Entrees available in mild, medium or hot (!) and Chef's Suggestions offer combinations for 2, 3 or 4 people. They also have a second location at the Rainbow Mall in Kihei.

WORLD CAFE   *American*
New Lahaina Center, 900 Front St. (661-1515) HOURS: Food service from 11-1am. SAMPLING: Burgers, fish tacos, ribs, chicken pita, burrito, stir-fry $6-10.75 Oysters, popcorn shrimp, mozarella sticks, pot stickers, nachos, jalapeno poppers, quesadillas, chili cheese waffle fries, salads $4.75-9.75 Vegetarian, Thai or create-your-own pizza from $7.75. Cake, ice cream, cheesecake all $3.50. COMMENTS: Restaurants by the pool aren't unusual on Maui, but this one has a pool *table!* Flat rate of $5 per hour til 7pm; $10 per hour at night. Live music on weekends, frequent happy hour specials and a $6 all-you-can-eat pizza buffet from 4-7pm Monday-Friday.

ZUSHI *Japanese*
Anchor Square, 888 Wainee St., (667-5142). Open 11am-1:30pm for lunch $4.75-6.24, and dinner 5-8pm for $6.72-12.40. Closed Sundays. COMMENTS: A little expensive for the fare and atmosphere. They recently moved from behind the Plaza to a more visible spot across from McDonald's.

MODERATE

ALOHA CANTINA *Mexican*
839 Front St. (661-8788) HOURS: Daily for breakfast 8-11am; Lunch/Dinner 11-10pm; pupus til 11. Live rock 'n roll music Thurs.-Sat. SAMPLING: Breakfast burritos, huevos rancheros, blueberry or mac nut pancakes, omelettes and French toast $5.95-6.95. Tostada, Caesar and Hawaiian chicken salads, Mexican pizza, quesadilla, flautas, nachos, ceviche or a "Cheeseburger in Paradise" from their sister restaurant down the street $5.95-9.95. Fresh fish, chicken, beef or shrimp fajitas; enchiladas; chile rellenos; burritos; fish, chicken or beef tacos; seafood enchilada and sauteed scallops and shrimp $8.95-15.95. COMMENTS: Both of the restaurants' "double-decks" overlook the ocean. Hurricane McShane's Coconut Bar in front has flavored margaritas, a dozen tequilas and both tropical and Mexican drink creations, So stop by to enjoy a Cantina-Rita and a plate of nachos with your hurricane. Huh? That's right! At this Front Street restaurant, diners get a little something extra with their meal. The hurricane winds tend to happen every 60 minutes or so, but they only bring the sound of heavy winds, thunder, rain pelting down on a tin roof and lightning. But don't worry, no actual gusts will be part of the experience!

COMPADRES ★ *Mexican*
Lahaina Cannery Mall. (661-7189). HOURS: 10am-10pm SAMPLING: Quesadillas Internacionales include Baja (Mexican shrimp in spicy BBQ sauce), Texas (fajita steak or chickens with Jack cheese) and Thai (chicken, Jack cheese, sprouts, peanuts, shredded carrots and peanut-chili sauce) $7.99-9.99. You can get the same flavors in the International Burrito Festivals as well as Hawaiian (teri chicken, beans & pineapple salsa), Oriental (stir-fried vegetables in oyster sauce), Jalisco (carnitas with whole beans) and Tijuana (Caesar salad with black beans & rice), all $5.99. Mexican pizza, tortilla soup, fajitas, nachos, chingalinga, six-layer dip and Caesar, cobb, taco and fajita salads are the unusual starters $3.99-10.99 while arroz con pollo, camarone (shrimp), tequila chicken, seafood enchilada, lobster burrito and a variety of Mexican egg dishes are some of the innovative entrees for $6.99-14.99. COMMENTS: We don't usually recommend many chain restaurants, but Compadres earns a star for its innovative menu and all-around good dining fare.

HECOCKS *American*
505 Front St. (661-8810) HOURS: 7am-10pm, bar 8am-2am SAMPLING: Eggs, pancakes, French toast $4.25-7.95. Sandwiches and burgers $4.75-7.50; dinner entrees of steak, lamb, ribs, fish & seafood $15.95-21.95; pastas with sausage, clams, vegetables or prawns $13.95-18.95. COMMENTS: More bar than restaurant; a waste of the ocean view. You can do better.

GEKKO RESTAURANT & SUSHI BAR   *Japanese-Sushi Bar*
Wharf Cinema Center, 658 Front St. (661-0955) HOURS: Lunch 11am-3pm, Sushi Bar 2-10pm, Dinner 5-10pm. SAMPLING: Lunch bentos, plate lunch, tempura, katsudon, oyakadon $7-8. Seafood salad, soba noodles, gyoza soup $5.95-8.95. Stir-fried eggplant, tofu dishes, Japanese pancake, shoyu chicken, soft shell crab, Dynamite $4-8.50. Teriyaki, tempura, broiled steak and fish dishes $15-20; traditional dinners (sukiyaki, yose nabe) for two or more at market price. Nigiri, makimono sushi and sashimi combinations $4.50-25. COMMENTS: Patio, sushi bar or inside seating.

KIMO'S ★   *American/Seafood*
845 Front St. (661-4811) HOURS: Lunch 11am-3pm. Dinner daily 5-10:30pm, bar until 1am. SAMPLING: Lunches $6.50-9.95 range from breast of chicken sandwich to reuben, grilled ham, swiss & turkey sandwich or burgers. Hot & chilled pupus, Hawaiian style, are available downstairs daily. Dinner at the bar available with a limited menu selection 5-11pm. Dinner entrees include Kimo's Caesar salad, freshly baked carrot muffins and sour herb rolls and steamed herb rice. Fresh fish of the day $19.95 prepared in one of five ways, beef, seafood or island favorites such as kushiyaki or Koloa ribs $14.95-17.95. A vegetarian pasta is available for $10.95. A keiki menu for guests 12 and under $4.50-5.95. COMMENTS: They have a waterfront location and, if you're really lucky, you'll get a table with a view. Our experience has been very good service and well prepared fresh fish. They must be doing something right because they've been doing it since 1977! This is where you find the original hula pie - it's still the biggest and the best and turns heads every time one of the whipped cream skyscrapers comes out of the kitchen. They also have a bar on the lower level and an ocean view which provides a pleasant sunset.

KOBE JAPANESE STEAK HOUSE ★   *Teppanyaki/Sushi Bar*
136 Dickenson (667-5555) HOURS: Dinner 5:30-9:30pm. SAMPLING: Teriyaki chicken $13.90, hibachi steak $19.90, sukiyaki steak $16.90. Seafood specials from $19.90, steak from $23.90. Dinners include soup, shrimp appetizer, vegetables and rice. COMMENTS: A sister of the Palm Springs and Honolulu restaurants, they offer teppan cooking (food is prepared on the grill in front of you) and the show is as good as the meal. Keiki menu offers either hibachi steak or chicken teriyaki $6.90-8.90. Sunset specials (served 5:30-6:30pm) $10.90-13.90. Sushi and sashimi items available individually or in chef-selected tray assortments. The sushi bar is very popular with local residents and they're very accommodating to the visitors. They'll make up your favorite sushi item if it is not on their menu.

LAHAINA COOLERS ★   *American*
180 Dickenson St., Dickenson Square, (661-7082) HOURS: Breakfast 7-11:15am, lunch 11:15am-5pm, dinner 5pm-midnight. SAMPLING: Four versions of Eggs Benedict and a black bean breakfast burrito are available for breakfast $3-8. Homemade pastas in appetizer or entree portions $5.50-9.00 include fettucini with chicken and mushrooms or smoked salmon, shrimp pesto linguini or penne carbonara. The evil jungle pasta with grilled chicken and spicy peanut sauce is their best seller and also comes as a pizza. Fresh fish tacos, Moroccan

chicken spinach enchilada and artichoke or sausage pizza combos are available for lunch or dinner. Mini crab cakes, spinach & feta cheese quesadilla and fried artichoke heart pupus or papaya chicken, Caesar, veggie and Greek salads run $3.95-7.50. Dinners come in larger sizes and offer additional selections of fresh fish and steak $5.50-18. The Riviera banana split of fried banana with ice cream and carmel sauce and their chocolate taco filled with tropical fruit and berry "salsa" are the don't miss desserts $4.90-5.50. COMMENTS: The new owners still maintain the great slogan, "Because Life is Too Short to Eat Boring Food" and have pretty much kept the same menu. The only changes are that they have added homemade pastas plus steak and fresh fish for dinner which is now served til midnight. We found the food items exotic and unique. The pizzas $9.90-10.75 are a single serving, ample for lunch, a little small for a hearty dinner eater.

LAHAINA FISH COMPANY   *Seafood-American*
831 Front St. (661-3472) HOURS: Lunch 12-3pm, dinner 5-10pm. SAMPLING: The lunch choices -- cheeseburger, chicken burger, fishburger, peel & eat shrimp or sashimi -- are all $8.95. For dinner, fish and shellfish are prepared Italian style (Alfredo, primavera) or in nightly Pacific Rim specials with teriyaki, pineapple salsa, sesame dijon or Kula corn lobster sauce $7.95-22.95. Hand carved steaks, stir-fry and chicken $8.95-22.95 COMMENTS: Pleasant setting on (in fact, right over) the ocean. Hammerheads Coffee Bar on the Front Street side offers coffee drinks and a limited selection of baked goods.

MOOSE McGILLYCUDDY'S   *American*
844 Front St., upper level of Mariner's Alley, a small shopping alley at the north end of town (667-7758) HOURS: Breakfast 7:30-11am ($1.99 Early Bird 7:30-8:30), lunch 11am-4pm, dinner 4-10pm ($8.95 Early Bird specials 4-6pm). SAMPLING: Breakfast meats and unusual egg preparations served in a quesadilla or on potato skins. The 21 omelettes include the 12-egg "Moose" for $19.95. Flavored pancakes, country biscuits and banana muffins $1.50-5.95. A variety of burger and sandwich combinations, chicken, tostada and garden salads plus fajitas, fettucini and fish tacos run in the $6-11 price range. Pupus include wings, nachos, quesadillas, skins, cheesey fries and mini chimichangas $3.95-9.95. Their clam or fish chowder is served in a hollowed out sourdough loaf for $5.95. Dinner entrees include steak, prime rib, fresh catch and Cajun fish or tequila chicken fettucini $9.95-13.95. The Mexican platter for two is $21.95. There's chocolate moose for dessert (what else?) and an extensive selection of fun, tropical drinks. COMMENTS: Recently completed extensive renovation that included moving the bar to the center and redecorating the dining area. This place really gets hopping at night with lots of young adults and live music that may be on the loud side for some.

OLD LAHAINA CAFE AND LUAU ★   *Hawaiian*
505 Front St. (661-3303) HOURS: Breakfast 7:30-11:30am, til 2pm on Sunday, lunch 12-3:30pm, dinner 6-10pm. SAMPLING: Breakfast options include Anahola granola, loco moco, French toast, Portuguese or luau omelette, Hawaiian pancakes $4.95-10.50. Daily plate lunches offer two choices each day ranging from chow fun to ahi tempura to beef stew for $6.95. Island fruits in a pineapple, crab filled papaya and calamari salad plus burgers and sandwiches of macadamia

smoked turkey, ahi salad and kalua pig run $5.95-10.95. Pupus available for lunch or dinner include coconut prawns, spring rolls, kalua pig won tons and sesame chicken wings $5.95-9.95. Dinners offer such local favorites as chicken lau lau, kalua pig & cabbage, Tahitian shrimp curry, huli huli chicken and a luau sampler $17.95-19.95 as well as Szechuan or teriyaki steak, Asian stir-fry and broccoli tofu $16.95-20.95. COMMENTS: Eat at the cafe and you can enjoy the music of the Old Lahaina Luau just outside. Open air, plantation-style setting right on the ocean. Early bird specials from 6-7pm offering fish, teri steak or shoyu-lime chicken with rice or potato and vegetable for $12.95.

PIONEER INN BAR & GRILL   *American*
Pioneer Inn (661-3636) HOURS: Breakfast, lunch and dinner. SAMPLING: Macadamia nut pancakes and cinnamon raisin bread French toast $7.25 & $7.95 are the breakfast specialties. Other items include eggs, fresh fruit, Portuguese sausage and Belgian waffles $1.95-8.95. Lunches offer soups, salads, sandwiches and "island style plates" $5.95-.$10.95. Pupus can be ordered individually or in a platter for two $21.95 for lunch or at the bar. Dinners include prime rib, beef brochette, fresh fish, seafood, pastas and Chicken Inviotto stuffed with ham, jack cheese, shiitake mushroom and black olives $11.95-22.95. COMMENTS: Dinner is served outside in the central Courtyard accompanied by live Hawaiian music.

PLANET HOLLYWOOD   ★ *California Cuisine*
744 Front St. (667-7877). HOURS: 11am-10:30pm, bar til midnight. SAMPLING: Texas nachos, cajun egg rolls, pizza bread and chicken crunch (breaded with Cap'n Crunch cereal!) are a few of the appetizers $5.95-6.75; pizzas run $9.50-10.50 and Caesar and Far East chicken salads are $7.95-12.95. Platters with fresh fish, ribs, steak, pork chops or teri chicken are $12.95-19.95, burgers $8.25-8.95. Thai shrimp, spicy chicken & tomato, penne primavera and Santa Fe chicken pastas are $9.95-13.95; chicken, beef and shrimp fajitas $12.95-13.95 and sandwiches include steak, club, cajun chicken, blackened ahi and a Parisian ham, chicken & swiss cheese $8.95-10.95. Be sure to save room for desserts like white chocolate bread pudding, caramel crunch pie, chocolate swirl cheesecake, ebony and ivory brownie or Arnold Schwarzenegger's mother's renowned Apple Strudel. COMMENTS: As everyone probably knows by now, shareholders of this project include Arnold Schwarzengger, Bruce Willis, Sylvester Stallone and Demi Moore among others. The food was actually better than expected, the Cap'n Crunch chicken was good, a fun idea and rather sweet tasting. They also did a good job on the pastas and pizzas. You can't go wrong on the desserts, the Ebony (dark chocolate) and Ivory (blond) brownie with chocolate and white chocolate ice cream, chocolate and caramel sauces, whipped cream and nuts was as rich as you'd expect and the other options were just as creative in flavor and texture. There's an extensive menu of specialty drinks named after famous films. Similar to Hard Rock Cafe, they feature a collection of movie memorabilia including Cleo, the man-eating plant from *Addams Family Values*, the 5-foot whale model from *Free Willy*, the ship's figurehead from the original *Mutiny on the Bounty* and the Joker's helicopter from *Batman*. The downstairs level is colorful and lively, the upstairs submarine room is very effective with dim lighting and cozy booths. TV monitors show films and videos. And no surprise here, you're also be able to buy T-shirts, watches, designer sunglasses, varsity

jackets ($225), beach towels or bags, leather jackets ($325) and even swim suits in their merchandise shop. The atmosphere alone merits a star.

SMOKEHOUSE BARBECUE   *American BBQ*
1307 Front St., near The Cannery (667-7005) HOURS: 11am-11pm. SAMPLING: Scallops, calamari, shrimp, onion rings, zucchini sticks $5.95-7.95. Sandwiches served 11am-4pm only: fresh fish, Louisiana hot link, charbroiled burgers or breast of chicken and smoked ham, turkey, beef or pork $5.45-7.95. BBQ ribs, chicken, hot link combinations or charbroiled steak, fish, chicken or burgers and smoked ribs and chicken. Dinners available a la carte $8.95-16.95 or complete with steak fries, coleslaw, cornbread and BBQ baked beans or rice $10.95-18.95. COMMENTS: Choice of baby back pork ribs or Kona beef ribs. Smoked and charbroiled meats are all from natural Hawaiian kiawe wood. Chocolate cake-style hula pie for dessert; full bar. Dining indoors or on their new oceanfront patio.

YAKINIKU TROPICANA   *Japanese/Korean*
843 Wainee St., Old Lahaina Center (667-4646) HOURS: 10am-10pm, sushi bar until 1am. SAMPLING: Soup, noodles, pot stew, broiled & steamed fish, yakiniku $7.95-18.95. Lunch specials (served til 3pm) include fish chun, shrimp tempura, beef, pork chop or chicken plate, fried man doo $7.50-9.50. Sushi and sashimi $4.25-8.50. COMMENTS: The menus are printed in English, Korean and Japanese and most of the employees speak Korean as their native language. Yakiniku means table grilled, so you'll be able to enjoy watching your own meal be prepared.

EXPENSIVE

AVALON ★   *Hawaiian Regional Cuisine*
844 Front St., (667-5559) HOURS: Lunch 11:30am-5pm and dinner 5-10pm. SAMPLING: A number of the dishes may be prepared to your liking: mild, medium or spicy. The lunch menu has many of the same items as dinner with slightly smaller portions and prices. You can also order Pasta Gerry, char-grilled chicken, fresh clams or shrimp & chicken on brown rice $6.95-15.95. Cheeseburger, fresh fish, chicken or avocado sandwiches are $8.95-11.95. For dinner, there's Asian pasta, BBQ lamb chops, NY steak and whole fresh opakapaka $23.95-29.95. Vegetarian selections include lemongrass or Chinese tofu salad, Gado Gado and stir-fried vegetables $9.95-14.95. An interesting array of starters includes summer rolls, satay, sugar snap peas, shrimp wonton and seared sashimi. Carmel Miranda, a fruit and ice cream platter, is Avalon's only dessert. COMMENTS: Mark Ellman, as owner/chef, continues in his fine tradition of Hawaiian Regional Cuisine. His Chili Seared Salmon Tiki Style is as much a visual as a culinary experience. A layered "tower" salad of mashed potatoes, eggplant, salmon, greens, island and tomato salsa, it is served with plum vinaigrette for $19.95. The $11.95 Gado Gado salad comes from the island of Bali and is a tasteful blend of romaine lettuce, cucumbers, tofu, steamed vegetables on a bed of brown rice topped with peanut sauce. Equally delicious is the Chinese tofu salad at $9.95. Both are large portions. Honey sake roasted Chinese duck with plum sauce and steamed buns is available on Fri.-Sat. nights $16.95-23.95. The

name Avalon, according to Celtic or Gaelic legend, is the West Pacific island paradise where King Arthur and other heroes went following death. The look here is '40's Hawaiian with antique aloha shirts adorning the walls, ceiling fans whirring and wonderful multi-colored oversized dishes. This one is a favorite of ours and we don't visit Maui without stopping by at least once. Word has it that Avalon will expand to add a brew pub in early 1997.

CHART HOUSE ★ *American*
1450 Front St. (661-0937). HOURS: Dinner 5-10pm. SAMPLING: Lobster cakes, coconut shrimp, garlic bread and sashimi appetizers $5.75-12.50. Lobster pot pie, steak, prime rib, crab, lobster, fresh fish, prawns & garlic steak, fresh salmon, grilled portobello mushroom with fettucine, Tuscan chicken with farfalle. Entrees include their unlimited fresh garden or Caesar salad, hot squaw bread, country-style bread, potatoes or wild rice $15.95-26.95. They also offer some good homemade desserts including mud pie, chocolate mousse and authentic key lime pie. Children's menu available. COMMENTS: There is a comfortable atmosphere with lots of wood and lava rock. The limited number of oceanview tables are a hot commodity and require that you arrive when they open. They provide one of the best keiki menus we've seen. The adult entree portions are huge! There is also a Chart House restaurant in Kahului and another in Wailea. Reservations accepted.

CHEZ PAUL ★ *French*
Five miles south of Lahaina at Olowalu (661-3843) HOURS: Two dinner seatings 6:30 and 8:30pm. Closed Sundays May-Nov. SAMPLING: Entrees include fresh fish poached in lobster sauce or champagne, scampi, lobster and duck with Dijon & breaded swiss cheese. Dinners include French bread, soup or salad and two vegetables. Escargot, seafood crepe, pate, lobster salad, artichoke and shrimp are available as appetizers. Save room for some very special desserts! COMMENTS: This small restaurant -- in what could be a tiny village in France -- has maintained a high popularity with excellent food and service. It's not surprising they have won numerous dining awards. The wine list is excellent, although expensive. Wines are also available by the glass. Reservations required. Their menu adds, "no pipes or cigar smoking and keep the cry babies at home."

DAVID PAUL'S LAHAINA GRILL ★ *New American*
127 Lahainaluna at the Lahaina Hotel (667-5117) HOURS: Nightly from 6pm. SAMPLING: The menu is described as New American Grill Cuisine with a Southwestern flair. The menu is constantly changing, but David's popular Tequila Shrimp and Firecracker Rice has become a permanent fixture. Kona coffee roasted lamb, Maui onion crusted seared ahi, roasted squab, goat cheese ravioli and kalua duck are other possible entrees $20.95-32.95; eggplant Napoleon, spicy crab cake and macadamia smoked salmon are good to start with for $9.95-14.95. COMMENTS: David Paul Johnson has won local and national awards since opening here in 1990. The seating area is attractively furnished with a crisp look to it. Black and white floors are contrasted with a beautifully detailed fresco blue/green ceiling and French impressionist art. While beautiful, it somehow lacks the cozy ambiance of one of our favorite restaurants just across the street, Gerard's. It has a masculine look, like the grill room of an elegant European

hotel. They have expanded their original dining area and recently added on a small room next door for private dining and special Chef's Dinners. The bar in the main restaurant is wide and suitable for dining and socializing. You can order appetizers and dinner or enjoy the seafood bar and late night menu until 11pm every evening. The food is excellent and David Paul's has a continually changing menu, which keeps your dining options interesting! When we were there, the menu offered a Caesar salad, which was excellent and an ample portion for two people. The pasta was delicately seasoned and the soft shelled crab was unusual: cooked and eaten shell and all! Shipped in from the east coast, these crabs are "harvested" when they are in the molting process so that their shell is very soft. It tastes like a crispy crust! The fresh grilled opakapaka was also a hearty portion accompanied by a tomato/onion zucchini sauce served finely chopped over eggplant. The tequila shrimp is available in mild, medium or hot. Medium proved to be plenty warm!

GERARD'S ★ *French*
In the lobby of the Plantation Inn at 174 Lahainaluna Rd. (661-8939) HOURS: 6-10pm. SAMPLING: The menu changes seasonally with entree selections that might include roasted Hawaiian snapper with peppers and orange & ginger butter sauce; lamb stew with Tedeschi red wine and spinach raviolis or medallions of venison with peppered sauce, poha berry compote, sweet potato and banana pie $24.50-32.50. Hors d'oeuvres (appetizers to you; pupus to us) offer shiitake and oyster mushrooms in puff pastry; lemon grass and curried risotto with grilled scallops and sauteed calamari with lime and ginger $8.50-18.50. Salads are just as intriguing with grilled quail and upcountry greens with hazelnut oil, croutons, pancetta and apple; Kona lobster with avocado with herb curry vinaigrette and white & green asparagus with shrimp and caviar $9.50-18.50. Desserts are all priced at $7.50 and include baked pineapple with ginger ice cream, chocolate mousse profiteroles, macadamia nut chocolate cake with star anise cream and exotic tropical fruit soup. COMMENTS: Dining at Gerard's is just as wonderful as it was years ago when it was in its old, small, hole-in-the-wall location up the street. The ambiance is equal to the fine cuisine. Crisply attired in country pastels, the restaurant offers indoor or outdoor seating. And although (like everyone) we are partial to Maui's sunset ocean views while dining, sitting beneath a mango tree on the veranda of the Plantation Inn while dining at Gerard's is hard to beat. A wine list features a range of moderate to expensive selections from California, France and the Pacific Northwest.

LONGHI'S ★ *Continental*
888 Front St. (667-2288) HOURS: 7:30am-10pm, breakfast served until 11:30 am, lunch until 4:30pm, dessert served until 11pm. SAMPLING: Fresh fruits, eggs Benedict or Florentine, baked fritatta, quiche, and freshly baked cinnamon rolls and pastries are available along with more traditional breakfast fare $2.50-11. Lunch pastas (canneloni, manicotti and fettucine variations) and entrees include smaller (cheaper!) versions of Longhi's signature dinners: Prawns amaretto or Venetian, shrimp or scallops Longhi and ahi torino $8-15. Among the sandwich offerings is Dona's favorite peking duck for $8.50 and salads feature toppings of chicken, shrimp or lobster $5-16. In addition to the ones already mentioned, a la carte dinner entrees also include filet Longhi, lamb chops

and several Italian preparations of chicken and veal $19-27, pastas from $14, vegetables $5-9. The dessert tray is hard to resist with ever-changing options like strawberry-rhubarb pie, kiwi glace, tiramisu cake, coconut haupia cream pie or espresso sambucca mousse, all $7. COMMENTS: In their now 20 years on Maui, Longhi's has become a legend in Lahaina. Part of the legend is the verbal menu, a great gimmick when it started, but after a while it was difficult to follow and intimidating if you didn't quite hear the prices or couldn't remember the third pasta from the top. It was one of those things that people either loved or they hated. So to appeal to both sides, Longhi's still maintains the verbal menu at night, but has added an intriguing new addition for breakfast and lunch: written menus! (What a concept!) People will probably go just to read them! That aside, the other reasons are: the to-die-for jalapeno, pizza and gorgonzola breads served with your meal; the casual setting with lots of windows open to view the bustling Lahaina streets; the accommodating breakfast hours that allow for both early risers (Christie) and the laziest of late sleepers (Dona) to enjoy the fresh baked goods and tasty egg dishes. Longhi's offers espresso and a good wine selection with valet parking nightly.

PACIFIC 'O   *Contemporary Pacific cuisine*
505 Front St. (667-4341) HOURS: Lunch 11am-4pm, dinner 5:30-10pm, pupus served until midnight. SAMPLING: Lunch includes penne pasta with smoked spicy shrimps, grilled chicken oriental salad, Diablo chicken sandwich and pizza with smoked shrimp, goat cheese and eggplant caviar $7.95-10.95. Dinner entrees offer Peking duck, scallops and shrimp in red curry coconut sauce, kiawe grilled NY steak, sesame crusted lamb, banana "imu style" fish and the award-winning Hapa Tempura with red and white fish in a double block design $21.50-24. COMMENTS: Unusual and artistic presentations. Pupus are served on a marble slab with sauces painted in colorful designs. The award-winning shrimp won tons are a must. A great ocean front location although the atmosphere is a bit casual for the pricey menu. The food is worthy of a star. It's just too bad that one of the two owners isn't more aware of good PR and customer service, hence, no star. Jazz on the Beach, Thurs.-Sat.

SCAROLES ★ *New York Style Italian*
930 Wainee St., Lahaina (661-4466) HOURS: Lunch Mon.-Fri. 11:30am-2pm; dinner 5:30-9pm nightly. SAMPLING: Lunch items are chicken picatta or marsala, veal or chicken parmesan and meatball sandwiches, homemade sausage lasagna and other pastas, appetizers soups and salads $7.95-12.95. Dinners start with stuffed clams, escargot, calamari, steamed mussels and mozarella marinara $8.95-12.95 or pastas prepared carbonara, primavera, pesto and Alfredo $13.95-16.95. Dinners feature shrimp scampi or fra diavolo; chicken parmigiana and saltimbocca, veal calvados or pizzaiola plus sausage & peppers and eggplant parmigiana $16.95-24.95. COMMENTS: Scaroles advertises itself as "The New York side of Lahaina" and we'd tend to agree. Located on the Kaanapali side of Lahaina the restaurant is an open air, smallish, but cozy, dining room for 30 inside and a table or two outdoors. A basic Italian black and white color scheme is the decor here. All entrees are served with homemade soup or salad and fabulous warm-from-the-oven onion rolls. Early Bird specials 5:30-6pm, $10.95. We're told by those who know that it is authentic New York Italian-style food.

KAANAPALI

INEXPENSIVE

BEACH BAR   *American*
Westin Maui (667-2525) Located atop the center island of the pool/deck area.
HOURS: 10am-6pm. SAMPLING: Services three pools with a limited pupu menu
that includes shrimp cocktail, chicken wings, chips & salsa and won tons.

BURRITO BROTHERS   *Mexican*
Located downstairs at the Lahaina side entrance to Kaanapali. (661-4500)
HOURS: Noon-11pm, bar til 2am. SAMPLING: Tacos and burritos with beef,
chicken, pork, fish or beef tongue $1.99-6. Pizzas, too, with combinations that
include Hawaiian, cheeseburger and a South Seas special with curry sauce,
bananas, onion, peppers, macadamia nuts and shrimp: small $10.99-16.99/large
$15.99-27.99. COMMENTS: They are owned by Luigi's restaurant upstairs,
hence the pizza menu.

CASTAWAY CAFE   *American*
Maui Kaanapali Villas Resort, 45 Kai Ala Dr. (661-9091) HOURS: Breakfast
7:30am-2pm; lunch 11am-5pm, pupus 2-9pm, dinner 5-9pm. SAMPLING: Egg
dishes, biscuits & gravy, macadamia, pineapple or banana pancakes, cinnamon-
raisin French toast $3.50-6.95. Caesar, tuna, paradise chicken salads $5.95-7.95;
burgers, patty melt, club, BLT, hot turkey, French dip and steak sandwiches
$5.50-8.95. Pupus include egg rolls, calamari or chicken strips, coconut shrimp,
sweet & sour chicken or shrimp, fish & chips $5.95-8.95 and dinners feature
shrimp or vegetable fettucine, Chinese pepper steak, prime rib, fried prawns,
macadamia chicken, vegetable or chicken stir-fry, sirloin steak $10.95-16.95.
COMMENTS: A cozy, poolside restaurant that's reminiscent of a beach cabana,
yet it's full-size with a patio that overlooks the lawn and the ocean. They offer
daily chef's specials and can accommodate special meal requirements or preparations.

COLONNADE CAFE   *American*
Westin Maui, Promenade Level overlooking lagoon of Koi fish with waterfalls
and tropical birds. HOURS: 6-11am for continental breakfast; 11am-3pm for
sandwiches, salads, and yogurt. COMMENTS: At 6pm this becomes the Sen Ju
Sushi Bar.

DELI PLANET   *American*
Embassy Suites Resort (661-2000) HOURS: 9am-10pm. SAMPLING: Deli
sandwiches include tuna or chicken salad, cheese, hot reuben or build your own
with choice of bread, cheese, meat and garnish. Alone or with salad plate or soup
$4.95-7.25. COMMENTS: Bottles of Chef Rey Baysa's award-winning orange-
mango barbeque sauce have recently become available for exclusive retail
purchase. Yum!

FOOD COURT (AT WHALERS VILLAGE)
The Food Court at Whalers Village has four outlets on the lower level: Pizza Paradiso has pizza, salads and submarine sandwiches (667-0333); Ganso Kawara Soba is a Japanese Noodle Shop (667-0815), Yakiniku Hahn serves Korean food (661-9798) and McDonald's offers its usual fare (667-6674).

GARDEN BAR   *American*
Westin Maui, located near the beach (667-2525) HOURS: 9am until midnight serving a poolside menu 11am until 6pm. Cocktails served. SAMPLING: Sandwiches, salads, burgers, pizzas, chicken wings, won tons and shrimp rolls. COMMENTS: Afternoon entertainment including a Friday hula show. Guitar music in the evenings.

KAANAPALI MIXED PLATE   *American-Hawaiian*
Kaanapali Beach Hotel (661-0011) HOURS/SAMPLING: Breakfast buffet 6-10:45am for $7.95; Ethnic lunch buffets feature a different theme each day: American, Japanese, Italian, Chinese, Hawaiian and mixed plate 11am-2pm for $7.95; prime rib dinner buffet 4-7pm $9.95, 7-9pm $11.95. COMMENTS: Pleasant coffee shop, decorated with donated momentos that reflect the diverse ethnic and cultural background of the hotel employees. A description of the display items and explanation of the cultural foods is featured in a souvenir booklet given at each table. All buffets include salad bar, beverages and dessert. The best value in Kaanapali, especially for the hearty appetite.

KAU KAU GRILL & BAR   *American*
Poolside at the Maui Marriott. (661-1200) HOURS: Early coffee 5:30am; continental breakfast 6am-7am, limited egg dishes until 11am. Lunch and snacks 11am-4pm; bar menu til 5. SAMPLING: Lunch menu includes cheeseburgers, pizzas by the slice, salads, and sandwiches. The more unusual offerings include chicken Caesar salad, roast turkey avocado tortilla roll, grilled mahi sandwich with spicy aioli, shrimp quesadilla and jalapeno poppers $6-6.50. COMMENTS: Daily specials (like veggie burrito or smoked turkey on a grilled roll) are $8.50 including a drink. A poolside Pizza Hut kiosk offers personal pan pizzas and a variety of mediums for $3.50-16.75 from 11am-7pm daily. The price of a cup of coffee ($2.25) may be an incentive to give it up! The cup (paper) is refillable all day, or purchase one of their travel cups and it is refillable with the beverage of your choice during your stay.

MADE IN THE SHADE   *American*
Royal Lahaina Resort (661-3611) HOURS: 11am-5pm. Variety of grilled burgers plus teri chicken, fresh fish, BLT and tuna sandwiches $4.75-7.25. Hot dogs $2.75-3.50; Caesar with chicken or fish $6.50-8. Chili or pasta salad $1.50; Nachos or pineapple fruit boat $6. COMMENTS: Poolside Hawaiian "hut."

THE MAKAI BAR ★ *American*
Maui Marriott (667-1200) HOURS: 4:30pm-midnight. Located lobby level, Lanai wing. COMMENTS: Open air cocktail lounge with sweeping ocean view of the island of Lana'i. Great gathering place with nice sunset vistas and live music nightly. Their pupu menu has proven very popular over the years with mini-roast

beef sandwiches, nachos, quesadillas, tako poke, sushi, sashimi, or ceviche priced affordably $1.50-6.50

MAUI YOGURT *American*
Whaler's Village (661-8843) HOURS: 8am-10pm. SAMPLING: Sandwiches such as cheese and egg salad, turkey or avocado and garden or fruit salads in the $4-5 range. COMMENTS: No seating in the restaurant, but a few tables outside. Call ahead and order a picnic lunch.

OHANA BAR AND GRILL *American-Italian*
Embassy Suites Resort (661-2000) HOURS: 11am-5pm daily, full bar. SAMPLING: If you are a guest of the hotel, this is where you'll find your morning breakfast cooked to order. They also offer poolside lunch selections that include burgers, sandwiches, salads, pizza and appetizers that feature their award-winning orange-mango BBQ sauce such as chicken wings, onion rings and onion blossom. $5.95-7.95.

ROYAL OCEAN TERRACE LOUNGE *American*
Royal Lahaina Resort (661-3611) HOURS: 11am-11pm, entertainment and happy hour 4-7pm, lite meals 4-10pm. SAMPLING: Appetizers of shrimp cocktail, buffalo wings, sashimi, pizza, kalua pork quesadilla and focaccia bread with grilled vegetables $6.95-10.25. Lite meals include Kula or Caesar salad (with seared ahi or cajun prawns), hamburger on Hawaiian sweetbread and Maui onions and reuben, mahi or prime rib sandwich $5.25-14.50. COMMENTS: Sunset torch lighting ceremony at 6:30pm followed by Hawaiian musical entertainment.

ROYAL SCOOP *American (Sandwiches/Ice Cream)*
Royal Lahaina Resort. (661-3611) HOURS: 6am-9pm. SAMPLING: Limited selection, but a few salad and sandwich items, coffee specialties, baked goods, shaved ice and, of course, ice cream $3-5! COMMENTS: Old-fashioned ice cream parlor, their fresh hot cones are made to order.

SEA DOGS *American*
Westin Maui (667-2525) Poolside snacks at a convenient "quick food" cart between the pool and the beach. HOURS: 7-10am; 10am-4pm. SAMPLING: Light breakfast until 10 then freshly baked pizza, sandwiches, salads and shaved ice until closing.

SHERATON MAUI LOUNGES
Sheraton Maui was not open as we go to press, but the newly renovated hotel was expected to resume operations in November, 1996. Lounges will include the Lagoon Bar, the Sundowner Bar and the Reef's Edge Lounge. The Honu Snack Shop will offer light snacks poolside.

MODERATE

BASIL TOMATOES   *Italian*
Royal Lahaina Resort (661-3611) HOURS: Dinner 5:30-10pm. SAMPLING: Antipasto selections of stuffed mushrooms, carpaccio, steamed artichoke, calamari, fried cheese and fried green tomatoes $5.99-9.99. Tomato & basil, Caesar, gorgonzola and panzanella salads $6.99-12.99; pastas with pesto, herbal, tomato or Alfredo sauce $9.99-16.99. Entrees include lasagna, seafood ravioli, scampi, veal or eggplant parmesan, chicken manicotti, steak, lamb, chicken, veal chop or mixed grill $15.99-26.99. Desserts range from Italian ices to banana crepe $3.49-5.99. COMMENTS: Good Italian fare has found a home in the old Moby Dick's location at the entrance to the Royal Lahaina. In fact, one of the entrees pays homage to the previous tenant: Basil Tomatoes' Seafood Pasta a la Moby Dick has shrimp, scallops, mahi and crab with Kaanapali sauce and bananas over linguine for $18.99.

BEACHCOMBERS   *Oriental-Polynesian*
Royal Lahaina Resort (661-3611) HOURS: Dinner nightly 5:30-10pm. SAMPLING: Crab cakes, tempura shrimp, onion rings and dim sum are the appetizers along with sashimi, shrimp cocktail and smoked salmon $5.25-9.95. Maui onion soup or Beachcomber's salad with Italian sausage, pepperoni, feta cheese and Maui onions $4.25-4.75. Grilled entrees include steak, lamb chops, prime rib, teri chicken, BBQ ribs and Mandarin roast duck $11.95-23.75. Seafood items offer mahi with Chinese spices, Thai salmon, scampi or Asian seafood pasta and Oriental dishes from the wok such as nutty chicken, beef, chicken or shrimp curry, lo mein and vegetarian stir-fry $11.95-19.50. Lahaina lime pie, Kula strawberry cheesecake, mac nut chocolate fudge cake and white chocolate gelato on homemade macadamia nut brittle are the desserts $3.75-4.50.

COOK'S AT THE BEACH ★   *American*
Westin Maui, north side of the swimming pool (667-2525) HOURS: Breakfast 6:30-11am; breakfast buffet 6:30-11am; lunch 11am-2pm and dinner 5-9pm. SAMPLING: Daily breakfast buffet is $17.50 adults, children $1.50 per year. Other breakfast menu items are limited, but include Egg Beaters fritatta, Continental breakfast, fresh fruits, omelettes and flavored pancakes $7.25-11.50. Lunch offers sandwiches, burgers and pizzas along with chicken quesadilla, won tons, spring rolls and award-winning Maui onion seafood gumbo served with Molokai sweetbread $5.95-11.95. Dinner features their prime rib buffet with a variety of salads, fresh catch, made-to-order shrimp pasta, special chef's entree and a very nice dessert cart for $26.95 adults, children $1.50 per year. Regular menu entrees include roasted chicken & spare ribs, stir-fry, shrimp curry, rib-eye steak and a variety of appetizers and salads. $16.50-23.95 COMMENTS: A good family restaurant with a varied assortment certain to please everyone. Fairly reasonable prices for a resort!

CORAL REEF RESTAURANT   *Hawaii-Pacifica*
Sheraton Maui, 2605 Kaanapali Parkway (661-0031) A la carte meat and fish entrees for dinner. The Sheraton was not open as we went to press, but was expected to resume operations in November, 1996.

HULA GRILL ★ *Hawaiian Regional/Seafood*
Whalers Village Shopping Center, on the beach (667-6636) HOURS: Dinner from 5:30pm, Barefoot Bar & Cafe from 11:30am, cocktails from 11am. SAMPLING: You can get many of the soups, salads and kiawe wood pizzas at both the Barefoot Bar and in the dining room. Dim sum is also available with mac nut & crab won tons, poke rolls, egg roll, summer rolls, coconut calamari and seafood potstickers $5.95-9.95. Entree salads and sandwiches are on the bar menu $6.95-11.95. Dinner entrees include teriyaki steak or ahi, crab & corn cakes, firecracker mahi, grilled chicken with jerk spice and tropical chutney, scampi, shrimp and scallop pasta and Hawaiian seafood gumbo $12.95-24.95. COMMENTS: The Hula Grill, formerly the location of El Crab Catcher, features Hawaiian Regional Cuisine focusing on Hawaiian fish and seafood designed by award-winning Chef Peter Merriman. Fresh fish entrees come with ginger and pineapple brown rice, meat dishes have garlic "smashed" potatoes. The casual oceanfront restaurant, reminiscent of a 1930's Dickey-style beach house, is surrounded by tropical gardens and ponds. The interior has a homey atmosphere with a cozy library room for a waiting area. Each room feels like part of a home and a collection of antique hula dolls are on display throughout. The Barefoot Bar is thatched and surrounded by "indoor" sand. There is an exhibition cooking line in front with a large kiawe grill/BBQ, an imu-style oven for the pizzas and a bar-counter to sit and eat and watch it all. This one had a slow start, but now the cuisine (and ambiance) are right up there with the best of 'em. Good kids menu, too!

KEKA'A TERRACE *American*
Sheraton Maui, 2605 Kaanapali Parkway (661-0031) HOURS: 6:30am-9:30pm. Buffet and a la carte breakfast. Lunch and dinner a la carte. Views of the ocean and the resort's tropical lagoons. The Sheraton was not open as we went to press, but was expected to resume operations in November, 1996.

LEILANI'S ★ *American-Seafood*
Whalers Village Shopping Center, on the beach (661-4495) HOURS: Beachside Grill 11:30am-11pm, dinner 5-10pm. SAMPLING: Fettucine pescatore $15.95, fresh island fish $17.95-19.95, ginger chicken $13.95, baby back pork ribs $15.95-19.95, prime rib $23.95. COMMENTS: Known for offering one of the best sunset viewing spots in Kaanapali, the outdoor lounge and terrace dining room overlook the beach. Leilani's has been here for years and is a good all around bet for family dining at Kaanapali. Leilani's specialties are prepared on lava rock broilers in koa wood ovens. The Beachside Grill, located on the lower level beachside of the restaurant, features pupus and casual menu fare like burgers, salads, sandwiches and Hawaiian local plates $2.50-9.95. There are two vegetarian items on the dinner menu (veggie brochettes; spinach, mushroom & cheese raviolis) both at $9.95. Children's menu. Reservations advised for dinner.

LUIGI'S PASTA PIZZARIA *Italian*
Kaanapali Resort, by the golf course (661-4500) HOURS: Daily 5:30pm-9:30pm, bar until 2am. SAMPLING: Greek or Caesar salad, seafood stuffed mushrooms, fried calamari, Italian sausage and fresh asparagus for starters $4.99-8.99. Entree selections of seafood pescatore, mixed grill, veal marsala, scampi, scallops or mahi mahi Alfredo and eggplant, veal or chicken parmesan $13.99-19.99. Pizza

combinations include Hawaiian, cheeseburger and a South Seas special with curry sauce, bananas, onion, peppers, macadamia nuts and shrimp: small $10.99-16.99/large $15.99-27.99. South Seas also available in pasta along with lasagna, manicotti and fettucini Alfredo with chicken and mushrooms $10.99-17.99. COMMENTS: Or how about a roasted garlic bulb baked in olive oil....? Your friends are gonna love you! (Same owners have Burrito Brothers downstairs and Basil Tomatoes at the Royal Lahaina.)

MOANA TERRACE ★ *American-Buffet*
Maui Marriott Hotel (667-1200) HOURS: 6:30am-10pm. SAMPLING: Breakfast 6:30-11:30am, $12.75 or $15.75 breakfast buffet 6:30am-11am, lunch 11:30-2pm, dinner 5-10pm, soup and salad bar 5pm-10pm, dinner buffets on Friday, Saturday and Sunday evenings 5-9pm. SAMPLING: Breakfasts feature eggs, breads, pancakes and oatmeal and offer a number of healthy alternatives. Several dinner entrees are available for lunch along with burgers, Pizza Hut pizza and sandwiches like roast beef & Maui onion, mahi with Chinese cabbage and shiitake mushrooms and grilled chicken breast with tomato, mozarella & peppers on focaccia bread $9.25-16.95. Dinner entrees include pesto grilled salmon, pesto & smoked chicken penne pasta, baby back ribs with mango BBQ sauce, firecracker shrimp & pasta as well as burgers and Pizza Hut pizza $9.25-18.95. Desserts include macadamia nut cheese pie, tiramisu, cheesecake and key lime pie $3.75-4.50. Friday dinner buffet is prime rib for $13.75 and Saturday they serve up an array of seafood for $21.95. Sunday is Italian pasta & sundae night for $11.25. Children 12 and under have a special menu with a dozen breakfast, lunch or dinner options. COMMENTS: Their set of menus is as long as a book! They have the most varied and changing assortment of meals, buffets, specials and options of any restaurant on Maui. The good news is that they do a good job on all, making this one of the best family values on the island. Seniors be sure to ask about AARP discounts on the buffets.

PAVILION *Blends Pacifica*
Hyatt Regency Maui, lower level (661-1234) HOURS: Breakfast 6-11:30am; lunch 11:30am-6pm. SAMPLING: Both their breakfast and lunch menu feature

"cuisine naturelle" which offers some healthy alternatives: egg white omelette, apple cinnamon oatmeal, strawberry crepes and chicken hash florentine $4.75-8.50 are available along with traditional breakfast fare $7.75-12. The healthy lunch choices are scallop salad, vegetable club, seared salmon Diablo and grilled chicken burger $8-10.75. Other options are Chinese chicken, cobb or shrimp Caesar salad, pizza, burgers, stir-fry, reuben, teri chicken or fruit and cream cheese on macadamia nut bread sandwiches $7.25-14. COMMENTS: A variety of smoothies and tropical drinks come with alcohol $6.50 or without $5. Flavors include peach, coconut, papaya, banana, strawberry, chocolate, macadamia nut, mocha and pineapple.

REILLEY'S   *Steaks & Seafood*
2290 Kaanapali Parkway, overlooking the golf course (667-7477) HOURS: Saturday and Sunday brunch 9:30am-2:30pm, lunch 11am-4pm, dinner 5-10pm. SAMPLING: Tuna in papaya, cobb and grilled chicken or seared ahi Caesar salads $7.95-9.95. Bacon & cheese, patty melt and mushroom & sour cream are among the burger selections $6.95-7.95. Pupus include calamari, nachos, steamed clams, Thai summer rolls, gyoza, onion strings and Reilley's steak pupu $4.95-8.95. Steaks are the signature dinner feature $15.95-26.95 along with fresh fish, seafood platter, Alaskan king crab, pastas, chicken and weekend prime rib $9.95-25. Save room for the brownie sundae or mint chocolate leprechaun pie $4.25-4.95. COMMENTS: Spacious and attractive pub atmosphere. Wine & beer and a selection of tropical, "Irish" and coffee drinks. Sandwiches are a cut above with a variety that includes BBQ or teri chicken breast, turkey, BLT, steak and Reuben $5.95-9.95. Weekend champagne brunch entrees are a la carte: egg dishes, crab cakes, French toast and Monte Cristo sandwich run $6.95-10.95.

ROYAL OCEAN TERRACE   *American*
Royal Lahaina Hotel (661-3611) HOURS: Breakfast 6-11am, and dinner 5pm-10pm. SAMPLING: Appetizers of shrimp cocktail, buffalo wings, sashimi, pizza, kalua pork quesadilla and focaccia bread with grilled vegetables $6.95-10.25. Lite meals offer Kula, cobb or Caesar salad (with seared ahi or cajun prawns), hamburger on Hawaiian sweetbread and Maui onions and reuben, mahi, turkey club or prime rib sandwich $5.25-14.50. Dinner entrees include filet mignon, porterhouse, prime rib, seared mahi, cajun prawns and wok-seared lasagna $15.50-24.50. COMMENTS: This is a very attractive, airy restaurant overlooking the pool and the ocean.

THE RUSTY HARPOON   *American*
Whalers Village (661-3123) HOURS: Breakfast 8-11am; lunch 11am-5pm; dinner 5pm-midnight; bistro menu 10pm-midnight; early bird special 4-6pm. SAMPLING: Their Belgian waffle bar offers coconut, fudge or maple syrups along with assorted fruit toppings, nuts, coconut, granola and even ice cream $8.95, omelettes and other breakfast items $2.95-13.95. Items available for lunch and dinner include potato skins, crab puffs, stuffed mushrooms, fried zucchini, onion blossom and onion rings $6.95-11.95; also shrimp Louie, spinach, tropical chicken and chef's salads $6.95-10.95. Cheese tortellini & ravioli, seafood fettucini and pan-fried lasagna are slightly higher at dinner, $2-5 over the lunch

range of $11.95-14.95. Spinach & goat cheese, Asian BBQ chicken, garlic prawn and other pizzas $7.95-8.95 are on the lunch menu along with several burgers and turkey, tuna melt, roast beef, cajun chicken, turkey reuben or seafood salad sandwiches $7.95-9.50. Dinner entrees include rack of lamb, pineapple teri chicken, prime rib, steaks and tempura or stuffed shrimp $16.95-24.95. Desserts offer cookies n' cream ice cream pie, strawberry shortcake, chocolate mousse, cheesecake and island high macadamia nut cream pie $4.95. Children's menu. COMMENTS: Pizzas, appetizers and coffee drinks (including flavored cappucino) are all available on the late night bistro menu. The Harpoon has added a sushi bar open from 5pm to midnight with several varieties of nigiri, roll and combination sushi from $5.50. The new owner's name of "Jerome E. Metcalfe's Rusty Harpoon and Tavern on Kaanapali Beach" adds a lot of words, but it looks like they've kept up their most popular traditions of the Belgian waffle bar and island high pies. The onion blossom is one of the popular new appetizers; pan-fried vegetarian lasagna is an unusual new entree.

SEN JU SUSHI BAR
Westin Maui at Kaanapali. (667-2525) HOURS: Daily 6-10pm. COMMENTS: The name Sen is for the owner of the Westin Maui, but it also means "a thousand" and Ju means happy times. The bar only seats seven, but there are bento-style sushi and sashimi trays that can be taken to the surrounding tables to be enjoyed in the Colonnade. Contemporary or traditional sushi from $4. They also offer hot sake, American and Japanese wine and beer.

TEPPAN-YAKI DAN   *Japanese*
Sheraton Maui, 2605 Kaanapali Parkway (661-0031) HOURS: Dinner only. SAMPLING: Japanese dinners prepared to order and grilled at your table. Menu will feature Hawai'i's local beef, fresh fish and vegetables. The Sheraton was not open as we went to press, but was expected to resume operations in November, 1996.

TIKI TERRACE   *American-Hawaiian*
Kaanapali Beach Hotel (661-0011) HOURS: Breakfast 7-11am, Sunday breakfast menu is served 7am-9am followed by Sunday brunch 9am-2pm and dinner 6-9:30pm. SAMPLING: Coconut crusted shrimp, chicken & beef satay, Maui onion lumpia, pipi kaula (marinated beef) plus soups and salads will start your meal for $3.95-8.95. Dinners include island bouillabaise, baked Hawaiian jumbo prawns, breast of chicken wrapped in taro leaf with coconut cream, veal chop filled with pohele fern shoots and shiitake mushrooms with sweet potato and several preparations for the catch of the day $17.95-24.95. They also offer a set meal modeled after the Native Hawaiian Wainae Diet with healthy Hawaiian preparations of pohele fern salad, poached chicken breast and fresh papaya for $17.95 A salad bar is offered with most entrees for $2.95 or on its own for $10.95. Hawaiian pineapple cake, papaya strudel and sweet potato taro pie are $3.95. COMMENTS: Complimentary hula show nightly with Hawaiian entertainment throughout the evening to enjoy while you dine. Their Sunday brunch is a great value and very popular with both visitors and residents.

EXPENSIVE

LAHAINA PROVISION COMPANY ★ *American*
Hyatt Regency Maui (661-1234) HOURS: Lunch 11:30-2pm; dinner 6-11pm. Chocoholic bar 6-11pm, lounge from 11am-11pm. SAMPLING: Appetizers are served all day: spring roll, onion rings, crab cakes, sate and shrimp Niihau $4.50-11.25; for dinner get them as a sampler for $18.75. The "Tropical Saladery" is a buffet of salads, vegetables, cold pastas and cheeses and includes a dessert bar for $14.75 or choose individual Caesar, Pacific Nicoise or hoisin duck salads $9.95. The Lahaina club has smoked chicken, avocado and Maui onion or try the grilled fish, burger, or crab cake sandwich $8.50-13. Dinner selections include prime rib, beef brochette, sweet chile shrimp, seafood mixed grill, vegetarian black bean & tofu cake or Hawaiian paella $18-30; sampler for two $58. COMMENTS: This restaurant is cleverly perched above the pool and on the edge of one of the Hyatt's waterfalls. Dinners here are very pleasant. Ask whether they have a children's Camp Hyatt menu or children can order most entrees on the menu at 1/2 price for 1/2 size. This place may be a favorite if you're a chocolate lover. They have a CHOCOHOLIC BAR that features rich ice cream with an incredible choice of chocolate temptations to top it. If you have dinner, it's an additional $5.95, but you can come later for dessert only and indulge for $7.95. This outrageous dessert is a definite Maui Best Bet! One of the best appetizers ever is their coconut shrimp! Reservations are recommended for dinner or dessert. Major credit cards are accepted.

LOKELANI ★ *American-Seafood*
Maui Marriott Resort (667-1200) HOURS: Dinner served 6-9pm. SAMPLING: All of the fish is market priced daily and your selection may be prepared in a variety of ways. Appetizers, soups, salads such as seafood chowder, seafood Caesar salad or mussels. Entrees $18-20, are by Maui standards fairly inexpensive given the very diverse selection. Sample Maalaea seafood pasta, Hunan barbequed wild boar, filet mignon with seared foie gras, baked ono, seared tiger prawns, rack of lamb. COMMENTS: Lokelani has won more than its share of dining awards at food festivals, chef's competitions and fund-raisers. Their early

JANORA BAYOT

bird special is probably one of the best values on the island. From 6-6:45 you can enjoy a complete prix fixe dinner with fish chowder or salad, grilled salmon or filet mignon or crusted chicken breast and macadamia nut cream cheese pie for $19.75. Their innovative coffee service is another special feature: the coffee is freshly brewed at your table and served with a "buffet" of sugars, cinnamon sticks, chocolate shavings and whipped cream - all good enough to eat!

NIKKO JAPANESE STEAK HOUSE   *Japanese*
Maui Marriott Resort (667-1200) HOURS: 6-9pm for dinner only. Samari Sunset Menu offers early bird prices from 6-6:30pm daily with complete dinner prices from $14.50-19.50. Regular entree prices are sesame chicken $21.95, mahi mahi $26.95, NY steak $26.95 and miso shrimp $26.95. Combinations, tempura and sushi & sashimi dinners run $21.95-39.95. All are served with shrimp or scallop appetizer, miso or tori soup, Nikko salad, steamed rice, teppan-yaki vegetables and Japanese green tea. Also included in the price is the "show." The chef works at your table and is adept at knife throwing and other dazzling cooking techniques. COMMENTS: Tempura, sushi and sashimi are new to the menu as are some intriguing desserts: the Marriott's signature chocolate macadamia nut pie, fresh fruit in plum and "white chocolate sushi" with ginger mango sauce. (It was yummy, but we're still trying to figure out how they made it!) Children's entrees are half price. The menu notes a 15% service charge is added to your bill.

NORTH BEACH GRILLE   *Pacific Rim*
Embassy Suites Resort (661-2000) HOURS: Dinner 5-10pm. SAMPLING: Shrimp cocktail with a citrus and sesame vinaigrette, seared blackened ahi and Rey's wings served with Chef Rey Baysa's award-winning orange-mango barbeque sauce $7.25-11.95. The sauce is also featured in the entrees of barbequed tiger prawns $19.95 and barbequed pork ribs $17.95. Other entrees include roast chicken, fisherman's platter, prime rib, fresh catch and a fajita platter $13.95-21.95. Pizzas are also available for $8.95-12.95. COMMENTS: North Beach Grille also features several buffet nights offering seafood on Saturdays, Italian on Wednesdays and a carved selection of prime rib and roast turkey on Fridays and Sundays $17.95-26.95. They are located right on the ocean (only a sidewalk separates you from the sand) and are one of the few restaurants to offer a salad bar.

SOUND OF THE FALLS *Sunday Brunch*
Westin Maui (667-2525) This elegant ocean front restaurant no longer serves dinner, but you can still experience the luxurious ambiance of its grand staircase, marble floors and cascading waterfalls while enjoying a sumptuous Sunday Champagne Brunch. HOURS: 10:30am-2pm. SAMPLING: Salads, yogurt, sushi, chilled fruit frappe, spiced shrimp, smoked fish with mini-bagels and cream cheese, eggs Benedict, pineapple-papaya blintz, tricolor seafood ravioli, pork ribs with plum sauce, chicken cordon bleu, wok-seared beef with oriental noodles, made-to-order omelettes, sushi & sashimi, breakfast pastries, croissants, strudels, white & dark chocolate fondue, chocolate-dipped strawberrries & truffles, petit fours, Hawaiian cheesecake and warm Molokai sweet bread pudding. COMMENTS: All-you-can-eat $22.95; $1.50 for every year of age for children under 12. A great price for such an indulgent splurge!

SPATS TRATTORIA ★ *Northern Italian*
Hyatt Regency Maui (661-1234) HOURS: Dinner daily 6-10pm. SAMPLING: Deep dish pizza, prosciutto with papaya, pizzelle (crispy miniature pizzas) and minestrone are some of the appetizers for $5-9.75. Entrees include seafood grill, veal piccata or scallopine, lasagna, chicken marsala, steak, gnocchi and cannelloni $13.75-26. Tiramisu, chocolate ganache cake, chocolate caramel torte for dessert $4.75-5.75. COMMENTS: The atmosphere is comfortable and homey, yet very classy, as in the parlor or drawing room of an old Italian mansion. Brass candelabras, sleek wood, beveled glass partitions and plush booths add to the distinctive ambiance. A gracious touch is a table at the entrance with small glasses of wine for sampling before you go in. A different bottle is offered each night. Tuscan flatbread accompanies the meal and is topped with cheese and herbs and arrives with a side of fresh pesto along with olive oil and herbs for dipping. Kids menu available at 1/2 portion for 1/2 price.

SWAN COURT ★ *Continental*
Hyatt Regency Maui (661-1234) HOURS: Breakfast buffet 6:30-11:30am, until 12:30pm on Sunday. Dinner 6-10pm daily. SAMPLING: Breakfast buffet includes fresh-squeezed orange juice, French toast, crepes, bread pudding, cereals, yogurt, breads & pastries, fresh fruits, egg dishes, potatoes, breakfast meats and omelettes $16.25. Also breakfast a la carte. Dinner appetizers include summer roll, BBQ sugar spice shrimp, crab cakes, dim sum, artichokes, wonton & seafood Napoleon, sushi tower and lasagnette of veal $10-14, plus Maui onion soup, lobster coconut bisque and spinach salad $6-8. Featured entrees are Thai spiced lobster & scallops, bouillabaisse, smoked char siu duck, Hunan marinated lamb chops and seared bison with Pailolo Channel shrimp $28-36. Classical chocolate souffle $10. COMMENTS: A pond of graceful swans, cascading waterfalls and a landscape of Oriental gardens create the atmosphere and view of the Swan Court. The ambiance alone is well worth the splurge for breakfast, our "best bet" for a daily breakfast buffet. The dinners are excellent and many unusual preparations are offered. Our only criticism is the proximity of other tables and noise seems to carry. Reservations are advised.

VILLA RESTAURANT AND VILLA TERRACE ★
American-Seafood/Asian Influences
Westin Maui (667-2525) HOURS: Dinner only 5:30-9pm. SAMPLING: Seafood is the specialty! "Lobster Maine-ia" offers a Maine lobster dinner for $26.95 ($39.95 with a filet). Appetizers have a bit of an Asian influence with their rice paper shrimp and lobster taco, crispy Thai chicken & lemongrass spring rolls and 1995 Taste of Lahaina Best of Show winner, tangled tiger prawns with chili cilantro garlic sauce $8-12. Crab bisque with cognac and fire roasted pepper & zucchini are soup and salad samples that run from $5-10. Entrees include Black Angus NY steak, lamb chops, seafood potpourri, macadamia nut crusted chicken or their excellent selection of fresh fish served with anything from papaya salsa to roasted peppers to sweet potato threads $22-29. From shutome to ulua, they generally have among the best selection of different types of fresh seafood in West Maui. COMMENTS: One of our best bets for fresh island fish and a beautiful setting. All tables look out onto the lagoon where swans and exotic ducks float along peacefully. You don't have to wait until Friday to enjoy the seafood buffet in the adjoining Villa Terrace, it's offered nightly for $27.95 from 6-9pm.

KAHANA - NAPILI - KAPALUA

LOUNGES

KAPALUA BAY RESORT - BAY LOUNGE ★ and LOBBY TERRACE
Kapalua Bay Resort (669-5656) HOURS: 5:30-10:00pm. (Music until 8:30) COMMENTS: Enjoy a fabulous sunset in this elegant setting. Live soft background music is provided. Hotel guests can enjoy complimentary coffee service in the Lobby Terrace daily 6:30-10:30am and tea service 3-5pm daily. An equally pleasant sunset can be enjoyed at The Bay Lounge, which is part of The Bay Club restaurant situated on a promontory overlooking the ocean. It's an idyllic setting from which to enjoy the scenic panorama along with pupus and cocktails. (You might want to indulge in one of their ice cream libations, such as a Bay Lounger with dark rum and fresh pineapple or the Bay Club Delight with Kahlua, Grand Marnier and Amaretto: about $6)

THE LOBBY LOUNGE AND LIBRARY
The Ritz-Carlton, Kapalua (669-6200) HOURS: Espresso bar 5:30-11am for coffee drinks and pastries. Noon to midnight for cocktails and pupus (4:30-9pm) including sashimi, shrimp cocktail, vegetable crudite, imported cheeses and exotic berries $6.50-13. Afternoon tea served 2:30-4:30pm, upon request, with advance reservations required. Finger sandwiches, scones with Devonshire cream, and tea pastries with pot of tea $14.75; light tea $10. Hawaiian entertainment 5-7pm.

THE ANUENUE LOUNGE
The Ritz-Carlton, Kapalua (669-6200) HOURS: Cocktails 5:30pm-midnight, dessert 8-10pm, Tuesday - Saturday, closed Sunday and Monday. Entertainment ranges from solo piano to a jazz duo. Located adjacent to The Anuenue Room restaurant.

RESTAURANTS-INEXPENSIVE

(THE) BEACH HOUSE *American*
The Ritz-Carlton, Kapalua (669-6200) HOURS: Lunch 11:30am-4:30pm. Bar service 11-5 with daily specialty drinks. SAMPLING: Lunch selections range from quesadilla, potsticker and tostada appetizers $4-13 to hot dogs, mahi, veggie and tuna pita sandwiches $5.25-11.50. COMMENTS: Located adjacent to Fleming Beach, this open-air restaurant utilizes more than 40 fully-grown coco palms to offer a natural roof.

(THE) COFFEE STORE *Coffee/pastries*
Napili Plaza (669-4170) HOURS: Daily 6:30am-8pm. Coffee drinks, with a few unusual selections including a banana mocha cooler or an Electric Brown Cow! Also quiche, muffins, scones, salads, veggie lasagna, garden burger or croissant sandwiches $1.95-8.50.

DOLLIES *American-Italian*
4310 Honoapiilani Hwy. at the Kahana Manor (669-0266) HOURS: 10 am-midnight. SAMPLING: A great assortment of sandwiches from tuna salad on pita bread, roast beef and provolone Italian sausage or BLT $4.95-8.25. Pasta dishes include linguini with meatballs, shrimp primavera, lasagna or shrimp and chicken with mushrooms $9.95-13.95. Pizza $7.95-20. COMMENTS: Good selection of beer with more than 40 domestic and imported. Wine and coffee drinks, too! Food to go. Very popular spot with local residents.

GAZEBO *American*
Napili Shores Resort, 5315 Lower Honoapiilani Hwy., (669-5621) HOURS: Both breakfast and lunch from 7:30am-2pm. SAMPLING: Breakfast offers an assortment of omelettes and egg dishes, but they are most popular for their macadamia nut pancakes (pineapple and banana run a close second) $4.50-6.95. Lunch selections include burgers, salads and sandwiches; including Monte Cristo, shrimp melt, chicken Monterey and patty melt $4.95-7.95. COMMENTS: "Paper-plate" casual and popular with Maui residents for the friendly atmosphere with a wonderful ocean view.

HONOLUA GENERAL STORE *American*
Past Kapalua as you drive through the golf course. Just above The Ritz-Carlton (669-6128) HOURS: 6am-8pm. SAMPLING: Breakfasts include pancakes, eggs and such. Lunches include four local plate lunches daily which might include stew or teri chicken $4.95-5.50, or a smaller portion called a hobo which is just a main dish and rice for $3.50. Sandwiches and grilled items $4.95. The spam masubi, a local favorite, is usually sold out by noon. COMMENTS: The Kapalua Hotel refurbished this once funky and local spot. The front portion displays an assortment of Kapalua clothing and some locally made food products as well as gourmet teas and coffees.

KAFE KAHANA *American*
Kahana Gateway (669-6699) HOURS: 7am-9pm. SAMPLING: Fresh fruit smoothies, a variety of coffee drinks (one called "Why Bother?" is made with

lowfat milk and decaf espresso) and freshly-squeezed juices $1.50-3.50. Salads, soups and sandwiches with choice of bread and fillings $2.75-6.75. Daily hot dishes. COMMENTS: Be sure to sample their freshly made cinnamon rolls, co-owner Steve Wolff also operates the Cinnamon Roll Fair in Kihei!

MAUI TACOS   *Healthy Mexican*
Napili Plaza (665-0222) HOURS: 10am-9pm, til 8pm on Sundays. SAMPLING: Potato enchiladas, hard or soft tacos, quesadillas, chimichangas and over a dozen varieties of special hand-held burritos $1.99-6.95. COMMENTS: Guacamole and salsa made fresh every day. No lard, no msg - they use only vegetable oil, fresh beans and lean meats. The complimentary salsa bar offers several choices with jalapenos, onions, cilantro, hot sauce and more. Good values! This the original with other outlets now in Lahaina Square, Kihei and Kaahumanu Food Court, all owned and operated by Mark Ellman of Avalon.

PICASSO CAFE   *Sandwiches*
Inside Posters Maui at 3600 Lower Honoapiilani Hwy., Honokowai (669-0958) HOURS: 6 am-7pm. SAMPLING: Made-to-order sandwiches named after famous Maui artists are all $5 and include Buffet (turkey), Nelson (ham), Lassen (tuna) and Wyland (roast beef). Salads $4, lasagne $5. COMMENTS: Coffee, juice and breakfast pastries as well as a mini-espresso bar.

PIZZA PEOPLE   *Italian*
Napili Plaza (669-7788) HOURS: 11am to midnight. SAMPLING: The usual pizza toppings plus extras like fresh broccoli, Maui onions, sweet banana peppers and pineapple with choice of tomato or pesto sauce and white, sesame seed or whole wheat crust. Medium and large $13.44-24. Also salads, breadsticks and active or dormant "Volcano" wings! COMMENTS: The dough is made fresh every day and hand-tossed the traditional way. Also at Lahaina Center.

SANSEI RESTAURANT AND SUSHI BAR ★   *Sushi-Japanese-Pacific Rim*
Kapalua Bay Hotel Shops (669-6286) HOURS: 5:30pm-2am (sushi til 1); Sundays til 11pm. They also have plans to open for lunch. SAMPLING: Spicy dijon chicken breast or shellfish and Thai pasta on Kula greens with citrus-ginger vinaigrette and pico de gallo; dynamite with scallops, zucchini and mushrooms; miso garlic prawns; seared ahi over Kula greens; Pacific Rim lomi lomi salmon with tri-color wonton chips and the "Kenny G Special" (snapper with fresh garlic, masago and ponzu) $5.25-13. They also have tempura, soft shell crab, pot-stickers, crispy duck (with homemade apricot chutney) and a selection of innovative sashimi and sushi with names like Bagel Roll, Paniolo and Pink Cadillac $3.50-12.50. COMMENTS: This used to be the Market Cafe and they've done a wonderful job transforming it into a comfortable and inviting sushi bar and small restaurant. They're serving up a new dining concept, too, offering sushi as well as a selection of traditional Japanese and innovative Pacific Rim dishes to share family-style with everyone at the table. (Kind of like Asian "tapas.") The small plates and small portions create a friendly, fun atmosphere, not the usual sedate and tranquil ambiance you'd expect from a traditional Japanese restaurant. If you don't like sushi bars, you'll like this one. And if you *love* them, this will probably be one of your favorites!

VILLAGE CAFE   *American*
Village Golf Course at the first hole. (669-1947) HOURS: Breakfast 7:30-11am; lunch 11:30am-3pm. SAMPLING: Breakfast sandwiches, quiche, French toast $3.50-4.95. Deli sandwiches plus fish, chicken, dogs and The Village Cheeseburger $5.50-6.50. Salads $3.95-6.95. COMMENTS: They serve Lappert's Kona Coffee (from 6:30am). We hear they make a great burger here! Let us know what you think!

MODERATE

BANYAN TREE   *Mediterranean*
The Ritz-Carlton, Kapalua HOURS: 11:30am-4pm for lunch. SAMPLING: Tropical libations and non-alcohol fruit smoothies. Food items include a prix fixe lunch for $18; appetizers of dim sum, quesadilla, black bean cake and bruschetta $6.50-10.50; pizzas $13-15; Caesar, spinach and Asian chicken salads $9-16 and entrees of mixed seafood grill, penne pasta, wok-fried snapper, sirloin burger or Thai chicken, mahi or BLT w/avocado sandwiches $8.50-22. COMMENTS: Located poolside, they offer a limited sandwich, pizza and appetizer menu by the pool $6.50-16.

BEACH CLUB   *American*
Kaanapali Shores Resort (667-2211) HOURS: Breakfast 7-11am, Lunch 11:30am-3pm, cafe menu (light fare) served 3-9:30pm, dinner 5:30-9:30pm. SAMPLING: Eggs, pancakes, French toast, fruit crepes $4.25-6.75. Hot and cold sandwiches, salads, chicken taquitos, cheese quesadillas and seafood melt $5.25-8.95. Cafe menu has burgers, salads and appetizers such as stuffed mushrooms, cajun ahi, cheese sticks, buffalo wings and scampi sampler $3.50-10.25. Dinners offer a selection of seafood, chicken, steak and pasta dishes $11.95-19.95. COMMENTS: While-they-last specials each evening $9.95-11.95. Keiki menu available for all meals. Full bar service and an extensive selection of specialty coffee drinks.

CHINA BOAT   *Cantonese-Szechuan-Mandarin*
4474 L. Honoapiilani, Kahana (669-5089) HOURS: Lunch 11:30-2pm, dinner 5-10pm. SAMPLING: Appetizers feature potstickers, shumai, mushroom garlic noodles and chinese pickles $3.75-8.75. Entrees include Kung Pao lobster, chicken & scallops; shrimp crabmeat; vegetable meatball and ginger onion halibut along with more familiar Chinese dishes $8.95-22.95. Lobster, Peking duck and whole fish up to $38.50. COMMENTS: They specialize in Chinese seafood and have an early bird special every evening from 5-6pm offering several choices that run $8.95-11.25 for a full dinner.

ERIK'S SEAFOOD GROTTO   *Seafood*
4242 Lower Honoapiilani Hwy. on the second floor of the Kahana Villas Condo (669-4806) HOURS: Lunch: 11:30am-2pm; dinner 5-10pm. SAMPLING: Lunch offers fish, chicken and steak sandwiches along with unusual salads like Mandarin chicken, seared ahi and three kinds of Caesar: chicken, mahi and snow crab $4.95-9.95. Dinners include soup or salad, starch and bread with entrees of BBQ shrimp, bouillabaisse, cioppino, lobster thermidor, scampi Olowalu, Coquille St.

Jacques with fresh fish, steaks and combinations $14.95-24.95. COMMENTS: They've only recently opened for lunch, a good idea and long overdue way to take advantage of that great ocean view from upstairs. Their early bird specials are more creative than most and offer Island Mahi "Oscar," lobster-stuffed boneless chicken breast and crab stuffed prawns in addition to NY steak or fresh fish for $11.95-13.95 from 5-6pm.

FISH AND GAMES SPORTS GRILL *Seafood*
Kahana Gateway (669-FISH) HOURS: Lunch 11am-3pm; dinner 6-10pm; late night menu 10:30pm-1am SAMPLING: Lunch at the Oyster Bar offers shrimp, sashimi, smoked salmon and, of course, Skookums, Kumamotos, Hama Hama Yearling, Miyagi and Blue Points $5.95-10.95! The main menu has clam or oyster chowder, cioppino, seared ahi, steamed clams or mussels, baked oysters, cajun chicken wings and BBQ rib appetizers for $6.95-9.95 and sandwiches that include cajun chicken, oyster po'boy, rib eye and *real* tuna $7.50-10.95. The dinner menu offers the same appetizer, soup and oyster bar items with the addition of Oysters Rockefeller, spicy crab cakes, cajun shrimp or ahi and wok-seared lobster claws $9.95-12.50. Salads offer grilled scallops or you can have a Caesar with cajun chicken, lobster claws, shrimp or salmon lox $5.95-11.95. Entrees feature rack of lamb or angus beef steaks $22.95-27.95, pastas with cioppino, scallops, mussels, clams, eggplant or fresh spinach $13.95-16.95 and live whole crab or crab legs, jumbo shrimp and live lobster $14.95-21.95 (some priced per pound). The late night menu offers fried seafood or chicken with fries, choice of Caesar, chef's tostada, fish sandwich, or pasta with lobster, chicken or fish $9.95-12.95. COMMENTS: A retail seafood market, sports bar and dining room with an exhibition kitchen. The sports bar offers state of the art equipment and satellite system. The oyster bar is unique and the fish market fresh. The wood and brass of the bar resembles a Gentlemen's club motif which is put to use several times a year with a "Smoker" featuring fine cigars, gourmet brews and a multi-course meal with wine.

JAMESON'S GRILL & BAR AT KAPALUA *Seafood-American*
200 Kapalua Drive, just across the road from the Kapalua Hotel and a short drive up Kapalua Drive (669-5653) HOURS: Lunch 11am-3pm, dinner 5-10pm, cocktails 11am-12:30am. SAMPLING: Fish, roast beef, chicken & steak sandwiches, burgers, salads, appetizers and pizzas $4.95-12.95. Dinner appetizers offer crab-stuffed mushrooms, calamari strips, Thai shrimp summer rolls, crab cakes, scampi and clams in Beck's beer broth $6.95-11.95, J.J.'s baked artichoke is still famous and still here for $8.95. Entrees include fresh catch, Black Angus meats, shrimp & scallop linguine, Chinatown duck with peppercorn sauce, rack of lamb, baked stuffed shrimp, sauteed scallops and poached opakapaka $13.95-23.95. COMMENTS: In May, 1996 Jameson's-by-the-Sea took over the Kapalua Grill & Bar offering diners the best of both. Familiar Grill & Bar items remain and popular Jameson dishes have been added. The wine list has been revamped and offers everything from the affordable to the impressive. A golf course and ocean view add to the plusses of this restaurant; outdoor dining is now available on a new patio overlooking the 18th hole. As before, tank tops are okay daytime attire, but not appropriate for evening. Dinner reservations suggested.

KOHO GRILL AND BAR ★ *American*
Napili Plaza, 5095 Napilihau St. (669-5299) HOURS: Daily 11 am-1am, lunch from 11am & dinner from 5pm. SAMPLING: Salads include chicken Caesar, Oriental chicken, taco, cobb or fajita $6.25-7.95; BLT, club, fish, turkey and chicken sandwiches $4.95-6.25; burgers, taco platters and plate lunches $5.75-7.95. Sizzling fajitas $7.25-7.95. Dinner entrees served with soup or salad include fish, steak, chicken stir-fry, ribs and fettucini primavera. Cinnamon apple or chocolate sundae, brownie or fried ice cream snow ball $3.45-4.50. COMMENTS: A diverse menu and affordable prices which boils down to great family dining. They also have a great keiki (kids) menu and knowing how fussy some kids can be, they'll even cut the crusts off the sandwiches! A few new salads and dinner entrees have livened up the menu. There is another Koho Grill and Bar in the Kaahumanu Center and the same owners also run the Plantation House in Kapalua and the SeaWatch restaurant in Wailea.

ORIENT EXPRESS *Thai-Chinese*
Napili Shores Resort, one mile before Kapalua (669-8077) HOURS: Dinner 5:30-10 pm. SAMPLING: Sizzling Szechuan beef, garlic shrimp, roasted duck curry, honey lemon chicken, spinach pork and seafood in a clay pot $10.50-17.50. COMMENTS: This restaurant is run by the same folks who operate Chez Paul (and Lobster Cove/Harry's Sushi Bar in Wailea). There is an early bird special for $11.95 from 5:30-6:30pm They use no MSG in their cooking. There is a Harry's Sushi & Pupu Bar located in the front of the restaurant which serves sushi, sashimi and Orient Express pupus and is open til "late."

PINEAPPLE HILL *Continental*
Up past Napili, turn left for Kapalua and you will see the entrance. (669-6129) HOURS: Dinner 5:30-9pm with cocktails from 4:30 pm. SAMPLING: Escargot, artichoke, stuffed mushrooms, won tons and their house specialty spring roll with assorted meats and seafoods fried and wrapped in a lettuce leaf are the appetizers. Chicken pineapple served in a pineapple boat and prawns Tahitian have been signature dishes for years and their Papeete steamed fish is a recent award-winner $16.95-24.95. Baked half chicken, prime rib, BBQ ribs, steak, scallops Provencale and linguine with pesto are other offerings $11.95-24.95. Dinners are served with soup or salad, vegetables and rolls. Baked Papaya Tahitian is the award-winning special dessert $4.95. Keiki menu available. COMMENTS: Pineapple Hill was once the home of plantation manager David Fleming. He was one of Maui's early agricultural pioneers who helped establish mango, lichee, pineapple and other exotic plants and trees. Just past Kapalua is the beach park bearing his name. He completed the plantation house in 1915 and planted those beautiful Norfolk pines which line the drive. It opened for dining in the early 1960s. Pineapple Hill has one of the loftiest settings for sunset viewing. We recommend enjoying cocktails out on the front lawn while watching the sun descend. Several recent reports indicate that both service and food have improved, although in the past we have had mixed reviews.

POOL TERRACE RESTAURANT AND BAR *International*
Kapalua Bay Hotel, poolside (669-5656) HOURS: Breakfast 6:30-10:30am, lunch 11am-5:30 pm. SAMPLING: Breakfast buffet $11.75-14-95 with choice of mimosa for $6. Eggs, cereal, fruit, pancakes with grilled banana, French toast with sweet bread rolled in coconut and macadamia nuts $4.75-8.75. Extended lunch offers starters of fried calamari, coconut prawns or shrimp summer rolls $5-14.50 plus Caesar, cobb, oriental chicken and fruit salads $5.25-9.75; burgers, pizza and sandwiches $8.25-14.50 and entrees of spaghetti with meatballs, short ribs, eggplant parmesan, mushroom raviolis and oriental chicken or shrimp stir-fry $10.50-14.75. COMMENTS: The beautiful location of this casual poolside setting features an ocean view from every seat. Good values, too.

SEA HOUSE *American*
5900 Lower Honoapiilani Rd., beachfront at Napili Kai Beach Club (669-1500) HOURS: Breakfast 8-11am, lunch 12-2pm, dinner 6-9pm. SAMPLING: Breakfast meats, eggs, Hawaiian sweet bread French toast, banana macadamia pancakes $3.95-8.95. Luncheon sandwiches include tuna melt, pastrami, chicken pita, seared ahi and Mexican turkey roll $5.25-8.95. Also calamari Provencal, island noodle salad, crab pizza, lemon chicken and shrimp scampi $6.95-8.95. Dinner entrees are served with chowder or salad, vegetable, rice or potato. Prime rib, herb-crusted pork loin, seafood brochette, lobster tail, rack of lamb, pecan-crusted chicken breast $12-24. Several items are offered in a light portion and there are keiki menus for lunch and dinner. COMMENTS: The day-of-the-week specials are a good value; it's hard to beat Thursday's lobster for $17.95! A nice oceanfront location is a plus too! Local entertainment most nights in the Whale Watcher's Bar. On Friday evening they offer a Polynesian Dinner Show performed by the children of the Napili Kai Foundation. $35 adults, $20 children.

TERRACE GRILL AND BAR *American*
4299 L. Honoapiilani Hwy., Sands of Kahana Resort (669-5399) HOURS: Breakfast 7:30-11am, lunch 11:30am-5pm, dinner 5:30-9pm. SAMPLING: Breakfast omelettes $5.25-6.95 and tropical flavored pancakes $4-5.50. Lunch menu offers French dip, fish, chicken, club sandwiches plus burgers or patty melt $5.50-8.95; Caesar, chicken and pineapple boat salads $5.95-7.95. Dinners start with chicken strips or wings, pot stickers, jalapeno poppers or calamari $5.95-6.95 then entrees of NY steak, ribs, macadamia or teri chicken, vegetable stir-fry, fresh catch, fish & chips, prime rib and pork chops $7.95-17.95. COMMENTS: Very quiet dining, this restaurant seems to be primarily used by the resort guests. A good selection of menu items; lunch items available at dinner too. Lunch and dinner specials; live music Fri.-Sat. and Tues. 5-7pm.

EXPENSIVE

ANUENUE ROOM ★ *Hawaiian Provencal Cuisine*
The Ritz-Carlton, Kapalua (669-6200) HOURS: Dinner served Tues.-Sat. 6pm-9:30pm; closed Sun.-Mon. SAMPLING: Their appetizer menu features dungeness crab cake, tea smoked duck, snails in crispy phyllo, seared foie gras and asparagus with tomato risotto $11-16. Soups and salads from $6.75-9.50. Entrees include chicken breast with marscapone risotto, carmelized salmon, sauteed John Dory, seared sea scallops, herbed veal loin, beef tenderloin and roasted lamb rack $23-32. They also offer menu of vegetarian selections for $16.50. The desserts round out a memorable meal. Unique in texture and flavor, they could be considered objet d'art! Selections might include chocolate-banana gateau, chocolate tarte with Asian pear won ton, apple-banana in phyllo pastry and mango tarte tatin with rum cream. COMMENTS: Superb service in an elegant, warm and cozy setting, spacious and comfortable, but "ritzy." Their food is marvelous too! Their name has changed from the traditional Grill used in other Ritz hotels to the Hawaiian word for "rainbow."

THE BAY CLUB ★ *French-Seafood*
At Kapalua near the entrance to the resort (669-8008 after 5 pm, 669-5656 before 5 pm) HOURS: Lunch 11am-2pm, dinner nightly 6-9pm, with pianist in the adjoining Bay Lounge until 10pm. SAMPLING: Lunches include Monte Cristo, shrimp & white cheddar, Philly steak and smoked salmon sandwiches along with cobb, Caesar and seafood salads tossed tableside $5.50-11.50. Dinner appetizers offer crab cakes, escargot or chilled oysters $9.75-12.50 with a la carte entrees of bouillabaisse, sauteed prawns & scallops, rack of lamb, steaks and fresh fish including their popular opakapaka with artichoke hearts and shiitake mushrooms $24-29. COMMENTS: Lunch dress code requires swimsuit coverup and, in the evening, dress shirts or jackets for men. No denim. The restaurant is located on a promontory overlooking the ocean offering a scenic panorama. A pianist in the adjoining lounge adds to the idyllic setting with romantic music. Extensive wine list with traditional fine dining menu. In the past, the food and service have been superb. After several changes in ownership and status over the last few years, both food and service had become inconsistent. Things seem to have settled down and we look forward to returning to this very special restaurant.

THE GARDEN RESTAURANT ★ *Continental (Hawaiian Influence)*
Kapalua Bay Resort Hotel (669-5656) HOURS: 6-9pm. SAMPLING: Appetizers of dim sum, seafood sampler, coconut smoked ahi, wok-roasted clams, sea scallops on avocado cake $9.75-14.75. Soups and salads including Kona lobster $5.75-18.75. Entrees feature Oriental-style mahi mahi, macadamia nut lamb, vegetable curry, pesto linguine with scallops, chicken with sugar cane, rum & papaya and wild boar wok. Their prix fixe dinner runs $39; $53 with selected wines. COMMENTS: Sunday Brunch Buffet 9:30am-1:30pm. Adults $24.95/$29.95 w/ champagne; children $1.50 per year. Arrive early or late (9:30-10 or 12-12:30) and pay $20.95/$25.95 w/champagne. Friday Seafood Buffet and Saturday Oriental Buffet 5:30-9:30pm run $26.95, Early Bird 5:30-6pm $21.95. Reservations recommended. Excellent food in a lovely dining room surrounded by ponds, hanging vines and a "waterfall" wall.

THE PLANTATION HOUSE ★ *Seafood-Continental*
2000 Plantation Club Drive, Kapalua (669-6299) HOURS: Breakfast/lunch 8am-3pm; dinner 6-10pm. SAMPLING: The breakfast/lunch menu offers either fare until 3pm. Eggs Benedict varieties with spinach, sausage, seared ahi, crab cake or smoked salmon plus omelettes, fruit, Mueselix and French toast $3-10. Burgers, chicken, tuna melt, reuben and club sandwiches and cobb, Caesar, shrimp, goat cheese and papaya shrimp boat salads $6.50-8. Dinners start with curried spinach potstickers, wonton Napoleon, scampi or honey-guava scallops $6-9. Entrees include several fresh fish preparations, sauteed prawns, pork chops, duck "under the influence," filet mignon, pepper-crusted NY steak and lamb chops $21-24. Pasta is $16-21. Additional appetizer and entree specials nightly. COMMENTS: The food is great and complimented by what is, no doubt, the best ocean view dining location in West Maui. Located in the clubhouse of the Plantation Golf Course, the management is well experienced with the dining scene on Maui. This restaurant is affiliated with the popular Koho Grill & Bar in Kahului and Napili and SeaWatch in Wailea. If you have a sweet tooth, don't miss the "Brownie to Da Max." It is sure to become the Hula Pie of the '90s. It is served in a huge dish and it is plenty big enough for two to enjoy. Plan to come a half hour or so before sunset to experience the view.

ROY'S KAHANA BAR AND GRILL ★ *Pacific Rim Cuisine*
4405 Honoapiilani Hwy., Kahana Gateway (669-6999) HOURS: Nightly from 6:30pm. SAMPLING: The menu specials changes nightly, so we really can't tell you what to expect! (Roy's always has individual pizzas made with Portuguese sausage & Maui onions, Chinese BBQ duck, bacon & tomato and grilled vegetable $5.95-7.50). Specials might include pork & beef lumpia, carmelized apple and walnut pizza, shrimp won tons, mushroom & shrimp risotto or green apple salad with pecans and bacon $5.50-8.75 or entrees like macadamia seared mahi, roasted chicken with cornbread stuffing and hoisin grilled ribs $17.50-25.50. All entrees are a la carte. For dessert, Roy's dark chocolate souffle is a must $6.50. COMMENTS: The food is as good as you've heard and Roy's is certainly deserving of it's many rave reviews and awards. He is one of the top chef's in the islands that have made Hawaiian Regional Cuisine (HRC) a trend of the 90's. However, the noise from the kitchen combined with the high ceilings make it difficult to carry on a conversation. With its consistently good cuisine, you'll never know what celebrity might be dropping by. Roy's Nicolina Restaurant is located next door and offers a different twist on nightly specials. The permanent menu is the same for both so check the listing below for appetizer and entree samplings. Roy's is planning to open in Kihei by 1997.

ROY'S NICOLINA ★ *Euro-Asian-Hawaiian Regional*
Kahana Gateway, 4405 Honoapiilani Hwy. (669-5000) HOURS: 5:30-9:30pm SAMPLING: Dim sum & appetizers offer potstickers, hibachi salmon, Thai lemongrass calamari, chow mein shrimp sticks, mushroom ravioli and carmelized onions & walnut tart $6.50-8.95. Flatbreads are a specialty and feature spinach ricotta, ginger chicken, spicy pineapple & cheddar and teri short ribs $5.95-7.50. Entrees include Chinese duck, seafood stir-fry and shrimp penne pasta $16.50-17.95 The menu here changes nightly based on what foods are the freshest available. One night's offerings might include duck quesadilla, shrimp toast, sour

cream & potato flatbread or parmesan eggplant and spinach salad to start $5.95-8.95, then lemongrass seared shutome with Thai peanut sauce, fajita beef linguine, spinach & blue cheese pork chops and sherry brown sugar mahi $19.95-24.75. COMMENTS: Named after Roy and Janne Yamaguchi's daughter, Nicole, this sister restaurant to Roy's is located right next door and has become just as popular in its own right. Much on the permanent menu is also on Roy's menu, but the flatbreads are an original creation and the nightly specials are different.

THE TERRACE ★ *Pacific Rim Cuisine*
The Ritz-Carlton, Kapalua HOURS: Breakfast 6:30-11:30am, dinner 5:30-10pm. SAMPLING: Breakfast buffet until 10:30 $12/17.50. A la carte items and full American, Japanese and Hawaiian breakfasts $5-15. Dinner appetizers include Peking duck quesadilla, Thai BBQ prawns, seared scallops and jasmine rice risotto $9-14.50. Grilled ahi, Asian chicken and Caesar salads or sirloin burger, chicken and smoked turkey sandwiches for a light meal $8-14. Entrees at $23.50 for chow mein noodles with clams and sea scallops, spicy shrimp pizza $16, crispy Chinese duck $23, or steamed snapper in ti leaves $27. Pineapple creme brulee, chocolate marquise and warm banana tart are a few of the desserts $7.50. They offer a series of themed buffets with hot dozens each of hot and cold items and a selection of desserts. There's Asian on Mon., Italian on Wed., seafood on Fri. and Paniolo on Sat., all $29. A little pricey, but the food is excellent and there's plenty of it! COMMENTS: Overlooking the courtyard and pool area. A very pleasant, informal atmosphere with sunset views.

KIHEI

INEXPENSIVE

ALEXANDER'S FISH, CHICKEN AND RIBS ★ *American*
1913 S. Kihei Rd. (874-0788) HOURS: 11am-9pm daily. SAMPLING: Meals $5.95-10.95. Mahi, oysters, calamari, clams, chicken, ono, and shrimp. Fish available by the piece. A la carte items include zucchini sticks, cornbread, french fries, rice, coleslaw and onion rings. Broiled items, too: shrimp, ono or chicken sandwich. They also have BBQ ribs. COMMENTS: They do a great job with basic fish and with some of the more unusual offerings as well. The oysters (like owner Don) were brought in from Puget Sound and they were fresh and tasty. The calamari was tender, not chewy and the fresh fish really was. Limited seating at the counter or at a few patio tables. (Or take out and have a picnic at the beach across the street!)

AROMA D'ITALIA ★ *Italian*
Island Surf Building, 1993 S. Kihei Rd./Auhana St. side (879-0133) HOURS: Lunch Mon-Fri 11:30am-2pm, dinner Mon-Sat 5-9pm. Closed Sunday. SAMPLING: Spaghetti, lasagna, cold pasta, Caesar salads and torpedo sandwiches including cold cuts, sausage, meatball, eggplant, hot pastrami, chicken parmigiana, veggie and prosciutto $4.50-9.50. Dinners offer several choices of spaghetti, ravioli and lasagna dishes as well as scampi, chicken or eggplant parmigiana $6.50-12.95. Tiramisu and freshly made cannoli for dessert $3.50-4.50. COMMENTS: They do not take credit cards and cannot serve liquor, but you can bring your own beer or wine and they'll provide the glasses. Dishes are made from scratch using owner Marie Akina's family recipes. Ample portions, flavorful sauces. A great and affordable dining option! An old-fashioned home-style restaurant that has a lot of aloha - even if it *is* Italian!

BOOMERS *American*
Kihei Gateway Plaza (875-8472) HOURS: 7am-8pm. SAMPLING: Boomer burgers and Boomer dogs, along with chicken, fish, reuben and cheese steak sandwiches $2.60-4.75. Tacos and burritos, plate lunches, deli sandwiches, and breakfast burritos and egg sandwiches $2.25-5.95. Pastries, quiche and Tongan pie $1.50-3.95. COMMENTS: Located in an area removed from the tourist traffic, this place probably appeals most to local residents. It is a self-service restaurant with a few tables. Nothing particularly inspired (except the prices), but if you've a family to feed or a budget to keep and want something other than McDonald's, stop by.

CASEY'S BAKEHOUSE ★ *Bakery/light lunches*
Kihei Commercial Center (879-7295) HOURS: Mon.-Fri. 7:30am-6pm, Sat. til 5pm., closed Sun. SAMPLING: Lunches all under $5: vegetarian lasagna, Caesar or pasta salads, fresh made hummus and roasted turkey, chicken parmesan or vegetarian sandwiches. Bread recipes come from previous owners (Pikake Bakery) and include Parmesana Tuscana, Maui onion with walnut, red potato with rosemary, Kalamata olive and sundried tomato. Low fat-sugar-honey-apple-

raisin-danish, bear claws, sticky buns, muffins and dried cranberry scones under $2 plus corn flake & coconut ranger cookies, white & chocolate biscotti and KC's secret recipe chocolate chip macadamia nut cookies. Dessert specialties of white chocolate mousse cake with raspberry glaze, mocha cheesecake, white chocolate pound cake, pear tarts, passion pecan pie, chocolate mousse cake or bars and chocolate mac nut tart run from $2.50 per slice, $19 for 8" and up. COMMENTS: You're going to have to look a little harder to find their Kihei location. (From the Piilani Hwy., you turn on Ohukai Rd. and drive behind Gas Express.) Casey A. Logsdon is the owner; this recent venture with his own bakery is the result of many award-winning years as pastry chef at Roy's (making chocolate souffle), Kapalua Bay Hotel and Four Seasons.

COCONUTS BAKERY & CAFE *Pastries/light meals*
1819 South Kihei Rd. in Kukui Mall (879-0261) HOURS: Sun.-Thurs. 7am-8pm., Fri. & Sat. until 9pm. COMMENTS: New owners really improved the variety and quality of this bakery. The emphasis is on the use of fresh island fruits in their muffins and pastries, also breads and cakes. A box lunch includes a sandwich, chips and a cookie for $4.95. They plan on adding a small deli soon.

(THE) COFFEE STORE *Coffee/pastries/light meals*
Azeka's Place II, 1279 S. Kihei Rd. (875-4244) HOURS: 6am-10pm. Coffee drinks, with a few unusual selections including a banana mocha cooler or an Electric Brown Cow! Also quiche, muffins, scones, salads, veggie lasagna, quesadillas, garden burger, panini or croissant sandwiches $1.95-8.50.

DENNY'S *American*
Kamaole Shopping Center (879-0604) HOURS: Open 24 hours. SAMPLING: Traditional Denny's burgers, sandwiches, salads and dinners plus island favorites like saimin, mahi sandwich, spam & eggs, local-style plate lunches and a new dessert special: macadamia nut caramel cream cheese pie. Fresh catch dinner includes soup or salad, potato, vegetable and rolls for $11.95. Prices from $4 (pancakes) to $12.75 (prime rib). Breakfast served anytime. Senior specials available. COMMENTS: The most unusual aspect of this Denny's is Gator's Good Times Tavern and the most unusual aspect of Gator's is its unique (and that's putting it mildly!) menu. The jalapeno poppers and made-to order hot potato chips are certainly interesting, but if you're game you can have a Skippy Burger with 5 oz. ground Roo (yes, it's what you think) or a Bar-B-Gator Sandwich (it, too, is what you think, smoked and spiced) both come on a grilled sweet bread bun for $6.75. You can also order a big bowl of gator gumbo for $4.75. Gator's is a sports bar that serves wine, beer and liquor from 8am to midnight and features pool tables, dart machines, foos ball, juke box and NTN Satellite trivia hook up. . . .not to mention gator and roo. (Actually gator is common, especially in New Orleans. It's grainy texture is like beef if it were white meat!)

DINA'S SAND WITCH *American*
145 North Kihei Rd., by Sugar Beach Condos (879-3262) HOURS: 11am-11pm. SAMPLING: Turkey, roast beef, club, reuben, spam and hoagie sandwiches $3.50-6.95, burrito, hot dogs, saimin, nachos, potato skins, salads $4.50-6.25.

HENRY'S BAR AND GRILL   *American*
Lipoa Shopping Center (879-2849) HOURS: 10am-1am. SAMPLING: Limited menu: chicken wings, BBQ beef, hamburgers and peel & eat shrimp $1.50-5.50. COMMENTS: A satellite with four televisions, one a big screen, for sporting events or your favorite soap opera. Dancing Wednesday-Friday.

HIROHACHI   *Japanese*
Kihei Town Center, 1881 South Kihei Rd.(875-7474) HOURS: Lunch 12-3pm; Dinner 5:30-10:30pm. Closed all day Tuesday, for lunch Sat.-Sun. SAMPLING: Set menu for lunch includes oyako Don, chicken katsu don, ten don, una don and tonkatsu or tempura teishoku $8.50-16. A variety of soba and udon noodle dishes $10.50-15.50. Dinners feature a variety of sashimi, sushi and sushi combinations from $3.75 to $28.50 for one. Vegetable and seafood rolls $4-13.50. Set dinner menu offers chicken or pork cutlet and sashimi or tempura assortments $15-28. COMMENTS: A large selection of sushi and sashimi.

INTERNATIONAL HOUSE OF PANCAKES   *American*
Azeka's Place Shopping Center on South Kihei Rd. (879-3445) HOURS: Sunday-Thursday 6am-10pm, Friday and Saturday 6am-midnight. SAMPLING: Breakfast, lunch, and dinner choices served anytime. The usual breakfast fare and sandwiches from $5. "Homestyle" dinners run from $12 and include soup or salad, roll and butter. COMMENTS: Children's menu. Crowded on weekends!

ISANA   *Yakiniku/Sushi*
Maui Isana Resort, 515 So. Kihei Rd. (874-5700) HOURS: Breakfast, lunch and dinner. SAMPLING/COMMENTS: Scheduled to open summer 1996 by the owners of Chun's Korean Barbecue in Lahaina. No details as we go to press except that they offer Korean BBQ items like Chun's plus yakinku-style cooking (at your table) and a sushi bar. Cocktails upstairs at the Karaoke Bar. Shuttle service for all major hotels and resorts.

KAIPUNI   *Japanese*
Lipoa Center, 41 East Lipoa St. (879-3854) HOURS: Mon.-Fri. 11am-9pm; Sat. 12-8pm. Closed Sun. SAMPLING: Sushi, noodles, Kushikatsu $2.75-8.75; tempura, Kaipuna plate $5.45-8.95, limited sandwiches and salads $3.50-4.75.

KAL BI HOUSE   *Korean*
1215 S. Kihei Rd., near Longs Drugs (874-8454) HOURS: Mon.-Sat. 9am-9pm. SAMPLING: Same menu for lunch and dinner with slightly lower lunch prices. Plate lunch special $6.25 served until 2pm. House special $8.50. Order mixed plate combination meals or separate entrees of BBQ short ribs, fried mandoo dumpling, Bi Beem Bap (Great name! It's rice, vegetables, chopped BBQ and fried eggs), hot spicy chicken, chicken katsu or fried oysters. Stews and soups include some more exotic selections including kim chee, small intestine or cuttle fish stew, seaweed soup and rice or Duk Man Doo Kook $6.74-7.99. (Editors note: These weird words just drive our computer spell-check system nuts!) COMMENTS: Recent renovations have added Oriental murals and rugs, Chinese fish bowl planters, Shoji screens and antique fans. All this and Korean music in the background!

KIHEI CAFFE   *Continental*
1945 S. Kihei Rd. (879-2230) HOURS: Breakfast 5am-2pm, Sun. til noon; lunch til 2:30pm. SAMPLING: Breakfast includes biscuits and gravy, cinnamon-raisin French toast, flavored pancakes, muesli and omelettes $3.95-6.50. Lunch selections range from couscous, tabouli, Greek and honey cashew chicken salads to tempeh burger, hot pastrami, mahi taco, kalua pig or foot long hot dog $4.95-6.95. COMMENTS: A popular restaurant for locals to hang out that visitors have begun discovering as well. Coffee drinks and fresh baked goods made daily. Picnic baskets with sandwiches, drinks, chips, fruit and cookies from $10.

MAUI TACOS   *Healthy Mexican*
Kamaole Beach Center (879-5005) HOURS: 10am-9pm. SAMPLING: Potato enchiladas, hard or soft tacos, quesadillas, chimichangas and over a dozen varieties of special hand-held burritos $1.99-6.95. COMMENTS: Guacamole and salsa made fresh every day. No lard, no msg - they use only vegetable oil, fresh beans and lean meats. The complimentary salsa bar offers several choices with jalapenos, onions, cilantro, hot sauce and more. Good values! The original is in Napili Plaza with other outlets now in Lahaina Square and Kaahumanu Food Court, all owned and operated by Mark Ellman of Avalon.

NEW YORK DELI   *American*
2395 S. Kihei Rd. (879-1115) HOURS: 8am-9pm; til 3am in the summer! SAMPLING: Tuna, roast beef, meatball or chicken parmesan hero, meatloaf, reuben, hot pastrami or corned beef sandwiches $5.75-5.95. Chef or Caesar salads, shrimp pasta, potato knishes and a variety of bagels $2.50-7.95. COMMENTS: Coffee drinks, Italian Cream Sodas and New York Egg Creams to help wash down the Manhattan cuisine. They also do catering.

OASIS POOL BAR   *American*
Maui Coast Hotel, 2259 S. Kihei Rd. (879-6284) HOURS: 11am-10pm. SAMPLING: Sashimi, calamari, chicken wings, Caesar or Polynesian salad, chili, fish & chips, burgers, tuna pita, club, chicken or fish sandwiches $4.20-8.40. Smoothies $3.75 COMMENTS: Family-owned and operated. Daily drink specials and live Hawaiian and contemporary entertainment nightly.

PAIR O' DICE   *Italian*
Kukui Mall, 1819 South Kihei Rd. (874-1968) HOURS: Mon.-Thurs 11am-9pm, Fri. & Sat. until 10pm, Sun. noon-9pm. SAMPLING: A hearty array of over 30 toppings can be enjoyed on whole wheat and thin or thick crust. Also available are entrees such as calzone, vegetarian lasagna or chicken parmesan. Pizza available in 12" size, beginning at $8.99, and large, 16", beginning at $11.99 or by the slice. COMMENTS: Pair O' Dice is the first we've seen that offers soy cheese as a topping alternative! This is a REALLY nice addition to the topping choices and is sure to be appreciated by anyone with sensitivity or allergies to dairy products. And those of you with family members that can't tolerate dairy no longer have to avoid pizza! (Oh yeah, we like the name too!)

PANDA EXPRESS   *Mandarin Chinese*
At Azeka Place II Shopping Center. HOURS: Daily 10:30am-9pm. SAMPLING:

Combination plates $3.99-7.99 for choice of 1-3 a la carte items (e.g. orange chicken, chop suey, sweet & sour pork) $3.79-8.49 each. Chef's specials: BBQ chicken, eggplant in garlic, Szechuan bean curd $3.79-8.49. COMMENTS: A chain of restaurants started in California. Also at the Kaahumanu Food Court.

PEGGY SUE'S   *Burgers And Such*
Azeka Place II, 1279 S. Kihei Rd. (875-8944) HOURS: Sun.-Thurs. 10am-9pm, til 10 Fri. & Sat. SAMPLING: The menu reflects the 50's diner/malt shop theme with sandwiches, burgers and hot dogs served with "the works" and a side of fries. Go for a Good Golly Miss Molly (teriyaki burger with pineapple), Earth Angel (garden burger), Bee-Bop a Lula (avocado burger) or La Bamba (guacamole burger) $5.95-6.95. Try a Sea Cruise (tuna), Splish Splash (mahi) or Funky Chicken sandwich or an avocado, Caesar or chicken salad $5.95-9.95. Ain't Nothing but a Hound Dog is priced at $4.95 and other Hot Diggity Dogs run $2.95-5.55. COMMENTS: They feature an original 1954 Seeburg juke box that operates from the box or by remote from the dining tables. Owners David and Cathy Tarbox relied on David's former occupation as a 1950's soda jerk in planning and decorating their restaurant and it looks like they had a great time doing it! The pink and blue decor gives the malt shop a suitable "Peggy Sue" look and there are plenty of cool, creamy selections including malts, milkshakes, egg creams, phosphates, sundaes and banana splits to keep the 50's tradition alive in the 90's.

PIZZA FRESH   *Italian*
2395 S. Kihei Rd. in Dolphin Plaza (879-1525) HOURS: Daily 3-9pm. SAMPLING: White or whole wheat crust pizza that they make and you bake. Available in four sizes, small to X-large and 50 toppings from which to choose $6.95-25.95. Also large salad $5.95, calzones $10.95 and cheesecake. COMMENTS: New options include sun-dried tomatoes and Alfredo sauce. Second outlet in Makawao. They also deliver!

ROYAL THAI CUISINE   *Thai*
1280 S. Kihei Rd. at Azeka's Shopping Center (874-0813) HOURS: Mon.-Fri. 11-3pm for lunch, daily 5-9pm for dinner. SAMPLING: Appetizers, soups, salads and entrees such as chicken cashew basil, Evil Prince chicken or garlic cabbage $4.50-8.25. COMMENTS: The prices are pretty decent, but the portions are a little small. Food was good, but nothing outstanding.

SHAKA SANDWICH AND PIZZA ★   *American-Italian*
Located behind Jack 'n the Box in Paradise Plaza on South Kihei Rd. across from Star Market (874-0331) HOURS: 10:30am-9pm. SAMPLING: Hot Philadelphia cheese steak sandwiches served with or without fried onions in small or large portions, cold hoagies $3.50-7.00. All sandwiches are served on their homemade Italian bread that has been a recipe passed down in the family for years. Pizza available in thin crust or thick square Sicilian pies. COMMENTS: If you like New York subway-style pizza you're in for a real treat. If you have no idea what New York subway-style pizza is, you're also in for a real treat. Their gourmet white cheese pizza with garlic and broccoli is outstanding. Don't miss stopping by for a piece of the pie!

SIGNATURES BREW PUB   *Burgers & Pizza*
41 East Lipoa (879-9001). HOURS: Nightly 4pm-1am. SAMPLING: "Upscale" burgers and pizza. Micro brewery and cigar bar. DEADLINE UPDATE! Not open as we go to press, but the name has changed to Hapa*s Brew Haus.

THE SPORTS PAGE GRILL AND BAR   *American*
2411 S. Kihei Rd. (879-0602) HOURS: 11am-midnight. SAMPLING: Portland Blazers Reuben, Utah Jazz Ham and Cheese, Robby Naish Tuna Salad, Pete Rose BLT (Bet, Lose, Trial), or Joe Montana Chicken Salad. COMMENTS: Got the idea? This is definitely the spot for the sports aficionados. With confident good humor their menu resembles a newspaper tabloid and reads, "You will be served in 5 minutes...or maybe 10 minutes...or maybe even 15 minutes...relax and enjoy yourself." It may take at least 15 minutes to read over the menu. The front page covers exotic beverages and a hearty selection of imported beers, followed on the inside by dugout dogs, champion burgers, sport fishing sandwiches, bowl games (otherwise known as salads), and "game favorite" sandwiches. Not much on the menu over $7.95. A big screen TV with remote monitors and satellite reception should ensure plenty of good conversation for the athletic enthusiast!

SUB STOP   *Subs and Salads*
Rainbow Mall, 2439 S. Kihei Rd (875-7782) HOURS: 8am-9pm. SAMPLING: Grilled chicken Caesar, Asian chicken, Wailea cobb, rotini pasta salads $2.69-5.29. Turkey, veggie, pastrami, cheesesteak, seafood and BBQ beef are among the sub choices available in single or double sizes $3.69-9.79. COMMENTS: Before he left the island, former Maui Prince and Hawaiian Regional Cuisine chef Roger Dikon bequeathed the owners with recipes for the Italian Combo, Combo Stop, Club Stop and Super Stopper - all loaded with extra meats.

SUDA SNACK SHOP   *Local Style*
61 S. Kihei Rd. by the gas station along S. Kihei Rd. (879-2668) HOURS: 6am-12:30pm (Closed Sunday). SAMPLING: Burgers $1.65-2.40, hot dogs $1.20-1.60, saimin $2.25-2.50, chow fun $2.50, bentos $3.75. COMMENTS: We were disappointed that this little "dive" wasn't one of the island's best kept secrets. The burgers were so-so, the french fries were pricey for the portion and the chow fun wasn't a meal, it was snack size. See you in Wailuku!

SURFER'S BAR & GRILL   *American*
61 South Kihei Rd., next to Suda's Store in Kihei. (879-8855) HOURS: Bar open noon-1:30am, food served noon-10pm. SAMPLING: Medium and large pizzas $10.95-18.95 or $2-3 a slice; buffalo wings, calamari, jalapeno poppers, onion rings, steak strips with mushroom and onion or calamari pupus $3.50-7.95. Surfer or Kowabunga burger, Kimboarder chicken, Hang Ten ahi, Big Kahuna turkey or Hookipa cheese & avocado sandwiches $4.95-7.50 and honey mustard baby back ribs, teri steak or chicken, roast pork with gravy and fresh fish $7.50-10.95. COMMENTS: A small, funky bar. Booth and patio seating; indoor and outdoor pool tables. Food to go. No personal checks or credit cards, dude.

SUSHI PARADISE   *Sushi/Sashimi*
1215 South Kihei Rd., Longs Drugs Kihei Center(879-3751) HOURS: Tues.-Sun.

6-9pm; closed Monday. SAMPLING: Sushi and sushi rolls $3-7.50; sushi or sashimi combinations, rainbow roll $15-25; dynamite or udon $6.75; sunomono salad $7.50. COMMENTS: Domestic and Japanese beer, hot and cold sake. Karaoke til 1am.

THAI CHEF   *Thai*
Rainbow Mall, 2439 S. Kihei Rd. HOURS: Lunch 11am-3pm; Mon.-Fri., dinner nightly 5-10pm. SAMPLING: Same menu as their Lahaina location with entrees such as Thai crisp noodles, sateh, green papaya salad and garlic squid $6.95-13.95. COMMENTS: A very lengthy menu ranging from noodle dishes to salads, seafoods, vegetarian fare and curry dishes. Entrees available in mild, medium or hot! Prices slightly higher than their original location in the Lahaina.

TOBI'S ICE CREAM AND SHAVE ICE   *American-local*
1913 South Kihei Rd. (879-7294) HOURS: 10am-7pm. SAMPLING: Garden burgers, sandwiches, chili dogs and Roselani Ice Cream $1.50-5.00. Also homemade ice cream pies, smoothies and frozen bananas. COMMENTS: This started as a family operation: the store was built by Tobi's father and run by Tobi and her mon, Puddie. It features an old woody surfboard that has been made into a table. New owner Mike took over from Tobi in December of '95 and plans to keep things as they were. It's the same menu and the same prices except he's upped the ante on the shave ice flavors - from 27 to 40! No credit cards.

MODERATE

BUZZ'S WHARF   *American-Seafood*
Maalaea Harbor (244-5426) HOURS: Lunch 11am-3pm; Dinner 5-9pm. SAMPLING: Lunches start with escargot, calamari, oysters, clams or artichoke plus Maui onion soup and assorted salads $4.95-9.95. Sandwiches, burgers, a variety of fresh catch preparations and teri steak or chicken, BBQ ribs, and prawns Tahitian $5.95-16.95. Dinner menu offers the same appetizers as lunch and for the same prices! In addition to the lunch entrees, dinners include oriental fried shrimp, scampi, scallops provencal, prime rib, NY steak and Chicken Pineapple Hill served in a pineapple boat $15.95-24.95. Baked papaya Tahitian, mud pie and Maui lime pie are the homemade desserts for $4.95. Entrees are served with salad, vegetables and bread. COMMENTS: Offers a scenic view of the Maalaea harbor activities. Sister restaurant to Kapalua's Pineapple Hill. Bar/lounge. Vegetarian entrees and a full page keiki menu. Try their specialty, Prawns Tahitian.

CANTON CHEF   *Cantonese-Szechuan*
Kamaole Shopping Center (879-1988) HOURS: Lunch 11-2pm and dinner 5-9pm. SAMPLING: Vegetable, chicken, beef, duck, seafood and pork dishes $6-12.

CHUCK'S   *American*
Kihei Town Center (879-4488 or 879-4489) HOURS: Lunch 11am-2:30pm and interim menu 2:30-5pm both served Mon.-Sat. Dinner nightly 5-10pm. SAMPLING: Lunch salads include taco or Caesar and sandwiches feature turkey, fish, French dip and burgers $4.95-9.95. or you can order a plate lunch, chicken-fried

steak or fresh fish $5.75-10.95. Dinner selections include rice or baked potato or fries and salad bar with homebaked seasoned bread. Steaks, prime rib, kalbi ribs, seafood brochette, pasta primavera, cajun mahi and shrimp $12.95-24.95. If you're still hungry, escargot, smoked marlin, cheese-stuffed jalapeno peppers and several preparations of shrimp are available as appetizers $4.95-7.25 or you can hold out for mud pie, hula pie, thunder cake, lemon coconut cake or hot apple pie $3.50-4.75. COMMENTS: Especially popular for its salad bar which is also available all day starting at $6.95. Pretty fair selection with eighteen items and six dressings. Early bird specials 5-6:30pm for $9.95. Children's menu.

FIVE PALMS BEACH GRILLE
Mana Kai Resort, 2960 S. Kihei Rd. (879-2607). We called the new owners repeatedly and they never did send us any information. It's too bad as this is one of Kihei's nicest beachfront dining locations.

FRESH ISLAND FISH   *American-Seafood*
Maalaea Harbor (244-9633) HOURS: 10am-4pm Mon.-Sat. SAMPLING: Menu changes daily. COMMENTS: This restaurant/seafood market is expensive for what you get. Better seafood dining can be found elsewhere.

GREEK BISTRO ★   *Greek*
Kai Nani Shopping Center, 2511 South Kihei Rd. (879-9330) HOURS: Dinner served 5-9:30pm. SAMPLING: Stuffed grape leaves, pita with tzaiziki, sauteed mushrooms, Greek salad $5.95-7.95. Lamb gyros, moussaka, pastichio and spanakopita served a la carte $12.95-14.95 or in combination in the Feast of the Gods platter for $16.95. Mediterranean specialties are served with vegetables and starch: prawns & scallops sauteed or in casserole, chicken or lamb souvlakia, steak, lamb chops, lamb kabobs or The Taste of Greece combination plate $14.95-21.95. Cheesecake or baklava for dessert $4. COMMENTS: This little restaurant is a delightful surprise. The Feast of the Gods is excellent and definitely the way to try a little of everything. Renovations have added some classic touches of wood to the bar and around the patio area giving this little garden hideaway the look of a quaint, but elegant European hotel. The seating has also been expanded. Check this one out!

HAMILTON'S BEACH CAFE   *Italian*
760 S. Kihei Rd., at the Menehune Shores Condominiums (879-6399) HOURS: Mon.-Sat. Breakfast 7am-noon; lunch 12-4pm; dinner 4-10pm. SAMPLING: Breakfast specials are "stuffed" French toast, sunrise sandwich, banana mac pancakes, sticky mac nut cinnamon roll and Spanish omelette $2.50-7.25. Lunch sandwiches are pastrami, teri chicken, burgers, mahi and macadamia nut smoked turkey and cheese $5.95-7.95 plus soups and salads. Dinners start with Italian nachos, hot wings or pizzas $4.95-6.95; spaghetti and linguini dishes come with marinara, clam, Alfredo or mizithra sauce $5.25-7.95. Entrees include veal and wild mushroom meatloaf, stuffed scampi, chicken Alfredo, mahi and steak $9.95-16.95. COMMENTS: Keiki spaghetti for $2.95. One of only a handful of island restaurants located right on the beach. The area in front of this resort complex was an ancient Hawaiian fish pond.

KAMAOLE BAR AND GRILL   *American-Sushi Bar*
Maui Coast Hotel, 2259 S. Kihei Rd. (874-6284) HOURS: 7am-10pm, Breakfast til 11am. Pupu Buffet 4-6pm Thurs-Sat; Sushi Bar 5-10pm (Closed Mondays) SAMPLING: Egg dishes, omelettes, banana-macadamia pancakes, sweetbread French toast and Japanese breakfast $5.25-11.95. Cobb, macadamia chicken, warm spinach, prawn or Caesar salads $5.95-9.95; Kalua pork quesadilla, crab won tons, fried calamari and spicy chicken wings $5.95-7.95. A good variety of sandwiches including Kalua pork, Philly cheesesteak, hot crab melt, Maui Coast club (with Portuguese sausage and turkey) and fresh ahi $5.95-9.95. Entrees are served after 4pm: Pork chops, garlic or spicy prawns, seafood fettucini or lasagna, stuffed chicken, scallops, grilled flank steak and pasta primavera $8.95-16.95. COMMENTS: The afternoon pupu buffet changes each week, but might include items like crab won tons, egg rolls, pot stickers, rolled sandwiches, stuffed jalapeno and veggie platter -- a great all-you-can-eat value for $5.95. The new sushi bar has it's own happy hour with selected sushi for $10 from 5-6:30.

KAI KU ONO BAR & GRILL   *Sandwiches & Pupus*
2511 S. Kihei Rd., at Kai Nani Village (875-1007) HOURS: Mon.-Wed. 11:30 am-midnight; from 4pm Mon.-Tues., Closed Sun., Lounge open til 1am. SAMPLING: All-day menu includes tuna melt, fresh fish, grilled chicken, reuben, BBQ beef and French dip sandwiches plus burgers, baby back ribs, fried chicken and pizzas $6.50-13.95. For pupus there are buffalo wings, oyster shooters, jalapeno poppers, BBQ baked beans, chili fries, onion rings, salad, shrimp basket veggie plate and fried zucchini or cheese sticks $3.50-5.95. COMMENTS: Pizzas are made with a fresh basil and garlic crust: the seafood pesto is a good choice. Pool tables, darts, games and big screen TV. Formerly La Bahia ("The Bay"), Kai Ku Ono means the same in Hawaiian.

LONE STAR COOKHOUSE   *BBQ/Smoked Meats*
1913 S. Kihei Rd. (875-2838) HOURS: 11am-midnight, dinner served 5-10pm. SAMPLING: Smoked BBQ plates of sausage, beef brisket, chicken, turkey legs, beef ribs with one, two or three meats and salad, corn on the cob, jalapeno corn muffin and ranch beans $8.95-11.95. Smoked beef brisket, sausage or chipped chicken sandwiches; baked potatoes with BBQ beef or BBQ chicken $4.95-6.95. Dinners come with coleslaw, potatoes and jalapeno muffin. Choices are: chicken fried steak, pork chops and charbroiled steaks $11.95-21.95. COMMENTS: Their meats are seasoned and slow-cooked for 16 hours in custom-built hardwood smokers; orders of ranch style beans are all-you-can-eat. Catering and take-out orders, too.

MARGARITA'S BEACH CANTINA   *Mexican*
101 N. Kihei Rd., Kealia Village (879-5275) HOURS: Food service 11:30am-10pm, bar open til midnight. SAMPLING: Quesadillas, nachos, shrimp brochette, taco or chicken salad, tostada $4.95-8.95. Burgers and sandwiches $6.95-8.95. Combination plates of enchiladas, tacos, chili relleno, tamales and tostadas $8.95-13.95. Specials include chimichanga, carnitas, steak tacos and fajitas $6.95-14.95. COMMENTS: Outdoor dining on their oceanview deck. Margaritas come in tropical flavors like mango, pineapple, guava, banana and coconut. Daily happy hour from 2:30-5:30pm has regular ones for $1. Bar features satellite TV

and electronic dart boards. Try their new pupu, fried pickles! They're cool and
crisp inside and coated with hot, crunchy dill breading on the outside.

RADIO CAIRO   *African*
2439 S. Kihei Rd., Suite 20-A, (879-4404) HOURS: Dinner 4-11pm; bar til 2am.
SAMPLING: Start with Negombo (fried whitebait with aioli & pepper sauce),
Marrakech Tik Dip (peas, beans & spices) or Sosaties (skewered lamb in spicy
apricot sauce) $6.95-7.75. Then try a salad from Morocco (orange, dates and
almonds) or Ceylon (banana, coconut, honey and lemon), some Mombassa
aromatic rice with coconut sambal, Couscous or Ujiji spiced cabbage $2.50-6.50.
The unusual and innovative entrees include Chicken Zambezia with coconut
sauce, Coco Verde Chicken with garlic, cashew, pine nut and coconut sauce,
Vegetal Ne Dovi (braised vegetables in Nigerian groundnut sauce), spicy
Mozambique prawns, Kenyan irio (potato) with vegetables in onion jungle sauce,
Salmon de Tangiers on a bed of chermoula sauce with Moroccan lemon $12.95-
19.95 or Zanzibar Seafood Hot Pot in an Afro-Portuguese tomato concasse
$23.95. For dessert try the vodoo mud cake served with spears! COMMENTS:
Needless to say, this is not your usual garden-variety jungle cuisine! And if the
samplings sounded intriguing, you'll want to try the Feast of Africa with twelve
courses of different dishes for $29.95 per person -- including Abysinnian coffee.
It's served for four or more, so grab three others who would enjoy a culinary
safari adventure! They offer wines from their private cellar and The Kalahari
Room is available for private dining and special occasions. The Radio Cairo
concept is based on several successful restaurants in Sidney, Australia. Scheduled
to open June, 1996

SILVERSWORD GOLF CLUB RESTAURANT   *American-French*
Located at the Silversword Golf Course (879-0515) HOURS: 11am-4:30pm for
lunch daily. SAMPLING: Roast beef, ham, turkey, tuna, corned beef, reuben,
pastrami, grilled cheese & bacon sandwiches plus hamburgers and soups. Lunch
entrees offer beef stroganoff, shrimp Silversword, mahi mahi, roast pork and beef
curry. All are affordably priced from $4.50-7.50. COMMENTS: Located on a
lofty setting with a pleasant view of Kihei and beyond Kaho'olawe and Molokini.

STELLA BLUES CAFE & DELI   *American*
Long's Center, 1215 S. Kihei Rd. (874-3779) HOURS: Breakfast, 8-11am,
Sunday til 2pm; lunch 11am-9pm, dinner 5-9pm SAMPLING: Breakfast eggs,
tofu scramble, banana macadamia pancakes, lox & bagel "Manhattan" $6.50-
7.75; Caesar or cobb salads and corned beef, eggplant, turkey, tofu and pastrami
melt sandwiches $6.50-7.75. Dinners include crab cakes, eggplant parmesan,
BBQ baby back ribs and fresh catch $11.50-17.95.

TONY ROMA'S   *American-Ribs*
Kukui Mall, 1819 S. Kihei Rd. Formerly Perry's Smorgy (875-6188) HOURS:
lunch 11am-4pm, dinner 4-11pm, til midnight Friday and Saturday. SAMPLING:
For lunch you can order BBQ chicken teriyaki, BBQ shrimp on a skewer, grilled
seafood or sandwiches like hot turkey, grilled sausage, Bayou chicken, cheese
steak or BBQ beef $4.99-10.99. Rib entrees or combos $7.99-12.99; Caesar,
cobb, Oriental chicken or chef salads $5.99-6.99; potato skins,

fried cheese and chicken skins $3.99-4.29. Same salads and appetizers at dinner at slightly higher prices. Baby backs, Carolina honeys, cajun style and bountiful beef ribs from $10.99-13.99; Roma feast, sampler and combos with BBQ shrimp or chicken, grilled mahi, steak and chicken $10.99-14.99. COMMENTS: Dinner menu always available. All BBQ, rib and grill entrees come with coleslaw and choice of baked potato, rice, French fries or ranch beans. Keiki menu available. Tony Roma's began in Florida and they now have locations all over the world. The Maui restaurant has done a nice job with their renovation adapting the previous decor to the brick and dark wood of the Roma's style while incorporating some Hawaiian touches. Separate bar; attractive piano is a focal point.

UKULELE GRILL *Continental-Hawaiian*
Maui Lu Resort, 575 South Kihei Rd. (875-1188) HOURS: Breakfast Mon.-Sat. 7-11am, til noon Sun., dinner 5:30-9pm nightly. Not open for lunch. SAMPLING: Breakfast quesadilla, burrito or pizza, frittata, Belgian waffles, Hawaiian French toast, pancakes, fruit plate, nutty granola parfait, eggs Benedict and saimin $3-9.25. Dinners start with kalua pig quesadilla, crab cakes with papaya salsa, ginger chicken lumpia or ahi poke Napoleon with wonton chips and lemon creme fraiche $5.50-9; Caesar and spinach salads or Maui onion chowder $3.75-5.50. A few of the entrees are orange hoisin BBQ chicken, salmon katsu wrapped in nori, seafood stir-fry, braised & grilled duck combo with sun-dried cherry sauce and grilled sweet miso and chili-marinated tiger prawns $15-22. COMMENTS: This is the newest venture from the Waterfront restaurant's Smith family. They've teamed with Chef Richard Matsumoto (from Raffles and SeaWatch) to bring innovative yet affordable cuisine to the Maui Lu Longhouse. Extensive menu for breakfast including a bottomless pot of coffee on the table. Contemporary and Hawaiian entertainment nightly.

EXPENSIVE

A PACIFIC CAFE-MAUI ★ *Hawaiian Regional Cuisine*
1279 S. Kihei Rd., Azeka Shopping Center (879-0069) HOURS: 5:30-10pm. SAMPLING: Tiger eye sushi tempura, kalua pork potstickers, firecracker salmon roll and shrimp & duck tacos are just a few of the ways to start your meal $7.50-9.75. Thai coconut curry soup (which is to die for), spinach bisque or warm seafood salad run $5.75-9.75. Wood grilled entrees include ahi steak, pork chops, rack of lamb and salmon $19-24 and specialties feature Chinese roasted duck, seared sea scallops, pan-seared mahi and rigatoni with seared beef tenderloin $16-23. After dinner indulgences range from macadamia nut profiteroles to triple chocolate peanut explosion at $6.25. COMMENTS: Jean-Marie Josselin, owner and chef of the highly acclaimed *A Pacific Cafe* in Kauai has also been very successful with this Maui branch. The menu changes regularly to take advantage of the foods as they come into season. They offer two separate dining areas, a wine room which seats up to 25, and an island bar. The tables are trimmed in koa wood with a copper inlay and the blonde rattan chairs are covered in tropical brocade. Lots of tables, but you don't feel crushed. As with their Kauai restaurant, the ceramic plates on which appetizers are presented are one-of-a-kind in varying sizes and shapes designed and hand-made by Chef Josselin's wife, Sophronia. They offer vintner and guest chef dinners once or twice a month.

ANTONIO'S   *Italian*
Longs Center, 1215 S. Kihei Rd. (875-8800) HOURS: Two seatings, 5:30pm, and 8:30pm. Closed Mondays. SAMPLING: Three course dinner $25, five-course dinner with antipasto, pasta, entree, salad and dessert $35. COMMENTS: Antonio features a varying menu of authentic Sicilian style Italian cuisine. You'll enter a little piece of his homeland when you walk through the door. Decor is simple, with bright checkered tablecloths and some amusing memorabilia along the walls. The main table is a long "U" shape with seating aimed at the dinner show, which is Antonio (imagine it as the Benihana of Sicily). Several tables for four are also available. The experience is rather like being invited into the home of a friend, as Antonio's chats and cooks, providing a leisurely dining experience. (Due to the length of the meal, we wouldn't recommend this one for kids.) The food is excellent and seconds are encouraged. No liquor license yet, but customers are welcome to bring their own wine. Antonio's enthusiasm for dining shines through. Eating a great tiramisu still makes his knees shake, but don't tell his mom that he has created some Sicilian recipes besides hers!

CARELLI'S ON THE BEACH   *Italian*
2980 S. Kihei Rd. at the Wailea Oceanfront Hotel (875-0001) HOURS: Dinner only 6-10pm, Rocco's Mangia bar menu until 11pm. SAMPLING: Pastas include fettucini with vegetables, seafood cannelone with two sauces, fresh gnocci, rigatoni, four-cheese ravioli $21-26. Entrees are cioppino, scampi, rack of lamb, filet mignon, veal and island fish $25-33. They also have wood-fired pizzas $13-16. COMMENTS: Menu changes seasonally; they open early (at 5:30) from Oct. 15-Jan. 31. A minimum food charge of $25 per person at the dining tables seems redundant when you look at the prices. Some of the food was worth it (the seared ahi was excellent; there were both Alfredo and marinara sauces on the cannelone and they used homemade sausage and Maui onions on the pizza), but other dishes were average and uninspiring. In any case, you're not really paying for the food as much as the wonderful ocean view and the equally wonderful view (if that's your thing) of the celebrity diners. They do seem to get more of their share of actors, producers, sports figures and directors, possibly because their chef, Lallo Scalera, was a personal chef to Michael and Janet Jackson.

KIHEI PRIME RIB AND SEAFOOD HOUSE ★   *American*
2511 South Kihei Rd., in the Nani Kai Village (879-1954) HOURS: Dinner 5-10pm; early bird specials 5-6pm. SAMPLING: Appetizers include baked artichoke, seared ahi, sauteed mushrooms, smoked salmon and lobster, mushroom & onion casserole $6.95-11.95. Entrees are prime rib, Tahitian prawns, fresh fish, cajun, macadamia or Polynesian chicken, rack of lamb, roasted duck, scallops au gratin, calamari filet, pork chops, steaks and scampi $19.95-24.95. COMMENTS: Dinners are served with fresh baked bread, choice of salad bar, Caesar or Greek salad and pasta or rice. The extensive salad bar has fresh fruit and a bread and cheese station. Their early bird is still one of the best values on the island. Polynesian chicken, prime rib or fresh fish are just $13.95-14.95 with bread, salad and pasta or rice. ($1.50 additional for the salad bar.) The second floor has a good ocean and sunset view. The high-beamed ceilings with the hanging plants compliment the gorgeous wood carvings done by Bruce Turnbull and paintings by a German artist, Sigrid. A long time Kihei favorite.

WATERFRONT ★   *Seafood*
At the Milowai Condo, Maalaea (244-9028) HOURS: Dinner 5-8:30pm. SAM-PLING: Fresh island fish prepared nine uniquely different ways $25-27, or select cioppino, baked prawns Wellington, scallops au gratin, Peking-style duck, veal scalloppine, teriyaki apple chicken, filet Diane or a daily offering of wild game $18.95-26.95. COMMENTS: A family operation, the Smith's have done a consistently excellent job ever since they opened, winning a number of awards and many deserving accolades. Fish preparations are particularly innovative prepared with shrimp, ginger and coconut milk; salsa, avocado and cilantro butter or "En Bastille": imprisoned in angel hair potato with scallions, mushrooms and tomatoes. Dinner entrees are all served with garden salad and a choice of four homemade dressings, vegetables and rice or potatoes. They have a great location to get their fish right off the boat at the Maalaea Harbor. Can't get it much fresher than that!

WAILEA-MAKENA

LOUNGES

BOTERO GALLERY
Grand Wailea Resort. HOURS: noon to midnight. The lobby bar is a beautiful setting and they do offer Hawaiian musical entertainment.

GAME IN THE BAR
Grand Wailea Resort, Spa Grande complex. HOURS: Bar service 6pm-midnight. "English" style Gentleman's Club atmosphere where you can play pool, shuffle-board or sip on a brandy pipe. Library room; cognacs and Davidoff cigar selection available.

GAMES ROOM
Four Season Resort HOURS: 9:30am-11pm. Pizzas, sandwiches, snacks, desserts and other food items available all day from the room service menu. Big screen, video games, table shuffleboard, pool tables and jukebox. Alcohol and smoke-free area on lower level near the health club. Fun for families!

GROTTO BAR
Grand Wailea Resort HOURS: 11-5pm. Dress code *required* here is a swim suit. Set in the midst of waterfalls, rock slides and channels, this is the kind of swim-up bar you've always heard about. They offer a variety of tropical drinks in a volcanic cavern-like setting.

LOBBY BAR AT KEA LANI
Kea Lani Hotel HOURS: 5-11pm, evening piano music 5:30-7:30pm; duo or trio from 8pm. Pupus include shrimp, seared ahi and hibachi kobe beef sashimi-style $15. Lounge overlooks the Pacific Ocean and tropical gardens and features a very different atmosphere with couches and overstuffed chairs.

LOBBY LOUNGE
Four Seasons Resort HOURS: 5pm-midnight; guitar music 8-11pm. Terrace adjoining the lobby overlooks the ocean and West Maui Mountains. Shrimp cocktail, pizza, quesadilla, chicken club, selection of cheeses and desserts run $6.50-15.

MOLOKINI LOUNGE ★
Maui Prince Hotel, Makena (874-1111) COMMENTS: A wonderful opportunity for a sunset view. Pupu menu 5-9:30pm daily, $5-12. Call to check on entertainment available in the lounge or in their lovely outdoor courtyard.

SUNSET TERRACE ★
Renaissance Wailea Beach Resort, on the lobby level (879-4900) HOURS: 5:30-10pm; til 11 Sun.-Mon. Pleasant evening entertainment seven nights a week ranges from contemporary and Hawaiian vocalists to hula. Pupus include chicken yakitori, wok-fried calamari, won tons, potstickers, egg rolls and pizza $5.75-10. Tropical drink menu $6.50.

VOLCANO BAR
Grand Wailea Resort (875-1234) HOURS: Food served 11am-5pm, bar open 10am-6pm. No entertainment. Burgers, hot dogs, nachos, shrimp in pita, tuna or turkey in a tortilla, club and submarine sandwiches and chicken Caesar salad $7-13.50. Keiki menu. Almost two dozen smoothie flavors and tropical fruit drinks.

INEXPENSIVE

BELLA LUNA   *Italian*
Diamond Resort. 555 Kaukahi St., Wailea (879-8255) COMMENTS: Although part of Diamond Resort, Bella Luna is privately owned. We used to like this restaurant on the upper level, but after repeated calls to get information, the owner told us that he didn't "want to bother with this." If giving people information about their restaurant is such a bother, then I guess we can't be bothered to recommend them.

MAKENA GOLF COURSE RESTAURANT   *American*
5415 Makena Alanui. At the Golf Course, just beyond Wailea (879-1154) HOURS: Lunch 10:30am-4pm, pupus 4-6:30pm. SAMPLING: Fruit, cobb, Caesar or chef's salads along with stir-fry, smoked chicken tostada, island curry or reuben, steak, fish or club sandwich $5.50-11.75 COMMENTS: Furnished in a tan and green theme, this open-air restaurant features an outstanding golf and ocean view.

MAUI ONION   *American*
Renaissance Wailea Beach Resort, poolside (879-4900) HOURS: Lunch 11am-6pm, bar open from 10am. SAMPLING: Sandwiches from the deli board or club, tuna melt, mahi or hamburger $6.50-10.75; Caesar, Chinese chicken, shrimp cobb and seared ahi salads $9-12.50. Maui onion rings, gazpacho, chicken & cheese quesadilla, spring rolls $5.25-6.50. Ice cream treats and hula pie $4-4.75. COMMENTS: We always hear great things about their onion rings and (some say Maui's best) burgers! Fashion show Wednesdays 12-1pm.

POLO BEACH GRILLE AND BAR   *American*
Kea Lani Hotel, poolside. (875-4100) HOURS: 11am-7pm. SAMPLING: Luncheon menu offers Chinese chicken, chicken walnut and local tuna salads, grilled chicken or mahi sandwich, croissant with smoked turkey, burgers, Maui onion rings, mango BBQ ribs and sashimi $6.50-13.50. COMMENTS: Bar service from 10:30am. Varied keiki menu $2.50-4.50.

SUB STOP   *Subs and Salads*
Wailea Shopping Village (875-1691) HOURS: 7am-8pm SAMPLING: Grilled chicken Caesar, Asian chicken, Wailea cobb, rotini pasta salads $2.69-5.29. Turkey, veggie, pastrami, cheesesteak, seafood and BBQ beef are among the sub choices available in single or double sizes $3.69-9.79. COMMENTS: Before he left the island, former Maui Prince and Hawaiian Regional Cuisine chef Roger Dikon bequeathed the owners with recipes for the Italian Combo, Combo Stop, Club Stop and Super Stopper - all loaded with extra meats. They also have soup, chili & rice and offer gourmet picnic boxes. This new (May, '96) outlet offers more frozen desserts than their Kihei store. The extra yogurt, ice cream and shave ice are to fill the void left by the previous tenants: Ed and Don's ice cream parlor that had been here for so many years.

MODERATE

CAFFE CIAO ★   *Italian*
Kea Lani (875-4100) HOURS: Lunch 11-5:30pm; Dinner 5:30-10pm. SAMPLING: Full bakery and deli serves capuccinos, deli salads and sandwiches, homemade sausages, antipasto items, Italian gelatos, breads and rich desserts. Indoor dining room or patio seating for lunch with items like bruschetta, calamari, rosemary chicken, gnocchi, lasagna noodles with spinach and ahi peppersteak $6-17. Pizzas with pepperoni, sausage, eggplants or truffles $12-16 are all baked in the outdoor brick pizza oven as are many of the lunch and dinner entrees. Pizzas are also available for dinner along with entrees of roast veal, salmon, short ribs, shrimp, t-bone steak and most of the lunch items $16-22. Antipasto, soups and pastas are also available for dinner $5-29. COMMENTS: Black and gold decor with high stools and tables in the deli which has been expanded to a full restaurant with a dining room next door and patio seating surrounding the brick pizza oven outside. While dining you can relax by reading one of a variety of complimentary newspapers, from the San Francisco Chronicle to the Australian News. The sausages are made in-house and they have several varieties, Italian, Portuguese, French and garlic, or try one of their unusual salami varieties including wild boar! They smoke their own salmon and produce

their own private label of products to sell at the deli: macadamia nut honey, peppercorn ketchup, Maui poha berry butter or pineapple jam. They also sell items imported from Italy. Jumbo oatmeal or chocolate chip cookies, freshly made cheese Danish croissants, macadamia nut pies, Italian tiramisu and banana nut bread are just a few of the items tempting the visitor. You can shop and eat at the same time - the best of both worlds!

CAFE KIOWAI *Polynesian-American*
Maui Prince Hotel, Makena (874-1111) HOURS: Breakfast 6-10:30am; lunch 11am-5pm, dinner 5:30-9pm. SAMPLING: Breakfast buffets: continental $11.95 or hot $17.95. A la carte omelettes, eggs Benedict, corned beef hash, French toast or fritatta $7.75-12. Start lunch with ahi Nicoise or southwestern chicken salad, pepper pot soup, chilled shrimp & oysters or seared ahi $5.25-12.75. Sandwiches include grilled mahi, roasted turkey, steak, hamburger or grilled chicken with bacon, cheddar & guacamole in a tortilla $7.75-11.25. Pizza, pasta, chicken katsu, seafood or chicken curry and saimin run $8-14.95; dessert choices are passion fruit cheesecake, raspberry lemon curd tart, chocolate macadamia nut brittle flan and Hawaiian chocolate cake with coconut and macadamias $4-5.50. Dinners begin with lemongrass prawns, chicken satay, seafood spring rolls, oysters, sashimi and Asian crab cake $6.95-12.50 or with Maui onion soup, assorted greens or Chinese chicken salad $5.50-6.50 or the salad bar for $12.95/-$7.95 with entree. Pizza, pasta or Asian noodle stir-fry $12.50-19; entrees of steak, herb chicken, filet & shrimp, lobster and fresh fish $17.95-29.50. COMMENTS: Friday seafood buffet $30; Saturday paniolo buffet $28. Keiki menu available. Kiowai pronounced "Key-oh-wy" means "fresh flowing water." A casual, open patio atmosphere. Try the passion fruit iced tea!

CAFE KULA *Upcountry Farmers Market & Deli*
Located at the Grand Wailea (875-1234) HOURS: 6am-3pm, lunch from 10:30. SAMPLING: Breakfasts include a tropical fruit sandwich on banana bread, strawberry crepe, apple strudel or smoked salmon on lava bread $4-7.50. Muesli, homemade granola and baked goods $2-4. Lite lunches offer tuna in papaya, seafood pasta, chef's, crab & shrimp or Oriental soba noodle salads, chilled salmon and tuna, turkey, ham or vegetarian sandwiches on lava bread $6.50-8.50. COMMENTS: Their original lava bread is slow rising bread, dipped in ice water so that when it bakes it explodes in small bubbles. (Like a volcano?) It also comes in cheese and spicy flavors. Coffee drinks and smoothies. Beer & wine.

CHART HOUSE ★ *American*
100 Wailea Ike Drive (879-2875) HOURS: Dinner 5-10pm. SAMPLING: Lobster cakes, coconut shrimp, garlic bread and sashimi appetizers $5.75-12.50. Lobster pot pie, steak, prime rib, crab, lobster, fresh fish, prawns & garlic steak, fresh salmon, grilled portobello mushroom with fettucine, Tuscan chicken with farfalle. Entrees include their unlimited fresh garden or Caesar salad, hot squaw bread, country-style bread, potatoes or wild rice $15.95-26.95. They also offer some good homemade desserts including mud pie, chocolate mousse and authentic key lime pie. COMMENTS: The Wailea Chart House will be offering some new, updated menus with different entrees like rack of lamb and porterhouse steak as

well as daily chef's specials. One of the best keiki menus we've seen and the adult entree portions are huge! Open-air setting with an ocean view. Other locations in Lahaina and Kahului.

FAIRWAY   *American-Continental*
100 Kaukahi St., at Wailea Golf Course Clubhouse (879-4060 or 879-3861) COMMENTS: We always thought this was a nice little hideaway and apparently, they want to keep it that way: we called the owner several times, but he never sent us any information. Oh, well, we can keep a secret: "Shhh, don't tell anyone to go there."

HARRY'S SUSHI AND PUPU BAR   *Japanese*
See Lobster Cove which follows. (879-7677)

HULA MOONS   *Seafood-American*
Aston Wailea Resort (879-1922) HOURS: Lunch 11am-5pm; Dinner 6-10pm (from 5:30 Sun.-Mon.). SAMPLING: Lunch appetizers include kalua pork spring rolls, Maui onion rings and tiger shrimp with pineapple cocktail sauce $3.95-9.95. Curried chicken, fresh fish, Caesar, Chinese chicken and fruit lau lau (in ti leaves) are some entree salads $6.95-10.95. A burger, hot dog, turkey club, grilled chicken, kalua pork and vegetable or tuna pita are the sandwiches and the entrees offer mahi tempura, saimin, grilled catch or sauteed shrimp in black bean sauce $6.95-12.95. Dinner appetizers are seared ahi, nori crostini, sesame tempura shrimp, oysters, Maui onion soup and a selection of salads $5-10.50. Choice of entrees are lemongrass grilled chicken breast, lilikoi duckling, pork medallions, T-bone steak, garlic shrimp, scallops and steamed vegetable basket $18-23. A new chocolate dessert bar was due to be added by summer, 1996. COMMENTS: Hula Moons is dedicated to the spirit of Don Blanding, Hawai'i's well known poet, artist and musician. "Hula Moons" was the title of one of his most popular books. The restaurant is located on the pool level and flickering torches and live Hawaiian music add to the ambiance of this ocean view restaurant. Hula moons provides both indoor or outdoor dining. Live entertainment evenings from 5:30-9pm.

LANAI TERRACE ★   *International*
Aston Wailea Resort (879-1922) HOURS: 6-11am for breakfast; 5-11pm for dinner, Sunday champagne brunch 11am-1:30pm. SAMPLING: Breakfast offers Belgian waffles, omelettes, eggs and meats, cinnamon French toast and banana or macadamia pancakes $5-11, full breakfasts $12.95-14.95. Their daily breakfast buffet runs $17 or select their continental buffet with pastries, fruits and juices for $13. Dinners start with soft shell crab tempura, steamed mussels, sashimi, tiger shrimp and Maui onion or artichoke soup $5-10. Entrees of pan-seared ahi, seafood fettucine, sauteed salmon, steak, shutome, free-range chicken and eggplant torta $15-19. You can enjoy the salad bar for $5 with an entree or $12 alone. Guava mousse cake, chocolate macadamia nut cake, creme brulee, almond tuille cup or cheesecake with an Oreo cookie crust are all $6. COMMENTS: Sunday Champagne Brunch includes entertainment $29. Theme buffets are Wednesday night for pasta $19.95, Friday night is seafood fare with four rotating menus at $28.95 and on Saturday night, the prime rib is $23.95. They do a very

good job on the brunch and buffets which is why they earn our star. (The ocean view doesn't hurt either!)

SANDCASTLE ★ *American*
3750 Wailea Alanui, Wailea Shopping Center (879-0606) HOURS: Lunch 11:30am-9pm; dinner from 5pm. SAMPLING: Lunch selections include soup, Caesar, spinach and cobb salads and tuna, chicken, reuben, Italian meatball, BLT, club, turkey and prime rib sandwiches $5.50-9.95. Dinner choices of fresh fish, prime rib, pork tenderloin, linguini with chicken, fried shrimp, boboli pizzas, stir-fry, osso bucco, seafood fettucini, spaghetti and steaks $9.95-21.95. COMMENTS: There are a good variety of selections and since they serve from their lunch menu all day, a good affordable dining option for families. The selection of sandwiches is great and the Monte Cristo is outstanding.

EXPENSIVE

BISTRO MOLOKINI ★ *"Light" Bistro Italian*
Grand Wailea Resort & Spa (875-1234) HOURS: Lunch 11:30am-3pm, light lunch 3-5:30pm; Dinner 5:30-10pm SAMPLING: Lunches start with minestrone or gazpacho, Nicoise, Greek, Caesar or spinach salad plus calamari, onion rings, shrimp cocktail and caprese, a mozzarella & tomato tower $6.25-15.25. Burger, chicken or ahi focaccia, clam, meat or chicken pasta, choice of pizzas $9.75-19.75. Dinner menu has the same appetizers as lunch with ahi tartare $12.50 and carpaccio $11.50 as well. Dinner pizzas, a larger selection of pastas and entrees of chicken saltimbocca, parmesan of veal & eggplant, grilled shrimp, herb crusted lamb chops, rib eye steak, grilled ahi Nicoise and fresh fish $27-31. COMMENTS: An open-air bistro overlooking the formal pool and the Pacific Ocean. (Pool service 11:30am-4:30pm). Exhibition kitchen and wood-burning oven. Casual shorts and shoes are acceptable. The menu is definitely Italian, but very light and innovative. Extensive wine list, beer and Italian sodas in unusual flavors like raspberry chocolate mint, kiwi banana, blueberry hazelnut and others. Children's menu available.

GRAND DINING ROOM ★ *Breakfast only*
Grand Wailea (875-1234) HOURS: 6:30-11am SAMPLING: Grand Breakfast Buffet $19; Nine-course traditional Japanese breakfast $22. A la carte menu offers tropical fruits, a basket of pastries, omelettes, eggs Benedict, banana mac-nut pancakes, turkey or corned beef hash. Swiss Birchermuesli, sweet bread French toast and a variety of breakfast meats $5.50-16. COMMENTS: Breakfast is now the only meal they serve in this elegant dining room so take advantage and pamper yourself.

HAKONE ★ *Japanese*
Maui Prince Resort, Makena (874-1111) HOURS: Dinner only, 6-9:30pm. SAMPLING: Dinners start at $22 for chicken karaage and range up to Hakone Gozen (a bento style assortment) $42. Broiled, steamed and deep fried dishes are offered a la carte $24. Nabemono selections of sukiyaki and sabu shabu are cooked at

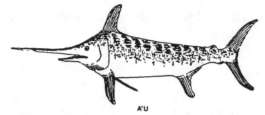

A'U

AHI

MAHI-MAHI

UKU

ONO

ULUA

HAPUPU'U

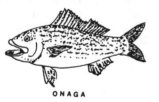

ONAGA

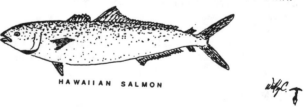

OPAKA PAKA

HAWAIIAN SALMON

your table and require a two person minimum by reservation $35. Hot and cold sake $7-12. COMMENTS: Authenticity is the key to this wonderful Japanese restaurant, from its construction (the wood, furnishings and even small nails were imported from Japan) to its food (the rice is flown in as well). The food and atmosphere are both wonderful here and, of course, the presentation of the food is artistic! Their Maui roll is a specialty here, made with smoked salmon, Maui onions and cucumbers. There is also a sushi bar, but with only 11 seats, it is definitely on a first-come basis.

HANA GION ★ *Japanese*
Renaissance Wailea Beach Resort (879-4900) HOURS: Open daily, except Thursday, 6-10pm, reservations are required for teppanyaki seating and recommended for restaurant dining. SAMPLING: Set dinners include teriyaki, tempura and teishoku combinations of chicken, beef, sashimi or shrimp as well as Nabemono (pot) dishes of sukiyaki, yosenabe, shabu shabu $24.50-35. Steaks, prawns, scallops, fish and chicken are prepared Teppanyaki-style $24-31 and Hana Gion specials range from $36 to $80 for an eleven course kaiseki meal (24 hour advance reservations requested). A sushi bar is also available. COMMENTS: The decor is as authentic as its cuisine. Woodwork, screens, stone flooring, bamboo trim, and decorative artifacts were all produced in Japan to exacting standards. In fact, parts of the dining area were actually constructed in Japan before dismantling them for shipment to the Renaissance Wailea. The name Gion originates from the Gion district of Kyoto. Traditional Japanese fare emphasizes freshness, subtle flavors and delicate preparations. The restaurant is designed to promote the feeling of privacy and intimacy. There is a main dining area with private dining rooms that seat four or six guests each. The sushi bar accommodates only ten.

HUMUHUMUNUKUNUKUA'PUA'A ★ *Seafood*
Grand Wailea Resort (875-1234) HOURS: Dinner only 5:30-10pm, bar open until 10:30pm. SAMPLING: The Pa'ina Bar has lobster, tako, ahi or clam poke and oysters $2.50 per pc./oz. to $52 lb. Sashimi, shrimp cocktail, spring rolls, BBQ ribs, clams with coconut pesto and one of the best appetizers we've ever had, Ahi Lemon Grass Traps $9-12.50. Mahi & clam chowder, spinach & pipikaula salad $7.50-9.50. Whole sizzling snapper, sauteed tiger prawns, bamboo steamed opakapaka lau lau, roasted ewa chicken $26-35 a la carte. Steaks and prime rib come with potato and vegetable $30-36. Side dishes include steamed or fried rice, baked potato or fries, wok vegetables $2.50-6 or kamameshi: rice with shrimp, clams and vegetables for $18. Desserts feature tropical creme brulee, macadamia nut carmel tart, banana & rum fudge hula pie, chocolate coconut paradise with mango vanilla anglaise and a sweet, dessert version of their fantastic traps appetizer in apple or banana $6-8.50. COMMENTS: Are you curious about the "traps"? The appetizer is made with strips of ahi rolled up with tiny vegetables, "trapped" by stalks of flavorful lemon grass and drizzled with spicy ponzu. The dessert substitutes apple or banana for the ahi and vegetables and uses powdered sugar, vanilla and chocolate sauces for the drizzles. There are several traps to an order and the presentation, flavor and texture make this a must-do-pupu! If you're curious about the restaurant's name, it is the Hawai'i state fish, the trigger fish.

Since the Hawaiian name is rather a mouthful, the eatery is affectionately and briefly referred to as Humuhumu. It is a wonderful dining location. Tucked in the front grounds of the resort it is situated on top of a saltwater pond filled with aquatic life. The huge saltwater tank that divides the bar area is worth stopping by to just admire. The restaurant floats on the lagoon and the thatched-roof and bamboo railings inspire exotic Robinson Crusoe fantasies. Given the prices of the a la carte entrees, the addition of a starter and a side dish or two, makes this a little bit more than just expensive fare. The ambiance alone, however, merits a star. They do offer smaller size portions for children 12 and under. Not very affordable family dining, but definitely a place to take the kids (or grownups) to look around. (Or just order some traps!)

JOE'S BAR & GRILL ★ *Gourmet American*
131 Wailea Ike Place, above the Wailea Tennis Club (875-7767) HOURS: Lunch 11am-2pm; Dinner 5:30-10pm. SAMPLING: Spinach, smoked chicken & corn salad with dried cranberries; grilled vegetables on focaccia bread or stuffed chicken sandwich with brie bacon and caramelized onions are some of the intriguing lunch offerings $8-14. Dinners start with grilled quail on pear salad, goat cheese tart, smoked salmon quesadilla and baked oysters with crab dip $6-12 and continue with seafood creole, pork chop with dried fruit compote, steak with caramelized onions and lobster pot pie $16-32. Apple walnut pie with cinnamon ice cream and warm chocolate glob are among the desserts $6. COMMENTS: This is the newest venture from Joe and (Chef) Bev Gannon of the Haliimaile General Store. Bev's food is as good as it reads, but nothing is overly-trendy. (She even takes the "goat" out of goat cheese!) Joe's background as a Hollywood producer-director and lighting designer sets the tone with the shiny hardwood floors, 43-foot cooper bar and individual geometric designs on the tables. The theater lighting is soft, yet strong enough to highlight the wall of show-biz memorabilia from Joe's days working with film, tv and music celebrities. All this and an ocean view, too!

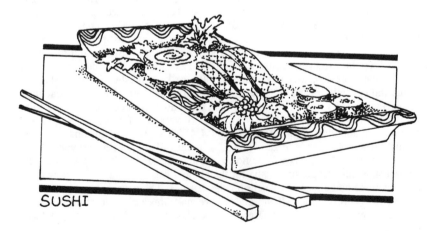

SUSHI

KEA LANI RESTAURANT ★ *Euro-Pacific Cuisine*
Kea Lani Hotel (875-4100) HOURS: Breakfast 6:30-11am, Dinner 5:30-10pm. SAMPLING: Breakfast buffet $17.95A, $10.95C plus a la carte items. (One traveling family told us that their package stay at the Kea Lani included the daily breakfast buffet and that with their teenage son the complimentary breakfast saved them huge amounts of money on their food travel budget! They also noted that the breakfast selections were diverse enough to keep their palates interested for the entire week.) A lengthy selection of salads, soups and appetizers (smoked pheasant with walnuts for one!) runs $7-17. The dinner menu changes seasonally and entrees might include rum and ginger duck, shrimp with polenta, napoleon of lobster, teppan-style scallops or poha & kiawe honey glazed range hen $25-38. White chocolate Cointreau terrine, sun-dried cherry napoleon, Asian banana flambe and fresh local pumpkin cheesecake are just a few of the desserts $7-8. COMMENTS: The Kea Lani features their own specialty line of gourmet products which they use in the restaurant and also sell at Caffe Ciao. They include garlic peppercorn catsup, guava catsup, banana nut bread and macadamia nut honey. They utilize fresh island ingredients and have their own herb garden at the hotel. The fine dining restaurant features 40-foot vaulted ceilings designed in a southern Mediterranean style and offers great ocean views. The menu is termed "Euro-Pacific" cuisine which is a combination of classic cooking styles of Europe with the flavors and foods of the Pacific. Once a month, Kea Lani Executive chef Steven Amaral hosts "Grand Chefs on Tour," a week-long culinary experience pairing a "grand" chef from the mainland with a Hawaiian chef of equal prominence in a series of dinners and cooking demonstrations. The program has been so successful, it has been extended through the end of 1997.

LE GUNJI ★ *Japanese*
555 Kaukahi St., located at the Diamond Resort (874-0500) HOURS: Two dinner seatings at 6pm and 7:30pm. Closed Wednesday. SAMPLING: A teppan-yaki restaurant offering set meals. The Diamond is $70 and includes fresh catch, lobster and filet mignon among the total of ten course; Mini-Diamond choices run $45-55, Steak is $50 and Seafood is $55. All offer a minimum of seven courses. COMMENTS: With $45 as the cheapest entree, this another on the mega-expensive borderline. The dining room is small and intimate with a beautiful garden courtyard located behind where the chef cooks. This Teppan-yaki is a bit different in that it is cooked with a French flair since their Chef Gunji Ito, from Osaka, previously cooked French cuisine. Seating hours change in the summer: 6:30 and 8pm from May through August. Reservations required. Shorts and sandals not permitted.

LOBSTER COVE-HARRY'S SUSHI BAR *Seafood-Japanese*
Located next to the Chart House in Wailea (879-7677) HOURS: Dining room 5:30-10pm; Harry's sushi bar til 1am. SAMPLING: Live Maine lobster, lobster tail and lobster thermidor $21-35. Seafood penne pasta, BBQ tiger prawns, filet mignon and a selection of fresh Hawaiian fish preparations $19.50-24. Appetizers and salads include fried seafood ravioli salad, steamed clams, crab & avocado salad and the signature "Bird Nest" lobster cake $5-11. COMMENTS: Harry's Sushi and Pupu Bar is operated by Harry Okumara and is located at the entrance

to Lobster Cove. We didn't stop by, but it was very busy! The menu offers maki sushi, nigiri sushi and sashimi with specialties like salmon Maui onion, eel avocado and lobster asparagus rolls $6-12.

PACIFIC GRILL   *East-West*
Four Seasons Resort (874-8000) HOURS: Breakfast 6-11:30am (buffet 6:30-11), lunch 11:30am-2:30pm, dinner 5:30-9:30pm. SAMPLING: Chocolate waffle, oatmeal brulee, sausage fritatta and Viennese pancakes are some innovative additions to traditional cereal, egg, meet and fruit choices $4.50-17. Buffet $15.75-19.75. Lunch salads include Caesar, chicken & macadamia cobb, shrimp or ahi Nicoise and Greek $6.25-16. A wonderful lobster salad & bacon sandwich tops a menu of sandwiches from $10.25-15.75 and entrees feature poached salmon, spaghettini, whole wheat rigatoni, spicy Japanese noodle & lemongrass shrimp and skewered lamb $12.75-16.50. The dinner menu offers both Pacific Rim and North American specialties. Pacific Rim starters include Vietnamese spring rolls, tempura calamari, crab & black Thai rice cakes and coconut lemon grass shrimp soup $5.50-14. Main courses offer wok seared salmon with spicy peanut sauce, sweet and sour stir-fried chicken, seafood stir-fry, steamed snapper with ginger and charred duck breast with Chinese pancakes and plum wine sauce $16-28. The more traditional western influences are embellished with a sampling of distinctive regional accents from Hawaii. These include Angus NY sirloin steak, lamb, T-bone steak, spinach fettucini and seafood stew $15.25-26. Also available are lite fare sandwiches from the lunch menu. COMMENTS: A pleasant dining environment with indoor or lana'i seating overlooking the pool and the ocean. All Four Seasons restaurants offer healthy alternative cuisine selections.

PALM COURT ★   *International-Buffet*
Reinassance Wailea Beach Resort (879-4900) HOURS: Breakfast a la carte and buffet 6am-11am. Sunday la carte only 6am-noon. Dinner 6-10pm. SAMPLING: Breakfast buffet $17A, $8.50C or eggs, pancakes, fruit and special sourdough French toast with marscapone cheese and guava jam $6-15; Dinner buffet every night: Mon/Pacific Rim, Tues & Sat/prime rib, Wed/Italian, Thurs/Southwestern, Fri/Seafood and Sun/Paniolo, all $28 except prime rib $30 & seafood $35. (Children 1/2 price.) A la carte menu has pot stickers, ginger chicken quesadilla, lobster & grapefruit or shrimp & cashew pizzas $6-16 and a salad bar for $12.50 ($7.50 with entree) Pastas include tri-color tortellini, spinach & pancetta and seafood with saimin noodles; sandwiches offer lemon peppered mahi, vegetarian focaccia and chicken club or you can choose an entree of fish & prawn brochette, kalbi beef steaks, wok-seared mahi or chicken with boursin cheese and crispy noodle cake $9.75-25. This open-air dining hall is festively decorated in reds and greens and offers evening breezes and an ocean view. Reservations are accepted only for a group of 5 or more. They no longer serve Sunday Brunch except on holidays.

PRINCE COURT ★   *Hawaiian Regional Cuisine*
Maui Prince Hotel, Makena (874-1111) HOURS: Dinner 6-9:30pm, (closed Tues. & Wed.), Champagne Sunday Brunch 9:30am-1pm. SAMPLING: Open-faced seafood lasagna, napoleon of foie gras, smoked Asian duck salad and shellfish

bisque are some of the appetizers, soups, and salads $5.50-12. Entrees include opakapaka on angel hair pasta with mango coulis creme; roasted rack of lamb with Maui onion chips and roasted macadamia nut crust, kiawe roasted Thai chicken with red coconut curry sauce, filet mignon & crab hash-stuffed lobster $19.95-34. The Chef's Tasting Menu offers a selection of entrees and appetizers that changes weekly. Items that might be found on the Sunday buffet include flavored pancakes and crepes, carved meats, chilled crab legs & shrimp, sashimi, smoked seafoods, Russian caviar salad, sweet & sour pork, beef stroganoff and seared ahi. The dessert table is a sumptuous fantasy that tastes as extravagant as it looks. A worthy indulgence for $31.95 (which is actually very reasonable considering you won't eat again til Tuesday!) Reservations required. COMMENTS: Hawaiian Regional Cuisine continues to be the "buzz" word in dining experiences in the islands. It is simply the opportunity to experience the many varied selections of fresh foods grown, raised or caught in the islands. The culinary cuisine of the Prince Court is an incredible blend of flavors which highlight the best and freshest Hawaiian produce, meats and fish. Beautifully situated, the dining room offers a splendid view of the both the ocean and landscaped hotel grounds. They have an excellent wine list with particularly good prices on champagne and wine selections. The Sunday brunch is still one of the island's best and in fact, one of the few still offered weekly!

RAFFLES' ★ *American/Hawaiian Regional*
Renaissance Wailea Beach Resort (879-4900) HOURS: Tuesday-Saturday 6:30-10pm. SAMPLING: By popular demand, they have added more grilled items like filet mignon, porterhouse and NY steaks as well as stuffed veal chops to Raffles' signature items: Crisped whole fish with coconut curry, seafood paella and papaya dijon rack of lamb $25-38. A three-course Hawaiian regional dinner with gingered lobster tiki or shiitake mushroom strudel; warm scallop salad or crab bisque and grilled ono with black bean & ginger sauce or pork chops with pineapple-onion relish is offered for $65 with wine, $53 without. COMMENTS: Raffles' is named for Sir Thomas Stamford Raffles (1781-1826), the British founder of the city of Singapore where Raffles' Hotel has become a legend. For over 100 years the Singapore establishment entertained seafaring merchants, literary giants and even royalty, and amid the splendor they sipped the drink created by Raffles -- the Singapore Sling. This restaurant has a special appeal for us, as it was one of the first we dined at during our first visit to Maui many years ago. It has been completely remodeled since then and, sadly, is one of the few fine dining restaurants left. But it has remained stalwart and stands as one of Maui's most elegant and romantic dining experiences.

RESTAURANT TAIKO *Japanese*
Diamond Resort, 555 Kaukahi St., Wailea (874-0500) HOURS: Breakfast 7-10am, lunch 11am-1:45pm, dinner 5:30-9pm. Closed Tuesday. SAMPLING: Set menus for breakfast offer both Japanese (fish, vegetables) or Western (eggs, meats) options $14-20 with limited a la carte items $3-9. Lunch also offers both styles with noodles, tempura and teriyaki chicken as well as spaghetti, shrimp curry and sandwiches $8-14. For dinner there are appetizers, steamed or vinegar dishes, stir-fry and deep-fried dishes, soup and rice offered a la carte for $6-25. Bordering the mega-expensive range, meals feature sliced beef, tempura and ahi

burger steak $35-40; Nabe dinners for two or more $40 per person and two dozen-course options for $65 & $95. There is also a choice of entrees prepared "Le Gunji" style at your table: Stuffed onaga with lobster, tiger shrimp, cornish game hen or steak $19-24. COMMENTS: Diamond Resort is an exclusive property that makes their fine restaurants available to the general public. The dining hall is large with cathedral-like ceilings and lots of attractive rockwork. Very simple, elegant decor. The Plumeria Counter is a small sushi bar that also features a la carte items from 5:30-8:30pm.

SEASIDE *American*
Four Seasons Resort (874-8000) HOURS: Lunch 11:30am-3pm, pupus 3-6pm, dinner 5:30-9:30pm. Sunset entertainment in the evenings. SAMPLING: Lunch or afternoon pupus offer summer rolls, teriyaki beef & chicken sate, jumbo shrimp, puna goat cheese rolled in eggplant $9.50-13. Also for lunch: poached albacore and roast turkey sandwiches, Caesar and Cobb salads $6.50-15. Grilled mahi mahi or ahi, burgers, hot dog, or chicken quesadilla $9-14. Dinner appetizers include crab cakes, rosemary skewered shrimp and smoked salmon roll $6.75-11.50; entrees from the grill feature a selection of unusual Hawaiian fish (nairigi, tombo, shutome) plus lobster, steak and pasta plus chicken, pork and lamb from the rotisserie $20-26.75. Cheesecake souffle, white & dark chocolate pate, apple or fruit tart and coconut cake are the choices for dessert $5.25-6.75. COMMENTS: You can't get a better ocean view than from this cliffside restaurant located right over the water.

SEASONS *Contemporary American with regional influences*
Four Seasons Resort (874-8000) HOURS: Dinner only 6-9:30pm, dancing until 10:30. SAMPLING: Pistou soup, lobster salad, and Kula yellow squash blossom with goat cheese fritters and green mango salad are among the starters for $11-22. Sauteed uku with hazelnut flavored artichoke sauce, crisped shutome with pancetta, medallions of veal loin, charbroiled onaga with ginger and roasted Barbarie duck with winter mango are just a few of the entrees $34-42. "Degustation Selections" offer multi-course prix-fixe menus for $62-95. If you can't make up your mind whether to have the warm pineapple tart, the lemon cream cappucino, the tiramisu or pikake sorbet for $10, you can order a trio for $16. COMMENTS: Terrace seating with an ocean view combined with background music performed by a jazz trio. The Four Seasons' Sunset Lounge offers nightly entertainment and dancing 6pm-1am. An elegant dining atmosphere and all new menu from famed Chef de Cuisine George Mavrothalassitis formerly of the renowned La Mer restaurant at Honolulu's Halekulani.

SEAWATCH ★ *Island Regional*
100 Wailea Golf Club Drive (875-8080) HOURS: Breakfast/lunch menu served 8am-3pm; grill menu 3-10pm; dinner 5:30-10pm. SAMPLING: Breakfast & lunch selections range from fresh fruit, egg dishes and Molokai French toast to burgers, pasta, stir-fry, fish tacos and salads like Caesar, cobb, Chinese chicken, shrimp & crabmeat and fruit $5.95-10.95. Dinners start with spring rolls, seafood potstickers, crab cakes, stuffed shrimp, wok-seared sashimi or spinach salad with grilled shrimp sate $8-9. Entrees include Asian pasta, miso chili glazed tiger prawns, rack of lamb, steaks and several fresh fish preparations $16-24.

COMMENTS: Breakfast and lunch options are relatively inexpensive, for a room with a view, too! And you can get lunch for breakfast or have breakfast for lunch! An elegant "grand hall" entrance with tall ceilings leads to the restaurant and several distinctive dining areas. The wide lanais offer the best views of Molokini, Kaho'olawe, Makena and Ma'alaea and the grill room is highlighted by giant glass doors and artwork from Arthur Johnson, a Big Island muralist. The lounge has a white baby grand piano as its centerpiece. Spacious seating; descriptive wine list. (Seawatch proprietors also own the two Koho Grill and Bars as well as the Plantation House Restaurant in Kapalua.)

MEGA-EXPENSIVE

KINCHA   *Japanese & Nouveau Continental*
Grand Wailea (875-1234) Hours: Dinner only, 6-10pm. COMMENTS: We had to invent the "mega-expensive" category, since just "expensive" really isn't descriptive enough for this very authentic Japanese restaurant. It appears the race is on for which Japanese restaurant in Wailea can charge the most for a meal and Kincha appears to be taking the lead with a per dinner per diner price of $300. No, that is not a typo, and it is dollars, not yen. (And believe it or not, the price has actually come down from the $500 dinner of a few years ago! The $500 Tokubetsu Kaiseki is still available by advance request and includes a tea ceremony, sushi and tempura prepared by a personal chef and served in their private Ozashiki-Tatami Room). Their Royal Kaiseki menu reads, "Set menu of finest, authentic Japanese food served on individual selected tableware." The Nishiki ("Golden Embroidery") runs $150 and includes homemade fruit wine, sakizuke, appetizer, clear broth soup, sashimi, broiled fish, boiled vegetable, deep fried course, vinegar course, cold wheat noodles, seasonal fruit, sweet dessert and the finest green tea. Add a steak course and shokuji for the Aya ("coloration") $200 and to that, add refreshing hassun and onmono for Miyabi

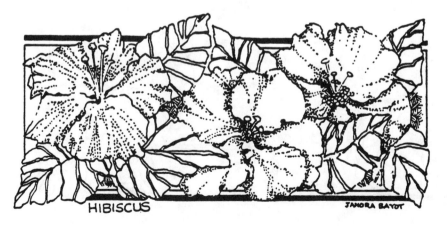

HIBISCUS

("elegance") $300. Multiple-course kaiseki dinners include sushi, tempura, lobster or broiled fish for $80-120. Kama'aina Kaiseki, an authentic Japanese full course dinner of eleven items offers sushi, tempura, chicken teriyaki or steak as an entree for $58. The Setsubun Kaiseki has more courses and several intricately designed items per course for $80. An a la carte menu ranges from $34-120 with a few minor offerings under $10. There is also a sushi bar (capacity 17) and a tempura bar (seats 15). Their children's menu is called "Keiki Kincha" which is a mini version of those above for $40. Entrees on the new Nouveau Continental menu seem relatively inexpensive at $30-34 each. Grilled Angus tenderloin and shrimp provencal with duchess potatoes; pan roasted supreme of muscovy duck with potato duck confit and sauce cassis; filet of salmon "en Papillote" in essence of chardonnay and fennel or sauteed snapper on wild mushroom bordelaise with roasted pinenut and rice croquettes are available along with appetizers of ginger glazed Pacific oysters; chilled tiger prawns or foie gras and apple mille feuille $15-18. Or you can start with veloute of lobster & asparagus; carpaccio of cucumber with field greens or salad of endive, frisee & honey walnuts $9-10. COMMENTS: While we may find these prices outrageous, the Japanese visitor may not be in for such a shock. We're told that a fine meal in Japan runs several hundred dollars or more. And although there are a number of food courses, the price is more reflective of the culinary artistry in preparation and display and the gracious ceremony with which it's presented. In any case, when you take the special private elevator to Kincha, you will feel as if you've just arrived in Japan. Created from 350 tons of rock from Mount Fuji, the restaurant features lush gardens and peaceful lagoons. Since the resort's Grand Dining Room is no longer open for dinner, Kincha now serves as the signature fine dining restaurant, offering not only a selection of exquisitely prepared Japanese and Continental meals, but a rare and special experience to go with them.

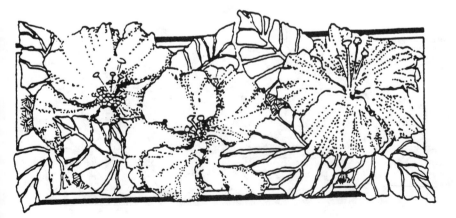

KAHULUI-WAILUKU

Along Lower Main Street in Wailuku are a number of local restaurants which are not often frequented by tourists and may well be one of the island's best kept secrets! Don't expect to find polished silver or extravagant decor, but do expect to find reasonable prices for large portions of food in a comfortable atmosphere. Note that many of these local restaurants may not accept credit cards. Dairy Queen, Pizza Hut, McDonald's, Burger King, and Jack in the Box are a few of the fast food restaurants in and around Kahului and the Maui Mall. These don't require elaboration.

INEXPENSIVE

While not restaurants, two of our favorite haunts bear mention here. The *Home Made Bakery* at 1005 Lower Main, open 5:30am-9pm daily, is an island institution. Recently remodeled and expanded, they have more than just donuts, you'll find unusual specialties such as empanadas, manju, and bread pudding. They began almost 40 years ago on Maui and do not add any preservatives to their made-from-scratch formulas. They are the home of the original Maui Crispy Manju and noted for their Maui Crunch bread. Some items available at island groceries. 244-7015.

Nearby is the *Four Sisters Bakery* on Vineyard and Hinano in Wailuku. It is run by Melen, Mila, Beth and Bobbie who arrived from the Philippines after helping their father run a Spanish Bakery in Manila for fifteen years. Not a large selection, but delicious and different items. One is a sweet bread filled with a cinnamon pudding, a sponge cake "sandwich," as well as cinnamon rolls and butter rolls. The only place you can purchase these delicacies is at their bakery or at the Saturday Swap Meet in Kahului. 244-9333. Open daily 5am-8pm.

A SAIGON CAFE ★ *Vietnamese*
1792 Main St. (243-9560) HOURS: Mon.-Sat. 10am-10pm, til 9pm on Sunday. SAMPLING: Spring or summer rolls and shrimp pops marinated and grilled on a sugar cane stick $33.50-6.95; lemon beef, lemon shrimps, chicken and green papaya salads $5.25-9.75. Clay pot, meatball, sirloin rolls, hot & sour, beef noodles and other soups, vermicelli noodle dishes, rice plates, wok fried noodles and vegetables, Saigon fondue (cooked at your table) and tofu, fish and chicken entrees. COMMENTS: If you haven't tried Vietnamese food, now is the time and this is the place! Very different from Chinese or Japanese, it is a refreshing combination of flavors that sets it apart. Lemon grass, cucumbers, sour garlic sauce, daikon pickles, fresh island basil and mint leaves are among the many distinctive ingredients used for seasoning dishes such as Ga Xao Xa Ot (curried chicken with lemon grass) or Bo Lui (grilled beef sirloin rolls). The most fun is Banh Hoi: choose from a variety of meats or seafood to fill with the above ingredients (along with bean sprouts and vermicelli cake noodle) in rice paper that you dip in hot water, then wrap! Thankfully, you don't have to be able to pronounce the food to enjoy it! They recently moved to the old Naokee Steak House

285

location and serve steaks on the menu in homage to the former tenant. A little hard to find; on our last check, they still didn't have a sign up. Simple atmosphere, great food -- a definite best bet!

AJIYOSHI OKAZUYA   *Japanese*
Kahului Industrial Area, 385 Hoohana St. 5-C (877-9080) HOURS: Mon.-Sat. 6am-2:30pm, Dinner 4-8:30pm SAMPLING: Egg & meat breakfasts $2.95-4.25. Lunch & Dinners: Chicken or pork served teriyaki or katsu style, fish or seafood tempura, sweet & sour meatball, BBQ beef, udon noodles, chow mein, chow fun, ramen katsu, yakitori, unagi don, bentos, sushi $4.50-8.85. COMMENTS: Entrees come with rice and choice of macaroni salad, stir-fry or Japanese vegetables.

AKI'S HAWAIIAN FOOD AND BAR   *Hawaiian*
309 N. Market, Wailuku (244-8122) HOURS: Mon.-Sat. 11am-10pm, Sunday 5-9pm. SAMPLING: Chicken hekka, Hawaiian favorites such as kalua pig with cabbage, pipikaula (beef), chicken long rice, saimin and a coconut milk soup $7-12. COMMENTS: Nightly dinners. A good stop if you want to try some local Hawaiian food. (Closed one Sunday each month so that the owner can enjoy her game of golf!)

ARCHIE'S   *Japanese*
1440 Lower Main St., Wailuku (244-9401) COMMENTS: We found their food good and their prices reasonable, but when we called for information for the last book they simply replied, "Archie no want to give you nothing." Archie seem's to have mellowed a bit. This time he let us know that he was in business for 28 years and as far as being in our book, he "never do that. We doing fine." Maybe we can get a menu for you *next* time.

ARTIE'S MEXICAN FOOD   *Mexican*
333 Dairy Road, next to Minit-Stop, Kahului (877-7113) HOURS: Mon.-Fri. 11am-7pm. SAMPLING: Chile relleno, taquitos, nachos, tostadas, tacos, enchiladas, burritos, quesadillas, taco salad $2.25-5.95. Chocolate taco ice cream $1.50. COMMENTS: After years of selling his salsa and chips retail, Artie's Mexican food is now available for lunch and dinner and for take out.

BACK STREET CAFE   *American*
335 Hoohana Blvd., #7A, Kahului (877-4088) HOURS: Mon.-Fri. breakfast 6:30-9:30am, lunch 10:30 am-2pm. SAMPLING: Salads and sandwiches. Daily homemade lunch specials $5. Take-out lunches available as are catering services. Very popular with the local residents. Free delivery Kahului/Wailuku.

BAMBOO RESTAURANT   *Local/Asian*
1032 Lower Main St. (244-1166) HOURS: Mon.-Sat., 10am-9pm, Half day on Sunday 10am-3pm. SAMPLING: Squid stir-fry, chicken katsu, monk fish, Kal bi ribs $6.95-14.

BEAK AND FIN *American*
Airport Triangle Building (871-0818) HOURS: We don't know! SAMPLING: We've called, we've stopped by, we've tried repeatedly to get information from this restaurant, but they're too busy, they forget or they're just not interested. Since we're too busy and no longer interested, our suggestion is to just forget 'em.

BENTOS AND BANQUETS BY BERNARD *Local-Take-out*
85 Church St., Wailuku (244-1124) HOURS: Mon.-Fri. Lunch 10am-1:30ish (Phone orders from 8am) SAMPLING: Roast pork, turkey burger, teri steak, Caesar salad and noodle dishes (choose two with potato macaroni salad for $5.75.) Weekly specials might include lasagna, mushroom chicken, beef chimichanga, pot roast, Chinese roast pork and oyster chicken $5.75-6. Salad and sandwich specials, too. COMMENTS: Small take-out shop; no seating. Good prices, large portions. Hawaiian plate on Fridays. They cater seven days a week offering both local and gourmet food. They also deliver -- for both take-out and catering.

CAFE SHRED *American*
1322 Lower Main St., Wailuku (244-8298) HOURS: Breakfast 7am-noon; Lunch 10:30am-2:30pm. SAMPLING: Egg and breakfast meat dishes, huevos rancheros, "Shredder Sandwich" with eggs, cheese, turkey and salsa on English muffin and "The Shredder" four-egg omelette with choice of fillings $3.95-4.95. Kula green salads, daily soups, fish, filet mignon, gourmet pastas and weekly specials like three different preparations of Cornish Game Hens $5.95. COMMENTS: Specialty coffees and exotic teas. Opened May '96, they plan to start serving dinner by the end of summer.

CHINA EXPRESS *Chinese*
At Safeway, 170 E. Kamehameha Ave., Kahului (877-3377) SAMPLING: Items in 1/2 pint, pint, quart, two quart size or pound. Plate lunches $3.49-5.69.

CHUM'S *Local Style*
1900 Main Street, Wailuku (244-1000) HOURS: Breakfast 6:30-11am, Sat.-Sun. til noon. Lunch/Dinner Sun.-Thurs. til 10pm, Fri.-Sat. til 10:30. SAMPLING: Homemade soups, saimin, stew. Local style meals include pork cutlet, teri chicken sandwich, beef tomato, mahi mahi, roast pork, fried chicken $5.70-7.25. Various chili dishes $2-5.25, teriyaki beef sticks $1 each. COMMENTS: A good option for a late evening snack after a movie in Kahului!

THE CLASS ACT ★ *Continental*
Maui Community College Campus, Kahului (242-1210) HOURS: Lunch only, Wednesday and Friday 11am-12:30pm. COMMENTS: This is one of Maui's best little finds. Insiders know they are in for a treat when they stop by for a four-course gourmet lunch for $10 prepared by the Food Service students of the Maui Community College. They shop, serve, clean and wait on the tables as well as offering a different menu each week. Each meal represents a different country or region like Italy, New Orleans, Morocco, Austria or Pacific Northwest. A heart healthy alternative, low in sodium and cholesterol, is offered at each meal. The

program is only offered during the school year, so be sure and call to check on availability and schedule a reservation. They suggest calling for reservations on Wednesday and Friday 8:30-10:30 am and reservations are taken up to two weeks in advance. The Class Act is located on the MCC campus adjacent to the upstairs cafeteria. Gourmet dinner once a term, cost is about $35.

(THE) COFFEE STORE   *Coffee/Pastries/Light meals*
Kaahumanu Center (871-6860) HOURS: Mon.-Fri. 7am-9pm; Saturday 7:30am-9pm; Sunday 9am-5pm. SAMPLING: Muffins $1.95, lasagna, $4.50, cheesecake, assorted pastries $2-3.75, pizzas $6.50-10, quiche $6.50. COMMENTS: They also have locations in Kihei and Napili. In addition to freshly roasted coffee and coffee drinks, they serve locally made fresh pasta dishes, croissants, salads and sandwiches. Voted as having the best capuccino on Maui in the "Best of Maui" contest conducted by the Maui News.

CUPIE'S   *American-Local*
134 W. Kamehameha Ave. (877-3055 or 871-6488) HOURS: Mon.-Sat. 6:30am-9pm for breakfast, lunch and dinner. SAMPLING: Breakfast served until 10:30, plate lunches, bento, mini bento and full menu served all day. This used to be one of those places where you sat in your car with the trays on your window, now it is a drive up to order "to go" or seating there. Plate lunches $5.45-6. Sandwiches, chow fun, beef teriyaki and broasted chicken.COMMENTS: This really is an old-fashioned place -- you can still get a grilled cheese sandwich for 99 cents!

DANI'S CATERING   *Local lunches-take out*
880 Kolu St. at Takamiya Market (242-6652) HOURS: Mon.-Fri. 10am-1pm SAMPLING: Daily menu has hamburgers, chicken cutlet or katsu, teriyaki beef, saimin, Chinese chicken or tossed salad with peanut dressing $1.95-3.50. Weekday specials include chicken curry, stuffed cabbage, roast pork with gravy, kalua pig, pork adobo and Hawaiian plate $4.50-5.95. COMMENTS: Eat in or to go lunches were recently reinstated here after a hiatus of three years.

EDO JAPAN (See Food Court at Kaahumanu Center)

FOOD COURT (AT KAAHUMANU CENTER)
The Queen's Market Food Court at Kaahumanu Center features seven upstairs restaurants near the main entrance. *Edo Japan* has teppanyaki plate dinners, rice bowls, saimin and sushi. *Yummy Korean BBQ* offers kal bi and BBQ meats, noodle and dumpling soups plus curries. *Cafe Little Siam* serves Thai curry, lemon grass beef, ginger chicken, spring and summer rolls and satay. *Panda Express* has Mandarin cuisine like orange chicken, spicy chicken with peanuts, chow mein and eggplant in garlic sauce. *Mama Brava's Italian* specialties include taco, teriyaki and "white" pizza, meat or veggie stuffed pizza, calzone, salads and hero sandwiches. *Maui Tacos* offers healthy Mexican. (For detailed description see Napili or Kihei listing.) There is also a *McDonald's* offering the usual fare.Prices $4-7 range. Minimum hours in the food court are 11am-9pm daily, although some may open earlier for breakfast and remain open later. (In 1997, a colorful carousel will be constructed in the middle of the Food Court, not only

for decoration, but rides for the kids as well.) Coffee and juice carts are nearby and there is an *Orange Julius/Arby's* downstairs. Also part of the mall are *Koho Grill & Bar* and *Sharktooth Brewery Steakhouse*. These last two are listed separately.

FUJIYA'S ★ *Japanese*
133 Market Street, Wailuku (244-0206) HOURS: Lunch 11am-2pm Mon.-Fri., dinner 5-9:30pm Mon.-Sat.; Closed Sunday. SAMPLING: Lunch: Fried or miso ahi or salmon, teriyaki or salted ika, miso butter fish $6.95-7.95. Noodles $4.25-5.25 Dinner: Tempura, teriyaki, donburi, curry, chicken or pork tofu $4.95-9.95; Sushi $4-8. Five combination dinner choices such as tempura with yakitori, shumai, tsukemono, miso soup and rice. Beer & sake available. COMMENTS: One of our best bets for Japanese food. Sushi lovers will appreciate their sushi bar where a large variety of selections are available at half the usual resort area price.

GOLDIE'S STORE ★ *Filipino*
1951 Vineyard St., Wailuku (242-5519) HOURS: Mon.-Sat. 9am-2pm SAMPLING: Pork & oeas, dinardaraan, lechon kawali and bihon guisado are the daily entrees $1.25-1.95. Each day offers a set selection of specials like pork adobo, chicken papaya, menudo, pinakbet, mungo beans, laing and some other interesting, but unpronouncable names $1.65-1.95. Lumpia is 3 for $1. They have desserts, too: Cascaron, kutsinta and bibingka pastries $1-1.60 plus strawberry parfait, leche flan, haupia or fruit salad $.95-1.45. COMMENTS: Self-serve buffet-style and as you can see, it doesn't get much cheaper! Lest you think you're sacrficing quality for such low prices, you should know that Goldie's just won for "Best Filipino" in the annual "Best of Maui" restaurant contest run by the Maui News.

HAMBURGER MARY'S *Mexican*
Corner of Main and Market St., Wailuku (244-7776) New owners bought Mary's around the time of our last book, but from the lack of response, it's apparent they weren't interested in being in our new book.

ICHIBAN THE RESTAURANT *Japanese*
Kahului Shopping Center (871-6977) HOURS: Breakfast 7am-2pm, Saturday 10:30am-2pm. Dinner 5pm-9pm, closed Sunday. SAMPLING: Luncheon menu offers chicken katsu, teriyaki chicken, or donburi and noodle meals $4.50-7.50. Shrimp tempura $6.95-9.95; Oxtail soup $6.95-7.95. Dinner combinations $11.95, stir-fry dishes $7.95, special combination plates $14.95, or steak and lobster $21.95. COMMENTS: Located in the older Kahului Center, this restaurant doesn't stand out as memorable for its food or ambiance.

INTERNATIONAL HOUSE OF PANCAKES *American*
Maui Mall, Kahului (871-4000) HOURS: Sun.-Thurs. 6 am-midnight, Fri. and Sat. until 2am. COMMENTS: A very large facility with a menu that is popular with all family members. Something for everyone and at reasonable prices. Breakfasts begin in the $5 range, dinners from $12.

KIM'S KITCHEN   *Local/Korean*
395F Dairy Road, Kahului (877-2434) HOURS: 9am-9pm; til 2pm. SAMPLING: BBQ, katsu, stir-fry, teriyaki and fried preparations of chicken, pork, steak, tofu, squid and shrimp Lunch $6.99-7.30/Dinner 6.99-9.50. Mixed plates $7.25-7.80. Noodle, stews and soups $6.25-9.25. COMMENTS: Formerly Song's II, this new outlet is now owned by her sister.

KOHO GRILL AND BAR ★   *American*
Kaahumanu Shopping Center, Kahului (877-5588) HOURS: Breakfast 7-11am, lunch from 11am & dinner from 5pm until 11pm, Thurs.-Fri. until midnight. SAMPLING: Create an omelette or a breakfast taco or try a skillet potato & egg dish, French toast, loco moco, or pancake sandwich $4.95-6.95. Salads include chicken Caesar, Oriental chicken, taco, cobb or fajita $6.25-7.95; BLT, club, fish, turkey and chicken sandwiches $4.95-6.25; burgers, taco platters and plate lunches $5.75-7.95. Sizzling fajitas $7.25-7.95. Dinner entrees served with soup or salad include fish, steak, chicken stir-fry, ribs and fettucini primavera. Cinnamon apple or chocolate sundae, brownie or fried ice cream snow ball $3.45-4.50. COMMENTS: A diverse menu and affordable prices which boils down to great family dining. They also have a great keiki (kids) menu and knowing how fussy some kids can be, they'll even cut the crusts off the sandwiches! A few new salads and dinner entrees have livened up the menu. One of only a few restaurants in the area open on Sundays, it's a convenient stop for a bite enroute to the airport. There is another Koho Grill and Bar at Napili Plaza and the same owners also run the Plantation House in Kapalua and the SeaWatch restaurant in Wailea.

LAS PINATAS OF MAUI   *Mexican*
395 Dairy Rd., Kahului (877-8707) HOURS: Mon.-Sat. 10:30am-7:30pm. SAMPLING: Nachos, tostados, hard & soft shell tacos, enchiladas, burritos, quesadillas, Mexican salads $2.05-5.55. Combination plates $5.95-6.95. COMMENTS: Owner Steve Waller reports that everything is made from scratch, from the beans to the salsa (two kinds, blended and smooth or chunky) and they use only 100% cholesterol free oils. A family operation, they wanted to keep the prices affordable, yet maintain a high standard. Vegetarian selections, too. Dine in or take out. A small, fast-food sized place; very convenient enroute to the airport.

LITTLE CAFE SIAM (See Food Court at Kaahumanu Center)

LUCY'S CYBER RESTAURANT & KATCHI KATCHI ESPRESSO BAR
American/Puerto Rican/Vegetarian
161 Alamaha St., Kahului Industrial Area (871-1135) HOURS: 10-2am SAMPLING: Same menu for lunch and dinner. Appetizers include jalapeno poppers, steak & onions with oyster sauce and Puerto Rican pasteles $3.95-8.95. Salads, burgers and sandwiches range from Philly steak to BLT to turkey, bacon and avocado to grilled cheese $4.50-8.95; Mahi mahi, steak, roast beef, manicotti crepes or spaghetti $5.95-10.50. Small vegetarian buffet every Sunday (6pm) and Monday (7pm) highlight a different ethnic food each week like Cuban, Russian or Irish for $15. COMMENTS: The casual kind of restaurant where you could probably get up and pour your own coffee (and pour some for the table next to

you while you're at it!) The bar does more business than the restaurant. Casual food, coffee drinks (including Puerto Rican coffee) along with darts, pool, a jukebox and a table of computers in "Lucy's Cyber Room" where you can surf the net.
(Lucy's Internet address is http://www.maui.net/ ~ lucys_pl or send E-Mail to lucyspl@maui.net)

MARKET STREET CAFE AND SAIMIN *Local*
318 North Market St., Wailuku (Former location of Sam Sato's) (249-0555). HOURS: Breakfast and Lunch 5:30am-2pm Mon.-Sat.; 6am-noon Sunday. SAMPLING: Belgian waffles with strawberries, sweet bread French toast, omelettes or set breakfast $3.75-4.50. Burgers, tuna, ham & egg and fried egg sandwiches; beef stew, roast pork, teriyaki, ribs and noodles $2.25-5.95. Daily specials include pork tofu, oxtail, kal bi, spaghetti and roast turkey $5.75-5.95. COMMENTS: Was the location for years of Sam Sato's and more recently it was Pupule Cafe. Market Street Cafe & Saimin opened April, 1996.

MAMA BRAVA (See Food Court at Kaahumanu Center)

MAMA DING'S PASTELES RESTAURANT ★ *Puerto Rican-Local*
255 E Alamaha St., Kahului (877-5796) HOURS: Breakfast/lunch 6:30am-2pm Mon.-Fri. You can have lunch at 7am and breakfast at 1pm! SAMPLING: Eggs Bermuda (2 eggs whipped with cream cheese and onion) served with potatoes or rice and toast $4.50 or a Puerto-Rican plate lunch $5.95 with pastele, gandule rice, empanadilla, choice of meat, bacalao salad and dessert. Other lunches run $2.95-5.75 including a homemade chorizo burger for $3.50. COMMENTS: Ready for a different breakfast? Skip IHOP and Denny's and try this cozy restaurant tucked away in the Kahului Industrial Area. Try a pastele which has an exterior of grated green banana and a filling of pork, vegetables and spices that is then steamed. Delicious! We've tried several of their breakfasts, all were good! No credit cards.

MAUI BAKE SHOP & DELI ★ *European Pastries-Deli*
2092 Vineyard St., Wailuku (242-0064) HOURS: Mon.-Fri. 5:30am-6:30pm, Sat. 7am-3pm. SAMPLING: They seem to be getting a thumbs up from visitors and tourists alike. An early morning arrival assures a greater selection from the many varied goodies. Some items are novelty desserts, shaped like pigs and chickens! This European style bakery is a combination of efforts between French chef Jose and his wife, Claire Fjuii Krall. They have pizzas, quiches, lasagna and sandwiches on French bread, soups, salads or croissant sandwiches $3-5.95. The big stone oven is still there, left over from the Yokouchi family that was in this location in the 1930s. Desserts include cakes, napoleons and other very fancy pastries. At Christmas holiday time check out their stollen gingerbread and yule logs, at Easter indulge in a marzipan egg. There are a few ice cream tables and chairs. Jose Krall began cooking in 1976 in France and trained in Belgium and France after that. He was Executive Pastry Chef at the Maui Prince in Wailea before opening this shop in Wailuku. Yum!

MAUI BAKERY, BAGELRY AND DELI *Light meals*
201 Dairy Rd., Kahului (871-4825) HOURS: 6:30am-5:30pm; closed Sunday. SAMPLING: Sandwiches come with soda and chips and are served on French bread. Also specialty baked goods like focaccia and pesto calzone. Salads include tuna, potato, egg, curry chicken and nine varieties of cream cheese toppings $3-6. Dessert items such as brownies, coffee cake and macaroons can round out your meal. COMMENTS: Freshly baked bagels come in a variety of flavors like strawberry, jalapeno and veggie.

MAUI COFFEE & CANDY FACTORY *Buffet*
Old Kahului Store Building, 55 Kaahumanu Ave., Kahului (871-0964) Not open as we go to press. All we could find out is that they plan to have a buffet and will sell retail coffee . . . .and presumably candy.

MAUI COFFEE ROASTERS (BEAN'S WORLD) *Light meals*
444 Hana Highway, Kahului (877-CUPS) HOURS: Mon.-Fri. 7:30am-6pm; Sat. 8am-5pm; Sun. 9am-3pm. SAMPLING: Veggie bagel, focaccia, basmato, falafel pita, crab salad or turkey sandwich, veggie burger, Caesar, tuna or Nicky salad (with brown & wild rice blend) $4.95-6.45. Also crab & red pepper quesadilla, ratatouille, eggplant subs and a variety of raviolis. Scones, chocolate croissants, brownies, coffee cake and muffins, too. $1.20-2.40 COMMENTS: Brightly and whimsically decorated with counter and table seating. Bean's World coffees feature Hawaiian, imported and flavored coffees, freshly roasted or retail sale or to order off the menu. Specialty drinks include granitas, rice milk, Maui juices, flavored teas and a variety of espressos, lattes and cappuccinos.

MAUI MALL
Not a food court, but there are several small food outlets in the mall: Restaurant Matsu has Japanese food including plate dishes, tempura, noodles, donburi (in a bowl over rice), sushi and bento lunches. There is also Siu's Chinese Kitchen, SW Bar-B-Q, a cafeteria-style Harvest House at Woolworth's and Tasaka Guri-Guri for a local type of creamy sherbet you can order with or without beans! (IHOP, Tiffany Luigi's and Stanton's are also at the mall and listed separately.)

MAUI TACOS (See Food Court at Kaahumanu Center)

MEL'S LUNCH TO YOU *Ethnic/Local*
1276 Lower Main St., at the Kanaloa Seafood Market, Wailuku (242-8271) HOURS: Lunch & delivery Mon.- Fri. 9am-1:30pm. SAMPLING: Select from over 10 dishes on their steam table; some daily entrees remain the same, others change weekly. The Hawaiian plate lunch and Friday seafood platter are popular as are the chicken yakitori, chow fun, pork tofu, chicken hekka and Filipino pork & (fresh, local) pumpkin. Wednesday's special is roasted turkey and they bring in fresh fish daily. Entrees run $5-6. Their bento boxes run $5.50 and you can select the three items to be included. COMMENTS: As soon as they opened we had some of our readers writing to let us know that this place is a find! They are located at the Kanaloa Seafood Market (244-0988) which sells exotic reef fish such as opelu, akule and oio.

MUSHROOM *Local*
2080 Vineyard, Wailuku (244-7117) HOURS: Lunch 10am-2pm and dinner 5-8:30pm. SAMPLING: Chinese pasta, calamari, beef stew, sauteed chicken, scallops, chicken and roast pork entrees all include rice, salad and soup $5-7.50. "Prepare your own" sandwiches, seafood or oxtail soup, local noodles, fried rice and daily specials like meat loaf, salmon steak, ham hock stew and chicken lau lau $3.25-6.25. COMMENTS: Owner Nagato Kato was with Kobe restaurant in Lahaina and Humuhumu at the Grand Wailea. This accommodating restaurant advises that if you're pressed for time you can call in your order 15 minutes before arrival and be served in minutes. They also want you to know that they love kids! Great local fare, one of the best reasons to come to Wailuku is to eat!

NAZO'S *Hawaiian-Local Style*
1063 Lower Main St., Wailuku, at Puuone Plaza (244-0529) HOURS: Mon.-Sat lunch 10am-2pm, dinner 5-9pm. SAMPLING: Sandwiches like egg salad or grilled ham and cheese $2.25. Entrees include soup or salad, rice or mashed potatoes, coffee, tea or fruit punch. Selections are liver with bacon, pork & squash, shrimp tempura, chicken papaya and pork adobo $5.50-7.25. Caesar or Oriental Chinese salads $3.75-6. Oxtail soup and Filipino specialties. Luau stew is featured on Wednesday, pig's feet on Thursday and Saturday. COMMENTS: A small, family-owned restaurant which is very affordable and prides themselves on their home-style cooking. They've added French fries to the menu by popular demand. Beer & wine, delivery and grilled fish, ahi and salmon bentos are all available.

NHU Y' RESTAURANT *Vietnamese*
1246 Lower Main St., Wailuku (244-2167) HOURS: Mon-Sat. 10am-3pm; 5-9:30pm (same menu all day) SAMPLING: Fried calamari, spring rolls and summer rolls with pork & shrimp and green papaya, lemon beef or lotus root salad $4.95-7.95. Specialties (with do-it-yourself vegetable summer rolls) include grilled pork meatballs, shrimp pops (on a sugar cane stick) and Vietnamese shrimp crepe $6.95-8.95. Beef, chicken or seafood noodle soup $5.75; beef stew $6.25, vermicelli noodles or rice plates with pork, shrimp and lemongrass beef or chicken $5.25-6.75. Stir-fry, lemongrass, egg noodle, sweet and sour entrees

selections as well as catfish, pork or shrimp in a clay pot. $5.95-8.75. Vietnamese fondue dishes with beef, shrimp and calamari are cooked at the table $7.25-13.75 They also have dessert: tapioca, dried longan, mungo bean and coconut redbean puddings $2-2.50. COMMENTS: This restaurant had changed hands (and names) four times since our last book. It's been difficult to keep up, but the good news is it has always been Vietnamese and the food, for the most part, has always been good. These new owners seem hospitable and gracious and we hope they'll be the ones that are here for our next edition. Opened May, 1996.

NORM'S CAFE   *Local style*
740 Lower Main St. (242-1667) HOURS: Breakfast and lunch Tues.-Sat 5am-2pm, Sun. 6am-2pm. Dinner Wed.-Thurs 5-8pm, Fri.-Sat. 5-9pm. SAMPLING: Local foods with okazuya. Local style "grinds" served with rice, macaroni salad, tossed green salad or coleslaw and includes roast pork, mahi, beef stew, beef tomato or roast pork $4.95-5.50. Dinners $7.95-12.95. Norm's sandwiches $2-7. Also noodles and salads.

OSAMU   *Japanese-Sushi*
270 Waiehu Beach Road, Wailuku (243-9323) Lunch Mon.-Fri. 10:30am-2pm, dinner Mon.-Sat. 5:30-9pm with sushi bar til 10. SAMPLING: Beef/ginger sauce, BBQ fish, potato koroke and several varieties of teriyaki, katsu, tempura and curry. For lunch $6-6.70; same items for dinner $6.75-8.75. Additional dinner items include sashimi combination, yosenabe and sukiyaki $9.20-12.95 COMMENTS: Meals include miso soup, rice and tsukemono. No liquor license, so bring your own. Owner Osamu Nishimiya was with the Westin Maui before opening his own restaurant in April, 1996.

PANDA EXPRESS (See Food Court at Kaahumanu Center)

RAMON'S   *Mexican*
2102 Vineyard St., Wailuku (244-7243) HOURS: Mon.-Sat. 10-10pm; Sundays 8am-2pm. SAMPLING: Homemade corned beef, pancakes, huevos rancheros, or con chorizo, Spanish omelette, loco moco for breakfast $3.95-5.95. Tostadas, burritos, taco salad, enchiladas, chile relleno, quesdilla $5.95-9.95 plus burgers, local plates. A la carte items run $1.75-5.95; fried ice cream for dessert at $3.95. COMMENTS: Opened in 1996 in the former Maui Boy location. They have plans to add an ice cream parlor and a bar/lounge with dancing.

SAIGON SANDWICHES   *French Sandwich Bakery*
1322 Lower Main, #A, Wailuku (244-8800) Mon.-Sat. 9am-6pm SAMPLING: Beef, ham, chicken, turkey, vegetarian, tofu, pate, steamed pork or Saigon special with ham, pate, steamed pork and head cheese $2.75-3.90. Oriental chicken salad, egg roll, chicken curry, spicy beef stew and wonton soup $5-5.25 and appetizers of spring roll, Vietnamese or tofu egg roll, papaya shrimp salad and soups $2.50-3.95. Also Vietnamese espresso $2 and an extensive selection of unusual desserts including taro, corn or beans with sweet rice and coconut syrup, apple banana with tapioca and coconut syrup and four fruit delight with lychee, mandarin orange, cherries and pineapple $2.15-2.25. COMMENTS: The French occupation of Vietnam lasted nearly ten decades, which was long enough

to have quite an influence on the cooking. Their meats are all marinated and the sandwiches served on freshly baked French bread or large croissants with pickled carrots and turnips. Breakfast and lunch picnic baskets are also available.

SAM SATO'S *Local Style-Hawaiian*
1750 Wili Pa Loop, Wailuku (244-7124) HOURS: Breakfast and lunch 7am-2pm; pastries served until 4pm. Closed Sunday. SAMPLING: Noodles are their specialty. Breakfast includes eggs or pancakes. Lunch options include combination plates $4.50-5.75 such as teriyaki beef, stew, chop steak or spare ribs. Sandwiches and burgers. Saimin and chow fun are served in small or large portions for $3-5.75. COMMENTS: The homemade pastries are wonderful. The peach, apple and coconut turnovers were fragrant and fresh. In addition to noodles they specialize in manju, a Japanese tea cake. It may come as a big surprise when you discover that these tasty morsels are actually filled with a mashed version of lima beans! COMMENTS: Located near the Wailuku post office in the Millyard.

SHIN SHIN CHINESE SEAFOOD *Northern Chinese*
752 Lower Main St., Wailuku (244-7788) HOURS: 10am-9pm; Lunch 10am-2:30pm SAMPLING: Two dozen lunch specials feature dishes off the main menu with rice and soup for $6.95. Almond, hot pepper or curry chicken; sweet and sour eggplant, mu shui pork; Mandarin, broccoli, Mongolian beef and roast pork with taro are a few choices for $6.50-7.50 Shrimp, squid, fish, crab and scallop dishes $10.50 plus soup, vegetables, sizzling platters, noodle and rice.

SIAM THAI *Thai*
123 N. Market St., Wailuku (244-3817) HOURS: Lunch Mon.-Sat. 11am-2:30pm; dinner nightly 5-9:30pm. Fresh spring rolls, sateh, green papaya salad, coconut or spicy soup $5.50-7.95 Eggplant tofu, red, green or yellow curry, Thai noodles, deep fried cornish game hen, Evil Prince, lemon beef or chicken $6.50-8.95. Ginger crispy fish, lobster tails or crab legs with bean sauce, garlic squid $8.95-15.95. COMMENTS: The white table cloths give this restaurant an elegant air. Very good Thai food although the competition is stiff with Saeng Thai just around the corner. You can't go wrong with any of the currys (just pick your favorite color!) or the Thai tapioca with coconut milk.

SIZZLER *American*
355 E. Kamehameha Hwy, Kahului (871-1120) HOURS: 6am-10pm, until 11pm Fri. and Sat. SAMPLING: Sirloin steak, sizzler steak, chicken dishes all in the $8-15 range. All-you-can-eat salad bar includes soup, salad and tostada bar for only $7.99 lunch, $8.99 dinner. A keiki (children's) menu offers special meals for $1.99 for ages 10 and under. COMMENTS: As Sizzlers go, this is one of the better ones. Attractive surroundings with a good selection of entrees at family prices and a very good salad bar.

STANTON'S *American*
Maui Mall, Kahului (877-3711) HOURS: Mon.-Thurs. 8am-6pm; Fri. til 9pm; Sat. 9-5:30; Sun. til 4pm. (Breakfast til 11:30am). SAMPLING: Enjoy a break-

fast burrito, tofu scramble, Belgian waffle, filled croissants, oatmeal, quiche $3.50-6.50. Ham, turkey, pastrami, chicken, crab, veggie, BLT, club and grilled focaccia sandwiches; pesto pasta, tabouli, Greek, three-bean and Caesar salads $4.25-7.95; quesadillas, boboli pizza, tofu burger, avocado sandwich plate $5.95. Cake, apple pie and cheesecake $2.75-3.25. COMMENTS: Steamed and iced coffee drinks; liqueur coffees and full bar. Gourmet teas, coffees and cigars for sale.

TC RESTAURANT (FORMERLY TASTY CRUST) ★ *Local Style*
1770 Mill St., Wailuku (244-0845) HOURS: Daily 5:30am-1:30pm for breakfast and lunch; Wed.-Sun. 5-10pm for dinner. SAMPLING: Unique and delicious crusty hotcakes are their specialty, two are a meal for $2.40. French toast $2, waffles $1.85. Omelettes and egg dishes $3-3.75. Spare ribs, fried shrimp, pork cutlet, chop suey, stew, fried chicken, roast beef $5.25-5.90 are served with rice and a salad. Sandwiches and hamburgers $1.60-4. COMMENTS: Local atmosphere and no frills, just good food at great prices. They've been called Tasty Crust since 1943, but the landlord felt it was time to take the old name back! TC Restaurant will be moving anyway -- to Las Vegas within the next four years -- but Clarence, the owner, promises to give us the secret of his legendary pancakes before he goes!

TIFFANY LUIGI'S *Italian*
Maui Mall, Kahului (871-9521) HOURS: Mon.-Sat. 11am-10pm; Sun. 11am-5pm. SAMPLING: Buffalo wings, stuffed mushrooms, steamed clams or mussels, dry mein, calamari steak pupu, potato skins, fried cheese and saimin for starters $4.99-7.49. Calamari, scampi, chicken or eggplant parmesan, tequila shrimp, steak and baby back ribs $8.99-15.99 a la carte or $11.99-18.99 with soup or salad and garlic bread. Lasagna, fettucini Alfredo, pasta primavera, pesto $5.99-12.99. Pizzas include clam & garlic, Hawaiian and calzone $5.99-11.49. Meatball, cajun chicken, steak, Italian sub and mahi sandwiches and a variety of burgers $6.49-8.99. COMMENTS: Hand-tossed pizza dough, homemade sausage and pastas made by their Italian chef. Good selection and large portions. Recent renovations have lightened and brightened the atmosphere. They have entertainment from 10pm-2am Tues.-Sat.

TIN YING *Chinese*
1088 Lower Main St., Wailuku (242-4371) HOURS: Daily 10am-9pm. SAMPLING: Selections include Hong Kong or Szechuan style with prices ranging from $5.75-16.95; appetizers from $3.60. Eat in or take out. COMMENTS: Okasuya style lunches at $2.95 include an entree and fried rice or noodles and are a real good value.

TOKYO TEI ★ *Japanese*
1063 E. Lower Main St., Wailuku. (242-9630) HOURS: Mon.-Sat. Lunch 11-1:30pm, dinner 5-8:30pm;. Sunday dinner served until 8pm. SAMPLING: Lunch specials include beef cutlet, sweet sour pork, teriyaki meat, omelettes and noodles $3.50-6.25. Teishoku trays include shrimp tempura, sashimi, fried fish, teriyaki pork or steak $9.25-10.25. Dinner selections offer hakata chicken, seafood platter, yaki tori, tempura, teriyaki steak, broiled salmon -- and a others that are

difficult to pronounce -- include rice, miso soup, namasu and ko-ko and run $6.25-9.25. COMMENTS: Small and cozy atmosphere. Take out meals also available; catering for 50 and over. Cocktails. Popular with both visitors and local residents and deservedly so. Winner of one of our top three awards for best local restaurants. Great food, great value, don't miss this one!

WEI WEI BARBECUE AND NOODLE HOUSE
Wailuku Millyard (242-7928) COMMENTS: We heard they had 24 types of noodles, dim sum and hanging ducks in the windows. We tried to find out more after their April opening, but they never sent us any information.

YUMMY KOREAN (See Food Court at Kaahumanu Center)

MODERATE

CHART HOUSE ★ *American-Seafood*
500 N. Puunene Ave., Kahului (877-2476) HOURS: Dinner 5-10pm. SAMPLING: Lobster cakes, coconut shrimp, garlic bread and sashimi appetizers $5.75-12.50. Lobster pot pie, steak, prime rib, crab, lobster, fresh fish, prawns & garlic steak, fresh salmon, grilled portobello mushroom with fettucine, Tuscan chicken with farfalle. Entrees include a small salad bar with pastas, fruit and Caesar salad plus hot squaw bread, country-style bread, potatoes or wild rice $15.95-26.95. They also offer some good homemade desserts including mud pie, chocolate mousse and authentic key lime pie. COMMENTS: Large portions, excellent children's menu. There is also a Chart House restaurant in Lahaina and another in Wailea so its usually a lot less crowded on this side of the island. A pleasant ocean view.

GRAND WAIKAPU GRILL *International*
Golf course at Waikapu, just outside of Wailuku. HOURS: Limited breakfast/full lunch 9am-4pm only. SAMPLING: Omelette or eggs $7-8.50. Curry beef stew, spaghetti, stir-fried noodles, fresh catch, Caesar salad, burgers and reuben, cajun chicken or club sandwiches $5.95-8.95. A pupu menu of spring rolls, calamari strips, cajun wings, soup and potstickers runs $3-6.25. Sundaes, brownie with ice cream and apple pie are available for dessert $2.50. COMMENTS: Small room in the sprawling Frank Lloyd Wright building makes you feel like you're on a cruise ship. The Sandalwood Restaurant just across the course is open for sandwiches and quick snacks. (Primarily for golfers.)

IMPERIAL TEPPANYAKI *Japanese*
Maui Palms Hotel, Kahului (877-0071) HOURS: Nightly from 5:30-8:30pm. SAMPLING: A buffet with different items prepared by teppanyaki chefs at the buffet. Entrees might include fried fish, teriyaki, tempura, chicken yakitori. From the salad bar sample sushi, sashimi, miso soup, tofu with ginger sauce, fried noodles, long rice and other local favorites including Mandarin mousse dessert. $16.95 Adults, $5.95 Children. COMMENTS: Reservations required.

LONE STAR COOKHOUSE *BBQ/Smoked meats*
1234 Lower Main St. (242-6616) HOURS: 11am-9pm. Dinner 5-9pm, Sun. 11am-7pm. SAMPLING: Smoked BBQ plates of sausage, beef brisket, chicken, turkey legs, beef ribs with one, two or three meats and salad, corn on the cob, jalapeno corn muffin and ranch beans $8.95-11.95. Smoked beef brisket, sausage or chipped chicken sandwiches; baked potatoes with BBQ beef or BBQ chicken $4.95-6.95. Dinners come with coleslaw, potatoes and jalapeno muffin. Choices are: chicken fried steak, pork chops and charbroiled steaks $11.95-21.95. COMMENTS: Their meats are seasoned and slow-cooked for 16 hours in custom-built hardwood smokers; orders of ranch style beans are all-you-can-eat. Catering and take-out orders, too. Evening Entertainment.

MARCOS GRILL & DELI *Italian*
444 Hana Highway (877-4446) HOURS: Breakfast Mon.-Fri 7am-10:45am, Sat. & Sun 7:30am-1pm. Lunch and dinner daily 10:45am-10pm. SAMPLING: Large selection of omelettes (like shrimp & eggplant) plus chocolate cinnamon French toast, granola with strawberries and bananas and chocolate chip, banana nut, strawberry and apple cinnamon pancakes $4.95-9.95. Later on you can order fried mozzarella, bruschetta, scampi, Italian poppers, gnocchi, calamari or Italian poppers $5.95-9.95. Caesar, Greek, oriental chicken and stuffed tomato salads plus a choice of pizzas $6.95-10-95. Deli, sub and grilled sandwiches like chicken or meatball parmigiano, Italian sausage, NY strip steak, hot pastrami, reuben and burgers $5.95-10.95. Entrees include vodka rigatoni, veggie lasagna, pasta penne, seafood rustica (in hollowed bread), homemade ravioli and mushroom chicken $12.95-21.95 COMMENTS: They're now twice their original size with more tables and a cocktail lounge with a big screen TV. The menu is diverse and interesting and we hear good reports on the gnocchi and some of the pastas. Although this is a family-run restaurant, there was very little on the lunch and dinner menu appropriate for kids. That's not necessarily a drawback (especially if you don't have kids). In any case, they have been successful and have become popular enough to be making plans for a second Kihei location due to open in February '97.

MING YUEN *Chinese*
162 Alamaha, Kahului (871-7787) HOURS: Lunch daily 11:30am-5pm, dinner 5-9pm. SAMPLING: Sharksfin and bird's nest soup, lemon, ginger or three mushroom chicken, mu shui pork, Mongolian beef, grandma's tofu, abalone with mushrooms, chili shrimps, hot Szechuan eggplant, seafood chow mein, egg fu yung and smoked tea duck are just a few of the Cantonese and Szechuan dishes $6-13.50. Dinner buffet every Saturday night from 5:30-8, $12.50 adult, $6.50 child, and a lunch buffet Mon.-Fri. 11am-1:30pm for $8.50. Both feature a diverse selection of ten rotating items from the menu. COMMENTS: A little off the beaten track, you'll find it tucked behind Safeway off Kamehameha Ave. in the industrial area. Not as inexpensive as some of the other local eateries, but they do a great job. And surprise! They also make what just might be the best chocolate mousse on the island (there's a secret ingredient) and the almond "tofu" with chilled lychees isn't bad either!

PAPAS -N- CHILES   *Mexican*

Lono Bldg., 33 Lono Ave. (871-2074) HOURS: Mon.-Sat. 11am-10pm; Sun. 5-10pm. SAMPLING: Caldo seven mares (soup with seven seafoods), enchiladas Mazatlan (with shrimps, bell peppers, mushrooms and guacamole), Pescado frito (a whole red snapper or opakapaka fried), calamari steak, scampi, steak ranchero, chile verde or colorado (with pork chunks) $8.95-13.95. Fish tacos, fajitas and traditional combination plates (taco, burrito, enchilada) served with rice and homemade beans $7.55-12.95. Lite lunches and a la carte items also available $3.95-5.95. COMMENTS: Family-operated restaurant with a menu that emphasizes fish and seafood. The refried beans are homemade with olive oil and chicken stock instead of lard and it really makes a big difference in the flavor! Service is attentive and friendly. Children's menu. Guitar player on the weekends.

RAINBOW DINING ROOM   *Meat & Seafood*

Maui Beach Hotel, Kahului. HOURS: Nightly 5:30-8:30pm SAMPLING: Prime rib, mahi mahi, baked salmon, teriyaki or honey-stung chicken, scampi, lobster, crab legs, seafood or chicken stir-fry, crab legs, rack of lamb $11.50-28.95. Calamari, onion rings, clams, sashimi, mushroom appetizers run $2.75-8. COMMENTS: Dinners include local-style salad bar, soup, rice or potato and vegetables. Children's portions available.

RED DRAGON CHINESE RESTAURANT   *Chinese*

Maui Beach Hotel, Kahului (877-0051) HOURS: 5:30-8:30pm, closed Mon. & Tues. SAMPLING: Cantonese buffet dinner with over fifteen selections which change nightly. Entrees may include haposai, chop suey, beef broccoli, roast duck, sweet and sour pork, lemon, ginger or smoked chicken. Pickle, soup, Mandarin orange and chow mein included $14.95 Adults, $7.50 Children includes tax & tip. Reservations required.

SAENG'S THAI ★   *Thai*

2119 Vineyard St., Wailuku (244-1567) HOURS: Lunch Mon.-Fri. 11am-2:30pm. Dinner nightly 5-9:30pm. SAMPLING: Mee krob, sateh, spring rolls and other appetizers $4.95-8.50; coconut or spicy soups and green papaya, beef, chicken and tofu salads $5.50-7.95; entrees of Thai ginger beef, chicken delight, sweet and sour pork or Evil Prince $7.50-9.95; seafood dishes include honey, Thai or garlic shrimps, seafood gumbo and crispy fish $8.50-13.95; Thai specialties are shrimps asparagus, cashew chicken and red, green, masman or pineapple shrimp curries $7.50-12.95. COMMENTS: This is one of the most attractive local restaurants in Wailuku. Owners Toh, Tom and Zach Douangphoumy have created a little Eden with lots of plants providing privacy between tables. They also know how to cook Thai. Traveling in India, Laos, Vietnam and Thailand in their youth they had an opportunity to sample a diversity of foods. This is the best of Maui's Thai cuisine. Not only was the service attentive, but the portions generous and every new dish better than the last. We were especially partial to the peanut sauce. Don't miss this one! Also a Lahaina location with the same menu.

SANDALWOOD CLUBHOUSE *American*
Golf course at Waikapu, just outside of Wailuku. (243-6000) HOURS: Full lunch 10am-3pm; sandwiches only 3-4:40pm; pupus only 4:30-6pm. SAMPLING: Pork chops with Maui onions and mushroom gravy, teriyaki chicken breast, loco moco, boboli tuna & shrimp pizza, fresh catch, Caesar salad, burgers and reuben, cajun chicken or club sandwiches $5.95-8.95. A pupu menu of onion rings, chicken or mahi fingers, won ton, cheese-stuffed shrimp, canned salmon, corned beef or Vienna sausage, calamari, cajun wings, soup and Texas toothpicks (slivered onion with jalapenos) runs $3-5.95. Sandalwood Mud Pie or apple pie are available for dessert $2.75-3.25. COMMENTS: Pleasant room set atop the golf course. Seating outside on the wide lanais offer an expansive view of Maui from a slightly different perspective than the usual beach front scenery. The Waikapu Grill, just across the course, is open to golfers and their guests.

SHARKTOOTH BREWERY STEAKHOUSE *Steak & Seafood*
Kaahumanu Center, 275 W. Kaahumanu Ave. (871-6689) HOURS: Mon.-Thurs. 11am-9pm; Fri.-Sat. til 10pm; Sun. 11:30am-9pm SAMPLING: Crab & artichoke dip, coconut shrimp, black & blue seared ahi, sauteed mushrooms and sashimi are some of the pupus for $3.95-8.95; BBQ or Thai chicken pizza $8.95, chicken or seared ahi Caesar, chili & rice (with Sharktooth ale), Thai chicken salad and a selection of plate lunches $4.50-8.95. Sharktooth beer beef ribs, pork chops, steaks, Hawaiian or BBQ chicken, ravioli or seafood pasta $10.95-18.95. Prime rib, veggie or teriyaki chicken sandwiches, fresh fish & chips and blackened seared ahi tacos $5.95-8.95. Mango fandango cheesecake or macadamia pound cake to follow $3.95 COMMENTS: Four hand-carfted ales brewed on the premises: Sharktooth (amber), Poi Dog (wheat), Hula Girl (pale) and Big Kahuna (brown) and the food is good, too! Hearty portions, especially the ribs. They also have a keiki menu ($4.25) that's suitable for coloring. Intriguing Techno-Hawaiian decor with sepia toned photos and antique display cases of memorabilia from the beer industry.

UPCOUNTRY

INEXPENSIVE

COURTYARD DELI *American-Continental*
3620 Baldwin Ave. #102A, Makawao (572-3456) HOURS: Sun.-Thurs 7am-5pm; Fri.-Sat. 7am-9pm. SAMPLING: Soups, garden burger, chicken tarragon salad and salad sample plate, smoked marlin sandwich or create your own $4.95-6.50. For breakfast try the tofu scramble, Belgian waffles, frittatas, breakfast burritos or special cinnamon custard French toast $3.95-6. (On Sundays, try them for brunch with a side order of live music served til noon.) Dinners served 5-9pm on Friday (a Pacific Rim choice of chicken, vegetarian or seafood) and Saturday for Indian cuisine $8-15. Live music both nights. COMMENTS: Also coffee drinks, freshly-baked desserts and imported chocolates. Indoor or outdoor seating in the courtyard terrace.

FEATHER CAFE   *Healthful & Vegetarian*
3682 Baldwin Ave., corner of Baldwin and Makawao in Makawao town (572-1101) HOURS: 8am-9pm, dinner specials 6:30-9pm. SAMPLING: Wild veggie, mock chicken, tuna with eggless mayonnaise and free-range turkey sandwiches; big bean burrito, tempeh or garden burger $3.75-6.75. Salads include Maui veggies with or without brown rice, "Rhapsody in Green" with romaine, spinach and other all green ingredients, spicy Thai tofu over brown rice, Moroccan-style with tabouli and hummus and free-range chicken with raisins and almonds in eggless curry mayonnaise over brown rice $4.50-7. They also serve natural muffins, granola with soy milk, fresh vegetable juices and coffee drinks $1.35-3.50. COMMENTS: Whenever possible and available, they use organic grains and locally-grown fresh produce. Vegetarian dinner specials feature international cuisine: German, Greek, Italian, Hungarian and Thai.

GRANDMA'S COFFEE HOUSE ★   *Local Style*
Located in Keokea (878-2140) HOURS: Wed.-Sat. 7am-8pm, Sun.-Tues. til 5pm. COMMENTS: This coffee house is run by Alfred Franco. Alfred is encouraging the return of the coffee industry in Upcountry Maui. Born and raised in Upcountry, his grandmother taught him how to roast the coffee beans to perfection. He does this several times a day in his 100 plus year-old coffee roasting machine that was brought from Philadelphia by his great-grandmother. The coffee is sold by the pound in a blend known as "Maui Coffees." Some of the beans used are grown on Molokaʻi which is part of Maui County. Prices are high, and there is no decaf available. (Grandmother never taught Alfred how to do that.) A few tables are an invitation to visitors to sit down, enjoy a cup of coffee, espresso, capuccino, or fresh fruit juice along with cinnamon rolls (get there early!), muffins and more, all fresh from the oven. A bit more of an appetite might require one of their fresh avocado sandwiches, a bowl of chili and rice or homemade Portuguese bean soup. Even hot dishes like chicken curry or baked salmon! Or you might want to pick up a "you-bake" pizza available from 4-8pm Wed.-Sat. They also sell their own coffee bean and chocolate Krunch Bar, made from Grandma's recipe, of course. With the popularity of this place among locals and visitors alike, it is tough for them to keep up with the demand for these goodies. So if you're hungry in Upcountry, be sure to stop in at Grandma's, just five miles before the Tedeschi Winery. (If you stop by, could you see if they have found Christie's coffee cup yet?) Alfred's goal is to put Keokea on the maps and minds of everyone. And he just may do it!

KITADA'S KAU KAU CORNER   *Local Style*
3617 Baldwin Avenue, Makawao (572-7241) HOURS: 6am-1:30pm daily except Sun. SAMPLING: French toast, eggs and omelettes $2.50-6.25. Small or large portions of beef or pork tofu, chopsteak, beef stew and spare ribs served with rice, macaroni salad and salted cabbage $3.75-5.25. Sandwiches and burgers $1.50-2.75. COMMENTS: Popular local eatery and with these prices and the variety of local plate lunches, you can see why.

KULA SANDALWOODS RESTAURANT
Haleakala Hwy. (878-3523) Different owners over the years, but one thing has not changed. Really poor communication! This year we did receive information on their lodgings, but nothing about the restaurant. We guess the concept of "free advertising" is beyond them.

MIXED PLATE *Local Style*
Pukalani Terrace Center (572-8258) HOURS: Daily 6am-1pm, breakfast and lunch, dinner; Fri. from 4-8pm. SAMPLING: Any of four breakfast specials $4.15; lunch has an Okazuya daily menu with wonton min, tofu patties, mochiko chicken, teriyaki steak and sushi. Specials might include lau lau, chicken hekka, mushroom chicken and kalua pork. Dinners offer curry stew, seafood, sweet sour spare ribs, halemalu chicken, butter fish, and chicken katsu from $5.

MAMA-SON'S *Korean BBQ*
Pukalani Terrace Shopping Center, 56 Pukalani St. (572-6213) HOURS: 10am-9pm.Closed Tuesday. SAMPLING: Breakfast items like saimin, udon, vegetable omelette, "omelrice" and oyako don buri are offered all day for $2.95-4.25. BBQ beef, chicken and pork, kal bi ribs, teri beef or chicken, curry rice, fried mandoo, bibim bap, bibim kook soo and meat jun can be ordered a la carte or in combo plates $4.95-6.95 and come with three scoops rice and three vegetables. Udon or saimin noodles run $3.35-5.95 and soups from oxtail to seaweed are $3.95-6.95. Dinners feature ribs, mahi mahi, and squid or seafood stir-fry $6.95-8.95. COMMENTS: Mama and John (son of Mama) opened their original award-winning restaurant in Hong Kong in 1976. Mama-son's opened June, 1996.

PIZZA FRESH *Italian*
1043 Makawao Ave., Unit 103 (572-2000) HOURS: Daily 3-9pm. SAMPLING: White or whole wheat crust pizza that they make and you bake. Available in four sizes, small to X-large and 50 toppings from which to choose $6.95-25.95. Also large salad $5.95, calzones $10.95 and cheesecake. COMMENTS: New options include sun-dried tomatoes and Alfredo sauce. Same owners as Kihei. They also deliver!

ROYAL KING'S GARDEN *Chinese*
Pukalani Shopping Center (572-7027) HOURS: Mon.-Sat. Lunch 11am-2pm; Dinner 4pm-9pm. Closed Sun. SAMPLING: Lunch specials include two entrees plus rice or chow mein and soda for $4.95. Dinners offer pot stickers, abalone soup, beef with broccoli, shrimp with ginger & onion, steamed fish, egg fu yung, crispy duck, pork hash, mu shu chicken, vegetarian cake noodle or chow mein $5.75-12.50. COMMENTS: No MSG. Former location of Fu Wah.

UPCOUNTRY CAFE *Local style*
7-2 Aewa Place, Pukalani (572-2395) This sounded like a great little find, but even though we called them several times, they apparently just couldn't "find" the time to supply us with any information.

MODERATE

CASANOVA ITALIAN RESTAURANT AND DELI   *Italian*
1188 Makawao Ave., Makawao (572-0220) HOURS: Lunch Mon.-Sat. 11am-2pm; dinner 5:30-9:30pm; deli 8am-6:30pm SAMPLING: The deli offers sandwiches with interesting combinations of lemon chicken, smoked salmon, roast peppers, mozzarella, eggplant, smoked ham, brie and pastrami plus Caesar, Greek and pasta salads $2.95-6.95. Breakfast pastries (lilikoi poppyseed cake, corn bread, blueberry scone, etc.), waffles, French toast and omelettes are served until 11:30 for $1.50-6.25. Coffee drinks include the "Ecoccino" -- a steamed rice dream and grain beverage, caffeine and dairy free. Restaurant lunches start with beef or salmon carpaccio, shrimp, calamari or clams $6-8. Caesar, Caprese, fresh fish or pear, walnut & gorgonzola salads $5-12. Cannelloni, lasagne and a choice of pasta/sauce combinations $8-10 and turkey, beef tenderloin, chicken and smoked ham sandwiches with a variety of cheeses and sauces come with salad and potatoes for $9-10. Dinners offer a larger selection of the lunch appetizers and salads $5-9 plus oven-baked fish, filet mignon, veal chop, roasted chicken and grilled seafood $16-23. Pastas include Rigatoni Beverly Hills (chicken and broccoli), Spaghetti Fradiavalo (seafood), "Maccheroni" with lamb, white and green linguini with mushrooms and spinach gnocchi $8-19. Pizzas and calzone are cooked in their wood-fired authentic Napoli style oven. The burning kiawe wood reaches and maintains a constant temperature of 700 degrees which creates the crispy crust on their pizza $10-15. COMMENTS: Another one of those restaurants that some people hate and others love although they seem to be winning more and more over to their side with good food and a variety of entertainment. (The cover charge is now waived for diners unless they are featuring a special celebrity concert). They have won accolades in Zagat and from Maui News' readers - let us know if you agree!

KULA LODGE   *"World Fusion With Local Ingredients"*
Five miles past Pukalani on Haleakala Highway (878-1535) HOURS: Breakfast 6:30-11:30am; Lunch 11:45-4:30pm, Dinner 5-9pm. SAMPLING: Breakfasts include tofu scramble, homemade corned beef hash, banana macadamia pancakes, upcountry granola and malted Belgian waffle $5.25-7.75. Lunches offer Kula onion & tomato, Asian ginger duck and papaya shrimp salads $4-7.50; Burgers, turkey melt, or club sandwich $7.50-10 and entrees of steamed salmon, Asian style crab cakes, grilled chicken, steak and fettucini Alfredo $12-25. Dinner appetizers include eggplant napoleon, steamed mussels, sauteed mushrooms, spring rolls and seared ahi $6.75-10 with entrees of duckling with raspberry sauce, sauteed shrimp and crab, rack of lamb Dijonnaise and seafood pasta $12-25. COMMENTS: Breakfast is the most popular meal of the day. An added benefit is the fireplace (a warming delight after a cold trip to the mountain top), panoramic view, and sunset cocktails. They recently added a brick patio amidst the sprawling cliffside garden. Children's portions available. They also offer vegetarian specials and make use of the varied types of organic produce grown in the Kula area.

MAUI MOUNTAIN COFFEE CO. CAFE   *American*
71 Baldwin Avenue, Paia (579-8477) HOURS: Breakfast 7-10:30/11am; lunch 11am-2:30pm. SAMPLING: Eggs, huevos rancheros, variety of omelettes, sweet bread French toast, and flavored pancakes including chocolate or pina colada $3.95-8.95. Specialties are shrimp, beef or vegetable stir-fry, fish tacos, hamburger on focaccia bun and herb-roasted half chicken $7.95-9.95. Sandwiches include roast beef, turkey, ham, vegetable or muffaletta -- an Italian style salami sandwich made popular in New Orleans $7.95-8.95. Asian chicken, Kula greens, fruit or pasta salad $6.95-8.95. COMMENTS: They also serve coffee drinks, granitas and chai tea along with an interesting selection of flavored cappuccinos and espressos -- vanilla, raspberry, caramel, hazelnut, orange and banana are just a few of the flavors that turn coffee into dessert. Opened June 1996.

POLLI'S   *Mexican*
1202 Makawao Ave., Makawao (572-7808) HOURS: Breakfast 7-10am, lunch and dinner 11am-10pm. SAMPLING: The usual eggs, pancakes, omelettes plus huevos rancheros and breakfast burrito $4.50-6.50. Mexican pizza, taquitos, jalapeno poppers, nachos, steak pupu $4.50-8.95. Chile relleno, tamale plate, stuffed quesadilla, seafood enchilada, chimichanga, fajitas, deluxe burritos, chili $5.50-14.95 Also menus for children $3.95 and gringos (burgers, BBQ chicken, steak and baby back ribs $6.50-15.95). COMMENTS: Black beans and chile verde sauce are two alternative menu options. They also have Polli's on Wheels, a mobile restaurant that brings their food to you every night from 4-9pm on South Kihei Road. (572-5315). Catering also available!

PUKALANI COUNTRY CLUB RESTAURANT   *American-Hawaiian*
360 Pukalani Rd. (572-1325) Turn right just before the shopping center at Pukalani and continue until the road ends. HOURS: Breakfast Mon.-Fri. 8-10:30am, lunch 10:30am-2pm, dinner 5-9pm. SAMPLING: Omelettes, pancakes, French toast, Belgian waffles or egg dishes with Kalua pig, tripe stew or lau lau and a side of rice or poi $3.35-5.55. For lunch there is Kalua pig, tripe stew, lau lau, pipi kaula, lomi salmon and chicken long rice $3.85-8.10. More tradiional fare includes a tuna melt, jumbo hot dog, burger, club or egg salad sandwich $4.10-6.35. Similar offerings at dinner at slightly higher prices along with steaks, breaded mahi or shrimp, fried chicken and teriyaki beef $7.45-12.70. COMMENTS: Lunch reservations are a must, as this is a popular place with the tour groups. Or eat lunch elsewhere and stop back on the way down from Upcountry for a drink, tropical sunset and a wonderful view. In addition to their authentic Hawaiian menu, they also have nightly specials and a salad bar at dinner. Keiki menu available.

STOPWATCH SPORTS BAR   *Italian/American*
1127 Makawao Ave. in Makawao (572-1380) HOURS: Daily 11am-2am. SAMPLING: Onion rings, won tons, cheese sticks, jalapeno poppers $3.25-5.75. Soups, salads, burgers and chicken, mahi or roast beef sandwiches $5.50-6.75. Entrees include fish and chips, grilled or fried chicken, mahi and scampi. $6.50-9 COMMENTS: The apple, banana cream and guava cheesecake are just a few of the home-baked pies made from scratch or you could try the Mudd Pie or sample

a chocolate sundae. The architecture was patterned after the old Nashiwa Bakery in Paia that was destroyed by a tidal wave. They're the only upcountry sports bar. The bar area has two big screens and four other TV's with satellite and cable.

EXPENSIVE

HALIIMAILE GENERAL STORE ★ *Hawai'i Regional & Continental*
Haliimaile Rd., Haliimaile (572-2666) HOURS: Lunch 11am-2:30pm, dinner 5:30-9:30pm, Sunday brunch 10am-2:30pm. Sushi bar Tues.-Sat. 5:30-9:30pm. SAMPLING: Their brunch menu is served a la carte and features Bev's signature boboli with crab dip, crab cakes Benedict, steak and egg hash, French toast, lox & bagel and omelettes $6-12 with brunch entrees of spinach, Chinese chicken or Nicoise salad and leg of lamb or chicken club sandwich $8-12 and a selection of desserts. Lunches offer all of the brunch entree items plus a cheese boboli, vegetable torte and blackened shrimp po' boy sandwich $4.50-12. Dinners start with sashimi Napoleon, fresh island fish cakes, Peking duck taco, shrimp lumpia and a marvelous brie & grape quesadilla with sweet pea guacamole $5-12. Innovative entrees include Szechuan barbecued salmon, coconut seafood curry, Hawaiian blackened chicken, lamb Hunan style and duck with port wine sauce and dried cherry, fresh cranberry, pecan crumble $16-24. Signature desserts ($6) are the macadamia nut fudge pie and the pina colada cheesecake which gave a new, literal meaning to the word "cheesecake" when it posed for the cover of *Food & Wine*, the only Hawai'i "dish" ever to do so! COMMENTS: This restaurant has put Haliimaile on the map collecting rave reviews and top ratings since it opened in October, 1988. The original structure dates back to the 1920s when it served as the General Store and hub of this community. The 5,000 square foot wood building has a main dining room and a sushi bar behind. The high ceiling is the original and the floors are refurbished hardwood. The intricately designed bar in the front dining room is surrounded by tall pine shelves and an exhibition kitchen. The menu changes seasonally, rotating to stress quality in the food availability and its preparation that includes the fresh herbs they cultivate in their own garden. The dinner menu features an innovative selection of dishes with unusual and creative preparations. The admirable wine list includes some nice ports, sherrys and cognacs. Our only previous complaint was the lack of choices for the traveling toddler in the group. Well, thanks go to Bev and Joe Gannon for adding a Haliimaile style peanut butter and jelly sandwich -- served on raisin bread, of course! This place has style! No complaints now. The food is exquisite and it's well worth the drive across the island.

MAKAWAO STEAK HOUSE *American*
3612 Baldwin, Makawao (572-8711) HOURS: Dinner only 5-10pm; Fri.-Sat. til 9:30pm. SAMPLING: Artichoke, crab cakes, escargot, dynamite and ahi spinach roll are some of the appetizers $5.75-6.75 and there are soups $3.75, dinner salads $5-6.75, or a la carte salads like Caesar with artichoke, salmon spinach and Chinese smoked fish for $10-12. Dinners are scampi, N.Y. steak, pork chop rosemary, beef picante, bouillabaise, ahi pasta, chicken Thai noodles, prime rib,

fresh fish and chicken zoie stuffed with creamed spinach $16.75-26. Dinners include choice of Portuguese bean soup, clam chowder or one of three salads. Fresh vegetables, potato or rice and breads complete the entree. COMMENTS: Cozy ambiance with wood paneling, curtains and a fireplace. Somewhat expensive for the area, but dinners are complete and the portions ample. A cut above a typical steakhouse menu. Hot bread, good spinach salad. Limited kids' menu: pizza, spaghetti or chicken $4.25-7.25.

PAIA/HAIKU

INEXPENSIVE to MODERATE

BANGKOK CUISINE *Thai*
120 Hana Highway in Paia (579-8979) HOURS: Lunch 11am-3pm, dinner 5-9:30pm. SAMPLING: Mee krob, sateh, summer rolls and stuffed chicken wings $5.50-9.50. Calamari, yum yai and green papaya salad; spicy or coconut soups $6.75-9.95. Evil Prince, garlic shrimp, red or green curry, Cornish game hen, chicken cashew basil, zucchini beef, Thai garlic pork or tofu delight with chicken $7.25-11.95, all available in mild, medium or hot. Tapioca, mud pie or white chocolate truffles for dessert $2.95-3.75 COMMENTS: Mike Kachornscrichol, who owned Siam Thai in Wailuku a couple of years back, is the owner of this family-run restaurant. They serve beer, cocktails and exotic drinks like the Bangkok Itch and the "infamous" Bangkok Devil. Coffee drinks, too.

CHARLEY'S *American-Italian*
142 Hana Highway in Paia (579-9453) HOURS: Breakfast 7am-1pm Sun. til 2:30), lunch 11:30am-2:30pm, dinner 5-10pm. SAMPLING: Breakfast taco or burrito, huevos rancheros, veggie Benedict, cinnamon vanilla French toast, omelettes, pancakes or build-your own breakfast $4-9.95. Lunch specials are country fried steak, fish & chips, fried chicken, chimichanga and hamburger steak $5.95-6.95. Sandwiches, salads, soups, burritos, burgers and chili $2.75-6.95. Dinners include pizza, calzone, lasagna, burgers, scampi, BBQ ribs, chicken marsala, beef brisket and smoked marlin $5.95-15.95. COMMENTS: They have a Big Screen (72 inch) television for sporting events by satellite. "Charley's smoker" is used to kiawe-smoke their ribs, brisket and marlin. Charley's began on Front Street in Lahaina as a granola type restaurant selling avocado sandwiches, carrot juice and the like. Charley's was named for the owners black and white great dane who roamed freely around the streets of Lahaina back in the old days. Charley and Charley's moved to Paia in 1971 and finally Charley P. Woofer restaurant and saloon was born. Charley, the dog, was named for the movie *Goodbye Charley* in which Debbie Reynolds was reincarnated as a great dane. The original Charley has been replaced by A.C. (after Charley) and Charley II. You'll find the story of Charley in its entirety on their menu!

CODY'S CANTINA *Mexican*
Old Haiku Cannery, Kokomo & Haiku Rd. in Haiku (575-7336) HOURS: Tuesday- Thursday & Sunday 12-10pm; Fri.-Sat. from 12noon-12midnight.

Closed Monday. SAMPLING: Tacos, quesadillas, enchiladas, burritos and taco salads with a variety of fillings, some including kalua pig or mahi mahi $2.25-5.50. Taco and enchilada combinations $5.50-6.50. Shrimp or Mexican salad, chili, upside down nachos, shrimp cocktail, roast chicken, shrimp melt, kalua pork sandwich $3.50-7.50. COMMENTS: Fri. & Sat. BBQ nights have steaks, fish, chicken, burgers and live entertainment. Full bar. Family-size chicken and ribs to take home $17-23. All food made fresh to order without animal fat.

HAIKU PIZZA & SUBS   *Italian*
Old Haiku Cannery, Kokomo & Haiku Rd. in Haiku (575-9211) HOURS: 11am-9pm. SAMPLING: So far there are 45 toppings for your pizza including unusual options like artichoke hearts, sun-dried tomatoes, Kula onions, smoked salmon, spinach, gorgonzola or feta cheese and baked tofu $12.95-18.95 or $2 by the slice. Meat, cheese and vegan subs $3.95-6.95. COMMENTS: Lunch special includes veggie or meat stuffed pizza or sub sandwich plus salad, soda and cookie for $5. They make all their own fresh pizza dough; it's even used by other pizza places! Soy cheese, whole wheat crust available. Their Haiku Bake Shoppe in front offers bread, rolls, brownies, danish, muffins, cheesecake, pies and cakes.

KIHATA RESTAURANT   *Japanese*
115 Hana Highway, Paia (579-9035) We tried to get an update, but no one here spoke English! We'll just have to presume that they are still closed on Monday, open for lunch Tues.-Sat. and dinner Tues.-Sun. 5-9pm. In our last book, their lunches included chicken katsu, noodle dishes, beef teriyaki for $5-8 and for dinner, Teishoku meals included miso soup, rice, shrimp tempura, chicken teriyaki and fish for $14-17. Also Bento lunches and sushi. We noted that they had good food, but that prices were slightly higher than similar restaurants in Wailuku. A cute local style restaurant that has been popular for years. However, unless someone different is taking the orders (than answering the phone), you might need to point to the menu item you want!

MAUI GROWN MARKET   *Sandwiches*
Hana Hwy. and Ulumalu in Haiku (572-1693) HOURS: Mon.-Sat. 6:30am-7pm; Sun. 7:30am-6pm. SAMPLING: Fresh soup daily and sandwiches ($5.50-6.25) that they claim to be the best on Maui or your money back! We haven't tried 'em yet, but they've got the right idea: all fresh ingredients like Maui onion and Maui sprouts and the condiments are all made from scratch from the mayo to the horseradish to the pesto. Hana box lunches include sandwich, chips, soda and a chocolate coconut "Dream Bar" $7.95. COMMENTS: They sound very confident and with all homemade ingredients, they may be justified. Try it and let us know if you had to ask for your money back!

MILAGROS FOOD CO.   *Tex-Mex*
#3 Baldwin Ave. on the corner of Hana Hwy., Paia (579-8755) HOURS: Breakfast 7-11:30am, lunch 11:30am-6pm, dinner 6-10:30pm. SAMPLING: Huevos rancheros, eggs Benedict, pancakes, French toast and granola for breakfast $3.95-6.95. Black bean nachos, pueblo grilled cheese with grilled chiles, charbroiled burgers and turkey melt for lunch $5.50-8.50. Appetizers

include Caesar and taco salads, grilled mussels, kalua pork taquitos and black bean feta quesadilla; entree menu has burritos, chili, fajitas and grilled fish with tomatillos $7.50-14.95. COMMENTS: Outside veranda; full bar with margaritas and micro beers. This is the only Maui restaurant with Santa Fe style Mexican food. It is owned by the same people as Peach's and Crumble bakery so they have a lot of the same desserts and will pack a box lunch for you while you're eating breakfast.

PAIA FISH MARKET RESTAURANT *American-Seafood*
101 Hana Highway, on the corner of Baldwin Ave. and Hana Highway in Paia (579-8030) HOURS: Lunch 11am-4:30pm and dinner 4:30-9pm. SAMPLING: Lunch and dinner selections similar to lunch plates. Lunches $9.95-14.95, dinners $14.95-16.95. A blackboard slate recounts the selections such as fish tacos, fish sandwich, fish chowder, shrimp fajitas, ahi burgers. Fresh fish is selected from the case and runs $10-16.95 for a dinner portion served with rice or home fries and coleslaw. Beer, wine and champagne. COMMENTS: This is the sixth restaurant for owner Warren Roberts from Malibu California. Our trial here was disappointing. Order at the counter and then pick up your meal and seat yourself at a half-dozen over-sized picnic tables. A dark interior at night with interesting and humorous artifacts lining the walls. The fish in the display looks fresh, but our filets of such fish as mahi or onaga were dried out when charbroiled. Our fish was accompanied by a pile of fried potatoes that filled up the plate. We were also disappointed in the selections for children. They sell fresh fish $11-14 lb.

PAUWELA CAFE *Healthy Homecooking*
Pauwela Cannery, 375 W. Kuiaha Rd., Haiku (575-9242) HOURS: 7am-3pm; Sun. 8am-2pm. SAMPLING: Breakfast is served throughout the day and includes hot-out-of-the-oven coffee cake, muffins, scones, breakfast breads and fruit cobbler $1.75-2.25. Also Eggs Chilaquile (corn tortillas layered with beans, cheese, chiles and egg custard), Pain Perdu (French bread baked in orange custard) and Belgian waffle served til 10am $4.25-4.75. Lunch selections include salads, black bean chili, veggie burrito, and kalua turkey with green chile pesto, tuna with capers & red peppers and ham & carmellized onion sandwiches $4-5.25. COMMENTS: Daily specials. Coffees, juices and smoothies. Keiki menu and take out available. Everything is made healthy and fresh with unbleached flour and raw sugar in all the baked goods. The lively artwork of Nancy Hoke dresses the walls of this cannery cafe, located on Highway 37 in the old Libby Pineapple Cannery, about 15 miles from Kahului. Built in 1918, it now houses many famous manufacturers of windsurf and surfing gear.

PEACH'S AND CRUMBLE *American-Healthy*
On Baldwin Ave. just off Hana Highway (579-8612) HOURS: Sat.-Wed 6:30am-6pm; Thurs.-Fri til 7:30pm. SAMPLING: Light meals, sandwiches and bakery items. Muffins, scones, cake squares and unusual baked items like carrot cake with guava filling, lilikoi cheesecake, "jungle bars" (dried organic bananas, coconut, macadamia nuts and passion fruit). Quiches, lasagna and Thai peanut salad. Sandwiches made on their own freshly baked bread $4-5.95. Box lunches $6.95. COMMENTS: A few counter seats. Full coffee and cappuccino bar. Their "Peach's and Crumble" (a niece's nickname) is their version of a peach cobbler.

PICNICS   *American-Healthy*
30 Baldwin Ave, a few blocks off the Hana Highway (579-8021) HOURS: Breakfast 7-11am, lunch 11am-7pm. SAMPLING: Breakfast croissant or burrito, Hawaiian pancakes, pancake sandwich, omelettes and set breakfasts $3.75-4.95. Plate lunches of teriyaki beef or chicken, roasted chicken, grilled fish or fish tacos include rice and salad for $6.95. Specialty is the spinach nutburger, but the mahi mahi supreme is just as good. Other hot sandwiches are calamari, cajun chicken or fish, BBQ beef or turkey and hamburgers $4.75-5.95. Turkey, avocado and swiss, tuna, veggie, roast beef and ham sandwiches $4.25-5.75. Chefs, chicken or fish Caesars and fruit salads $3.95-6.95. Excursion box lunch meals include choice of sandwich, drink, cookie, chips and fruit run $7.95-15.95 for one, $19.95 for two, $49 for 2-4 people. COMMENTS: Coffee drinks and fresh baked pastries plus frozen yogurt and banana splits. A very popular place to pick up some lunch goodies for the road to Hana or Haleakala. (In fact, their newsprint menu contains a map, and Guide to Hana with information about Hana's parks, bridges and points of interest.) Anything on their menu is available to go and everything is ready from 7am. No need to call ahead, just stop by enroute.

THE VEGAN RESTAURANT   *American-Vegetarian*
115 Baldwin Ave., a few blocks off the Hana Highway (579-9144) HOURS: 4-8:30pm. SAMPLING: Serves only vegetarian foods. Salad platters available in small or side portions $3.50-4.95, their vegan burger $4.95, Mexican fiesta combo $5.95, or entrees with selections varying daily $8.95. COMMENTS: It is hard to believe with the wealth of restaurants that this is the only one that's strictly vegetarian. It opened in late 1989 with an aim to create foods with tastes and textures to resemble meat products, but without the use of animal products or cholesterol in any of their food. Vegan is a non-profit organization that has been doing vegetarian nutrition seminars for more than six years before opening this restaurant. Seating for a dozen people. Catering also available. The menu stays pretty constant and there has not been a price change in six years!

309

WUNDERBAR   *German-Continental*
89 Hana Highway, Paia (579-8808) HOURS: Breakfast and lunch 7:30am-5pm, dinner 5-10pm. SAMPLING: Eggs Benedict with ham, veggie or cajun fish, omelettes, muesli, breakfast burrito and pancakes $4.45-9.95. Caesar, Greek or spinach salad, nachos, pastas, bratwurst & sauerkraut, coconut shrimp, crab cakes, calamari, burger and turkey, fish or chicken sandwich $6.75-9.95. Similar appetizers on dinner menu plus buffalo wings, kiawe smoked marlin, German kraut salad and avocado salad with fish or chicken $3.95-11.95. Pastas include marinara, primavera, carbonara, cajun and pesto or with seafood or smoked marlin $8.75-15.95. Entrees include beef stroganoff, seafood in lemon sauce, steak, pork chops, pizza, couscous chicken and chicken cordon bleu, or try German preparations of sauteed pork loin, veal with paprika cream sauce and German sausages $12.95-19.95. Desserts change frequently, but might feature Bavarian chocolate cake or chocolate mousse cake. They also plan to serve fresh strawberry and chocolate crepes. COMMENTS: The interior is cozy and warm with a friendly, family-style atmosphere. It has the feel of a European Inn. The bar and dining room are decorated with memorabilia such as a black forest clock, an old piano from Vienna, big railway signs and beer ads. The homecooked food is hearty and just a little bit different, but would certainly satisfy the meat and potatoes palate. Good, healthy preparations made with Maui grown produce, Kula beef and fresh fish from the H&P Fishmarket across the street. The desserts are made European-style, rich but not overwhelmingly sweet. There are cocktails, wine and beer on tap. They also serve the only German beer on Maui, but due to popularity, it might not be in stock. Entertainment on Friday nights.

EXPENSIVE

MAMA'S FISH HOUSE ★   *Continental-Seafood*
On Highway 36 just 1 1/2 miles past Paia at Kuau, look for the ship's flagpole and the angel fish sign. (579-8488) HOURS: Lunch 11am-2:30pm, pupus 2:30-5pm, dinner 5-9:30pm. SAMPLING: Menu and specials change daily to reflect the day's catch. Lunches might include steamed clams, fish chowder, sauteed seafood or grilled ahi salad, ginger teriyaki chicken, ahi club sandwich, filet mignon and a selection of fresh fish $9.95-23.95. Pupus of crab cakes, shrimp won tons, grilled mushrooms and seared sashimi run $9.95-14.95. Dinner entrees might be bouillabaise, Polynesian lobster, shrimp Hawaiian, seafood stuffed fish, honey-mustard BBQ mahi and a dozen other preparations of fresh fish for $20.95-36.95. Meals begin with a warm loaf of fresh poppy seed bread and end with a dessert tray that includes macadamia cheesecake, banana or mango crisp, pineapple almond tart or Kuau pie, a chocolate mousse with melted carmel in graham cracker and Oreo cookie crust. Nightly prix fixe menu with soup or salad, entree, dessert and coffee or tea for $45. Full bar service, reservations suggested. COMMENTS: Mama's opened in 1973 making it one of the island's oldest restaurants and one of the few that consistently offers an outstanding variety of excellently prepared foods. It really is a beach house, right on the ocean, with just the kind of atmosphere you expect to find in Hawai'i. Mama's mission was "to serve creative seafood dishes with that elusive taste of Maui island cooking." And it appears she has meet her mission! Expensive, but if you're looking for great Hawaiian seafood, put this one on your "must do" list.

HANA

INEXPENSIVE

CAFE AT HANA GARDENLAND *Light and healthy*
Located just before Hana at the Gardenland. (248-7340) HOURS: Daily 9am-6pm. SAMPLING: Everything on the menu served all day except waffles (with fresh fruit and real maple syrup) til 11. Otherwise order what you like of steamed eggs and salsa, granola with fresh island fruit, ambrosia cream with fruit and walnuts, smoked turkey sandwich, lasagna, boboli pizza, pesto or four cheese pasta, quiche $3.75-8.95. Lighter options include bagels, homemade banana bread, soup and garlic potato salad $2.75-3.50. Fresh squeezed orange juice and lemonade, fresh fruit smoothies or espresso drinks are sure to quench your thirst after that long drive. COMMENTS: Hillary Rodham Clinton and daughter Chelsea visited Maui in 1993 and enjoyed their first meal so much, they came back every day while they vacationed in Hana. (Apparently, steamed eggs and salsa was the First Lady's favorite.) While dining, pick up one of their whole coconuts and send it on home as a postcard. So, follow in the foot steps of the White House family. Good food and a relaxing atmosphere -- inside the nursery!

ALSO IN HANA:

HANA RANCH STORE: Open daily, ready-made sandwiches and hot dogs.

HASEGAWA GENERAL STORE: Open daily, a little bit of everything!! Hasegawa Store will have a new building within two years built on the site of the old building that was destroyed by fire. In the meantime, they are starting a new line of Hana coffee and other Hana products.

TUTU'S: Hana Bay, 8:30-4pm. Sandwiches, plate lunches. (People have been known to drive for miles for their haupia ice cream!)

MODERATE Nothing in Hana qualifies for this price range.

EXPENSIVE

HANA RANCH RESTAURANT *American*
Downtown Hana. (248-8255) HOURS: Lunch 11:30am-2pm, dinner 6-8:30pm. SAMPLING: Buffet luncheon with salad bar, teriyaki chicken, BBQ beef ribs, ranch beans, baked potato, pineapple coleslaw and beverage $8.95. Dinner entrees include mango BBQ smoked ribs, teriyaki chicken, NY steak, prawns and pasta, seafood combination and lobster $20.95-34.95. Wednesday is Pizza & Pasta night with a special menu of pizzas $8.50-18.50, spaghetti and lasagne $8.95-9.50 and appetizers of fried mozzarella, calamari, onion rings, sauteed jalapenos, Caesar salad and salad bar $3.50-10.95. Ice cream desserts or a "Banana Pizza" $3.25-7.50. COMMENTS: Attire is casual. Full bar service. Dinner reservations recommended.

HOTEL HANA MAUI DINING ROOM   *Continental*
(248-8211) HOURS: Breakfast 7:30-10am, lunch 11:30am-2pm, dinner 6-9pm.
SAMPLING: Breakfasts of fruit, eggs, hash, loco moco, waffles, French toast
or special recipe taro pancakes $8.50-14.50. Lunches start with pizza, brie
quesadilla or sashimi with entrees of chicken, steak, pasta or fish plus Oriental
chicken, fruit or smoked turkey salads and seafood pita, cajun ahi, or Hana club
sandwiches. $7.50-16.50. Dinner appetizers include crab cakes, escargot, scampi,
ahi carpaccio, prawn satay and pesto scallops $10-15.50. Entrees offer prime rib,
steak, pork loin, Thai chicken, lasagne primavera and choice of fresh catch
preparations $20.50-31. Nightly prix fixe of appetizer, soup or salad and entree
$40. Special buffet and Hawaiian dinner show on Sundays $29.95A, 13.95C.
COMMENTS: Children's menu with a good choice of mini-dinners $4.50-9.50.
From 11:30am-1:30pm, the Hotel offers a BBQ lunch at Hamoa Beach. The
"beach party" menu includes grilled sandwiches, hot entrees, sides and beverage
for $15.95A, $10.95C. Good, basic food served with light and tasty sauces.
Prices are a little high, but when you're the only fine dining place in town, I
guess you're entitled!

SUNSETS AND NIGHTLIFE

Here are a few suggestions as to what to do when and after the sun goes down
on Maui. These locations usually offer entertainment, however, call to see what
they are offering and which night, as it varies. Check *This Week* or the "Scene"
section of the Thursday edition of the *Maui News,* which lists current late night
happenings. Another good source for what's happening is *The Maui Bulletin,*
another free publication found around town.

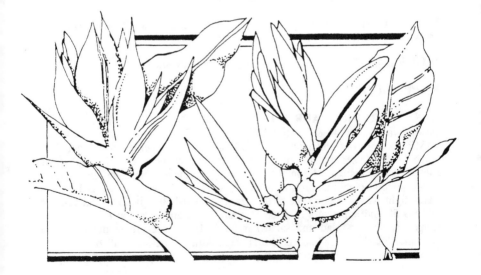

SUNSET WATCHING SUGGESTIONS

The Plantation House Restaurant, Kapalua
The SeaWatch Restaurant in Wailea
On the front lawn of the Pineapple Hill Restaurant, Kapalua
Enjoying pupus from the lobby bar of the Kapalua Bay Resort
Jameson's Grill and Bar at Kapalua
On the promontory at the Bay Club, Kapalua
Enroute down from Haleakala, at the Pukalani Country Club
The Fairway at the Wailea Golf Course (try an ice cream drink)
Relaxing in the lobby bar at the Renaissance Wailea Beach Resort
From the sea wall on Front Street
On a sunset cruise as you sail back into the harbor

NIGHT SPOTS & ENTERTAINMENT

Consult the "Scene" section of the *Maui News*, Thursday edition, to see who is playing when and where. The following spots generally offer entertainment, but as everything else, things change quickly!

Karaoke entertainment is still very popular at a number of restaurant/lounges. Karaoke is where a member of the audience selects a song that has music only, no words. They are given a sheet with the words and they sing along. There is usually a fee to entertain. Lahaina Broiler has karaoke nightly, Stopwatch and others do it periodically.

LAHAINA - KAANAPALI - KAPALUA AREA

Lahaina: Moose McGillycuddy's is always hopping for the young crowd. Lahaina Broiler, Kobe Japanese Steakhouse, Sunrise Cafe and Il Bucaniere all have musical entertainment. World Cafe, Cheeseburger in Paradise and Aloha Cantina have rock and roll and BJ's Chicago Pizzeria offers Hawaiian music as well. *Blue Tropix Nightclub* in Lahaina is just that, the only club on the west side and definitely the hottest night spot. A weekly schedule of entertainment changes each night from reggae to retro to dance parties. Open Thurs.-Mon. 8pm-2am; no cover til 9pm.

Kaanapali: The Makai Bar at the Marriott features entertainment and a very small dance floor. Both Hula Grill and Leilani's offer live Hawaiian music at the Whalers Village. The Royal Lahaina Resort, Napili Kai Beach Club and Kaanapali Beach Hotel also have Hawaiian music.

KIHEI - WAILEA - MAKENA AREA NIGHT SPOTS

The Inu Inu Lounge at the Aston Wailea Resort is a prime spot for evening entertainment in South Maui. In Makena, The Maui Prince always has something in their Molokini Lounge. Lone Star Cookhouse has country music in both their Kihei and Kahului locations. Kahale Beach Club is a small jazz club next to Kihei

Foodland and Ukulele Grill at the Maui Lu has a variety of nightly entertainment including Hawaiian. Oasis at the Maui Coast has entertainment by the pool. *Tsunami*, the high-tech place to be, is at the Grand Wailea. It features laser and neon lights, and a 10,000 square foot dance floor. Open 9pm-1am Sun.-Wed., Thurs. til 2am and Fri.-Sat. til 4am with $5 and $10 cover charge respectively. Top 40 music with a disc jockey.

ELSEWHERE

Casanova's in Makawao has a dance floor and features blues, jazz, western, disco and a bit of anything else. Sharktooth at Kaahumanu Center, Wunderbar in Paia and Stopwatch in Makawao have live music primarily on weekends.

BEACHES

INTRODUCTION

If you are looking for a variety of beautiful, uncrowded tropical beaches, nearly perfect weather year round and sparkling clear waters at enjoyable temperatures, Maui will not disappoint you.

With beaches that range from small to long, white sand to black sand or rock, or more exotic shades of green or salt and pepper. Many are well developed, a few (at least for a little longer) remain remote and unspoiled. There is something for everyone, from the lay-on-the-beach-under-a-palm-tree type, to the explorer-adventurer will not want for the appropriate beach. The Maui Visitors Bureau reports that there are 81 accessible beaches, 30 with public facilities around an island that spans 120 linear miles.

Maui's beaches are publicly owned and most have right-of-way access, however, the access is sometimes tricky to find and parking may be a problem! Parking areas are provided at most developed beaches, but are generally limited to 30 cars or less, making an early arrival at the more popular beaches a good idea. In the undeveloped areas you will have to wedge along the roadside. It is vital that you leave nothing of importance in your car as theft, especially at some of the remoter locations, is high.

We figured we had a story for the television show, Unsolved Mysteries. A few years ago we noted the posting of Beach Access signs. Each one was numbered. We decided that this may be of help to the users of this guide and we planned on cross referencing them with the information on each beach. We spoke to no fewer than 16 people in the Department of Land and Natural Resources, State Parks Department, County Parks Department, the Office of Economic Development and a handful more. The first dozen people had never heard of the numbered signs, the next few had heard of them, but didn't know what they were for or who had even placed them. Finally, one individual seemed to be "in the know" and offered to send us a County Shoreline Access Guide 1994. Now this is quite a nice map, and we'd recommend you send for one from The Office of Economic Development, County of Maui, 200 South High Street, Wailuku, HI 96793. While this map tells about facilities and accesses for each beach, the numbers it lists have nothing to do with the access signs, they are just numbers that correspond with the illustration on the map. We speculated as to the reason for these access numbered signs, which by the way, do not follow any sequential order. Perhaps it was for emergency vehicles? To specifically identify which access at which beach might be helpful. At long last we discovered from Jeff Chang that the beaches wre numbered to match a 1994 map. However, the map was so popular they ran out and it is now out of print! The only solution seems to be driving the island and manually writing down each sign number. We decided we didn't want to do that, so we aren't going to be able to help you with this one. Actually we decided that the menehunes posted these beach access numbers, just to drive these authors nuts.

At the larger developed beaches, a variety of facilities are provided. Many have convenient rinse-off showers, drinking water, restrooms, and picnic areas. A few have children's play or swim areas. The beaches near the major resorts often have rental equipment available for snorkeling, sailing, boogie boarding, and even underwater cameras. These beaches are generally clean and well maintained. Above Kapalua and below Wailea, where the beaches are undeveloped, expect to find no signs to mark the location, no facilities, and sometimes less cleanliness.

Since virtually all of Maui's good beaches are located on the leeward side of East and West Maui, you can expect sunny weather most of the time. This is because the mountains trap the moisture in the almost constant trade winds. Truly cloudy or bad weather in these areas is rare but when the weather is poor in one area, a short drive may put you back into the sun again. Swells from all directions reach Maui's shores. The three basic swell sources are the east and north-east trade winds, the North Pacific lows, and the South Pacific lows. The trades cause easterly swells of relatively low heights of 2-6 feet throughout most of the year. A stormy, persistent trade wind episode may cause swells of 8-12 feet and occasionally 10-15 feet on exposed eastern shores. Since the main resort areas are on leeward West and East Maui, they are protected.

North Maui and Hana are exposed to these conditions however, along with strong ocean currents, therefore very few beaches in these areas are considered safe for casual swimming.

Kona winds generated by southern hemisphere storms cause southerly swells that affect leeward Maui. This usually happens in the summer and will last for several days. Surf heights over eight feet are not common, but many of the resort areas have beaches with fairly steep drop offs causing rather sharp shore breaks. Although it may appear fun to play in these waves, many minor to moderate injuries are recorded at these times. Resorts will post red warning flags along the beach during times of unsafe surf conditions. Most beaches are affected during this time causing water turbidity and poor snorkeling conditions. At a few places, such as Lahaina, Olowalu and Maalaea, these conditions create good surfing.

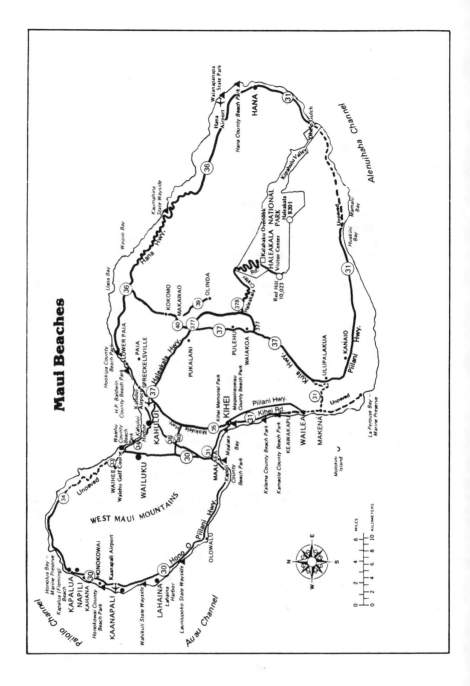

Maui Beaches

Northerly swells caused by winter storms northeast of the island are not common, but can cause large surf, particularly on the northern beaches, such as Baldwin, Kanaha and Hookipa Beach Parks.

Winter North Pacific storms generate high surf along the northwestern and northern shores of Maui. This is the source of the winter surf in Mokuleia Bay (Slaughterhouse), renowned for body surfing, and in Honolua Bay which is internationally known for surfing.

Land and sea breezes are local winds blowing from opposite directions at different times depending on the temperature difference between land and sea. The interaction of daytime sea breezes and trade winds, in the Wailea-Makena area particularly, produce almost daily light cloudiness in the afternoon and may bring showers. This is also somewhat true of the Honokowai to Kapalua region.

Oceanic tidal and trade wind currents are not a problem for the swimmer or snorkeler in the main resort areas from Makena to Kapalua except under unusual conditions such as Kona storms. Beaches outside of the resort areas should be treated with due caution since there are very few considered safe for casual swimming and snorkeling except by knowledgeable, experienced persons.

Maui's ocean playgrounds are probably the most benign in the world. There is no fire coral, jelly fish are rare, and sharks are well fed by the abundant marine life and rarely come into shore. However, you should always exercise good judgement and reasonable caution when at the beach.

1. "Never turn your back to the sea" is an old Hawaiian saying. Don't be caught off guard, waves come in sets with spells of calm in between.

2. Use the buddy system, never swim or snorkel alone.

3. If you are unsure of your abilities, use flotation devices attached to your body, such as a life vest or inflatable vest. Never rely on an air mattress or similar device from which you may become separated.

4. Study the ocean before you enter; look for rocks, breakers or currents.

5. Duck or dive beneath breaking waves before they reach you.

6. Never swim against a strong current, swim across it.

7. Know your limits.

8. Small children should be allowed to play near or in the surf ONLY with close supervision and should wear flotation devices.

9. When exploring tidal pools or reefs, always wear protective footwear and keep an eye on the ocean. Also, protect your hands.

10. When swimming around coral, be careful where you put your hands and feet. Urchin stings can be painful and coral cuts can be dangerous.

11. Respect the yellow and red flag warnings when placed on the developed beaches. They are there to advise you of unsafe conditions.

Paradise Publications has endeavored to provide current and accurate information on Maui's beautiful beaches, however remember, nature is unpredictable and weather, beach and current conditions can change. Enjoy your day at the beach, but utilize good judgement. Paradise Publications cannot be held responsible for accidents or injuries incurred.

Surface water temperature varies little with a mean temperature of 73.0 in January and 80.2 in August. Minimum and maximum range from 68 to 84 degrees. This is an almost ideal temperature (refreshing, but not cold) for swimming and you will find most resort pools cooler than the ocean.

BEST BETS
On South Maui our favorite beaches are Makena for its unspoiled beauty, Maluaka for its deep fine sand and beautiful coral, Wailea and Ulua-Mokapu for their great beaches, good snorkeling and beautiful resorts, and Keawakapu and Kamaole II which offer gentler offshore slopes where swimming is excellent. A good place for small children is the park at the end of Hauoli Street in Maalaea, just past the Makani A Kai condos. There are two small, sandy-bottomed pools protected by reefs on either side of the small rock jetty.

On West Maui, Kapalua offers a well protected bay with very good swimming and snorkeling. Hanakaoo Beach has a gentle offshore slope and the park has lots of parking, good facilities, numerous activities, and is next to the Hyatt. Olowalu has easy access and excellent snorkeling. An excellent place for small children to play in the sand and water is at Pu'unoa Beach, which is well protected by a large offshore reef.

SPINNER DOLPHINS

BEACH INDEX

MAALAEA TO LAHAINA

The beaches are described in order from Maalaea to Lahaina and are easy to spot from Honoapiilani Highway. They are all narrow and usually lined by Kiawe trees, however, they have gentle slopes to deeper water and the ocean is generally calmer and warmer than in other areas. The offshore coral reefs offer excellent snorkeling in calm weather, which is most of the time. These beaches are popular because of their convenient access and facilities as well as good swimming and snorkeling conditions.

PAPALAUA STATE WAYSIDE PARK

As you descend from the sea cliffs on your way from Maalaea you will see an undeveloped tropical shoreline stretch before you. At the foot of the cliffs at mile marker 11, Papalaua Park is marked by an easily seen sign. There are picnic tables, BBQ grills, and portable restrooms. The beach is long, (about 1/2 mile) and narrow and lined with Kiawe trees that almost reach the water's edge in places. The trees provide plenty of shady areas for this beautiful beach. Good swimming and fair snorkeling, popular picnicking area.

UKUMEHAME BEACH PARK

The entrance to the park is near mile marker 12, but there is no identifying sign. There is off-street paved parking for about 12 cars. Five concrete picnic tables. This is also a narrow 1/2 mile long sand beach with lots of Kiawe trees providing shade. Good swimming, fair snorkeling.

OLOWALU BEACH ★

About 2/10 mile before and after mile marker 14 you will see a large, but narrow stand of Kiawe trees between the road and the beach, followed by a few palm trees, then a few more scattered Kiawe trees. Parking is alongside the road. No facilities. This narrow sand beach slopes gently out to water four or five feet deep making it good for swimming and beach playing. There are extensive coral formations starting right offshore and continuing out a quarter mile or more, and a fair amount of fish expecting handouts. The ocean is generally warmer and calmer than elsewhere, making it a popular snorkeling spot.

AWALUA BEACH

The beach at mile marker 16 may be cobble stone or sand depending on the time of year and the prevailing conditions. No facilities. At times when Kona storms create a good southern swell, this becomes a very popular surfing spot for a few days until the swells subside.

LAUNIUPOKO STATE WAYSIDE PARK

This well-marked beach park near mile marker 18 offers a large paved parking area, restrooms, many picnic tables, BBQ grills, rinse-off showers, drinking water, pay phone, and a large grassy area with trees, all of which makes for a good picnic spot. There is a large man-made wading pool constructed of large boulders centered in the park. (Sand has accumulated to the extent that even at high tide there is no water in the pool). To the right is a rocky beach and to the left is a 200-yard dark sand beach with fairly gentle slope. It looks nice, but signs posted warn "Sharks have been seen in the shallow water off this beach. Entry into the water is discouraged." This area is rumored to be a shark breeding ground with shark fishing done here in the past. There is also a no alcohol sign posted. For some reason the beach does not seem to be used for much besides picnicking! However, a couple hundred yards offshore is good snorkeling and you may see snorkel excursions visit this shoreline when the weather prohibits a trip to Lana'i.

PUAMANA BEACH PARK
Well marked beach park near mile marker 19, just south of the Puamana Resort complex. Parking for 20 cars in paved parking area, with additional parking along the highway. Nice grassy park with seven picnic tables and plenty of shade trees. At the park itself there is no sandy beach, only a large pebble beach. The only beach is a narrow 200 yards long white sand beach just north of the park and fronting Puamana Resort. Fairly gentle slope to shallow water.

LAHAINA TO KAANAPALI

LAHAINA BEACH
There is a large public parking lot across from the 505 Front Street shopping center with easy access to the beach through the mall. There is also on-street parking near the Lahaina Shores with public right-of-way to the beach at the south end of the complex. Restrooms and showers are only available at the resort. The Lahaina Sailing Center is located on the beach. This narrow sand beach fronts the Lahaina Shores and 505 Front Street and is protected by a reef 30-50 yards out. The beach is generally sandy offshore with a gentle slope. The water stays fairly shallow out to the reef and contains some interesting coral formations. The area offers fair snorkeling in clear water on calm days. A good place for beginning snorkelers and children, but not good for swimming due to shallow water and abundant coral.

PUUNOA BEACH ★
The beach is at the north end of Lahaina between Kai Pali Rd. and the old Mala Wharf and can be seen as you leave Lahaina on Front St. Southern access: Take Kai Pali Rd. off Front St. Parking for about 20 cars along the road which is the entrance for the Puunoa Beach Estates. Public Beach access sign with concrete sidewalk to the beach. Mid beach access: Take Puunoa Place off Front St. at the Public Beach access sign. Parking for about four cars at the end of the road which ends at the beach. A rinse off hose here is the only facility for the beach. North access: Take Mala Wharf off Front St. Parking for approximately 20 cars along the road just before the entrance to the Mala boat launching parking area.

This narrow, dense, darker sand beach is about 300 yards long and well protected by a reef approximately 100-150 yards offshore. The beach slopes gently to water only 3-4 feet deep. Unfortunately, rock and coral near the surface make swimming unadvised. There are areas of the beach clear of coral 10 - 15 feet out where children can play safely in the calm, shallow water. At high tide there are more fish to see while snorkeling. This continues to be a favorite with our children because of the calm, warm water.

WAHIKULI STATE WAYSIDE PARK

There are three paved off-street parking areas between Lahaina and Kaanapali. Many covered picnic tables, restrooms, showers, and BBQ grills are provided. The first and third parking areas are marked but have no beach. The second unmarked area has an excellent, darker sand beach with a gentle slope to deeper water. There is some shelf rock in places but it's rounded and smooth and not a problem. With the handy facilities, trees for shade, and the nice beach, this is a good, and popular, spot for sunning, swimming, and picnicking.

HANAKAOO BEACH PARK ★

Off Honoapiilani Highway, immediately south of the Hyatt Regency, there is a large, well-marked, off-street parking area. The park has rinse-off showers, restroom, and picnic tables. Wide, darker sand beach with gentle slope to deeper water. This is a popular area because of the easy parking, facilities, good beach, shallow water and good swimming, and you are right next to the Hyatt.

HANAKAOO BEACH ★ (Kaanapali Beach)

The beach fronts the Hyatt Regency, Marriott, Kaanapali Alii, Westin Maui, Whaler's Shopping Center and condos, Kaanapali Beach Hotel, and the Sheraton, and is known as Kaanapali Beach. Access is through the Kaanapali Resort area. Turn off Honoapiilani Highway at either of the first two entrances. This area was not designed with non-guest use in mind, and parking is definitely a problem.

A) The Hyatt end of the beach is only a short walk from the large parking area of Hanakaoo Beach Park.
B) Public right-of-way with parking for 10 cars at the left of the Hyatt's lower parking lot.
C) Public right-of-way between the Hyatt and Marriott, no parking.
D) Public right-of-way between Marriott and Kaanapali Alii with parking for 11 cars only.
E) Public right-of-way between Kaanapali Alii and Westin Maui, no parking.
F) Public right-of-way between Kaanapali Beach Resort and the Sheraton with parking for 11 cars only.
G) The Whalers Shopping Center has a three-story pay parking lot, but with beach access only through the complex.
H) There is no on-street parking anywhere in the Kaanapali Resort complex.

The Hyatt, Marriott, Westin Maui, and Sheraton all have restrooms, showers, bars, and rental equipment. There is a beautiful, long, wide, white sand beach with an abrupt drop-off to deep water. There are small areas of offshore coral from the Hyatt to the Westin Maui at times, but no true offshore reef. Great swimming and good wave playing with the exception of two or three points along the beach where the waves consistently break fairly hard. In the winter, snorkeling can be fair off the Westin Maui when the coral is exposed underwater. The best snorkeling is at Black Rock, fronting the Sheraton Hotel. The water is almost always clear and fairly calm, with many types of nearly tame fish due to the popularity of hand feeding by snorkelers. (Bread, frozen peas and packaged dry noodles seem popular.) Not much colorful coral. The best entrance to the water is from the beach alongside Black Rock.

ALII KAHEKILI NUI 'AHUMAHI BEACH PARK ★
Previouly we referred to it as KAANAPALI BEACH - South End
This beach begins at the north side of Black Rock and runs for over a mile to the north fronting the Royal Lahaina Resort and the Maui Kaanapali Villas. Turn off Honoapiilani Road at the last Kaanapali exit at the stop light by the Maui Kaanapali Villas. This new beach park has been developed just north of these two resorts.

Kahekili was the last ruler of Maui. This park, which pays tribute to him, is lovely. The park's name, which is quite a mouthful, translates to "Feather Cloaked Nightly Thunderer." Kahekili ruled 1766-1793.

The beach park is open 6 am - 6:30 pm with plenty of paved parking spaces. There are paviliooions with dining tables, a very pleasant grassy lawn area dotted with BBQ's and mroe tables. A rinse off shower is available. There is a gate which is locked nightly. This area was formerly the Kaanapali airport. It has been cloed for a number o years now and future hotel and condo development is planned. However, current building and zoning restrictions have put any major development on hold.

This wide, (usually) white sand beach has a steep drop-off to deep water and is usually calm - a good place to swim. Snorkeling around Black Rock is almost always good.

KAHANA - NAPILI - KAPALUA AND BEYOND

KAANAPALI BEACH (North End)
This section of beach fronts the Mahana Resort, Maui Kai, Embassy Suites, Kaanapali Shores, Papakea, Maui Sands and Paki Maui from south to north, and ends at the Honokowai Beach Park. Access is generally only through the resorts. Most of the resorts have rinse-off showers convenient to the beach, however, no other facilities are available. This is a long, narrow, white sand beach which is fronted by a close-in reef. All the resorts except the Kaanapali Shores and Embassy Suites have retaining walls along the beach. The Kaanapali Shores has, over the last couple of years, suffered considerable erosion of its once wide beach and has recently completed an expensive new under-the-sand retaining wall in an effort to stabilize and restore it. There is also a cleared area through the coral in front of the resort. This is the only good swimming area on the north section of the beach and is the only good access through the reef for snorkeling.

The reef comes into shore at the south end of Papakea and again at the Honokowai Beach Park. At low tide the reef fronting Papakea can be walked on like a wide sidewalk. (See GENERAL INFORMATION - Children, for night walking on the reef.) The reef is generally only 10-20 yards offshore and the area between is very shallow with much coral and rock making it undesirable for swimming and snorkeling. The middle section of beach, fronting the old Kaanapali Airport, is slated for future development.

HONOKOWAI BEACH PARK
Turn off the Honoapiilani Hwy. on the first side street past the airport (at the Honokowai sign) and get onto Lower Honoapiilani Hwy., which parallels the ocean. The park is across the street from the Honokowai Grocery Store (a pay phone is available there). There is paved off-street parking for 30 cars. There are 11 picnic tables, 5 BBQ pits, restrooms, showers, and a grassy park with shade trees. The white sand beach is lined by a wide shelf of beach rock. Between the shelf rock and reef there is a narrow, shallow pool with a sandy bottom which is a good swimming area for small children. There is a break in the reef at the north end of the beach where you can get snorkeling access to the outside reef. Water sport equipment for rent at the Honokowai Store.

KAHANA BEACH
In front of the Kahana Beach Condominiums, Sands of Kahana, Royal Kahana, Valley Isle Resort and Hololani from south to north on Lower Honoapiilani Hwy. There is limited off-road parking at the south end of the beach. Other access would be through the condos. The only facilities available are at the condos, usually rinse-off showers. There are several grocery stores, one at the Valley Isle Resort, the other at the Hololani condos. This white sand beach varies from narrow to wide and its offshore area is shallow with rock and sand, semi-protected by reef. Good swimming, fair snorkeling. The beach may be cool and windy in the afternoons.

During the past years, from about 1989, this area has been particularly plagued by the unexplained green algae bloom which tends to concentrate here due to the wind, current and shoreline continues. The beach is frequently unappealing for swimming and beach use due to the amount of slimy green algae on the beach and in the water. One possible cause of this unsightly mess may be the nitrates and other chemicals which are used for agriculture and golf course maintainence, flowing into the ocean. The county is continuing to investigate and may find it necessary to institute some controls.

KEONENUI BEACH ★
The beach is in front of and surrounded by the Kahana Sunset with no convenient public access. A lovely wide crescent of white sand with a fairly gentle slope to water's edge, then fairly steep slope to deeper water. The beach is set in a small shallow cove, about 150 yards wide, which affords some protection. At times, especially in winter, rough seas come into the beach. When calm (most of the time), this is an excellent swimming and play area with fair snorkeling.

ALAELOA BEACH ("The Cove")
This miniature, jewel-like cove is surrounded by low sea cliffs. The small, approximately 25-30 yard long, white sand beach has a gentle slope with scattered rocks leading into sparkling clear waters. Pavilion and lounge chair area for use by Alaeloa guests. Good swimming and snorkeling with very clear and calm waters except when storm-generated waves come in. Fortunately, or unfortunately, depending on your point of view, this small cove is surrounded by the Alaeloa residential area which has no on or off-street public parking, therefore, public access to this beach is very difficult.

NAPILI BAY ★

There are two public accesses to this beautiful beach. There is a small, easily missed, public right-of-way and Napili Beach sign just past the Napili Shores at Napili Place Street. On-street parking at sign for Napili Surf Beach Resort. The public beach right-of-way sign shows the entrance to the beach. Public telephone in parking lot of Napili Surf. The second entrance is at the public beach right-of-way and Napili Sunset, Hale Napili, and Napili Bay signs on Hui Street. On-street parking and pay phone at entrance to beach walk. This is a long, wide crescent of white sand between two rocky points. The offshore slope is moderately steep. Usually very safe for swimming and snorkeling except during winter storms when large waves occasionally come into the bay. At the south end of the beach are a series of shallow, sandy tide pools which make an excellent place for children, but only under close supervision. Coral formations 30 - 40 yards offshore can provide fair snorkeling on calm days especially at the northern end of the beach and decent boogie boarding with mild swells. No public facilities along the beach. A grocery store is past the second entrance at the Napili Village Hotel.

KAPALUA BEACH ★

Just past the Napili Kai Beach Club you will see a public beach right-of-way sign. Off-street parking area for about 30 - 40 cars. Showers and restrooms. A beautiful crescent of white sand between two rocky points. The beach has a gentle slope to deeper water, maximum about 15 feet. From the left point, a reef arcs toward the long right point creating a very sheltered bay, probably the nicest and safest swimming beach on Maui. Shade is provided by numerous palm trees lining the back shore area. Above the beach are the lovely grounds of the Kapalua Bay Resort. Swimming is almost always excellent with plenty of play area for children. Snorkeling is usually good with many different kinds of fish and interesting coral. It is no surprise that this beach has been selected as one of the top ten beaches in the world. For many years local knew this beach as "Flemings Beach" and called D.T. Fleming's Beach "Stables." *REMEMBER* parking is limited, so arrive early!

NAMALU BAY ★

Park at Kapalua Beach and take the concrete path along the beach, up through the hotel's grounds, and out to the point of land separating Kapalua Bay from Namalu Bay. This small bay has a shoreline of large lava boulders, no beaches. On calm days snorkeling is very good and entry and exit over the rocks is easy. This little known spot is definitely worth the short walk down the trail.

ONELOA BEACH

Enter at the public right-of-way sign just past the Kapalua Bay Resort. Paved off-street parking for 12 - 15 cars only, no other facilities. Long, straight white sand beach with a shallow sand bar that extends to the surfline. The beach is posted with a warning sign "No swimming at time of high surf due to dangerous currents." This area tends to get windy and cloudy in the afternoons, especially in the winter months. We have usually found this beach deserted.

D. T. FLEMING BEACH PARK
The County maintains a life guard on this beach. The Ritz-Carlton operates The Beach House Restaurant. Off-street parking for 70 cars. Public showers. Private restrooms by the Beach House rstaurant. The long white sand beach is steep with an offshore sand bar which may cause dangerous water conditions when swells hit the beach. This beach was named for David Thomas Fleming (1881-1955), who became manager of the Honolua Ranch in 1912. Under his guidance, the Baldwin cattle ranch was converted to a pineapple plantation. His home is now the Pineapple Hill restaurant at Kapalua. Once called "Stables Beach" as the Fleming family kept their horses at this site into the 1950's.

MOKULEIA BEACH ★ (Slaughterhouse)
On Highway 30, past D. T. Fleming Beach Park, look for cars parked along the roadside and the Mokuleia-Honolua Marine Reserve sign. Park your car and hike down one of the steep dirt and rock trails - they're not difficult. There are no facilities. The wide, white sand beach has a gentle slope to deep water and is bordered by two rocky points and is situated at the foot of steep cliffs. The left middle part of the beach is usually clear of coral and rocks even in winter when the beach is subject to erosion. During the winter this is *THE* bodysurfing spot, especially when the surf is heavy, however, dangerous water conditions also exist. This area is only for the strong, experienced swimmer. The summer is generally much better for swimming and snorkeling. In the past couple of years, this has become a very popular beach. Snorkeling is fair to good, especially around the left rocky point where there is a reef. Okay in winter when the ocean is calm and visibility good. NOTE: The beach is known as Slaughterhouse because of the once existing slaughterhouse on the cliffs above the beach, not because of what the ocean can do to body surfers in the winter when the big ones are coming in! Remember this is part of the Honolua-Mokuleia Bay Marine Life Conservation District - look but don't disturb or take.

HONOLUA BAY ★
The next bay past Slaughterhouse is Honolua Bay. Watch for a dirt side road on the left. Park here and walk in along the road. There is no beach, just cobblestone with irregular patches of sand and an old concrete boat ramp in the middle. Excellent snorkeling in summer, spring, and fall especially in the morning, but in winter only on the calmest days. In summer on calm days the bay resembles a large glassy pond and in our opinion, this is the best snorkeling on Maui. Note: After a heavy rainfall, the water may be turbid for several days before it returns to its sparkling clear condition again. You can enter at the boat ramp or over the rocks and follow the reefs either left or right. Remember this is a Marine Life Conservation area, so look but don't disturb. There is an interesting phenomenon affecting the bay. As fresh water runoff percolates into the bay, a shimmering boundary layer (usually about three feet below the surface) is created between the fresh and salt waters. Depending on the amount of runoff it may be very apparent or disappear entirely. It is less prevalent on the right side of the bay. Honolua Bay is also an internationally known winter surfing spot. Storm generated waves come thundering in around the right point creating perfect waves and tubes. A good vantage point to watch the action is the cliffs at the right point of the bay, accessible by car on a short dirt road off the main highway.

KIHEI

The Kihei beaches aren't quite as beautiful as Wailea's. They don't have the nicely landscaped parking areas, or the large, beautiful resort complexes (this is condo country). They do offer increased facilities such as BBQs, picnic tables, drinking water, and grassy play areas. The Kamaole I, II and III beaches even have lifeguards. The beaches are listed in order from Maalaea Bay to Wailea.

MAALAEA BAY BEACH
This gently curving white sand beach stretches three miles from the Maalaea boat harbor to Kihei. For the most part, the beach is backed by low sand dunes and large generally wet, sand flats. Public access is from many areas along South Kihei Road. There are no facilities. Casual beach activities are best early in the morning before the strong, mid-morning, prevailing winds begin to sweep across the isthmus. Due to the length of the beach and the hard-packed sand near the water, this has become a popular place to jog. Windsurfing is popular in the afternoons.

The beach begins in front of the last three condominiums in Maalaea, the Kana'I A Nalu, Hono Kai and the Makani A Kai. Just past the Makani A Kai on Hauoli Street is a public park and beach access. There is a good section of beach here with a fairly gentle drop off. Also there are two small, sandy-bottomed pools, protected by the reef on either side of the small man-made rock jetty. These are good play areas for kids. The waves remain fairly calm, except at high tide or high surf conditions. The best snorkeling is out from the beach here, but the conditions are extremely variable, from fairly clear to fairly murky, depending on the time of year and prevailing conditions. Snorkeling is usually better in the winter months. The beach from this point to North Kihei is generally fronted by shelf rock or reef and is not good for swimming, but excellent for a lengthy beach walk! The beach becomes excellent for swimming and other beach activities in front of the North Kihei condos. Snorkeling is fair. A beach activity center is located on the beach at the Kealia Beach Center.

MAI POINA OE IAU BEACH PARK
On South Kihei Road, fronting Maui Lu Resort. Paved parking for 8 cars at the Pavilion (numerous other areas to park are along the road). 5 picnic tables, restrooms, showers. This is actually part of the previous beach. In-shore bottom generally sandy with patches of rock, fronted by shallow reef. Swimming and snorkeling are best in the morning before the early afternoon winds come up. Popular windsurfing area in the afternoon.

KAONOULULU BEACH PARK
Located across the street from the Kihei Bay Surf. Off-road parking for 20 cars, restrooms, drinking water, rinse-off showers, picnic tables, and four BBQ grills. Very small beach, well protected by close-in reef.

KAWILIKI POU PARK
Located at the end of Waipulani Street. Paved off-street parking for 30 cars, restrooms, large grassy area, and public tennis courts. Fronts Laule'a, Luana Kai

and the Maui Sunset Hotel. Tall, graceful palms line the shoreline. Narrow sandy beach generally strewn with seaweed and coral rubble. (See GENERAL INFORMATION - Children, for frog hunting information)

KAWILILIPOA AND WAIMAHAIKAI AREAS
Any of the cross streets off South Kihei Road will take you down toward the beach where public right-of-ways are marked. Limited parking, usually on street. No facilities. The whole shoreline from Kalama Park to Waipulani Street (3 - 4 miles) is an area of uninterrupted beaches lined by residential housing and small condo complexes. Narrow sandy beaches with lots of coral rubble from the fronting reefs.

KALAMA BEACH PARK
Well-marked, 36-acre park with 12 pavilions, 3 restrooms, showers, picnic tables, BBQ grills, playground apparatus, soccer field, baseball field, tennis courts, volleyball and basketball courts. Lots of grassy area. There is no beach (in winter), only a large boulder breakwater. Good view of the cinder cone in Makena, Molokini, Kahoolawe, Lanai, and West Maui.

KAMAOLE I
Well-marked beach across from the Kamaole Beach Club. Off-street parking for 30 cars. Facilities include picnic tables, restrooms, rinse-off showers, rental equipment, children's swimming area, and lifeguard. Long, white, sandy beach offering good swimming, poor to fair snorkeling. NOTE: The small pocket of sand between rock outcroppings at the right end of the beach is known as Young's Beach. It is also accessible from Kaiau Street with parking for about 20 cars. Public right-of-way sign at end of Kaiau Street.

KAMAOLE II
Located across from the Kai Nani shopping and restaurant complex. On-street parking, restrooms, rinse-off showers, rental equipment, and lifeguard. White sand beach between two rocky points with sharp drop-off to overhead depths. Good swimming, poor to fair snorkeling.

KAMAOLE III ★
Well-marked beach across from the Kamaole Sands Condominiums. Off-street parking, picnic tables, BBQ's, restrooms, rinse-off showers, drinking water, playground equipment, a grassy play area, and a lifeguard. 200-yard long, narrow (in winter) white sand beach with some rocky areas along the beach, and a few submerged rocks. Good swimming, fair snorkeling around rocks at south end of the beach. Kamaole II and III are very popular beaches with locals and tourists because of the nice beaches and easy access.

WAILEA

This area generally has small, lovely, white sand beaches which have marked public access. Parking is off-street in well maintained parking areas, and restrooms as well as rinse-off showers are provided. You won't recognize this area from a few years ago. The new Grand Hyatt Wailea, Kea Lani and Four Seasons Resorts, along with the renovated Renaissance Wailea Beach and Aston Wailea Resort, have transformed this once under developed area into a world class resort destination riviling Kaanapali, and even surpassing Kaanapali in some ways.

KEAWAKAPU BEACH ★

There are two convenient public accesses to this very nice but generally underused beach. There is paved parking for 50 cars across the street from the beach, about 2/10 mile south of Mana Kai Resort. Look for the beach access sign on the left as you travel south. There are two small crescent shaped, white sand beaches separated by a small rocky point. Good swimming, off-shore sandy bottom, fair snorkeling around rocks at far north end. There are rinse-off showers and a restaurant at the Mana Kai which is right on the beach. Access to southern end of beach - go straight at left turn-off to Wailea, road says "Dead End." Parking for about 30 cars. Rinse-off showers. Beautiful, very gently sloping white sand beach with good swimming. Snorkeling off rocks on left. Popular scuba diving spot. Four hundred yards off shore in 80-85 feet of water there is supposed to be an artificial reef of 150 car bodies.

MOKAPU BEACH ★

A public access sign (Ulua/Mokapu Beaches) is near the Rennaisance Resort. Small parking area, restrooms and showers. Rental equipment at nearby Wailea Resort Activities Center at Renaissance. Beautiful white sand beach. Excellent swimming. Good snorkeling in mornings around the rocks which divide the two beaches. The best snorkeling is on the Ulua beach side.

ULUA BEACH ★

A public access sign located near the Rennaissance Beach Resort. Small paved parking area with a short walk to beach. Showers and rest rooms. Rental equipment is only a short walk away at the Wailea Ocean Activities Center. Beautiful white sand beach fronting the Elua Resort complex. Ulua and Mokapu Beaches are separated by a narrow point of rocks. The area around the beaches is beautifully landscaped because of the resorts. The beach is semi-protected and has a sandy offshore bottom. Good swimming, usually very good snorkeling in the mornings around the lava flow between the beaches. Parking is limited!

WAILEA BEACH ★

One half mile south of the Inter-Continental Resort there is a public beach access sign and a paved road down to a landscaped parking area for about 40 cars. Restrooms and rinse-off showers. Rental sailboats and windsurfing boards are available. Beautiful wide crescent of gently sloping white sand. Gentle offshore slope. Good swimming. Snorkeling is only fair to the left (south) around the rocks (moderate currents and not much coral or many fish). The new Kea Lani resort is situated on this beachfront.

POLO BEACH

Just past the Kea Lani Resot turn right at the Wailea Golf Club-Fairway Restaurant sign and head down to the Polo Beach Resort condominiums. The public access sign is easy to spot. Parking for 40 cars in paved parking area. Showers and restrooms. The beaches are a short walk on a paved sidewalk and down a short flight of stairs. There are actually two beaches, 400 foot long north beach and 200 foot long south beach, separated by 150 feet of large rocks. The beaches slope begins gently, then continues more steeply off-shore and is not well protected. This combination can cause swift beach backwash which is particularly concentrated at two or three points and also a rough shore break, especially in the afternoons. The beach is dotted with large rocks. Fair swimming, generally poor snorkeling.

MAKENA

This area includes the beaches south of Polo Beach, out to La Perouse Bay (past this point, you either hike or need to have a four-wheel drive). The Makena beaches are relatively undeveloped and relatively unspoiled, and not always easy to find. There are few signs, confusing roads, and some beaches are not visible from the road. Generally, no facilities and parking where you can find it. The nearest grocery is at the Wailea Shopping Center. We hope our directions will help you find these sometimes hard-to-find, but very lovely, nearly pristine beaches.

PALAUEA BEACH

As you leave Wailea, there is a four-corner intersection with a sign on the left for the Wailea Golf Club, and on the right for the Polo Beach Condos. 8/10 mile past here turn onto the second right turnoff at the small "Paipu Beach" sign. At roads end (about 1/10 mile), park under the trees. Poolenalena Beach lies in front of you. Walk several hundred feet back towards Polo Beach over a small hill (Haloa Point) and you will see Palauea Beach stretching out before you. A beautiful beach, largely unkown to tourists. The area above the beach at the south end has been developed with pricey residential homes.

If you drive down to the Polo Beach Condos instead, you can continue on Old Makena Road which will loop back to Makena Alanui Road after about a mile. Palauea Beach lays along this road, but is not visible through the trees. There is a break in the fence .35 miles from Polo Beach with a well worn path to the beach. Although this is all private and posted land, the path and the number of cars parked alongside the road seems to indicate that this beautiful white sand beach is getting much more public use than in the past. Good swimming. No facilities. Both Palauea and Poolenalena beaches have the same conditions as Polo Beach with shallow offshore slope then a steep dropoff which causes fairly strong backwash in places and tends to cause a strong shore break in the afternoon.

POOLENALENA BEACH

See directions for Palauea Beach. This is a lovely wide, white sand beach with gentle slope offering good swimming. This used to be a popular local camping spot, however no camping signs are now posted.

331

UPCOUNTRY ROAD 1.4 miles from Polo Beach. Currently closed.

PAIPU BEACH (Chang's Beach)
Continue another 2/10 to 3/10 miles on Makena Alanui Rd., past Poolenalena and you will come to the Makena Surf Town Houses (about 1.2 miles from the Wailea Golf Club sign). This development surrounds Chang's Beach, however, there is a public beach access sign and paved parking for about 20 cars. It's a short walk down a concrete path to the beach. A rinse-off shower is provided. This small but sandy beach is used mostly by guests of the Makena Surf.

ULUPIKUNUI BEACH
Turn right just past the Makena Surf and immediately park off the road. Walk down to the beach at the left end of the complex. The beach is 75-100 feet of rock strewn sand and is not too attractive, but is well protected.

FIVE GRAVES
From the Makena Surf, continue down Old Makena Road another 2/10 mile to the entrance of Five Graves. There is ample parking. The 19th century graves are visible from Makena Rd. just a couple hundred feet past the entrance. There is no beach, but this is a good scuba and snorkeling site. Follow the trail down to the shore where you'll see a good entrance to the water.

MAKENA LANDING - PAPIPI BEACH
Continue another 2/10 mile on Old Makena Rd. to Makena Landing on the right. There is off-street parking for 22 cars. The beach is located at the entrance and is about 75-100 feet with gentle slope, sometimes rock strewn. Not very attractive and is used mostly for fishing, but snorkeling can be good if you enter at the beach and follow the shore to the right. Restrooms and showers available. Instead of turning right onto Old Makena Road at the Makena Surf, continue straight and follow the signs to the Makena Golf Course. About 9/10 mile past the Makena Surf there is another turnoff onto Old Makena Rd. At the stop sign at the bottom of the hill, you can turn right and end up back at Makena Landing or turn left and head for Maluaka Beach. 2/10 mile past the stop sign you will see the old Keawalai Church U.C.C. and cemetery. Sunday services continue to be held here. Along the road is a pay phone.

MALUAKA BEACH ★ (Naupaka)
3/10 mile past the stop sign there is a turnaround and public entrance to this beach on the right. There are a few parking places near the entrance along the road, however, the main parking lot with restrooms and showers is located a short walk back up the road. The resort above the beach is the Maui Prince. This gorgeous 200-yard beach is set between a couple of rock promontories. The very fine white sand beach is wide with a gentle slope to deeper water. Snorkeling can be good in the morning until about noon when the wind picks up. There are interesting coral formations at the south end with unusual abstract shapes, and large coral heads of different sizes. Coral in shades of pink, blue, green, purple and lavender can be spotted. There are enough fish to make it interesting, but not an abundance. In the afternoon when the wind comes up, so do the swells, providing good boogieboarding and wave playing.

ONEULI BEACH (Black Sand Beach)
On Old Makena Hwy., past the Maui Prince Resort, just past the intersection of the old road is a dirt road turnoff. A 4-wheel drive or a high ground clearance vehicle is a good idea for the very rutted 3/10 mile to the beach. The beach is coarse black sand and the entire length of the beach is lined by an exposed reef. No facilities.

ONELOA BEACH ★ (Makena Beach)
The entrance for the north end of the beach is at the second dirt road to the right off Old Makena Hwy. after the intersection of the old road. It is 3/10 mile from the turnoff to the beach and parking area with room for quite a few cars. The old, very rutted dirt road has been replaced by a graded and somewhat graveled road. This very lovely white sand beach is long (3/4 mile) and wide and is the last major undeveloped beach on the leeward side of the island. Community effort is continuing in their attempt to prevent further development of this beach. The 360-foot cinder cone (Pu'u Olai) at the north end of the beach separates Oneloa from Puuolai Beach. The beach has a quick, sharp drop off and rough shore break particularly in the afternoon. Body surfing is sometimes good. Snorkeling around the rocky point at the cinder cone is only poor to fair with not much to see, and not for beginners due to the usually strong north to south current.

PUUOLAI BEACH (Little Makena)
Take the first Oneloa Beach entrance, and park at Oneloa Beach. From there, you hike over the cinder cone. There is a flat, white sand beach, with a shallow sandy bottom which is semi-protected by a shallow cove. The shore break is usually gentle and swimming is good. Bodysurfing sometimes. Snorkeling is only poor to fair around the point on the left. Watch for strong currents. Although definitely illegal, beach activities here tend to be au naturel.

AHIHI-KINAU ★ (NATURAL RESERVE AREA)
About 3/4 mile past Makena Beach, a sign indicates the reserve. There is a small, 6-foot wide, sandy beach alongside the remnants of an old concrete boat ramp. Although it's located in a small cove and is well protected, the beach and cove are very shallow with many urchins. There is also very limited parking here. Up around the curve in the road is a large parking area. It's a short walk to the shore on a crushed lava rock trail. Another couple hundred feet to a very small (3 foot) and partially hidden sand and pebble beach that makes a better entrance to the water than over the rocks. There is excellent snorkeling directly off shore to the right and left. Remember, this is a marine reserve - look, but don't disturb. No facilities.

LA PEROUSE BAY
2 miles past Ahihi-Kinau, over a road carved through Maui's most recent lava flow, is the end of the road unless you have a 4-wheel drive. The "road" is extremely rough and we would recommend a hike rather than a ride. It's about 3 or 4 miles from road's end at La Perouse Bay to the Kanaio beaches. If you hike, wear good hiking shoes as you'll be walking over stretches of sharp lava rock. There are a series of small beaches, actually only pockets of sand of various compositions, with fairly deep offshore waters and strong currents.

WAILUKU - KAHULUI

Beaches along this whole side of the island are usually poor for swimming and snorkeling. The weather is generally windy or cloudy in winter and very hot in summer. Due to the weather, type of beaches, and distance from the major tourist areas on the other side of the island, these beaches don't attract many tourists (except Hookipa, which is internationally known for wind surfing).

WAIHEE BEACH PARK

From Wailuku take Kahekili Highway about three miles to Waihee and turn right onto Halewaiu Road, then proceed about one-half mile to the Waihee Municipal Golf Course. From there, a park access road takes you into the park. Paved off-street parking, restrooms, showers, and picnic tables. This is a long, narrow, brown sand beach strewn with coral rubble from Waihee Reef. This is one of the longest and widest reefs on Maui and is about one thousand feet wide. The area between the beach and reef is moderately shallow with good areas for swimming and snorkeling when the ocean is calm. Winter surf or storm conditions can produce strong alongshore currents. Do not swim or snorkel at the left end of the beach as there is a large channel through the reef which usually produces a very strong rip current. This area is generally windy.

KANAHA BEACH PARK

Just before reaching the Kahului Airport, turn left, then right on reaching Ahahao Street. The far south area of the park has been landscaped and includes BBQs, picnic tables, restrooms, and showers. Paved off-street parking is provided. The beach is long (about one mile) and wide with a shallow offshore bottom composed of sand and rock. Plenty of thorny Kiawe trees in the area make footwear essential. The main attraction of the park is its peaceful setting and view, so picnicking and sunbathing are the primary activities. Swimming would appeal mainly to children. Surfing can be good here.

WINDSURFING

H. A. BALDWIN PARK

The park is located about 1.5 miles past Spreckelville on the Hana Highway. There is a large off-street parking area, a large pavilion with kitchen facilities, picnic tables, BBQs, and a tent camping area. There are also restrooms, showers, a baseball and a soccer field. The beach is long and wide with a steep slope to overhead depths. This is a very popular park because of the facilities. The very consistent, although usually small, shore break is good for bodysurfing. Swimming is poor. There are two areas where exposed beach rock provides a relatively calm place for children to play.

HOOKIPA BEACH PARK

Located about two miles past Lower Paia on the Hana Highway. Restrooms, showers, four pavilions with BBQ's and picnic tables, paved off-street parking, and a tent camping area is provided. Small, white sand beach fronted by a wide shelf of beach rock. The offshore bottom is a mixture of reef and patches of sand. Swimming is not advised. The area is popular for the generally good and, at times (during winter), very good surfing. Hookipa is internationally known for its excellent windsurfing conditions. This is also a good place to come and watch both of these water sports.

HANA

WAIANAPANAPA STATE PARK

About four miles before you reach Hana on the Hana Highway is Waianapanapa State Park. There is a trail from the parking lot down to the ocean. The beach is not of sand, but of millions of small, smooth, black volcanic stones. Ocean activities are generally unsafe. There is a lava tunnel at the end of the beach that runs about 50 feet and opens into the ocean. Other well marked paths in the park lead to more caves and fresh water pools. An abundance of mosquitos breed in the grotto area and bug repellent is strongly advised.

HANA BEACH PARK

If you make it to Hana, you will have no difficulty finding this beach on the shoreline of Hana Bay. Facilities include a pavilion with picnic tables, restrooms and showers, and also Tutu's snack bar. About a 200-yard beach lies between old concrete pilings on the left and the wharf on the right. Gentle offshore slope and gentle shore break even during heavy outer surf. This is the safest swimming beach on this end of the island. Snorkeling is fair to good on calm days between the pier and the lighthouse. Staying inshore is a must, as beyond the lighthouse the currents are very strong and flow seaward.

KAIHALULU BEACH (Red Sand Beach)

This reddish sand beach is in a small cove on the other side of Kauiki Hill from Hana Bay and is accessible by trail. At the Hana Bay intersection follow the road up to the school. A dirt path leads past the school and disappears into the jungle, then almost vanishes as it goes through an old cemetery, then continues out onto a scenic promontory. The ground here is covered with marble-sized pine cones which make for slippery footing. As the trail leads to the left and over the edge of the cliff, it changes to a very crumbly rock/dirt mixture that is unstable at best.

You may wonder why you're doing this as the trail becomes two feet wide and slopes to the edge of a 60 foot cliff in one place. The trail down to the beach can be quite hazardous. Visitors and Hana residents alike have been injured seriously. It is definitely not for the squeamish, those with less than good agility or youngsters. And when carrying beach paraphernalia, extra caution is needed. The effort is rewarded as you descend into a lovely cove bordered by high cliffs and almost enclosed by a natural lava barrier seaward. The beach is formed primarily from red volcanic cinder, hence its name. Good swimming, but stay away from the opening at the left end because of rip currents. Although definitely illegal, beach activities here may be au naturel at times. The Hotel Hana Maui has plans to improve the access to this beach sometime in the future.

KOKI BEACH PARK
This beach is reached by traveling 1.5 miles past the Hasegawa Store toward Ohe'o Gulch. Look for Haneoo Road where the sign will read "Koki Park - Hamoa Beach - Hamoa Village." This beach is unsafe for swimming and the signs posted warn "Dangerous Current."

HAMOA BEACH ★
This gorgeous beach has been very attractively landscaped and developed by the Hotel Hana Maui in a way that adds to the surrounding lushness. The long white sand beach is in a very tropical setting and surrounded by a low sea cliff. To reach it, travel toward Ohe'o Gulch after passing through Hana. Look for the sign 1.5 miles past Hasegawa store that says "Koki Park - Hamoa Beach - Hamoa Village." There are two entrances down steps from the road. Parking is limited to along the roadside. The left side of the beach is calmer, and offers the best snorkeling. Because it is unprotected from the open ocean, there is good surfing and bodysurfing, but also strong alongshore and rip currents are created at times of heavy seas. The Hana Hotel maintains the grounds and offers restrooms, changing area, and beach paraphernalia for the guests. There is an outdoor rinse-off shower for non-hotel guests. Hay wagons bring the guests to the beach for the hotel's weekly luau.

RECREATION
AND TOURS

INTRODUCTION

Maui's ideal climate, diverse land environments, and benign leeward ocean have led to an astounding range of land, sea and air activities. With such a variety of things to do during your limited vacation time, we suggest browsing through this chapter and choosing those activities that sound most enjoyable. The following suggestions should get you started.

REMEMBER! If you are making your vacation recreation plans from the mainland, you'll need to use the (808) area code. This is the area code for all phone numbers unless stated otherwise. When you are in Hawai'i you do not need to use this area code. Wherever possible we have also listed fax numbers, (which also require an (808) prefix and toll free 1-800 phone numbers. If you are a person with a disability, see the General Information chapter topic on the Physically Impaired for additional information.

Maui is abloom with street corner hawkers selling any and every form of recreational activity. In fact, these editors find it quite unpleasant that every nook (including the corner of one Front Street ice cream parlor) has been filled with an activity booth. You should be aware that there are several kinds of activity vendors. Some activity booths are what they appear to be. They explain the various activities and can book you on your choice. Be aware that they may have favorites. This is fine, recommendations are helpful, but if this is based on how much commission they receive from a certain tour operator, then they may not be giving you the full picture. Concierge desks at the major hotels and resort can also book your activities. Most of these (although we'd guess probably all of them) also receive commissions. Those which are affiliated with the resort property will no doubt give you the best service since they are a reflection of the resort. However, some activity desks at hotels, condos and the like are merely a concession. They rent the space, just as do the activity booths on Front Street, hence, the educated and informed visitor is ahead of the game in any case. The prices will be about the same, although there are those like Tom Barefoot's Cashback Tours who offer a 10% discount on every tour.

The other kind of tour activity broker is the one that *appears* to have the best deal. Half price on a helicopter trip or $50 off on a luau. These are the folks that are using the activity as "bait." The "catch" is that you must attend some sort of breakfast meeting or tour of a property. Their aim is to sell you a timeshare unit on Maui. A time share is a week of time which you purchase once each year at a specific property. In a sense, you own 1/52 of a condominium. The cost is in the thousands of dollars. You can put your week into a pool by joining one of several organizations and trade with someone else. In this way you could get a week at some other location around the world. In addition to the purchase price you pay a yearly or monthly maintenance fee. It appears to us that this is a great deal for the condo owner/developer. For example, they charge you $15,000 a week for your one-bedroom oceanview condo. Then they find another 51 folks to do the same and *voila*, they have just made $780,000 for a condo that would sell for perhaps $210,000. A lot of people do own time shares and love them. You may be interested in learning more about them, so you could take advantage of one of these opportunities and have a free meal and save on an activity. If you have plenty of time and more patience than we do, then attending one of these sessions, even if you aren't interested in a time share, may be worth your while to save money on an excursion. However, the time share programs we have attended have proven full of very high pressure sales tactics. The Activity Owners Association of Hawai'i regulates these booths. For information contact them at 1-800-398-9698.

We haven't tried this one, but one dive shop, Boss Frog's, promises that when you rent a set of snorkel gear for two for a week (at $10-25) you also get a free snorkel sail to Molokini or the Coral Gardens. (Apparently, one free trip for each person renting gear - no "double occupancy" clause!) Their ad claims, "no gimmicks, no last minute tickets, no time share, no mule rides. Believe it." Lahaina 661-3333 ext. 8, or Kihei 875-4477 ext. 8., Napili 669-4949 ext. 8.

The final option is to book the tour yourself by calling one of the numbers listed in this chapter. Ask your questions and inquire if they have any specials or discounts. Since there is not a middle man to take a commission, you might be pleasantly surprised! In any case, it certainly won't hurt to ask. Enough of our editorial comments, now on to why you're reading this chapter: To be an informed and educated visitor! (P.S. We do not get commissions, nor do we sell timeshares!)

BEST BETS

To see and experience the real Maui, take a hike with guide Ken Schmitt.

For spectacular scenery and lots of fresh air, try the 38-mile coast down the world's largest dormant volcano on a bicycle or one of several other Upcountry bicycle trips.

For great snorkeling try Honolua Bay, Namalu, Ahihi Kinau, or Olowalu.

Enjoy a romantic starlight evening sail aboard the *America II*.

Experience the thrill of a real sailing experience aboard *World Class*.

Take a helicopter tour and get a super spectacular view of Maui.

Golf at one of Maui's excellent courses.

Sail to Lana'i and snorkel Hulopo'e Beach with the Trilogy Cruise.

If the whales are in residence, take advantage of a whale watching excursion to view these beautiful mammals a bit more closely. An estimated 1,500 whales winter each year in the waters surrounding Maui.

For an underwater thrill consider an introductory scuba adventure, no experience necessary. Or sample a newer arrival to the Maui aquatic scene, Snuba!

For those who like to stay dry in the water, take a submarine trip to view the underwater sights off Lahaina.

For a wet and wild water tour, plus snorkeling, try a raft trip.

If you're really adventurous, consider parasailing (during the summer when the whales have gone back north!), sea kayaking, or try scuba kayaking at Kapalua.

For great scenery at a great price, drive yourself to Hana and visit the Pools of O'heo at Haleakala National Park-Kipahulu or to Upcountry and Haleakala.

OCEAN ACTIVITIES
SNORKELING

Maui offers exceptionally clear waters, warm ocean temperatures and abundant sea life with safe areas (no adverse water conditions) for snorkeling. If you are a complete novice, most of the resorts and excursion boats offer snorkeling lessons. From the youngest to the oldest, everyone can enjoy this sport that needs little experience and there is no need to dive to see all the splendors of the sea. If you are unsure of your abilities, the use of a floatation device may be of assistance. Be forewarned that the combination of tropical sun and the refreshing coolness of the ocean can deceive those paddling blissfully on the surface, and result in a badly burned backside. Water resistant sunscreens are available locally and are recommended.

Equipment is readily available at resorts and dive shops, and as you can see, much less expensive at the dive shops (even better are the weekly rates). For a listing of dive shops see Scuba Diving. All snorkeling boat trips provide equipment as a part of their package. Some offer prescription masks.

If you plan on doing a lot of snorkeling, the purchase of your own equipment should be considered. Good quality gear is available at all the dive shops. Less expensive sets can be purchased at Longs or Costco.

TYPICAL RENTAL PRICES - MASK-FINS-SNORKEL FOR 24 HOURS:

Maui Dive Shop in Kihei - $7.50-10
Boss Frog's in Lahaina, Napili and Kihei - $1.50-$10 depending on equipment
Hyatt Regency Resort at Kaanapali - $15 per day, 8 am-6 pm only

WEEKLY RATES

Snorkel Bob's in Lahaina and Kihei charges $15 per set per week. Silicon set $19-29 per week, prescription masks $39.
Auntie Snorkel and Uncle Boogie in Kihei (Rainbow Mall) charges $9.95 per week for regular gear, $14.95 for silicon set.

Most major dive shops can fit you with a prescription mask, as long as your vision impairment is not too severe. (Editor's note: As a contact wearer with a strong prescription, I wear my soft lenses with a good fitting mask.)

Good snorkeling spots, if not right in front of your hotel or condo, are only a few minutes' drive away. The following are our favorites, each for a special reason.

WEST MAUI

Black Rock - At the Sheraton in the Kaanapali Resort. Pay for parking at Whalers Village and walk down the beach. Clear water and a variety of tame fish - these fish expect handouts!

Kapalua Bay - Public park with off street parking, restrooms and showers. A well protected bay and beautiful beach amid the grounds of the Kapalua Resort. Limited coral and some large coral heads, fair for fish watching. Arrive early as parking is very limited!

Namalu Bay - Park at Kapalua Bay, walk over from Kapalua Bay to the bay which fronts the grounds of the resort. Difficult entry, very good on calm days.

Honolua Bay - No facilities, park alongside the road and walk a 1/4 mile to the bay, but the best snorkeling on Maui, anytime but winter.

Olowalu - At mile marker 14, about 5 miles south of Lahaina. Generally calm and warmer waters with ample parking along the roadside. Very good snorkeling. If you find a pearl earring, let us know, we *STILL* have the match!

EAST MAUI

Ulua-Mokapu Beach - Well-marked public beach park in Wailea with restrooms and showers. Good snorkeling on the Ulua side of the rocky point separating these two picturesque and beautiful beaches.

Maluaka Beach - Located in Makena, no facilities and along the road parking. Good coral formations and a fair amount of fish at the left end of the beach.

Ahihi Kinau Natural Reserve - Approximately five miles past Wailea. No facilities. This is not a very crowded spot and you may feel a little alone here, but the snorkeling is great with lots of coral and a good variety of fish.

Generally at all locations the best snorkeling is in the morning until about 1 pm, when the wind picks up. For more information on each area and other locations, refer to the BEACHES chapter.

A good way to become acquainted with Maui's sea life is a guided snorkeling adventure with *Ann Fielding*, marine biologist and author of *Hawaiian Reefs and Tidepools and Underwater Guide to Hawai'i*. She takes small groups (minimum 2, maximum 6) to the best location, but generally Honolua Bay in summer and Ahihi Kinau in winter. These morning (8 am - noon) excursions begin with an introductory discussion on Hawaiian marine life, identification and ecology which is followed by snorkeling. Floatation devices, snorkel gear and refreshments are provided for the $45 fee. Call ahead for your reservation at 572-8437.

You may feel the urge to rent an underwater camera to photograph some of the unusual and beautiful fish you've seen, and by all means try it, but remember, underwater fish photography is a real art. The disposable underwater cameras are a fun and inexpensive and available everywhere, but your resulting photos may be disappointing.

There are several video tapes of Maui's marine life available at the island bookstores if you want a permanent record of the fish you've seen. Several of the sea excursions offer video camera rentals.

There are two other great places to snorkel, however, you need a boat to reach them. Fortunately, a large variety of charter services will be happy to assist.

Molokini Crater - This small semicircular island is the remnant of a volcano. Located about 8 miles off Maalaea Harbor, it affords good snorkeling in the crater area. These waters are a marine reserve and the island is a bird sanctuary.

Molokini is usually a 1/2 day excursion with a continental breakfast and lunch provided. Costs are $40 - $100 for adults, $25 - $60 (plus tax) for children under 12. (You may find rates even lower during a price war.)

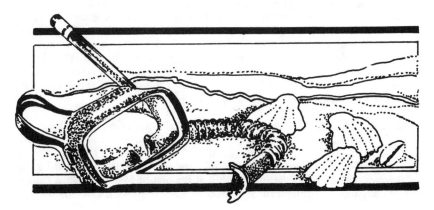

Hulopo'e Beach, Lana'i - This is one our favorites. Located on the island of Lana'i, it's worth the trip for the beautiful beach and the abundant coral and fish. We saw a school of fish here that was so large that from the shore it appeared to be a huge moving reef. After swimming through the school and returning to shore we were informed that large predatory fish like to hang out around these schools! Lana'i is usually a full-day excursion with continental breakfast, BBQ lunch and a optional island tour. $79 - $149 for adults, $35 and up for youth under age 12. Half-day trips are available on the *Navatek*.

A variety of snorkel/sail/tour options are available for snorkeling along East and West Maui's coastline, Molokini, Moloka'i or Lana'i. Your first decision is choosing between a large or small group tour. Large groups go out in substantial monohull or catamaran motor yachts of 60 - 90 feet in length. They get you there comfortably and fast, but without the intimate sailing experience of a smaller, less crowded boat. There are also many sleek sailboats (monohull, catamaran or trimaran) that you can share with 4 to 24 people or charter privately. Another option for a Maui sea excursions is the Zodiac type rafts that use 20 - 23 foot inflatable rafts powered by two large outboards. These rides can be rough, wet and wild.

All tours provide snorkel gear with floatation devices, if needed, and instruction. Food and refreshments are provided to varying degrees. *Navatek* provides a state-of-the-art ride on their half-day Lana'i trip. Trilogy is a long-time favorite of ours. For a list of outings, see the section on Sea Excursions.

MOLOKINI... again
Molokini is a 10,000 year old dormant volcano with only one crescent shaped portion of the crater rim now providing a sanctuary for marine and bird life. The crater on the inside of the island offers a water depth of 10 - 50 feet, a 76 degree temperature and visibility sometimes as much as 150 feet on the outer perimeter creating a fish bowl effect. Molokini has been making a slow comeback. Our first trip to the crescent shaped crater was in the days when only two or three boats operated trips. It was truly picture perfect. However, for several years after the detonation of some submerged bombs by the Navy, the aquatic life was sparse. The many tour boats dropping anchors further damaged and destroyed the reef. While it hasn't been restored to the way it was during our first excursions, now many years ago, it is now returning to a much improved condition. Fortunately, concerned boat operators were granted semi-permanent concrete mooring anchors, thereby preventing further reef damage. Most trips are taken in the morning, some do offer afternoon trips, but expect rougher ocean conditions. On occasion even the morning trips are forced to snorkel at an alternative site, usually La Perouse.

According to legend, the islet of Molokini was created as the result of a jealous rage. Pele had a dream lover, Lohiau, who lived in Ma'alaea, located to the north of Makena. Lohiau married a mo'o (lizard) and Pele was so angry she bisected the lizard. The head became Molokini islet and the tail became Pu'u O La'i at Makena. Pu'u O La'i is the rounded hill at the end of Makena. (Dona calls it "the nubby thing" - which probably is not an ancient Hawaiian word.)

We recommend **Blue Water Rafting** ★for those die-hard snorkelers who would enjoy their early bird arrival to the crater with the opportunity to explore three different Molokini dive locations. They currently offer four small group adventures on their 6 and 24 passenger rafts. They offer a Molokini Express, which is a two hour trip. They arrive at the crater first and snorkel the best spot before the big boats come in. Then it's a stop at the far crater wall for a second snorkeling opportunity. The trip includes beverages and gear for $39. Their Molokini Deluxe trip is 3 1/2 hours. You snorkel at the reef's end, Enenui, and the famous wall on the backside. Trip includes lunch, beverages and snorkel gear $55 adults/$45 youth. Their 4 hour Kanaio Coast trip is an opportunity to snorkel at some remote coves along the Maui coastline. Trip includes lunch, beverages and gear. The 5 1/2 Kanaio Coast/Molokini trip is a combination trip with three stops at Molokini to snorkel as well as snorkeling along the Kanaio coast. Trip includes breakfast, lunch, beverages and gear. $99 adults/$85 youth. Call 879-RAFT.

The **Four Winds** departs daily from Maalaea to Molokini. The half-day excursion is 7:30 - 12:30 with a maximum of 112 passengers. Booking directly may save you some money on this one. Unfortunately, at capacity the boat can be a little bit crowded. One of several boats operated by Maui Classic Charters, this one has a few unique options. They offer a BBQ as compared to a very similar basic (buffet) deli lunch and the breakfast is a varied selection of fresh bagels and cream cheese with jellies. A nice change from the old Danish! Also fresh pineapple and orange slices. The BBQ lunch is cooked on board on three grills on the back of the boat...lunch selections include Mahi Mahi, burger or chicken breast. All very good, and a nice selection of condiments for the burgers. Beer, wine and soda included as well. Lay-out of the boat is nice, but it lacks seating except on the top deck. An optional activity is Snuba which takes six people at a time with air tanks carried on rafts which float at the surface ($39). You can go down to a depth of twenty feet. Call 879-8188.

A good option for those preferring a larger, more ferry-type boat is the 92' motor yacht **The Prince Kuhio**. Phone 242-8777 or 1-800-468-1287.

Navatek is also a good trip for the landlubber. This high-tech boat provides a smooth, even ride. More detailed information follows. Phone 661-8787.

The Pride of Maui ★ 65' catamaran featuring a large indoor cabin and outdoor sundecks, and hot fresh water shower. They offer daily departures at 8 am from the Maalaea Harbor for morning dives at two destinations, Molokini and "Turtle Town" (Pu'u O La'i). Depending on weather conditions, snorkel location may be Olowalu or Coral Gardens. Phone 875-0955. Also see SEA EXCURSIONS for more information.

The Coon family's *Trilogy* operation also offers a Molokini snorkel aboard their 44' trimaran cutter **Trilogy IV**. Adults $75, Children $37.50, they serve breakfast enroute, a snack and then a BBQ chicken lunch. Departs Maalaea. For information phone 661-4743 or 1-800-874-2666.

SCUBA DIVING

Maui, with nearby Molokini, Kaho'olawe, Lana'i and Moloka'i, offers many excellent diving locations. A large variety of dive operations offer scuba excursions, instruction, certification and rental equipment.

If you are a novice, a great way to get hooked is an introductory dive. No experience is necessary. Instruction, equipment and dive, all for $34.95 - $95, averages about $60. Dives are available from boats, or less expensive from the beach. A beginning beach dive may be advisable for the less confident aquatic explorer. For those who are certified but rusty, refresher dives are available.

The mainstay of Maui diving is the two-tank dive, two dive sites with one tank each. Prices depend on location and include all equipment. A trip runs about $90. If the bug bites and you wish to get certified, the typical course is five days, eight hours each day, at an average cost of $350 plus books. One dive shop suggested that visitors with limited time, do "PADI" dive preparation on the mainland and they can then be certified on Maui in just two days. Classes are generally no more than 6 persons, or if you prefer private lessons, they run slightly more. Advanced open water courses are available in deep diving, search and recovery, underwater navigation and night diving (at a few shops). If you wish to rent equipment only, a complete scuba package runs $25 per day, wet suit is an additional $5.

The larger resorts also offer complimentary introductory instruction and some can arrange certification courses and excursions. Many of the dive operators utilize boats specifically designed for diving.

Information, equipment, instruction and excursions can be obtained at the following dive shops and charter operators. As you can see by the number of listings, diving is very popular around Maui.

SCUBA DIVING

In addition to the following there are ten Maui Dive Shops and Ocean Activities and Beach Activities of Maui have outlets in a variety of locations.

WEST MAUI

Aquatic Charters &
Underwater Video
Kihei
879-0976

American Institute
of Diving, Lahaina
667-5129

Beach Activities
of Maui, 661-5552

Beach Activities of Maui
at Kapalua
Kapalua Bay Hotel
669-4664

Boss Frogman's
Lahaina (Wainee St.
by Foodland)
661-3333
Napili Plaza 669-4949
Kihei (Dolphin Plaza)
875-4477

Captain Nemo's
150 Dickenson ST.
Lahaina, HI
1-800-367-8088
Lahaina 661-5555

Dive Maui, Inc.
Lahaina, 667-2080

Extended Horizons
P.O. Box 10785
Lahaina, 667-0611

Hawaiian Reef Divers
156 Lahainaluna
Lahaina, 667-7647

Lahaina Divers
143 Dickenson
Lahaina, 667-7496
1-800-998-3483

*Ocean Activities
at Maui Marriott
661-3631/667-1200

SOUTH MAUI

Bill's Scuba Shack
Kihei, 879-3483

Ed Robinson's
Diving Adventures
Kihei, 879-3584
1-800-635-1273

Makena Coast Charters
Kihei, 874-1273

Maui Dive Shop
Azeka Center, Kihei
879-3388

Maui Sun Divers
Kihei, 879-3631 or
879-3337

Mike Severns
Kihei, 879-6596

Molokini Divers
1993 S. Kihei Rd
879-0055

Ocean Activities
1847 S. Kihei Rd. #203, Kihei
879-4485

AROUND THE ISLAND
*These have multiple locations around Maui. We have listed their main locations.

345

Kapalua Dive Company is featuring a Kayak Scuba Dive that was developed out of necessity in the summer of 1990. The Kapalua area coastline offers some of the finest diving on the West Coast of Maui, however, entry over lava rock was not feasible. "The Scrambler" offers the means to reach terrific dive spots while not creating the noise or potential anchor damage of a full size dive vessel. "The Scrambler" kayak was designed by Tim Niemier, Olympic Kayak coach. It weighs 35 lbs., is approximately 11 feet long, made of recyclable polyurethane and is described as a sit-on-top, self-scupping kayak. The paddler is not tied, strapped or sealed inside the kayak, therefore, if it should roll, the paddler is free to swim to the side, roll the kayak back upright and climb aboard. The term self scupping refers to the design which allows water to drain free of the topside without any procedures on the part of the paddler. This makes the kayak unsink-able. Departing from Kapalua Bay, each diver paddles his or her own kayak (although a double kayak is available for tight knit buddy teams) along the rugged and scenic Kapalua coastline for 15 to 20 minutes prior to reaching one of two different dive sites. Trips are limited to a maximum of four divers, price is $89 per person. Also available are Underwater Scooter Dives, night dives, snorkeling, sailing and windsurfing. Call direct to the Beach Activities of Maui at Kapalua at 669-4664.

Books of interest available at dive shops or area bookstores:
Diving and Snorkeling Guide to the Hawaiian Islands by Doug Wallin, $11.95
Diving Hawaii by Steve Rosenberg, 128 pages, $19.95
The Diver's Guide to Maui by Chuck Thorne. $9.95

SNUBA

One of the newer water recreations available is Snuba which is a combination of snorkeling and scuba diving, allowing the freedom of underwater exploration without the heavy equipment of scuba diving. In brief, the snuba diver has a mask and an air hose that is connected to the surface. Two vessels currently offer Snuba excursions, The Pride of Maui, phone 875-0955 and The Four Winds, phone 879-8188. Cost is $40 in addition to the cruise fee.

SEA EXCURSIONS

Maui offers a bountiful choice for those desiring to spend some time in and on the ocean. Boats available for sea expeditions range from a three-masted schoo-ner, to spacious trimarans and large motor yachts, to the zodiac type rafts for the more adventurous. Your choice is a large group trip or a more pampered small group excursion with a maximum of six people. Two of the most popular snorkeling excursions are to Molokini and Lana'i. Most sailboats motor to these islands and, depending on wind conditions, sail at least part of the return trip. All provide snorkel equipment. Food and beverage service varies and is reflected in the price. Many sailboats are available for hourly, full day or longer private charters. Note: Due to weather conditions, your trip to Molokini may, at the last minute, be altered to another location, usually along the Southern shore of Maui.

One of the nicest new additions to a number of boats is the option of a freshwater shower! Some of them even have solar heated their water which provides a refreshing rinse off after your saltwater snorkel/swim.

Excursion boats seem to have a way of sailing off into the sunset. The number of new ones is as startling as the number of operations that have disappeared since our last edition.

As mentioned previously, competition to Molokini has become fierce. Twenty to thirty boats a day now arrive to snorkel in this area. Many more boats now take trips to Lana'i as well.

Currently only Princess Cruises offers inter-island transportation to Moloka'i.

In the following list, phone numbers of the excursion companies are included in case personal booking is desired, however, most activity desks can also book your reservation. The best deal with an activity operator is ***Tom Barefoot's Cashback Tours*** who can book most boats and offers a 10% refund. They are located in Lahaina at 834 Front St. and can be reached at 661-8889.

PRICES PER PERSON WILL RUN YOU ACCORDINGLY
TAX NOT INCLUDED:

 Full day trip to Lana'i $79 - $149
 Club Lana'i $69
 1/2 day trip to Molokini (3 - 6 hours) $39 - $99
 1/2 day Maui coastline (3 - 4 hours) $40- $65
 Full day Maui coastline $80 - $90
 Sunset sails (1 1/2 - 2 hrs.) $30 - $50
 Whale watching (3 hrs./seasonal) $30 - $50
 Private charters $75 per hour and up, $400 per day and up
 Dinner cruise $50 - $85

HUMUHUMUNUKUNUKUAPUAA

347

SEA EXCURSIONS -

CHARTER LISTING

ADVENTURE ONE - Powerboat - 25 passengers for a Molokini snorkel with food $49.95 plus tax, whale watch seasonal. Departs Maalaea at 7 am. Phone 242-7683, 1-800-356-8989.

FIRST CHARTERS ★ - *World Class*, a 65' MacGregor Yacht departs in the afternoon tradewinds for a performance sail. 1 1/2 hours of true sailing with beverages available. Departs 12 pm and 2 pm. The performance sail runs $35. Whale watches seasonally $25, sunset sail $45. A new "Voyage to Lana'i" trip is available Monday thru Friday. Check-in at 9:15 with a depart at 10 am at Kaanapali Beach (an almost civilized hour for Dona!) and arrival at Manele Bay by noon. A leisurely picnic lunch consists of sub sandwiches, potato or pasta salad, chips, fruit, cookies and soft drinks and it is followed by a chance to snorkel at the pristine Hulopo'e Bay Marine Sanctuary. Equipment and instruction is included. Depart Manele Bay at 3:30 and enjoy champagne, beer and mai tai's enroute back to Maui, arriving by 6 pm. Cost is $129 per person. Private charters and overnight charters are also available and can include catered meals. *World Class* is a real find, but will appeal to a very specific kind of traveler. It's nothing like any of the other visitor boats, this is a yacht! It should appeal to people who REALLY like to sail, and for the more adventurous types. If you enjoy sailing, don't miss this one. It is reportedly the fastest charter yacht in the islands. Feel that wind in your face, yee ha! Phone 667-7733, FAX 667-0314.

AMERICA II - Built to compete in the 1987 America's Cup races in Fremantle, Australia, *America II* was skippered by John Kollius. Although she lost to Dennis Connor of the *Stars & Stripes,* Connor did go on to bring the cup home for the U.S. Enjoy a snorkeling and sailing experience on this 12 meter class yacht. Sails include soda, juice, water and snacks. Beer and wine may be brought on board. Whale watches in season, snorkel/sails during off whale season. Sunset sails available all year. An innovative addition is their Starlight Sail from 7:30-9:30 four days a week. All two hour sails are $24.95, $12 for children 6-12 years. Snorkel/sails include gear and continental breakfast $39.95 adults, $19.95 for children 6-12 years. Infants 5 and under, one free per paying adult. Phone 667-2195 or FAX 661-1107.

BEACH ACTIVITIES OF MAUI - In addition to windsurfing lessons, they offer a variety of small boat rentals including Hobie Cat, pedal boats, one and two person kayaks, and UFO floats. Introductory and certified scuba dives are available. They also operate the *Teralani,* a 53 foot, catamaran. They offer daily excursions that include picnic/snorkel sails and sunset cruises. Seasonal whale watches $37. Picnic snorkel sail $69 adults, $35 for children 5-12 years, free for children under age 5, champagne sunset sail $35 adults, $30 teens, $25 children. Periodically they also offer a Vintner Sail, $37, which features wines from Northern California, Oregon and Washington. Vintner Representatives accompany the sail. PO Box 10056, Lahaina, HI 96761. Phone 661-5500. FAX 661-0448.

BLUE WATER RAFTING ★ - 3 1/2 hr. Molokini snorkel, 3 different sites in the crater, 2 hr. Molokini snorkel, 1 site. Departs Kihei Launch ramp in their zodiac rafts. Max. 6-24 passenger. Four trips available: Kanaio Coast/Molokini 5 1/2 hours $99 adults/$85 youth. Kanaio Coast 4 hours $75 adults/$65 kids. Molokini Deluxe 3 1/2 hours $55 adults/$45 youth. Molokini Express 2 hours $39. All trips include snorkel gear and beverages. Breakfast and/or lunch included on 3-5 hour trips. See review in "Snorkeling" and following excursion listings. Limited seating. 24 hour notice required on all cancellations or rescheduling. Phone 879-RAFT.

CAPT. NEMO'S - Maui's only PADI 5-star IDC dive shop and vendor for scuba activities. They no longer operate their own boat. They can book your trip for a morning snorkel, sunset sail, whale watch, introductory or certified scuba dive. Scuba dive prices $49-$129. Phone 661-5555, 1-800-367-8088.

CLUB LANA'I - See description following excursion listings. Day trip to private beach on Lana'i. $89 price for adults is all inclusive. $69 for individuals 13-20 years, $29 for children under age 13. Scuba diving available for certified and non-certified divers $49 (1 tank dive). Phone 871-1144.

EXPEDITIONS ★ - Ferry service from Lahaina to Lana'i five times daily. $50 round trip adult, $40 child. 661-3756. If you'd like to explore Lana'i on your own, you can take the early morning ferry boat over and return on the late afternoon trip. From the dock it is a moderate, but easy walk to Manele Bay and the adjacent Manele Bay Resort. There is a shuttle that runs between the dock and the Manele Resort and the Koele Lodge, which is restricted to golf and resort guests. From the dock to Lana'i City is a shuttle service that charges $10 round trip. Expeditions offers a day package for two persons. Options include boat trip plus car $175, boat trip plus jeep $228, boat trip plus van $255. Lana'i City Service operates a Dollar rental car outlet, contact them at 244-9538. Rental car $60, or Jeep $119. Expeditions reservations and information phone 565-7227.

FROGMAN - Frogman began operations in 1986 and departs Maalaea Harbor each morning for a Molokini Snorkel and Scuba Adventure. The trip include breakfast, lunch, beverages, equipment and instruction. During season, they also offer an afternoon whale watch. They also have rental equipment of everything from boogie boards, to surfboards or Hana tape tours at their Boss Frog's Snorkel Shop at 888 Wainee across from McDonald's in Lahaina or at 2396 S. Kihei Rd., behind Pizza Hut in Dolphin Plaza in Kihei and their newest location at Napili Plaza. They operate two catamarans, *Frogman* and *Seabird*. Scuba dive from $49.95, Molokini and Turtle Reef $79. Seasonal two hours whale watch $20 adults, $15 youth 4-12 years. Phone 1-800-700FROG or 661-3333.

FRIENDLY CHARTERS - *Maalaea Kai II*, 44' trimaran, takes a max. of 37 people on a Molokini snorkel/cruise $49.95 adults and children. Seasonal whale watching $20 adults, $16 children. Afternoon snorkel sail $33 adults, $23 children 12 and under. Private charters available. Maalaea Harbor. (Check visitor publications for $10 off discount on Molokini snorkel.) Phone 871-0985.

349

GEMINI CHARTERS - 64' glass bottom catamaran. The *Gemini* is a 64' catamaran with glass-bottom viewports and departs daily from Kaanapali Beach in front of the Westin Maui. *Gemini* offers year round picnic snorkel sails for $69 adults, under 12 $40. This trip includes snorkel equipment including prescription masks, flotation devices, snorkel instruction, a fresh water shower (this is great!) and a hot buffet lunch including mahi mahi, teriyaki chicken, vegetarian rice, vegetable platter and dip, soft drinks, beer and wine. From mid-April to mid-December, Gemini offers a Champagne Sunset Sail $40 adults, under 12 $25. During July and August, Friday night is Teen Sail night, the trip is only open to 14-19 year olds and includes sailing swimming, hot pizza and music. $30 per person. During Whale Season, Gemini offers a morning and an afternoon Whale Watch with a Marine Naturalist on board and an underwater hydrophone to listen to the whales singing, $40 adults, under 12 $30. They offer a keiki snorkel as a part of their Kamp Kaanapali program at the Maui Westin. They also can arrange for private charters. Gemini Charters, PO Box 10846, Lahaina, Maui, HI 96761. For reservations call 661-2591.

HAWAII OCEAN RAFTING - Their 14 passenger raft takes guests on a 1/2 day snorkel lanai trip five days each week. $69 adult, $39 child. A 3/4 day snorkel to Lana'i runs $95 adults and $55 children. Full day circumnavigation of Lanai or Moloka'i at $119. A 2 /1 hour afternoon snorkel is $29 adults, $19 children. Private charter available. Phone 667-2191.

HAWAIIAN RAFTING ADVENTURES
DESTINATION PACIFIC - 1223 Front St., Lahaina. In their RAIV (Rigid, Aluminum Inflatable Vessels) you can enjoy a full day expedition, circumnavigating the island of Lana'i. Includes a BBQ lunch served in a sea cave. Continental breakfast and snorkel gear also provided. Adults $120, $100 for children 4-12. Their half-day expedition crosses the Auau Channel and includes continental breakfast, snacks and beverages. Adults $59, $45 for children 4-12. Seasonal two hour, half day and full day whale watching or whale watch/snorkel combinations. Also available are one tank introductory dives, two tank certified dives, one tank night dive, open water certification. $79-325. Six hour private charter $1,200. For reservations or information phone 661-7333.

ISLAND MARINE ACTIVITIES - They offer three vessels that depart from the Lahaina Harbor. The *Lahaina Princess*, a 65' touring yacht, 149 passengers maximum; the *Maui Princess,* a 150 passenger 118' touring yacht and the *Lin Wa* a 65' glassbottom Chinese Junk, maximum capacity 137 people. The *Lin Wa* was built in Honolulu in 1979 with a steel hull fashioned to resemble a Chinese Junk. The *Lin Wa* offers cocktail cruises, whale watching and dinner cruises. Apparently the *Lahaina Princess* is the only boat which does a Molokini trip and departs from Lahaina. (They also offer a Molokini trip aboard the *Leilani* which departs Maalaea Harbor). Either Molokini trip is $59 adults, $39 children. Aboard the *Maui Princess* you can travel in their air-conditioned cabin to the island of Moloka'i. They make two round trips daily. A combination air/land package is available for the day-tripper. You can have a day to enjoy the Kalaupapa Trail Hike and Settlement Tour ($139 adults) or visit the settlement by flying in ($189 adults) or travel to the settlement with a guided mule tour ($225 adults). All tours to Moloka'i peninsula require that you must be age 16 or older. Other packages include a visit to the wildlife safari, a cruise-drive package, a golf package, a narrated van tour, or an overnight stay at one of four Moloka'i properties. $94-154 adults/$50-104 children. Call 661-8397 or 1-800-833-5800.

KAMEHAMEHA SAILS, INC. - *King Kamehameha*, 40' Woody Brown catamaran built in Hawaii for Hawaiian waters. Snorkel/sail, sunset sail, whale watching, private charter from Lahaina Harbor. A small catamaran, maximum 15 people, with limited padded seating around the wheel area and a big net out front. You may have recognized it by the big picture of King Kamehameha on the sail! Owner Tom Warren has been sailing on various charter boats since 1969 and purchased the *Kamehameha* in 1977. A congenial captain and a fun, casual atmosphere. While he takes a maximum of 15 guests, it is usually less, which allows for a pleasantly intimate sailing experience. Minimal snacks provided or bring your own. A morning 2 hour whale watch (in season) and snorkel tour $40 per person, an afternoon 3 hour whale watch (in season) and snorkel sail $50, sunset sail and seasonal whale watch $40 per person. Phone 661-4522.

KAPALUA KAI ★ - They have been operating out of Whalers Village but expect to resume services out of Kapalua by November 1996. This 53 foot wing-masted catamaran, 49 passenger, offers plenty of shaded area in their open air cabin, a glass bottom viewing area. Snorkel trip $10:30 am-3 pm, Adults $69 and children $35. It includes a buffet lunch catered by Hula Grill which includes smoked turkey and a salad bar featuring kula greens. Their sunset sail is $39 adults, $20 children and offers finger sandwiches, veggie platter, fresh fruit platter. They sail the whole time through the sunset! Both tours have a premium bar. Their food is about the best you'll find. Call 665-0344.

KAULANA - 65' power catamaran, departs Lahaina Harbor. Sunset sail departs 5-5:30 pm and returns 7-7:30 pm Tuesday - Saturday. Cold hors d'oeuvres, beer, wine, mai tai's, juice, soft drinks, rum and vodka mixers. Live music. Adults $39, $19 for children 4-6 years, under 4 are free. Their dolphin daywatch is a half day snorkel and cruise to Lana'i. They operate this during non-whale watching season. Departs 9:30 am and returns 2 pm. Includes beverages, deli-style lunch, snorkel equipment. $69 adults, $35 for children 4-16 years. During whale season, whale-watch cruises are operated three times daily for a two hour trip. $32 adults, $19 children. Kaulana can also arrange resort/hotel pickup of guests for an additional fee. This vessel also ferries visitors to Club Lana'i. Phone 871-1144.

KIELE V - 55' catamaran, 4 hr. snorkel/sail and also an afternoon sail. Contact Hyatt Regency, Kaanapali. Phone 661-1234 ext. 3104.

MAKENA BOAT PARTNERS - *Kai Kanani*, 46' catamaran, departs from the Maui Prince Hotel. Molokini picnic/snorkel cruise $65 adults, children $40. Afternoon seasonal whale watching $30 adults, $20 children. Phone 879-7218.

MAUI CLASSIC CHARTERS - *Lavengro*, a 60' gast rigged Schooner built in 1926, does Molokini snorkel sail. Includes continental breakfast, deli-style lunch, snorkel gear and instruction, complimentary beer, wine and soda. $59 adult, $40 children (any age). *Four Winds*, a 53' double deck glass bottom catamaran, has BBQ grills, waterslide. Morning snorkel to Molokini includes continental breakfast and BBQ lunch and runs adults $69, child $45. Afternoon snorkel to Molokini or Coral Gardens during non-whale watching season $39.95 adults, $29.95 for children 3-12 years. December-May they offer whale watching during their afternoon snorkel. Both boats depart from Maalaea harbor, phone 879-8177 or 879-8188.

MAUI DIVE SHOP - Books boating activities. They have a number of shops (10 at this count). Here are a couple: Kihei Town Center 879-1919, Azeka II 879-3388, and Lahaina 661-5388.

MAUI-MOLOKAI SEA CRUISES - *Prince Kuhio*, 92' motor yacht. Whale watching, private charters, 1/2 day Molokini, departs Maalaea. This boat has the benefits of a larger vessel with more comforts, but with a bigger capacity, there are a lot more people! Rates are $75 for adults and $40 for children for their Molokini trip. Whale watching runs $30 adults and $20 for children. Phone 242-8777 or 1-800-468-1287.

NAVATEK - Described in their brochure as "travel beyond the usual." This $3 million cruise vessel will definitely catch your eye. The technology of this new vessel offers a revolutionary smooth ride as a result of a SWATH design (Small Water Plane Twin Hull) which is the result of 13 years of research focussed on minimizing ship motions. (According to literature on the *Navatek*, SWATH technology was actually born in the 1800's, but the first patent was not issued until 1942 in the U.S.) The ship rides above the water rather than on it. The main cabin is air conditioned, offers a full service bar and special viewing area with amphitheater seating. The *Navatek* system was designed by Steven Loui, a Honolulu shipbuilder. *Navatek I* is based in Honolulu, and version II was built in 1994 in the Honolulu shipyard as well. The cruise ship is 82 feet long and 36 feet wide, can carry 149 passengers plus crew and has a cruising speed of 22 knots. There are two full decks offering 3,250 square feet of space including an enclosed main deck and an open observation deck with amphitheater bow seating, tanning areas, lounge chairs, restrooms, a hot shower, a service bar and full commercial kitchen.

Their Maui Sunset Odyssey Dinner Cruise currently operates five nights each week. They offer an alternating dinner menu. Two nights weekly they feature a "Romance Cruise" with Pacific Rim cuisine. The current menu includes local fish wrapped in tea leaf with mango butter paired with New York sirloin and caramelized onions. The standard menu offers roasted striploin of beef with bernaise sauce and kiawe grilled prawns. $85 for adults, $42.50 for children 5-11 years.

"Lana'i Voyage of Discovery" is a half-day adventure to Lana'i to visit scenic points around the island including Shipwreck Beach, Pu'u Pehe Rock and Shark Fin Rock. Your day begins early (before 7 am) when a tender shuttles you out from the Lahaina Harbor to the Navatek where a waffle bar breakfast is being prepared. The hot Belgian waffles with fruit toppings (peaches, blueberries and strawberries), syrups (guava, passion strawberry and cane) whipped cream, nuts, and assorted fruits are breakfast fare. After circumnavigating Lana'i, the boat anchors at Nanahoa (also called Five Needles) about 9 am. The snorkeling is good, but not great, but it is a spot seldom seem by visitors. Lunch is served about 10:30 am (sounds early, but believe us, you'll be hungry!). Lunch includes grilled herb chicken, hamburgers and veggie burgers, various salads, chips and dips, and homemade cookies. If you'd like to sample a cruise ship, then the *Navatek II* comes close. Rates are $127.25 for adults, $64 for children and it includes breakfast and lunch with snorkeling at Nanahoa (Five Needles aka Pinnacles). Seasonal whale watches January 1 through mid-April. $55 for adults and $35 for children 5-11 years. Children under five are free.

The *Navatek II* folks have a new boat in the waters off Lahaina. It is a 48' rigid hull inflatable which is supported on large neoprene pontoons. The *Maui Nui Explorer* (and her sister boat on Kaua'i the *Na Pali Explorer*) are mounted on Scarab ocean racing hulls and powered by twin Volvo turbo supercharged diesels which each generate 230 horsepower. This provides a significantly different kind of boating experience than the *Navatek II*. Needless to say, the *Maui Nui Explorer* gets to where it is going pretty quickly, cruising at 25 knots and with the potential of 33 knots. The new boat will circumnavigate the island of Lana'i with stops for swimming and snorkeling, weather permitting. Other days the boat may travel to the north shore of Moloka'i. The trip around Lana'i take six hours. Travel time from Lahaina to Lana'i can be handled in 20 minutes under good weather and ocean conditions. Trip includes continental breakfast and deli-style lunch. $116 adults, $85 for children 8-12 years.

For you land-lubbers with dreams of the sea, but a stomach for the earth beneath your feet, *Navatek* may be the one for you! For information and reservations phone 661-8787.

OCEAN ACTIVITIES - Departures from Maalaea and Lahaina Harbor aboard the 37' Trolleycraft *No Ka Oi III* for deep sea sport fishing. Sail aboard the 65' catamaran *Wailea Kai* for Molokini picnic snorkel. Half day morning Molokini snorkel cruise or an afternoon snorkel/sail on the 65' power cat *Maka Kai*. Whale season and party boat fishing are seasonal. Phone 879-4485 or 1-800-798-0652.

OCEAN ENTERPRISES - 6 passenger cabin cruisers, snorkeling, scuba, sportfishing. Call 879-7067 or 874-9303.

OCEAN RIDERS - "Adventure Rafting" on one of their rigid hull, inflatable rafts, 15 - 18 people max. They feature unusual destinations (depends on daily weather conditions). Reefs of Kaho'olawe, Moloka'i's cliffs or Lana'i. Seasonal whale watching. Departs Mala Wharf in Lahaina. Phone 661-3586.

PACIFIC WHALE FOUNDATION CRUISES - *Whale One*, 53' motor vessel, Maalaea. They do a Molokini and Turtle Arches snorkel picnic. Departs 7 am and returns at noon. Adults $39.50, children $33. In the afternoon they provide a Molokini or Coral Gardens cruise, the site depending on weather and ocean conditions. Departs 1 pm, returns 4:30 pm. $28.50 adults, $23.50 children. *Whale Two*, 50' sailing ketch, departs Lahaina Harbor. Depart Lahaina at 10 am for a four hour snorkel sail. $38.50 adults, $30.25 children. The afternoon sailing adventure departs at 3 pm and returns at 5 pm. Adults $22.50, children $17. *Manute'a*, 50' sailing catamaran, departs Lahaina harbor. Depart at 8 am for their Lana'i wild dolphin and snorkel adventure. Travel to Lana'i and enjoy a tropical breakfast, buffet lunch and a chance to snorkel. They also make home-made ice cream, cranked by the crew! $65 adults, $34.50 children. In the evening the *Manute'a* offers a sunset dinner sail for $59.50 adults and children. Seasonal whale watching on all boats. A portion of each ticket is donated to Pacific Whale Foundation. Phone 879-8811.

PARAGON SAILING CHARTERS -The *Paragon* is a 47' catamaran built in California and is presently the only one of its kind (that we know of) featuring new construction techniques and a hull designed paired with a state-of-the-art rotating carbon fiber mast. The Cabin House offers sunshade and shelter and trampolines offer outside lounging. They sail from Maalaea Harbor offering a morning snorkel-sail that begins with a 7:30 am departure and a light breakfast as you head toward Molokini. Snorkel gear is provided and they also have small size gear for children. A fresh hot/cold water shower is located on top of the swim ladder for refreshment after your swim and before a buffet lunch. Maximum 49 passengers. The 5 hour Molokini Sail & Snorkel includes continental breakfast, buffet lunch, beer, wine, sodas, juices and coffee. They offer two hours of snorkeling paired with three hours of "high performance sailing." The trip runs $69 adults, $32 for children under 12 (ages two and under free).

The afternoon 3 hour "Speed Sail & Snorkel Coral Gardens" trip includes snorkeling followed by a speed run in excess of 20 knots. Adults $39, $19.50 for children under 12. The trip includes hors d'oeuvres and beverages. Snorkel gear provided with both trips. Write RR2, Box 43, Kula, HI 96790. Reservations phone 244-2087 or FAX 878-3933.

THE PRIDE OF MAUI ★ - 65' catamaran featuring a large indoor cabin and outdoor sundecks. They offer daily departures at 8 am from the Maalaea Harbor for morning dives at two destinations, an option not offered by most other companies. They stop at Molokini and "Turtle Town" (Pu'u O La'i). Depending on weather conditions, snorkel location may be Olowalu or Coral Gardens. Whale watching available. Handicap access, freshwater showers, glass bottom viewing, slide, underwater video cameras available for rent. Built with a 149 passenger maximum, they limit their trips to 110 guests. The morning snorkel includes breakfast, lunch, beverages, equipment. Adults are $70, Juniors (13-18 years) $60, $40 for children 4-12 years. Afternoon Molokini Snorkel Cruise (4 hours) is offered Tuesday, Thursday, Friday and Saturday. Adults $40/youth $20. It includes appetizers, beverages and gear. (Editors note: The afternoon sails, on any excursion, can be a rougher and windier trip.) The Sunset Cocktail Cruise is a two hour excursion, currently offered Wednesdays from 5-7 pm. Price is $30 adults/$15 youth and it includes beverages and snacks. Seasonal Whale Watching $25 adults/$15 youth. Scuba certified dives are available. Snuba available for an additional fee.

They also offer an afternoon snorkel trip 2:30-6:30 to Molokini or Coral Gardens. Adults $32, $16 for children 5-12 years. Lunch is optional. A third option is their two hour evening sunset sail and whale watching during that season as well. $54 couple, $28 adult, $18 junior, $12 child. Includes sunset cocktails, appetizers, soda and prize giveaways. Additional beer, wine, mai tai's and Margaritas available for small fee. Phone 875-0955.

U-DRIVE BOAT RENTALS/SEA ESCAPE - You-drive 16' zodiac raft and 17' Boston whalers for rent by the hour, half day or full day. Call 879-3721.

SCOTCH MIST CHARTERS - *Scotch Mist II* is a Santa Cruz 50' sailboat, which takes 23 people max on West Maui 1/2 day snorkel/sail, or champagne sunset sail, or private charters. Whale watching seasonal. Departs Lahaina Harbor. Phone 661-0386.

TRILOGY EXCURSIONS ★ - *Trilogy I*, 64' trimaran, *Trilogy II*, catamaran, and *Trilogy III*, a 51' catamaran, do full-day snorkel/picnic/sightseeing tours to Lana'i. A definite best bet. *Trilogy IV*, a 44' trimaran, does 1/2-day sail/snorkel to Molokini. $149 all day, 6:45-4 pm, Lana'i departs Lahaina Harbor. $75 half day to Molokini, 6:45 am-1 pm, departs Maalaea. Afternoon Maui coastal cruise, 1:30-5 pm, for $45, departs Maalaea. Call 661-4743 or 1-800-874-2666. See review following excursion listings.

WHALE MIST - 36' monohull sailboat. Whale watch/sunset cruise, snorkeling trip goes to area off shore from Launiupoko Beach. Three hour coral reef snorkel $39, deli lunch cruise $59, sunset cruise $39. An interesting specialty cruise is their introduction to sailing, $99 per person. This is a six hour, hands-on, primer on sailing under the tutelage of Captain Bill Pritchard with maximum 6 passengers. Lahaina Harbor. Phone 667-2833.

WINDJAMMER CRUISES MAUI - *Spirit of Windjammer*, a 70' three-masted schooner offers 2-hour Maui coastline dinner cruise at $69 adults, $34.50 children, seasonal whale watching $34.95. Three two hour daily sails are available. Transportation available from West Maui for $15 and South Maui for $30. Departs Lahaina. Maximum 91 passengers. Phone 667-8600.

ZIP-PURR - 47' catamaran, departs Kaanapali Beach. Built by owner/captain Mike Turkington. Morning snorkel sail along Maui's coastline with 2-3 snorkeling stops. Sunset cocktail sail, seasonal whale watch. Phone 667-2299.

BLUE WATER ADVENTURES!
While Molokini continues to be a much touted snorkeling spot, those seeking something a little different should sign up with *Blue Water Rafting* ★ for their *Kanaio Coast of Maui* trip along Maui's southern shore. The area past Makena is geologically one of Maui's youngest and the coastline is only accessible by foot. However, a trip on the zodiac raft will get you up close to see the beautiful and unusual scenic wonders of Mother Nature. Natural lava arches, pinnacles and caves are explored with the picturesque slopes of Haleakala providing a magnificent backdrop. Our chosen day for the expedition proved to be an exhilarating wet one! The ocean conditions were somewhat rougher than desired, but our hearty group agreed to push forward. With spray from the ocean drenching us, one of the more witty members of our group donned his snorkel and mask which worked admirably at keeping the water out of his eyes! The scenic vistas were fabulous and the boat was able to maneuver through one of the arches and up close to the cliffs which appeared to have been sculpted by a fine artisan. There was a brief stop for some mid-morning nourishment and a snorkel at La Perouse before returning to Kihei. This is a trip that can be best experienced only in this manner. To the best of our knowledge, only Blue Water Rafting is offering this trip. The 5 1/2 hour trip includes snorkeling with sea turtles. So, for an unusual and exciting Maui adventure, check this one out! Phone 879-7238.

A TRIP TO LANA'I
It appears that the Coon family knows not to mess with a good thing. The morning boat trip over to Lana'i still starts earlier than most would like, but once underway with warm (yes, still homemade by the Coons) cinnamon rolls and a mug (the ceramic kind, no styrofoam here!) of hot chocolate or coffee, it seems all worth the effort. Don't forget to bring the camera! Two boats bring about 60 guests to the island each day for snorkeling, sun and fun at Manele Bay. With the additional number of people on the trip, they have now divided the snorkeling and Lana'i island tour in two. One boat load walks to the beach and snorkels, tours the island and eats. Beginning snorkelers are carefully instructed before entering the ocean. The other group tours the island, snorkels and then eats at a second "sitting." If you would prefer, you can also skip the tour of Lana'i City and snorkel even longer. The chicken is cooked on the grill by the ship's captain and served on china-type plates. It is accompanied by a delicious stir-fry, and fresh rolls, but Mrs. Coon still isn't giving out the secret ingredients for her salad dressing to anyone. The eating area is a series of picnic tables covered with heavy naugahyde cloth and shaded by an awning. Plans are for a new BBQ and pavilion during the next couple of years. The meal is followed up by some sweet Lana'i pineapple, but save room for homemade ice cream on the sail back home. Leftovers from the meal are deposited nearby and you might catch a glimpse of the "wild" cats dining side by side with the "wild" turkeys! Unfortunately the Coon brothers don't get out of the office much any more to skipper the boats, but our Captain was energetic and really seemed to enjoy the trip as much as the rest of us. This is a very special outing and well worth considering as a part of your island holiday. $125 - $149 for this all day trip (6:45 am-4 pm). Trilogy offers a video of a sample day on their cruises. Although it shows probably a little more aquatic life than you'd actually see on a given day, it certainly is a good way to sample before you buy. Phone 661-4743 or 1-800-874-2666.

CLUB LANA'I
This is a one-of-a-kind operation on Maui and the closest thing the visitor will find to Gilligan's Island. It began operating in 1987, closed and then reopened in the spring of 1992. Things have changed little since they opened originally. The current going rate is $69 adults, $35 children, for a trip that departs the Lahaina Harbor aboard the Kaulana at 7:30 am and returns at 3:30 pm. Enroute there is a continental breakfast of donuts and coffee and, once you arrive, it is a full day of choosing whatever you want to do. There is biking and kayaking and plenty of time to do nothing at all but enjoy a hammock. The craftmaking in the little huts is gone, apparently they have a more casual theme where they demonstrate coconut cutting or the like along the beach for guests to watch. Lunch is a very heavy meal which includes mahi, teriyaki beef and BBQ chicken, served with vegetables, rice, fruit, a salad bar, French bread and dessert. They serve iced tea and punch and they still serve their special Lana'i Tais at the bar. Most of the guests take advantage of the coastline snorkeling (weather permitting), which leaves plenty of room for the remaining guests to pick out the perfect hammock. Keep an eye out for Mary Ann and the professor! Phone 871-1144.

DINNER CRUISES - SUNSET CRUISES

Sunset cruises are quite popular on Maui with their free flowing mai tai's, congenial passengers, tropical nights, and Hawaiian music which entertains while the boat cruises along the coastline. In the past couple of years, most of the dinner cruises seem to have sunk. In our opinion, this is just as well. Dinner aboard the smaller catamarans was most definitely not haute cuisine. The food was prepared ahead of time and usually tepid by the time it was served. Balancing a plate on your lap was anything but leisurely dining. Two dinner cruises which have survived are those which serve a sit down meal on a larger vessel. Dinner cruises typically last about two hours and prices run $60-85. Samples of dinners listed may vary. All in all, don't expect the kind of food quality you'd experience at one of the islands land-locked restaurants. The sunset cruises are far more numerous than dinner cruises and are a pleasant way to enjoy a Maui evening and run in the $30-40 range.

DINNER CRUISES
The *Lahaina Princess* departs the Lahaina Harbor nightly at 6:30 for a two hour dinner cruise. The tables below are set up for dinner and this reviewer found it a bit confining. It can be compared with a dining car on a train, tables on both sides and nice big windows to look out. Live music is soft rock.

On the top deck was an open air cocktail lounge which is pleasant, but the space fills quickly and if you don't arrive first, there is only standing room. Dinner includes BBQ pork ribs, chicken, corn on the cob, baked beans, baked potato, coleslaw and peel your own shrimp. While not a very inventive menu, it is an "all you can eat." The dancing area can accommodate about three couples maximum. We can recommend it, but not very enthusiastically. Adults $69, children $35. Departs Lahaina Harbor. From O'ahu toll free 1-800-533-6899, from Mainland toll free 1-800-833-5800, local reservations and information 661-8397.

The *Navatek II* offers the smoothest ride with their state-of-the-art vessel and with an on board kitchen, the most freshly prepared food. Enjoy contemporary live music while dining on a full course dinner. Their Maui Sunset Odyssey Dinner Cruise currently operates five nights each week. They offer an alternating dinner menu. Two nights weekly they feature a "Romance Cruise" with Pacific Rim cuisine. The current menu includes local fish wrapped in ti leaf with mango butter paired with New York sirloin and caramelized onions. The standard menu offers roasted striploin of beef with bernaise sauce and kiawe grilled prawns. $85 for adults, $42.50 for children 5-11 years. Departs about 5:30, times may change seasonally.

They serve a glass of non-alcoholic punch as you board and then alcoholic drinks are served after you are out of the harbor. The dining area is nice with tall, wide windows on both sides making it easy to see out either side even across other people and tables. The brass backed chairs have a deco-ish design. The experience was first class, with good food, but again not quite up to restaurant standards. The technology of this new vessel promises an incredibly smooth ride, another wonderful benefit. If you can live with the price and figure you are paying the price of new technology, it is a pleasant evening out. 661-8787. See additional description under SEA EXCURSIONS.

Pacific Whale Foundation offers the "Taste of Maui," a sunset dinner sail aboard the *Manute'a* out of Lahaina Harbor. Live Hawaiian musical entertainment. (Editorial opinion: A plus for them. Why go on a Hawaiian sunset or dinner cruise to hear rock & roll?) Beverages and tropical drinks served from an open bar. Four entrees are available for dinner: sauteed mahi mahi with tropical Hawaiian shoyu mushroom sauce, broiled double breast of chicken skewered on Maui Sugar Cane with tropical fruit salsa, pepper crusted New York Steak with Madagascar peppercorn sauce or vegetarian lasagna with roasted eggplant and sundried tomatoes. Dinner includes wine. Dessert and Kona coffee follow. Maximum of 17 couples per evening. Departs 5 pm, returns 7 pm. Adults/children $59.50. Call 879-8811.

Spirit of Windjammer - A 70' three masted schooner with table seating, and an open bar. Hawaiian music provided by Ernie Paiva and his brother Damian with a couple of hula dancers (who also serve as your waitresses) finishing the evening with a hula. The crew was nice and the seating up top was comfortable. The food was very good, as dinner cruises go, with an all you can eat, but not a buffet. You simply ask for seconds or thirds and it will be served to you. Dinner began with a basket of rolls followed by a salad topped with mandarin oranges and almonds. The prime rib was surprisingly tender and the chicken breast cooked on the barbecue grill proved very good with lemon butter sauce, accompanied by rice, fresh fruit and a dessert of cheesecake topped with a flavored fruit sauce. Two complimentary drinks are included. The food is prepared in the on-board galley, which makes the food a step above. The dinner cruise runs $65 for adults, children 3-12 years half price. It rates a marginal thumbs up. Phone 661-8600.

SUNSET CRUISES
The true sailing enthusiast should investigate the *World Class* and *America II*
The *Gemini* was pleasant and comfortable. It's a really tough choice, but there
is a quality trip for any visitor.

Gemini - This 64' glass bottom catamaran is used by the Westin and departs from
Kaanapali Beach. They offer a champagne sunset sail nightly from 5-6:30 pm
which includes pupus, beer and wine and non-alcoholic beverages. The sunset
cruise costs $35 for adults. This is a glass bottom catamaran with long tables and
padded seats inside. The wide passage area is all around, accessible steps and
ample headroom make it a comfortable boat. There are viewports on each side
(glass bottom windows) and big side windows. No music or entertainment, just
a good chance to wind down on a pleasant sail. The *Gemini* also does snorkel
sails. Phone 661-2591.

Kaulana - Departing from the Lahaina Harbor this vessel offers good seating
areas on benches on top and on the sides. Musical entertainment included
Hawaiian and contemporary music, and there was room to dance. Pupus and an
open bar. Daily 5 - 7 pm (times change with the seasons). $39 adults, $19 kids
ages 4-16 years. An enjoyable, comfortable trip aboard this 65' power catamaran.
Operated by the folks that run Club Lana'i. Phone 871-1144.

King Kamehameha - A small catamaran, maximum 15 people, with limited
padded seating around the wheel area and a big net out front. You may have
recognized it by the big picture of King Kamehameha on the sail! Owner Tom
Warren has been sailing on various charter boats since 1969 and purchased the
Kamehameha in 1977. This is a BYOB and limited snacks provided. $40 per
person for a two hour sail. A good option if you're seeking a smaller boat. Phone
661-4522.

Scotch Mist - 23 passenger max. Trips daily. Beer, wine, soft drinks, no pupus,
just chips. $35 adults, $25 for kids under age 12. Departs Lahaina Harbor. Phone
661-0386.

Teralani -- A 53', catamaran offers a sunset sail for $35. They also periodically
do a Vintner Sail for $37 which features wines from Northern California, Oregon
and Washington. Vintner representatives accompany the sail. 970 Limahana
Place, Suite 204, Lahaina, HI 96761. Phone 661-5500.

Wailea Kai - Sunset cruises available by private arrangement. Phone 879-4485.

Whale Mist - 36' monohull sailboat, max. 18, whale watch/sunset cruise, $39
adults. Depart Lahaina, slip #6. Phone 667-2833.

World Class ★- First Class Charters offers an evening sailing cruise aboard the
yacht *World Class*. This is another branch of the Sunshine Helicopter family.
This is a quality operation with brand new, very sleek yachts.

The World Class yachts are 65' MacGregor with a beautiful, plush interior! Some tours include beverages, others offer them for sale. Departures vary. $45 adult. This cruise is a real find to a very specific kind of traveler. This is an opportunity to enjoy a real sailing experience aboard an outstanding yacht. These trips should appeal to the more adventurous types. The boat glides through the water making a very fast, but smooth ride! If you enjoy sailing, don't miss this one. Phone 667-7733 or FAX 667-0314.

Zip-purr - Owned by Julie and Mike "Turk" Turkington. Mike built this 47' sailboat and is its captain. While it can carry a maximum of 49 passengers, they prefer to book no more than 35 - 40. They do their two hour sunset cruise daily and ALWAYS sail, even though it can be a bit rough, which should appeal to the sporty types. There is no entertainment. A nice padded seating area inside and benches at various spots. They pick up at different areas, depending on the weather. They put out a line to troll and while on board a fish was hooked which was exciting. Adults run $39.95, teens are $30 and children are $25. Hot and cold appetizer buffet is served. Phone 667-2299.

SUBMARINE TOURS

The *Atlantis Submarine* tours the underwater world beyond Lahaina's harbor. Excursions last approximately two hours. The underwater submarine tour lasts approximately 45 minutes, except the Discover Dive, which is approximately 30 minutes in length. Atlantis' children rates apply to those youths 12 years and younger. Children must be at least 36 inches tall to ride aboard *Atlantis*. The *Atlantis* adventures include an ocean cruise out to the dive site (whale watching in season) and complimentary beverages. The dive descends to a depth of 120 feet. The Maui Odyssey Adventure includes transportation from major hotels. $89 adults, $39 child. The Maui Expedition Adventure is offered during non-peak hours at a discounted rate of $79 adults, $39 children. The Maui Discovery Adventure is a late afternoon special and is a 30 minute tour. $69 adults, $39 children. Combination packages include the Royal Lahaina Luau and Submarine Tour ($99 adults, $49 children) and a helicopter and submarine combination trip, prices vary depending on helicopter flight path. They also do Japanese narrated

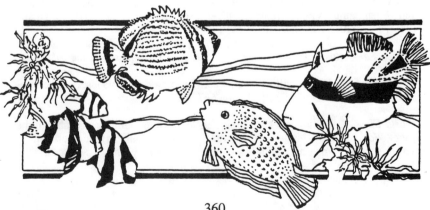

tours. The fully submersible submarine is an 80 ton, 65 foot touring vessel that accommodates 46 passengers. They operate eight dives daily beginning at their Pioneer Inn shop, which also affords you plenty of time to shop for logo items from polo shirts, to visors, beach bottles, jelly beans or beach towels. There is a short boat ride to reach the submarine and quite surprisingly it suddenly emerges out of the middle of the depths of the Pacific. Then you step across from the tender and load onto the submarine. The seats are lined up on both sides in front of 1/2 a porthole. The submarine submerges about 100 feet. The area is a little close, but the temperature is kept cool and comfortable. There are plenty of fish, and fish cards at each station help you identify them. Rocks and coral formations resemble an environ that is somehow extra-terrestrial. Call 667-2224.

The **Reef Dancer** (formerly *Nautilus*) is a semi-submersible, meaning it only partially submerges, so at any time you can go up on deck for some fresh air, or if you feel a bit claustrophobic. It departs at least 5 times a day, times change seasonally. The bottom is six feet below the surface and they cruise around about 5 feet from the ocean floor off of Puamana. The total trip is an hour, but once you are underway, you begin viewing, while the *Atlantis* does require some coordinating to get from the dock to the submarine. The *Reef Dancer* seats are more comfortable, allowing for a bit more room to walk around. One of the crew scuba dives out to hold up items for the guests to view. $29.95 adults, $15.95 for children 6-12 years, 5 and under are free. Call 667-2133 or FAX 661-1107.

The **SeaView** is a 56' semi-submersible vessel. (Formerly the Maui "E" ticket). The *SeaView* Adventure cruises are three 2 hour fully narrated viewing and swim snorkel cruises which depart daily from the Lahaina harbor. This trip offers the opportunity to stay dry in air conditioned comfort or just jump in for an up-close and personal view. They also have free use of ocean kayaks and viewing boards. Adults $39, $20 for children 4-12 years and children under 4 are free. 661-5550.

The *Atlantis* does have clearer viewing since they are down so deep and have infra-red lights. The *Reef Dancer* makes use of sunlight, which at times can be bright, other times cause the water to be hazy. In brief, the *Reef Dancer* is more like dry snorkeling and the *Atlantis* more like dry scuba diving. The *Atlantis* has a smoother, plane-like motion, while the *Reef Dancer* is more like a helicopter, bobbing and rocking as it maneuvers. The *Atlantis* does provide the submarine experience, but you pay the price. The *Reef Dancer* (currently running a special at $29.95), is substantially less expensive than the *Atlantis*. For ten dollars more you can have a two hour trip on *SeaView* (versus one hour on *Reef Dancer*) and a chance to snorkel, too. If you are a snorkeler, you won't see much through the viewing windows on the *Reef Dancer* than you would if you were swimming. But if you are unable or unwilling to get wet, then one of these trips may be an option to consider.

WHALE WATCHING

Every year beginning November 15 and continuing until April 15 (official whale season), the humpback whales arrive in the warm waters off the Hawaiian Islands for breeding, and their own sort of vacation! The sighting of a whale can be an awesome and memorable experience with the humpbacks, small as whales go, measuring some 40 - 50 feet and weighing in at 30 tons. The panoramic vistas as you drive over the Pali and down the beachfront road to Lahaina afford some excellent opportunities to catch sight of one of these splendid marine mammals. However, PLEASE pull off the road and enjoy the view. Many accidents are caused by distracted drivers. For an even closer view, there are plenty of boat trips (kayaks, too). Although most every boat operator does whale watching tours in season, you may want to check into the one sponsored by Pacific Whale Foundation 879-8811. As they are a research group, they are very well informed and knowledgeable about the whales. You can report your sightings by calling the Whale Watch Hotline at 879-8811. Also refer to SEA EXCURSIONS.

DEEP SEA FISHING

Deep sea fishing off Maui is among the finest in the world and no licenses are required for either trolling or bottom fishing. All gear is provided. Fish that might be lured to your bait include the Pacific Blue, Black or Striped Marlin (Au) weighing up to 2,000 lbs., Yellow Fin Tuna (Ahi) up to 300 lbs., Jack Crevalle (Ulua) to 100 lbs., Bonita-Skipjack (Aku) to 40 lbs., Dolphin Fish (Mahi) to 90 lbs., Wahoo (Ono) to 90 lbs., Mackerel (Opelu), Amerjack (Kahala), Grey Snapper (Uku), Red Snapper (Onaga), and Pink Snapper (Opakapaka). Boats generally offer half or full-day fishing trips on a share or private basis with prices running from $60 - $110 shared or $325 - $550 private for a half day (4 hr.), and $85 - $135 shared or $500 - $800 private for a full-day (8 hr). Some are willing to take non-fishing passengers along at half price. Most boats take 4 - 6 on a shared basis, however several can handle larger groups.

FINDING A CHARTER: Your local activity center may be able to direct you to a particular boat that they favor, or you could go down to the docks at the Lahaina or Maalaea Harbor in the afternoon and browse around. There are also a number of activity booths at both harbors that can be consulted. When reserving a spot, be aware that some boats will give full refunds only if 48-hour notice is given for cancellation. If you want to take children fishing, many have restrictions for those under age 12. If you are a serious fisherman, you might consider entering one of the numerous tournaments. Some charters offer tournament packages. Following are a list of just some of the charter fishing boats. While not a scientific study, Finest Kind and Exact (both operated by Finest Kind, Inc.) have managed to be consistently mentioned in the local newspaper for regular catches of very large fish.

A WORD OF ADVICE: The young man had a grin that reached from ear to ear as he stood on the pier in Maalaea, holding up his small ahi for a snapshot of his big catch. The surprise came when the deck hand returned it to the ice chest and continued on with his work. The family all stood, unsure what to do. It appeared that the fish was to remain on board, while the family had envisioned a nice fresh fish dinner. One family member spoke up and a very unhappy crew member sliced a small filet, tossed it into a sack and handed it to the young man. Unlike sportsfishing charters in some parts of the country, the fish caught on board generally remain the property of the boat. The pay to captain and crew is minimal and it is the selling of the boat's catch that subsidizes their income. Many vacationers booking a fishing excursion are unaware of this fact. There seems to be no written law for how fishing charters in Hawaii handle this, at least everyone we talked to had different answers. Many of the brochures lead one to believe that you keep your fish, and they neglect to mention that it may be only a filet of fish. Occasionally you may find a head boat which operates under a different sort of guideline. In this situation, you pay for your bait, gear, and boat time and then keep the fish. In any case, be sure you check when you book your trip about just what and how much fish will be yours to keep. If the person at the activity desk assures you that you keep your catch, don't leave it there, also check with the captain when you board. Communication is the key word and have a mahi mahi day! (As thorough editors we checked and Carol Ann of Carol Ann charters who told us that on board her vessel, you DO get to keep your fish!)

LAHAINA HARBOR

ABSOLUTE SPORTFISHING
Absolute, 31' Bertram sportfisher
Charter: 8 hr. $675; 6 hr. $550
4 hr. $450, bottom fishing 4 hr/$300
Recording 669-1449/
Westin Maui 661-2591

AERIAL SPORTFISHING
CHARTERS *Aerial II and III*
8 hr $660-650; 6 hr $500-550
4 hours $400-450. 667-9089

FINEST KIND, INC.
Exact, 31' Bertram; *Finest Kind*, 37'
Merritt; *Reel Hooker*, 35' Bertram
$135 full day per person
$110 for 3/4 day per person
PO Box 10481, Lahaina, HI 96761
Maximum 6 people, 661-0338

HINATEA SPORTFISHING
Hinatea, 41' Hataras
PO Box 5375, Lahaina, HI 96761
Full day $135 shared boat
6 hours $110 shared boat
Slip #27-Lahaina Harbor, 667-7548

ISLANDER II SPORTFISHING
36' Uniflite, 667-6625

KAANAPALI SPORTFISHING
Desperado 31' Bertram
Shared boat 3/4 day $110
Shared boat full day $135
Private charters $400-600
Bring your favorite lunch and beverage. Alcohol is permitted, no bottles or bananas (bottles can get broken and bananas are bad luck!!).

LAHAINA CHARTERS
Broadbill, 36' Harcraft (max 6)
Judy Ann II, 43' Delta (max 8)
Alohilani, 28' Topaz (max 6)
4 hr $300-360; 6 hr $400-450
8 hours $450-550. Max. 6 people
PO Box 12, Lahaina, HI 96761
667-6672

LUCKEY STRIKE CHARTERS
Kanoa, 31' Uniflite, max. 6
Luckey Strike II, 50' Delta
Shared boat: 4 hours $75; 6 hours
$110; 8 hours $130
Private charters/bottom fishing.
PO Box 1502, Lahaina, HI 96767
661-4606

ROBOLO-ONE FISHING
Bottom fishing: 1/2 day shared $80
Entire boat: 1/2 day $275, Full day
$500; Plug casting: 1/2 day $300
Trolling: 1/2 day $300
Departs Lahaina 661-0480

MAALAEA HARBOR

CAROL ANN CHARTERS
33' Bertram, max. 6
Shared boat:
4 hours $95
6 hours $135
8 hours $150
Private:
4 hours $435
6 hours $535
8 hours $635
Departs Maalaea
877-2181

RASCAL
SPORTFISHING CHARTERS
Rascal, Bertram 31'
Shared boat:
4 hours $85
6 hours $100
8 hours $125
Private charter
4 hours $375
6 hours $475
8 hours $575
Slip #13 Maalaea, 874-8633

OCEAN ACTIVITIES CENTER
No Ka Oi III, 37' Trolley Craft
Shared: 6 hours $115; 8 hours $140
Private: 6 hours $535; 8 hours $635
Departs Maalaea, 879-4485

KIHIKIHI   JBay

SMALL BOAT SAILING

Small boat sailing is available at a number of locations with rentals, usually the 14', sometimes 16' and 18', Hobie Cat. Lasers are also available. Typical rental prices are $35 - $50 per hour and lessons are available. Most of the resorts have sailing centers with rental facilities on the beaches.

FOR MORE INFORMATION ON RENTALS CONTACT:

Beach Activities Pavilion. Rental equipment for windsurfing, kayaking, surfing. Also Hobie Cat, pedal boats and laser sailboats. Phone 661-5552.

West Maui Sailing School. Also windsurfing, kayak and snorkel equipment. (667-5545) Daily scheduled lessons or personalized lessons. They also have sea cycles: two seaters with two sets of independent pedals. A large snorkeling selection, in-line skates, surfboards and body boards, too.

WINDSURFING

Windsurfing is a sport that is increasing astronomically in popularity. Hookipa Beach Park on Maui is one of the best windsurfing sites in the world. This is due to the consistently ideal wind and surf conditions, however, this is definitely NOT the spot for beginners. For the novice, boardsailing beginner group lessons run $40 - 60 an hour, which generally involves instruction on a dry land simulator before you get wet with easy to use beginners equipment. Equipment and/or lessons are available from the following:

Alan Cadiz' Hawaiian Sailboarding Techniques - 425 Koloa St., Kahului. Alan Cadiz and his staff of professional instructors offer a full range of small group and private lessons for beginner or expert. They specialize in one-on-one instruction tailored to each person's ability, travel schedule, budget and goals. Phone 871-5423 or 1-800-968-5423 or FAX 871-6943.

Cort Larned Windsurfing School - Group & private lessons for all levels. Beginning group 2 1/2 hours or private 1 hour $70; three day lesson package $165, five day $250. Also rental equipment via their Maui Windsurf Co. 520 Keolani Place, Kahului. Phone 877-4816 or 1-800-872-0999 U.S. and Canada.

Hawaiian Island Surf and Sport - Pro shop, sales, service, rentals and instruction. Three hour group (up to 3 students) beginner lessons or advanced water start $69. Private instruction $49 for 75 minutes or three lessons $139. (8:30 am-noon). 415 Dairy Road. Phone 871-4981 or toll free 1-800-231-6958.

Hi-Tech Surf Equipment - Sales and Rentals. Kahului 877-2111, Paia 579-9297. Also Shapers at Kaahumanu Center. Call 877-SURF.

Kaanapali Windsurfing School - Beginner lesson 1 1/2 hour $49. Rental equipment per hour $20, $45 for three hours, $65 for 5 hours. Equipment for beginners to intermediate. Located at Whalers Village, Kaanapali. Call 667-1964.

Maui Windsurfari - Offers packages which include accommodations, rental car, windsurfing equipment and excursions. Many of their vacation rentals are unusual with close proximity to windsurfing locations. 871-7766 or 1-800-736-6284. http://windsurfar.com

Sailboards Maui - 397 Dairy Road, Kahului. Typical costs are $49 for full day, $275 for 7 days. Rental includes board, universal mast, boom, sail and soft car rack. They offer insurance or you pay for broken, lost or stolen equipment. They also have surfboard rentals. Phone 871-7954.

Second Wind - Proshop rental, used and new sales. Private lessons $45 per hour, $49 for two hour class. They also have a travel desk to assist with making your accommodation and car rental plans. Phone 877-7467 or 1-800-936-7787. web page http://www.maui.net/ ~ secwind/index.html

Windsurfing West Maui - Provides windsurfing lessons and equipment. 415 Dairy Rd. in Kahului. Also operates Maui Windsurfing. Rents vans with racks and hangers for boards and equipment. Phone 877-0090 or 1-800-870-4084.

Some resorts offer their guests free clinics. Rental by the hour can get expensive at $20 per hour and $40 - $65 per four hours. A better rate is $45 for all day.

Books of interest available at local bookstores: *Hawaiian Windsurfing Guide* $15.95.

SURFING

Honolua Bay is one of the best surfing spots in Hawaii, and undoubtedly the best on Maui, with waves up to 15 feet on a good winter day and perfect tubes. A spectacular vantage point is on the cliffs above the bay. In the summer this bay is calm and, as it is a Marine Reserve, offers excellent snorkeling.

Also in this area is Punalau Beach (just past Honolua) and Honokeana Bay off Ka'eleki'i Point (just north of the Alaeloa residential area). In the Lahaina area there are breaks north and south of the harbor and periodically good waves at Awalua Beach (mile marker 16).

On the north shore Hookipa Beach Park, Kanaha Beach, and Baldwin all have good surfing at times. In the Hana area there is Hamoa Beach. There are a couple of good spots in Maalaea Bay and at Kalama Beach Park.

Conditions change daily - even from morning to afternoon - around the island. Check with local board rental outlets for current daily conditions.

Hawaiian Sailboarding Techniques - 444 Hana Hwy., Kahului. HST goes "surf-surfari" to wherever the best place for learning happens to be that particular day. Small groups and private instruction available for beginners wanting to cruise the waves their first time out, also intermediate and advanced lessons. Current rates for longboard surfing class is $60 each two hours, three people per class maximum, includes surfboard. Phone 871-5423. FAX 871-6943. 1-800-968-5423.

Maui Surfing School - Andrea Thomas originated the "Learn to Surf in One Lesson" and has taught thousands of people between the ages of 3 and 70. She's been teaching on Maui since 1980 and offers private and group lessons specializing in the beginner and the coward. Board rentals available. Lahaina Harbor. Phone 875-0625.

Books of interest available at local bookstores: *Surfin'ary: A Dictionary of Surfing Terms and Surfspeak. $17.95. Surfer's Guide to Hawaii* (Hawaii Gets all the Breaks!) by Greg Ambrose. 156 pp, $12.95. *The History of Surfing* $27.95.

BODY SURFING

Mokuleia (Slaughterhouse) Beach has the best body surfing especially in the winter. This is not a place for weak swimmers or the inexperienced. When the surf is up, it can be downright dangerous. The high surf after a Kona storm brings fair body surfing conditions, better boogie boarding, to some beaches on leeward Maui.

JET SKIING

Thrillcraft activities, which include parasailing and jetskiing have been banned during whale season. The "open season" for participating in jet skiing recreation is May 16th until December 14th.

Currently the only jet ski operation, *Pacific Jet Ski Rental*, is at the south end of Kaanapali Beach at Hanakaoo Beach Park. They have two and three passenger wave runners. Rental prices are per jet ski, not per person. Super Jet - Wave Runner: 1/2 hr. $45, 1 hr. $65, two people max. Waverunner III: 1/2 hr. $55, 1 hr. $76, three people max. An additional charge of $10 per person is charged if more than two people use the Super Jet or Waverunner and if more than three people use the Waverunner III. Hawaiian law requires a person be 15 years old to operate a machine by himself. Younger persons can ride as a passenger on the waverunner with someone who is at least 15 years of age. All renters are fitted with a life vest. Open Monday thru Saturday 9 am - 4 pm (weather permitting) and closed on Sunday. Phone 667-2066.

PARASAILING

The parasail "season" on Maui is May 16 - December 14th due to the restrictions during whale season. For those that aren't familiar with this aquatic experience, parasailing is a skyward adventure where you are hooked to a parachute and attached to a tow line behind a boat and soon are floating high in the air with a bird's eye view of Maui. The flight lasts 8 to 10 minutes which may be either too long or too short for some! Prices $32.50-$50. Some allow an "observer" (friend) to go along for an extra fee.

367

Lahaina Para-sail - 1 and 2 seaters. Cost is $30-46.50. Observers $15. Phone 661-4887.

Parasail Kaanapali - Departs from Mala Wharf. $35.65 for 10 minute ride at 1,000 feet up. Phone 669-6555.

UFO Parasail - Observers can go for $17. Departs in front of Whalers Village. They use a new wrinkle, a self-contained "winch" boat. You get started standing on the boat and as your parachute fills, you are reeled out 400-800 feet. When it comes time to descend, you're simply reeled back in. $37 early bird, $42 standard, $52 deluxe. Phone 661-7836, FAX 667-0373.

West Maui Para-sail - Lahaina Harbor, Slip #15. Uses "Skyrider," a two passenger aerial recliner as well as harness flights. Dry take-off and landing. Boat departs every 30 minutes with six passengers. They use a 800 ft. line so passengers are over 400 feet above the water. Call for reservations. $48 regular or $39 for early bird (first flight of the day). Phone 661-4060.

WATERSKIING

Hawaii Island Watercraft, Inc. dba *Kaanapali Waterski*. Located at Whaler's Village on Kaanapali Beach. Waterskiing runs $25 for 15 minutes, 30 minutes will cost $50, 60 minutes is $80. Also available are the aqua sled (banana boat), private coastal tours and seasonal whale watching. Phone 667-1964.

KAYAKING

Kaanapali Windsurfing School - Kayak rentals: 1 hour $15 one person, $25 two persons. Kayak tour 9 am-noon, $65 includes snorkel, lunch, pickup in Kaanapali or Lahaina. Phone 667-1964.

Kelii's Kayaking -South Shore of Maui (Turtle Adventure) 2 1/2 hours $55, 4 1/2 hours $85. North Shore or West Shore of Maui 2 1/2 hours $55, 4 1/2 hours $85. Maui Sunset 2 1/2 hours $55. Custom tours on request. Call 874-7652.

Maui Kayaks - Instruction for the novice (experienced paddler can join) in a half or full day guided trip along the Kihei coast. Contact: Bill Pray, Maui Kayaks, 50 Waiohuli St., Kihei, Maui 96753. Phone 874-3536.

South Pacific Kayaks - Rainbow Mall at 2439 S. Kihei Rd. They offer introductory paddle and snorkel excursions with short paddling distances combined with offshore snorkeling 2 1/2-3 hrs. $55, departures from both West and South Maui. Maui Hiking Adventures half day $55, full day $85. Marine Reserve Explorer, turtle, dolphin and whale watch travels along the southern coast with time for snorkeling and a deli lunch. 6 1/2 hours $85. Also available are single and double kayaks as well as car racks, life vests, snorkel gear, boogie boards and more. Phone 875-4848.

Tradewind Kayaks - 2 1/2 hour "Wet Your Okole" is an introductory shoreline kayak and snorkel trip $55. Their barefoot special is offered in the winter, "Tharr She Blows" is a 2 1/2 hour whale watching adventure. $49. Their "Marine Reserve Experience" is a trip to La Perouse along the Kinao lava flow. This 4 1/2 hour excursion runs $75. Their "Exotic Tropical Sunset" is a two hour trip for $45. Phone 879-2247.

LAND ACTIVITIES

LAND TOURS

Land excursions on Maui are centered upon two major attractions, Hana and the O'heo Valley, and Haleakala Crater. Lesser attractions are trips to the Iao Valley or around West Maui. You can do all of this by car (refer to the WHERE TO STAY - WHAT TO SEE chapter), however, with a tour you can sit back and enjoy the scenery while a professional guide discourses on the history, flora, fauna and geography of the area. The single most important item on any tour is a good guide/driver and, unfortunately, the luck of the draw prevails here.

Another, somewhat expensive option, is a personalized custom tour. A local resident will join you, in your car, for a tour of whatever or wherever you choose. You can do the driving or sign on your guide with your rental car company to do the driving. This may allow you the opportunity to linger at those places you enjoy the most, without following the pace of a group. Your guide may also be able to take you to locations the tour vans don't include. ***Rent-a-Local*** recommends a 24 hour advance reservation, 877-4042 or from the mainland 1-800-228-6284.

Driving to Hana and back requires a full day and can be very grueling, so this is one trip we recommend you consider taking a tour. A Haleakala Crater tour spans 5-6 hours and can be enjoyed at sunrise (3 am departure), midday or sunset. The West Maui and Iao Valley trips are half-day ventures. Only vans travel the road to Hana, however, large buses as well as vans are available for other trips. (Be aware that some vans may not be air conditioned.) Prices are competitive and those listed here are correct at time of publication. Some trips include the cost of meals, others do not. Also available are one day tours to the outer islands. The day begins with an early morning departure to the Big Island, O'ahu or Kaua'i. Some excursions provide a guided ground tour, others offer a rental car to explore the island on your own.

Akina Aloha Tours - This family owned business has been operating exclusively on Maui for over 78 years. They specialize in ground transportations to groups, charters and families for tours of Upcountry and Haleakala in their Belgium-made VanHool buses, mini buses, vans, sedans and late vintage limousines. Multi-language interpreters are available. 1-800-800-3989. 879-2828. FAX 879-0523.

Arthur's Limo Service - They provide tours to Haleakala and Hana in their luxury limousine. $69.50 per hour (2 hour minimum) plus tax and tip. Phone 871-5555 or 1-800-345-4667 inter-island or from Mainland.

Ekahi Tours - 532 Keolani Place, Kahului, HI 96732. Tours of Hana $75 adult, $55 child, Sunrise Haleakala $55 adult, $45 child via van. Other areas charter for $65 per hour. A new exploration was recently added to the Ekahi tours roster. The Kahakuloa Valley tour is an opportunity to enjoy a cultural experience at a Hawaiian *kuleana* (parcel of land) which is part of an *ahupua'a* (land division extending from the uplands to the oceans), located along the northwest coast of Maui. According to background information provided to us from Ekahi Tours, "The Kahakuloa Valley is inhabited by some of the same families of past generations of Hawaiians who were the original settlers 1,500 years ago and is the only village in existence that still has a working *Konohiki*." A *Konohiki* is the caretaker of the *ahupua'a* and oversees the land and fishing rights. Oliver Dukelow is a Hawaiian (formerly a policeman) who cultivates taro. Dukelow provides guests with background into the plants, taro farming and the Hawaiian lifestyle. The half day trip runs $60 adults and $50 children. Phone 877-9775.

Kawika's 'Aina Tour Company - 505 Front Street, Suite 231, Lahaina, HI 96761. Tours are offered to Kahakuloa, a remote village on Maui's north shore. Tours are $80 per person. They also offer sunrise and sunset tours to Haleakala, $80 per person, and all day trips to Hana, $100 per person. Phone 667-2204.

Rent-a-Local - Discover Maui in your car with an island resident as your guide. Explore the destinations of your choice. $195 for two people, 8 hours, (plus your own gas). Phone 877-4042 or 1-800-228-6284.

Polynesian Adventure - Haleakala Sunrise $51.04 adult, $35.46 child, includes tax. Haleakala Day trip $54.17 adults, $36.46 child. Hana $67.71 adult, $44.27 child. They also offer one day trips to Kaua'i, The Big Island of Hawaii, or

O'ahu. These one day, one island trips run $165.63 adults, $160.42 child. They also do a Hana Grand Adventure which is a land/helicopter tour. Phone 877-4242 or 1-800-622-3011 from Mainland U.S.

Robert's Hawaii Tours - Offers land tours in their big air conditioned buses or vans. They depart to all scenic areas from Kahului, Kihei, Wailea, and the West Maui Hotels. Tours include: Kula/Iao Valley/Lahaina; Iao Valley/Lahaina; Haleakala/Iao Valley/Lahaina; Iao Valley/Haleakala Crater; Hana Highlights; Haleakala. Prices vary depending on tour, departure and arrival location. Phone 871-6226 or 1-800-767-7551 U.S. Mainland.

Sugar Cane Train - The Lahaina Kaanapali and Pacific Railroad is affectionately referred to as The Sugar Cane Train. In Lahaina in 1862, the harvesting of sugar cane was one of the island's biggest industries. More than 45,000 tons were produced from 5,000 acres. The Lahaina Kaanapali & Pacific Railroad began in 1882, replacing the slower method (mules and steers) of hauling sugar cane between the harvest area and the Pioneer Sugar Mill. This allowed a greater area of cane to be planted as well. By the 1900's the railroad was also transporting an ever-increasing number of workers to their jobs. In 1970 the Sugar Cane Train was once again brought back to life, but financial difficulties silenced the train whistle once more. In 1973, Mr. Willes B. Kyele purchased the railroad and brought life back to its engines. Currently two trains operate daily on a three foot narrow gauge railroad between 8 am and 6 pm. The trains are pulled by two steam locomotives, "Anaka" and "Myrtle." The locomotives were built in 1943 and were restored to resemble those that were used in Hawaii at the beginning of the 20th century. The singing conductor will guide you through history as you wind through the cane fields of Lahaina. The train makes six round trips daily with one way fares for adults $9, round trip is $13.50. Children 3-12 years are $5 one way, $7 round trip. Their main depot is located just outside of Lahaina, turn at the Pizza Hut sign. The Kaanapali Station is located across the highway from the resort area. The free Kaanapali trolley picks up at the Whalers Village and drops off at this station. The Puukolii boarding platform and parking lot is located on the Kapalua side of Kaanapali. They offer several package options: The Hawaiian Experience is a round trip train ride and Hawaiian Domed Experience Theater movie $17.50 adults and $9.25 children. The Land/Sea Adventure is a round trip train ride plus a one hour tour on a submarine. Their Lahaina Town Tour includes a round trip train ride plus tickets to three Lahaina museums. $17.50 adults, $7 children. Be sure to purchase your return tickets early as they often sell out quickly. 661-0089 has recorded information. Reservations needed for groups of 12 or more. Phone 661-0080.

Temptation Tours ★ - If you'd really like to pamper yourself, then enjoy the luxury of a tour by these folks. Working in conjunction with Blue Hawaiian Helicopter they provide a unique option to either Hana or Upcountry Maui. The "Hana Sky-trek" is their ultimate package that begins with a helicopter trip to Hana, a tour of the town and Wainapanapa in a luxury van, an elegant lunch and then drive back to Kahului. Or the reverse trip where you drive to Hana and fly back, $199. The Hana picnic is a round trip in their 6-8 passenger limo van for $110, or with the Hana Ultimate substitute lunch at the Hotel Hana Maui for

$139. The Jungle Express is a Hana tour which includes round trip travel by small airplane from Kahului airport to the Hana airport. Then a van tour of Hana before your flight back to Kahului for $249. The Haleakala Day Tour begins with an ascent up Haleakala in their luxury limo-van, to the eucalyptus forests an pastureland of the Thompson Ranch. An hour and a half to enjoy the view on horseback is followed by elegant lunch at the Silver Cloud Ranch. Price is $159 for the all day excursion. Or choose an upcountry adventure which offers a trip to the summit of Haleakala, a tour through the Kula area with lunch at Makawao with a chance to visit the galleries there. This 8 hour trip runs $115. Also available is a Haleakala Sunrise Tour for $150. Phone 877-8888.

Trans Hawaiian - A day trip to Hana $65 adult $42.50 children. It departs 8 am and returns to hotels between 5 and 6:30 pm. A no host lunch is available in Hana. Haleakala sunrise or morning tour $49 adult, $31.75 for children under 12. (Fare does not include Haleakala National Park entrance fee of $4.50 per person.) Phone 877-7308 or 1-800-231-6984. Japanese language phone number 871-7940.

ART CLASSES AND ART TOURS

Maui Art Tours offers visitors an opportunity to visit the homes and studios of three or four of Maui's fine artists, meet them and watch them work. This unique day-long adventure is provided in a luxury air-conditioned car and includes a gourmet lunch. Cost is $200 per person. P.O. Box 1058, Makawao, HI 96768. Phone 572-3453.

Hui Noeau Arts Center near Makawao offers art classes. Phone 572-6560 and the *Art School of Kapalua* also offers art education. Phone 665-0007.

The Aston Wailea Resort offers the *Ho'olokahi Hawaiian Cultural Program*. These classes include lectures and workshops on Hawaiian culture. Activities vary throughout the year. The Hana Ka Lima is an arts and crafts exhibition, currently held every Friday at the resort from 9 am - 2 pm. The exhibition features Maui artisans displaying, demonstrating and selling their creations throughout the lobby of the resort. It is open to the public free of charge. The resort's Cultural Presentation Series features biweekly classes in a rich variety of subjects. In addition to learning the finer points of haku lei weaving, Hawaiian quilt making, and hula, guests can enrich their understanding of Hawaiian Sovereignty, Pidgin English, the Hawaiian Moon Calendar, Herbal Healing, Feather Work, the Hawaiian Green Sea Turtle and the Humpback Whale. There is a small fee for non-resort guests which includes refreshments. Ho'olokahi, which means "to create unity" was instituted in 1993. The goal of the program is to preserve and perpetuate the Hawaiian culture. Contact the director of Hawaiian activities at the Aston Wailea Resort 874-7822.

Enjoy a self-guided tour of the wonderful art galleries in Lahaina. Friday Night is Art Night with many free activities and a chance to meet some of the artists in person. Underneath the Banyan tree are exhibits by local, amateur and profession-als. The old courthouse also has art galleries featuring local artists.

THEATER AND THE ARTS

With the opening of the *Maui Arts and Cultural Center* in May 1994, new doors of opportunity have opened for theater on Maui. However, Maui clearly has a history of strong community support and involvement of many long-time performing arts organizations. The individual theater groups will now be performing at the cultural center as well as their individual locations. The center's ticket office is 242-SHOW. Check the paper for performances of the *Maui Symphony*. They periodically have 40-minute concerts for children as a part of their Youth Education Performances. Also performances by the *Valley Isle Symphony Orchestra*.

Maui Community Theatre produces dramatic performances at the Historic Iao Theatre in Wailuku. This is another non-profit organization which has been in existence in varying forms since the 1920's. Then, it was two different theatre groups, the Maui Players and Little Theatre of Maui. In 1931, these two organizations joined forces to create the Maui Community Theatre. The Maui Onstage's production schedule continued through the 1930's but was interrupted during the war years and not rekindled until 1971 when a group of Maui citizens reactivated the organization. In 1972, Maui Onstage took up residency in the Maui County Fair Grounds' Territorial Building, until the fall of 1984 when it, along with all the props, costumes, light and sound equipment, was destroyed by fire. They reorganized and moved to their present home in the newly renovated historic Iao Theatre on Market Street. Phone 242-6969.

The Baldwin High School Performing Arts Learning Center (Baldwin Theatre Guild) offers six main stage productions each year. Generally they do a musical, a children's show, a dramatic presentation, a summer musical and an annual revue. The group was formed in 1964 when interested students expressed a desire to organize and perform theatrical productions. Over the years, hundreds of students have been a part of this organization. Workshops are held at various times during the month and in addition to the performances, the guild also offers its members involvement in other social activities, such as dances or picnics. For information on performances phone 243-5673 or check the local paper.

Theatre Theatre Maui (TTM) is a nonprofit organization founded in 1991 whose mission is to offer all West Side residents the opportunity to experience a full spectrum of live, hands-on theatre. They generally offer one adult and three children productions. TTM offers summer workshops for children which culminate in an annual production, usually held in July. They are partially funded through grants from the County of Maui and private foundations. Look for adult productions held in the spring at West Maui hotels. Phone 661-1168.

The *Maui Academy of Performing Arts* clearly has it all when it comes to entertainment. An educational and performing arts organization for youth and adults, the Academy is located in its own building on the grounds of the Maui Arts and Cultural Center. They offer community theatre performances, special events, dance, drama and voice classes, and special drama and dance workshops for youth and adults. Open to the public. For more information on any of the current programs or daily schedule, call the Academy offices at 244-8760.

ASTRONOMY

The rooftop of the Hyatt Regency is home to "Big Blue," the 16-inch recreational telescope. Three times each evening a maximum of ten people head to the hotel's rooftop for a guided tour of the stars with Maui's own Director of Astronomy. Cost is $12 for adults, $6 for children 12 and under. For reservations contact the Hyatt Regency Maui at 661-1234 ext. 3225.

BIKE TOURS

The Hawaiian Islands offer an endless array of spectacular air, sea and land tours, but only on Maui is there an experience quite like the bicycle ride down from the 10,000 foot summit of the world's largest dormant volcano. Bob Kiger, better known as Cruiser Bob, was the originator of the Haleakala downhill. Cruiser Bob is reported to have made 96 individual bike runs himself to thoroughly test all aspects of the route before the first paying customers attempted the trip. Cruiser Bob's operations are now *pau* (Hawaiian for over), but there are a number of companies still operating Haleakala downhill trips.

Each tour company differs slightly in its adaptation of the trip, but the principal is the same, to provide the ultimate in biking experiences. For the very early riser (2-3 am) you can see the sunrise from the crater before biking down. Later morning expeditions are available as well. Your day will begin with a van pickup at your hotel for a narrated trip to the Haleakala summit along with safety information for the trip down. The temperature at the summit can be as much as 30 degrees cooler than sea level, so appropriate wear would include a sweater or sweatshirt. General requirements are for riders to wear closed-toe rubber soled shoes, sun glasses or prescription lenses (not all helmets have visors). A height requirement of about 5 feet is requested by some and no pregnant women are allowed on the trip. Bikers must also sign an acknowledgement of risk and safety consideration form. For the descent, riders are equipped with windbreaker jackets, gloves, helmets and specially designed bicycles with heavy duty brakes. Dress in layers - the temperature change can be dramatic!

A leader will escort you down the mountain curves with the van providing a rear escort. Somewhere along the way will be a meal break. Some tours provide picnics, others include a sit-down meal at the lodge in Kula or elsewhere. Actual biking time will run about 3 hours for the 38-mile downhill trip. The additional time, about 5 hours for the entire trip, is spent commuting to the summit, meals, and the trip from the volcano's base back to your hotel. Prices for the various tours are competitive and reservations should be made in advance.

We biked down with Maui Downhill and opted for the "late" 7 am trip. We found them to be very careful, courteous and professional. Unfortunately they don't have control over the weather and the day we chose was clear on the drive up, fogged in and misty at the summit and a torrential downpour for more than half of the 38 miles down. Due to the weather, we couldn't enjoy much of the scenery going down, but probably wouldn't have had much time to gander as it is important to keep your eyes on the road! The leader set a fairly slow pace, not much of a thrill for the biking speedster, but safe and comfortable for most. At any time we were invited to hop in the van, but ours was a hearty group and after a stop to gear up in rain slickers, we all continued on. Our leader also advised that if the weather posed any kind of risk, he would load us on the van. The weather broke just long enough for us to enjoy sandwiches or salads at the Sunrise Market and to bask in the sun's momentary warmth. In radio contact with the group just ahead of us we were advised that the rain promised to await us just a little farther down the volcanic slope. As predicted, the drizzle continued as we biked down through the cowboy town of Makawao. We arrived in Paia only a little wetter for the experience.

Chris's Bike Adventures - They offer some unusual bike expeditions and interesting options. These bike rides take riders around upcountry, not just down it. They use 21 speed mountain bikes and provide helmets, gloves and weather gear. All tours include a tour host. All tours beginning in the morning, last 6-8 hours, and include breakfast and lunch. All afternoon tours include a snack and run 4-5 hours. Bike at your own pace. The Haleakala Wine Trek travels (22 miles) to the Tedeschi Winery and beyond to the remote lava fields above La Perouse. Includes crater viewing and short hike, a continental breakfast and picnic lunch. Sunrise, full day and half day trips available. $89 full day, $59 half day. The Wilder Side of Haleakala (46 miles) is the above trip plus some biking along the wilder, remote backside of Haleakala $115. Other trips including hiking or hiking/biking combinations are available as well as biking expeditions to neighbor islands. Phone 871-2453

Cruiser Bob's - The legendary creator of the Haleakala downhill bike trip is gone. He packed up and closed his doors.

Haleakala Mountain Bikes - 1043 Makawao Ave., Makawao, HI 96768. They have a sunrise special $64.95, Haleakala Express $4.95 and a "Take Away Bikes" plan which includes a Hollywood style bike rack for your own car and equipment. Phone 572-2200.

Maui Downhill - Transportation from your hotel/condo. Trips include the 38 mile sunrise tour with breakfast at Kula Lodge or Kula Sandalwood is $115.20, 38 mile day tour with picnic lunch at Sunrise Market runs $110.40, the 38 mile day midday tour with light lunch at Sunrise Market costs $95.04, the 22 miles sunrise tour runs is $79.68, 22 mile day tour is $48-59. The day trip begins with a continental breakfast at the base yard before departure up the mountain and a picnic lunch at the Sunrise Market (and protea gardens) on the way down. Must be over 12 years. Phone 871-2155 or 1-800-535-2453 in U.S.

Maui Mountain Cruisers - Pickup provided from Kaanapali, Lahaina, Kahului and Kihei. Minimum age is 12 years, minimum height is 4'1". Closed toe shoes and protective eyewear (sunglasses or prescription glasses). Sunrise tour $99 includes a continental breakfast prior to the tour and breakfast at Kula Sandalwoods. The midday tour runs $86.40 and includes a continental breakfast before the trip with lunch at Sunrise Market, located halfway down Haleakala. Phone 572-0195, FAX 871-5791 or 1-800-232-MAUI in U.S.

Mountain Riders - They offer a guided Haleakala Volcano Downhill tour, 38 miles for $99. A Haleakala Bicycle Wine Tour is a self-paced midday tour of about 8 hours in duration. $89. The Sunrise 22 mile downhill meets in Makawao at 4 am and is self-paced. $59. Trips one and two include round trip transportation to and from hotels and condos in their vans and use of helmets, gloves and rain gear. They also include continental breakfast and a sit down breakfast at Casanova or lunch at the Sunrise Protea flower farm. Call 242-9739.

BIKE SALES AND RENTALS

Bikes and mopeds are an ambitious and fun way to get around the resort areas, although you can rent a car for less than a moped. Available by the hour, day or week, they can be rented at several convenient locations.

A & B Rentals - 3481 Honoapiilani Hwy. at the ABC store in Honokowai. They have mopeds, bicycles, beach equipment, surfing and boogie boards, snorkel gear, fishing poles and underwater cameras. Mopeds run $24 for 24 hours, bikes $10 day or $50 week. Mountain bikes $15-60. Phone 669-0027.

Kukui Activity Center - Kukui Activity Center. 1819 S. Kihei Rd. Bicycles $12 day, $65 week. Mopeds $27.50 - 24 hours. They also rent used cars, jeeps and trucks. Phone 875-1151.

South Maui Bicycles - 1913 S. Kihei Rd. They sell and rent mountain, off-road and road bikes. Phone 874-0068.

GOLF

Maui's golf courses have set for themselves a high standard of excellence. Many are consistantly ranked among the top in the United States and the World by prominent golf magazines.

Not only do they provide some very challenging play, but they also offer distractingly beautiful scenery. Most of the major resorts offer golf packages and for the avid player, this may be an economical plan.

Delmar Golf College at Kaanapali Golf Course offers golf instruction for the beginner or the advanced. Their "curriculum" includes video analysis, half and all day schools, beginner clinics, private lessons and any of the above paired with 9 or 18 holes of play on the Kaanapali Golf Course. Call 661-0488 or 661-9249.

KAANAPALI

The Kaanapali Resort offers two championship courses. Green fees are $100 for 18 holes, cart included for resort guests. Green fees for non-guests $120. Twilight rate $60. Residents $50. Located at the Southern entrance to the Kaanapali resort area is the Royal Kaanapali driving range. Club rental $27. Phone 661-3691.

Golf on Maui

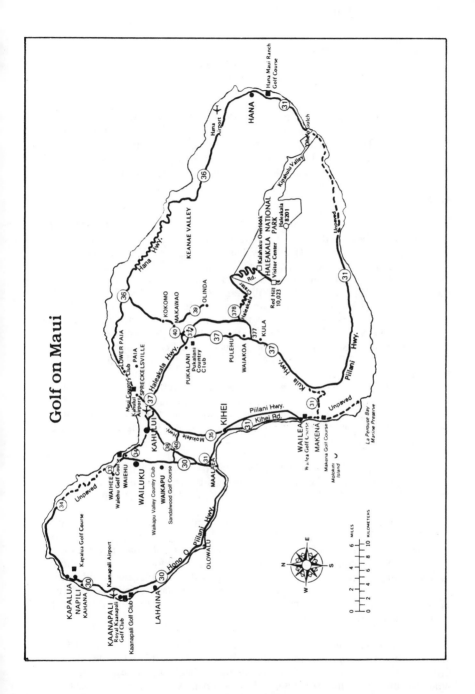

The North Course has been attracting celebrities since its inaugural when Bing Crosby played in the opening of the first nine holes. Designed by Robert Trent Jones, this 6,305 yard course places heavy emphasis on putting skills. At par 72, it is rated 70 for men and 71.4 for women.

The South Course first opened in 1970 as an executive course and was reopened in 1977 as a regular championship course after revisions by golf architect Arthur Snyder. At 6,205 yards and par 72 it requires accuracy as opposed to distance, with narrower fairways and more small, hilly greens than the North Course. As an added attraction, the Sugar Cane Train passes by along the 4th hole.

KAPALUA

The Kapalua Resort features the Bay Course, Village Course and Plantation Course. Green fees for the Bay and Village Course: $115 includes cart; registered guests of Kapalua Bay Hotel & Villas, The Kapalua Villas and The Ritz-Carlton, Kapalua $75; Maui resident $47; Twilight play 2 pm - 6 pm runs $62. Green Fees for the Planation Course: Standard $125, registered guests of Kapalua Bay Hotel & Villas, The Kapalua Villas and The Ritz-Carlton, Kapalua $80. Twilight play $69. Replay on any of the courses, the same day is $25-30. Club and shoe rentals available. Practice range is open 8 am - 4:30 pm, $5 per bucket. Guests may reserve tee-off times up to 7 days in advance. Non-guest reservations 4 days in advance. Special golf events include the GTE Hawaiian Tel Hall of Fame Championship (May), Kapalua Clambake (June), Lincoln-Mercury Kapalua International (November) In 1992, Golf Digest ranked The Plantation Course #4 among resort courses in the U.S. and all three courses were listed in Hawaii's top 7. One day golf school includes instruction and lunch at Jameson's Grill and Bar at Kapalua for $225. Also available are video golf lessons to analyze your swing, and playing lessons are offered. Daily clinics are available Monday-Thursday 4-5 pm. Clinic fee is $20. Phone 669-8044.

Kapalua recently restored one of the game's lost traditions with the establishment of the Caddie Program. This reflects Kapalua's desire to kindle interest in the game among Maui's youth and restore the player/caddie relationship.

Kapalua has demonstrated its dedication to the land. All three golf courses are Certified Audubon Cooperative Sanctuaries. Kapalua's courses received this Sanctuary designation by meeting the stringent environmental standards set forth by the New York Audubon Cooperative Sanctuary System for water conservation, habitat enhancement, public involvement, integrated pest management and more. An environmental awareness program, "Eagles and Birdies at Kapalua" encourages players to identify the many birds (23 varieties) they are likely to encounter during their rounds at Kapalua.

The Bay Course, under the design of Arnold Palmer, opened in late 1975, sprawls from sea level to the mountain's edge. This beautiful and scenic par 72, 6,600 yard course has a distinctly Hawaiian flavor. With its picturesque signature hole extending onto an ocean-framed black lava peninsula, The Bay Course is an excellent example of a premier resort golf course.

The Village Course opened in 1981 and sweeps inland along the pineapple fields and statuesque pine trees. At par 71 and 6,632 yards, designer Arnold Palmer and course architect Ed Seay are reported to have given this course a European flavor. Resembling the mountainous countryside of Scotland, this course is reputed to be the most difficult and demanding in Hawaii and one of the most challenging in the world.

The Plantation Course opened in May 1991. It was designed by Coore and Crenshaw of Austin, Texas and is the home of the Lincoln-Mercury Kapalua International held each November. The 18-hole championship is situated on 240 acres north of the Village Course. The 7,263 yard course has a par 73. The course features expansive greens, deep valleys and expansive fairways.

KIHEI

The Silversword Golf Course, a non-resort course, offers a 6,800 yard par 71, 18-hole course located off Piilani Highway near Lipoa Street. Green fees, which are currently $69, includes shared cart. Rider (non-golfer) $15. Golf Special April thru December 18, $57. Twi-lite (no guarantee on 18 holes, after 1 pm; must be in barn by 6 pm), $44, Twi-light April thru December 18, $42. $15 for same day replay. Rental clubs $22, rental shoes $10. Driving range offers a bucket of balls for $3, open 8 am-9 pm, except Saturday and Sunday nights, Thursdays noon - 9 pm. Phone 874-0777.

MAKENA

Makena offers two courses. The original 18-hole course opened at the same time as the Maui Prince resort in 1991-1992. The second 18 holes opened November 1993. It is a bit confusing, but what they have done is taken the original 18 holes, divided it in two, and added an additional 9 holes to each course. Both courses were designed by Robert Trent Jones. Resort guests $80; twilight $60 (after 2 pm). All others $120; twilight $70. $35 for same day replay. Fees include cart. King Cobra club rental $35. Phone 879-3344.

The South Course is a more classic open style course that leads to the ocean. The large cactus which abound in this area were imported to feed the cattle which were once ranched in this area. This course is 6,168 yards with a par 72.

The North Course is a narrower course that travels along the slopes of Haleakala offering some spectacular panoramic views. The North Course has a par 72 and is 6151 yards.

WAILEA

The Wailea resort offers the challenging Orange, Blue and Gold Courses. Current green fees for the Blue or Emerald course is $125; for resort guests $85. Play on the Gold Course is $90 for Wailea Guests; $130 for non-resort guests. Golf Pro Don Pasquariello offers morning clinics, afternoon golf school 2-4 hours or private lessons. Phone 875-5111 or FAX 875-5114.

The Emerald Course opened in December 1994, designed by Robert Trent Jones, Jr. It is a par-72 layout and 6,825 yards. It was designed to provide a tropical garden experience. Originally this course was the Orange Course, but was completely revamped and redesigned to be enjoyable for golfers of all caliber, the course also boasts spectacular scenery. The fourth hole has a great oceanview. Definitely worth packing a camera along with your clubs.

The Blue Course is par 72 and 6,758 yards from the championship tees. A creation of Arthur Jack Snyder, it opened in 1972. Four lakes and 74 bunkers provide added hazards along with the exceptional scenery. The 16th hole is especially lovely with numerous people stopping to snap a picture from this magnificent vantage point.

The Gold Course, is par 72, stretching 7,070 yards across the lower slopes of Haleakala, affording exquisite views of the Pacific Ocean. Designed by golf course architect Robert Trent Jones Jr., it opened January 1, 1994. Jones design concept was to create a classical, rugged style of golf - that takes advantage of the natural sloping terrain.

WAIKAPU

Waikapu Sandalwood Golf Course is a par 72, and a 5,162-6,469 yard course, depending on your choice of the blue, white or red tee-offs. Mandatory cart fee is included. Non-player is extra charge. Regular $75, Rental clubs $30, rental shoes $5, Hawaii resident $35. Phone 242-4653 or FAX 242-8089.

The Grand Waikapu Resort Country offers a special Golf and Spa package. A $200 all inclusive package offers a round of 18-holes plus use of the golf course spa facilities. (Special rate of $120 for guests of selected hotels.) The ladies facilities include jacuzzi, sauna, showers, TV, lounge and juice bar. The men's feature a furo (Japanese bath) sauna, showers, lounge area. What a way to finish your day of golf! Spa hours daily from 11 am - 7 pm. In 1949 Frank Lloyd Wright designed a luxury home for the Windfohr family in Fort Worth, Texas. The home was never built. In 1952, Raul Bailleres, a Cabinet Member of the

Mexican Government, had the Windfohr design modified for a site on an Acapulco cliffside. Unfortunately, the Dailleres' suffered the loss of their son, and the project was abandoned. In 1957, Marilyn Monroe and her husband Arthur Miller, requested Mr. Wright design a country home for them in Connecticut. Mr. Wright, being fond of this particular design, again modified the original for Monroe and Miller. However, once again the project was abandoned. The design was ultimately purchased for Taliesen West by the Grand Waikapu Country Club owners and has been constructed as the Grand Waikapu Country Club. The Grand Waikapu Country Club clubhouse is tri-level with two thirds of the building underground, and measuring 74,788 square feet. Phone 244-7888.

SPRECKELSVILLE

The Maui Country Club is a private course which invites visitors to play on Mondays. Call on Sunday after 9 am to schedule Monday tee times. It originally opened in 1925. The front 9 holes have a par 37 as do the back nine. Green fees are $45 cart included for 9 or 18 holes. Phone 877-0616.

PUKALANI

Pukalani Country Club and Golf Course is nestled on 160 acres along the slopes of Haleakala and affords a tremendous panoramic view of Central Maui and the ocean from every hole. Designed by Bob Baldock, the first 9 holes opened in 1980. Nine additional holes have been added making a par 72, 6,692 yard course. Green fees are $50 before noon, $40 after noon for 18 holes, $27 for nine holes, anytime, cart included. Phone 572-1314.

WAILUKU

The Waiehu Municipal Course, which is north of Wailuku, opened with nine holes in 1929 and an additional 9 holes were added later. The mens course is 5330 yards par 72, women's course is 5511 yards par 71. Green fees are $25 weekdays and $30 weekends and holidays. A cart is optional. $7.50 per person for 9 holes, $15 per person for 18 holes. Phone 243-7400 or pro shop 244-5934.

THE ISLAND OF LANA'I

Two 18-hole courses are offered on Lana'i, *The Challenge at Manele* and *The Experience at Koele* courses. Non-guests are charged $150 for either course. A day package which includes round-trip transportation via the Expeditions out of Lahaina, green fees and Lana'i island transfers is available, (808) 565-7227. Trilogy Excursions can be reached at 1-800-874-2666 or 661-4743. They also offers a golf surf & turf package at the Challenge at Manele course. See the Lana'i section of this guide for course descriptions.

MINIATURE GOLF

The course is 18-holes on the roof of the *Embassy Suites Resort* at Kaanapali from 9 am-9 pm daily. Adults $5; $2.50 ages 12 & under. Call 661-2000.

TENNIS

Tennis facilities abound on Maui. Many condos and major hotels offer tennis facilities, also, there are quite a few very well kept public courts. They are, of course, most popular during early morning and early evening hours.

PUBLIC COURTS

Haliimaile - One court by the baseball park.

Hana - Hana Ball Park, one double lighted court.

Kahului - Maui Community College (Kaahumanu and Wakea Ave.) has 2 unlighted courts. Kahului Community Center (Onehee and Uhu St.) has two lighted courts. The Kahului War Memorial Complex has four lighted courts, located at Kaahumanu and Kanaloa Ave. Phone 243-7389.

Wailuku - Wellspark has 7 lighted courts, S. Market St. and Wells St. Phone 243-7389.

Kihei - Kalama Park has four lighted courts. Six unlighted courts in park fronting Maui Sunset condos. Phone 879-4364.

Lahaina - Lahaina Civic Center has five lighted courts and there are four lighted courts at Malu-ulu-olele Park. Phone 661-4685.

Makawao - Eddie Tam Memorial Center has two lighted courts. Phone 572-8122.

Pukalani - Pukalani Community Center has two lighted courts, located across from the Pukalani Shopping Center. Phone 572-8122.

PRIVATE COURTS WITH FACILITIES OPEN TO PUBLIC

Hyatt Regency, Kaanapali. Six unlighted courts. 7 am-dusk. Guests $10 and $12 for non-guests. Phone 661-1234 ext. 3174.

Kapalua Bay Hotel, Kapalua. Offers the Tennis Garden with 10 courts, 4 are lighted. Tennis attire required at all times. Guests $10 per day, non-guest $12. 669-5677. They also have a Village Tennis Center with 10 courts, 5 are lighted. Charge is $10 per day for resort guests, non-guests $12. Phone 665-0112.

Makena Tennis Club, 5415 Makena Alanui, Makena Resort. Two lighted courts. Resort guests $16 per hour, non-guests $18 or per person rate of $12 all day. Phone 879-8777.

Maui Marriott Resort, Kaanapali. Guests $10 per person per day and non-guests $12 per person per day. Five courts, three are lighted. 7 am-8 pm. Phone 667-1200.

Royal Lahaina, Kaanapali. Has the 2nd largest facility on the island with 11 courts, 6 lighted and 1 stadium court. It is now privately owned and no longer a part of the hotel, but it still works in conjunction with them. Rates are $5-7.50 all day or $30 per week for unlimited play. They have complete facilities including private lessons, ball machine, clinics, and pro shop. They underwent renovations in late 1995. Phone 661-3611.

Wailea Tennis Club, Wailea. Has fourteen courts, 3 lighted, 3 grass. Grass for Wailea Resort Guests $20 per hour, non-guests $25 per hour. Regular courts same price for one hour, more time if space is available at no extra charge. They offer summer workshops for kids. Phone 879-1958.

RESORT COURTS RESTRICTED TO GUESTS

Hale Kamaole, Hotel Hana Maui, Kaanapali Alii, Kaanapali Plantation, Kaanapali Shores, Kaanapali Royal, Kahana Villa, Kamaole Sands, Kihei Akahi, Kihei Alii Kai, Kihei Bay Surf, Kuleana, Maalaea Surf, Mahana, Makena Surf, Maui Hill, Maui Islander, Maui Lu Resort, Maui Vista, Papakea, Puamana, Royal Kahana, Sands of Kahana, Shores of Maui, The Whaler.

HORSEBACK RIDING

Historically, the first six horses arrived on the islands in 1803 from Baja California. These wild mustangs were named "Lio" by the Hawaiians, which means "open eyes wide in terror." They roamed and multiplied along the volcanic slopes of Maui and the Big Island until they numbered 11,000. They adjusted quickly to the rough terrain and had a reputation for terrific stamina. Today these ponies, also known as Kanaka ponies or Mauna Loa ponies, are all but extinct with fewer than a dozen purebreds still in existence.

Lush waterfalls, pineapple fields stretching up the mountain's flanks, cane fields, kukui nut forests and Haleakala's huge crater are all scenic environs that can be enjoyed on horseback. Beginner, intermediate or experienced rides lasting from 1-2 hours or up to three days. Most stables have age restrictions.

Adventures on Horseback - A 6 hour "Waterfall Adventure Ride" outside Haiku is $170 per person and includes lunch and gear. Enjoy the cliffs of North Maui, the slopes of Haleakala, the old Hana Highway, rainforest streams and secluded waterfalls. Breakfast, picnic lunch, and swimming. Maximum 6 riders. Children 16 years of age or older are welcome provided they have prior riding experience. Phone 242-7445. Office phone 572-6211.

Crater Bound - They offer a new feature in 1996, a Maui Mule Ride into Haleakala Crater. See Crater Bound listing which follows under "Hiking." Phone 878-1743.

Hotel Hana Maui - Guided trail rides around the 4,500 acre working cattle ranch on open range, shoreline, rain forest and mountains. Maximum 10 riders. Phone 248-8211.

Ironwoods Ranch - Follow Honoapiilani Highway 11 miles north of Lahaina, entrance near exit for Napili where a van picks you up. Trips are available for beginning, intermediate or advanced riders in either English or Western style. Rides tour the Honolua Planation and the West Maui foothills. $75-135. Phone 669-4991 or 669-4702.

Makena Stables - 7299 South Makena Rd. Owner operated since 1983 by Patrick and Helaine Borge, their horses were personally raised and trained. They match each person to their horse by ability and offer help and lessons as needed. All of their rides are on Ulupalakua Ranch, a 20,000 acre open range ranch which overlooks the Ahihi-Kinau Reserve, La Perouse Bay and the lava flows. Introductory two hour ride is 1 1/2 hours of riding with a 1/2 hour refreshment break. This ride travels up to Kalua O Lapa, the vent where the last lava flow on Maui erupted. It offers panoramic views of the south slopes of Haleakala, La Perouse Bay and the islands of Kahoolawe, Molokini, Lana'i and Moloka'i. Currently only available one morning a week for $99. Three hour rides are designed for the intermediate to experienced rider. This trip continues up the slopes of Ulupalakua Ranch to the cinder hills overlooking La Perouse Bay. The variety and terrain of the trails are more challenging. Morning rides include snack breaks with fresh fruit, pastries and beverage. Sunset rides include a break for beverages, Maui chips and cookies. $115-130. Their La Perouse Bay Lunch ride leaves in the morning and tours the south slope of Haleakala through Ulupalakua Ranch. A leisurely picnic lunch is enjoyed by La Perouse Bay. Offered only once a week by request for groups of four to six advanced riders. $160. Children 12-14 years with experience are welcome when accompanied by an adult. All riding is Western style. All rides are physically strenuous and they recommend that all riders be in good physical condition. Weight limit is 205 lb. All rides are guided. Maximum of six riders. Phone 879-0244.

Mendes Ranch - Journey into an actual working cattle ranch in the heart of West Maui. After a western-style open pit BBQ, take off with Sunshine Helicopters for a full tour of West Maui. The Paniolo Horseback Adventure includes lunch, but no helicopter tour, runs $130. With helicopter tour $219. Offered Monday through Saturday, weight limit 250 pounds, minimum age 11 years, Western or Hawaiian Saddle Style. Phone: Horseback only: 871-5222. Combination tour: 871-0722.

Ohe'o Stables - 3 hour ride once daily with snacks and soda $95. 6-8 people along the backslope of Haleakala in the Kipahulu District. Stables located 25 minutes past Hana on County Road 31. Phone 667-2222.

Pony Express Tours - Has trips across Haleakala Ranch, the largest working cattle ranch on Maui and into Haleakala Crater. Haleakala Ranch treks are one hour introductory, two hour intermediate and advanced rides and run $35-60. Trips available Monday through Friday. Trips into Haleakala Crater are 7.5 miles and 12 mile trips $120-150. Phone 667-2202 and 667-2200.

Seahorse Ranch - 7 persons or less, 3-1/2 hour ride with lunch at a waterfall offered Monday - Saturday runs $99. Highway 340 Waiehu at 10 mile marker. Phone 244-9862.

Thompson Riding Stables - Located on Thompson Rd. in Kula, the Thompson Ranch was established in 1902. Located at the 3,700 foot elevation they offer trail and crater tours, sunset and picnic rides. Child under age 4 can ride with adult. 1 1/2 hour $45, 2 hour picnic $55, 2 hour sunset without food $50. Phone 878-1910 or 244-7412.

POLO

Polo season on Maui is April thru November (excluding July). You'll find Polo events every Sunday (during the season) in Makawao with the Maui Polo Club at the arena located at 377 Haleakala Highway. Gates open at noon, game starts at 1 pm. Tickets are $3 for adults, under age 12 are free. Weekly activities may include a practice, a club game or events such as the Oskie Rice Memorial Polo Cup or the Annual Rocking Kapalaia Ranch Cup. Call Emiliano at 572-4915 for more information.

HIKING

Maui offers many excellent hiking opportunities for the experienced hiker, or for a family outing. Comprehensive hiking information is available from several excellent references (see ORDERING INFORMATION). Craig Chisholm and his wife Eila were the pioneers in the field of Hawaiian hiking information with the 1975 release of *Hawaiian Hiking Trails*, and it has been continually updated. They recently began work on separate island hiking guides and have added *Kaua'i Hiking Trails*. The Chisholm's books are attractively done with beautiful color photographs in the frontpiece, and easy to follow U.S. Geological maps for each of the hikes. Throughout the text are black and white photos. These books are thoroughly researched by the authors and very accurate. The *Hawaiian Hiking Trails* book has six trails described for Maui.

The first edition of Robert Smith's *Hiking Maui* was published in September 1977. He continues to update his book every couple of years. He also has books for the other islands. The books are compact in size with a color cover and a scattering of black and white photographs. The Maui edition covers 27 trails.

Kathy Morey writes *Maui Trails* which is published by Wilderness Press. There are over 50 trails listed in the hiking table of contents, however, some are really more walks than hikes. It has plenty of easy-to-use maps. Also guides for Oahu, Kaua'i and The Big Island.

We're not going to even attempt to cover the many hiking trails available on Maui, but would like to share with you several guided and non-guided hiking experiences which we have enjoyed.

There are many interesting and diverse hiking opportunities on Maui. They vary from hiking in a volcanic crater, strolling among a grove of eucalyptus, exploring a rocky shoreline or walking through a tropical rainforest.

The ***Lahaina Pali Trail*** was recently refurbished. It traverses from sea level to an elevation on the *Kealaloloa Ridge* of 1600 feet. The Lahaina Pali Trail was built originally as a foot path and then used as a horse trail. (While horses were introduced to the islands in 1803, their use was restricted to chiefs or alii until the middle of the century.) Portions of the old trail were well preserved. Today, access to the trailhead is possible through the courtesy of the Wailuku Agribusiness Company. An interesting and informative guide for the trail and the area is provided by the Na Ala Hele Statewide Trail and Access Program, a Division of Forestry and Wildlife. It corresponds to markers along the trail and provides some fascinating historical narratives. For example, in by-gone days robbers would wait along the trail, ready to pounce on unsuspecting travelers. If you'd like information on the trail, the free booklet or would be interested in volunteering for trail maintenance call 871-2521.

Another interesting hike is at the Pu'u O La'i Cinder cone, the red-earth hillock which juts out to the sea just beyond the cover fronting the Maui Prince Hotel. It is one of Haleakala's craters (under which is a large cave), and is said to be the sacred dwelling place of Mano, the ancestral shark deity. To reach the top of the cinder cone, turn right on the first dirt path after the hotel, then pass giant cacti and dry brush to reach the hiking trail. The short 15 minute hike uphill offers a rewarding sight of the coast - a black sand beach just below the hill, and broad white beaches and black lava contrasting with the lush greens of the Makena Golf Course.

With permission of Craig Chisholm, the following is one of his favorite hikes. The Waihee Ridge hike requires 3 1/2 hours, round trip and is 4.5 miles. It traverses from an elevation of 1,050 feet to a high point of 2,563. This is one of just a few hikes of the excellent hikes covered in Chisholm's ***Hawaiian Hiking Trails*** guide.

*West Maui's valleys, deeper and more rugged than East Maui's, show that erosion has had a longer time to work without interruption by volcanic building. The Waihee Ridge Trail leads up onto a ridge above such deep valleys, offering spectacular scenery. Waihee Ridge, preserved from erosion by exceptionally durable lava, climbs gradually from pasture land and guava thickets up into wetter areas of West Maui where there is still much native vegetation. There are fine views of the waterfalls in the Makamakaole Valley, the Waihee Valley, central Maui, and, finally, Mount Eke. There is no drinkable water along the route, but the trail is well-marked and in good shape. Choose a dry day. **ROUTE:** Drive northwest about four miles from Wailuku along the coastline to Waihee. Continue from Waihee Elementary School 2.7 miles farther northwest, to a paved turnoff, on the left, leading to the Boy Scouts' Camp Maluhia. Turn there and drive up 0.9 miles. The trailhead is at a parking area on the left side of the road, before reaching the Scout camp, and is probably marked by a brown "Na Ala Hele" sign. Go through the cattle fence at the first of three stiles, designed, no doubt* *in Hell's seventh circle for the torment of gluttons. A right of way easement leads for 0.3 miles straight southwest up the hill through private pasture to the boundary of the West Maui Forest Reserve, which is marked by a fence with a second narrow stile. Note the differences in vegetation delineated by the fence. Beyond the fence the shady path, which is also a dirt road, is flanked by planted Norfolk Island pine on the left and invading guava on the right. The road soon disappears as the trail swings right to sidehill up the slope. Just as the trail turns left on a switchback, there is a fine view of a double waterfall in the Makamakaole Valley, to the north. The trail continues a switchbacking ascent along the ridgeline, passing good views of the deep Waihee Valley, Mount Eke, waterfalls, and central Maui across to Haleakala. At about 1.6 miles the trail rounds a corner, passes between Norfolk Island pine, and comes to a small, open swampy area. The trail crosses it and switchbacks up to the top of Lanilili. Note and avoid the deep sinkholes along the trail climbing up Lanilili. The trail ends at the two and a quarter mile mark, a good place for a picnic. There are fine views of Mt. Eke to the southwest and down to wild rain-soaked peat swamps, forested ridges, and steep valleys of the West Maui Natural Area Reserve, Kahakuloa Section. Return as you came. (Hawaiian Hiking Trails* is available from Paradise Publications. See Ordering Information at the back of this book.)

Among the most incredible adventures to be experienced on Maui is one, or more, of the fifty hikes your personal guide **Ken Schmitt** and his staff have available. These hikes, for 4 - 8 people only, can encompass waterfalls and pools, ridges with panoramic views, rock formations, spectacular redwood forests (yes, there are!), the incomparable Haleakala Crater or ancient structures found in East Maui. Arriving on Maui in 1979, Ken has spent much of that time living, exploring and subsisting out-of-doors and experiencing the "Natural Energy" of this island. This soft spoken man offers a wealth of detailed knowledge on the legends, flora, fauna and geography of Maui's many diverse areas. Ken has traversed the island nearly 400 times and established his fifty day hikes after considerable exploration. His favorites are the 8 and 12 mile crater hikes which he says offer unique, incredible beauty and magic, unlike anywhere else in the world. The early Hawaiians considered Haleakala to be the vortex of one of the strongest natural power points on earth.

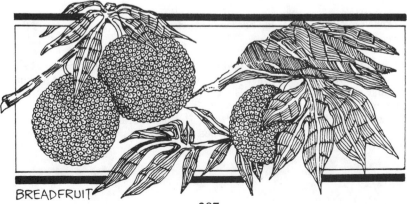

BREADFRUIT

Ken has expanded from a one-man operation to a number of experienced guides. John Jasinski specializes in marine biology, and is especially knowledgeable in music and aviation. Lono Hunter is a political science, philosophy and economics major and his thesis was on the Hawaiian sovereignty movement. Cathy Davenport is an archeologist and is working on her masters in anthropology. Dr. Renate Gassmann-Duvall grew up in Berlin and is a veterinarian as well as an ornithologist. Helga Fieder, from Germany, is a botanist who lived with native tribes of the Amazon for several years studying tropical rain forest plants.

The hikes are tailored to the desires and capabilities of the individual or group and run 1/2 or full day (5 - 12 hours). They range from very easy for the inexperienced to fairly rugged. These outtings are more than mere hikes, however, as Ken and his staff specialize specially-arranged tours emphasizing the teaching of the natural history of Maui and the Hawaiian islands. Tours run $70 - $110 fee (children are less).

Hikers are supplied with waterproof day packs, picnic lunch, specially designed Japanese fishing slippers, wild fruit and, of course, the incredible knowledge of Ken. Tours include transportation to the trails from their meeting spots in new, air-conditioned tour vans.

Ken and his staff can be reached at *Hike Maui*, 879-5270, FAX 876-0308 or by writing **Ken Schmitt**, P.O. Box 330969, Kahului, Maui, HI 96733. Here is a sample of the excursions you might be able to enjoy with Ken and crew!

UPCOUNTRY MAUI
Poli Poli Springs Recreational Area is ideally situated on the leeward slopes of Haleakala. Cool crisp mountain air provides a temperate climate for hiking and the trails are suitable for the entire family. Since the weather can be cool, warm attire and rain apparel should be included in your day or night pack, however, the clouds often clear and treat visitors to a sunny and very mild afternoon. To get to the turn off, go just past the Kula Botanical Gardens and turn on Waipoli Rd., or go 3/10 mile past the junction of Hwy 37 and Hwy 277. Follow the paved, steep and windy road approximately eight miles. The last portion is graded, but rain quickly makes the roads impassable for all but 4-wheel drive vehicles.

WARNING: Rental car agencies are not responsible for damage done to cars that travel this road.

We have found it passable in a car with high clearance only if the road has been recently graded and is dry. Once you reach the park there is a graveled parking area and a grassy camping area. There are two BBQ's and the luxury of a flush toilet in a small outhouse. Drinking water is available. Trail options include a .8 mile trek to the Redwood Forest, a 6 mile Haleakala Trail, 4.8 mile loop trail, 1.0 mile to the cave shelter and 1.5 miles to Plum Trail.

The 4.8 mile loop is a very easy trail and with frequent snack stops, even our three year old was able to make it the entire distance. There is an array of lush foliage and plums may be ripe if you arrive during June and July. The clouds can roll quickly in, causing it to be pleasant and warm one minute and cool the next, as well as creating some interesting lighting effects amongst the trees. The cave shelter, is a bit of a disappointment. It is a shallow cavern and reaching it meant a descent down a steep incline of loose gravel that was too difficult for our young ones. The eucalyptus was especially fragrant as the fallen leaves crunched underneath our tennis shoes. An area along the trail that had been freshly rutted by wild boars demonstrated the incredible power of these animals. On one trip we heard a rustling in the bushes nearby followed by grunting sounds. We have been told that while you definitely want to avoid the wild boars, they are accustomed to being hunted and will also choose to avoid you. Apparently we were down wind of them and since they have poor eyesight we passed by quietly without them noticing us and without seeing them.

HALEAKALA
A hike, once again with Ken Schmitt, is a thrill for all the senses. Not only does he pack a great lunch and yummy snacks, but the hike provides beauty for the eyes, cool, fresh air for the lungs, tantalizing scents for the nose, peace and serenity for the ears, and an opportunity to touch and get in touch with Maui's natural beauty. We chose a trip to Haleakala to see the awesome crater up close. The trip was an 8-mile hike down Switchback (Halemauu) Trail to the Holua cabin and back. The first mile of the trek was over somewhat rocky, but fairly level, terrain. The next mile seemed like three as we descended seemingly endless hairpin twists down the side of the crater with changing panoramic vistas at each turn. Sometimes fog would eerily sweep in, hovering around and obscuring the view completely, only to soon move away. The vegetation (following a period of heavy rains) was exceptionally lush. All the greenery seemed quite out of place in the usually rather desolate crater.

We continued along the crater floor and past the Holua cabin to reach the Holua lava tube. The small opening was not marked and could be easily overlooked. A small sign advised the use of lights inside the cave. We prepared our flashlights and bundled up for the cooler temperatures to be encountered below. A ladder set by the park service provides access. Once at the base of the ladder, the cavern was large, cool and dark. While there were several directions that lead quickly to dead ends, Ken took us further down the main tube. The cavern was so large that seldom did we have to do more than occasionally duck. Once inside we turned out the lights to enjoy a few moments of the quiet darkness. The tube travels about 100 yards with a gradual ascent to daylight. As daylight peeks down through the dark shaft, it appears the end is in sight. Another turn in the tunnel reveals not the end, but a natural altar-like flat rock piled with assorted stones. Light cascading through a hole in the ceiling casts an almost supernatural glow to eyes now accustomed to the darkness. The effect is to create a luminescence on the stones making them appear to be statues set in a natural cathedral. A very awesome experience. Returning to the cabin, we picnicked on the grounds while very friendly nene geese begged for handouts. Ken advised against feeding them as the park rangers prefer these geese not become dependent on human handouts.

After a rest in the warm sun, we retraced our path back up Switchback Trail to the van and continued on to enjoy the summit before heading back to town. Other more strenuous and lengthy crater ventures include the Sliding Sands Trail and one that traverses down the side of the volcano through the Kaupo Gap. Available through Paradise Publications are two excellent photo-filled books from K.C. Publications. *Haleakala* and *Hawai'i Volcanos*. See Order information.

Sierra Club Maui Group of the Hawaii Chapter invites the public to join their guided hikes. This is a wonderful and affordable way to enjoy Maui with a knowledgeable group of people. There are several weekend outings every month. They offer a variety of hikes, introductory, youth and educational. Donations are accepted. The main office Sierra Club, Hawaii Chapter is in Honolulu (808) 538-6616. On Maui call 573-4147 for voice mail information and schedules.

The Hawaii Nature Center, 875 Iao Valley Road, Wailuku, Maui, HI 96793. This is a statewide, private, non-profit organization with a hands-on approach to outdoor education adventures for children and families. Iao Valley is their field site on Maui, the main center is on Makiki on Oahu. They offer fun and educational themed hikes for children with their Saturday program "Keiki Nature Adventure." Children must wear closed toe shoes and be accompanied by an adult. They also need to bring water, a snack, sunscreen, insect repellent and other items that may be necessary for a specific hike. Reservations are required. $3 for members, $5 for non-members. Phone 244-6500.

The Waikamoi Preserve, Box 1716, Makawao, Maui, HI 96768. For reservations call 572-7849 or FAX 572-1375. On the second Saturday of every month hikes are conducted on this 5,230 acre Nature Conservancy Preserve located on the northeast slope of Haleakala. The preserve was established in 1983 in cooperation with Haleakala Ranch Company and protects vital habitat for 14 native Hawaiian birds, eight of which are endangered. Vegetation types range from dense rain forests to open shrub and grasslands to introduced pine tree plantations. The area is remote and very rugged with many steep gulches. The area is named after a stream that runs through the property. Along with a waiver and release form, they will provide you with an information sheet on hiking dates, work party dates as well as background on the native and introduced birds of the area and a brochure on the many island areas throughout the Hawaiian chain that are under their protection. Elevation in the Waikamoi Preserve ranges from 4,400-9,000 feet and annual rainfall varies from 50-200 inches per year. Temperature ranges are 35-70 degrees. The hike begins at Hosmer's Grove in Haleakala National Park at 9 am and finishes around noon at the same location. They recommend binoculars, cameras as well as warm rain gear and non-canvas shoes. The Nature Conservancy is a non-profit Environmental Awareness Group which has under its protection 13,000 acres of habitat critical to the survival of many of Hawaii's native plants and animals. A donation is appreciated. Reservations are required.

On Moloka'i, the Nature Conservancy also runs monthly tours at the Kamakoau Preserve (a rain forest preserve). The Moloka'i address is PO Box 220, Kualapuu, Moloka'i, HI 96757. Phone (808) 553-5236.

Haleakala National Park offers guided hikes to two different areas on Tuesday and Friday mornings, 9 am. The hikes are free of charge, but admission to the National Park is $4. Verify days and times with the ranger office at 572-9306.

A reminder! Hiking off established trails without a knowledgeable guide is *definitely* not advised, however, the following sources will help you find and enjoy many established hikes. *Hawaiian Hiking Trails* by Craig Chisholm, 128 pages, $15.95, has nearly 50 hiking trails throughout the islands, seven of these are on Maui. Robert Smith's book *Hiking Maui* 160 pages, $10.95, will guide you on 27 fairly accessible trails throughout Maui. *Hawaii, Naturally* is an environmentally oriented guide to the wonders and pleasures of the Islands by David Zurick, 206 pp, $12.95. (See ORDERING INFORMATION).

There are a number of other folks who do island hikes. Some do overnight trips or have canoe or kayaking as a part of their trips, and one also offers mule trips!

Crater Bound, PO Box 265, Kula, HI 96790. Craig Moore offers tours and hikes into Haleakala Crater, overnight camping in Haleakala and/or Kipahulu, a combination hiking adventure which includes packing gear into Haleakala Crater by mules and new in 1996 is their Maui Mule Ride into Haleakala. There are hikes of Haleakala crater that vary between 3 miles, 8 miles and 12 miles. $80-110. Overnight camping trips of one or two nights $100-$500. The mule rides will be offered in two different lengths, both beginning and ending at the summit of Haleakala. The Aloha Ride is two hours and departs at 8 am and returns at 1 pm. It descends from 10,000 feet to 8,300 feet in elevation and covers approximately six miles. $80. The Paniolo Ride is six hours and departs at 9:30 am. It includes lunch and descends from 10,000 feet to 7,300 feet in elevation and a chance to view scenic points of interest such as central crater, the bottomless pit, Pele's paint pot and Pele's pig pen. $110. In 1990 Crater Bound received a Kahili Award from the Hawai'i Visitors Bureau for demonstrating aloha spirit and perpetuating the essence of Hawaii. Phone 878-1743 or FAX 878-1743.

Hana Cave Tours by Island Spelunkers. PO Box 40, Hana, HI. Chuck Thorne has a brand new, unique hiking tour. Four days each week you have the opportunity to trek 1-1/2 hours through Maui's largest lava tube. It traverses miles and miles underground. Call for tour times, rates, and other information. Limited to spelunkers age 12 and older. Phone Chuck 8 am-8 pm Hawaii time: 248-7308.

Hawaiian Heart of the Jungle Journeys, PO Box 1567 Makawao, HI 96768. Solomon or one of his staff will tailor-make your eco-adventure. Solomon has a degree in forestry and apparently does impressive bird calls. Rates are $125 per day for two people, $45 for each additional person and $25 for children under 12 years. In addition to Maui expeditions, he can also lead your trek on an inter-island excursion to Kaua'i or the Big Island. Phone 572-6982.

Mango Mitch Ecotours. They offer one, three and five day island safari ecotours. Explore tropical rainforests, coastal beaches, volcanic craters, and/or lava flows. Hiking, kayaking and snorkeling are among the activities. Cost ranges from $81 for a one day trip to $560 per person for a five day trip. Phone 872-4888.

Maui Hiking Safaris, PO Box 11198, Lahaina, HI 96761. Randy Warner offers half and full day hikes to the valleys of East or West Maui, or to La Perouse Bay. Half day trips $49, full day $79. Custom hikes to meet the needs of the hikers run $50 per hour, four hour minimum with up to four guests. All hikes include narration on Hawaiiana and volcanology, identification of flora, waterproof day packs and rain parkas. Hikes range from 5-9 hours including riding time and rendezvous with guide in Kahului. Maximum of six clients, minimum of two. Complimentary soda after the hike. Phone 573-1716.

CAMPING

Camping, hiking and activity package tours are offered from *Pacific Quest Outdoor Adventures* on Kaua'i, Moloka'i, The Big Island and Maui. Eight day (two islands) to fourteen day (four island) trips are offered year round and include inns, camping, meals, local air and ground transportation, natural and cultural history tours. Trips begin at $1,400. PO Box 205, Haleiawa, HI 96712. Phone 638-8338, FAX 638-8255. Toll Free 1-800-367-8047 ext. 523. (They also offer New Zealand packages).

MAUI COUNTY PARKS

County permits are available for the two county parks, H.A. Baldwin and Rainbow Park, can be obtained by writing the Dept. of Parks and Recreation, County of Maui, 1580 Kaahumanu Ave., Wailuku, Maui, HI 96793. Phone 243-7389. Maximum length of stay is three consecutive nights per campsite. Fee per night is currently $3 per adult and 50 cents per child below age 18.

H.A. Baldwin Beach Park - This county park is a grassy fenced area near the roadside. It is located near Lower Paia on the Hana Highway and has tent camping space, restrooms and outdoor showers.

Rainbow Park - Located in Paia. Facilities: Restrooms.

BREADFRUIT

STATE PARKS

There are only two State Parks on Maui where camping is allowed. A permit is required from the Division of State Parks at 54 South High Street, Wailuku, HI 96793. Phone 984-8109.

There is currently no charge for tent camping, but a permit is required. The two campsites on Maui are Polipoli and Wainapanapa. Permits are issued between 8 am and 4 pm on weekdays only. The maximum length of stay is five consecutive nights and they do have a limit on the number of campers per campsite. You will need to provide names and ID numbers of those camping. ID numbers consist of Social Security Number, Driver's License, State ID or Passport.

Poli Poli Springs Recreational Area - Located in Upcountry, this state park has one cabin and offers tent camping. This is a wooded, two-acre area at the 6,200 foot elevation on Haleakala's west slope and requires four wheel drives to reach. Extensive hiking trails offer sweeping views of Maui and the other islands in clear weather. Seasonal bird and pig hunting. Nights are cold, in winter below freezing. No showers. Toilets, picnic tables. The single cabin sleeps 10 and has bunk beds, water, cold shower, kitchenware. Sheets and towels can be picked up along with the key. See additional description in the hiking section which precedes.

Wainapanapa State Park - Located near Hana. Tent camping, 12 cabins. More information on this location can be found under WHERE TO STAY - HANA. Restrooms, picnic tables, outdoor showers. This is a remote volcanic coastline covering 120 acres. Shore fishing, hiking, marine study, forests, caves, blow holes, black sand beach and heiau. The park covers 7.8 acres. BRING MOSQUI-TO REPELLENT!

For information on other day use state park camps, see BEACHES.

NATIONAL PARKS

The most recent information we have received states that a permit is not currently required to camp at either Hosmer's Grove or O'heo. A maximum stay of three nights is allowed. For information on camping within the Haleakala Crater, contact them at PO Box 369, Makawao, HI 96768 or phone 572-9306 for the latest data. For information on use of one of the three cabins located in the Haleakala Crater, please refer to the Upcountry accommodations section of this book. Haleakala National Park Information (recording) 572-9306; Haleakala Weather 871-5054; Ohe'o Headquarters Ranger Station (10 am-4 pm) 248-7375.

Hosmer Grove - Haleakala National Park. Tent camping. No permit required. Located at the 7,000 foot elevation on the slope of Haleakala. Cooking area with grill, pit toilets, water, picnic tables.

Pools of 'Ohe'o. - Haleakala National Park, Kipahulu District, just outside of Hana. Tent camping. No permit required. Chemical toilets, picnic tables, BBQ grills, bring your own water. Currently there are no rental companies offering camping vehicles. Car rental agencies prohibit use of cars or vans for camping.

ARCHERY

Valley Isle Archers holds weekly meetings in Kahului at the National Guard Armory each Wednesday, visitors are welcome. An annual competitive shoot is held each year in June on Kamehameha Day - actually a three day weekend event. Call John at Maui Sporting Goods in Wailuku at 244-3880 or 877-5555.

BOWLING

Aloha Bowling Center in Wailuku is Maui's only alley. Located at 1710 Kaahumanu, Wailuku. They are open daily from 9 am. They have twenty lanes with an automatic scoring system. They also have a room for use for parties and meetings. Rates are $2.50 per person per game (seniors 55 and older $2 between 9 am and 5 pm. Shoe rental is $1.50 per pair. The Aloha Bar & Grill has plate lunches, casual snacks and is open the same hours as the bowling alley.

FITNESS CENTERS, HEALTH RETREATS, SPAS

If you are interested in keeping in shape and you have no fitness center at your resort, there are several fitness centers that welcome drop in guests:
Valley Isle Fitness Center, Lahaina Square, (667-7474)
Valley Isle Fitness Center, Wailuku Industrial Park, (242-6851)
Valley Isle Fitness Center, Lipoa Shopping Center in Kihei (874-2844)
Powerhouse Gym, Kihei Commercial Center, 300 Ohukai Rd., C-112 in Kihei (879-1326)

Grand Wailea Resort and Spa invites non-guests to their luxurious spa. Price is $30 admission, $100 per day to use facilities with various added fees for massage and extras. 875-1234. If you'd like a sneak peak at what to expect at this grand

WILIWILI

of grand spas, here is Dona Early's first-hand report from the land of Ahhhs: "As soon as you arrive at the magical, underground autonomous 'city' of the Grand Wailea Resort Spa, you'll know you're not in Kansas anymore. *Spa Grande - designed with Italian marble, original artwork, Venetian chandeliers, mahogany millwork and inlaid gold - offers two full floors of invigorating fitness, rich luxury, soothing relaxation and stimulating rejuvenation. Whether you need your rusty joints oiled and massaged, your body freshened and reshaped, or you just want to come out with your mane washed and conditioned with yummy essences of coconut and mango, Spa Grande is the place to point your ruby slippers. This magical city takes you around the globe with a blend of European, Japanese and America spa philosophies and treatments, but it's the Hawaiian Regional Regime that makes this spa unique. Cleanse with the Hawaiian Salt Glo Scrub, heal and cleanse with a Ti Leaf or Alii Honey Steam Wrap and relax with the healing Lomi Lomi massage or Hawaiian Limu Rejuvenator body masque. Then soak in a soothing bath of seaweed or fragrant tropical enzymes, sit under an indoor waterfall to massage and relieve tired back muscles or refresh under an 'ordinary' shower with extraordinary mango shower gel. And what's the password to enter this jewel-like kingdom and enjoy such a multi-faceted experience? Why - "Pamper me" - of course!*

Maui Visions Vacations - 680 E. Kuiaha Rd., Haiku, Maui, HI 96708. They offer eco-adventures, wellness and Hawaiian culture. Adventures include dolphin and whale encounters, sea kayaking, paragliding or mountain biking. Their all-inclusive rejuvenation adventure retreats include ground transportation, seven nights lodging, healthy meals, morning movement programs, daily guided nature outings, massage/bodywork treatment and evening entertainment. Individuals $2000, couples $3500. Phone 572-2161.

Spa Luna - In Makawao, offers facials, facial and body muscle toning, body wraps, hydrotherapy, massage, sauna, waxing, lymphatic cleansing, reflexology, acupuncture, tai chi classes, yoga classes and wellness workshops. Located at 1156 Makawao Avenue in a remodeled historic building. Call 572-1300.

The Strong, Stretched and Centered Fitness Body/Mind Institute is offered by Gloria Keeling. The six week health and fitness retreats are designed for personal wellness as well as fitness instruction certification. Gloria explains that this is a program where people learn completely new lifestyles and learn how to teach those lifestyles to others. The $5,036 cost includes 240 hours of training, workbooks, T-shirt, 30 minute massage weekly, shared housing and meals, including taxes and gratuities. Airfare, shuttles, and spa service gratuities not included. Cost is $450 for a single room. P.O. Box 758, Paia, HI 96779. Phone 575-2178.

The exquisite setting of the ***Hotel Hana-Maui*** combined with their Wellness Center offers a range of health related activities. Complimentary guest activities include twice daily aquacise classes. Step aerobics and yoga are offered at a nominal fee. Personal training is available by the hour. Nature walks, nutritional counseling, and even creative visualization are available. Other wellness activity packages include the Ali'i Massage Sampler, The Wellness Sampler, and The Great Outdoors-Hana Style package.

HUNTING

Contact Bob Caires, owner/guide of **Hunting Adventures of Maui, Inc.**, 1745 Kapakalua Rd., Haiku, Maui, HI 96708. Year round hunting season. Game includes Spanish Goat (*kao*) and Wild Boar (*Pua'a*). Hunting on 100,000 acres of privately owned ranches with all equipment provided. Rates: Goat $450 one person, $375 second and third person each. Boar $500 one person, $400 second and third person each. Non-hunters $100. Three persons maximum. Includes sunrise-sunset hunt, food, beverages, four wheel drive transportation, clothing, boots, packs, meat storage and packing for home shipment, Kahului airport pick up. Rifle rentals and taxidermy available. Also available are sightseeing safaris. A non-resident hunting license is required. Cost is $95. Phone 572-8214.

RUNNING

Maui is a scenic delight for runners. **Valley Isle Road Runners** can provide up-to-date information on island running events. Event schedules call 871-6441.

SPORTING CLAYS

There are a couple of Sporting Clay locations on Maui. Papaka Sporting Clays in South Maui and West Maui Clays at the other end of the island. We requested, but never received information from either. Here is the little that we do know: Papaka Sporting Clays. 1295 South Kihei Rd., Suite 3006, Kihei, HI 96753. Call 879-5649.

TRAMPOLINE

Okay, this one has us confused! Should it be considered an air activity or a land activity? We guess it is a little bit of both!! A new Lahaina activity is *"The Sky's The Limit's Ultimate Trampoline."* Located in the courtyard of the Lahaina Marketplace, owners Sharon Friemoth and Rex Padgett promise more than a mere trampoline experience. You are harnessed and attached to bungee safety devices, enabling the jumper (if they so desire) to jump up to twenty-five feet in the air, performing backflips and somersaulting in mid-air. The activity is available to anyone between 30 and 240 pounds. Cost is $6 per jumping session and $8.95 for an individual video, or jump, video and a tee-shirt for $24.95. Hours are daily from 9:30 am-9:30 pm. Phone 283-6042.

AIR TOURS

SMALL PLANE FLIGHTSEEING

Flightseeing trips are available via small plane. American Pacific Air and Paragon Air are charter companies, no scheduled flightseeing tours are offered. Trips are arranged by customer request and could include Hana and Haleakala as well as island flights to Mauna Loa on the Big Island, O'ahu, Kaho'olawe, Lana'i or Moloka'i. Small plane trips are less expensive than a helicopter tour, but you won't get as close to the scenery.

American Pacific Air - Len Cooper, owner has a 4-passenger aircraft at $88 per hour or 6-passenger twin engine planes at $185 per hour. Phone 871-8115 or 878-6366.

Paragon Air - Twenty-four hour charter service to all islands, five and nine passenger planes. Excursions are quite different than those offered on a helicopter tour. Their Kilauea volcano trip is a 2 1/2 hour narrated flight that travels to Hana along the picturesque coastline before traveling the 33 miles across the Alenuihah channel to the Big Island of Hawaii. Departs from Kahului, Kapalua and Hana. Combine this with a helicopter tour over the Kilauea Volcano before returning by charter flight to Maui. Or plan a trip to Moloka'i with a tour of the Kalaupapa peninsula or fly to Lana'i for a round of golf. PO Box 575 Kahului, HI 96732. 244-3356 or 1-800-428-1231, FAX 871-8300.

BIPLANE TOURS

Biplane Barnstormers - Open-cockpit scenic tours for one or two people in their bright red reproduction of a 1935 Waco biplane. It's just as you'd imagine - you soar high above the island, but not so high you can't tip your wing or wave a friendly "shaka" (Hang Loose!) to the beachgoers, picnickers or snorkelers below. There you are ... "Flying Down to Ohe'o" ... the wind in your face, goggles pressed against your nose, leather helmet jauntily strapped under your chin- all you need is a long flowing scarf trailing behind the plane! Twenty minute basic flight, minimum 2 passengers $49.50 each, 30 minute 1 passenger $125 or 2 passengers $150. West Maui Circumnavigation, 45 minutes, 1-2 passengers $220. East Maui Circumnavigation, 60 minutes 1-2 passengers $320. East Maui/Haleakala, 75 minutes, 1-2 passengers $350. Aerobatic, 30 minutes, 1 passenger only $175. Pilot's Dream, 60 minutes (they perform takeoff and landing and you fly it) 1 passenger $300. They fly seven days a week 8 am-4 pm. The aerobatics ride takes passengers through loops, spins, rolls - even hammerhead stalls! Whether adventurous, nostalgic of just curious, you can say, "Hello, Good Biplane," by calling Cora at 878-2860.

HANG GLIDING

Hang Gliding Maui - Motorized hang-gliding flights. A 45 minute flight with 24 exposure film from a wing mounted camera, $150. Each additional 15 minutes is $30. Maximum weight for passenger/student is 200 lbs. Tandem hang gliding flights available from $250. Maximum weight is 185 lbs. Phone 572-6557.

Proflyght - Hawaii Paragliding School offers orientation clinics for experienced pilots new to flying the Hawaiian islands. Tours, covering all of Hawaii and 1-2 international tours are planned each year. Scott and Steve Amy are top ranked pilots and have been teaching paragliding for six year. They boast an outstanding safety record. Out of 500 tandem flights there have been no injuries. They have gracefully taken people as old as 68 and as young as 5. Tandem rates $50-225. Solo rates are $30 per hour. Certification Course SPR (solo paragliding rating) $950. They also sell new and used equipment. Phone 874-5433. FAX 878-6869. E-Mail at (gliding@maui.net).

HELICOPTER TOURS

The price of an hour helicopter excursion may make you think twice. After all it could be a week's worth of groceries at home. We had visited Maui for 7 years before we finally decided to see what everyone else was raving about. It proved to be the ultimate island excursion. When choosing a special activity for your Maui holiday, we'd suggest putting a helicopter flight at the top of the list. (When you get home you can eat beans for a month!) Adjectives cannot describe the thrill of a helicopter flight above majestic Maui. Among the most popular tours is the Haleakala Crater/Hana trip which contrasts the desolate volcanic crater with the lush vegetation of the Hana area. Maui's innermost secrets unfold as the camera's shutter works frantically to capture the memories (one roll is simply not enough) and pilots narrate as you pass by waterfalls cascading into cool mountain pools. Truly an outstanding experience. Keeping up with the prices is impossible. Listed are standard fares, and we hope you'll be delighted to learn of some special discount rates when you call (directly to the helicopter company) for reservations. Currently all helicopters depart from the Kahului heliport. Most companies include a video of your trip.

For your information in choosing a helicopter tour, you should know that there are several different types of helicopters with different seating configurations. The Hughes 500 is a four passenger with two passengers in front and two in the back, so each passenger has their own window. The Bell Jet Ranger is a four passenger with one passenger in front next to the pilot and three in the back seat. The AStar has two passengers in the front and four passengers in the rear seat.

Air Maui - Owners Steven and Penni Eggi relocated to Maui after Hurricane Iniki, and currently offer flights ranging from 30-60 minutes. Six passenger AStar aircraft. Steve has been flying 26 years and has logged 20,000 hours flying in a helicopter. A family operation, the office staff and crew range from brothers and mothers to best friends. Flights include West Maui, 30 minutes, $99. West Maui Deluxe, 50 minutes, $139. Hana/Haleakala, 45 minutes $129; Hana/Haleakala Deluxe, 60 minutes, $179. Circle Island 65-70 minutes, $189. Phone 877-7005.

Alexair - Features four passenger Hughes 500 helicopters. Hana/Haleakala 45 minute special $119. Other flights range from 20 minute West Maui for $69 to circle of Maui with ground stop for $240. Phone 871-0792 or 1-800-462-2281.

Blue Hawaiian - Six passenger AStar. Hana/Haleakala, 45 minutes, $130; Hana/Haleakala Deluxe, 60 minutes, $165; Moloka'i/West Maui 65 minutes, $180; Complete Island Special 65 minutes, $180; Complete Island 1 hour 40 minutes, $220; Sky Trek, a half day event which combines a 40 minute Hana/Haleakala Deluxe flight with Temptation Tour's guided limousine van tour along the road to Hana, $220 per person. Sunset Spectacular, 1 hour 35 minutes, an extended Hana/Haleakala Deluxe Tour to include landing at the best vantage point to view the sunset and enjoy refreshments, $195 per person. Phone 871-8844, FAX 871-6971. Toll free 1-800-745-BLUE.

Hawaii Helicopters Inc. - 6-passenger AStar jet turbine helicopters. Trips include 30 minutes rainforest and Hookipa beach flight, sunset or sunrise trips, West Maui/Moloka'i, a 2 1/2 hour air and ground excursion which includes a champagne picnic at Wainapanapa Park in Hana. Rainbow Special to east Maui, 45 minutes, $129. Valley Isle Deluxe, 55-60 minutes, $179. West Maui & Moloka'i, 60 minutes, $179. Heli-Trek (air and ground tour) 5 hours, $199. Other trips $129-249. Phone 877-3900.

Sunshine Helicopters Inc. ★ - Maui's most experienced pilots fly you with comfort in their "Black Beauties" -- Sunshine's 1993-1994 AStar helicopters featuring state-of-the-art audio and video systems. Three external cameras and one cockpit camera capture live video of your actual flight including passenger reactions. Air conditioned comfort and recordable CD players on board make for a pleasurable ride into our nations largest rainforest "above the rest." West Maui Deluxe tour $99; Hana Haleakala Special $129; Circle Island Special $179; Circle Island Special with beverage stop at Nu'u, an ancient Hawiian temple ruin overlook) $209; Hana/Haleakala with Nu'u Stop $159; Hana Grand Adventure, a combination van tour to Hana with lunch at Hamoa beach and swim stop plus a 40 minute helicopter tour of Hana and rainforest. Video. $199; a Paniolo Horseback Combination with a 30 minute flight and a 3 1/2 hour ranch horseback ride $229. We've flown with Sunshine on a number of occasions and can recommend their courteous ground crew along with their engaging and informative pilots. Journey into an actual working cattle ranch in the heart of West Maui. After a western-style open pit BBQ, take off with Sunshine Helicopters for a full tour of West Maui $219. Offered Monday through Saturday, weight limit for horseback riding 250 pounds, minimum age 11 years, Western or Hawaiian Saddle Style. Morning Limo-Trek departs 7:30 am and evening Limo-Trek departs 11:30 am. Includes a 40 minute helicopter flight with video, lunch at the Hotel Hana Maui and 3 1/2 hour Silver Cloud Limousine tour with open bar, $249. The Limo-Trek Extended tour includes the above, plus time to explore and swim at the Pools of O'heo. $299 per person. Phone 871-0722 or 1-800-544-2520.

Windward Aviation - They fly the McDonnell Douglas Notar. A no tail rotor helicopter that they advertise as the worlds quietest. They also offer a Doors Off tour in which you put on a flight suit and helmet then get ready with your camera loaded. Current rates include a West Maui 25 minute flight $120, a Haleakala or East Maui 45 minute flight for $150, a combo 60 minute tour for $179 and a Moloka'i 60 minute excursion for $199. Private rental $750 per hour. For more information call 877-3368.

THE ISLAND
OF LANA‘I - COUNTY OF MAUI

INTRODUCTION

The meaning of Lana‘i seems to be steeped in mystery, at least this was our experience. Several guidebooks report that the name means "swelling" or "hump." In discussions with local residents we were told it meant the obvious interpretation of "porch" or "balcony," perhaps because Lana‘i is, in a rather nebulous fashion, is the balcony of Maui. So, with no definitive answer we will continue the search, but, in the meantime, come enjoy this little piece of Paradise.

Just before and just following the turn of the century, Lana‘i was a bustling sheep and cattle ranch. Beginning in the 1920s, Dole transformed Lana‘i into the largest single pineapple plantation in the world. The 1990s have brought Lana‘i into the visitor industry with the opening of two new elegant and classy resorts, the country-style Lodge at Koele in Lana‘i City and the seashore resort at Manele Bay. Under the helm of David Murdock, the metamorphosis has been a positive one with young people returning to the island to work in the new tourism industry.

Cattle are again dotting the landscape and a new piggery has been developed as the silver-blue fields of pineapple rapidly fade into extinction.

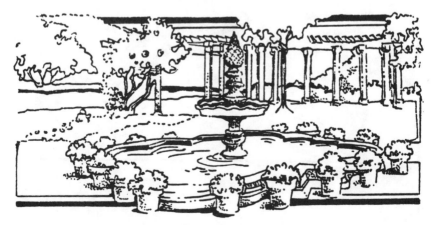

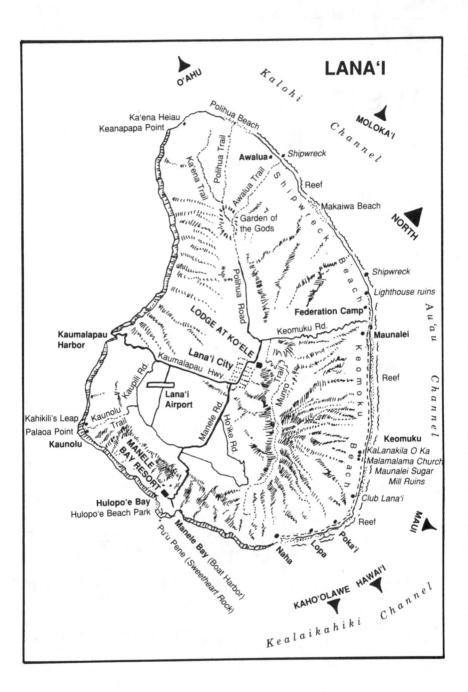

LANA'I

O'AHU

MOLOKA'I

Kalohi Channel

Ka'ena Heiau
Keanapapa Point

Polihua Beach

Awalua • Shipwreck

NORTH

Reef

Makaiwa Beach

Garden of
the Gods

Shipwreck Beach

Shipwreck

Lighthouse ruins

Federation Camp

Keomuku Rd.

Maunalei

LODGE AT KO'ELE

Kaumalapau
Harbor

Lana'i City

Kaumalapau Hwy.

Reef

Au'au Channel

Lana'i
Airport

Kaupili Rd.

Munro Trail

Keomuku Beach

Manele Rd.

Kahikili's Leap
Palaoa Point
Kaunolu

Kaunolu
Trail

Ho'ike Rd.

Keomuku
KaLanakila O Ka
Malamalama Church
Maunalei Sugar
Mill Ruins

MANELE
BAY RESORT

Club Lana'i

Reef

MAUI

Hulopo'e Bay
Hulopo'e Beach Park

Manele Bay (Boat Harbor)

Pu'u Pene (Sweetheart Rock)

Naha

Lopa

Poka'i

KAHO'OLAWE

HAWAI'I

Kealaikahiki Channel

While each isle has its own nickname, it appears that Lana'i has outgrown hers. "The Pineapple Isle" no longer bears much symbolism for an island which has transformed from an agricultural setting to an oasis within an oasis for the lucky tourist. While in the past it had been a wonderful retreat, much of what was good about Lana'i has not changed. The slow pace of the isle has not been as significantly altered by the arrival of the mega-resort as one might imagine. What new term of endearment will be vested upon the isle? The Isle of Relaxation, Pine Isle, The Island Less Traveled, The Isle of Enchantment? Time will tell, or perhaps the tourist bureau will!

With the continuing construction of luxury homes in the Koele district on 68 acres, and plans for 350 homes at Manele, the rich and famous will very shortly (if not already) be anteing up to purchase a vacation home on Lana'i.

As with each Hawaiian Island, Lana'i is unique. The price for a stay at the two resorts may be steep, but if you want to really indulge, read on! A truly luxurious and relaxing island get-away that is only eight miles, (but in many ways, 30 years removed) from Maui, Lana'i will simply enchant you.

LANA'I - GEOGRAPHY AND CLIMATE

Lana'i is 140 square miles, making it the sixth largest of the eight major Hawaiian islands. It is situated eight miles to the west of Maui and seven miles south of Moloka'i.

It is likely that millions of years ago, when the glaciers were larger and the seas much lower, that Maui, Lana'i, Moloka'i and Kaho'olawe comprised one enormous island. This is further substantiated by the fact that the channels between the islands are more shallow and the slopes of the islands visibly more gradual than on the outer coastlines of the islands.

The island of Lana'i was formed by a single shield volcano. A ridge runs along the eastern half of the island and forms its most notable feature. This large, raised hump is dotted with majestic Norfolk pines. The summit of the island is Lanaihale, located at an elevation of 3,370 feet. A rather strenuous hike along the Munro Trail provides access to this summit where you will be treated to the only location in Hawai'i where you can view (on a clear day) five other Hawaiian islands. Maunalei and Hauola are Lana'i's two deepest gulches. Today the Maunalei Gulch continues to supply the island with its water. The center of the island, once a caldera, is now the Palawai Basin and has been used as both farm and ranch land.

Lana'i has one city, cleverly dubbed Lana'i City. Located at an elevation of about 1,700 feet, it can be much cooler, and wetter, than the coastline. It is the hub of the island, or what hub there is, and visitors will soon learn that all roads lead to Lana'i City. The island population in 1994 was about 2,600, with almost everyone a resident of Lana'i City. The houses are generally small, mostly roofed with tin and the yards are abloom with fruits and flowers.

Rainfall along the coastline is limited, only 4 or 5 inches a year. The heart of the island and Lana'i City, however, may have rainfall of 20 inches or more, and the higher slopes receive 45 to 60 inches annually. The weather in Lana'i City might range from 80 degree days in September with lows in the mid-sixties, to cooler January temperatures in the low 70s, dropping an additional 10 degrees at night. The coastline can be warmer by 10 degrees or more. Pineapples and pines, not palms, were the predominant vegetation on the island. At its peak in the 1970s, there were 15,000 acres of pineapple in cultivation. Castle & Cook made the decision in the 1980's to diversify the island and enter the tourist industry in a big way. The pineapple fields have been reduced to only about 100 - 120 acres, simply enough for local consumption. The production of hay and alfalfa is well underway, and some fields are spotted with Black Angus cattle. Other acreage has been converted to an organic garden for use by the Manele and Koele restaurants. A piggery and a chicken house have also been established with an aim of making Lana'i more self-sufficient.

The island flower is very unusual. The Kaunaoa is more a vine in appearance than a flower and there are two varieties. One grows in the uplands and the other near the ocean. The ocean species have a softer vine with more vivid hues of yellow and orange than the mountainous counterparts. Strands of the vine are twisted and adorned with local greens and flowers to make beautiful and unusual leis. The mountain vines make a stiffer lei and, we were told, are used for leis for decorating animals. One of the best places to spot this plant is along the drive down to Keomuku and Shipwreck Beach or along the shoreline.

Driving around Lana'i you will note that it is a very arid island. Water supply has always been a problem and most of the greenery is supplied by the Norfolk pines which dot the island.

HISTORY OF LANA'I

The historical tales of the island of Lana'i are intriguing, filled with darkness and evil. As legend has it, in ancient times the island of Lana'i was uninhabited except for evil spirits. It is said that in the olden days, those who went to Lana'i never returned and that the island was tabu (or *kapu* in Hawaiian). Hawaiians banished wrong-doers to Lana'i as punishment for their crimes. The story continues that around the 16th century on West Maui there was a chief named Kaka'alanaeo. He had a son named Kaulula'au who was willful and spoiled. The people became furious with his many misdeeds and finally rebelled and demanded that Kaulula'au be put on trial by the ancient laws. The verdict was guilty and, according to the ancient laws, his punishment was death. His father begged for his life and it was agreed that Kaulula'au would be banished to the island of Lana'i. He was set ashore near the Maunalei Gulch, the only source of potable water on the island. His father promised him that if he could banish the evil spirits from Lana'i, he could then set a bonfire as a signal and his father and the warriors would return for him. And, as luck would have it, Kaulula'au managed to trick the evil spirits and send them over to Kaho'olawe. He signaled his father and returned to Maui, heralded now as a hero. (Be sure you take time to view the beautiful, large murals on either side of the entrance at the Manele Bay Hotel.

One depicts the fallen son being taken by canoe to Lana'i. The other shows Kaulula'au, head held high in victory, standing over his signal bonfire.) At this time in history, Maui was reaching its population zenith and Hawaiians relocated to Lana'i with settlements near Keomuku and inland as well.

The first archeological studies were done in 1921 by Kenneth Emory from the anthropology department of the Bishop Museum and he published his work in 1923. (Hardcover reprints of the book are available at Walden bookstores on Maui.) Kenneth Emory found many ancient villages and artifacts which had been, for the most part, undisturbed for hundreds of years. He found the area of Kaunolu to be Lana'i's richest archaeological region filled with house sites and remnants of a successful fishing village. He also ventured to the eastern coastline and explored Naha and Keomuku. He noted eleven heiaus, found relics including old stone game boards and discovered a network of trails and petroglyphs. Before the construction on the two new resorts began, the first archeological team since 1921 arrived. Villages were studied and ashes from old fires were analyzed. The findings showed that the ashes dated from 900 A.D., much later than the other islands which were inhabited as early as 40 or 50 B.C. One of the earliest heiaus, The Halulu Heiau, is in the Kaunolu area, and it is thought that this region may have been one of the earliest Hawaiian settlements.

While the Hawaiian population increased throughout the archipelago, Lana'i was left largely uninhabited until the 1500s. Two of Captain Cook's ships, *The Discovery* and *The Resolution*, reported a visit to Lana'i. They found the Hawaiians friendly along the windward coastal area where they replenished their supplies of food and water. In talking with the islanders they estimated that the population was approximately 10,000. They observed and noted that the island was a dry dustbowl and that the people fished and grew some taro. About this same time, chiefs of Maui became worried that the people on Lana'i might become too powerful. So they divided Lana'i into 13 ohanas (ohana means family, but this refers more to regions) and put a konahiki in charge of each -- this way insuring that no one chief would be too powerful. These district names are still used today. They are Kaa Paomai, Mahana, Maunalei, Kamoku, Kaunolu, Kalulu, Kealiakapu, Kealiaaupuni, Palawai, Kamao, Pawili and Kaohai.

Six months after the island was visited by Cook's vessels, a tragic event happened that would change life on Lana'i forever. Inter-island battles among the island chiefs were not uncommon, but until this time Lana'i had remained unaffected. In 1778 Kalaniopu'u, the chief on the Big Island, launched an unsuccessful attack on Lahaina, Maui. He retreated, then turned and attacked central Maui. Here again his warriors were overcome. As they returned to the Big Island in great anger, he passed the island of Kaho'olawe, which was loyal to the Maui chieftains. In retaliation, Kalaniopu'u's warriors massacred the entire population on Kaho'olawe. Bolstered by his victory, Kalaniopu'u turned once again to assault Lahaina and again was defeated. Now enraged, Kalaniopu'u and his warriors chose to strike the leeward coastal villages of Lana'i. Lana'i's warriors were unprepared and retreated to the Ho'okia Ridge to have a better location from which to launch their counterattack. However, without access to food and water, the Lana'i warriors soon weakened and Kalanaiopu'u moved quickly to crush them. The Big Island warriors continued around Lana'i and systematically destroyed all the villages. Kalaniopu'u returned to the Big Island of Hawai'i and there, seven months later, he died and his lieutenant, Kamehameha came to rule.

During the rule of Kamehameha the population increased. The king and his warriors would visit Kaunolu Bay on Lana'i's southwestern coastline. Here Kahekili is said to have leaped from a cliff above the sea into the Pacific waters, proving his loyalty to the king. Other warriors were then challenged to follow his example and the area continues to be referred to as Kahekili's Leap.

The elders from the Church of Jesus Christ of Latter Day Saints acquired land on Lana'i from one of the chiefs in 1855. In 1860 Walter Murray Gibson came to Lana'i with the intent of establishing a Mormon colony called the City of Joseph in the Palawai Basin. Gibson had been instrumental in assisting Kamehameha. He served on his cabinet and was among the advisors for the construction of the Iolani Palace. He purchased 20,000 acres of land on Lana'i and obtained leases on more. By 1863 there were about 600 Mormons living on Lana'i. In 1864, when the church elders arrived to visit, they discovered that Walter had purchased additional lands with the church money, but had listed ownership under his own name, and he wasn't willing to release them. He was quickly expelled from the church and the Mormons went on to develop their church on O'ahu. As owner of 26,000 acres Gibson first established the Lana'i Sheep Ranch which later became the Lana'i Ranch. In 1867 the population was 394 people (the 600 Mormons had departed earlier), 18,000 goats and 10,000 sheep. In 1870 Gibson attempted a cooperative farm, but this operation soon proved unsuccessful. By 1875 Gibson was controlling 90 percent of the island for ranch or farming operations. In 1874, Gibson's daughter, Talula, married Frederick Harrison Hayselden, formerly of England and Australia, and by the early 1880s Frederick was managing the ranch. Walter Gibson died in San Francisco in 1888 and ownership of the land transferred to his daughter, Talula Hayselden, and his son-in-law Frederick.

By 1894 the Lana'i Ranch now ran 40,000 sheep, 200 horses, 600 head of cattle in addition to large herds of goats, hogs and wild turkeys. However, by 1898 the ranch was in debt, but the sugar industry looked promising. The Hayseldens established the Maunalei Sugar Company on the island's windward coast. They begin by building three wells and a wharf at Kahalepalaoa for shipment of the cane to Olowalu on Maui for grinding. A railroad was also built between the wharf and Keomuku along with a two-story building, a store, boarding house, camp houses and barracks.

In 1802, a Chinese entrepreneur spent only one season attempting sugar cultivation in Naha from wild sugar cane. The Maunalei Sugar Company in nearby Keomuku did little better, lasting only a little more than two years. The Hayseldens constructed a six mile train track for transporting their sugar cane. However, they failed to respect the local culture and custom. Stones from an ancient heiau (temple) were used to build part of the railroad bed and then the disasters began. Their Japanese workers fell sick and many died. The ever important supply of drinking water went brackish and rain did not fall. Company records show the closure was due to lack of labor and water. The local population knew otherwise: Fred and Talula Hayselden soon left Lana'i. On Lana'i we heard a report that the Maunalei Plantation House was transported to Maui and became Pioneer Inn, but this was not accurate. We did some extensive research with the historical societies to search out the answer. Apparently some years ago the Honolulu Star-Bulletin printed an article to this effect. G. Alan Freeland, son of Pioneer Inn's founder George Freeland, spoke with Lawrence Gay, the owner of most of Lana'i at the turn of the century, and was told that when the construction of the Pioneer Hotel was completed, the similar-designed building on the island of Lana'i was still standing.

In 1902 Charles Gay (a member of the Robinson family from Ni'ihau) and George Munro visited the island of Lana'i and Gay acquired the island at public auction for $108,000. He enlarged his holdings further through various land leases. Gay began making major improvements and bringing cattle from Kaua'i and Ni'ihau to his new ranch on Lana'i. In 1903 Gay purchased the remaining holdings from the Hayseldens and through land leases and other avenues became the sole owner of the entire island. By 1909 financial difficulties forced Charles Gay to loose all but 600 acres of his farmland. On the remaining acres he planted pineapples and operated a piggery while moving his family from Koele to Keomuku.

In 1909 a group of businessmen that included Robert Shingle, Cecil Brown, Frank Thompson and others, purchased most of the island from Charles Gay for $375,000 and formed the Lana'i Ranch Company. At that time there were 22,500 sheep, 250 head of cattle, and 150 horses. They changed the emphasis from sheep to cattle and spent $200,000 on ranch improvements. However, because the large herds were allowed to graze the entire island, destroying what vegetation was available, the cattle industry was soon floundering. The island population had dwindled to only 102 at the turn of the twentieth century with fifty people living in Koele (means farming) and the rest along the windward coastline in Keomuku. There were only thirteen men to work the entire cattle ranch, which was an insufficient number to manage the 40,000 head of beef on land that was over-grazed by the cattle, pigs and goats that roamed freely.

George Munro, a New Zealander by birth who had visited the island in 1902, was asked to return by the new owners to manage the ranch. Soon after arrival he began instituting much needed changes. He ordered sections of the range fenced and restricted the cattle to certain areas while allowing other areas to regrow. He also ordered the wild pigs and goats to be rounded up and destroyed. In 1911 the large three million gallon storm water reservoir, now the beautiful reflecting pond, was built. In 1912 an effort to destroy the goat population began in earnest. The first year 5,000 goats were killed and an additional 3,300 more were destroyed by 1916. (It wasn't until the 1940s that the last pigs and goats were captured.) Sheep dogs were introduced to assist the cowboys.

Water continued to be a major concern. An amateur naturalist, Munro noted that the Cook Island pine tree outside his home seemed to capture the mist that traveled past the island. Today, as in the days of Munro, there is only one Cook

Island pine tree on the island. The tree planted in 1875 by Frederick Hayselden is the same one that stood outside of Munro's home and has become a noted Lana'i landmark. It remains a stately sight right outside the Koele Lodge. From that pine an idea was born, and Munro ordered the paniolos (Hawaiian cowboys) to carry a bag of Norfolk Pine seeds. They poked a small hole in the sack and, as they traveled the island on horseback, they left a trail of pines. The result is an island of more pine than palm. In 1914 the automobile age arrived on Lana'i in the form of a single 1910 Model T owned by George Munro.

By 1917 there were 4,000 head of cattle and 2,600 sheep, but profits were slim and the Lana'i Ranch Company sold its land to the Baldwin family for $588,000 and George Munro remained as foreman. The ranch slowly became more profitable. In 1920 Axis deer were introduced on Lana'i from Moloka'i and a pipeline was constructed from Maunalei Gulch to provide additional sources of fresh water.

In 1920 James Dole came to Lana'i, liked what he saw, and purchased the island in 1922 for $1.1 million from Alexander & Baldwin. George Munro was retained as manager. Castle & Cooke acquired one third ownership in the Hawaiian Pineapple Company soon after. The Kaumalapua harbor was dredged and a breakwater constructed in preparation for shipment of pineapple to O'ahu for processing. Lana'i developed into the single largest pineapple plantation in the world, which produced 90% of the United States' total pineapples. The company was called Hawaiian Pineapple Company until 1960 when the name was changed to Dole Corporation. In 1986 David Murdock became the major stockholder of Castle and Cooke and the chairman of the board. Today the company is called Dole Company Foods. Also in the 1920s the community of Lana'i City began. The houses were very small, only large enough for the workers, as families were discouraged. The workers arrived from Japan, Korea and the Philippines. The last residents left the Palawai Valley and moved to Lana'i City between 1917 and 1929.

KOELE LODGE

The population of Lana'i soared to 3,000 by 1930. In the 1950s larger homes, located below Fraser Avenue were built to accommodate the workers and their families and in the 1950s employees were given the option of purchasing their homes fee simple. In 1923 Dole realized the need to provide a center for entertaining island guests and had "The Clubhouse" constructed. Today it is known as Hotel Lana'i. The dining room provided meals for guests as well as for the nurses and patients from the plantation hospital. Also constructed in the center of town was Dole Park. The building in the middle was once a bowling alley, pool hall and restaurant until the late 1970s when it was made into a meeting hall. As a part of the development of Lana'i, David Murdock had a large new community center built, complete with swimming pool. It's located a block away from the park. Today less than 100 Lana'ians are part- or full-blooded Hawaiian.

The word Manele means "soap berry plant" or is the word used for a hand carried chair, a "sedan." The Manele boat harbor was once a small black sand beach and a fishing shrine found here indicates it was used by the early Hawaiians. You can spot the old pepe (cattle) ramp that Charles Gay used for loading his steers onto freighters.

In the 1970s E.E. Black was contracted to build the breakwater. It is traditional for any new project in Hawai'i to be blessed at the onset, but E.E. Black chose to forego the blessing. After only 20 feet of breakwater were constructed, the huge crane fell in the ocean and the people then refused to work. After great effort, another crane was brought over to lift the first from the ocean, but by the time it was recovered, the saltwater had taken its toll and it was worthless. Before resuming construction, E.E. Black held a blessing ceremony, the people returned to work, and the breakwater was completed without further incident.

GETTING THERE

To reach Lana'i you may travel by air or sea. The Lana'i airport is serviced by IslandAir and Hawaiian Airlines (See Transportation under General Information Chapter.) Airfare is about $60 one way from Lana'i to O'ahu. By boat you can travel a cool and comfortable 45 minutes from the Lahaina harbor aboard *Expeditions*. For a $25 one-way ticket, (children $20), you can have a scenic tour spotting dolphins, flying fish, and whales during the winter season. It is a pleasant way to travel, and much more affordable for a family than air transportation. The boat travels round trip five times daily to Manele Harbor where a shuttle van will pick you up for transport to the Manele Bay Hotel and from there up to Koele Lodge. Reservations are advised as space is limited. They can also arrange an overnight or golf package. Phone (808) 661-3756.

GETTING AROUND LANA'I

For guests of the hotel or those with golf reservations, there is a complimentary shuttle every hour between the Lodge at Koele and Manele Bay Hotel. (Non-guests are $10 per person, one-way to lodge; Manele Bay is a relatively short walk). Beginning on Friday afternoon at 3 pm, the schedule increases to every half hour until Sunday afternoon. Depending on how busy they are, they run mini-vans or larger size school type buses. (Lana'i City Service has no regular schedule, but if you ask your Expeditions captain to have them meet you at the harbor, they will take you to Lana'i City for $5 per person, one-way. Resort guests can inquire with the hotel van driver regarding a drop off in Lana'i City. Bikes are available at Koele for guests to use or enjoy a brisk 15 - 20 minute walk to downtown Lana'i City. For further independent exploration there is one rental car company. Since many of the island's roads are unimproved and even a small rainshower can render dirt roads impassable, most guests are advised to rent one of the 4-wheel drive Jeeps. A 4 x 4 Geo Tracker currently costs $109 per day, a 4 x 4 Wrangler is $119, a 15 passenger van will set you back $175 and a Huyandai Excel compact is $59.99. Major car repairs require that the unit be transferred by barge to Honolulu, hence the inflated rates. The rental car company notes that given the unique terrain of the island, they are not able to obtain (and therefore cannot provide) insurance of any kind on rental vehicles. Renters take full responsibility for the vehicle whether it is damaged by the renter, a second or a third party. Rental arrangements can be made through the concierge or contact Lanai City Service (A division of Dollar Rent A Car) (808) 244-9538 or (808) 565-7227. FAX (808) 565-7087.

Rabaca's Limousine Services offers hourly charter rates as well as airport transfers. Neal Rabaca provides 24 hour limousine service in his seven passenger Mercury Grand Marquis. One way transfers between the resort hotels and the airport run $10 per person, two person minimum. Charter, hourly rates begin at $147 for a minimum of two hours. Island tours are also available. 1-800-475-6838 or FAX (808) 565-6670. PO Box 304, Lanai City, HI 96763.

LANA'I ACCOMMODATIONS

There are currently three choices for hotel accommodations. Lana'i's original Hotel Lana'i and the two luxury hotels, Manele Bay Hotel and the Lodge at Koele. More on these three accommodations in the following sections.

CAMPING ON LANA'I

Tent camping is available at Hulopo'e Bay. Permits are issued by Lana'i Company, Inc., at PO Box 310 , Lana'i City, Lana'i, HI 96762. Phone (808) 565-8206.

PRIVATE HOMES

Lana'i Realty has rentals at The Villas at Koele, Homes at Pualani Ridge and Homes at Manele. (808) 565-4800.

BED AND BREAKFAST

Lucille Graham operates the island's only registered bed and breakfast facility, *Lana'i Bed & Breakfast*. She rents out two rooms of her three bedroom plantation style home. One room offers a queen size bed and the other a double plus a single bed. The two guest rooms share a full bathroom with a shower or the additional half bath (although she tells us that seldom are both rooms rented at the same time.) Unlike many bed & breakfasts, there is no minimums stay. Lucille might start your day off with her popular buttermilk oatmeal pancakes and then set you on your way with beach towels, snorkeling equipment and a jug of water. We've heard wonderful things about her hospitality and personal touches!

Room rates are $55 for a single person, $65 for double occupancy. Extra adult in a room is $25, extra child is $10. Prices do not include the room tax. Contact Lucille at Lana'i Bed & Breakfast, Box 956, Lana'i City, HI 96763. Phone (808) 565-6378. Her residence is at 312 Mahana Place in Lana'i City.

Another couple, Michael and Susan Hunter operate *"Dreams Come True"* offering rooms in their home/art studio at 547 - 12th St. They also have a separate fully furnished home (2 bedroom plus separate cottage) with outside tubs and showers, and enclosed fenced yard, for $190 for six, including tax. The second home can be rented as a bed and breakfast for a larger group. Continental breakfast provided. Single rate $55, double $75, triple (adults) $95, children $10 per night. Airport pick up and drop off. A truck and a jeepster are available for rent. PO Box 525, Lana'i City, HI 96763. Phone (808) 565-6961, toll free 1-800-566-6961

For other information you might wish to contact the local visitor information center at Destination Lana'i, PO Box 700, Lana'i City, 96763 (808) 565-7600, FAX (808) 565-9316.

LANA'I RESORTS, HOTELS AND RESTAURANTS

HOTEL LANA'I
Hotel Lana'i, built in 1923, is also run by Lana'i Company, Inc. Before the opening of the new resorts, this ten-room hotel had the only accommodations on the island. You'll still find it a quiet and comfortable accommodation with very basic rooms. Rooms run $95, $135 for cottages. Children ages eight and under are free in room with parents. You'll want to book as far in advance as possible. For information or reservations write: Hotel Lana'i, PO Box A-199, Lana'i, HI 96763. (808) 565-4700, FAX (808) 565-4713 or toll free 1-800-321-4666.

The restaurant at the Hotel Lana'i is a popular place for island residents and it offers the only bar in town. Hours are 7:30 am-10 am for breakfast, lunch is served 11:30 am-1:30 pm and dinner 5:30 pm-9 pm The bar closes at 9 pm Breakfast fare runs $6.25-$8. Lunches include an assortment of sandwiches or plate lunches $6-$9. A pleasant addition to their dinner menu is the option of several sandwiches for the less hearty appetite or children in your group. Sandwiches $7.50-$9. Dinner entrees $16-20.

THE MANELE BAY HOTEL ★
The resort is spread across the cliffside of Hulopo'e Beach like an enormous Mediterranean Villa. It is a strikingly beautiful building with a pale blue tile roof. There are four buildings in the East wing and five in the West wing, and each is slightly different. The rooms line sprawling walkways which meander through five lush courtyard gardens, each with a unique theme. The gardens include The

Hawaiian, The Bromelaid, The Chinese, the Japanese and The Kaamaina Gardens. The original resort plan called for a 450 room hotel directly on the beach, but was revised to the current structure with 250 rooms on the cliff alongside the beach. Behind the resort is the newest 18 hole golf course, The Challenge of Manele, which encompasses 138 acres along the ocean.

The *Hulopo'e Court* is the more casual of the two dining rooms and serves breakfast and dinner, with a children's menu available. Breakfasts include entrees $12-$22 such as smoked salmon on toasted bagel, catch of the day, poached egg with paprika Hollandaise or homemade corned beef hash and poached eggs. Side orders such as rice, sausage or potatoes $2.50-3.50. Pancakes, waffles or French toast run $9.50. Their dinner menu features Contemporary Hawaiian Regional Cuisine and features the culinary talents of Executive Chef Philippe Padovani. Appetizers run $9.50 and up and include pan fried crab cake, seared ahi with spicy crust or Chinese spring rolls. Soups or salads $6.50-$9. Fresh pasta is available in appetizer or entree size portions $14-$20. Appetizers, soups and salads are considered "First Courses" and run $11 and up. Main courses include Pan fried Lana'i venison with Moloka'i sweet potato puree $42, poached pali kali with julienne cucumbers $35, pan fried onaga $33, sauteed Moana duck liver terrine $36, roasted squab breast with marmalade of onions $34. Adding a beverage, soup or salad and dessert will make this elegant dining experience an expensive one.

The Ihalani, is the formal dining room at the Manele Bay Hotel. They feature French Mediterranean selections with Executive Chef Philippe Padovani heading the kitchen. They have two menus each evening that run from soup to dessert.

A sample dinner might be as follows: Vine ripe tomato petals, summer vegetable salad, Pan Fried Onaga with sugar snap peas in creamy curry sauce, followed by sauteed veal rib eye served with woodland mushroom sauce and a ragout of vegetables. A selection of gourmet cheese and walnut bread is followed by the dessert of the evening. Price per person is in the range of $75-95. We haven't had the opportunity to dine here, so let us know if you do!

Hale Aheahe, which means House of Gentle Breezes, is located off the upper main lobby. There is an indoor lounge and outdoor veranda from which to enjoy nightly entertainment. The Pool Grill opens at 11 am and serves sandwiches and salads and a children's menu is also available here. Sandwiches, salads and "Hawaiian Favorites" run $10-$17.

In many of the areas the ceilings have been given very special attention. In the main dining room are huge floral paintings, in the Hale Aheahe lounge you'll see fish and starfish. The resort took advantage of the undiscovered talent of the island residents and much of the artwork was done by local residents.

If you're thinking that maybe too much lying in the sun and fine food will affect your waistline, then hurry into the fitness studio. Open 6 am - 8 pm there is plenty of equipment, then treat yourself to a steam room, massage, pedicure or facial.

This place is truly an island get-away. If our stay was any indication, then celebrities have quickly found Lana'i to be a convenient and luxurious retreat. Both Kevin Costner and Billy Crystal were guests during our brief stay.

We enjoyed the proximity to the beachfront, but the pool seemed the place to be and lounges were filled by mid-afternoon. It seems here on Lana'i, there is no reason to hurry. The pool water is slightly warm, yet delightfully refreshing. Attendants from the adjoining restaurant circulate, taking drink and sandwich orders. The poolside restaurant was a little pricey, but the portions large and even the fish sandwich featured the fresh catch. We noted with appreciation that they provided a more economical children's menu here as well as in their main dining rooms.

The rooms are spacious, a bit larger than the standard rooms at Koele and each wing differs slightly in decorating style. Our wing had bright, bold yellow wall coverings and bedspreads accented with very traditional furniture. The bathroom amenities thoughtfully included suntan lotion and moisturizer in a little net bag to take along to the pool or beach. Rooms have a private butler service, mini-refrigerator. Reservation information is available from Manele Bay Hotel, PO Box 310, Lana'i City, HI 96763. Phone 1-800-321-4666. *Room rates are as follows: Terrace Room $250, Garden Room $295, Ocean View $400, Ocean Front $450, Ocean Mini-Suite $700, Ocean Front Suite $750. Other Suites $900-2,000.*

LODGE AT KOELE ★

The Lodge at Koele is not what a visitor might expect to find in Hawai'i. Guests arrive via a stately drive lined with Norfolk pine to this Victorian era resort that typifies turn of the century elegance. The inscription on the ceiling of the entry was painted by artist John Wullbrandt and translates "In the center of the Pacific is Hawai'i. In the center of Hawai'i is Lana'i, In the heart of Lana'i is Koele" and Lana'i may quickly find its way into your heart as well.

The rug in the entry is circa 1880, made of Tibetan wool. The Great Hall features enormous natural stone fireplaces that hint at the cooler evening temperatures here in upcountry Lana'i. The twin fireplaces on either side of the lobby are the largest in the state of Hawaii and the Lodge itself sets the record for being Hawai'i's biggest wooden structure. The high beamed ceilings give the room a spacious character, yet the atmosphere is welcoming and the comfortable furnishings invite you to sit and linger. Designer Joszi Meskan of San Francisco spent more than two years securing the many beautiful artifacts from around the world. A descriptive list is available from the concierge. The Great Hall's rug was handmade in Thailand for the resort and utilizes 75 different colors. Some of the furniture are replicas, but many pieces are antiques, including the huge altar desk where steaming morning coffee awaits the guests. Be sure to notice the two exotic chandeliers, with playful carved monkeys amid the leaves, designed for the great hall by Joszi Meskan. The large portrait on one end of the Great Hall is of Madame Yerken, painted by Belgian artist Jan Van Boern in 1852. An intricately stenciled border runs around the perimeter of the ceiling with antelope, deer and wild turkeys. Another more subtle stenciling is done around the floors. The skylights are beautiful, etched glass. The furnishings are covered in lush brocade

413

tapestries and suede upholstery in hues of burgundy, blues and greens. The room is accented with fresh flowers, many of them orchids grown in the greenhouse located beyond the reflecting pool. The woodwork is finely carved, with pineapples often featured. At the end of an exhausting day of vacationing, there is nothing like curling up in the big overstuffed armchair next to a crackling fire with an after dinner drink to enjoy the evening entertainment, play a game of checkers or visit with local women as they demonstrate Hawaiian quilting. Green is the color theme throughout the resort with the bellman, concierge and front desk staff crisply attired in pine green suits.

Surrounding the main building is a wonderful veranda with comfortable rattan furniture accented by Hawaiian quilted pillows. (Similar pillows, by the way, are for sale through the concierge, $100 each.) Huge trees hug the building and the view of the horses and fields beyond has a tranquilizing effect. The setting is truly picture perfect.

Several public rooms surround the Great Hall. The library overlooks spacious lawns and offers newspapers from around the world as well as books, backgammon and chess. The trophy room also has an assortment of board games and an interesting, but very uncomfortable, English horn chair. Both of these rooms have fireplaces which can be lit at the request of the guests. A music room and tea room on the other side of the lobby host afternoon tea served daily between 3 - 5 pm and pupus (appetizers) from 5 - 7 pm. A slide show depicting the history of Lana'i is offered several times a week.

Adjoining the Great Hall is the Terrace Dining Room, open for breakfast, lunch and dinner. The food is excellent and the service outstanding. In fact, the restaurants at the Lodge at Koele could very possibly be the best in all of Hawai'i. (According to the readers of *Conde Nast Traveler*, they are - not only the #1 restaurant in Hawai'i, but also in the top ten in America!) We were also very pleased that they provided a children's menu which offered a varied dinner selection priced $5 - $7. The formal dining room, open for dinner only, is tucked away in the corner of the resort and requires a jacket and tie for the gentlemen. Restaurant Executive chef, Edwin Goto, makes excellent use of the five acre organic farm to ensure the freshest ingredients in his meal preparations. Herbs, white eggplant, purple turnips, and yellow teardrop tomatoes are among the interesting and varied crops. Simple foods with unusual ingredients and elegant presentations are the key here.

Breakfast at the Terrace Dining Room is changeable, but it might include Lana'i Axis deer sausage, Kaunolu bananas on coconut cream, zucchini omelette of Lana'i farm fresh eggs with basil and Gruyere cheese, or sweet rice waffle $4.75-$12.25. Lunch is another dining experience extraordinaire. Sample a toasted sandwich of lobster, avocado and Gruyere cheese $13.75, Koele cobb salad $11.50, or cilantro pasta salad with grilled scallops $14.50. Dinner (served 6-9:30 pm) entrees offer special daily features such as veal osso bucco or select from their standard menu between a grilled chuck burger with cheddar cheese $9.50, or grilled lamb and Japanese eggplant sandwich $15.25. The Golf Clubhouse at Koele serves lunch and has proven popular with the local residents and visitors alike, with their selection of quality meals at prices more reasonable than the lodge. Samples include a grilled fresh fish sandwich $8, grilled sandwich of three cheeses with vine ripe tomatoes $5.25, saimin with char sui $4.50 or Chinese chicken salad $7.

This was once the site of the farming community known as Koele and the pine lined driveway was planted in the 1920s and led to the 20 or 30 homes in this area. Only two remain on the property and are owned by the Richardson family, descendants of the early Lana'i paniolos. The church was moved to the front grounds of the Lodge and a small schoolhouse is being restored and converted into a museum. The grounds of this country manor are sprawling and exquisitely landscaped. More than a mile of lush garden pathways and an orchid house can be enjoyed while strolling the grounds. The large reflecting pond was once the reservoir for the town of Koele. There are plenty of activities to be enjoyed from strolling the grounds to swimming or just relaxing in the jacuzzi. (See WHAT TO DO for more information.) In fact, it is so relaxing and so lovely that we didn't even miss the beach. But if you're hankering for some sand and sun, it is only a 25 minute shuttle trip to the shore.

The elegant, uniformed staff are efficient, very friendly and courteous. We were impressed with the quality of service at the Lodge. It is also pleasing to know that the development of the tourist industry on Lana'i has meant a return of many of the island's young people.

There are 102 guests rooms at the Lodge and they are artistically decorated in three different fresh, bright color schemes. The artwork that lines the corridors was done by some of the many talented Lana'i residents and each floor has a different theme. The beds feature a pineapple motif and were custom made in Italy, then handpainted by Lana'i artisans. The floral pictures on each door were painted by the postmaster's wife! The bathrooms have Italian tile floors and vivid blue marble counter tops. Room amenities are thoughtfully packaged and include an array of fine toiletries. There are in-room televisions with video recorders and a couple of beautifully carved walking sticks in the closet tempt the guest to enjoy one of those leisurely walks around the grounds.

Choose Garden Rooms ($350) which are located on the ground floor and the Koele Rooms ($295), which are the same size, are on the second floor. The Plantation Rooms ($450) are slightly larger. Plantation Suites ($825) have a wrap around lanai and a separate living and sleeping area with a murphy bed in the living room. The Plantation Room and Plantation Suite can be combined into one large living area. The Norfolk, Terrace Junior or Plantation Suites $600-$825 provide separate living room and sleeping areas, and oversized lanai. These rooms are located along the balcony above the Great Hall and are the only guest rooms that are air conditioned. The Fireplace Suites runs $975-1,100. They are slightly larger than the regular rooms and just as beautifully decorated. Whether your luggage needs packing, a bath needs to be drawn, a dinner reservation is required or a suit needs pressing, the butler is ready to assist. The butlers are schooled for a year and must pass rigorous testing before being licensed. Honeymoon Package, Golf Package, Tennis package and other adventure option *packages are available.* Reservation information is available from Rock Resorts, Inc., PO Box 774, Lana'i City, HI 96763. Phone 565-7300.

As much as we enjoyed the Manele Bay Hotel, we found something very appealing about this Lodge in upcountry. Perhaps it was because the service was so superb, perhaps it was because the air was so fresh, perhaps it was the comfortable and homey quality of the great hall, or perhaps it was because we truly were in the heart of Lana'i. This resort had a special quality, and both kids and adults in our group were enchanted. Our visit will long be a fond memory... that is until we visit once again!

SHOPPING - LOCAL EATING

There are three grocery stores from which to choose. *Richard's*, which has the honor of being on Lana'i since 1946, and the small *Pine Isle Market*. Since everything must be brought in by barge, prices are steep. Don't be surprised if they are closed for noontime siesta and closed for the day by 6 pm. *International Food & Clothing* is the only food store open on Sundays until 1:30. Pineapples are available for sale at all three groceries. We suggest you purchase one and sample the difference between the mainland version of this fruit and the field ripped variety. Pineapples already boxed and ready to take home are at the airport gift shop *"Pineapple Landing."*

One of the limited local style fast food restaurants is *Tanegawa's*. Open daily for breakfast and lunch, and now also open for dinner. You can select a sandwich or burger $2-$3.50, plate lunches $4-$6 and breakfasts $4 - $6. The fare is filling and the atmosphere charmingly rustic. Next door is the only other casual dining spot in Lana'i City. The *Blue Ginger* serves up some of the best, freshly made pastries in town. (The hotel's bakery in Lana'i City delivers ono fresh breads daily to Lana'i grocery stores.) Blue Ginger opens at 5:30 am for breakfasts which are surprisingly diverse for such an early hour! They offer eggs, pancakes or waffles with blueberries, strawberries or macadamia nuts. Lunch include sand

MANELE BAY RESORT

wiches, local style plate lunches and saimin, dinners include steak, seafood and pizza. Prices are moderate. There are now three restaurants on Lana'i open for three meals a day, and Blue Ginger serves in-between meal hours too! HOURS: 5:30 am - 9 pm. Phone: (808) 565-6363.

The *Hotel Lana'i* has a restaurant, see description listed under the Hotel Lana'i section. The Lodge at Koele and the Manele Bay Hotel both have small sundry gift shops. There are also shopping excursions available to Lahaina. Leaving the Manele Harbor aboard *Expeditions*, you can arrange for a day of shopping in Lahaina town. Cost is $25 per person one way.

Across the park is an art gallery called *Heart of Lana'i Gallery* operated by Denise, a water color artist who also teaches classes at the gallery. This is the beginning of Lana'i's cultural center. Work by Lana'i artists and other island artists are on display. Just another building down is the workshop where island residents can come to pursue their artistic abilities.

RECREATION ON LANA'I

GOLF

There are a number of selections for the golfer on Lana'i. At Koele there is the 18-hole *Experience at Koele* course, another, older 9-hole course and one stupendous 18-hole putting course is also adjacent the Lodge. The *Challenge at Manele* is the newest 18 hole course.

Golfers and non-golfers of all ages will delight in the executive 18-hole putting green at Koele, beautifully manicured course with assorted sand traps and pools lined with tropical flowers and sculptures. Putt-putt will never be the same again! No charge. Course rates for the 18-hole Challenge of Manele or Koele Experience is $150 for non-guests and $99 for hotel guests.

The *Challenge of Manele*, designed by Jack Nicklaus and Greg Norman, is the island's newest course and opened on December 25, 1993. Built on several hundred acres of lava out-croppings among natural kiawe and ilima trees, this links-style golf course features three holes constructed on the cliffs of Hulopo'e Bay using the Pacific Ocean as a dramatic water hazard.

The 18-hole *Experience at Koele* was designed by Greg Norman and Ted Robinson. From a golfer's standpoint, Greg Norman assures the golfing guest that this course will require both skill and strategy and adds that it is the only course in Hawaii with Bent grass greens. The beauty of the course, he continues, with its lush natural terrain -- marked by thick stands of Norfolk pines -- and panoramic views will make concentrating on the game difficult for even the most expert golfer. The signature 8th hole of the Experience at Koele has a truly inspired setting. This is a 390 yard par 4 with a dramatic 200 foot drop in elevation from tee to green. The course is laid out on a multi-tiered plan. The upper seven holes meet the lower eleven at this sublime tee. From the top of the bluff at the eighth tee is a view so stunning that our first thought was that this could be right out of Shangri-la. The mist floats by this enchanted valley, filled with lush vegetation and with a lovely lagoon. The lagoon at one time had served as a back up reservoir for the old cattle ranch. Now, while we are not golf aficionados, this single hole was enough to at least consider taking up the sport! The Experience at Koele was recently rated #1 in the world in the 1996 Readers' Poll of the World's Best Golf Courses in *Conde Nast Traveler*. Charges for either the Experience at Koele or the Challenge of Manele is $75 for resort guests, $130 for non-resort guests. A restaurant at the Golf Clubhouse offers some good luncheon selections.

The Cavendish, a 9 hole, 36 par, 3,071 yard course, (complimentary for guests of either resort) is located at the front of the Koele Lodge and was the island's first.

TENNIS

There are plexipave courts at both Koele and Manele Bay. These are complimentary for use by hotel guests. Lessons are available at an extra charge. There is also a public court at Lana'i School in Lana'i City.

THEATER

In February 1993 the Lanai Playhouse refurbishment was complete and it opened as Lana'i's movie theater.

HORSEBACK RIDING

The Lodge at Koele has an impressive stable. A variety of rides are available from a 15 minute children's ride to one or two hour treks through the plantation, along wooded trails or more experienced riders can enjoy longer trips with a stop for lunch. The two-hour Paniolo Trail ride ($65) travels up through guava groves and patches of Ironwood tree. Here the rider will enjoy the spectacular views of Maui and Molokai and have the opportunity to glimpse Axis deer, quail, wild turkeys and cattle and pass through the dryland forest of Kanepu'u. Also available are the one-hour Plantation Trail Ride ($35) and the Paniolo Lunch Ride which is a three hour trip ($90). Private trail rides can also be scheduled ($95 per two hours). Riders must wear long pants and sport shoes and children must be at least nine years of age and four feet in height to ride. Riders must be twelve years or older to sign up for the Paniolo rides. Maximum weight of riders is 250 lbs. Safety helmets are provided for all riders. The horse drawn buggy is another equine activity. Reservations can be made through the concierge at either hotel.

WEDDINGS

Lana'i may well be one of the most romantic places on earth. The Lana'i Wedding is available through the resorts. The wedding package includes a garden setting at Manele Bay Hotel or a gazebo at the Lodge at Koele, minister, bouguet and bridal leis, souvenir book. $1,000. Lana'i Honeymoon package runs $200.

HIKING

Walking sticks are provided in all the rooms at the Lodge at Koele for guest usage. It's almost impossible to resist strolling around the pastoral grounds. Near the Koele Lodge are two small houses. These were originally located where the orchid house is now. The Richardson families live here; their ancestors were among the early Lana'i paniolos. You can stroll around the front grounds to view the enormous Cook Island pine or enjoy watching guests try their hand at lawn bowling, croquet or miniature golf. Walk down to the horse stables or peek inside the old church. The stables are new, but the church was relocated due to the construction of the Lodge. A small school was also moved and it is currently being restored and perhaps will one day house Lana'i's first museum.

The Munro Trail is a 9 mile loop trek along the ridge of Lana'i. The view from the 3,370 ft. summit of Lanaihale can be spectacular on a clear day. This route can be tackled by four-wheel drive vehicles, but only during very dry conditions. For the adventurous, there is also the High Pasture Loop, the Old Cowboy Trail, Eucalyptus Ladder or Beyond the Blue Screen. A light to moderate weight raincoat might be a good idea to take along if you're planning on hiking. The concierge can provide you with a map showing the various routes. Picnics can be provided by the hotel.

MISCELLANEOUS

Lawn bowling and both English and American croquet fields surround the Lodge at Koele. Guests can also borrow a mountain bike and ride into town, around the resort paths, or in the early morning or early evening they are allowed to ride along the golf course paths. One evening we followed one of the garden paths behind the putting green that led to a very steep golf cart track from the lower nine holes to the upper nine. It was so steep, in fact, that it proved quite a challenge to just walk the bikes up. After the journey up, we were delighted to find an ample supply of water and cups that reappeared every couple of holes on the golf course. Once on top we traveled around a few holes of the golf course which were fairly level. We were pleasantly surprised to find ourselves at the tee off for the 8th hole of the golf course, and as previously described, it was an inspired location. We then attempted to ride down from the tee to the green. The path down was so steep that it required brakes on full force to go slow enough to maintain control! Beyond is another picturesque lagoon and more golf cart trails to follow, again, on flat ground. The walk into town takes about 15 minutes at a fairly brisk pace, but only about 5 minutes by bike. Biking is a good option for seeing Lana'i City or if you want to sample some of Lana'i's local eateries. Guests of the resorts can drive down and spend the day at Club Lana'i. See Maui section - WHAT TO DO for Club Lana'i description. $68 adults, $25 youth.

Both resorts have wonderful swimming pools. The Koele pool, flanked by two bubbling jacuzzi was seldom busy. The Manele pool is slightly larger and, at a lower elevation than Koele, became quite hot during the afternoon. The adjacent poolside restaurant provided refreshing drinks and light food fare. Guests at the resorts have pool privileges at both facilities.

Scuba diving, fishing expeditions, raft trips and other ocean excursions can be arranged through the concierge at either resort. Half day raft trips (2 1/2 hr.) run $40 - $60. Half day sailing and snorkeling trips are run by Trilogy Excursions.

At both resorts, a sheet describing the activities for the next day is left in the room with the evening maid service.

LODGE AT KOELE -- Tea is served in the Music Room each afternoon and in the evening there are complimentary pupus, also available in the Tea Room (aka "bar". The Music Room has an array of interesting musical instruments lining the walls and the grand piano may be used by the guests. In the Trophy Rooms are board games and the library has books. Complimentary video tapes are available at the concierge for guests to view in their rooms. At night there is varied musical entertainment in the Great Hall. The twin fireplaces are ablaze and the overstuffed chairs invite you to slow down and relax. The fireplaces are lit, upon request, in the library, music or trophy room. This may be as close to heaven on earth as you can get.

MANELE BAY HOTEL - Manele also has varied daily activities. A tour of the resort is available and there is afternoon and evening entertainment in the lower lobby and the bar. Complimentary video tapes are available for guest use in their rooms and complimentary morning coffee is a pleasurable experience in the Orchid Lounge or Coral Lounge.

ART

If you're a resident or a visitor and interested in pursuing your artistic talents, you can register for the *Lana'i Art Program.* Classes are taught by local and visiting artists and might include a variety of paint medias or even craft classes such as bead making. For registration or other information phone (808) 565-7503. The *Lana'i Visiting Artist Program* offers arts and culture to guests of both hotels with a lineup of literary, culinary, and performing artists who come to the island to share their talents in an informal living room setting. Past participants in the program include playwright Wendy Wasserstein, Chef Bradley Ogden, Dr. Oliver Sacks, former Presidential Press Secretary Marlin Fitzwater, jazz guitarist Charlie Byrd, producer David Wolper, author Richard Preston (*The Hot Zone*), humor columnist Dave Barry, novelist Paul Theroux, singer Cleo Laine, Pulitzer Prize-winning writer Jane Smiley, humorists Garrison Keillor and Calvin Trillin, authors John McPhee and Susan Isaacs, and pianist Andre Watts. All events are free of charge. For further information about the program, contact Lana'i Company at 1-800-321-4666 or 808-548-3700.

RESORT TOURS

Both Manele and Koele offer complimentary tours daily of their resorts. Just sign up at the concierge. The tour of Koele is especially informative and discusses the many unique pieces of art gracing the lobby, making it a worthwhile 30 minutes.

WHAT TO SEE

There are only three paved roads on Lana'i outside of Lana'i City, no stop lights, and very few street signs once you leave town. After driving around on even a dry day, we assure you that they aren't kidding when they recommend a four-wheel drive. On rainy days, you can be fairly certain you'll get stuck in the mud and muck! You can fairly well see all of Lana'i in a long day, but if you want to slow down, do some hiking, or simply sit in the sun on a quiet beach, there is plenty to occupy you for days. Either of the resorts can provide you with a map and advice. We were pleased that Pete Agliamo forfeited a day of fishing to act as a tour guide. Born in the Philippines, he has lived for 43 years on the island and worked for Dole driving pineapple trucks. Besides being an active fisherman he has hunted around the island for years and was a most knowledgeable guide. Leaving the driving to him was a delight as we cruised along the dirt roads and "talked story." Along the road to the Garden of the Gods we asked him if he was taking a short cut. Judging by the fact that we were zooming between pastures with cattle and abandoned pineapple fields with no street signs at all, we were certain we'd taken the back way, but he assured us we were on the main road. It seemed to us that it wouldn't be all that hard to get lost on Lana'i! Since there are no local quick marts, be sure you pack plenty of water and bring along a picnic, because we're sure you'll find the perfect spot to enjoy it.

We headed east and were pleasantly surprised to find the road to the *Garden of the Gods* was smooth, packed dirt that was free of ruts. (However this may not always be the case.) A 20 minute ride took us through a stand of ironwoods before we reached the large carved stone announcing our arrival in the Garden of the Gods, which was named in 1935. (It happened that the stone had been carved by Pete's daughter!) We arrived during mid-day, but the best time to see this lunar-like and rather mystical place is early morning or late evening. In the early morning, on a clear day, you can see the faint outline of Honolulu's sky-scrapers and a sharp eye can observe Axis deer out foraging. The rays of the sun in the early evening cast strange shadows on the amber baked earth and huge monolithic rocks and your imagination can do the rest.

GARDEN OF THE GODS

Interestingly enough, here, in what seems to be the middle of nowhere, with no one in sight, and a peaceful stillness, (except for the occasional call of a bird or the wind brushing against your cheek) are street signs! One indicates Awailua Rd. which is a very rugged and steep dirt path down to the ocean. Most of these roads are used by the local residents for fishing or hunting. Be advised, if you attempt to start down, there may be no place to turn around should you change your mind.

Follow Polihua Road and you'll arrive at a stretch of white sandy beach with rolling sand dunes. According to Lawrence Kainoahou Gay, in his account entitled "True Stories of the Island of Lana'i," the word Polihua means Poli (cover or bay) and hua (eggs). He reports that in this area turtles would visit to lay their eggs above the high water mark. He had seen turtles, in days gone by, that were large enough to carry three people! This beach is not recommended for safe swimming or other water activities. The Kaena Road winds down to a very isolated area called Kaena Iki Point, which is the site of one of Lana'i's largest Heiaus.

Shipwreck Beach, or Kaiolohia, on Lana'i's northeast coast, is about a half hour drive along a paved road from the Lodge at Koele. Enroute down you'll note that there are many little rock piles. At first glance they appear to be some relic of the distant past, however, they began to appear in the 1960's, a product of tourists and/or residents and have no historical or other significance. The road is lined with scrub brush, and as you begin the descent to the shoreline you catch a glimpse of the World War II liberty ship. Be sure to keep an eye out for pheasant, deer, turkeys and the small Franklin partridges.

At the bottom of the road you can choose to go left to Shipwreck Beach or continue straight and follow the coastline on the unpaved, dusty and very rugged Awalua Road to *Club Lana'i*. Club Lana'i is a day resort that shuttles visitors from Lahaina, Maui to the leeward shores of Lana'i for a day of relaxation and recreation--sort of a Hawaiian version of Gilligan's Island. It's a bit of a drive and slow going. Four wheel drive vehicles are advised. It is about five miles down the road to Keomuku. There are still remnants of the failed Maunalei Sugar Company near Keomuku, and a Japanese cemetery, also a memento of the failed sugar company. The beaches are wonderful for sunbathing or picnicking, but not advisable for swimming. Beyond are Naha and Lopa, two uninhabited old villages. The old Kalanakila a ka Malamalama church, located near Keomuku, is in the process of being renovated. There are also some ancient Hawaiian trails at Naha. The road ends at Naha and you'll have to drive back by the same route.

If you're headed for Shipwreck Beach, go left. (The old sign that said "Federation Camp." is gone.) This is Lapahiki Road, and while dry and bumpy during our drive, we understand a little precipitation can make it impassable except in a four-wheel drive. The dirt road is lined by Kiawe trees and deserted little houses. This is a getaway spot for the local residents, although there is no fresh water. The reef along Kaiolohia Beach is very wide, but the surf can be high and treacherous. During a storm, waves come crashing down over the liberty ship that now sits on the reef.

This was one of three Navy L.C.M. ships that were not shipwrecked, but purposely grounded in 1941-1942. The other two have disappeared after losing their battle to the ocean. Barges are also towed over, anchored and left to rot as well. The channel between here and Moloka'i is called Kolohi, which means mischievous and unpredictable. The channel between Lana'i and Maui is the 'Au'au channel which means to bathe. There were several ships that were wrecked here or on other parts of the island. In the 1820s the British ship *Alderman Wood* went aground; in 1826 the American ship *London* was wrecked off Lana'i. In 1931 George A. Crozier's *Charlotte C.* foundered somewhere along the beach. The 34 foot yawl called *Tradewind* was wrecked off the mouth of the Maunalei Valley on August 6, 1834 while cruising from Honolulu to Lahaina. There is a remnant of an old lighthouse and also some old petroglyph sites nearby. The concierge desk can give you a list of petroglyphs around the island. Please respect these sights. The beach is unsafe for swimming, but you might see some people shorefishing. Sometimes after storms, interesting shells, old bottles and assorted artifacts are washed up along the shoreline. One area you probably won't visit is Pohaku "O" which roughly translates to mean "rock." This is in the Mahana region of Lana'i on the island's leeward side. The rocks here resemble tombstones and were avoided by the early Hawaiians as a place of evil. If the breezes are favorable, the wind blowing by the rock creates an "O" sound that changes with the wind, which is the reason this rock received its evil connotations.

For another adventure, leave Lana'i City and follow Kaumalapau Highway past the small airport and continue on another five minutes toward Kaumalapau Harbor. It's paved all the way! The harbor isn't much to see, but the drive down to the water shows the dramatically different landscape of Lana'i's windward coastline. Here you can see the sharply cut rocky shoreline that drops steeply into the ocean, in some places more than 1,500 feet. The Kaunolu Bay can be accessed from the Kaumalapau Highway along a very, very rugged road. Follow the road just a bit further and you'll reach the harbor. The bulk of the island's materials come in by barge which were also the method used to take the thousands of tons of pineapples to O'ahu for processing. Each pineapple crate weighed seven tons and a barge could haul 170 crates at a time. Today, pineapple production has become too expensive on Lana'i. Hawai'i is finding it hard to compete with countries such as the Philippines, where people are willing to work at a much lower daily wage and the fruit can be grown and processed for much less. In the past, freight was brought to Lana'i aboard the barges returning from Honolulu after delivering the pineapple. Today the Young Brothers have the contract for freight delivery.

Hulopo'e Beach is a splendid marine reserve. Along a crescent of white sandy beach is Hulopo'e Beach which fronts Manele Bay Hotel. It is also Lanai's best swimming beach. As with all beaches, be aware of surf conditions. There are attendants at the beach kiosk who can provide beach safety information. Although netting and spearfishing are not allowed, shorefishing is permitted. The best snorkeling is in the mornings before the surf picks up. Across the bay from the Manele Bay Hotel are a series of tidal pools. When the tide drifts down, sea creatures emerge making this a great spot for exploration. The Lodge at Koele and Manele Bay Hotel offer a handy "Tide Pool Guide" prepared by Kathleen Kapalka. It notes that the Hulopoʻe Bay and tide pool areas are both part of a marine life conservation district which was set up in 1976. Also included in the conservation district are Manele Bay and Puʻupehe Cove and as such, all animals and plants (dead or alive) are protected from collection or harm. The color brochure is an easy-to-follow guide to your personal tour of these wonderful tidal areas. Mollusks, arthropods, marine vertebrates, annelids, echinoderms, marine invertebrates and marine plants are described and illustrated. Safety tips and conservation tips include the fact that suntanning oils are detrimental and should be cleansed from the hands before reaching into the pools. This is an excellent brochure which will make your tidal pool adventure a valuable learning experience. Note: Reef shoes are available at the hotel's beach kiosk for resort guests, a recommended protection when prowling around the rocky shoreline.

Climb up the bluff and you will be rewarded with a great view of Maui and Kahoʻolawe. A large monolithic rock sits off the bluff. This is Puʻupehe (often referred to as Sweetheart Rock) that carries a poignant local legend. As with most oral history, legends tend to take on the special character of the storyteller. Such is the story of Puʻupehe. We asked three people about the legend and heard three different versions. One made the hero into a jealous lover, the other a thoughtful one. So here is our interpretation. There was a strong handsome young Hawaiian man whose true love was a beautiful Hawaiian woman. They made a sea cave near Puʻupehe rock their lover's retreat. One day the man journeyed inland to replenish their supplies, leaving his love in the sea cave. He had gone some distance when he sensed an impending storm. He hurriedly returned to the sea cave, but the storm preceded him and his love had drowned in the cave. He was devastated. Using superhuman strength he carried her to the top of the monolithic rock called Puʻupehe and buried her there before jumping to his death. Whether there is truth to this legend is uncertain, but some years back a scientist did scale the top of the peak, which was no easy task, to investigate. No bones or other evidence was found. However, we were told that in ancient times, the bones were removed and hidden separately away. And so ends this sad tale of lost love.

Manele Bay is a quaint boat port which offers excellent snorkeling just beyond the breakwater. When the surf at Hulopoʻe is too strong, Lanaʻi tour boats often anchor here for snorkeling.

WILDLIFE

You'll notice very quickly that there are many, many birds on Lana'i, a far greater number than on Maui. Fortunately for the birds, Lana'i does not have the mongoose as a predator. Wild turkeys, the last non-native animal to be introduced to Lana'i, are hunted in early November for about two weeks. They are easily spotted, but we understand as soon as the 1st of November appears (the turkeys must have calendars) they disappear until promptly after Thanksgiving. These wild birds look very lean and don't appear to make a very succulent Thanksgiving dinner. The easiest place to spot them is down near the Manele boat harbor where a group of turkeys and a pack of wild cats together enjoy the leftovers from the Trilogy boat's daily picnics. Pheasant are also hunted seasonally. Wild goats were rounded up and captured years ago. The only island pigs are in the piggery where they are raised for island consumption. Pronghorn antelope, introduced in 1959, have now been hunted to extinction. Twelve Axis deer were introduced by George Munro and have adapted well to Lana'i. It is estimated that there are some 3,000 - 6,000 animals and, given the fact that they produce offspring twice yearly, the numbers are ever growing. In fact deer far outnumber Lana'i's human population. The deer run a mere 110 - 160 pounds and are hunted almost year round. It is easiest to spot these lean, quick deer in the early mornings or late evenings bounding across fields, but during the day they seek sheltered, shaded areas. There are still a few remaining mouflon sheep, which have distinctive and beautiful curved horns. You'll note many of the houses in Lana'i City are decorated with arrays of horns and antlers across their porch or on a garage wall.

BEACHES

Along Lana'i's Northern Shore is Polihua. There is an interesting stretch of long sand dunes. This coast is often very windy, and some days the blowing sand is intense. The surf conditions are dangerous and swimming should not be attempted, ever. Also along the Northern Shore is the area from Awalua to Naha. The beaches are narrow and the offshore waters are shallow with a wide reef. However, the water is often murky. Swimming and snorkeling are not recommended.

Surf conditions can be dangerous. Lopa on the Eastern shore is a narrow white sand beach that can be enjoyed for picnicking and sunbathing.

Along the Western coastline is Kaunola, a rocky shore with no sandy beach and no safe entry or exit. Conditions can be dangerous. Swimming is not advised at any time. Also on the Western shore is Kaumalapau Harbor, the deep water harbor used for shipping. Water activities are not recommended at any time.

The southern coastline affords the safest ocean conditions. Manele Bay is the small boat harbor, but water activity is not recommended due to heavy boat traffic. Hulopoe Bay is the island's best and most beautiful white sand beach. It is located in front of the Manele Bay Hotel. It is popular for swimming, surfing, boogie-boarding and snorkeling. The tidepools make for fun exploration and, although a marine preserve, shore fishing is permitted. On summer weekends the camping area is often filled with local residents. However, large swells, and high surf conditions can exist. During times of high surf, undertows become very strong. Entry is hazardous during these conditions. During these times it is not safe to stand or play even in the shore break, as severe injury can occur. Be aware of water safety signs. There are no lifeguards on duty, however, there are attendants at the resort's beach kiosk who might be able to answer questions you have. Never swim alone and always exercise good water safety judgement.

CHILDCARE

The Manele Bay Hotel and The Lodge at Koele offer a *Pilialoha Adventure Program* for youth aged 5-16 years. Pilialoha means close friendship and beloved companion. The half day program, either 9 am-12:30 pm or 11:30 am-3 pm is $35 per child and includes lunch. A full day, 9am - 3pm program, runs $55 including lunch. Their evening program is available only on Friday and Saturday evenings and includes dinner at $50 per child. During holidays they may add additional evening programs. Children ages 3-5 years may join the program when appropriate and when accompanied by an attendant. There is an individual care fee of $10 in addition to the regular program rate. Daytime activities include scavenger hunts, exploring petroglyphs, learning about dolphins and whales, putting at the golf course, snorkeling lessons, or tide pool exploration. Evening activities range from a beach party or ice cream social to making your own videos and a luau night. Advanced registration is required, it is suggested that you make your plans with the concierge the day prior. Private babysitting is also available through the concierge at $10 per hour, each additional child at $5 per hour.

There are many activities your child can also enjoy on Lana'i. A Pilialoha staff member can accompany your child for an additional $20 fee. Tennis lessons, half or full hour for youths 5-14 years. Golf lessons at the Challenge of Manele, either private or semi-private. On Saturdays a complimentary golf clinic is available for youths aged 8 and up. Children five and up can enjoy a pony ride for $10, children 9 and up are invited on the one hour Plantation horseback excursion for $35 and youth ages 12 and up can have private horseback riding lessons or take the two hour Paniolo ride. A five hour excursion on Trilogy is offered for youth ages 5 and up for $40. Snorkeling lessons at the Manele Bay Pool for those 8 years and up. Spinning Dolphin Fishing Charter is available for half day excursions for children 12 and up $85.

RECOMMENDED READING

An excellent account of the history of the island is *True Stories of the Island of Lana'i* by Lawrence Kainoahou Gay, the son of Charles Gay. First published in 1965 and reprinted in 1981 it is available for $12 at the resort gift shops on Lana'i and probably could be obtained through bookstores on the neighboring islands as well.

RECOMMENDED READING

Ashdown, Inez. *Ke Alaloa O Maui. Authentic History and Legends of the Valley Isle*. Hawaii: Kama'aina Historians. 1971.

Ashdown, Inez. *Stories of Old Lahaina*. Honolulu: Hawaiian Service. 1976.

Barrow, Terence. *Incredible Hawaii*. Vermont: Charles Tuttle Co. 1974.

Begley, Bryan. *Taro in Hawaii*. Honolulu: The Oriental Publishing Co. 1979.

Bird, Isabella. *Six Months in the Sandwich Islands*. Tokyo: Tuttle. 1988

Boom, Bob and Christensen, Chris. *Important Hawaiian Place Names*. Hawaii: Bob Boom Books. 1978.

Chisholm, Craig. *Hawaiian Hiking Trails*. Oregon: Fernglen Press. 1994.

Christensen, Jack Shields. *Instant Hawaiian*. Hawaii: The Robert Boom Co. 1971.

Clark, John. *Beaches of Maui County*. Honolulu: University Press of Hawaii. 1980.

Daws, Gavan. *The Illustrated Atlas of Hawaii*. Australia: Island Heritage. 1980.

Echos of Our Song. Honolulu: University of Hawaii Press.

Fielding, Ann. *Hawaiian Reefs and Tidepools*. Hawaii: Oriental Pub. Co.

Haraguchi, Paul. *Weather in Hawaiian Waters*. 1983.

Hawaii Island Paradise. California: Wide World Publishing. 1987.

Hazama, Dorothy. *The Ancient Hawaiians*. Honolulu: Hogarth Press.

Judd, Gerrit. *Hawaii, an Informal History*. New York: Collier Books. 1961.

Kaye, Glen. *Hawaiian Volcanos*. Nevada: K.C. Publications, 1987.

Kepler, Angela. *Maui's Hana Highway*. Honolulu: Mutual Publishing. 1987

Kepler, Cameron B. and Angela Kay. *Haleakala, A Guide to the Mountain*. Honolulu: Mutual Publishing. 1988.

Kyselka, Will and Lanterman, Ray. *Maui, How it Came to Be*. Honolulu: The University Press of Hawaii. 1980.

Lahaina Historical Guide. Tokyo: Maui Historical Society. 1971.

Lahaina Restoration Foundation, *Story of Lahaina*. Lahaina: 1980.

London, Jack. *Stories of Hawaii*. Honolulu: Mutual Publishing. 1965.

Mack, Jim. *Haleakala and The Story Behind the Scenery*. Nevada: K.C. Publications, 1984.

Mrantz, Maxine. *Whaling Days in Old Hawaii*. Honolulu: Aloha Graphics. 1976.

Na Mele O Hawai'i Nei. Honolulu: University of Hawaii Press. 1970

Nickerson, Roy. *Lahaina, Royal Capital of Hawaii*. 1980.

On The Hana Coast. Hong Kong: Emphasis Int'l Ltd. and Carl Lundquist. 1987.

Pukui, Mary K. et al. *The Pocket Hawaiian Dictionary*. Honolulu: The University of Hawaii Press. 1975.

Randall, John. *Underwater Guide to Hawaiian Reef Fishes*. Hawaii: Treasures of Time. 1981.

Smith, Robert. *Hiking Maui*. California. 1990.

Stevenson, Robert Louis. *Travels in Hawaii*. Honolulu: University of Hawaii Press. 1973.

Tabrah, Ruth. *Maui The Romantic Island*. Nevada: KC Publications. 1985.

Thorne, Chuck. *50 Locations for Scuba & Snorkeling*. 1983.

Titcomb, M. *Native Use of Fish in Hawaii*. Honolulu: University of Hawaii Press. 1952.

Twain, Mark. *Letters from Mark Twain*. Hawaii: U. of Hawaii Press. 1966.

Twain, Mark. *Mark Twain in Hawaii*. Colorado: Outdoor Books. 1986.

Wallin, Doug. *Exotic Fishes and Coral of Hawaii and the Pacific*. 1974.

Westervelt, H. *Myths and Legends of Hawaii*. Honolulu: Mutual. 1987.

Wisniewski, Richard A. *The Rise and Fall of the Hawaiian Kingdom*. Honolulu: Pacific Basin Enterprises. 1979.

> *"One cannot determine in advance to love a particular woman,*
> *nor can one so determine to love Hawaii.*
> *One sees, and one loves or does not love.*
> *With Hawaii it seems always to be love at first sight.*
> *Those for whom the islands were made,*
> *or who were made for the islands,*
> *are swept off their feet in the first moments of meeting,*
> *embrace and are embraced."*

Jack London

RECOMMENDED READING FOR CHILDREN

Adair, Dick. *The Story of Aloha Bear*. Honolulu: Island Heritage. 1986.

Adair, Dick. *Aloha Bear and the Meaning of Aloha*. Honolulu: Island Heritage. 1987.

Feeney, Stephanie. *Hawaii is a Rainbow*. Honolulu: University of Hawaii Press. 1985.

Feeney, Stephanie and Fielding, Ann. *Sand to Sea: Marine Life of Hawaii*. Honolulu: University of Hawaii Press. 1989.

Kahalewai, Marilyn. *Maui Mouse's Supper*. Honolulu: Bess Press. 1988.

Kahalewai, Marilyn. *Whose Slippers are Those?* Honolulu: Besss Press. 1988.

Knudsen, Eric A. *Spooky Stuffs*. Aiea, Hawaii: Island Heritage Publishing. 1989.

Laird, Donivee Martin. *The Three Little Hawaiian Pigs and the Magic Shark*. Honolulu: Barnaby Books. 1994.

Laird, Donivee Martin. *'Ula Li'i and the Magic Shark*. Honolulu: Barnaby Books. 1985.

Laird, Donivee Martin. *Wili Wai Kula and the Three Mongooses*. Honolulu: Barnaby Books. 1983.

Laird, Donivee Martin. *Keaka and the Lilikoi Vine*. Honolulu: Barnaby Books. 1982.

Land-Nellist, Cassandra. *A Child's First Book About Hawaii*. Hawaii: Press Pacifica. 1987.

McBarnet, Gill. *A Whale's Tale*. Hawaii: Ruwanga Trading. 1988.

McBarnet, Gill. *Fountain of Fire*. Hawaii: Ruwanga Trading. 1987.

McBarnet, Gill. *Goodnight Gecko*. Hawaii: Ruwanga Trading. 1991.

McBarnet, Gill. *The Whale Who Wanted to be Small*. Hawaii: Ruwanga Trading. 1985.

McBarnet, Gill. *The Wonderful Journey*. Hawaii: Ruwanga Trading. 1986.

McBride, Leslie R. *About Hawaii's Volcanoes*. Hilo: Petroglyph Press. 1986.

Pape, Donna L. *Hawaii Puzzle Book*. Honolulu: Bess Press. 1984.

Swanson, Helen. *Angel of Rainbow Gulch*. Honolulu: 1992.

Thompson, Vivian. *Hawaiian Tales of Heroes and Champions*. Honolulu: University of Hawaii Press. 1986.

Tune, Suelyn Ching. *How Maui Slowed the Sun*. Honolulu: University of Hawaii Press. 1988.

Wagenman, Mark A. *The Adventures of Aloha Bear and Maui the Whale*. Honolulu: Island Heritage. 1989.

Warren, Bonnie. *Aloha from Hawaii!* Honolulu: Warren Associates. 1987.

Williams, Julie Stewart. *And the Birds Appeared*. Honolulu: University of Hawaii Press. 1988.

Williams, Julie et. al. *Maui Goes Fishing*. Honolulu: University of Hawaii Press. 1991.

Von Tempski, Armine. *Bright Spurs*. Honolulu: Oxbow Press. 1946

Von Tempski, Armine. *Judy of the Islands*. Honolulu: Oxbow Press. 1941

Von Tempski, Armine. *Pam's Paradise Ranch*. Honolulu: Oxbow Press. 1940.

SUGAR TRAIN

INDEX

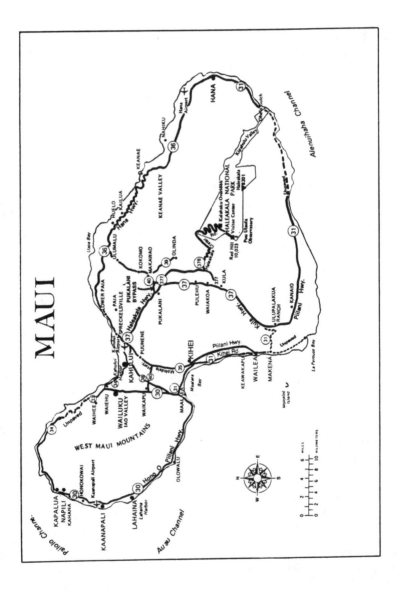

ORDERING INFORMATION: Available from Paradise Publications are books and videos to enhance your travel library and assist with your travel plans, or provide a special gift for someone who is planning a trip! Prices are subject to change without notice.

MAUI AND LANA'I: Making the Most of Your Family Vacation
by Christie Stilson & Dona Early. This completely revised guide is packed with information on over 150 condos & hotels, 200 restaurants, 50 great beaches, sights to see and travel tips for the valley island. The island of Lana'i is included. Here the visitor will enjoy fine dining, local eateries, remote beaches, wonderful hikes and peaceful enchantment. *"A down-to-earth, nuts-and-bolts companion with answers to most any question."* L.A.Times. Over 400 pgs, maps, $15.00, 7th ed. 1997.

KAUA'I, A PARADISE FAMILY GUIDE: Making the Most of Your Family Vacation
by Dona Early & Christie Stilson. Completely revised and rewritten since Hurricane Iniki, this information packed guide describes island accommodations, restaurants, secluded beaches, plus recreation and tour options. "If you need a 'how to do it' book to guide your next to Kaua'i, here's the one." 300 pages, multi-indexed, maps, illustrations, $15.00. Fourth edition. Copyright 1996.

HAWAI'I: THE BIG ISLAND, A PARADISE FAMILY GUIDE
by John Penisten. Outstanding for its completeness, this well-organized guide provides useful information for people of every budget and life-style. Each chapter features the author's personal recommendations and "best bets." In addition to comprehensive information island accommodations, you will find a full range of water, land and activities and tours from which to choose. Then enjoy dining at one of the more than 250 restaurants which range from local style drive-ins to fine dining establishments. Sights, beaches, and travel tips. 300 pgs. $15.00 4th ed. 1997.

UPDATE NEWSLETTERS! *THE MAUI UPDATE, THE KAUA'I UPDATE,* and *HAWAI'I: THE BIG ISLAND UPDATE* are quarterly newsletters published by Paradise Publications that highlight the most current island events. Each features late breaking tips on the newest restaurants, island activities or special, not-to-be missed events. Each newsletter available at the single issue price of $2.50 or a yearly subscription (four issues) rate of $10. Canada $12 per year.

FREE! A free copy of Paradise Publication's quarterly newsletter, ***THE BIG ISLAND UPDATE***, is available by writing Paradise Publications (Attention: Newsletter Dept.) 8110 S.W. Wareham, Suite 306, Portland, OR 97223, and enclosing a self-addressed, stamped, #10 envelope.

MAPS! A great addition to your travels is a full-color topographical maps by cartographer James A. Bier. Maps are available for $3.95 each for the islands of O'ahu, Maui, Kaua'i, Lana'i & Moloka'i and the Big Island of Hawai'i. ***MORE MAPS!*** *Haleakala,* Earth Press Topographical Map is a must-purchase if you are planning to enjoy this park in-depth. Water resistant, too! $3.95

VIEWBOOKS Doug Peebles is quite possibly Hawai'i's best photographer, and his finest photography has been showcased in these full-color paperback books. Ideal for the armchair traveler or trip planner, these affordable pictorial guides are wonderful souveniers and great gifts. Choose from these five: HAWAII (Big Island), MAUI, KAUA'I, O'AHU, VOLCANOES. Each is 10 x 13. 32 pages, $7.95.

THE NEW CUISINE OF HAWAII. This 150 page hardcover cookbook is subtitled "Recipes from the Twelve Celebrated Chefs of Hawaii Regional Cuisine" and that about sums it up. The culinary wizardry of Roger Dikon, Mark Ellman, and others are shared in this fascinating cookbook. Color photographs highlight each chef's magic touch. 1994. $30.

COOKING WITH ALOHA. Discover the flavors and smells of the Hawaiian islands in your own kitchen with this easy-to-follow cookbook. Appetizers to desserts are covered. An inexpensive guide to cooking your favorite Hawaiian foods. 9 x 12, paperback, 184 pages, $9.95.

A TASTE OF ALOHA and **ANOTHER TASTE OF ALOHA**. Each of these cookbooks have already becoming classics. A Taste of Aloha premiered in 1983 and is nearly 400 pages of island favorites, reflecting the influence that each new of the many ethnic groups introduced to the island. Another Taste of Aloha has all new recipes reflects the trend toward a low-fat lifestyle. Both cookbooks are hardbound. $21.95 each.

MAJESTIC MOLOKAI. Explore Hawaii's "Friendly Isle" with this attractive and information-filled book. Discover the beauty and splendor of this island. 144 pages, plus hundreds of color photographs. $14.95

HAWAIIAN HIKING TRAILS by Craig Chisholm. This very attractive and accurate guide details 49 of Hawaii's best hiking trails. Hikes for every level of ability. Includes photography, topographical maps, and detailed directions. An excellent book for discovering Hawai'i's great outdoors! 152 pgs., $15.95. 1994. **KAUAI HIKING TRAILS.** Fernglen Press produces this quality 160 page book features color photographs, topographical maps and detailed directions to Kaua'i's best hiking trails. $12.95. 1991.

HIKING MAUI by Robert Smith. Discover 27 hiking areas all around Maui. 5 x 8 paperback, 160 pages. $10.95. Also by Robert Smith. **HIKING KAUA'I**, over 40 hiking trails throughout Kaua'i. 116 pages, $10.95. **HIKING HAWAII (The Big Island)**, 157 pages, $10.95. Black & white photographs and maps. Compact and easy-to-use.

DIVING AND SNORKELING GUIDE TO THE HAWAIIAN ISLANDS. 6 x 9. 108 pages. 24 maps. 1991. $11.95.

DIVERS GUIDE TO MAUI A popular guide for many years, written by local resident Chuck Thorne. A comprehensive guide to over 50 locations for snorkeling and diving on Maui. $9.95.

NEW POCKET HAWAIIAN DICTIONARY. Resolve just what those Hawaiian words mean and how to pronounce them! $4.95.

MAUI REMEMBERS: A LOCAL HISTORY. This is an outstanding historical guide to the Valley Isle. It covers some interesting aspects of island history. This 167 page paperback volume is accented with hundreds of sepia photographs. Fascinating and informative. 11 x 14. $22.95.

COMPUTER/VIDEO   *(All Videos are VHS format)*

HAWAIIAN POSTCARDS This is a screen saver program for you computer. Enjoy a little piece of Hawai'i everyday. Postcards of Hawai'i's most famous vistas flash past. Fun! $8.95 MacIntosh or PC.

HAWAIIAN PARADISE -- by International Video Network. More than a travel log, this is one of the best of many, many videos we have reviewed. The journey covers all six of the major Hawaiian islands, Kaua'i, Hawai'i, Lana'i, Moloka'i, Maui and O'ahu. The narrative begins with the formation of the Hawaiian islands and deviates from the average video by exploring the culture, legend, lore and history of the island. The lover of Hawai'i will learn new and interesting island facts and points of history and the new-comer to Hawaii will be thrilled with this visual taste of the islands. The next best thing to being there. $29.95. 90 minutes.

FOREVER HAWAII -- This 60 minute, video portrait features all six major Hawaiian islands. It includes breathtaking views from the snowcapped peaks of Mauna Kea to the bustling city of Waikiki, from the magnificent Waimea Canyon to the spectacular Halakeala Crater. A lasting memento. 1992. $24.95. **FOREVER MAUI** -- An in-depth visit to Maui with scenic shots and interesting stories about the Valley Isle. An excellent video for the first time, or even the returning Maui visitor. $19.95. **FLIGHT OF THE CANYON BIRD** -- An inspired view of the Garden Island of Kaua'i from a bird's eye perspective; an outstanding 30 minute piece of cinematography. This short feature presentation explores the lush tropical rainforests surrounding Waialeale (the wettest spot on earth), the awesome Waimea Canyon and the Napili Coastline. The narration explores the geologic and historic beginnings of the island. A lasting memento or gift! Each tape is 30 minutes. Cost $19.95 per tape.

KUMU HULA: KEEPERS OF A CULTURE -- This 85-minute tape, funded by the Hawaii State Foundation on Culture & Arts, is beautifully filmed and includes hulas from troupes on various islands and explores the unique qualities of hula as well as the history. $29.95. **HULA - LESSONS ONE AND TWO** -- "Lovely Hula Hands" and "Little Brown Gal" are taught by Carol "Kalola" Lorenzo who explains the basic steps. fun and interesting video for the whole family. 30 minutes. $29.95.

SHIPPING: In the Continental U.S.-- Please add $4 for 1 to 2 items (books or videos). Each additional item over 2, please add $.50. Orders shipped promptly by US First class mail If you'd prefer items shipped bookrate mail, we'll be happy to quote you shipping costs. Canadian Orders -- Please add $4 for the first book and $1 each additional book/tape. Orders shipped U.S. airmail. Federal Express or overnight mail services are available. Include your check or money order/Visa or Mastercard information and send to: **PARADISE PUBLICATIONS, 8110 S.W. Wareham, Portland, OR 97223** -- Phone or FAX (503) 246-1555

HAWAI'I, THE BIG ISLAND,

5th Edition
Making the Most of Your Family Vacation

John Penisten

$15.00

This is the must-have guide to the islands for every family traveling to Hawai'i. In this, the fifth edition of *Hawai'i, The Big Island,* author John Penisten highlights the best hotels and restaurants for families as well as the best beaches and day-trip destinations. Fully updated with the most current information by one of the best-known and most respected travel writers in the business, this is *the* book to make your trip to Hawai'i truly a trip to paradise.

**Available now
from Prima**

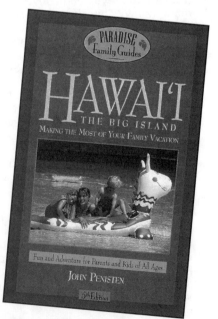

KAUA'I

Making the Most of Your Family Vacation

Dona Early and Christie Stilson

$15.00

Here is the complete traveler's reference and guide to the tropical paradise of Kaua'i. Completely revised and updated to reflect changes in accommodations, scenery, roads, and more following the hurricane that ravaged Kaua'i in 1992. With an emphasis on family travel (and an eye on the family budget!), this book provides travelers with all they need to know about this sun-drenched get-away such as more than 125 restaurants and recommendations; Hawaiian language and history; accommodations for all budgets; and recreational opportunities in Paradise.

**Available now
from Prima**

Walt Disney World® with Kids, 1998

Kim Wright Wiley

U.S. $14.00 / Can. $18.95
ISBN 0-7615-0808-2
paperback / 368 pages

Millions of families travel to Walt Disney World every year, but even "the happiest place on earth" can be exhausting and expensive without a knowledgeable guide. Author Kim Wright Wiley to the rescue! The nation's leading expert on traveling to Walt Disney World with kids in tow, she tells parents how to plan a wonderful, carefree vacation the kids will never forget with tips on the best hotels and restaurants for kids, smart ways to beat the crowds, and ratings for the most kid-pleasing rides.

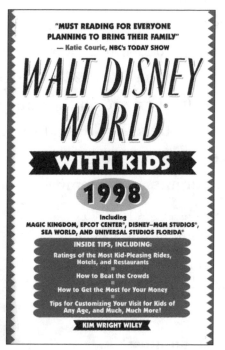

To order, call (800) 632-8676 or visit us online at www.primapublishing.com

Disneyland® & Southern California with Kids, 1998–1999

Carey Simon

U.S. $14.00 / Can. $18.95
ISBN 0-7615-1242-X
paperback / 272 pages

Disneyland & Southern California with Kids is an essential guide to "kid-proofing" a visit to Southern California's many attractions. Not simply a guide to Disneyland, this book offers advice for parents and children headed to Knott's Berry Farm, Universal Studios, Magic Mountain, the San Diego Zoo, and many other Southland attractions. Also included are tips on finding restaurants and hotels with "kid appeal,"

ways to save money on the Disneyland trip, plus parades, fireworks, and special shows that first-timers frequently miss.

To order, call (800) 632-8676 or visit us online at www.primapublishing.com

To Order Books

Please send me the following items:

Quantity	Title	Unit Price	Total
_____	**Disneyland & Southern California with Kids**	$ _14.00_	$ _____
_____	**Walt Disney World with Kids, 1998**	$ _14.00_	$ _____
_____	_____	$ _____	$ _____
_____	_____	$ _____	$ _____
_____	_____	$ _____	$ _____

	Subtotal	$ _____
	Deduct 10% when ordering 3–5 books	$ _____
	7.25% Sales Tax (CA only)	$ _____
	8.25% Sales Tax (TN only)	$ _____
	5% Sales Tax (MD and IN only)	$ _____
	7% G.S.T. Tax (Canada only)	$ _____
	Shipping and Handling*	$ _____
	Total Order	$ _____

*Shipping and Handling depend on Subtotal.

Subtotal	Shipping/Handling
$0.00–$14.99	$3.00
$15.00–$29.99	$4.00
$30.00–$49.99	$6.00
$50.00–$99.99	$10.00
$100.00–$199.99	$13.50
$200.00+	Call for Quote

Foreign and all Priority Request orders:
Call Order Entry department
for price quote at 916-632-4400

This chart represents the total retail price of books only (before applicable discounts are taken).

By Telephone: With American Express, MC or Visa, call 800-632-8676 or 916-632-4400.   Mon–Fri, 8:30-4:30.
WWW: http://www.primapublishing.com

By Internet E-mail: sales@primapub.com
By Mail: Just fill out the information below and send with your remittance to:

**Prima Publishing
P.O. Box 1260BK
Rocklin, CA 95677**

Name _____

Address_____

City _____ State _____ ZIP_____

MC/Visa#_____ Exp. _____

Check/money order enclosed for $_____ Payable to Prima Publishing

Daytime telephone _____

Signature _____